International Business
A Global Perspective

International Business
A Global Perspective

M a r i o s   I.   K a t s i o l o u d e s

American University of Sharjah, UAE

and

S p y r o s   H a d j i d a k i s

Intercollege, Nicosia-Cyprus

AMSTERDAM • BOSTON • HEIDELBERG • LONDON
NEW YORK • OXFORD • PARIS • SAN DIEGO
SAN FRANCISCO • SINGAPORE • SYDNEY • TOKYO

Butterworth-Heinemann is an imprint of Elsevier

Butterworth-Heinemann is an imprint of Elsevier
30 Corporate Drive, Suite 400, Burlington, MA 01803, USA
Linacre House, Jordan Hill, Oxford OX2 8DP, UK

⊗ Recognizing the importance of preserving what has been written, Elsevier
prints its books on acid-free paper whenever possible.

Library of Congress Cataloging-in-Publication Data
Katsioloudes, Marios I.
  International business : a global perspective / Marios I. Katsioloudes and Spyros
Hadjidakis.
    p. cm.
  ISBN 0-7506-7983-2
  1. International trade.   2. International business enterprises.   3. International
finance.   4. Globalization–Economic aspects. I. Hadjidakis, Spyros. II. Title.
  HF1379.K38 2006
  338.8′8–dc22

                                                                          2006035890

British Library Cataloguing in Publication Data
A catalogue record for this book is available from the British Library

ISBN 13: 978–0–7506–7983–1
ISBN 10: 0–7506–7983–2

> For information on all Butterworth-Heinemann publications
> visit our web site at http://books.elsevier.com

Typeset by Integra Software Services Pvt. Ltd, Pondicherry, India
www.integra-india.com

Printed in the United States of America

07 08 09 10 11   10 9 8 7 6 5 4 3 2 1

This book is dedicated to our families and to all the people of the world, irrespective of color, religion, gender and social status.

Contents

1

2

3

9

10

11

12

13

14

15

16

Preface

In the shadow of globalization and all the other world developments we have decided to write a book on international business from a global perspective, and not just from the European, the American, the German, or the Japanese point of view. We have included a lot of primary information that were based on interviews of several individuals from around the world, and also from our own international experience as educators, researchers, and consultants. Several chapters were written by specialists in their own field and their contributions are extremely valuable to the final version of the book.

The book consists of two parts. The first part consists of sixteen chapters, with the last four being a practical application of how it is to do business in certain regions of the world.

Each chapter begins with an Opening Case and a stimulating question. The main body of each chapter consists of a theoretical framework that results from primary and/or secondary data, and the chapter ends with a Closing Case with a stimulating question. Chapter summary and review and discussion questions are found at the end of each chapter, and practical tips are found in some chapters, wherever appropriate.

The second part consists of six comprehensive cases addressing international issues ranging from human resources management, culture, to marketing, family businesses and national development.

The book is accompanied by an instructor's manual with PowerPoint presentation slides, and a test bank with true or false, multiple choice, and critical thinking questions.

The unique features of the book are:

- the opening and closing cases in each chapter with one OR MORE thought provoking question for each case;
- the answers in some chapters of people interviewed from the government, business, and other sectors;
- the reference on women issues and their contribution to international business issues in some chapters;
- the global approach found throughout the book;

- the last four chapters which address international business issues in various geographic areas of the world; and
- the length of the book which consists of sixteen chapters.

This book is an anthology of chapters written by a number of experts in their respective fields and we are sincerely grateful and thankful for their contribution. These colleagues are:

- Dr George Baourakis of the Mediterranean Agronomic Institute of Chania, Crete-Greece, responsible for Chapters 8 and 9.
- Dr John L. Haverty of Saint Joseph's University, Philadelphia, USA, responsible for Chapter 10.
- Professor Harry Kogetsidis of Intercollege, Nicosia, Cyprus, responsible for Chapter 11.
- Dr Marie-France Waxin of the American University of Sharjah, Sharjah, UAE, responsible for Chapter 12.
- Dr Alkis Thrasou of Intercollege, Nicosia, Cyprus, responsible for Chapter 13.
- Dr Rumen Gechev of the University of National and World Economy, Sofia, Bulgaria, responsible for Chapters 14 and 16.
- Professor Christina Ioannou of Intercollege, Nicosia, Cyprus, responsible for Chapter 15.

Our gratitude goes to the following people who have contributed their case studies: Dr Marie-France Waxin; Dr Robert Bateman; Dr Donelda McKechnie; Dr James Grant; Dr Zeinab Karake-Shalhoub; and Ms Mona Fahmi all of the American University of Sharjah, UAE; Dr Gary Kritz of Seton Hall University and Dr Samuel Wathen of Coastal Carolina University, USA and Dr Virginia Bodolica of the Université du Québec en Outaouais, Canada.

Special thanks go to Mr Anthos Shiekkeris and Dr Maria Michaelidis, both at Intercollege, Nicosia, Cyprus, for their contributions in earlier versions of Chapter 12.

Special thanks also go to Michael G. Papaioannou of International Capital Markets Department, International Monetary Fund, who has endorsed our book.

Furthermore, our sincere and honest appreciation goes to Maggie Smith and Dennis McGonagle, of the Elsevier Group, for their patience, guidance and, above all, professionalism throughout this project. Our thanks go to all the anonymous reviewers of the manuscript and all the interviewees who have been very willing to provide us with useful information for inclusion in some chapters. Finally, we would also like to thank the project manager,

Kalpalathika Rajan, and the copy editor Abiramavalli R. of Integra Software Services, India for the successful completion of this book.

Dr Marios I. Katsioloudes,
American University of Sharjah, UAE
Dr Spyros Hadjidakis,
Intercollege, Nicosia-Cyprus
June 2006

Part A: Chapters

1

Challenges in International Business

Objectives

Through this chapter, the student will be exposed to:

- Today's world of business
- What is international business
- Why companies go international
- The participants in international business
- The global perspective of international business
- Why study international business
- The framework of this textbook.

Opening Case

FAMAGUSTA, Inc. in Manila, Philippines

FAMAGUSTA, Inc. (a fictitious name) is a large, non-US-based multinational corporation (MNC) that has set up its new office in Manila. With the help of a few previous connections and more than a little good fortune, you land your first contract within a relatively short period of time. The job involves providing professional consultation and technical support on a joint venture project with a local corporation. You will be working in the offices of the Philippine company, scoping and designing the project, managing the implementation phase, and working with their domestic personnel to get the job done. Your contract specifies an interim review after the design phase is completed, but top management assures you that it is just a formality—they definitely want to work with you for the whole project. You review the facilities and résumés of both management and technical staff and everything looks fine. No problem, you tell yourself as you tackle the project enthusiastically.

At first everything is great. You are given your own office and are told by the chief executive officer (CEO) to work directly with the executive vice president (EVP) for the division; he seems highly supportive and tells you to call on him at any time for whatever you might need. Although the working environment is relaxed by American and European standards, the staff works long hours and everyone is unfailingly polite. You soon find yourself enjoying the change of pace and the congenial aspects of the Filipino workplace.

Until, that is, you become aware that the project is slowly but surely falling behind schedule. Being the accountable party, you know it is up to you to address the problem. After some quiet background investigation, you pinpoint the source of the problem: the manager of a mission-critical department who appears to be horrendously incompetent. An old lady nearing retirement by the name of Mrs. Santos has been with the company her entire career. The analysis shows clearly that the problem lies in her use of outdated methods and her resistance to certain innovative aspects of the project. Although your interactions with her have always been courteous, you begin to wonder if she's trying to sabotage your efforts.

In an effort to attack the problem you approach the EVP to discuss the issue. You come in well prepared for the meeting, with hard copy documentation tracing the bottleneck to Mrs. Santos's inept management. Thus, you are a bit surprised that he doesn't seem to share your concern for the issue. Although he listens intently to what you have to say, he gives oblique answers to your questions and seems to be avoiding the issue. But you know better than to press too hard and quickly back off. At the end of the meeting, which was much shorter than you anticipated, it is clear that he thinks you can work around Mrs. Santos and that he does not share your concern about the problem.

You do your best to keep the project on track, and keep looking the other way. However, the problems continue to pile up and get even worse over the next few weeks. Murphy seems to lurk around every corner, and every time you have to put out a fire the origin seems to lie in the same place: the inefficient department head. You have lunch with a couple of her key employees and pump them for information. Although what they tell you about operational matters confirms what you already know about inefficiency, it also becomes clear that they see no way of changing dear old Mrs. Santos's way of doing things. When asked hard questions about project objectives and what could be done to ease the bottlenecks, they shrug their shoulders and laugh in a nervous, almost incongruous fashion.

Finally, at a key staff meeting just before you must file your interim report, the issue comes to a head. The EVP is there, but primarily as an observer—as the big shot expat consultant, you are chairing the meeting. You present the project as it has proceeded to date, doing your best to paint a positive picture, even going out of your way to compliment some of the technical staff who have done outstanding jobs. But you feel that you can no longer avoid the hard fact that important deadlines are about to be missed. It also seems clear to you that 90 percent of the problems lie in that one particular department.

When Mrs. Santos takes the floor to summarize her department's work on the project, however, she paints a glowing picture. Things are really moving along, targets are being met and exceeded, everything is copacetic indeed. You can't believe what you are hearing! You know that everyone in the room must know that she is basically covering up, and can't help being upset in that she is downright contradicting what you have been saying and trying to bring to everyone's attention.

Responding to your gut instincts and knowing for a fact that the data support your position, you take a deep breath before asking a series of hard questions that leave Mrs. Santos with very little wriggle room. She gives evasive answers, and everyone else around the table suddenly becomes quite uncomfortable. People are shifting around in their chairs and looking out of the windows—a drastic shift in mood. You immediately realize that you have made a major blunder, but it's too late to back off, so you press ahead. After her third circular and evasive answer, the EVP clears his throat rather loudly, then interrupts: "Perhaps we should move on with the meeting. These little details can be worked out later."

Within a month the project has fallen completely off track, precisely as you would have predicted. However, rather than taking action to put things back on track, top management decides to rethink the whole project, including their collaboration with the outside consultant (that being you). At the recommendation of the EVP, they pull the plug entirely after the design phase. They thank you for doing such a good job on the project design, reassure you they are anxious to work with you in the future, and cancel the project as it was their contractual prerogative to do. In parting, the EVP tells you: "Our staff feels that they can really carry this out on our own, and management agrees. Your work has been first-rate, but you know things can change. Call me if you ever need a reference."

Note: The case is strategically placed in this chapter for the simple reason of sensitizing and exposing the readers very early on to international business with the cultural perspective in mind. More in-depth discussion on culture will take place in Chapter 2.

Question: What do you think really happened in this case? What is Mrs. Santos's position in the company? What issues of international business are found in this case? What do you think the consultant should have done?

Source: The case was compiled by the author.

Today's World of Business

International business differs from domestic business by degrees. Although laws, cultures, and economic conditions differ within countries, such differences are usually less marked than those among countries. Even though there are limitations on the movement of goods and services and the resources to produce them within countries, these limitations are usually less pronounced within than among countries.

Most countries vary internally, causing companies to alter their business practices from one region to another. Take the United States, where taxes and legal requirements differ among states and municipalities. This is why many companies place their headquarters in the business-friendly state of Delaware. Certain products also enjoy greater acceptance in some areas than in others, as seen in the higher per capita demand for bottled water in California than in the Midwest. Some tastes differ regionally as well; for instance, people in parts of the Midwest prefer white-looking dressed chickens to the yellow-looking ones that people prefer elsewhere. In some areas of the United States, there are non-English-language radio and television programs. And because income levels vary, purchasing power is higher in some areas than in others.

But some countries have much greater internal variation than do others. Geographic and economic barriers in some countries can inhibit people's movements from one region to another, thus limiting their personal interactions. Decentralized laws and government programs may increase regional separation. Linguistic, religious, and ethnic differences within a country usually preclude the fusing of the population into a homogeneous state, which means that business cannot be conducted in the same way throughout the country. For example, for all the reasons just given, India is a much more diverse country to do business in than Denmark.

Despite all the differences among regions within countries, this diversity is small when compared to the differences among countries. To successfully conduct business abroad, companies must often adopt practices other than what they are accustomed to domestically. Differences in the legal—political, economic, and cultural environment all may necessitate a company's altering every type of business activity, from production and accounting to finance and marketing.

Legal–Political Environment. Despite some differences in regional or municipal laws within a country, overriding national laws link a whole country together. Yes, different countries adhere to various treaties; still, every country in the world is a sovereign entity with its own laws and political systems. These laws dictate what businesses can exist, how they can be organized, their tax liabilities, the minimum wages they must pay to employees, how much they may cooperate with competitors, and how they must price their goods and services.

Companies that do business internationally are subject to the laws of each country in which they operate. When laws differ greatly from those at home, a firm may encounter substantial operating problems abroad. For example, Blockbuster Video closed down its German operations because of the strict laws prohibiting retail establishments from being open Saturday afternoons, Sundays, and all evenings. These limitations reduced the company's ability to generate sufficient revenue through impulse rentals from people who do not plan well ahead to view a videotape.[1]

Political relationships between countries also influence what companies can do internationally. For example, China forced Coca-Cola to drop a multi-million-dollar advertising campaign because the ads used the voice of a Taiwanese singer who publicly supports Taiwanese independence.[2]

In some areas of the world most laws are codified. In others, such as the United Kingdom, there is a common law heritage in which precedents set the rules. In still other countries, like Saudi Arabia, a state religion dictates what is legal. Political systems range across a spectrum from dictatorships to democracies, and democracies vary substantially. For instance, Switzerland and the United States are both frequently held to be models of democracy. In the former, however, the general population votes on most legislation, whereas in the latter, representatives enact legislation. In terms of business operations, companies wishing to have specific legislation enacted may thus lobby public officials in the United States but must influence general public opinion in Switzerland.

Economic Environment. People in rich countries, such as the United States, Canada, and Sweden, earn on average about 100 times more than those in such poor countries as Burkina Faso, Bangladesh, and the Democratic Republic of Congo. In fact, the average income in most of the countries is very low. A number of conditions correlate substantially with countries' economic levels, even though some countries are exceptions.

Generally, poor countries have smaller markets on a per capita basis, less educated populations, higher unemployment or underemployment, poor health conditions, greater supply problems, higher political risk, and more foreign exchange problems. We shall offer just a few examples of how these conditions affect international business.

In terms of market size on a per capita basis, the United States has almost 100 times as many cars as India has, despite India's much larger population. Where much of a nation's population is uneducated (e.g., in Bhutan, Chad, and Ethiopia, less than 25 percent of children between the ages of 6 and 17 are enrolled in school), companies often have to respond by providing workers with additional training, using more supervisors, depending more on the transfer of management personnel from abroad, and simplifying work-related duties. They may also have to alter and simplify instructions for the use of products, and they may have very little market for certain types of products, such as books and magazines. The life expectancy in the richer countries is more than 70 years whereas that in poorer countries is less than 50 years. Among the reasons for the difference are inadequate access to food, nutritional education, and medical care. The situation in poor countries affects companies' productivity through employee work absences and lack of stamina on the job. Inadequate infrastructure (such as roads, ports, electrical power, and communications facilities) in poor countries causes supply problems. The problems occur because countries sell too little abroad to earn enough to buy all the needed machinery and replacement parts abroad. In turn, companies therein incur added production costs because of production downtime and the longer time required to transport their supplies and finished goods. Because of poverty in poorer countries, there is a greater incidence of civil disorder and a greater tendency for governments to treat foreign firms as scapegoats for the economic ills their citizens face. Finally, poorer countries are more apt than richer countries to depend on primary goods, such as raw materials and agricultural products, to earn income abroad. The prices of these primary products have not risen as rapidly as have prices of services and manufactured products. Further, the prices tend to fluctuate greatly from one year to another because of climatic conditions and business cycles. Exporters to these economies thus face variations from year to year in their ability to sell and receive payment for goods and services.

Cultural Environment. "Culture" refers to the specific learned norms of society based on attitudes, values, beliefs, and frameworks for processing information and tasks. These norms vary from one country to another, and they are reflected in attitudes toward certain products, advertising, work and relationships among the people of a given society. For example, different countries have different norms regarding the extent of worker participation and decision making within their organizations. Cultural differences are also reflected in the acceptance of certain products. Pork products, for instance, have almost no acceptance in predominantly Muslim societies, nor do meats of any kind in predominantly Hindu societies. Cold cereals are extremely popular in Ireland, but not in Spain.

It is interesting to note the international trade activity with the major importers and exporters as evidence of intense international business

Exhibit 1.1

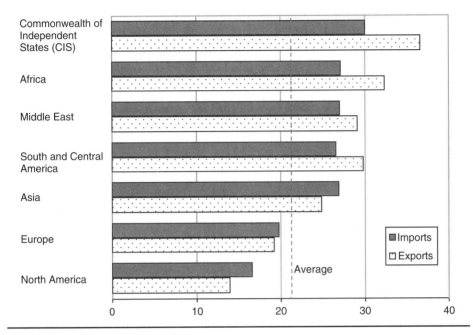

World Merchandise Trade by Region, 2004 (Annual Percentage Change in Dollar Values)

Source: http://www.wto.org/english/res_e/statis_e/its2005_e/chp_0_e/ch5.xls.

transactions among countries. Exhibit 1.1 indicates the leading exporters and importers in world merchandize trade by region.

More on culture and its impact on international business will be addressed in Chapter 2. The section below addresses definitional issues of international business.

What is International Business?

We should ask ourselves, what is international business? International business is all commercial transactions—private and governmental—between two or more countries. Private companies undertake such transactions for profit; governments may or may not do the same in their transactions. These transactions include sales, investments, and transportation. Why should we study international business? A simple answer is that international business comprises a large and growing portion of the world's total business. Today, global events and competition affect almost all companies—large or small—because most sell output to and secure supplies from foreign countries. Many companies also compete against products and services that come from abroad. A more complex answer is that a company operating in the international business field will engage in modes of business, such as exporting and importing, that differ from those it is accustomed to on a domestic level.

Another definition of "international business" refers to profit-related activities conducted across national boundaries. The environment for those business activities within which the international manager functions is shaped by major developments in the world. Such developments are globalization; the various regional trading blocs such as the European Union with the introduction of the Euro as its legally tradable currency; the North American Free Trade Agreement (NAFTA); the Commonwealth of Independent States (CIS); information technology; workforce diversity; the status of the emerging economies of China, India, Mexico and Brazil; and the unstable political situation in various parts of the world, such as the one in Afghanistan, the Middle East, and in various parts of Africa.

Furthermore, an international business is any firm that engages in international trade or investment. A firm does not have to become a multinational enterprise, investing directly in operations in other countries, to engage in international business, although multinational enterprises are international businesses. All a firm has to do is export or import products from other countries. As the world shifts toward a truly integrated global economy, more firms, both large and small, are becoming international businesses. What does this shift toward a global economy mean for managers within an international business?

As their organizations increasingly engage in cross-border trade and investment, it means managers need to recognize that the task of managing an international business differs from that of managing a purely domestic business in many ways. One such fundamental difference is the fact that countries are different. As already mentioned, countries differ in their culture, political systems, economic systems, legal systems, and levels of economic development. Despite all the talk about the emerging "global village" and despite the trend toward globalization of markets and production, these fundamental differences still remain and are very profound and enduring.

Differences between countries require that an international business vary its practices country by country. Marketing a product in Great Britain may require a different approach than marketing the same product in China; managing Italian workers might require different skills than managing Japanese workers; maintaining close relations with a particular level of government may be very important in Greece and irrelevant in Germany; the business strategy pursued in Sweden might not work in Singapore; and so on. Managers in an international business must not only be sensitive to these differences, but they must also adopt the appropriate policies and strategies for coping with them. The Opening Case reviews Famagusta, Inc.'s business in Manila, Philippines, and shows what happens when managers do not consider country differences.

Another way in which international business differs from domestic business is the greater complexity of managing an international business. In addition to confronting the problems that arise from the differences between countries, a manager in an international business confronts a range of issues that the manager in a domestic business never encounters. An international business must decide where in the world to site its production activities to minimize costs and to maximize the value added. Then it must decide how best to coordinate and control its globally dispersed production activities. An international business also must decide which foreign markets to enter and which to avoid. It also must choose the appropriate mode for entering a particular foreign country. A series of questions should be asked: Is it best to export its product to the foreign country? Should the firm allow a local company to produce its product under license in that country? Should the firm enter into a joint venture with a local firm to produce its product in that country? Or should the firm set up a wholly owned subsidiary to serve the market in that country? Obviously, the choice of entry mode is critical, because it has major implications for the long-term health of the firm.

Conducting business transactions across national borders requires an understanding of the rules governing the international trading and investment system. Managers in an international business must also deal with government restrictions on international trade and investment. They must find ways to work within the limits imposed by specific governmental interventions. Furthermore, even though many governments are nominally committed to free trade, they often intervene to regulate cross-border trade and investment. Managers within international business must develop strategies and policies for dealing with such interventions.

Cross-border transactions also require that money be converted from the firm's home currency into a foreign currency and vice versa. Since currency exchange rates vary in response to changing economic conditions, an international business must develop policies for dealing with exchange rate movements. A firm that adopts a wrong policy can lose large amounts of money, while a firm that adopts the right policy can increase the profitability of its international transactions.

Overall, managing an international business is different from managing a purely domestic business for the following reasons:

1. Because of different cultural, political, economic, and legal systems, and so on, countries are different.
2. The issues at the international business level are more complex than those at the domestic level.

3. International business transactions involve converting money into different currencies.
4. International business must find ways to work within the limitations and constraints imposed by the various governments.

When a company operates internationally, it has to face foreign conditions in addition to facing domestic ones, making its external environment more diverse. Physical, societal, and competitive trends in the external environment influence a firm's operations. Even if you never have direct international business responsibilities, you may find it useful to understand some of its complexities. Companies' international operations and governmental regulation of business affect company profits, employment security and wages, consumer prices, and national security. A better understanding of international business may assist you in making more informed decisions, such as where you want to work and what governmental policies you want to support.

Why Do Companies Go International?

When operating internationally, a company should consider its mission (what it will seek to do and become over the years; what is the purpose of the company's existence?); its objectives (what is the company trying to accomplish according to its mission?); and strategies (means to achieve its objectives). These concepts will be further addressed in Chapter 7.

Companies engage in international business in order to:

- Minimize competitive risk
- Acquire resources
- Expand sales
- Diversify sources of sales and supplies.

Minimize Competitive Risk. Many companies enter into international business for defensive reasons. They want to protect themselves against domestic companies that might gain advantages in foreign markets, and then use that advantage in the domestic market. Company X may fear that Company Y will generate large profits from a foreign market if left alone to serve that market. Company Y then might use those profits to improve its competitive position domestically. Thus, companies, being afraid of such activities, may enter a foreign market primarily to prevent a competitor from gaining advantages.

Acquire Resources. Manufacturers and distributors seek out products, services, and components produced in foreign countries. They also look for foreign capital, technologies, and information they can use at home. Sometimes they do this to reduce their costs. For example, Nike relies on cheap manufacturing operations in Southeast Asian countries to make its products. Acquiring resources may enable a company to improve its product quality and differentiate itself from competitors, potentially increasing market share and profits. Although a company may initially use domestic resources to expand abroad, once the foreign operations are in place, the foreign earnings may then serve as resources for domestic operations; for example, McDonald's used the strong financial performance of its foreign operations to invest in more resources for domestic growth.[3]

Expand Sales. By reaching international markets, companies increase their sales faster than when they focus on a single market, that being the domestic one. These sales depend on the consumers' interest in the product and their ability to purchase the product.

Ordinarily, higher sales mean higher profits and that in itself is a motive for companies to go international. Many of the world's largest companies derive over half their sales from outside their home country, such as BASF of Germany, Electrolux of Sweden, Gillette and Coca-Cola of the United States, Michelin of France, Philips of the Netherlands, Sony of Japan, Nestle of Switzerland.

Diversify Sources of Sales and Supplies. In order to minimize fluctuations in sales and profits, many companies may look for foreign markets to take advantage of the business cycle differences among countries. Sales increase in a country that is expanding economically and decrease in another that is in recession. Consequently, companies may be able to avoid the full impact of price fluctuations or shortages in any one country, by obtaining supplies of the same product or component from different countries.

In addition to the aforementioned reasons for international business, there are some additional factors that have contributed to the increased international business activities in more recent years. These factors, which are sometimes interrelated, are (1) increase in global competition; (2) the development and expansion of technology; (3) the liberalization of cross-border movements; and (4) the development of supporting services.

Increase in Global Competition. Many companies, of any size, decide to compete internationally because new products quickly become known globally; companies can produce in different countries; and the suppliers, competitors, and customers of domestic companies have become international as well.

Development and Expansion of Technology. Even in 1970, there was no Internet as it is known today, no commercial transatlantic supersonic travel, no faxing or e-mailing, no teleconferencing or overseas direct-dial telephone service, and no sales over the Internet (electronic commerce; e-commerce sales). All these technological advancements have enabled more and more companies to be exposed to an increased number of international business activities. Transportation and communication costs are more conducive for international business operations.

Liberalization of Cross-Border Movements. Lower governmental barriers to the movement of goods, services, and resources (financial, human, informational, physical) enable companies to take better advantage of international opportunities. The European Union, the NAFTA, and other regional economic blocs throughout the world provide fewer restrictions on cross-border movements than they did a decade or two ago.

Development of Supporting Services. Companies and governments of various countries, alike, have developed services that ease international business. Mail, which is a government monopoly, could be transferred by an airline other than that of the country of origin, with a stamp of the country of origin, and could go through many different countries before it could reach its final destination. Also, banking institutions have developed efficient and effective means for companies to receive payment for their foreign sales. The banks can assist in the payment of any currency through various international business transactions, upon the receipt of goods and/or services.

It is interesting to note how one international businessman replied to the question: "Why do you engage in international business?" His answer appears to be like a mission statement that indirectly addresses the issue as to why they engage in international business. His response appears in the box below:

> Arriva Plc has a vision to become the leading provider of public transport services in Europe, as the mainland European market is open to competition. We believe that we can assist this process and provide added value to transport authorities who are facing competitive tendering for the first time. This can be achieved by the application of best practice and avoidance of "worst mistakes," which we have seen in different countries, and this provides an exciting opportunity to help to develop the opening of European markets in a structured manner. Arriva also recognises and fully respects the cultural diversity of different countries and relishes the international challenge of creating value for our customers and shareholders alike.
>
> *Source: David Martin, Managing Director, International Arriva Passenger Services, United Kingdom; Interview, April 4, 2002.*

Dr. Robert Moran, a well-known academic of international management, professor emeritus at Thunderbird, the Graduate International Management School, in Phoenix, Arizona, USA, responded in the following manner:

Companies go international to cross their cultural boundaries and grow in every aspect possible. Of course these companies go abroad to experience higher sales and profits, but they should be ready and well prepared to face all types of other challenges, such as socio-cultural issues. To me, this is the biggest challenge of all. If these international firms learn how to cope with the culture of that particular foreign market, they will have a higher probability of succeeding in that market, and they will be respected globally.

Source: Dr. Robert Moran, Professor of International Management, Emeritus, Thunderbird, the Graduate International Management School, Arizona, USA; Interview, April 20, 2002.

The Participants in International Business

Companies of all types and sizes, and in all types of industries, enter into international business transactions. Manufacturing companies, service companies, and retail companies all search for customers outside their countries. As mentioned earlier, an international company is a business that engages directly in any form of international business activity such as exporting, importing, or international production. No matter what the nature of the international business transactions, there are different types of international companies, and we will take a closer look at them in the following pages.

Small companies are becoming increasingly active in international trade and investment. Companies are having quicker turnaround times with regard to exports and are growing faster as a result of increased international business activities.[4] Because of improved technological advancements; electronic distribution is a cheap and effective method for many small businesses. Some small businesses are reaching out to customers exclusively through the World Wide Web (WWW). Despite all these technological amenities, many small businesses that are capable of exporting have not yet begun to do so. There are certain myths that keep small businesses from exporting: there is no export financing available for small businesses; small businesses have no place to turn for export advice; the licensing requirements needed for exporting are not worth the effort; only large companies can export successfully; small businesses do not have the right people to assist in exporting; small businesses find it difficult to research and identify international markets; and so on.

Despite all these, small businesses play a vital role in their national economies—through employment, new job creation, development of new products and services, and international operations, typically exporting. Although many small businesses are affected by globalism only to the extent they face competing products from abroad, potential offshore customers, thanks to the burgeoning number of trade shows, are welcoming an increasing number of entrepreneurs and federal and state export initiatives. Furthermore, one quarter of all exporting companies employ fewer than 100 people. As small companies expand abroad, international management skills become an important asset to managers other than those in large corporations. The problem is that most small businesses cannot afford to create an international division, and many entrepreneurs are too independent to relinquish power to someone else. But it is very time-consuming for an entrepreneur to learn about trade regulations and business practices in other countries, or to travel abroad to negotiate and finalize a business deal. They are often unable to take the time away from the domestic business and so may turn to export management companies to handle all the details.

Because most small businesses are limited by their resources to exporting, they are pursuing other strategies. One of these strategies is franchising, which is ideal for small businesses because of the low investment needed in capital and personnel to establish franchise outlets.

Multinational corporations vary in size, being as small as a security firm or as large as a car manufacturer. The units of large international companies can function either rather independently or as parts of a tightly integrated global network. Independent operations tend to have a good understanding of local culture and are often able to adapt quickly to changing local market conditions. On the other hand, firms that operate as global networks often find it easier to respond to changing conditions by shifting production, marketing, and other activities among national units. Depending on the type of business, either structure can be appropriate.

The multinational corporations' economic and political muscle makes them highly visible. Large companies generate a large number of jobs, greater investment, and significant tax revenue for the areas in which they operate. On the other hand, the downsizing of large international companies, or the closing of factories throughout the world, makes these companies visible as well. Furthermore, these companies' transactions involve large amounts of money. For example, in 1998, Daimler-Benz of Germany announced a merger with Chrysler of the United States, which was valued at $40 billion; in the same year, Exxon and Mobil, two global petroleum companies, created a merger worth $86 billion.

Around the world, MNCs are already giants and growing even more gigantic. These big, traditional manufacturing enterprises, with their long planning horizons, are leading the drive toward globalization. Increasingly, too, we are seeing service organizations go global—financial institutions such as Citigroup, retailers such as Wal-Mart, telecommunications companies such as MCI-WorldCom. Leadership in global trends comes from the close involvement of these companies in cross-boundary relationships with suppliers, customers, and venture partners.[5] Conglomerates such as Thailand's Chraroen Pokphand, with revenues of $7.6 billion, have chosen to go global through alliances with foreign players such as Nynex in the telecom market and Wal-Mart in retailing. Some American MNCs (e.g., Exxon Mobil Oil and Hoover) earn most of their sales outside the United States; Daimler-Chrysler, IBM, and Coca-Cola earn more than half their profits outside the United States. In addition, many nonprofit organizations—called multinational enterprises (MNEs)—such as the Red Cross in Switzerland and the Roman Catholic Church in Italy operate globally.

Because many MNCs have become complex conglomerates, it is difficult to identify which companies are the parents of which, or which companies own various other companies or properties around the world. Although American MNCs own many foreign firms, a significant number of large American firms are owned by foreign MNCs. Many of these foreign-owned firms have familiar American names, so they are assumed to be American firms—for example, RCA is owned by Thompson SA of France; Vaseline is owned by Unilever, a UK–Dutch company; Tropicana Orange Juice is owned by Canada's Seagram; and Green Giant is owned by Grand Metropolitan in England.

Exhibit 1.2 shows the first 50 out of the total of the Fortune Global 500 for 2005, as a sample of MNCs. The exhibit is limited to the first 50 MNCs. These MNCs are manufacturers, service providers, and/or distributors, and their location varies from being in the United States, Germany, the United Kingdom, Japan, the Netherlands, France, Italy, Switzerland, China, etc. They are found everywhere in the world and most of them are global in nature.

Exhibit 1.2

Fortune Global 500 (2005)

Rank	Company	Revenues ($ millions)	Profits ($ millions)
1	Wal-Mart Stores	287,989.0	10,267.0
2	BP	285,059.0	15,371.0
3	Exxon Mobil	270,772.0	25,330.0
4	Royal Dutch/Shell Group	268,690.0	18,183.0
5	General Motors	193,517.0	2,805.0
6	DaimlerChrysler	176,687.5	3,067.1
7	Toyota Motor	172,616.3	10,898.2
8	Ford Motor	172,233.0	3,487.0
9	General Electric	152,866.0	16,819.0
10	Total	152,609.5	11,955.0

(continued)

Exhibit 1.2 *continued*

Rank	Company	Revenues ($ millions)	Profits ($ millions)
11	ChevronTexaco	147,967.0	13,328.0
12	ConocoPhillips	121,663.0	8,129.0
13	AXA	121,606.3	3,133.0
14	Allianz	118,937.2	2,735.0
15	Volkswagen	110,648.7	842.0
16	Citigroup	108,276.0	17,046.0
17	ING Group	105,886.4	7,422.8
18	Nippon Telegraph & Telephone	100,545.3	6,608.0
19	American Intl. Group	97,987.0	9,731.0
20	Intl. Business Machines	96,293.0	8,430.0
21	Siemens	91,493.2	4,144.6
22	Carrefour	90,381.7	1,724.8
23	Hitachi	83,993.9	479.2
24	Assicurazioni Generali	83,267.6	1,635.1
25	Matsushita Electric Industrial	81,077.7	544.1
26	McKesson	80,514.6	−156.7
27	Honda Motor	80,486.6	4,523.9
28	Hewlett-Packard	79,905.0	3,497.0
29	Nissan Motor	79,799.6	4,766.6
30	Fortis	75,518.1	4,177.2
31	Sinopec	75,076.7	1,268.9
32	Berkshire Hathaway	74,382.0	7,308.0
33	ENI	74,227.7	9,047.1
34	Home Depot	73,094.0	5,001.0
35	Aviva	73,025.2	1,936.8
36	HSBC Holdings	72,550.0	11,840.0
37	Deutsche Telekom	71,988.9	5,763.6
38	Verizon Communications	71,563.3	7,830.7
39	Samsung Electronics	71,555.9	9,419.5
40	State Grid	71,290.2	694.0
41	Peugeot	70,641.9	1,687.8
42	Metro	70,159.3	1,028.6
43	Nestlé	69,825.7	5,405.4
44	US. Postal Service	68,996.0	3,065.0
45	BNP Paribas	68,654.4	5,805.9
46	China National Petroleum	67,723.8	8,757.1
47	Sony	66,618.0	1,524.5
48	Cardinal Health	65,130.6	1,474.5
49	Royal Ahold	64,675.6	−542.3
50	Altria Group	64,440.0	9,416.0

Source: http://money.cnn.com/magazines/fortune/global50.

The Global Perspective of International Business

People around the globe are more connected to each other than ever before. Information and money too flow more quickly than ever before. Goods and services produced in one part of the world are increasingly available in all parts of the world. International communication is commonplace. This phenomenon has been titled "globalization." The era of globalization is fast becoming the preferred term for describing the current times.

Because we are thoughtful people concerned about world affairs, our job is to pick up "globalization," examine it from all sides, dissect it, figure out what makes it tick, and then nurture and promote the good parts and mitigate or slow down the bad parts. Globalization is much like fire. Fire itself is neither good nor bad. Used properly, it can cook food, sterilize equipment, form iron, and heat our homes. Used carelessly, fire can destroy lives, towns, and forests in an instant. Globalization can be incredibly empowering and incredibly coercive. It can democratize opportunity and democratize panic. It makes the whales bigger and the minnows stronger. It leaves you behind faster and faster, and it catches up on you faster and faster. While it is homogenizing cultures, it is also enabling people to share their unique individuality farther and wider.

Globalization has dangers and an ugly dark side. But it can also bring tremendous opportunities and benefits. Just as capitalism requires a network of governing systems to keep it from devouring societies, globalization requires vigilance and the rule of law.

The term "globalization" was first coined in the 1980s, but the concept stretches back decades, even centuries, if you count the trading empires built by Spain, Portugal, Britain, and Holland. Some would say the world was as globalized 100 years ago as it is today, with international trade and migration. But the 1930s depression put paid to that. Nation-states drew back into their shells on realizing that international markets could deliver untold misery in the form of poverty and unemployment. The resolve of Western states to build and strengthen international ties in the aftermath of World War II laid the groundwork for today's globalization. It has brought diminishing national borders and the fusing of individual markets. The fall of protectionist barriers has stimulated free movement of capital and paved the way for companies to set up several bases around the world. The rise of the Internet and recent advances in telecommunications have boosted the already surging train. For consumers and avowed capitalists, this is largely a good thing. Vigorous trade has made for greater spending, rising living standards, and a growth in international travel. And that is just the tip of it. Supporters of globalization say it has promoted information exchange, led to a greater understanding of other cultures, and allowed democracy to triumph over autocracy.[6]

On the other hand, critics say the West's gain has been at the expense of developing countries. The already meager share of the global income of the poorest people in the world has dropped from 2.3 to 1.4 percent in the last 10–15 years. But even in the developed world, not everyone has been a winner. The freedoms granted by globalization are leading to increased insecurity in the workplace. Manual workers in particular are under threat as companies shift their production lines overseas to low-wage economies. National cultures and identities are also under threat, thanks to the spread of satellite TV, international media networks, and increased personal travel. In French cinemas, around 70 percent of filmgoers watch Hollywood movies. At the heart of their concern is the fact that huge transnational companies are becoming more powerful and influential than democratically elected governments, putting shareholder interests above those of communities and even customers.

Ecological campaigners say corporations are disregarding the environment in the stampede for megaprofits and marketplace supremacy. Human rights groups say corporate power is restricting individual freedom. Even business people behind small firms have sympathy for the movement, afraid as they are that global economies of scale will put them out of work. But the mere fact that the debate can take place simultaneously across countries and continents may well show that the global village is already here.

Just as the Depression, the cold war era, the Space Age, and the Roaring Twenties are used to describe particular periods of history, globalization describes the political, economic, and cultural atmosphere of today. Although some people think of globalization as primarily a synonym for global business, it is much more than that. The same forces that allow businesses to operate as if national borders did not exist also allow social activists, labor organizers, journalists, academics, and many others to work on a global stage.

Globalization refers to the shift toward a more integrated and interdependent world economy. Globalization has two main components: the globalization of markets and the globalization of production. Globalization is not a phenomenon. It is not just some passing trend. Today it is an overarching international system shaping the domestic politics and foreign relations of virtually every country, and we need to understand it as such.

The globalization of markets refers to the merging of historically distinct and separate markets into one huge global marketplace. It has been argued for some time that the tastes and preferences of consumers in different nations are beginning to converge on some global norm, thereby helping to create a global market.[7] The global acceptance of consumer products such as Citicorp credit cards, Coca-Cola, Levi's jeans, Sony Walkmans, Nintendo game players, and McDonald's hamburgers are all considered as prototypical examples of this trend. By offering a standardized product worldwide, they are helping to create a global market.

In many global markets, the same firms frequently confront each other as competitors in nation after nation. Coca-Cola's rivalry with Pepsi is a global one, as are rivalries between Ford and Toyota, Boeing and Airbus, Caterpillar and Komatsu, and Nintendo and Sega. As rivals follow rivals around the world, these multinational enterprises emerge as an important driver of the convergence of different national markets into a single, and increasingly homogenous, global marketplace.

The globalization of production refers to the tendency among firms to source goods and services from locations around the globe to take advantage of national differences in the cost and quality of factors of production (such as labor, energy, land, and capital). By doing so, companies hope to lower their overall cost structure and/or improve the quality or functionality of their product offering, thereby allowing them to compete more effectively. Consider the Boeing Company's latest commercial jet airliner, the 777. The 777 contains 132,500 major component parts that are produced around the world by 545 suppliers. Eight Japanese suppliers make parts for the fuselage, doors, and wings; a supplier in Singapore makes the doors for the nose landing gear; three suppliers in Italy manufacture wing flaps; and so on.[8] Part of Boeing's rationale for outsourcing so much production to foreign suppliers is that these suppliers are the best in the world at performing their particular activity. The result of having a global web of suppliers is a better final product, which enhances the chances of Boeing winning a greater share of total orders for aircraft than its global rival, Airbus. Boeing also outsources some production to foreign countries to increase its chance of winning significant orders from airliners based in that country.

> To emphasize on the magnitude of globalization, Exhibit 1.3 indicates the growth in trade by selected regions in the world.

Why Study International Business?

International business affects the activities of every consumer, every worker, company, and government all over the world, whether they are in Cyprus, Iceland, the United States, Australia, Brazil, Nepal, Nigeria, or Russia. Falling trade barriers, increasing competition, and converging consumer tastes are creating global markets for many different products and/or services. Consumers throughout the world enjoy greater product selection at better prices than ever before. Workers often find themselves competing for

Exhibit 1.3

Growth in the Volume of World Merchandise Trade by Selected Region, 2000–2004 (Annual percentage change)

Exports				Imports		
2000–2004	2003	2004		2000–2004	2003	2004
4.0	5.0	9.0	World	4.5	5.5	10.0
0.0	1.0	7.5	North America	3.5	4.5	10.5
6.5	6.0	13.0	South and Central America	1.5	1.5	17.5
3.0	2.0	6.5	Europe	2.5	3.0	6.5
3.0	1.5	6.5	European Union (25)	2.0	2.5	6.0
9.5	13.0	13.0	Commonwealth of Independent States (CIS)	15.0	13.0	15.0
8.0	11.5	14.0	Asia	8.0	13.0	14.5
3.0	5.0	10.5	Japan	3.5	7.0	7.0
6.5	10.5	14.5	Six East Asian traders	4.5	5.5	14.5

Source: http://www.wto.org/english/res_e/statis_e/its2005_e/section1_e/i02.xls.

jobs against workers in another country thousands of miles away. Companies directly involved in international production or marketing confront cultures, political systems, and economic systems that can differ greatly from their own. Local, regional, and national governments work to attract jobs by offering incentives for companies to locate in specific places.

Each of us experiences the result of dozens of international business transactions every day. You wear a Gap T-shirt made in Egypt; you drive your Japanese Toyota that was assembled in Kentucky, USA, with parts manufactured in 120 different countries; you wear Nike shoes assembled in China, with parts coming from many different countries; you drink your coffee at the local café in your hometown in Nicosia, Cyprus, with coffee beans harvested in Brazil or Kenya, etc.

You don't even have to set foot out of your own hometown to be affected by international business. Through e-commerce you can make an international business transaction, for example, purchase a Sony CD player from Tokyo, Japan, by using your credit card, while you are in Moscow, Russia.

As students of international business, you are consumers, one day you might be working for a company that could be involved directly or indirectly in international business and you will definitely be somewhere, whether it is your own country or another country. You definitely know someone who comes from another country, or you know someone who knows someone from another country, and so on and so forth. By studying international business you will become a more intelligent consumer, a more selective applicant/candidate for a job, a more open-minded and knowledgeable "student" of the world around you, and more sensitive toward other cultures.

Some international business trends will continue in the future. One is the pressure on international management to keep pace with the increasing amount of international business and the intensifying competition in the world, both from large trading blocs and from the new developed economies (NDEs). Companies around the world are making serious commitments to meet that competition with considerable international investment.

Another future trend will be the increasingly complex nature of the overall business environment. In a more interdependent world, rapid and unpredictable changes in political, economic, technological, regulatory, and financial variables will provide constant pressures to adapt to compete. To benefit from future opportunities, astute managers will maintain a global orientation; i.e., they will view the world as one giant market where "cooperation and interdependence, not conflict and independence, are prerequisites for survival."[9]

To deal with globalization more effectively, international business people will have to increasingly organize their MNCs in such a way as to see the world as one market, operate as "stateless" corporations, and cross boundaries to secure functions or resources in the most efficient way. Such corporations produce truly multinational products. For example, a sports car is financed in Japan, designed in Italy, and assembled in the United States, Mexico, and France, using advanced electronic components invented in the United States and fabricated in Japan.[10] The term headquarters is becoming immaterial; headquarters now cross boundaries whenever expedient, either to sites where operations dictate or to rootless and scattered but integrated networks of information.[11] The latter form of organization—described as "delayered, downsized, and operating through a network of market-sensitive business units"—will have a great impact on the structure of international business.[12]

International business people/managers play a powerful role in determining the relative competitiveness of various countries in the global arena. Managers' skills and biases, based on their administrative heritage, will subtly influence strategies and resource allocation. They will be faced with "more cultures to understand, more social responsibilities to master, more time pressures to juggle, and more relationships to rethink."[13]

Since we are operating in this global village, more and more international business opportunities will be made available to us; thus we need to be well prepared to face these challenges and take advantage of them.

For all the aforementioned reasons, studying international business becomes a must, more now than ever before.

Furthermore, we find it extremely helpful to present a number of facts that directly or indirectly relate to international business and have an impact on our lives. Some of these facts are given below:[14]

- A third of the world's obese people live in the developing world.
- The United States and Britain have the highest teen pregnancy rates in the developed world.
- China has 44 million missing women.
- Brazil has more Avon ladies than it has members in its armed forces.
- British supermarkets know more about their customers than the British government does.
- One in five of the world's people live on less than $1 a day.
- There are 44 million child laborers in India.
- People in industrialized countries consume between 6 and 7 kg of food additives every year.
- The golfer Tiger Woods is the world's highest paid sportsman. He earns $78 million a year or $148 every second.
- There are 67,000 people employed in the lobbying industry in Washington DC—125 for each elected member of Congress.
- Cars kill two people every minute.
- More people can identify the golden arches of McDonalds than the Christian cross.
- In Kenya, bribery payments make up a third of the average household budget.
- The world's trade in illegal drugs is estimated to be worth around $400 billion—about the same as the world's legal pharmaceutical industry.
- Every day, one in five of the world's population—some 800 million people—go hungry.
- A third of the world's population is at war.
- The world's oil reserves could be exhausted by 2040.
- Eighty-two percent of the world's smokers live in developing countries.
- Some 30 million people in Africa are HIV-positive.
- America spends $10 billion on pornography every year—the same amount it spends on foreign aid.
- There are 27 million slaves in the world today.

Practical Tips

Building a successful business is hard. Building a successful international business is even harder and more challenging. Most of the work will be devoted to finding customers, which will be the firm's toughest job. The firm has to do the following, among others, to become successful internationally.

Identify the Target Market. The first step in developing the firm's strategy is to isolate the best target market for its product and/or service. The firm's sales efforts will be most effective if they focus on a group of prospects with common characteristics and similar problems. The firm's executives should start identifying on paper their ideal customer or client. Developing a list of all the characteristics the firm is expecting to find in good customers or clients and also the characteristics that make the product and/or service valuable to them could be a good idea. Defining the market target in writing is very helpful.

Find the Most Appealing Customer Benefit. Exactly what is the most compelling problem for prospects in the firm's target market? Why is the firm's product and/or service the best solution to their problem? Answering these two questions reveals the customer benefit(s) to stress in the firm's sales approach.

Develop a Motivating Offer. The firm should develop two or three offers that motivate prospects to take buying action immediately. For example, could the firm use a special discounted price offer with a deadline? Are there bonuses the firm can add if prospects order or sign up before the deadline? Could the firm combine both into a "special price plus bonus" offer? The firm should decide which offer on the list is the most powerful and use it in the firm's sales material and/or presentation. Remember, a special offer providing obvious value always increases the firm's volume of business. It is a proven technique to overcome buyer resistance and procrastination. A special offer also provides a logical reason in the buyer's mind to justify what may actually be an impulsive decision to buy now.

Decide How to Publicize the Firm's Business. The firm must decide how to introduce itself to prospects in this market. Will they use classified or display ads in print publications or on the Internet? Will they use direct mail? Is broadcast media, such as radio or TV, appropriate and cost-effective? What networking can the firm participate in locally or on the Internet to draw attention to the firm's business? What other methods of promotion can the firm use? The firm should prioritize each method on its list and develop an action plan with deadlines for implementing them.

Establish a Plan to Promote Customer Loyalty. Decide what the firm will do to cultivate customers so they continue to do business with the firm and give the firm referrals. For example, the firm could call its customers or clients immediately after a transaction and thank them for their business. Ask them if they are pleased with what they have received. If they express satisfaction, then it is the right time to ask for referrals.

All the aforementioned steps could easily apply to the local market of a firm, but they increasingly become more complex when applied in the international arena; thus, the firm's executives should be more sensitive to the peculiarities of the foreign market and the people's preferences and culture of the particular country.

Furthermore, there are more activities an international firm might do to outsell its competition abroad:

Price. Can you offer a lower price? Can you offer a higher price and increase the perceived value of your product? Do you offer easier payment options than your competition?

Packaging. Can you package your product more attractively? Do the colors of your package relate to your product? Can you package your product into a smaller or larger package?

Delivery. Can you offer cheaper shipping? Do you have a high enough profit margin to offer free shipping? Can you ship your products faster?

Benefits. Can you offer more benefits than your competition? Are your benefits stronger? Do you have believable proof that supports your claims?

Quality. Is your product built and tested to last longer than your competition? Can you improve the overall quality of your product?

Performance. Can you make your product faster at solving your customers' problem? Is your product easier to use than your competitors'?

Features. Can you offer more product features than your competition? Do your features support the benefits you offer?

Availability. Is your product always available or do you have to backorder it? Can your product suppliers drop ship to your customers?

Extras. Do you provide free bonuses when your customers buy your product? Are your bonuses more valuable than your competitors' bonuses?

Service. Do you offer your customers free 24-hour customer service? Can you provide free product repair? Does your competition make their customers talk to a machine?

Proof. Can you provide more proof than your competition that your product is reliable? Can you provide stronger testimonials or endorsements?

Again, for all these activities, the international executives should be extremely cautious and sensitive to the idiosyncrasies of the country they are going to conduct business in and respect the preferences and behavior of the people of that particular culture.

Closing Case

Terminalmarkets.com[15]

From Wall Street stockbroker to vegetable importer to Internet entrepreneur, Sinan Talgat has trusted his serendipitous career wherever it has led him.

It all started with a mango farm venture in South America. A friend persuaded Talgat to sell the produce in New York. So he solicited interested buyers at Hunts Point Terminal Produce Cooperative in the Bronx, which is the largest produce marketplace in the world. But El Niño hit Ecuador hard, wiping out the mango crop and Talgat's chances.

Still, the produce market intrigued Talgat. To him, Hunts Point was "like the floor of the New York Stock Exchange." He formed Fortune Fruit Ltd. and imported fresh basil and asparagus. But the stockbroker in him kept wondering: Is there a more efficient way to do this? A way that more closely resembles a securities exchange?

Six months ago, Talgat developed his strategy for Terminalmarkets.com, a fruit and vegetable exchange for the global wholesale produce industry and a culmination of all his past experience. He plans to have the site operating in three months.

A terminal marketplace that handles perishable items including produce, meat, and flowers, it forms the hub in the supply chain that takes the product from the farm to the consumer. Every city has one.

About $18 billion worth of produce currently travels through various terminal markets. No one wholesaler controls more than 1 percent of the market. "The market is completely fragmented and completely inefficient," Talgat says.

New York-based Terminalmarkets.com will serve all the major players in the wholesale produce industry. The site will provide wholesale produce buyers, producers, and truckers with timely and improved price information, reducing all their transaction costs. Wholesalers will sort of act as market makers, and selling will be based on supply and demand.

Buyers will be able to determine all sellers currently carrying the product, request prices from these sellers, compare prices on a single page, examine seller reputations, and complete transactions.

Terminalmarkets.com has already signed up 60 percent of the wholesalers at Hunts Point, which, as a whole, generates almost $2 billion in annual revenues. Talgat reports that wholesalers in the terminal markets in Boston, Philadelphia, Baltimore, and St. Louis have asked to link up with Terminalmarkets.com.

The site will also include an auction site for surplus produce, industry news reports, third-party inspection services, an employment board, and a truck brokerage service. Terminalmarkets.com will generate revenues through transaction fees.

Question: What issues of international business are being addressed in this case? Do you think that Talgat's idea was a good one or not? Why?

Chapter Summary

International business differs from domestic business in many different ways. When a company decides to go international many factors need to be taken into consideration in respect to the other countries' environment, such as the legal–political, economic, and cultural environments. International business is defined as all commercial transactions—private and governmental—between two or more countries. Another definition of international business refers to profit-related activities conducted across national boundaries. This chapter addresses the reasons as to why companies go international: in order to minimize competitive risk; acquire resources; expand sales; and diversify sources of sales and supplies. Furthermore, some additional factors have contributed to the increased international business activities in more recent years, which sometimes are interrelated. These are increase in global competition; the development and expansion of technology; the liberalization of cross-border movements; and the development of supporting services.

The participants in international business vary from small businesses to multinational corporations in this global environment in which people around the globe are more connected to each other than ever before. This globalization of markets refers to the merging of historically distinct and separate markets into one huge global marketplace, which creates the globalization of production. Thus there is a tendency among firms to source goods and services from locations around the globe to take advantage of national differences in the cost and quality of factors of production.

We study international business so that we can become more educated consumers and more knowledgeable about international events that have an impact on us on a daily basis. Since we are operating in this global village, more and more international business opportunities will become available; thus we need to be well prepared to face these challenges and to take advantage of them.

Review and Discussion Questions

1. What is the nature of today's global business environment? How does this environment facilitate international business activities? Provide examples.
2. How do the legal–political, economic, and cultural environmental differences within a country affect a firm's international business transactions? Provide examples.
3. What is international business? How does the management of an international business differ from that of a domestic one? Provide examples with specific firms and countries in mind.

4. Provide the reasons as to why companies go international. What additional factors contribute to the increased international business activities in the recent years?
5. Who are the participants in the international business?
6. Why do small businesses become increasingly active in international trade and investment? Provide examples.
7. How do multinational corporations—MNCs—get involved in international business? How do they differ from small businesses?
8. Define globalization. What are the pros and cons of globalization? Provide examples.
9. What is the globalization of markets? Of production? Provide examples.
10. Why do we study international business? Why has studying it become more important today than ever before?

Endnotes

1. Cacilie Rohwedder, "Blockbuster Hits Eject Button as Stores in Germany See Video-Rental Sales Sag," *Wall Street Journal* (January 16, 1998), p. B9A.
2. James Kynge and Mure Dickie, "Coca-Cola Ad Touches Raw Nerve in China," *Financial Times* (May 25, 2000), p. 14.
3. Richard Tomkins, "McDonald's Makes Skeptics Eat Their Words," *Financial Times* (March 11, 1996), p. 17.
4. "It's a Small World," *Entrepreneur Magazine* (February 1997), p. 39.
5. Rosabeth Moss Kanter, "Need for Global Orientation," *Management International Review* 30 (1990/1991), pp. 5–18.
6. BBC News, "Globalisation: What on Earth Is it About?" (Thursday 14, September, 2000).
7. T. Levitt, "The Globalization of Markets," *Harvard Business Review* (May–June 1983), pp. 92–102.
8. I. Metthee, "Playing a Large Part," *Seattle Post-Intelligencer* (April 9, 1994), p. 13.
9. R. Reich, "The Myth of 'Made in the USA,'" *Wall Street Journal* (July 5, 1991).
10. W. J. Holstein, "The Stateless Corporation," *Business Week* (May 16, 1990), pp. 98–105.
11. C. C. Snow, R. E. Miles, and H. J. Coleman, Jr., "Managing 21st Century Network Organizations," *Organizational Dynamics* (Winter 1992), pp. 5–20.
12. L. Uvhitelle, "US Businesses Link to Mother Country," *New York Times* (May 21, 1989), pp. 1, 12.
13. Rosabeth Moss Kanter, "Transcending Business Boundaries: 12,000 World Managers View Change," *Harvard Business Review* (May–June 1991), pp. 151–164.
14. Jessica Williams, *50 Facts that Should Change the World*, Icon Books, 2004.
15. www.inc.com/going_global/advice/17991.html. Last accessed: April 7, 2002.

The Culture Challenge in International Business

Objectives

Through this chapter, the student will be exposed to:

- What is culture
- The elements of culture
- The study of cultural differences
- Culture in the workplace
- Cross-cultural management and training.

Opening Case

Culture Gap

Global: With its domestic operations in trouble, Gap isn't getting much help from abroad. If any retail brand looked like a sure bet internationally, it was the Gap, the 3700-store clothing chain that has proliferated like kudzu across the United States. With an image as American as Levi's or Coke, the company figured it would be an easy sell.

Banking on success, Gap bragged about becoming "the world's head-quarters for khakis" in 1998. However, Gap was in for a serious surprise. Domestically, Gap was in trouble. Not only were the fourth-quarter profits expected to fall by 37 percent down $262 million from a year ago, but also same-store sales fell off by 12 percent in January: Gap needed all the help it could get and so it turned toward its stores outside the United States for rescue. However, Gap's international business was suffering equally. Same-store sales in Gap's 525 international stores fell an estimated 10 percent in January and were off by about 5 percent in the past half-year. The company cryptically acknowledged to analysts last year that in Germany and France it hasn't been able "to work out the economics." It is cutting international store growth to 20–25 percent this year from 41 percent in the year just ended. The company's international operating margin (net before interest and taxes, as a percent of sales) declined to 10 percent in fiscal year 2001 compared to 12 percent in 1999; these margins were far less than the company's overall profit margin at 16 percent in fiscal 2001.

What went wrong? Gap fell because of the belief that it could apply uniform merchandising and marketing in all its stores around the world. In Japan, for example, the tags on Gap's clothing are in English. Also, Gap employees cheerfully greet customers with the casual Japanese version of "hi," something not welcomed by the mannerly Japanese.

Additionally, despite Americanization, the Japanese seem to be more interested in bargains. Uniqlo, Gap's 480-store rival owned by Fast Retailing Co., cheaply sources its fashions from China and undercuts the Gap on price. In Harajuku, the heart of the Japanese fashion world, Uniqlo sells denim jackets for $25, half the price of similar jackets at a nearby Gap. Even monolithic Wal-Mart has figured out how to tailor its merchandise and suppliers to the locale, whether in the United States or abroad. In Beijing, Wal-Mart sells 20-pound moon cakes to coincide with Chinese lunar year holidays. Given the challenge of Byzantine retailing laws overseas, such customization is a big help. In Europe, for instance, retailers need special permission to build stores larger than 40,000 square feet.

Interestingly, however, some foreign tastes flow backward. Gap experimented in two of its Old Navy stores in the United States with Japanese punk fashions that included plaid shirts with ripped-off sleeves that were reattached with safety pins. However, the trend was not to the liking of Americans and never caught on.

In 1999 Mickey S. Drexler merged domestic and international operations and installed Kenneth Pilot, the former head of Gap's outlet business, to run worldwide merchandising. Pilot had replaced son of Gap's founder Donald Fisher when he quit. Looks like it may be time for Gap to drop the jingoism.

Question: What was Gap's difficulty? What should Gap do?

Source: *Forbes*, 3/19/2001, Vol. 167 Issue 7, p. 62, and www.gapinc.com.

This chapter's Opening Case describes the way in which a lack of understanding of the local culture might create problems for companies operating in countries other than their own. No matter how big these companies may be, they can ignore the cultural aspect in their international operations only at their own risk. Cultural differences and the unique ways of life that accompany them necessitate that managers develop international expertise to enable them to successfully manage according to the different environments in the countries in which they operate. This dynamic environment consists of political, sociocultural, economic, legal, and technological factors that influence the strategy, functions, and processes of any international business.

A critical skill that international business managers must have is a working knowledge of the cultural variables that could influence their managerial decisions. In other words, they need to be culturally sensitive, possessing a healthy respect for another individual's culture. This is what cross-cultural literacy is all about: an understanding of how cultural differences across and within nations can affect the way in which business is practiced.

The cultural insensitivity of managers who underestimated the significance of cultural factors led them to failure in their international operations. Cultural sensitivity requires the ability to understand the perspective of those living in other, different societies and the willingness to practice cultural empathy, putting oneself in another's shoes.

International managers can benefit greatly from understanding the nature, dimensions, and variables that constitute a country's culture and how these affect work and organizational processes. Such cultural awareness enables managers to develop appropriate policies and functions for planning, leading, controlling, and organizing in an international setting. Such an adaptation process is necessary in order to realistically and successfully formulate and implement organizational objectives and strategies. Also, such cultural adaptation greatly contributes to an increase in workforce diversity around the globe.

In Chapter 1 we discussed the global issues and challenges that international business is confronted with. Because countries are different from one another, international business is different from any other type of business and thus we stress the need for cross-cultural literacy in this chapter. Despite the dynamic technological developments of the twenty-first century—global communications, rapid transportation—and the concept of the "global village" becoming a reality, we are still faced with tremendous differences across cultures. For example, Westerners, including Americans, assume that because people of other cultures might be using Western products like McDonald's, Levi's jeans, Microsoft software, BMW, BP, Shell, Coca-Cola, or are listening to Western music and watching Western movies, they also accept the other elements of Western culture. However, this could not be further from reality. Many Islamic militants responsible for various terrorist attacks against Western ideals were using some, if not all, of the aforementioned Western goods and services. Furthermore, many cultures are in the process of changing their outlook and status vis-à-vis the role of women in their society, for example, the countries of Saudi Arabia and the United Arab Emirates.

What Is Culture?

In everyday usage, the term "culture" refers to the finer things in life, such as the fine arts, literature, and philosophy. Under this very narrow definition of culture, the "cultured person" is one who prefers Handel to hard rock; can distinguish between the artistic styles of Monet and Manet; prefers pheasant under glass to grits and red-eye gravy, and 12-year-old Chivas Regal to Budweiser; and spends his/her time reading Aristotle or Marx, rather than watching wrestling on television. For the anthropologist, however, the term culture has a much broader meaning that goes far beyond mere personal refinements. The only requirement for being cultured is to be human, and therefore all people have culture.

The term culture has been defined in many different ways. Even among anthropologists, who claim culture as their guiding conceptual principle, there is no agreed-upon single definition of the term culture. In fact, Kroeber and Kluckhohn (1952)[1] identified over 160 definitions of culture. One of the earliest, most widely cited definitions of culture, offered by E. B. Tylor (1871) over a century ago, is "that complex whole which includes knowledge, belief, art, morals, law, custom, and any other capabilities and habits acquired by man as a member of society."[2] More recently, Kluckhohn and Kelly (1945)[3] have referred to culture as "all the historically created designs for living, explicit and implicit, rational, irrational, and non-rational, which exist at any given time as potential guides for the behavior of men." Also, Herskovits (1955) spoke of culture as being "the man-made part of the environment,"[4] while Downs (1971) defined culture as being "a mental map which guides us in our relations to our surroundings and to other people."[5]

Running the risk of adding to the confusion, we will offer yet another definition: Culture is everything that people have, think, and do as members of their society. The three verbs in this definition—have, think, and do—can help us identify the three major structural components of culture. This means that in order for a person to have something, some material object must be present. When people think, ideas, values, attitudes, and beliefs are present. When people do, they behave in certain socially prescribed ways. Thus culture is made up of (1) material objects; (2) ideas, values, and attitudes; and (3) normative or expected patterns of behavior. The final component of this working definition, "as members of society," tells us that culture is shared by at least two individuals and, of course, real societies are much larger than that. Thus, it is crucial that international business managers look at groupings of individuals within a society.

Before entering the discussion of culture's impact on organizations it is necessary to address yet another topic, that of cultural universals. The term "cultural universals" refers to the idea that all cultures of the world—despite their many differences—not only face a number of common issues, but also share a number of common characteristics. Even the most casual perusal of an introductory book in cultural anthropology leads us to the conclusion that there are many societies around the globe, each with its own unique culture. Although determining the number of cultures that exists today largely depends on how culture is defined, anthropologists approximate that there are 850 separate and distinct cultures in the continent of Africa alone, illustrating the large amount of cultural variability, the importance of which is even greater than the number of cultures around the world. The great number of differences between cultures illustrates how flexible and adaptable humans are in relation to other animals, for each culture has arrived at different solutions to the universal human problems that face all societies.

As we encounter the many different cultural patterns found throughout the world, there is a natural tendency to become overwhelmed by the magnitude of the differences and overlook the commonalities. Even anthropologists, when describing "their people," tend to emphasize the uniqueness of each culture and only rarely look at the similarities between them. But all societies, if they are to survive, are confronted with fundamental universal needs that must be satisfied, and when cultures develop ways of meeting those needs, general cultural characteristics emerge. At a very concrete level, differences in the details of cultural patterns exist because different societies have developed different ways of meeting these universal societal needs. Yet, at a higher level of abstraction, a number of commonalities exist because all cultures have worked out solutions to certain problems facing all human populations. Let us briefly examine the needs that all cultures must satisfy and the universal cultural patterns that emerge while attempting to satisfy such needs.

Economic Systems

One of the most obvious and immediate needs of a society is to meet the basic physiological requirements of its people. To stay alive, all humans need a certain minimal caloric intake; potable water; and to varying degrees, protection from the elements in terms of clothing and shelter. No society in the world has access to an infinite supply of such basic resources as food, water, clothing, and housing materials. Since these commodities are always in finite supply, each society must develop systematic ways of producing, distributing, and consuming these essential resources. Thus emerges society's need to develop an economic system.

To illustrate the principle of cultural universals, we can look at just one component of all economic systems: forms of distribution of resources. In addition to working out patterned ways of producing basic material goods (or procuring them from the immediate environment), all societies must ensure that these goods are distributed to all those members of society whose very survival depends on receiving them. In the United States most goods and services are distributed according to the capitalistic mode, based on the principle of "each according to his/her capacity to pay." On the other hand, in socialist countries like China and Cuba, goods and services are distributed according to a very different principle—"each according to his/her need"—even though in China this principle is changing.

These two well-known systems of distribution hardly exhaust the range of possibilities found in the world. The Pygmies of Central Africa distribute goods by a system known as "silent barter," in which the trading partners, in an attempt to attain true reciprocity, avoid face-to-face contact during the exchange. The Bushmen of present-day Namibia in South West Africa distribute the meat of hunted animals according to the principle of kinship—each share of meat is determined by how one is related to the hunter. However, whatever particular form the system of distribution might take, there are no societies, at least not for long, that have failed to develop and adhere to a well-understood, systematic pattern of distribution.

Marriage and Family Systems

For a society to continue over time it is imperative that it develop systematic procedures for mating, childbearing, and education. Failure to do so would result in the end of that particular society in a very short time. No society permits random mating, for all societies have worked out rules for determining who can marry whom, under what conditions, and according to what procedures. In other words, all societies have patterned systems of marriage. And because human infants (as compared to the young of other species) have a particularly long period of dependency on adults, there arises the need for every society to develop systematic ways of meeting the needs of dependent children. If the basic needs of dependent children are not satisfied, they will not survive to adulthood, and consequently, the very survival of society would be in jeopardy. Thus, it is safe to say that all societies, in order to survive, have patterns of childbearing and family institutions.

Educational Institutions

In addition to ensuring that the basic physical needs of its children are met, a society must see to it that these children learn the way of life of this particular society. Rather than expecting each new child to rediscover for himself/herself all the accumulated knowledge of the past, a society must have an organized way of passing on its cultural heritage from one generation to another. This universal societal need for cultural transmission gives rise to some form of educational system in each society.

Social Control Systems

If societies are to survive, they must establish some ways of preserving social order. This means that all societies must develop mechanisms that ensure that most of its people obey most of its laws at least most of the time. If this need is not met, people will violate each other's rights to such an extent that anarchy will prevail.

Certainly, different societies meet this need for social order in different ways. In the United States, for example, behavior control rests on a number of formal mechanisms, such as a written constitution; local, state, and federal laws; and an elaborate system of courts, penal institutions, and police, among other things. Many small-scale, technologically simple societies have less formal means of controlling the behavior of their members. Regardless of the specific methods used, one thing is certain: every society has a system of coercing people to obey the rules laid out by society, and these are called social control systems.

Supernatural Belief Systems

All societies have a certain degree of control over their social and physical environments. There are a number of things that all people in a society can understand and predict. For example, a heavy object when dropped into a lake will sink to the bottom; if I have five dollars or euros or yen or dirhams and give you two, I will have only three left; the sun always rises from the east and sets in the west. However, there are still many things that we cannot explain or predict with any degree of certainty. Why does one child develop a fatal disease while his/her playmate does not? Why do tornadoes destroy some houses and leave others unharmed? Why do safe drivers die in auto accidents while careless ones do not? Such questions have no apparent answers, for they cannot be explained by either our conventional systems of justice or rationality. Therefore, societies must develop systems for explaining "unexplainable" occurrences. The way that people do this is by relying on various types of supernatural explanations such as magic, religion, witchcraft, sorcery, and astrology. Thus all societies, despite variations in form and content, have systems of supernatural beliefs, which serve to explain otherwise inexplicable phenomena.

Thus, despite the great variety in the details of cultural features found throughout the world, all cultures, because they must satisfy certain universal needs, have a number of traits in common. This basic anthropological principle of cultural universals can be an important tool for helping those working in international business better understand and appreciate culturally different business environments. Greater empathy for cultural differences—an important if not crucial condition for increased knowledge—can be attained by avoiding concentrating solely on the apparent differences between cultures, without appreciating their underlying commonalities as well.

Robinson states:

> [T]he successful international manager is one who sees and feels the similarity of structure of all societies. The same set of variables are seen to operate, although their relative weights may be very different. This capacity is far more important than possession of specific area expertise, which may be gained quite rapidly if one already has an ability to see similarities and ask the right questions—those that will provide the appropriate values or weights for the relevant variables. Such an individual can very quickly orient himself on the sociocultural map.[6]

In other words, we are less likely to prejudge or be critical of different practices, ideas, or behavioral patterns if we can appreciate the notion that they simply represent different solutions to the same basic human problems facing all cultures of the world, including our own.

Culture gives people a sense of who they are, of belonging, of how they should behave, and of what they should be doing. Culture impacts behavior, morale, and productivity at work as well, and it includes values and patterns that influence company attitudes and actions.

Culture is often considered the driving force behind human behavior everywhere. The concept has become the context to explain politics, economics, progress, and failures.

Huntington states that the new world will not experience conflicts that will be attributed to ideologies or economics, but to culture, which will be the dominating source of conflict.[7]

Culture and its Elements

The following elements of culture can be a useful means for better understanding culture itself, and for studying any group of people, whether they live in Dubai, or in the Greek islands, in the city of Paris, or in Siberia.

Dress and Appearance. This includes the outward garments and adornments, or lack thereof, as well as body decorations that tend to be distinctive by culture. We are aware of the Japanese kimono, the Native American headband, the African headdress, the Polynesian sarong, the Englishman's bowler and umbrella, and the cowboy's hat. Some tribes smear their faces for battle, while some women use cosmetics to manifest different ideals of beauty. Many subcultures wear distinctive clothing: the formal look for business, the jeans of the youth throughout the world, and uniforms that segregate everyone from students to police, to firemen, to military generals. In the military subculture or microculture, customs and regulations determine the dress of the day, length of hair, and equipment to be worn.

Communication and Language. The communication system, verbal and nonverbal, distinguishes one group from another. Apart from the multitude of "foreign" languages, some nations have 15 or more major spoken languages (within one language group there are dialects, accents, slang, jargon, and other such variations). Spoken language or verbal communication is the part of a culture's communication system that is embodied in its spoken and written vocabulary. It is the most obvious difference we notice when traveling in another country.

Linguistically different segments of a population are often culturally, socially, and politically distinct. For instance, Malaysia's population comprises Malay (60 percent), Chinese (30 percent), and Indian (10 percent). Malay is the official national language, but each ethnic group speaks its own language and continues its traditions. The United Kingdom includes England, Northern Ireland, Scotland, and Wales—each of which has its own language and traditions. Recently, Scotland vigorously renewed its drive for independence, and Ireland's native language, Gaelic, is staging a comeback on Irish television and Gaelic-language schools. In Cyprus, Greek is the national language, but Turkish is also spoken due to the presence of a Turkish minority, while English is used widely due to the fact that Cyprus was a British colony. English is used by only 5 percent of the world population, but it is used as lingua franca third or "link" language that is understood by two parties who speak different languages. For example, companies such as Philips NY (a Netherlands-based electronics firm) and Asea Brown Boveri AG (a Swiss-based industrial giant) use English for all internal correspondence. Japan-based Sony and Matsushita also use English in their work abroad.

Even firms that seriously take into consideration the multilinguistic environment of international business are likely to face many hazards along the way. In fact, literature is filled with examples of problems US firms have had in their international advertising campaigns due to sloppy translations. For example, US firms have advertised cigarettes with low "asphalt" (instead of tar), computer "underwear" (instead of soft wear), and "wet sheep" (instead of hydraulic rams). As amusing as these examples may seem, such translation errors have cost US firms millions of dollars in losses over the years, not to mention the damage done to their credibility and reputation.

It is important to note, however, that US firms are not the only ones to commit linguistic mistakes. Even when people think they know English, they frequently convey messages they do not particularly intend to send.

- A sign in a Romanian hotel informing the English-speaking guests that the elevator was not working read, "The lift is being fixed. For the next few days we regret that you will be unbearable."
- A sign in the window of a Parisian dress shop said, "Come inside and have a fit."
- Reporting to his firm's headquarters, an African representative of an electronics firm referred to the "throat-cutting competition" when in fact he meant "cut-throat."
- Japan-based Kinki Tourist Company changed its name in English-speaking markets after people called looking for "kinky" sex tours.
- Braniff Airlines' English-language slogan "Fly in Leather" was translated into "Fly naked" in Spanish.

On the other hand, unspoken language or nonverbal communication communicates through unspoken cues, including hand gestures, facial expressions, physical greetings, eye contact, and the manipulation of personal space. Italians, Greeks, Arabs, and Venezuelans, for example, animate conversations with lively hand gestures and other body movements. The Japanese and Koreans, although more reserved, communicate just as much information through their own unspoken languages.

Most unspoken language is subtle and takes time to recognize and interpret. Physical gestures, for example, often convey different meanings in different cultures: the thumbs-up sign is vulgar in Italy and Greece but means "all right" or even "great" in the United States. Former US president George Bush once gave a backward peace sign with his fore- and middle fingers (meaning "peace" or "victory" in the United States) to a crowd in Australia. He was unaware that he was sending a message similar to that given with a middle finger in the United States.

Sense of Self and Space. The comfort one has with oneself can be expressed differently according to each culture. Self-identity and appreciation can be manifested by humble bearing in one place and macho behavior in another. Independence and creativity are countered in other cultures by group cooperation and conformity. For example, Americans and the British have a sense of space that requires more distance between individuals, while Latins, Arabs, and the Vietnamese stand closer together. Also, some cultures are very structured and formal, while others are more flexible and informal. Some cultures are very closed and determine one's place very precisely, while others are more open and changing. Each culture validates itself in a unique way.

Food and Feeding Habits. The manner in which food is selected, prepared, presented, and eaten often differs by culture. For example, one man's pet could be another person's delicacy. Similarly, Americans love beef, yet it is forbidden to Hindus, while pork, which is widely consumed by the Chinese, is forbidden in Muslim and Jewish cultures. Many restaurants cater to diverse diets and offer "national" dishes to meet varied cultural tastes. Feeding habits also differ, and the range goes from hands and chopsticks to full sets of cutlery. Even when cultures use a utensil such as a fork, one can distinguish a European from an American by which hand holds the fork. Subcultures, too, can be analyzed from this perspective, such as the executive's dining room, the worker's submarine sandwich, the ladies' tearoom, and the vegetarian's restaurant.

Time and Time Consciousness. Sense of time differs by culture; some are exact and others are relative. Generally, Germans are precise about the clock, while many Latins are more casual. In some cultures, promptness is determined by age or status; thus, in some countries subordinates are expected to be on time for staff meetings, while executives are the last to arrive. Some subcultures, like the military, have their own system of 24 hours—1.00 p.m. civilian time becomes 1300 hours in military time. In such cultures, promptness is rewarded, and in battles all watches are synchronized. On the other hand, there are people in some other cultures who do not bother with hours or minutes, but manage their days by sunrise and sunset.

Managers often experience much conflict and frustration because of differences in the concept of time around the world, that is the differences in temporal values. To Americans and Western Europeans, for example, time is a valuable and limited resource, to be saved, scheduled, and spent with precision, lest it be wasted. The clock is always running—time is money, and therefore deadlines and schedules have to be promptly met. When others are not on time for meetings, Germans and Americans feel insulted; when meetings digress from their purpose, they tend to become impatient.

In many parts of the world, however, people view time from different and longer duration perspectives, often based on religious beliefs (such as reincarnation, in which time does not end at death), on a belief in destiny, or on pervasive social attitudes. In Latin America, for example, a common attitude toward time is *manana*, a word that literally means "tomorrow"; a Latin American person using this word, however, usually means an indefinite time, in the near future. Similarly, the word *bukra* in Arabic can mean "tomorrow" or "some time in the future." Although Americans usually regard a deadline as a firm commitment, Arabs often regard a deadline imposed on them as an insult. They feel that important things take a long time and therefore cannot be rushed; to ask an Arab to rush something would imply that you have not given him an important task or that you assume that he will not treat that task with respect. International managers have to be careful about not offending people or losing contacts or employee cooperation because of a misunderstanding about the local perception of time.

Relationships. This refers to social structure, which embodies a culture's fundamental organization including its groups and institutions, its system of social positions and their relationships, and the process by which its resources are distributed. Consequently, social structure affects business decisions ranging from production-site selection to advertising methods and the costs of doing business in a country.

Cultures fix human and organizational relationships by age, gender, status, and degree of kindred, as well as by wealth, power, and wisdom. The family unit is the most common expression of this characteristic, and the arrangement may go from small to large—in a Hindu household, the joint family includes under one roof a mother, father, children, parents, uncles, aunts, and cousins. In fact, one's physical location in such houses may also be determined with males on one side of the house and females on the other.

Gender. Socially learned traits associated with, and expected of, men or women or another social group association refers to such socially learned behaviors and attitudes as styles of dress and activity preferences. Many countries have still not made any progress toward equality between men and women in the workplace. For instance, countries operating under Islamic law sometimes segregate women and men in schools, universities, and social activities, and restrict women to certain professions. Sometimes they are allowed to be teachers or physicians but only for female students or patients, respectively. Saudi Arabia, Iran, and, most recently, Afghanistan (Taliban rulers) are some of the examples of countries where there is or was discrimination against women.

In Japan, women have traditionally been denied equal opportunity in the workplace. While men held nearly all positions of responsibility, women generally served as office clerks and administrative assistants until their mid to late twenties when they were expected to marry and stay at home tending to family needs. Although this is still largely true, there has been some progress in expanding the role of women in Japan's business community. Exhibit 2.1 shows the percentage of women who are owners of businesses in selected countries including Japan. The exhibit shows that greater gender equality prevails in the United States, Australia, Canada, and Germany, despite the fact that women in these countries still earn less money than men in similar positions.

Social values are another dimension of social structure that determine peoples' relationships within a culture, and more specifically within the work environment. Charles Hampden-Turner and Fons Trompenaar[8] researched value dimensions; the work was spread over a ten-year period, with 15,000 managers from 28 countries representing 47 national cultures. These dimensions that affect daily business activities, with the descriptions and the placement of nine of the countries in approximate relative order, are given in Exhibit 2.2.

Exhibit 2.1

Percentage of Women who own Businesses in Selected Countries

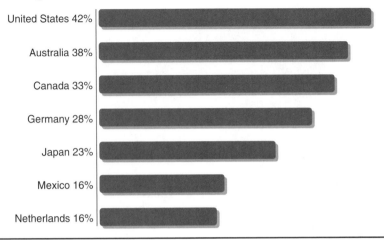

Source: Compiled by the author.

If we view the placement of these countries along a range from personal to societal, based on each dimension, some interesting patterns emerge. One can see from the exhibit that the same countries tend to be at similar positions on all dimensions, with the exception of emotional orientation.

In Trompenaar's dimension of universalism versus particularism, the universalistic approach applies rules and systems objectively, without consideration for individual circumstances, whereas the particularistic approach, more common in Asia and in Spain for example, not only puts the obligation toward relationships first but is also more subjective. Trompenaar found that people in particularistic societies are more likely to pass on inside information to a friend than those in universalistic societies.

In the neutral versus affective dimension, the focus is on the emotional orientation of relationships. The Italians, Mexicans, and the Chinese, for example, would openly express emotions even in a business situation whereas the British and the Japanese would consider such displays unprofessional; in turn they would be regarded as hard to "read."

As for involvement in relationships, people tend to be either specific or diffuse (or somewhere along that dimension). Managers in specific-oriented cultures—United States, United Kingdom, France—separate work from personal issues and relationships; they compartmentalize their work and private lives and are more open and direct. In diffuse-oriented cultures like Sweden and China, there is a spillover from work into the realm of personal relationships and vice versa.

The achievement versus ascription dimension examines the source of power and status in society. In an achievement society, the source of status

Exhibit 2.2

Trompenaar's Value Dimensions

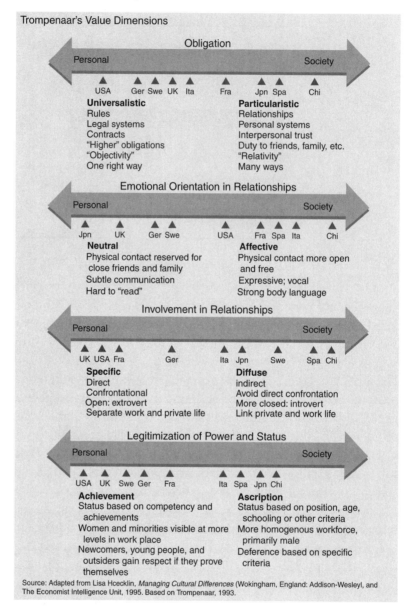

Trompenaar's Value Dimensions

Obligation

Personal ←→ Society

USA Ger Swe UK Ita Fra Jpn Spa Chi

Universalistic
Rules
Legal systems
Contracts
"Higher" obligations
"Objectivity"
One right way

Particularistic
Relationships
Personal systems
Interpersonal trust
Duty to friends, family, etc.
"Relativity"
Many ways

Emotional Orientation in Relationships

Personal ←→ Society

Jpn UK Ger Swe USA Fra Spa Ita Chi

Neutral
Physical contact reserved for
 close friends and family
Subtle communication
Hard to "read"

Affective
Physical contact more open
 and free
Expressive; vocal
Strong body language

Involvement in Relationships

Personal ←→ Society

UK USA Fra Ger Ita Jpn Swe Spa Chi

Specific
Direct
Confrontational
Open: extrovert
Separate work and private life

Diffuse
indirect
Avoid direct confrontation
More closed: introvert
Link private and work life

Legitimization of Power and Status

Personal ←→ Society

USA UK Swe Ger Fra Ita Spa Jpn Chi

Achievement
Status based on competency and
 achievements
Women and minorities visible at more
 levels in work place
Newcomers, young people, and
 outsiders gain respect if they prove
 themselves

Ascription
Status based on position, age,
 schooling or other criteria
More homogenous workforce,
 primarily male
Deference based on specific
 criteria

Source: Adapted from Lisa Hcecklin, *Managing Cultural Differences* (Wokingham, England: Addison-Wesleyl, and The Economist Intelligence Unit, 1995. Based on Trompenaar, 1993.

and influence is based on individual achievement—how well one performs the job and what level of education and experience one has to offer. Therefore, women, minorities, and young people usually have equal opportunity to attain positions based on their achievements. In an ascription-oriented society, people ascribe status on the basis of class, age, gender, and so on; one is more likely to be born into a position of influence. Hiring in Indonesia, for example, is more likely to be based on who you are than hiring for a position in Germany or Australia. From all this it becomes clear that a lot of what goes on at work can be explained by differences in people's innate value systems. Awareness of such differences and how they influence work behavior can be very useful to the international manager.

Beliefs and Attitudes. Possibly the most difficult classification is determining the major belief themes of a people, and how this and other factors influence their attitudes toward themselves, others, and what happens in their world. People in all cultures seem to have a concern for the supernatural that is evident in their different religions and religious practices. Primitive cultures, for example, have a belief in spiritual beings labeled by us as "animism." Religious traditions in various cultures consciously or unconsciously influence our attitudes toward life, death, and the hereafter. Western culture seems to be largely influenced by the Judeo-Christian–Islamic traditions, while Eastern or Asian cultures have been dominated by Buddhism, Confucianism, Taoism, and Hinduism. Religion, to a degree, expresses the philosophy of a people about important facets of life—it is influenced by culture and vice versa. In fact, human values often derive from religious beliefs. Different religions take different views of work, savings, and material goods. An understanding of religious beliefs will help the international manager understand why companies from certain cultures are more competitive than companies from other cultures. It also helps us understand why some countries develop more slowly than others do. Knowing how religion affects business practices is especially important in countries with a religious form of government such as Iran.

While there are thousands of religions in the world today, four dominate: Christianity, Islam, Hinduism, and Buddhism. Along with Confucianism, all these religions will be reviewed, with a special emphasis on their business implications. Exhibit 2.3 shows the major religions of the world ranked in terms of the number of adherents.

Christianity. Christianity is the most widely practiced religion in the world, with about 2 billion people identifying themselves as Christians and a vast majority of them living in the Americas and in Europe. Christianity grew out of Judaism and, like Judaism, it is a monotheistic religion (monotheism is the belief in one god). A religious division in the eleventh century led to the establishment of two major Christian organizations—the Roman Catholic Church and the Orthodox Church. Today the Roman Catholic Church accounts for over half of all Christians, most of whom are found in southern Europe and Latin America. The Orthodox Church, while less influential, is still of major importance in several countries (e.g., Greece, Russia, and most of Eastern Europe).

In the sixteenth century, the split in the Roman Catholic Church resulted in Protestantism. Under Protestantism several denominations emerged, such

Exhibit 2.3

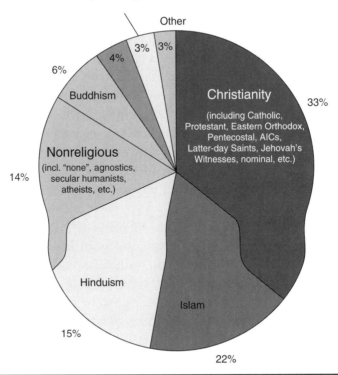

Major Religions of the World

Christianity: 2 billion; Islam: 1.3 billion; Hinduism: 900 million; Secular/Nonreligious/Agnostic! Atheist: 850 million; Buddhism: 360 million; Chinese traditional religion: 225 million; primal-indigenous: 190 million; Sikhism: 23 million; Yoruba religion: 20 million; Juche: 19 million; Spiritism: 14 million; Judaism: 14 million; Baha'i: 6 million; Jainism: 4 million; Shinto: 4 million; Cao Dai: 3 million; Tenrikyo: 2.4 million; Neo-Paganism: 1 million; Unitarian-Universalism: 800 thousand; Scientology: 750 thousand; Rastafarianism: 700 thousand; Zoroastrianism: 150 thousand. *Source: www.adherents.com.*

as Baptist, Methodist, and Calvinist. Protestantism, according to Max Weber, has had the most economic implications.

In 1904 he made the connection between Protestantism and capitalism. He noted that capitalism appeared in Western Europe and that Protestant ethics emphasized the importance of hard work and wealth creation and frugality, and this was the underlying value system that facilitated the development of capitalism. The combination of hard work by the Protestants and the accumulation of wealth for further expansion and investments prepared the way for the development of capitalism in Europe and eventually in the United States.

Islam. Islam is the second largest religion in the world and it has its roots in both Judaism and Christianity. Muslims–Islam's believers—inhabit more than 35 countries stretching from the northwest coast of Africa to the

Middle East, to China and Malaysia. Islam is a religion that provides a social structure for Muslims, and their number is approximately 1.3 billion. The ritualistic nature of everyday life in a Muslim country is striking to a Western visitor. Muslims pray five times a day, and many Muslim women dress in a certain manner, and the consumption of either pig meat or alcohol is strictly forbidden. In the past twenty years or so , a movement has developed within Islam, that of Islamic fundamentalism. In the West, Islamic fundamentalism is being associated with militants, terrorists, and violent activities. This movement has been created in some traditional Islamic societies because of the modernization that is taking place in these countries, and derives from Western ideologies of liberal democracy, materialism, equal rights for women, and the Western attitudes toward, marriage, sex, and alcohol. Such influences have created a social gap. The believers of Western culture, who live mainly in urban areas, have benefited financially, whereas the majority of people in these countries, who live in both urban and rural areas and who have not adopted some of these Western values, are financially impoverished.

In several Islamic countries, fundamentalists are using their political power to try and make Islamic law (as set down in the Koran) the law of the land. In this context, Islam is not just a religion; it is also the source of law, and, overall, a way of life that determines social behavior. Muslims believe that every human endeavor is within the framework of faith, because they believe that the only purpose of any activity is to do "inshallah," God's will. Iran is a country with a fundamentalist political structure, and Afghanistan with its Taliban government was one till recently. Algeria, Egypt, Pakistan, and Saudi Arabia are some other countries where Islamic fundamentalism is gaining ground.

In economic and financial terms, Islam allows people to make a profit, as long as that profit is earned justly and is not based on the exploitation of others. The profits should also be used for charitable activities and for helping the poor. One economic principle in Islam prohibits the payment or receiving of interest, which is considered usury.

For a Muslim the acceptance of interest payments is considered a sin. It is gradually becoming a law, and evidence of this is that Pakistan's Federal Shariá Court, the highest Islamic lawmaking body in that country, pronounced interest to be un-Islamic, and therefore illegal, and demanded that the government amend all financial laws accordingly.[9]

Traditionally, however, the Arab World has had a very different attitude toward finance and profit and toward financial matters, as compared to Western practices. This has not changed despite the impact of the Western world on some parts of the region. This is found in the avoidance of interest on capital, and profit sharing, which is based on the avoidance of usury, an Islamic tenet.[10]

A characteristic feature of Islamic finance is profit and loss that are based on Zakat, which derives from a social provision.[11] Furthermore, these traditional concepts have created some contemporary institutions. The first Islamic Bank in the region was the Dubai Islamic Bank, which was established in 1975 and operates on a profit-sharing model, where the bank acts as the lender and a coinvestor.[12]

Overall, it is not easy for Westerners to understand the Islamic notions on corporate citizenship, since many Muslims are considered to be terrorists. We must understand though that Islam is a way of life. Many Muslims see Islam as the religion of trade and business, making no distinction between men and women and seeing no contradiction between profit and moral acts. The Holy Koran provides tenets on financial and business matters in general.[13]

Applying this to the banking and financial system of an Islamic country might discourage international businesses and investors. When an Islamic bank lends money to a business, rather than charging that business interest on the loan, it takes a share in the profits that are derived from the investment. Similarly, when a business deposits money at an Islamic bank in a savings account, the deposit is treated as an equity investment in whatever activity the bank uses the capital for. Consequently, the depositor receives a share in the profit from the bank's investment.

Hinduism. Hinduism is a major religion with approximately 900 million followers, most of whom are found on the Indian subcontinent. It originated about 4000 years ago and is considered the world's oldest major religion. Hindus believe that there is a moral force in society that requires the acceptance of certain responsibilities, called *dharma*. They believe in reincarnation or rebirth into a different body after death. Hindus also believe in *karma*, the spiritual progression of each person's soul. A person's *karma* is affected by the way he/she lives. Another dimension of Hinduism is *nirvana*, which is a state of complete spiritual perfection. Many Hindus believe that the way to achieve *nirvana* is to lead a severe ascetic lifestyle of material and physical self-denial, devoting life to a spiritual rather than material quest.

Max Weber also argued that the ascetic principles found in Hinduism do not encourage the kind of entrepreneurial activity needed in the pursuit of wealth that is found in Protestantism.[14] According to Weber, traditional Hindu values emphasize that individuals should not be judged by their material achievements, but by their spiritual achievements. Overall, we must be very careful not to read too much into Weber's position, simply because there are millions of hardworking Hindu businessmen and -women in India who form the backbone of this country's emerging economy.

Buddhism. Buddhism was founded about 2600 years ago in India by a Hindu prince named Siddhartha Gautama. He taught that by extinguishing desire, his followers could attain enlightenment and escape the cycle of existence into *nirvana*. By opening his teaching to everyone, he opposed the caste system. Because Buddhist monks are involved in various activities in their geographic regions and in political and social decisions, international managers working in these areas need to be aware of what these religious leaders are doing. A Buddhist teaching is that if people have no desires, they will not suffer. This is important to marketers and production managers because if Buddhists and Hindus have no desires, they have little motive for achievement and for the acquisition of material goods. Today, Buddhism has approximately 360 million followers, mostly in nations such as China, Tibet, Korea, Vietnam, Thailand, and Japan.

Confucianism. Kung-fu-dz (Confucius in English) began teaching his ideas in China nearly 2500 years ago. Today, China houses most of the 350 million followers worldwide. Confucianism has also spread in countries such as Vietnam, Japan, Singapore, and South Korea. South Korean business practices reflect Confucian thought in their rigid organizational structure and great respect for authority. Korean employees do not question strict chains of command, but non-Koreans often feel very differently. Attempts were made to apply this type of management to foreign subsidiaries in other countries, such as Vietnam. This resulted in confrontations between US executives and workers in Vietnam. Confucianism is built around a comprehensive ethical code that sets down guidelines for relationships with others. High moral and ethical conduct and loyalty to others are very essential teachings of Confucianism.[15]

In modern organizations based on Confucian cultures, the loyalty that binds employees to the heads of their organization can reduce the conflict between management and labor that we find in class-conscious societies such as Britain. According to this religion, loyalty to one's superiors, such as an employee's loyalty to management, is not blind loyalty. On the other hand, management is obliged to reward the loyalty of subordinates by bestowing blessings on them. For example, the employees of a Japanese organization are loyal to the company's leadership, and in return, the leaders bestow on their employees the "blessing" of lifetime employment. The business implications of this cultural practice are that the lack of mobility between companies implied by the lifetime employment system suggests that over the years managers and workers build up knowledge, experience, and a network of interpersonal business contacts. All of these can assist managers and workers in performing their jobs more effectively and in cooperating with others in the organization, consequently making the organization more profitable.

Another concept found in Confucian ethics is the importance of honesty. Thinkers of this religion believe that dishonesty does not pay in the long run. When companies can trust each other not to break contractual obligations, the costs of doing business are lowered; thus the terms of cooperative agreements are not violated. For example, the close ties between the automobile companies and their component parts suppliers in Japan are facilitated by a combination of trust and reciprocal obligations. These close relationships allow the auto manufacturers and their suppliers to cooperate on issues such as inventory and quality control, design, and on-time delivery. This explains to an extent the Japanese auto companies' competitive advantage.[16]

The Study of Cultural Differences

There are two universally acceptable ways of studying cultural differences: the Kluckhohn–Strodtbeck framework and the Hofstede framework. The analysis of both would assist international managers better understand the way organizations function within their own cultural framework.

The Kluckhohn–Strodtbeck framework[17] compares cultures along six cultural dimensions. The following six questions assist the international manager in studying any given culture and in comparing it to a different one:

1. Do people believe that their environment controls them, that they control the environment, or that they are part of nature?
2. Do people focus on past events, on the present, or on the future?
3. Are people easily controlled and not to be trusted, or can they be trusted to act freely and responsibly?
4. Do people desire accomplishments in life, carefree lives, or spiritual lives?
5. Do people believe that individuals or groups are responsible for each person's welfare?
6. Do people prefer to conduct most activities in private or in public?

Another useful framework for understanding how basic values underlie organizational behavior and for the understanding of different cultures is the one proposed by Hofstede. The framework is the result of his research in the 1980s on more than 116,000 IBM employees in 50 countries. Hofstede proposes four value dimensions:

1. Power distance
2. Uncertainty avoidance
3. Individualism
4. Masculinity.[18]

Power distance, the first value dimension, is the level of acceptance by a society of the unequal distribution of power in organizations. In the workplace, inequalities in power are normal, as evidenced in hierarchical boss–subordinate relationships. However, the extent to which subordinates accept unequal power is socially determined. In countries in which people display high power distance (such as Malaysia, the Philippines, and Mexico), employees acknowledge the boss's authority simply by respecting that individual's formal position in the hierarchy, and they seldom bypass the chain of command. This respectful response results, predictably, in a centralized structure and in autocratic leadership. In countries where people display low power distance (such as Austria, Denmark, and Israel), superiors and subordinates are apt to regard one another as equal in power, resulting in more harmony and cooperation. Clearly, an autocratic management style is not likely to be well received in low power distance countries. Exhibit 2.4 portrays these results.

The second value dimension, uncertainty avoidance, refers to the extent to which people in a society feel threatened by ambiguous situations. Countries with a high level of uncertainty avoidance (such as Japan, Portugal, and Greece) tend to have strict laws and procedures to which their people adhere closely, and a strong sense of nationalism prevails. In a business context, this value results in formal rules and procedures designed to provide more security and greater career stability. Managers have a propensity for low-risk decisions, employees exhibit little aggressiveness, and lifetime employment is common. In countries with lower levels of uncertainty avoidance (such as Denmark, Great Britain, and, to a lesser extent, the United States), nationalism is less pronounced, and protests and other such activities are tolerated. Consequently, company activities are less structured and less formal, with some managers taking more risks, and there is high job mobility. Exhibit 2.5 shows the above-mentioned results.

The third of Hofstede's value dimensions, individualism, refers to the tendency of people to look after themselves and their immediate family only and neglect the needs of society. In countries that prize individualism (such as the United States, Great Britain, and Australia), democracy, individual initiative, and achievement are highly valued; the relationship of the individual to organizations is one of independence on an emotional level, if not on an economic level.

Exhibit 2.4

Exhibit 2.5

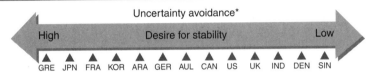

In countries such as Pakistan and Panama where low individualism prevails—that is where collectivism predominates—one finds tight social frameworks, emotional dependence on belonging to "the organization," and a strong belief in group decisions. People from a collectivist country, like Japan, believe in the will of the group rather than that of the individual, and their pervasive collectivism exerts control over individual members through social pressure and the fear of humiliation. Such a society values harmony and saving face whereas individualistic cultures generally emphasize self-respect, autonomy, and independence. Hiring and promotion practices in collectivist societies are based on paternalism rather than achievement or personal capabilities, which are valued in individualistic societies. Other management practices (such as the use of quality circles in Japanese factories) reflect the emphasis on group decision-making processes in collectivist societies. Exhibit 2.6 shows the value dimension of individualism.

Hofstede's findings indicate that most countries scoring high on individualism have both a higher gross national product and a more liberal political system than those scoring low on individualism—that is there is a strong relationship among individualism, wealth, and a political system with balanced power. Other studies have found that the output of individuals working in a group setting differs between individualistic and collectivist societies. In the United States, a highly individualistic culture, social loafing is common—that is people tend to perform less when working as part of a group than when working alone. In a comparative study between the United States and China, a highly collectivist society, Earley found that the Chinese did not exhibit as much social loafing as the Americans.[19] This result can be attributed to Chinese cultural values, which subordinate personal interests to the greater goal of helping the group succeed.

Exhibit 2.6

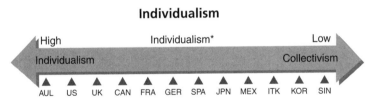

Exhibit 2.7

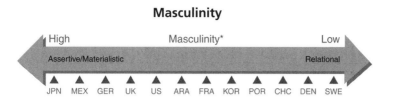

The fourth value dimension, masculinity, refers to the degree of tradition-ally "masculine" values—assertiveness, materialism, and a lack of concern for others—that prevail in a society. In comparison, femininity emphasizes "feminine" values—a concern for others, for relationships, and for the qual-ity of life. In highly masculine societies (e.g., Japan and Austria), women are generally expected to stay at home and raise a family. In organizations, one finds considerable job stress, and organizational interests generally encroach on employees' private lives. In countries with low masculinity (such as Switzerland and New Zealand), one finds less conflict and job stress, more women in high-level jobs, and a reduced need for assertiveness. According to Hofstede's research, the United States lies somewhat in the middle. American women typically are encouraged to work and are usually able to get some support for childcare (through daycare centers and maternity leaves). (See Exhibit 2.7 for a diagrammatic representation of masculinity.)

The four cultural dimensions proposed by Hofstede do not operate in iso-lation; rather they are interdependent and interrelated—and thus complex—in their impact on attitudes and behaviors within the work environment. Again, international managers must remember that the evaluation of an entire country on the basis of any one cultural value dimension is a gen-eralization and thus a possible oversimplification, for variations may occur according to subcultures, regions, and individuals. An interesting exercise would be to replicate Hofstede's study in this new millennium and see whether the countries studied have remained the same within the same cat-egories. It can be assumed that many countries have shifted from one value dimension to another, due to the complexity of the business environment, globalization, technological advancements, multiculturalism, the brain drain phenomenon, the counter brain drain phenomenon, and many others. (See Exhibit 2.8 for the abbreviations for countries.)

Culture in the Workplace

The effects of culture on specific management functions are particularly noticeable when we attempt to impose our own values and beliefs on those from another society. For example, American managers plan activities,

Exhibit 2.8

Abbreviations for Countries and Regions in Value Dimension Graphics

ARA	Arab countries (Egypt, Lebanon, Libya, Kuwait, Iraq, Saudi Arabia, UAE.)	JAM	Jamaica
ARG	Argentina	JPN	Japan
AUL	Australia	KOR	South Korea
AUT	Austria	MAL	Malaysia
BRA	Brazil	MEX	Mexico
CAN	Canada	NET	Netherlands
CHL	Chile	NZL	New Zealand
COL	Colombia	PAK	Pakistan
COS	Costa Rica	PAN	Panama
DEN	Denmark	PER	Peru
EAF	East Africa (Kenya, Ethiopia, Zambia)	PHI	Philippines
EQA	Ecuador	POR	Portugal
FIN	Finland	SAF	South Africa
FRA	France	SAL	El Salvador
GBR	Great Britain	SIN	
GER	Germany	SPA	
GRE	Greece	SWE	
GUA	Guatemala	SWI	
HOK	Hong Kong	TAI	
IDO	Indonesia	THA	
IND	India	TUR	
IRA	Iran	URU	
IRE	Ireland	USA	
ISR	Israel	VEN	
ITA	Italy	WAF	
		YUG	

schedule them, and judge their timely completion based on the belief that people influence and control the future, rather than assuming that events will occur only at the will of Allah, as managers in an Islamic nation might believe. Many people in the world understand and relate to others only in terms of their own culture. This unconscious reference point of one's own cultural values is called a self-reference criterion.

An international manager, as a first step in cultural sensitivity, should understand his/her own culture. This awareness helps guard against adopting either a parochial or an ethnocentric attitude. Parochialism occurs when a German, for example, expects those from or in another country to automatically fall into patterns of behavior common in Germany. Ethnocentrism describes the attitude of those who operate from the assumption that their ways of doing things are best no matter where or under what conditions they are applied. Companies, both large and small, have demonstrated this lack of cultural sensitivity in countless subtle ways, with disastrous effects. After studying his/her own culture, the manager's next step toward establishing effective cross-cultural relations is to develop cultural sensitivity, as we have already mentioned earlier in this chapter. International managers not only must be aware of cultural variables and their effects on behavior in the workplace but also must appreciate cultural diversity and should understand how to build constructive working relationships anywhere in the world.

Cross-cultural Management and Training

International managers play a powerful role in determining the relative competitiveness of various countries in the global arena. Managers' skills and biases, based on their administrative heritage, will have a subtle influence on strategies and resource allocation. They will be faced with more cultures to understand, more social responsibilities to master, more time pressures to juggle, and more relationships to rethink.[20] Because an international manager is confronted with all these challenges, it is clear that his or her preparation for cross-cultural interactions is critical.

Both cross-cultural adjustment problems and practical differences in everyday life present challenges for expatriates and their families. Examples are evident from a 1998 survey of expatriates when they ranked the countries that presented the most challenging assignments to them, along with some comments from their experiences:

- *Brazil*: Expatriates stress that cell phones are essential because home phones do not work.
- *China*: Adjustment is a continuing problem for expatriates; one complained that at his welcome banquet he was served duck tongue and pigeon head.
- *India*: Returning executives complain that the pervasiveness of poverty and street children is overwhelming.
- *Indonesia*: Here you need to plan ahead financially because landlords typically demand rent two to three years in advance.
- *Japan*: Expatriates and their families remain concerned that although there is excellent medical care, Japanese doctors reveal little to their patients.

After these five countries, expatriates ranked Russia, Mexico, Saudi Arabia, South Korea, and France as being challenging to adjust to as well.

Even though cross-cultural training has proved to be effective, less than a third of expatriates are given such training. In a 1997 study by Harvey of 332 US expatriates (dual-career couples), the respondents stated that their multinational corporations (MNCs) had not provided them with sufficient training or social support during the international assignment.[21] Much of the rationale for this lack of training is an assumption that managerial skills and processes are universal. In a simplistic way, a manager's domestic track record is used as the major selection criterion for an overseas assignment.

Although training in language and practical affairs is quite straightforward, cross-cultural training is not; it is complex and deals with deep-rooted behaviors. The actual process of cross-cultural training should result in the expatriate learning both content and skills that will improve interactions with host-country individuals, thus reducing misunderstandings and inappropriate behaviors.

Culture Shock. The goal of this training is to ease the adjustment to the new environment by reducing culture shock—a state of disorientation and anxiety about not knowing how to behave in an unfamiliar culture. The cause of culture shock is the trauma people experience in new and different cultures, where they lose the familiar signs and cues that they had used to interact in daily life and where they must learn to cope with a great number of new cultural cues and expectations. Subculture shock, which is similar to culture shock, though usually less extreme, is the experience of subculture shock. This occurs when a manager is transferred to another part of the country where there are cultural differences—essentially from what he/she perceives to be a "majority" culture to a "minority" one. The shock comes from feeling like an "immigrant" in one's own country and being unprepared for such differences. For example, when someone moves from the northern part of France to the southern part, where people are friendlier, hospitable, and have a Mediterranean temperament. MNCs worldwide are filled with managers who fear dealing with the management of cultural differences—the diverse set of assumptions and expectations that people from different backgrounds bring into the workplace. When locally hired employees and expatriates, or headquarters-based, employees are combined, there are many opportunities for misunderstanding, frustration, and lost business.

The question "What type of skills, training, and experiences do you think stimulates executives to think and act globally?" was posed to a number of executives to find out what mindset their organizations have in terms of expatriates' work. Here are their responses:

First of all, I feel one of the most important skills is an appreciation and understanding of other cultures. In many cultures, a global manager knows it is not just the product that sells but how it is introduced and how you go about keeping your relationships with customers. Working in a diverse organization, knowing another language and having international experience are helpful in developing a global manager. More important than being technically oriented to a product is knowing how to measure the buying power of various cultures and understanding the dynamics of negotiating globally. I feel knowing other languages plays a crucial role in developing international negotiation skills.

Source: Spyros Charalambous, Logistics Manager, Carlsberg, Cyprus.

Unless you have experienced the world outside of your own country, it may be more challenging to be able to think and act globally. Those experiences influence a global manager more than anything else does. Also, being part of a multi-nationally diverse management team gives global managers the arena to really think globally.

Source: David Marshall, International Human Resource Manager, Nokia.

Practical Tips

Most managers in MNCs fall under one of two categories: those who deny that culture is an "issue" and therefore refuse to talk about cultural differences because they worry that it will drive their multicultural workforce apart or those who are afraid to tackle the issue, too busy with "more important" issues, or do not know where to begin. There are four vital areas to look at when an MNC is assessing its approach to manage a given culture:

- There are certain consequences when culture is not managed. These might be lack of timely information sharing, derogatory name-calling of cultural "others," inability to enter a new market, loss of market share, lack of trust between the organization and its cultural counterparts, inability to recruit and retain quality employees, low productivity, and so on. For example, one US-based MNC suffered a high turnover rate in several countries, from both relocated American expatriate managers and locally recruited managers. The American expatriates returned to the United States prematurely and some left the company. None had received any preparation about the impact of cultural differences on their jobs or lives. Local managers complained of a lack of timely

information from the US headquarters and opposed the US "company way" of dealing with customers.
- There are also certain common defenses that are being used to justify refraining from managing culture. "If we focus on differences, it will drive us apart." "Culture doesn't matter—we're all human and have the same goal." "Language is the only barrier—if we speak their language, there would be no misunderstandings. If I become too effective in this culture, I run the risk of being alienated by the home office."

The argument that "all people are motivated by the same things" was dispelled in the company that insisted all salespeople be compensated on the US model of 50 percent commission and 50 percent salary. The Japanese wanted 100 percent salary. The eventual compromise was 80 percent salary and 20 percent commission. Still, the Japanese sales staff was so demotivated that sales volume and market share eroded. After three years, the Americans accepted the original 100 percent salary compensation. This delay in trusting the local Japanese managers cost the US company hundreds of millions of dollars in lost revenues.

- International managers should possess the necessary attitudes and skills for managing culture. Be open to clarifying with your colleagues the assumptions, expectations, and behaviors you consider "common sense." Are they the same? Be willing to break some rules considered to be sacred at headquarters. Be willing to learn management and communication skills that are effective in the target culture and practice them.

One Japanese corporation with extensive US operations devoted one year to developing a set of values for doing business in ways that respected both cultures. This blending of values resulted in a synergy that improved operations, management–employee relations, recruitment, and customer service.

- There are some obvious benefits from managing culture. An international manager will develop allies among the local managers; he/she will enjoy a successful term as a manager in a foreign country or on a project in which he/she will be dealing with managers from other countries; and eventually, the MNC will increase its market share.

The opportunities to put these ideas into practice are many, and the benefits of managing cultural differences, compared to the consequences of not managing them, should convince the international manager to deal wisely with cultural issues.

Furthermore, in light of the new global environment, international managers must be culturally literate and they can learn from the best. Each part of the world excels in a different literacy area. Some Asian cultures, for example, teach us about personal literacy through their ability to understand paradox and ambiguity. Latin American cultures teach us about social literacy by modeling how to build relationships in less-organized, constantly changing environments. From European cultures, we learn cultural literacy based on centuries of living and working cross-culturally. In North America, we learn business literacy by building change-ready, technology-savvy, high-performance organizations in a results-oriented culture. It is also vital to understand how your culture influences how you relate to technology. Americans love new technology; they like quick action and excel at creating new things. They tend to abandon ideas that do not show a rapid return on investment. The Japanese, on the other hand, are more comfortable with incremental improvements.

When it comes to presentations, what works in one culture does not necessarily translate well—on a cultural level—to the rest of the world. To avoid a culture clash overseas and to ensure a positive connection, the following guidelines should be followed when planning a presentation for an international audience. Identify the decision makers? In many cultures, especially Asian ones, the most powerful people who make the final decisions are typically not present at formal presentations. In this, and in other similar cases, presenters need to connect equally with all members of the audience and not expect quick decisions.

If senior people are present, the presenters may want to direct most of their remarks to them, yet make eye contact with others in the audience. Also, it must be known that "yes" among the British means "maybe" and that among Asians, if said immediately, probably means "no." Communicate the essentials. Doing the homework includes knowing how much information the audience needs to hear. Speakers often become so absorbed in researching topics that they fail to realize which essentials can get the point across. Typically, the presenter could be on track if he/she shares only 2 percent of his/her knowledge with the audience.

While many cultures respond well to lots of detail, the presenters should avoid presenting too many details and unnecessary data for fear of clouding the central message. Set the pace. The presentation should be paced at a rate that is consistent with the culture. South Americans, for example, are usually energetic and passionate and like presentations to proceed at a fast clip. This varies tremendously from Europeans who prefer more time to assimilate information. When in doubt, the presenters should use silence by taking a break, checking for comprehension, and then continuity. Respect personal space. How much the presenters physically interact with their audience depends on the culture's definition of suitable audience distance. Americanss, for example, are used to seeing speakers go into audiences and ask impromptu questions. More formal British audiences would be appalled by such informality. This same sensitivity should apply to how close you stand next to someone. People in Latin American and Mediterranean countries have no problem with touching and standing close to others, while some Europeans may not appreciate such intimacy. Watch color cues. In selecting visuals, the presenters should be aware that in certain cultures different colors have different meanings. For example, in Japan white symbolizes death. Similarly, in some Latin countries yellow has negative connotations. Rephrase questions. Particularly where language barriers may exist, the presenters should make sure they fully understand the audience's questions. Even if a translator is present, always rephrase the questions, which will buy the presenters more time to formulate in-depth answers. Presenters should be more flexible to accommodate some cultures, which allows more floor time per questioner, than others. Hold the jokes. Humor rarely translates well from culture to culture. Projecting a cordial nature is appropriate everywhere, but avoid phrases with a political/religious flavor that might offend the audience.

The following section presents a case that shows how foreigners adjust to the American culture. It demonstrates a reverse perspective as to what other people do to understand the American culture, which in many instances is a puzzle for foreign managers.

Closing Case

Adjusting to the American Culture

A group of Arab oil workers sent to Texas for training found American teaching methods impersonal. Several Japanese workers at a US manufacturing plant had to learn how to put courtesy aside and interrupt conversations when there was trouble. Executives of a Swiss-based multinational company could not understand why its American managers demanded more autonomy than their European counterparts.

To all these people, America is a foreign country with a strange corporate culture. Just as Americans doing business abroad must grapple with unfamiliar social and commercial practices, so too must a growing number of European, Asian, and Latin American managers of US subsidiaries struggle with diversity. "Most people think that culture is manners, food, dress, arts and crafts," says Clifford Clarke, president of IRI International, a Redwood City, California, consulting company. "They don't realize that how you motivate a guy is culturally determined. Every managerial task is culturally determined." Occasionally, transferees find that behavior suitable at home may irritate coworkers here. A recent training film portrays a Japanese employee living in the United States angering an American colleague by repeatedly apologizing for a late report; the American expects explanations and solutions. "In America, if you talk around things, people get frustrated with you," says Lennie Copeland, who helped produce the film.

Jose Carlos Villates, a business manager for animal health products at American Cyanamid Company, also had a problem with office protocol. In Puerto Rico and the Dominican Republic, where he was raised, businesspeople would begin meetings with relaxed chitchat. At the company's headquarters in Wayne, New Jersey, however, he says he picks up "signals or body language" that Americans find such sociability a waste of time. Even after 15 months in the United States, Villates feels uncomfortable plunging abruptly into business. "It strikes us as cold-blooded," he says. Europeans, on the other hand, can be flummoxed by "a deceiving appearance of informality," says French-born Andre Rude, who counsels international tranferees at Hewlett-Packard in Palo Alto, California. "They don't realize the urgency of the request and find themselves in trouble" when work isn't done on time.

Question: How would you go about adjusting to the American culture based on the various scenarios presented above?

Source: Compiled by the author.

Chapter Summary

At the beginning of this chapter we have presented a number of definitions on culture, starting from some earlier ones and ending by presenting some more recent ones. All of these definitions lead to the conclusion that despite the cultural differences, cultures face a number of common issues and characteristics.

We have also addressed the needs that all cultures must satisfy and the universal cultural patterns that emerge while attempting to satisfy such needs. Such needs deal with economic systems, marriage and family systems, educational institutions, social control systems, and the so-called supernatural belief systems.

The following elements can be useful in understanding culture better: dress and appearance; communication and language; sense of self and space; food and feeding habits; time and time consciousness; relationships; gender; social values. Furthermore, Trompenaar's value dimensions were presented as an additional tool for analyzing culture. The Kluckhohn–Strodtbeck and Hofstede frameworks were also presented. Their analysis assists international managers better understand the way organizations function within their own culture.

The most important world religions, namely Christianity, Islam, Hinduism, and Buddhism were presented with their philosophies and what impact they have on international business.

A number of cross-cultural management and training issues were presented and a potpourri of practical tips was recommended for international business managers to follow.

Review and Discussion Questions

1. Define culture. Which definition in your opinion, is the most appropriate and why? Provide examples?
2. Which needs must be satisfied by culture? Briefly explain each and provide examples.
3. Present culture and its elements. Provide examples and relate them to international business.
4. What is the role of each major religion in conducting international business? What do Christianity, Islam, Hinduism, and Buddhism declare in terms of business?
5. Describe Trompenaar's value dimensions and discuss their use in international business.
6. Compare and contrast the Kluckhohn–Strodtbeck and Hofstede frameworks and their application in understanding culture.
7. What is parochialism? Culture shock? Ethnocentrism? Provide examples.
8. What do we mean by cross-cultural management and training?
9. How would you train an international business manager?
10. Which practical tips would you provide as the most appropriate when it comes to international business, and why?

Endnotes

1. A. L. Kroeber and Clyde Kluckhohn, *Culture: A Critical Review of Concepts and Definitions* (New York: Vintage Books, 1952).
2. E. B. Tylor, *Primitive Culture* (London: Murray, 1871).
3. Kluckhohn, C. and Kelly, W. H. "The concept of culture." In R. Linton (ed.), *The Science of Man in the World Culture*, pp. 78–105 (New York: Columbia University Press, 1945).
4. Melville J. Herskovits, *Cultural Anthropology*, p. 569 (New York: Alfred A. Knopf, 1955).
5. James F. Downs, *Cultures in crisis* (Beverly Hills, California: Glencoe Press, 1971).
6. R. D. Robinson, *Internationalization of Business: An Introduction* (New York: Dryden Press, 1983).
7. Lawrence E. Harrison, Samuel P. Huntington (eds), *Culture Matters: How Values Shape Human Progress* (New York: Basic Books, 2001).

8. Charles Hampden-Turner, "Fons Trompenaars," *Building Cross-Cultural Competence* (Yale University Press, 2001. Based also on Trompenaars' work in 1993).

9. http://en.wikipedia.org/wiki/Islamic_studies.

10. S. Ismail, *Rethinking Islamist politics: Culture, the State and Islamism* (London/New York: I.B. Tauris, 2003).

11. Ibid.

12. K. Hutchings and D. Weir, "Guanxi and Wasta: A Comparison." *Thunderbird International Business Review*, Vol. 48(1), pp. 141–156. January–February, 2006.

13. S. Abuznaid, "Islam and Management: What Can Be Learned?" *Thunderbird International Business Review*, Vol. 48(1), pp. 125–139. January–February, 2006.

14. M. Weber, *The Protestant Ethic and the Spirit of Capitalism* (New York: Charles Scribner's Sons, 1958, original 1904–1905).

15. Charles W. Hill, *International Business. Competing in the Global Marketplace*, 6th edn (McGraw-Hill International Edition, 2007).

16. See R. Dore, *Taking Japan Seriously*, and C. W. L. Hill, "Transaction Cost Economizing as a Source of Comparative Advantage: The Case of Japan," *Organization Science* 6 (1995).

17. F. Kluckhohn and F. L. Strodtbeck, *Variations in Value Orientations* (New York: Harper & Row, 1961).

18. G. Hofstede, "The Cultural Relativity of Organizational Practices and Theories," *Journal of International Business Studies* (Fall 1983), pp. 75–89, and G. Hofstede, *Cultures and Organizations: Software of the Mind* (New York: McGraw-Hill, 1997).

19. P. C. Earley, "Social loafing and collectivism: A comparison of the United States and the People's Republic of China," *Administrative Science Quarterly*, Vol. 34, pp. 565–581, 1989.

20. P. Harris, R. Moran and S. Moran, *Managing Cultural Differences: Global Leadership Strategies for the 21st Century*, 6th edn (The Elsevier Press, 2006).

21. M. Harvey, "Dual Career Expatriates: Expectations, Adjustment, and Satisfaction with International Relocation," *Journal of International Business Studies*, Vol. 28(3), pp. 627–658 (3rd Qtr., 1997).

Theories of International Trade and International Investment

Objectives

Through this chapter, the student will be exposed to:

- International trade in general and its importance
- Mercantilism
- Adam Smith and the theory of absolute advantage
- David Ricardo and the theory of comparative advantage
- The Heckscher–Ohlin (H-O, factor proportions) model
- Raymond Vernon and the product life cycle theory of trade
- Contemporary trade theories
- Porter's diamond.

Opening Case

Cyprus and Trade

Throughout its history, Cyprus, an island in the eastern Mediterranean Sea, has been heavily involved in trade. Cyprus traded with the Phoenicians, the Venetians, the Arabs, the Assyrians, the Romans, and the Greeks. It is a country with approximately 800,000 inhabitants, with the majority being Greek-Cypriots and a minority Turkish-Cypriots, Armenians, and Maronites (a sect of the Catholic Church that originated in Lebanon).

From the Neolithic period to the middle Bronze Age, ca. 7500–1600 BC, we know of the first Cypriots who inhabited the island and were involved in the trade of pottery and copper. By ca. 1700 BC, there was a mass export of pottery to Syria and Palestine. During the late Bronze Age, ca. 1600–1050 BC, the island emerged as a commercial center, with trade exchanges intensifying with Egypt and the Levant, especially with the emporium of Ugarit on the north Syrian coast. Cypriot pottery, apart from copper, now enjoyed a wide circulation overseas. Commercial enterprise encouraged the growth of large mercantile cities on the east and southeast coasts of the island.

From 1250 BC onward, Cyprus became embroiled in the general collapse of Bronze Age civilizations in the eastern Mediterranean. Peaceful commerce was interrupted by piracy; among Mycenaean visitors, the merchant was replaced by the soldier of fortune.

The Iron Age, ca. 1050–300 BC, around 8th Century, was a time of recovery and of rapidly widening horizons for trade with Cyprus. Contact with the Aegean was restored, and eastward trade flourished once again.

During the Hellenistic and the Roman period, ca. 300 BC–AD 330, Cyprus continued to trade mainly with Egypt and the other provinces under the Roman Empire.

Under the Greco-Roman period, 50 BC–AD 395, and the Byzantine period, 395–1191, Cyprus expanded its trade activities, especially with regard to pottery, copper, and bronze products in most of Europe, North Africa, and the Middle East all the way to Persia (what is known as Iran today) and India.

There were a number of rulers in Cyprus since 1184, ranging from the Lusignan Dynasty (1192–1489) to the Venetian Occupation (1489–1571), to the Turkish Occupation, as an Ottoman province (1571–1878). Then, Cyprus came under the British Administration from 1878 to 1960, when it gained its independence from the British Crown. During all these periods, Cyprus was heavily involved in trade, mainly with the native lands of its rulers and the other lands they had occupied.

In 1960, the newly formed government of Cyprus inherited an economy that exhibited most of the symptoms of underdevelopment. The productive base of the country was inadequate and economic activity was dependent on unstable factors; agriculture was the dominant sector in economic activity and accounted for 16 percent of the gross domestic product (GDP) and 45 percent of gainful employment; manufacturing activity was essentially restricted to the processing of locally produced agricultural raw materials; tourism had not yet taken off; exports had the characteristic structure of underdeveloped countries, with primary commodities such as minerals (53 percent of the total) and agricultural products (32 percent of the total) dominating; hidden unemployment and underemployment were widespread and mass emigration was taking place; financial capital was flowing out of the country, a clear indication of the existing uncertainty.

The Government of Cyprus through a number of five-year plans started working on the recovery of the economy, and the years between independence in 1960 and the Turkish Invasion in 1974 were characterized by sustained growth, accompanied by conditions of external and internal economic stability. The GDP grew at an average annual rate of about 7 percent in real terms. Agricultural production doubled, while industrial production and exports of goods and services more than trebled. Tourism became the single largest foreign exchange earner. Fixed capital formation increased from 18 percent of GDP in 1961 to 28.5 percent in 1973. Exports from 1960 to 1973 were worth 1 billion US dollars and the main exports were agricultural products, wine, and citrus to the United Kingdom, Germany, Greece, the Scandinavian countries, and clothing and shoes to the Middle East. Total imports for the same period were twice the amount of exports. Imports were in terms of heavy machinery and equipment, vehicles, electric appliances, and other raw materials, from the United Kingdom, other European countries, and the United States.

In 1974, the rapid and sustained economic development was utterly disrupted by the Turkish Invasion and the occupation of about one third of the territory of the country by the Turkish army. Under this situation, the Government of Cyprus adopted a short-term campaign of providing relief to the 200,000 refugees displaced by the Turkish Army, and from a medium- and long-term perspective, it was considered essential to arrest the economic slide and lay the foundations for economic recovery and the creation of new employment opportunities. Both objectives necessitated the adoption of expansionary fiscal and monetary policies and the promotion of labor-intensive projects.

The progress of the economy is indicated by the impressive rate of growth, which over the period 1975–1981 averaged 10 percent per annum in real terms. This emanated primarily from the foreign demand for goods and services, which grew on average by 15 percent in constant prices. The impressive growth performance was based on a number of exogenous and endogenous factors. Exogenous factors, such as the booming Arab markets, the Lebanese crisis of 1975, favorable weather, and high international market prices for some of the major Cyprus agricultural products, provided the impetus that lifted the economy. An additional element was foreign aid, which helped bridge the financing gap. Internally, the aggressive and expansionary fiscal and monetary policies, the entrepreneurial ability, which exploited the arising export opportunities, the acceptance by trade unions of a substantial cut in wage levels, and the diligence and work ethic of the people formed the front that led the economy to the path of recovery.

From 1974 to 2001, Cyprus, among other actions, reduced the import tariffs in the context of the implementation of the Customs Union Agreement with the EU. Exports as well as services increased, and Cyprus is slowly but surely becoming a center for offering services to offshore companies from all over the world and a hub of consulting companies and private institutions of higher learning. The average ratio of exports to the gross national product (GNP) from 1981 to 2001 was 17.8 percent, an increase of 5 percent from the decade prior to 1981.

Today, Cyprus is a full member of the EU (since May 1, 2004). Furthermore, the trade relations of Cyprus with the EU, Eastern Europe, Russia, China, Japan, and the United States have strengthened in the last ten years, and being a member of the WTO has enhanced this island's trade prospects in the world. The EU is the major trading partner of Cyprus and in that the Ministry of Commerce, Industry and Tourism provides various incentives and assistance, including an insurance scheme for exports, a scheme for financial aid to manufacturers/exporters for market research abroad, the organization of trade missions and visits of foreign importers and journalists to Cyprus, the participation in trade fairs and specialized exhibitions abroad, the advertising of Cypriot products abroad, the research of export markets, the dissemination of trade and economic information, and the operation of the Cyprus Trade Centers abroad, such as in Austria, Belgium, the Czech and Slovak republics, France, Germany, Greece, Japan, Kuwait, Russia, Sweden, the United Arab Emirates, the United Kingdom, and the United States.

Question: After reading this chapter can you determine whether the trade theories helped you better understand the trade issues facing Cyprus throughout its history? What do you think Cyprus should do in terms of enhancing its trade horizon? Do you think that EU membership will help the island's trade activities?

Sources: Panteli, Stavros, *The Making of Modern Cyprus. From Obscurity to Statehood*, Interworld Publications, 1990; Press and Information Office, Cyprus, 1996; Press and Information Office, The Almanac of Cyprus, 1996; Mr. John Shiekkeris, Trade Senior Officer, Ministry of Commerce, Industry and Tourism, Government of Cyprus, Interview, April 15, 2002.

International Trade in General and its Importance

Countries are linked in many different ways, whether it is through political, social, cultural, or commercial events and activities. One such link is international trade, which is the exchange of goods and services between people, organizations, and countries. In the last five decades, trade among nations has grown in great proportions,[1] and it is freer now than ever before. This exchange takes place because of differences in the costs of production between countries and because it increases the economic welfare of each country by widening the range of goods and services available for consumption.

For as long as countries and businesses have been in existence, international trade has been a vital means of the countries' and businesses' economies. Why does international trade take place and how does it affect the countries' and businesses' existence and viability? Does trade take place between countries or between companies? What is the importance of international trade theories within the framework of a country's competitiveness? Does international trade improve the welfare of a country's citizens? Why do students of international business need to study international trade? All these questions will be discussed within the context of this chapter, and hopefully students will have a better understanding of international trade and its implications in today's global environment. A number of international trade theories will be discussed to ensure that the readers appreciate the contributions of these trade theorists to the field of international trade throughout the years. Furthermore, the students will be challenged to determine whether these trade theories are applicable to today's global exchange of goods and services.

Mercantilism

Mercantilism is an economic and cultural philosophy of the sixteenth and seventeenth centuries, reflecting the emergence of economies based on commerce. Mercantilists attached great importance to the attainment of a net inflow of precious metals and imports were discouraged by duties. The policy was also marked by aggressive nationalism toward overseas colonies. This trade theory stated that the government should establish economic policies that promoted exports and discouraged imports, so that the trade surplus created should be paid for in gold and silver. This was a time of state building, when national monarchs sought to consolidate and extend their own power, and to enhance the power and prestige of their states, by all available means. Mercantilism, or "economic state building," commonly involved extensive governmental intervention in economic life with the objective of fostering the growth of national commerce and industry. Tax exemptions, loans, subsidies, and other forms of state aid encouraged newly established industries, and elaborate regulative schemes were instituted to control their development and assure the quality of their products.

Mercantilist Doctrines: The measures taken by Jean Baptiste Colbert (1619–1683), the greatest of all mercantilist statesmen, as finance minister to Louis XIV of France, are typical.[2] A central aim of *colbertisme* (the common

French synonym for mercantilism) was to increase the taxable wealth of the kingdom so that the monarch would have sufficient revenue to support his ambitious policies of political consolidation and territorial expansion. A second purpose of Colbert's program was to expand industrial production with a view to achieving self-sufficiency and a consequent reduction in necessary imports of goods and services from abroad. French exports, on the other hand, were to be increased to the point where they exceeded imports, thus bringing about the "favorable balance of trade" so much desired by virtually all mercantilists. The result would be a net influx of bullion (gold and silver). This was desired because it was assumed that commerce would be stimulated by an increase in monetary circulation. In addition, nations without domestic gold or silver mines could hope to acquire the reserves of precious metals needed to provide the "sinews of war" only by this means. In an age when bank credit and paper money were still undeveloped, the supply of bullion assumed a disproportionate importance. Colbert and his mercantilist contemporaries seem also to have believed that the total quantity of commerce in the world was fixed or, at any rate, only slowly changing.[3] Consequently, a nation could increase its share only at the expense of its rivals. This meant that mercantilist statesmen were ready to resort to any means, even including actual warfare, to advance their trading interests or to injure those of their competitors.

Mercantilist rivalries extended to the colonial field. Countries sought colonies as markets for their manufactures, as sources of food and raw materials, and as outlets for surplus population. The colony was to complement, rather than compete with, the home economy. Each colonizing power was determined to reserve to itself the entire benefit of trade with its own overseas possessions, and foreign interlopers were excluded as much as possible. Spain and Portugal attempted to enforce almost complete monopolies of trade with their colonies, while France, England, and especially the Netherlands tried to apply more flexible policies. The English Navigation Acts, from 1651 onward, aimed at creating a monopoly of the carrying trade between Britain's colonies and the rest of the world.

In Central Europe, where overseas trade and colonial expansion were less emphasized, a different type of mercantilism grew up, chiefly in Austria and Prussia. This was known as cameralism because it was heavily oriented toward filling the royal treasury (Kammer). Encouragement was given to new industries. Immigrants—particularly those having special economic capabilities—were welcomed. Model farms were established to improve agricultural methods and to promote the use of better crops and livestock strains. Taxation was reformed so as to foster new investment and population growth, and efforts were made to decrease dependence on imports.

Critics of Mercantilism: Toward the middle of the eighteenth century there developed widespread criticism of mercantilist assumptions and there were attacks on the restrictive policies that stemmed from them. The reformers placed their faith in the maxim of the French liberal economist and administrator Vincent de Gournay (1712–1759): "laissez faire, laissez passer," which may be freely translated as "leave things alone, let goods pass." This free-trade philosophy was developed further by Francois Quesnay (1694–1774) and his followers, the French physiocrats, who protested against mercantilist preoccupation with industry and commerce and the consequent neglect of agriculture. They believed that new wealth arose only in agriculture and extractive industries, and so opposed encouragement of "sterile" urban pursuits. But the most devastating attacks on the mercantile system were those of David Hume (1711–1776)—who proved that bullionism was self-defeating because it was necessarily inflationary—and, above all, of Adam Smith (1723–1790), whose *Wealth of Nations* was published in 1776. While admitting that the navigation acts had gone far to make England mistress of the seas, Smith condemned most forms of government intervention in economic life on the ground that the free competitive market was, in the long run, a far more effective regulator. Coming simultaneously with the revolt of the 13 American colonies (provoked in substantial part by Britain's efforts to tighten its mercantilist regulations after the Seven Years' War), Smith's writings had a tremendous impact on the thought and action of subsequent generations. Only in the twentieth and the twenty-first centuries, in response to problems of war economy and pressures for full employment, has there been a revival of "neomercantilist"—that is protectionist, interventionist, nationalist, populationist—policies.

Although the era of mercantilism ended in the last part of the seventeenth century, this theory's arguments still have applications today. Nations encourage more exports than imports of goods and services so that they can have a more favorable trade balance. In other words, exports bring revenues to a country, and imports cause a nation to pay.

Adam Smith and the Theory of Absolute Advantage

Why can't countries rely on the goods and services they produce, and be self-sufficient? In Adam Smith's (1723–1790) writings we find many of the answers to the aforementioned question. Smith's major work, *An Inquiry into the Nature and Causes of the Wealth of Nations*, which appeared in 1776, became the foundation upon which was constructed the whole subsequent tradition of English classical economics. Smith was primarily concerned with the factors that led to increased wealth in a community and he rejected the physiocrat's view of the preeminent position of agriculture, recognizing the parallel contribution of the manufacturing industry. He began his analysis by means of a sketch of a primitive society of hunters.

If it cost twice the labor to kill a beaver as it does to kill a deer, one beaver would exchange for two deer. Labor was the fundamental measure of value, though actual prices of commodities were determined by supply and demand on the market. There were two elements in the problem of increasing wealth: (a) the skill of the labor force and (b) the proportion of productive to unproductive labor. (According to Smith, the service industries did not contribute to real wealth.) The key to (a) was the division of labor.

To illustrate his point, he quoted the example of the manufacture of pins. If one man were given the task of carrying out all the operations of pin manufacture—drawing the wire, cutting, head fitting, and sharpening—his output would be increased hundredfold. The size of the output need only be limited by the size of its market. The key to (b) was the accumulation of capital. Not only did this enable plant and machinery to be created to assist labor, but it also enabled labor to be employed. Capital for the latter was the wages fund. The workers must be fed and clothed during the period of production in advance of the income earned from their own efforts. Smith believed that the economic system was harmonious and required minimum of government interference (laissez-faire). Although each individual was motivated by self-interest, they acted for the good of the whole, guided by a "hidden hand" made possible by the free play of competition.

Free competition was the essential ingredient of the efficient economy. However, from his *Wealth of Nations* it is clear that not only did his scholarship range widely over the fields of history and contemporary business, but that, at the same time, he was a very practical man. He was quite aware, for instance, of the forces that were at work to limit competition: "People of the same trade seldom meet together even for merriment and diversion, but the conversation ends in a conspiracy against the public, or on some contrivance to raise prices."[4] In his discussions on public finance, he laid down four principles of taxation: (a) equality (taxes proportionate to ability to pay); (b) certainty; (c) convenience; and (d) economy.

On the basis of the aforementioned discussion and his contributions to international trade, he developed the theory of absolute advantage. According to this theory, a country can produce some goods more efficiently than other countries. This is based on the fact that a country's advantage would be either natural (climate and natural resources) or acquired (technology and skills) in the production of goods. Smith extended his division of labor in the production process to a division of labor and specialized product across countries. Each country would specialize in a product for which it was uniquely suited. More would be produced for less. Thus, a country with absolute advantage could produce more in total and exchange products—trade—for goods that were cheaper in price than those produced at home.

Exhibit 3.1

Absolute Advantage

Country	Olive oil	Shoes
Spain	2	4
Italy	4	2

The example in Exhibit 3.1 illustrates the theory of absolute advantage. The relative efficiency of each country in the production of the two products is measured by comparing the number of man-hours needed to produce 1 unit of each product.

Spain has an absolute advantage in the production of olive oil. It requires fewer man-hours (2 being less than 4) for Spain to produce 1 unit of olive oil. Italy, on the other hand, has an absolute advantage in the production of shoes. It requires fewer man-hours (2 being less than 4) for Italy to produce 1 unit of shoes. Spain is obviously more efficient in the production of olive oil. It takes Italy 4 man-hours to produce 1 unit of olive oil whereas it takes Spain only 2 man-hours to produce the same unit of olive oil. Italy takes twice as many man-hours to produce the same output. Italy needs 2 man-hours to produce 1 unit of shoes that takes Spain 4 man-hours to produce. Spain therefore requires 2 more man-hours than Italy to produce the same unit of shoes. The two countries are exactly opposite in relative efficiency of production.

David Ricardo and the Theory of Comparative Advantage

David Ricardo took the logic of absolute advantage in production one step further to explain how countries could exploit their own advantages and gain from international trade.

Ricardo had little formal education. At the early age of 14, however, he was already working in the money market. He succeeded in making a fortune on the stock exchange, sufficient for him to be able to retire at 42. Not surprisingly, many of his earlier publications were concerned with money and banking. In 1815 he published his *Essay on the Influence of the Low Price of Corn on the Profits of the Stock*, which was the prototype for his most important work. This first appeared in 1817 under the title of the *Principles of Political Economy and Taxation*, a work that was to dominate English classical economics for the following half-century. In his *Principles*[5] Ricardo was basically concerned about determining the laws that regulate the distribution (between the different classes of landowners, capitalists, and labor) of the produce of industry. His approach was to construct a theoretical model that abstracted from the complexities of an actual economy so as to attempt to reveal the major important influences at work within it. His economy was predominantly agricultural. With demand rising as a result of increasing population, and a level of subsistence that tended, by custom, to rise also over time, more and more less-fertile land had to be brought into cultivation. The return (in terms of the output of corn) of each further addition of capital and labor to more land fell. This process continued until it was no longer considered sufficiently profitable to bring any additional plots of land under cultivation. However, opportunity costs and profits must be the same on all land, whether or not it was marginal. Labor cost was the same wherever it was applied. If profits were higher at one place than at another, it would encourage capital to be invested at the place of high return, until by the process of diminishing returns, profit fell into line with profits elsewhere. Therefore, as costs and profits were the same throughout, a surplus was earned on the nonmarginal land, and this was rent.

The consequence of this was that as the population expanded and more less-fertile land was brought under cultivation, profits became squeezed between the increasing proportion of total output that went in rent and the basic minimum level of subsistence allocated to the wages of labor. Ricardo assumed that prices were determined principally by the quantity of labor used during production. However, he recognized that capital costs did nevertheless also have an influence on prices and that the effect of a rise in wages on relative prices depended on the proportion of these two factors of production in the various commodities. With a rise in wages, capital-intensive goods became cheaper than labor-intensive goods, with a consequent shift in the demand and output in favor of the former.

In the theory of international trade Ricardo stated explicitly for the first time the law of comparative costs. This theory of comparative advantage can best be illustrated by means of the example of two countries (Spain and Italy) producing two commodities, shoes and olive oil. If the relative cost of shoes to olive oil is the same in both countries, then no trade will take place because there is no gain to be had by exchanging olive oil (or shoes) for shoes (or olive oil) produced abroad for that produced at home. Trade will take place where cost differences exist. These can be of two kinds. First, if olive oil is cheap in Spain and shoes in Italy, Spain will specialize in olive oil and Italy in shoes, and exchange will take place to their mutual advantage. Second, the theory of comparative advantage states the condition under which trade will take place, even though both commodities may be produced more cheaply in one country than in another (Exhibit 3.2).

Italy exports 1 unit of olive oil to Spain, and imports in exchange 120/100 units of shoes. If Italy had devoted the 80 man-hours employed in making

Exhibit 3.2

Comparative Advantage

Country	Olive oil	Shoes
Spain	120*	100
Italy	80	90

* *Man hours per unit of olive oil*

olive oil for exports to making cloth, it would have produced only 80/90 units of shoes. Italy therefore gains from the trade by the difference ((120/100)–(80/90)) in the units of shoes. As long as Italy can exchange olive oil for shoes at a rate higher than 80/90, it will gain from the trade. If Spain exports 1 unit of shoes to Italy, it will obtain in exchange 90/80 units of olive oil. If the 100 man-hours required by Spain to produce 1 unit of shoes had been devoted to the home production of olive oil, only 100/120 units of olive oil would be obtained. The gain from trade therefore is ((90/80)–(100/120)) units of olive oil. If Spain can exchange shoes for olive oil at a rate higher than 100/120, it will gain from the trade. Within the range of exchange of olive oil for shoes of 120/100 and 80/90, both countries therefore benefit.

The theory of comparative advantage survives as an important part of the theory of international trade today. Overall, comparative advantage according to Ricardo was based on what was given up or traded off in producing one product instead of the other.

The Heckscher–Ohlin (Factor Proportions) Model

The previous model was developed in the nineteenth century, primarily by David Ricardo. It considers only one factor of production—labor. The Heckscher–Ohlin (H-O) model, also known as factor proportions theory, expands on the Ricardian model by allowing multiple factors of production. The H-O model was originally developed in the 1920s by two Swedish economists, Eli Heckscher and his student Bertil Ohlin, who received the Nobel Prize in Economics in 1977. The H-O model incorporates a number of realistic characteristics of production that are left out of the simple Ricardian model. Recall that in the simple Ricardian model only one factor of production, labor, is needed to produce goods and services. The productivity of labor is assumed to vary across countries, which implies a difference in technology between nations. It was the difference in technology that motivated advantageous international trade in the model.

The standard H-O model[6] begins by expanding the number of factors of production from one to two. The model assumes that labor and capital are used in the production of two final goods. Here, capital refers to the physical machines and equipment that is used in production. Thus, machine tools, conveyers, trucks, forklifts, computers, office buildings, office supplies, and much more are considered capital.

All productive capital must be owned by someone. In a capitalist economy most of the physical capital is owned by individuals and businesses. In a socialist economy productive capital would be owned by the government. In most economies today, the government owns some of the productive capital but private citizens and businesses own most of the capital. Any person who owns common stock issued by a business has an ownership share in that company and is entitled to dividends or income based on the profitability of the company. As such, the person is a capitalist, that is an owner of capital.

The H-O model assumes private ownership of capital. Use of capital in production generates income for the owner. We will refer to that income as capital "rents." Thus, workers earn "wages" for their efforts in production whereas the capital owner earns rents.

The assumption of two productive factors, capital and labor, allows for the introduction of another realistic feature in production: that of differing factor proportions both across and within industries. When one considers a range of industries in a country it is easy to convince oneself that the proportion of capital to labor used varies considerably. For example, steel production generally involves a large number of expensive machines and equipment spread over perhaps hundreds of acres of land, but also uses relatively few workers. In the tomato industry, in contrast, harvesting requires hundreds of migrant workers to handpick and collect each fruit from the vine. The amount of machinery used in this process is relatively small.

In the H-O model we define the ratio of the quantity of capital to the quantity of labor in a production process as the capital–labor ratio. We imagine, and therefore assume, that different industries, producing different goods, have different capital–labor ratios. It is this ratio (or proportion) of one factor to another that gives the model its generic name: the factor proportions model.

In a model in which each country produces two goods, an assumption must be made as to which industry has the higher capital–labor ratio. Thus, if the two goods that a country can produce are steel and clothing, and if steel production uses more capital per unit of labor than is used in clothing production, then we would say steel production is capital-intensive relative to clothing production. Also, if steel production is capital-intensive, then it implies that clothing production must be labor-intensive relative to steel.

Another realistic characteristic of the world is that countries have different quantities, or endowments, of capital and labor available for use in the production process. Thus, some countries like the United States are well endowed with physical capital relative to its labor force. In contrast, many less developed countries have very little physical capital but are well endowed with a large labor force. We use the ratio of the aggregate endowment of capital to the aggregate endowment of labor to define the relative factor abundancy between countries. Thus, if, for example, the United States has a larger ratio of aggregate capital per unit of labor than France, we would say that the United States is capital-abundant relative to France. By implication, France would have a larger ratio of aggregate labor per unit of capital and thus France would be labor-abundant relative to the United States.

The H-O model assumes that the only difference between countries is found in the relative endowments of factors of production. It is ultimately shown that trade will occur, trade will be nationally advantageous, and trade will have characterizable effects upon prices, wages, and rents when the nations differ in their relative factor endowments and when different industries use factors in different proportions.

It is worth emphasizing a fundamental distinction between the H-O model and the Ricardian model. The Ricardian model assumes that production technologies differ between countries whereas the H-O model assumes that production technologies are the same. The reason for the identical technology assumption in the H-O model is perhaps not so much because it is believed that technologies are really the same, although a case can be made for that. Instead, the assumption is useful because it enables us to see precisely how differences in resource endowments are sufficient to cause trade and it shows what impacts will arise entirely due to these differences.

The Main Results of the H-O Model: The H-O theorem predicts the pattern of trade between countries based on the characteristics of the countries. The H-O theorem says that a capital-abundant country will export capital-intensive goods while the labor-abundant countries will export labor-intensive goods. Here is why.

A capital-abundant country is one that is well endowed with capital in comparison with another country. This gives the country a propensity for producing the goods that use relatively more capital in the production process, that is capital-intensive goods. As a result, if these two countries were not trading initially, that is they were in autarky, the price of the capital-intensive good in the capital-abundant country would be bid down (due to its extra supply) relative to the price of the good in the other country. Similarly, in the labor-abundant country the price of the labor-intensive good would be bid down relative to the price of the good in the capital-abundant country. These relative factor costs would lead countries to excel in the production and export of products that used their abundant, and therefore cheaper, production factors.[7]

Once trade is allowed, profit-seeking firms will move their products to the markets that temporarily result in higher price. Thus the capital-abundant country will export the capital-intensive good since the price will be temporarily higher in the other country. Likewise, the labor-abundant country will export the labor-intensive good. Trade flows will rise until the price of both goods are equalized in the two markets.

The H-O theorem demonstrates that differences in resource endowments[8] as defined by national abundancies are one reason that international trade may occur.

Overall, the H-O factor proportions theory of comparative advantage states that international commerce compensates for the uneven geographic distribution of productive resources, that traded commodities are really bundles of factors (land, labor, and capital), and that the exchange of commodities internationally is therefore indirect arbitrage, transferring the services of otherwise immobile factors of production from locations where these factors are abundant to locations where they are scarce. Under some circumstances, this indirect arbitrage can completely eliminate price differences. Despite new models in trade theory, the H-O theory is still extraordinarily useful: pedagogically, in correcting the assumptions of the partial equilibrium with regard to labor supply and wage rates; politically, in showing that although tariffs and quotas have redistributive effects, they reduce efficiency; and, empirically, in explaining important aspects of the pattern of international trade.

Raymond Vernon and the Product Life Cycle Theory of Trade

Many theories of trade, like the theory of comparative advantage where one country trades with another because it has a comparative advantage in producing the good it is selling to the other country, put emphasis almost exclusively on cost.

Raymond Vernon, through his published article "International Investment and International Trade in the Product Life Cycle," in 1966[9] does not completely agree with these theories and introduces a new one that puts emphasis on information, uncertainty, and scale economies rather than comparative cost. He studies the whole life cycle of high-income or labor-saving products through this point of view: the invention of a new product, the maturing product, and the standardized product, each stage implying a different type of trade. While discussing Vernon's model, Louis T. Wells, Jr., states: "the model claims that many products go through a trade cycle, during which the United States is initially an exporter, then loses its export markets and may finally become an importer of the product."[10] Warren

Keagan, a marketing scholar, on the other hand, refers to the international product life cycle in the following manner: "The international product life cycle model suggests that many products go through a cycle during which high-income, mass consumption countries are initially exporters, then lose their export markets, and finally become importers of the product."[11] These are clear instances where trade cycle and product life cycle have been defined almost identically in the international context.

There could be several possible explanations for the interchangeable use of the product cycle and product life cycle concepts. One explanation is that the product cycle, developed by economists as part of the international framework, was initially unknown to marketers when they developed the product life cycle concept.[12] Another possibility is that marketers, in order to extend the product life cycle concept to international markets, borrowed the product cycle concept from economists who employed the concept to explain the patterns of international trade. The interchangeable use has created conceptual fuzziness in the literature and has overshadowed the differences between the two.

Product Cycle and Product Life Cycle: The purpose of the following section is to make a distinction between the product cycle and product life cycle concepts, to clarify the relationship between the two, and to redefine the international product life cycle (IPLC). Raymond Vernon, attempting to explain patterns of international trade, observed a circular phenomenon in the composition of trade between countries in the world market. Advanced countries, which have the ability and the competence to innovate besides having high-income levels, and engage in mass consumption become initial exporters of goods. However, they lose their exports initially to developing countries and subsequently to less developed countries and eventually become importers of these goods. Vernon's hypothesis was an attempt to advance the trade theory beyond the static framework of the comparative advantage of David Ricardo and other classical economists. It explored hitherto ignored or unexplained areas of international trade theory such as timing of innovation, effects of scale economies, and the role of uncertainty and ignorance in trade patterns. His intent was not to propose a theory of product life cycle as commonly understood by marketing theorists.

The product life cycle concept, typically expressed as an "S"-shaped curve in marketing literature, is based on the analogy of the human biological cycle.[13] Products, like living organisms, go through stages of birth, development, growth, maturity, decline, and demise. To be meaningful, the product life cycle concept has to be used in conjunction with its counterpart, market evolution, which consists of various stages of market development. Philip Kotler links both product life cycle and market stages in his concept of market evolution.[14]

The product life cycle concept identifies four stages that the trade patterns go through. Louis Wells identifies these four phases as follows:

1. United States exports strength
2. Foreign production starts
3. Foreign production becomes competitive in export markets
4. Import competition begins.[15]

The product cycle is a macro-level attempt to generalize patterns of trade between nations based on empirical data. It offers innovation and economies of scale as predominant explanatory variables. Vernon hypothesized a circular pattern of trade composition that occurs between trading partners in different stages of economic growth.

Unlike the product cycle with its macro orientation, the product life cycle concept in marketing theory is a micro-level explanation of stages of the life cycle a product or service goes through in the context of its market life. Sales volume and profits become the critical micro variables in the product life cycle framework. In the introductory stage of a product's life, sales are typically slow and profits negative. In the growth stage, both sales and profits rise at a rapid rate. During maturity, sales volume may continue to rise at a declining rate and profit may stay high. In the decline state, both sales and profit decrease.[16] Sales and profits are the principal variables for marketing decisions. The product life cycle is essentially a tool for firms to design marketing mix strategies for different states of the life span of a product or service.

Vernon stresses the degree of standardization as evidence of maturation of the product. A mature product typically may become standardized across international markets. The yardstick for maturity in the product life cycle approach is the rate of sales growth. Changes in this rate mark the transition from one stage of the product life cycle to the next.

An interesting example of these differing perceptions of maturity can be found in the market for personal computers. In the past decade, many facets of the computer hardware and software products became standardized either through strength of market leaders such as IBM and Microsoft or by the joint efforts of industry, users, and/or government to establish standards. Currently this market has standards but is not mature as yet. It is rapidly expanding domestically as well as globally. Using Vernon's yardstick of maturity, the computer industry is in a mature stage of product cycle whereas it is still in the growth stage according to the product life cycle approach.

Vernon's product cycle model is fundamentally production-oriented and does not focus on consumer-oriented sociocultural and behavioral variables. Vernon's framework is based on industrial goods in manufacturing sectors and virtually ignores trade in intangibles such as services or brand names.

While it provides a broad, long-term macro frame or reference, it is not particularly valuable in making micro-level and short-term managerial decisions in firms. His approach is more likely to provide insights for national policy formulation at macro levels.

Traditional definition of demand in economics has two important components: willingness to buy and the ability to pay. Vernon's hypothesis deals with the ability to pay as indicated by one's level of income. The product cycle hypothesis does not refer to the willingness to buy, which is a function of culture. Culture influences greatly the willingness to buy through changes in values, norms, attitudes, business customs, and practices. The product life cycle model factors in on these variables in marketing mix decisions, which are aimed at stimulating the consumer's willingness to buy. Marketers believe in the role, freedom, and ability of the marketing mix to alter consumer behavior patterns and the expectations of consumers' demand shifts.

Interest in a product and its acceptance or rejection will depend upon its cultural relevance. For instance, nonkosher meat products many not have market prospects in Israel. If products are not culturally acceptable, the international product cycle concept has little relevance.

Another striking difference between Vernon's perception of the international product cycle and marketers' view of the product life cycle is that the former focuses mainly on inventions and new products. It overlooks the tried and well-established products in the domestic market, which do not enter international markets to take advantage of the economies of scale. Firms that manufacture these products have had ample opportunities for growth in the domestic market and they do not think of the international market until the market for their products reaches maturity. McDonald's, Pizza Hut, and Kentucky Fried Chicken did not go international until the domestic markets were nearly saturated. The product life cycle concept is generally a tool for making decisions relating to domestic markets.

The International Product Life Cycle: The usage of the phrase "international product life cycle" (IPLC) has been anything but standard and the term can be precisely defined to remove it from the shadow of the product cycle or the trade cycle concepts in the international context. The IPLC can be defined as market life span stages the product goes through in international markets sequentially, simultaneously, or asynchronously. The sequential stages are introduction, growth, maturity, decline, and extinction in the international markets. When a product is positioned in different international markets at the same time and is going through similar life cycle stages, the cycle process is simultaneous. The life cycle stages are asynchronous when the product is in different stages in different international markets at the same time. The life cycle stage in which a product can be positioned is influenced by macro variables indigenous to country markets. Stanton and others cite examples of this phenomenon. Steel-belted auto radial tires had reached the saturation level in Western Europe when they were being discovered by the US market. Thus it was in the maturity stage in Western Europe and introductory stage in the United States.[17]

There are two major differences between the product life cycle and the IPLC. The first relates to rejuvenation or rebirth in international markets of a product that is in decline domestically for market-related reasons or is close to extinction. The consumption of cigarettes in the US market has been rapidly declining due to health consciousness of consumers and changes in public policy toward smoking. But the markets for American cigarettes are expanding in China, Eastern Europe, and Russia. The handloom-produced "Bleeding Madras" fabrics were almost extinct in the Indian domestic market when they gained a new lease of life after being introduced as a fashion product for summer wear in the United States. Finding new international markets can rejuvenate products that have reached the declining stage in the domestic market.

The second difference is that if a culture-specific product is designed for the international market, it can attain a new dimension of the product life cycle that is not possible in the domestic market. For example, fast food outlets like Burger King and McDonald's can design a product for cultures permeated by Buddhist or Hindu vegetarian values. This product can succeed and go through product life stages in international markets and still not be acceptable in domestic markets. The IPLC is clearly different from the product cycle concept that is essentially circular and from the product life cycle concept with its numerous variations.

Overall, Vernon's theory suggests that MNCs typically develop new products in their home countries, utilizing local resources and technologies to respond to local market needs, and then diffuse the innovations around the world step by step, first to countries that are close to the stage of development achieved by the home country (such as Europe for US-based multinationals), and then to lesser developed countries.

Contemporary Trade Theories

Globalization is a phenomenon that has remade the economy and trade balance of virtually every nation, reshaped almost every industry, and touched billions of lives, often in surprising and ambiguous ways. The stories filling the front pages in recent weeks—about economic crisis and contagion in Argentina, Uruguay, and Brazil, about President Bush getting the trade bill[18] he wanted—are all part of the same story, the largest story of our times: what globalization has done, or has failed to do in terms of trade, and which is the dominant trade country in the world. No nation has ever developed over the long term without trade. East Asia is the most recent example. Since the mid-1970s, Japan, Korea, Taiwan, China, and their neighbors have lifted 300 million people out of poverty, chiefly through trade. The United States, Germany, France, and Japan all became wealthy and powerful nations behind the barriers of protectionism. East Asia built its export industry by protecting its markets and banks from foreign competition and by requiring investors to buy local products and build local know-how. These are all practices discouraged or made illegal by the rules of trade today.

Furthermore, with its heated rhetoric and threats of retaliation, the transatlantic fight over President Bush's decision to raise tariffs against steel may look like just another trade dispute.[19] But Pascal Lamy, trade commissioner for the European Union, is using the steel spat to make the EU the new rule maker for international trade. This and similar recent headlines set the stage for contemporary trade theories and their relevance to today's world trade dominance.

Earlier in this chapter we have seen that factor abundance leads to comparative advantage. Perhaps this theory overlooks an important point. When factors are abundant, it might lead to inefficient use of that factor as there is little incentive to use this factor in an efficient way. For example, the logging industry in British Columbia, in Canada, has experienced little innovational activity (e.g., diversification into the recycling business); this industry is complacent and stagnant because its primary resource is available plentifully. By contrast, if factors are scarce, firms have a strong incentive to make efficient use of the available resources, and be innovative. There are numerous examples of cases where scarcity has led to innovation. Japan's scarcity has delivered us the just-in-time production. In the North Sea, oil platforms are expensive to build and maintain; their scarcity has led to the development of horizontal drilling to reach distant undersea oil reservoirs. Short building seasons in Sweden have led to prefabricated houses.

Porter's Diamond of National Advantage

Michael Porter (1990),[20] a Harvard business professor, believes that standard classical theories on comparative advantage are inadequate. He studied 100 firms in ten developed nations to learn if a nation's dominance in an industry can be explained more adequately by variables other than the factors of production on which the theories of comparative advantage and the H-O theory are based.

According to Porter, a nation attains a competitive advantage if its firms are competitive. Firms become competitive through innovation. Innovation can include technical improvements to the product or to the production process. He proposed a model that provides conditions that have to be met for a firm to be internationally competitive and successful. This model

Exhibit 3.3

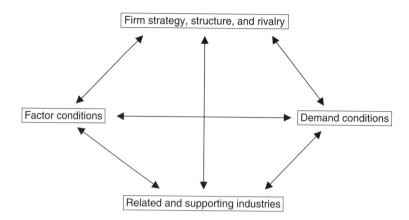

Porter's Diamond

focuses on four primary conditions that he arranged in a diamond-shaped diagram—Exhibit 3.3—(hence the name "Porter's diamond"). These four key elements to international entrepreneurial success are:

- Factor conditions (i.e., the nation's position in factors of production, such as skilled labor and infrastructure)
- Demand conditions (i.e., sophisticated customers in home market)
- Related and supporting industries (i.e., the importance of clustering)
- Firm strategy, structure, and rivalry (i.e., conditions for organization of companies, and the nature of domestic rivalry).

Factor Conditions

Factor conditions refer to inputs used as factors of production—such as labor, land, natural resources, capital, and infrastructure. This sounds similar to standard economic theory, but Porter argues that the "key" factors of production (or specialized factors) are created, not inherited. Specialized factors of production are skilled labor, capital, and infrastructure. Furthermore, "nonkey" factors or general use factors, such as unskilled labor and raw materials, can be obtained by any company and, hence, do not generate sustained competitive advantage. However, specialized factors involve heavy, sustained investment. They are more difficult to duplicate and eventually this leads to a competitive advantage, because if other firms cannot easily duplicate these factors, they are valuable. Porter argues that a lack of resources often actually helps countries to become competitive (call it selected factor disadvantage); thus, abundance generates waste and scarcity generates an innovative mindset. Such countries are forced to innovate to overcome their problem of scarce resources. How true is this? Switzerland was the first country to experience labor shortages. They abandoned labor-intensive watches and concentrated on innovative/high-end watches. Japan has high-priced land so its factory space is at a premium. This lead to just-in-time inventory techniques—Japanese firms cannot have a lot of stock taking up space, so to cope with the potential of not having goods around when they need it, they innovated traditional inventory techniques. Sweden has a short building season and high construction costs. These two things combined created a need for prefabricated houses. In several Middle Eastern countries, due to the climatic conditions—lots of sun, limited rain fall, scarcity of water—the need to use solar energy for heating up water became a necessity.

Demand Conditions

Porter states that a sophisticated domestic market is an important element in producing competitiveness. Firms that face a sophisticated domestic market are likely to sell superior products because the market demands high quality and a close proximity to such consumers enables the firm to better understand the needs and desires of the customers (this same argument can be used to explain the first stage of the IPLC theory when a product is just initially being developed; after it has been perfected, it does not have to be so close to the discriminating consumers). If the nation's discriminating values spread to other countries, the local firms become competitive in the global market. One example is the French wine industry. The French are sophisticated wine consumers. These consumers force, help, and expect French wineries to produce high-quality wines. The Italian consumers are sophisticated in terms of leather products; thus they force, help, and expect the Italian leather industry to produce high-quality leather products.

Related and Supporting Industries

Porter continues with his theory by stating that a set of strongly related and supporting industries is important for firms to be competitive. This includes suppliers and related industries. This usually occurs at a regional level as opposed to a national level. Examples include Silicon Valley in the United States, Detroit (for the auto industry), and Italy (leather shoes and other leather goods industry). The phenomenon of competitors (and upstream and/or downstream industries) locating in the same area is known as clustering or agglomeration. What are the advantages and disadvantages of locating within a cluster? Some advantages to locating close to your rivals may be:

- Potential technology knowledge spillovers
- An association of a region on the part of consumers with a product and high quality and therefore some market power
- An association of a region on the part of applicable labor force.

Some disadvantages to locating close to your rivals are:

- Potential poaching of your employees by rival companies
- Obvious increase in competition possibly decreasing markups.

Firm Strategy, Structure, and Rivalry

1. Strategy

   (a) *Capital Markets*: Domestic capital markets affect the strategy of firms. Some countries' capital markets have a long-run outlook, while others have a short-run outlook. Industries vary in how long the long run is. Countries with a short-run outlook (like the United States) will tend to be more competitive in industries where investment is short-term (like the computer industry). Countries with a long-run outlook (like Switzerland) will tend to be more competitive in industries where investment is long-term (like the pharmaceutical industry).

   (b) *Individuals' Career Choices*: Individuals base their career decisions on opportunities and prestige. A country will be competitive in an industry whose key personnel hold positions that are considered prestigious.

2. Structure

   Porter argues that the best management styles vary among industries. Some countries may be oriented toward a particular style of management. Those countries will tend to be more competitive in industries for which that style of management is suited. For example, Germany tends to have a hierarchical management structure comprising managers with strong technical backgrounds and Italy has smaller, family-run firms.

3. Rivalry

   Porter states that intense competition spurs innovation. Competition is particularly fierce in Japan, where many companies compete vigorously in most industries. International competition is not as intense and motivating. With international competition, there are enough differences between companies and their environments to provide handy excuses to managers who were outperformed by their competitors.

The Diamond as a System: Overall, Porter's theory states that if the elements in the diamond are increasingly present, trade increases. Furthermore, these elements in the diamond constitute a system and are self-reinforcing. Domestic rivalry for final goods stimulates the emergence of an industry that provides specialized intermediate goods. Keen domestic competition leads to more sophisticated consumers who come to expect upgrading and innovation. The diamond promotes clustering. Porter emphasizes the role of chance in the model. Random events can either benefit or harm a firm's competitive position. These can be anything like major technological breakthroughs or inventions, acts of war and destruction, or dramatic shifts in exchange rates. One might wonder how agglomeration becomes self-reinforcing.

- When there is a large industry presence in an area, it will increase the supply of specific factors (i.e., workers with industry-specific training) since they will tend to get higher returns and will face less risk of losing employment.
- Upstream firms (i.e., those that supply intermediate inputs) will invest in the area. They will also wish to save on transport costs, tariffs, interfirm communication costs, inventories, and so on.
- Downstream firms (i.e., those that use the industry's product as an input) will also invest in the area. This causes additional savings of the type listed before.
- Attracted by the good set of specific factors, upstream and downstream firms, producers in related industries (i.e., those that use similar inputs or whose goods are purchased by the same set of customers) will also invest. This will trigger subsequent rounds of investment.

Implications for Governments: The government plays an important role in Porter's diamond model. Like everybody else, Porter argues that there are some things that governments do that they shouldn't and other things that they do not do but should.

He says, "Government's proper role as a pusher and challenger...is to encourage or even push firms to raise their aspirations and move to a higher level of competitive prowess even though this may be an unsettling and even unpleasant process."[21]

Governments can influence all four of Porter's determinants through a variety of actions such as:

- subsidies to firms, either directly (money) or indirectly (through infrastructure)
- tax codes applicable to corporation, business, or property ownership
- educational policies that affect the skill level of workers
- establishment of technical standards and product standards, including environmental regulations
- government's purchase of goods and services
- antitrust regulation.

Moreover, Porter has emphasized the role of chance in the model. Random events can either benefit or harm a firm's competitive position. Typically, such events are:

- major technological breakthroughs or inventions
- political decisions by foreign governments
- acts of war and destruction
- dramatic shifts in exchange rates
- sudden price shocks affecting input goods (such as the oil price shock in the early 1970s)
- sudden surges or drops in world demand or sudden shifts in consumer preferences.

Although Porter's diamond theory is renowned, it has been criticized on the following points:

1. It focuses too strongly on developed economies.
2. The government's role can be both positive and negative. Even well-intentioned government actions can occasionally fail by cushioning domestic industries and making them less internationally competitive.
3. Chance is difficult to predict. Situations can change very quickly and unexpectedly.
4. Porter says that firms, not countries, compete in international markets. This means that national comparative advantage must be understood at the level of a firm rather than at the level of a country.
5. Porter describes four distinct stages of national competitive development:
    - Factor-driven (e.g., Singapore)
    - Investment-driven (e.g., Korea)
    - Innovation-driven (e.g., Japan, Italy, Sweden)

- Wealth-driven (e.g., Great Britain, with the United States and Germany somewhere between innovation-driven and wealth-driven), which is characterized by decline.

6. Porter argues that only outward foreign direct investment (FDI) is valuable in creating competitive advantage and inbound FDI does not increase domestic competition significantly because the domestic firms lack the capability to defend their own markets and face a process of market share erosion and decline. However, there seems to be little empirical evidence to support this claim.

7. Porter contends that reliance on natural resources alone is insufficient. Canada is an example that does not fit this description, as is apparent by the success of Canadian MNCs like Alcan and Norando.

8. The Porter model does not adequately address the role of MNCs. There seems to be ample evidence that the diamond is influenced by factors outside the home country.

It is obvious that Porter's diamond model continued on Ricardo's and H-O's theories but a final criticism is that Porter's evidence is anecdotal and there is no empirical proof as yet.[22]

The following questions were posed to Mr. Bill Bogle, the chief operating officer of Genesis Machinery Products, Inc., during an interview:

What products are you trading and with which countries? What criteria have you used in exporting to the countries you are exporting to and what steps have you taken in becoming familiar with these countries? Do you import? If yes, what and from where?

Our company manufactures capital equipment used in the manufacturing of injectable drugs. We export our product to Europe, South America, Asia, as well as Canada, Mexico and the Caribbean. Our primary export customers tend to be the large pharmaceutical companies or their foreign affiliates. Since the majority of our equipment is used in a highly regulated industry, the technical requirements usually take precedence to other commercial concerns and we tend to achieve our best results with those customer facilities that are running high-speed operations. We are currently designing new equipment that will be available in November of this year and that takes our same high speed technology and applies it to less complicated machines with lower output so that we can target host country national companies predominantly in Asia but also in other markets.

Like most other businesses, our success depends upon the relationships that we have built over the years with companies and individuals that specialize in our industry. We are represented in many countries by people whose trust has been earned over time. The only way to effectively develop business in the countries in which we work is to go there and meet with people face to face on

(Continued)

their terms. To this end, I have done business personally visiting customers and representatives in twenty-eight countries.

Our experience with importation is much more limited but part of a critical element of our business plan. We are formalizing an agreement with an Italian company that has a testing technology that complements the work that we do in the industry. We will represent them in the US as well as provide service and spare parts for their equipment. This increases our contacts with the technical experts in our target industry as well as provides us with lucrative aftermarket income.

Source: Interview with Mr. Bill Bogle, Chief Operating Officer of Genesis Machinery Products, Inc., located in Exton, Pennsylvania. September 9, 2002.

Note: Genesis is the world's leading manufacturer of capping equipment for pharmaceutical companies that are manufacturing injectable drugs.

Practical Tips

Both nations and individuals benefit from trade when they perceive an advantage in the production of some product or service. All nations have finite resources, whether natural or manufactured, such as capital, labor, and technical ability. Nations can benefit when they put these resources to the most efficient use, and all nations do some things more efficiently than they do other things. Ideally, nations would produce only the goods that they can produce efficiently and import those they cannot produce efficiently from more efficient producers. This would benefit both nations.

Many nations have established agencies throughout their land to assist individual firms take the right steps in engaging in international trade. Such an agency is the Trade Information Center (TIC) in the United States. The TIC is a comprehensive resource for information on all US Federal Government export assistance programs. The center is operated by the International Trade Administration of the US Department of Commerce for the 20 federal agencies comprising the Trade Promotion Coordinating Committee (TPCC). These agencies are responsible for managing the US Government's export promotion programs and activities.

The TIC, the first stop for US exporters in the federal government, provides, among other things, the following:

- Referrals and information on all US Federal Government export assistance programs. Interested parties can view the TIC's *Export Programs Guide: A Business Guide to Federal Export Assistance*. This manuscript describes the resources available from the 20 federal agencies that help US companies develop their export potential.

- General export counseling. New-to-export firms should start with the TIC's Frequently Asked Questions to find answers to the most commonly asked exporting questions and links to the most-used resources. *Export America*, another publication, publishes articles of interest written by international trade specialists.
- Sources of international market research and trade leads. The Internet Guide to Export Trade Leads, a list of web sites that provides trade lead information.
- Calendar of overseas and domestic trade events and activities. Interested firms can access the Commercial Service Calendar to learn about international trade events supported by one or more US government agencies.
- Sources of export finance. The *Alternative Trade Finance Guide* could be searched to view a state-by-state list of service providers nationwide, including those that specialize in meeting the unconventional needs of US exporters.
- Advice on export licenses and controls.
- Country-specific export counseling and assistance for Western Europe, Asia, the western hemisphere, Africa, and the Near East on commercial laws, regulations, business practices, distribution channels, business travel, and other market information.
- Import tariffs/taxes and customs procedures and assistance in overcoming commercial difficulties in doing business abroad.

Furthermore, there are agencies at the local, that is county, level where interested firms can obtain information on exporting. Such an agency is the Chester County International Trade Council (CCITC), in the county of Chester in the state of Pennsylvania, USA. Established in 1999, the CCITC is an economic development initiative of the Chester County Economic Development Council and serves as the Chester County "arm" of the Delaware River Port Authority's (DRPA) Export Development initiative. The CCITC receives funding from DRPA to deliver export assistance services to small to medium-sized companies located in Chester County. The CCITC is staffed by a program manager and an international trade specialist and receives guidance and expertise from its volunteer 33-member Advisory Board.

The mission of the CCITC is to contribute to the vitality of the regional economy by directly assisting businesses in international commerce. Its activities and services are designed to facilitate the export sales of Chester County companies. Offered in partnership with DRPA, CCITC services are available to all Chester County companies and include:

- individualized export/import counseling
- expertise and mentoring form the CCITC Advisory Board
- educational seminars and networking events
- in-depth marketing research
- market access grants (MAG) designed to subsidize business travel to develop new overseas markets
- official access point for Pennsylvania's 17 Overseas Trade Offices, which provide customized services to PA companies
- recruitment, organization, and assistance with foreign trade show participation and in-bound trade and buying missions
- assistance with federal and state export financing programs
- videoconferencing equipment to facilitate business meetings with overseas contacts
- access to pro bono legal consultation via the CCITC Advisory Board and the DRPA Legal Assistance Program.

Overall, the CCITC's activities center around the goals of awareness raising, capacity building, and networking for local companies in order to facilitate increased trade activities, mainly, exports.

Closing Case

Trading Coffee

After oil, coffee is the most traded commodity and the largest source of export earnings in the developing world. Yet coffee farmers are hurting. They are paid record-low prices, due both to a global market glut and to modest consumption growth. Some analysts say coffee, like any other commodity, is simply subject to the swings of a competitive market. This notion is cold comfort to countries such as Nicaragua and Burundi, which rely heavily on coffee exports. The coffee cartel of the 1980s failed. What now? Producing countries are urging coffee companies to help find ways to stabilize the market, including a fund to help small farmers.

Because coffee bushes are perennials, production may keep rising for two to three years in the face of falling prices. In the last five years, production grew an average 3 percent annually, adding 9 million bags of excess supply to the unprecedented 27 million bags already in stock. Over the same period, total consumption grew at only 1.5 percent. Further, per capita consumption of coffee in importing countries—where young people are more inclined to soft drinks—actually decreased.

An estimated 100 million people directly depend on coffee for their livelihoods, including farmers and their families, coffee pickers, market intermediaries, and industry employees. And almost 25 million people are coffee farmers, most of them cultivating less than 10 hectares apiece in about 80 countries in Africa, Asia, Latin America, and the Caribbean. These small landholders provide around 70 percent of the world's coffee supply.

Unskilled labor accounts for more than 60 percent of the total production cost on coffee farms. This characteristic, plus coffee's ease of cultivation, makes coffee production very attractive for poorer countries such as Vietnam, whose government decided in the early 1990s to promote coffee production and export. In 2000, Vietnam became the world's second largest coffee producer, displacing Colombia.

Five traders dominate 48 percent of the world market, five importers manage 46 percent of the total coffee exports, and five roasters control 55 percent of this volume. In Germany, Kraft Jacobs Suchard and Tchibo/Eduscho control 56 percent, and in Japan, Ueshimo Coffee and Key Coffee hold 43 percent of the market. US brands Maxwell House (Kraft Foods) and Folgers (Procter & Gamble) represent 56 percent of the US market.

Most coffee is still consumed at breakfast in homes and restaurants; the ubiquitous Starbucks Coffee Company buys less than 1 percent of the world's coffee supply. One of the reasons Starbucks profits in its niche is because the price of coffee is a small component of the final product's price. Even if Starbucks adjusts its final price when coffee prices change, these changes are so small they do not affect demand.

International prices have fallen by two thirds since 1997, and no significant recovery is expected any time soon. As a consequence of low price and low demand, farmers have become poorer. Nongovernmental organizations (NGOs) such as TransFair had led a "fair trade" campaign to increase the price paid to small growers. Under this initiative, small cooperatives themselves distribute the coffee they grow, and consumers are encouraged to patronize companies that buy this coffee. Certified importers pay the fair trade price ($1.26 per pound). Certified roasters pay TransFair a licensing fee of 10 cents per pound of green coffee to use its fair trade-certified label. Yet a minuscule 0.2 percent of the coffee consumed in the United States and 0.9 percent of that consumed in the European Union is sold under the certification program.

Other suggested remedies include persuading MNCs to set up a fund that helps small farmers improve quality and productivity and enter more lucrative specialty—coffee niches.

Sources: *The Coffee Book: Anatomy of an Industry from Crop to Last Drop* (New York: New Press, 1999) by Gregory Dicum and Nina Luttinger; International Coffee Organization; Food and Agriculture Organization of the United Nations; Starbucks Corporation, annual report; TransFair USA.

Question: What issues of international trade are addressed in this case? What international trade theories are implied?

Chapter Summary

This chapter addressed issues of international trade by presenting a definition of international trade that states that international trade is the exchange of goods and services between people, organizations, and countries. This exchange takes place because of differences in costs of production between countries and because it increases the economic welfare of each country by widening the range of goods and services available for consumption. Then, the economic and cultural philosophy of mercantilism was discussed, which back in the sixteenth and seventeenth centuries stated that governments should establish economic policies that promoted exports and discouraged imports so that the trade surplus created could be paid for in gold and silver. Although this trade theory has been criticized, it has some applications today in that nations encourage more exports of goods and services than imports, so that they have a more favorable trade balance.

Adam Smith's theory of absolute advantage was then discussed, which appeared in his major work *Wealth of Nations* in 1776. According to this theory, a country can produce some goods more efficiently that other countries. Thus, a country with absolute advantage could produce more in total and exchange products—trade—for goods that were cheaper in price than those produced at home.

Then came David Ricardo who took the logic of absolute advantages in production one step further to explain how countries could exploit their own advantages and gain from international trade. This theory states that it makes sense for a country to specialize in the production of those goods that it produces most efficiently and to buy the goods it produces less efficiently from other countries, even if this means buying goods from other countries that it could produce more efficiently itself. Overall, comparative advantage according to Ricardo was based on what was given up or traded off in producing one product instead of the other.

The H-O or factor proportions theory expands on the Ricardian model by allowing multiple factors of production, not just labor, but capital as well. This theory predicts that countries will export those goods that make intensive use of factors that are locally abundant, while importing goods that make intensive use of factors that are locally scarce.

The product life cycle theory introduced by Raymond Vernon in the 1960s suggests that trade patterns are influenced by where a new product is. In other words, this theory tells us that where a new product is introduced is important for trading.

Then came Porter's diamond of national advantage as a contemporary trade theory, which was developed in the late 1980s and states that the pattern of trade is influenced by four attributes of a nation, namely, factor conditions, demand conditions, related and supporting industries and strategy, and structure of rivalry among firms.

Review and Discussion Questions

1. Describe the trade theory of mercantilism, give examples, and then see if it applies in any way to today's international trade environment. Support your answer with examples.
2. Compare and contrast the theories of absolute and comparative advantage. How do they stand today? Does one stand more than the other? Why or why not? Support your answer with examples.
3. What is your opinion of the Heckscher—Ohlin-factor proportions—theory? Does it have any implications today? Yes. No. Why?
4. How would you evaluate Vernon's product life cycle theory? What are the differences and similarities between the product cycle and the product life cycle?
5. What do the contemporary trade theories state? Provide examples.
6. What are the implications and criticisms of Porter's diamond of national advantage theory? Support your answer with examples.
7. In the Reverse Perspective Situation, Trading Coffee, what do you think a government's intervention ought to be in the trade of coffee?
8. In the Opening Case, Cyprus and Trade, what do you think countries similar to Cyprus, for example Malta, should do to expand their trade horizons?

Endnotes

1. United Nations and UNCTAD, "World Investment Report: Cross-Border Mergers and Acquisitions and Development, 2000," in *The Global Competitiveness Report* (Oxford University Press, 2000).
2. Cole, C. W., *French Mercantilist Doctrines Before Colbert (1931) and Colbert and a Century of French Mercantilism* (2 Vols, 1939).
3. Hecksher, E. F., *Mercantilism* (2 Vols, 1956).
4. Adam Smith, *An Inquiry into the Nature and Causes of the Wealth of Nations*, Chapter X, Part 2, published by Regency Publishing (Washington, 1998).
5. David Ricardo, "The Principles of Political Economy and Taxation," in William R. Allen (ed.) *International Trade Theory: Hume to Ohlin* (New York: Randon House, 1965).
6. The "standard" H-O model refers to the case of two countries, two goods and two factors of production. The H-O model has been extended to a many country, many goods and many factors case but most of the exposition in this text, and by economists in general, is in reference to the standard case.
7. Eli Heckscher, Heckscher-Ohlin Trade Theory (Cambridge, MA: MIT Press, 1991).
8. Ibid., "The Effect of Foreign Trade on the Distribution of Income," *Economist Tidskrift*, XXI, pp. 497–512 (1919); and Bertil Ohlin, *Interregional and International Trade* (Cambridge, MA: Harvard University Press, 1933).

9. Raymond Vernon, "International Investment and International Trade in the Product Cycle," *Quarterly Journal of Economics*, May 1966.
10. Louis T. Wells, Jr, "A Product Life Cycle for International Trade?" *Journal of Marketing*, July 1968.
11. Warren Keegan, *Global Marketing Management* (4th edn) (Englewood Cliffs, NJ: Prentice Hall).
12. Sak Onkvisit and John J. Shaw, "An Examination of International Product Life Cycle and its Application Within Marketing," *Columbia Journal of World Business*, Fall 1983.
13. Nariman K. Dhalla and Sonia Yuspeh, "Forget the Product Life Cycle Concept!" *Harvard Business Review*, January–February 1976.
14. Philip Kotler, *Marketing Management* (6th edn), pp. 369–373 (Englewood Cliffs, NJ: Prentice Hall, Inc.).
15. Wells, "A Product Life Cycle for International Trade?."
16. Ibid.
17. William J. Stanton, Michael J. Etzel and Bruce J. Walker, *Fundamentals of Marketing* (9th edn), p. 200 (New York, NY: McGraw Hill).
18. Tina Rosenberg, "The Free-Trade Fix," *The New York Times Magazine*, 18 August, 2002.
19. Stephan Richter, "Is This Europe's Hour to Lead on Free Trade?" *New York Times*, 1 April, 2002.
20. Michael Porter, *The Competitive Advantage of Nations* (New York: Free Press, 1990).
21. Ibid.
22. John., H., Dunning, *The Globalization of Business*, p. 106 (London: Routledge, 1993).

4

The Monetary System in the International Arena

Objectives

Through this chapter, the student will be exposed to:

- Explain a country's balance of payments accounts
- Understand how balance of payments deficits are financed
- Identify the factors affecting exchange rates
- Distinguish between fixed and flexible exchange rates
- Explain the international impact of domestic monetary and fiscal policies
- Grasp the importance of international policy coordination.

Opening Case

Euro versus the Dollar

The interest rate on a one-year Treasury bill in the United States is 2 percent and in Europe 6 percent. Provided that, in the absence of any significant news, markets do not expect a change in the dollar/euro exchange rate, US investors can increase their returns by selling US Treasury bills and buying European Treasury bills. In order to invest in Europe they must first change dollars into euros. The increased demand for euros causes an appreciation of the euro in relation to the dollar or, alternatively, the dollar depreciates against the euro. The rise in the value of the euro is now generating expectations of depreciation as markets now consider that the euro is overvalued.

US investors are having second thoughts as to the realization of capital gains if they shift their funds to Europe.

If markets expect the euro to fall by 3 percent, the return on the European Treasury bill will be 3 percent (6 percent minus 3 percent depreciation). Interest rates are still higher by 1 percent but less capital will flow toward Europe as US investors see that the returns on their investment are now lower than previously. As long as markets are convinced that the euro will appreciate, capital will flow into Europe. When markets believe that the overvalued euro will depreciate by 4 percent, returns are equalized and there are no further incentives to shift funds out of the United States and into Europe.

When financial markets are closely linked, higher interest rates in one country create expectations of depreciation. The argument can be pursued even further. Suppose that expectations are not taken into account and US investors shift their funds into Europe. Once they cash in on their capital gains, they will need to repatriate their profits. In doing so, the demand for dollars increases and the dollar appreciates relative to the euro or, alternatively, the euro depreciates against the dollar.

Question: What would you advise investors, and more specifically, US investors, to do in terms of investing in Europe? What financial aspects do these investors need to look at before deciding to invest in Europe?

Source: Compiled by Dr. Spyros Hadjidakis, Associate Professor of Economics and Finance, School of Business, Intercollege, Nicosia-Cyprus; Adjunct Professor of Economics, University of Maryland University College in Europe.

International Transactions

It has become a cliché to say that we now live in one world—ready or not. What happens in Europe, the United States, or any other country influences other countries, and events abroad have repercussions at home. Trillions of dollars worth of goods and services—American computers, German cars, Japanese DVDs, French wines, Italian clothes—are traded across international borders each year. A vastly larger volume of international transactions—trade in stocks, bonds, and bank deposits—take place in the global economy at the speed of light.

Chapter 3 examined the basic principles of product specialization and the exchange of goods among countries without taking into account the monetary aspect of international transactions. In other words, it focused on the real aspect whereby the price of one good is expressed in units of the other good and not in monetary units.

Buying goods, services, or assets from foreign countries is complicated by the fact that countries use different monetary systems. In order for these transactions to take place, there must be some way to change domestic into foreign money and vice versa. The foreign exchange market is where these transactions take place. Its participants include banks and other financial institutions, consumers, business firms, and governments.

Balance of Payments

The balance of payments is a summary statement of all transactions that take place between a country and the rest of the world during a given period of time (usually a year). One of the main uses of the balance of payments accounts is to provide information regarding the demand and supply of foreign exchange. In other words, and for a given time period (a year), the balance of payments summarizes a country's transactions that require payments to other countries and transactions that require payments from other countries.

The balance of payments uses a double-entry system of bookkeeping. Transactions are recorded as debits and credits. From the standpoint of the home country, a debit (−) transaction is a flow for which the home country must pay and requires the supply of the home currency. Examples of debit transactions are:

- Imports of goods and services
- Transfers to foreign residents (also known as remittances)
- Acquisition of long-term assets or reduction of a long-term liability (i.e., stocks, bonds, real capital)
- Acquisition of a short-term asset or reduction of a short-term liability (i.e., bank deposits, cash or short-term bonds such as treasury bills).

From the standpoint of the home country, a credit (+) transaction is a flow for which the home country is paid and increases the demand for the home currency by foreign residents. Examples of credit transactions are:

- Exports of goods and services
- Transfers from foreign residents
- Sale of a long-term asset or increase of a long-term liability
- Sale of a short-term asset or increase of a short-term liability.

It is important to realize that every transaction involves two opposite flows of equal value, that is each transaction gives rise to both debit and

Exhibit 4.1

Hypothetical Balance of Payments

Credit ($)		Debit($)	
Exports of goods	1200	Imports of goods	1500
Exports of services	300	Imports of services	200
Transfers	200	Transfers	100
Imports of capital	300	Exports of capital	200
Total receipts	2000	Total payments	2000

credit entries.[1] Consequently, the balance of payments must always balance in the accounting sense. These issues are explained in Exhibit 4.1.

As explained above, credit includes all transactions that give rise to foreign exchange inflows whereas debit includes all transactions causing foreign exchange outflows. Consequently, exports of goods and services are placed on the credit side. On the other hand, imports of goods and services are placed on the debit side. The "Transfers" entry on the credit side refers to unilateral transactions or transfers (i.e., it does not require a corresponding payment abroad) and mainly includes remittances from home residents working abroad and aid from abroad. Equivalently, the "Transfers" entry on the debit side includes remittances paid to home or foreign residents (such as remittances to home students studying abroad) and aid abroad.

International transactions are not limited to the exchange of goods and services but also include flows of capital for lending or investment purposes. For example, the purchase of bonds or company stock from foreign residents involves an inflow of capital and is placed on the credit side. On the other hand, the purchase of such assets abroad is placed on the debit side because it creates demand for foreign exchange.

In Exhibit 4.1 total credits are equal to total debits according to double-entry bookkeeping. For example, "exports of goods" is a credit entry and is only one side of the transaction. The other side refers to the way the transaction is paid. Whether it is paid through lending or cash, it will appear as a debit entry.

The equality of credit and debit entries can also be seen from a different angle. A country, as an individual, cannot pay more than it receives during a specified time period unless it borrows or sells assets. The latter transactions are credit entries in the balance of payments accounts. By the same token, a country's receipts cannot be higher than its payments without a corresponding increase in assets, other claims, or lending or without a corresponding decrease in its liabilities. These transactions appear as debit entries in the balance of payments accounts.

Current and Capital Accounts

All transactions are placed into specific categories. The simplest break-down is between the current account and the capital account. The current account records all transactions involving goods and services. The capital account records all transactions involving short-term and long-term assets. Exhibit 4.2 shows the different categories originating from the hypothetical balance of payments account of Exhibit 4.1.

If we consider only the goods sector, the difference between imports and exports of goods gives the trade balance, which is −300 in our example, that is imports of goods are greater than exports and in this case we have a trade deficit. Had exports of goods been greater than imports, the trade balance would have a positive sign and we would have a trade surplus.

One of the most important categories of the balance of payments is the current account. It includes goods, services (tourism, banking, insurance, brokerage services, transport), transfers, receipts of interest, profit and divi-dends earned by investments abroad, and, equivalently, payments of interest, profit, and dividends to investments by foreign residents in the home country (not shown in Exhibit 4.2). In our example, there is a current account deficit (−100), which is less than the trade deficit, that is the trade deficit is par-tially offset from the surplus in services and transfers. Obviously, Exhibit 4.2 could also have included the services and transfers balance. In our example, the balance in both categories is in surplus that, as mentioned above, par-tially finances the trade balance. The services balance is also known as the invisible trade balance.

Transactions in assets, termed the capital account of the balance of pay-ments, consist of the purchase and sale of physical assets like land and build-ings together with borrowing and lending. Included in the capital account are items like trade credit (i.e., the settlement of debts at a future date),

Exhibit 4.2

Balance of Payments Breakdown

			Credit ($)	Debit ($)
1.	Goods		1200	1500
	Trade balance	−300		
2.	Services		300	200
3.	Transfers		200	100
	Current account	−100	1700	1800
4.	Capital movements	100	300	200
	Capital account			
	Balance of Payments	−	2000	2000

lending by banks, and the purchase and sale of securities like company stock, corporate bonds, government long-term bonds, and short-term bonds such as Treasury bills. The purchase of home country assets by foreign residents is known as inward investment or capital inflow, since funds flow into the home country, while the purchase of foreign assets by home country residents is termed outward investment or capital outflow. Transactions in physical assets are known as direct investment while borrowing, lending, and transactions in securities are termed indirect or portfolio investment.

In Exhibit 4.2, the capital account is in surplus, which exactly offsets the current account deficit so that the balance of payments is zero. If there is a current account surplus, then there must be a corresponding capital account deficit.

A current account deficit means that the home country's current payments abroad for goods, services, and transfers are greater than the corresponding receipts. The home country must either resort to foreign lending or reduce its claims from abroad or draw from its foreign exchange reserves in order to finance the current account deficit. In our example, there is a capital account surplus of 100 (an excess of capital inflows over outflows). Therefore, the country in question either borrowed from abroad or reduced its foreign claims or used up part of its foreign exchange reserves.

In case of a current account surplus the process is reversed. Current receipts are greater than current payments and the home country can either lend abroad or increase its foreign claims or increase its foreign exchange reserves.

The question arising from the above analysis is "what does a balance of payments deficit or surplus really mean?" This question is answered in the section below.

Balance of Payments Disequilibrium

It should be stressed from the outset that a deficit or a surplus in the balance of payments is an economic and not an accounting concept since, in the accounting sense, the balance of payments should always be zero. From an economic point of view, the existence of balance of payments deficits or surpluses is a frequent phenomenon.

The key in understanding balance of payments imbalances is the distinction between autonomous and offsetting or accommodating transactions. Autonomous transactions are independent of the balance of payments in the sense that they are affected by factors outside the balance of payments statement. These include exports, imports, transfers, public transactions, and net capital movements. Imports and exports are the result of cost differences among countries (i.e., international competitiveness). Transfers and public transactions are based on military, political, or humanitarian considerations (i.e., military aid or humanitarian aid following natural disasters). Capital movements are dependent on expectations about returns on foreign investments (i.e., interest rate and exchange rate considerations).

On the other hand, transactions occurring in order to compensate for differences between payments and receipts arising from a country's autonomous transactions are called accommodating (offsetting) transactions. In effect, they are balancing transactions, which finance payments imbalances associated with autonomous transactions. For example, suppose a country's autonomous transactions are the following:

- Exports: $40 billion
- Imports: $50 billion
- Transfer receipts: $4 billion
- Foreign aid receipts: $2 billion
- Net capital inflow: $2 billion.

According to the information above, payments are $50 billion (imports) while receipts are only $48 billion $(40+4+2+2)$. The country in question has a disequilibrium of $2 billion, which, in effect, is a balance of payments deficit. In order to correct the situation, this country must undertake a $2 billion financing or accommodating transactions to account for the difference between payments and receipts. Consequently, the existence of accommodating or financing transactions is evidence of balance of payments disequilibrium.

Exhibit 4.3 is a simplified version of the US balance of payments for the year 2003.[2] A positive sign (+) denotes credits, that is exports of goods and services, income receipts, transfers to the United States, capital inflows—increase in foreign-owned assets (US liabilities) or decrease in US-owned assets (US claims). On the other hand, a negative sign (−) denotes debits, that is imports of goods and services, income payments, transfer payments, capital outflows—decrease in foreign-owned assets (US liabilities) or increase in US-owned assets (US claims). You will notice that a third account—the Official Reserves Account—appears in the balance of payments statement. It shows the change in the country's foreign exchange reserves that are needed to balance the current and capital accounts. You can also observe that the United States ran a balance of payments deficit in the year 2004, equal to the difference between the sum of all debits and all credits in the current and capital accounts. A deficit means that the Federal Reserve (i.e., the US Central Bank) draws foreign exchange reserves. This increase in reserves is a credit item in the balance of payments. In other words, a deficit is financed by either an increase in the holdings of US dollars by foreign governments or a reduction in the United States' foreign exchange reserves. The Federal Reserve sells some of its reserves in order to buy dollars in the foreign

Exhibit 4.3

US Balance of Payments Account, 2004 ($ million)

1. **Current account**

Exports of goods	+807,536	
Imports of goods	−1,472,926	
Balance of trade		−665,390
Exports of services (business, travel, etc.)	+343,912	
Imports of services (business, travel, etc.)	−296,105	
Income received from foreign residents	+379,527	
Income payments to foreign residents	−349,088	
Invisible trade balance		+78,246
Transfers, net	−80,930	
Balance on current account		−668,074

2. **Capital account**

Capital inflow	+1,440,105	
Capital outflow	−855,509	
Balance on capital account		+584,596
Errors and omissions (statistical discrepancy)	85,126	

3. **Official reserves account**

Decrease in reserves		+1,648
		0

Source: US Bureau of Economic Analysis, *Survey of Current Business*, http://www.bea.gov/bea/ newsrelarchive/2005/trans305.xls.

exchange market. Selling reserves is a credit item in the balance of payments since funds that are drawn from reserves is an inflow to the balance of payments (and an outflow from the official reserves account). The opposite would hold true in the case of a balance of payments surplus.

Finally, the item statistical discrepancy (or errors and omissions) is used to balance the sum of credits and debits of all accounts. This happens because the flows on both sides of each transaction are not correctly recorded mainly because certain entries are underestimated or overestimated or the flow of goods, services, or capital is hidden from government officials and is never recorded. For example, if there are restrictions on capital outflows, there is a tendency for home residents to hide the export of foreign currency; consequently, the capital outflow is never recorded.

The Foreign Exchange Market

Economic analysis tends to neglect the accounting procedures of the balance of payments and concentrates on the fundamental economic and financial

Exhibit 4.4

Selected Euro Exchange Rates, as on 21 December, 2005 (all currencies quoted against the euro)

€1.00 =	1.1872 US dollars
€1.00 =	139.18 Japanese yen
€1.00 =	7.4575 Danish kronas
€1.00 =	0.67895 pounds sterling
€1.00 =	9.43 Swedish kronas
€1.00 =	1.5529 Swiss francs
€1.00 =	8.0495 Norwegian kronas
€1.00 =	0.5735 Cyprus pound
€1.00 =	28.954 Czech koruna
€1.00 =	15.6466 Esthonian croon
€1.00 =	251.19 Hungarian forint
€1.00 =	3.4528 Lithuanian litas
€1.00 =	0.6965 Latvian lats
€1.00 =	0.4293 Maltese liras
€1.00 =	3.8883 Polish zloty
€1.00 =	239.64 Slovenian tolar
€1.00 =	37.851 Slovakian koruna
€1.00 =	3.66196 New Romanian leu
€1.00 =	1.6184 Australian dollars
€1.00 =	1.3918 Canadian dollars
€1.00 =	9.20377 Hong Kong dollars
€1.00 =	1209.04 South Korean won

Source: European Central Bank, http://ecb.int/stats/exchange.

relationships emanating from these procedures. The foreign exchange market, where different national currencies are bought and sold, provides that link.

The exchange rate is the price of one nation's currency in terms of another's. Exhibit 4.4 shows exchange rates between the euro and selected currencies on December 21, 2005. For example, €1 buys 1.1872 US dollars, 139.18 Japanese yen, or 0.67895 pounds sterling. Exhibit 4.5 shows dollar exchange rates with selected currencies on January 7, 2004 and January 7, 2006.

It is important to emphasize that the exchange rate is a relative price, that is it can be expressed in either direction—if the euro rises against the US dollar, the US dollar falls against the euro. One way is to express the foreign currency in terms of the domestic currency. In other words, we ask how much foreign currency exchanges for one unit of the domestic currency, as is the format in Exhibit 4.4 for the euro, and in columns 3 and 5 of Exhibit 4.5 for the US dollar. This is known as indirect quotation of the

Exhibit 4.5

Dollar Exchange Rates, January 7, 2004 and January 7, 2006

Currency	January 7, 2004		January 7, 2006	
	$/1 unit	Units/$1	$/1 unit	Units/$1
Australian dollar	0.768498	1.30124	0.751698	1.330328
Canadian dollar	0.776156	1.284	0.855358	1.1691
Swiss franc	0.807428	1.2385	0.781616	1.2794
Euro	0.789578	1.2665	0.828912	1.2064
Pound sterling	1.8193	0.549662	1.76449	0.566733
Hong Kong dollar	0.128803	7.7638	0.129021	7.7507
Japanese yen	0.0094171	106.19	0.00872144	114.66

Source: http://www.x-rates.com.

exchange rate. In this case, if the exchange rate of the domestic currency falls (rises), it means that its value also falls (rises), that is it depreciates (appreciates). Therefore, we can say that the value of the domestic currency has fallen (risen) or the exchange rate (of the domestic currency) has fallen (risen).

Alternatively, in direct quotation we can express the prices of all other currencies in terms of the domestic currency (columns 2 and 4 in Exhibit 4.5). In this case we are trying to determine how much, in dollars, it costs to buy one euro, one Swiss franc, and so on. We are quoting the price of the foreign currency in each case, that is the domestic currency is expressed in terms of the foreign currency. In direct quotation, if the exchange rate rises (falls), that is it costs more (less) US dollars to buy one euro, the value of the US dollar has fallen (risen)—the dollar has depreciated (appreciated). Thus, an increase (decrease) in the exchange rate of the domestic currency means that its value has fallen (risen).

An example from Exhibit 4.4 should put things into perspective. If $1.1872 = €1 in indirect quotation, the direct quotation can be calculated as the reciprocal: if we divide €1 by the above indirect quotation, we get $1/1.2138 = 0.84232$, that is €0.84232 = $1. In terms of the direct quotation, if the euro fell (rose), the exchange rate would rise (fall)—it would cost a higher (lower) proportion of the euro to buy one US dollar. Conversely, if we were to use the indirect quotation, if the euro fell (rose), the exchange rate would fall (rise)—it would cost fewer (more) euros to buy one US dollar. According to the dollar/euro exchange rate from Exhibit 4.4, a product costing €25 in Europe would cost $29.68 (25 × 1.1872); a product costing $50 would cost €42.12 (50/1.1872). All major financial newspapers (*Wall Street Journal, Financial Times*) express exchange rates both in direct and in indirect quotation.[3]

We have mentioned that the dollar may depreciate or appreciate. The rate of depreciation or appreciation is the percentage change in the value of the dollar over a specified time period. In terms of Exhibit 4.5, the euro/dollar exchange rate was €1.2665 = $1 on January 7, 2004 and €1.2064 = $1 on January 7, 2006. Using the percentage change formula we can calculate the change in the value of the dollar in terms of the euro:

$$\frac{\text{Current value} - \text{previous value}}{\text{Previous value}} \times 100 = \frac{1.2064 - 1.2665}{1.2665} \times 100 = -4.75$$

Since the percentage change is negative, the dollar has depreciated by 4.75 percent against the euro during the January 2004–2006 period. We can see from Exhibit 4.5 that the dollar has appreciated with respect to the remaining currencies, with the exception of the Canadian dollar, between January 2004 and January 2006.

To put things into perspective, an exchange rate is quoted with a trading margin or spread. In other words, two exchange rates are quoted. For example, the dollar may be quoted as $1 = €1.0186–1.0196. This is known as the bid—ask spread where the bid is the rate at which market traders buy the home currency; the ask rate is the price at which market traders sell the home currency. The difference between the two represents trading costs and profits. A small spread indicates the absence of relative risk (i.e., the exchange rate is not expected to fluctuate) while the opposite holds true in the case of a large spread. Spreads are often quoted as basis points where a point corresponds to 0.0001. In the above example, the spread is 1.0196 − 1.0186 = 0.001 = 1 basis point. The midpoint is the average of the bid and ask rates (sometimes also known as fixing) and gives a single exchange rate. The exchange rates quoted in Exhibits 4.4 and 4.5 are midpoint figures. In the above example, the midpoint is 1.0191. The bid—ask spread can very easily be converted into direct quotation if we divide $1 by the indirect quotation. In this case, the meaning of bid and ask rates is reversed.

From the information provided in Exhibits 4.4 and 4.5, it is possible to calculate, through the euro or the dollar, the exchange rate between any pair of currencies listed in the two tables, that is it is possible to calculate the cross rate, which is an exchange rate calculated from two other rates. For example, in Exhibit 4.5, the exchange rate of the Swiss franc against the pound sterling can be derived from the pound sterling/US dollar and the Swiss franc/US dollar exchange rates. On January 7, 2006, the sterling/dollar rate was 0.566733 pound sterling = $1 and the Swiss franc/dollar rate was 1.2794 Swiss francs = $1. To derive the Swiss franc against the pound sterling rate, we divide the pound/dollar rate by the Swiss/dollar franc rate. Thus, 1 Swiss franc is 0.44297 pounds sterling (0.566733/1.2794). The *Financial Times* and the *Wall Street Journal* publish the cross exchange rates of major currencies daily.

Exchange Rates in the Business Context

To understand the importance of the foreign exchange rate of a currency, it would be useful to consider the role of the dollar exchange rate in the business environment. Needless to say, the reverse would hold true for euro. To illustrate this point, let us imagine that an American firm exports hand tools to Europe. Let us further assume that the sale price of each hand tool is $10 in the United States and the exchange rate is €1.1 = $1. Consequently, the sale price in Europe is €11.

If the exchange rate rose to €1.2 = $1, the sale price of the hand tool in the United States would still be $10 and the American firm would have to raise the sale price from €11 to €12. However, this implies that the sale price of the hand tool in Europe rises and the American firm suffers a loss in sales.

If, on the other hand, the exchange rate falls to €0.95 = $1, the American firm can reduce the price of the hand tool to €9.5. This means that the American firm acquires a competitive advantage and its sales in Europe increase. Therefore, as a general rule, a lower exchange rate for the dollar increases American exports.

Conversely, American importers of European goods will have to pay European suppliers in euros. The sale price of European goods in the United States will depend on the price charged by European suppliers and on the euro/dollar exchange rate. For example, assume that an American firm imports computers from Europe at a price of €500 per computer. If the exchange rate were at €1 = $1, the firm would charge $500 per computer. In the case of a rise in foreign exchange rate, say €1.2 = $1, the firm could afford a cut in the price of computers to $417. Consequently, as a general rule, a high exchange rate reduces the dollar price of imported goods whereas a low exchange rate increases the dollar price of imported goods. We can therefore say that a low exchange rate will increase American exports and decrease imports (a trade surplus) whereas a high exchange rate will decrease American exports and increase imports (a trade deficit).

The same analysis holds true for financial assets and services. A low exchange rate will attract European investors because they can now buy a larger quantity of assets (real property, stocks, bonds) with the same amount of euros; a high exchange rate will make it easier for Americans to invest in Europe. More European tourists will visit the United States if the exchange rate is low since euros can buy more goods and services. On the other hand, a high exchange rate will encourage Americans to travel to Europe since more euros can be obtained for every dollar.

The above analysis implicitly assumed a spot exchange rate, that is the exchange rate at which transactions are settled immediately (within two working days). Alternatively, a forward exchange rate[4] refers to the rate on a contract to exchange currencies in 30, 60, 90, or 180 days. A firm, for example, may sign a contract with a bank to buy, say, euros for US dollars 90 days from now at a predetermined exchange rate, which is called the 90-day forward rate. Such forward contracts are used to reduce exchange rate risk.

For example, an American importer of European goods is expecting a shipment in 90 days. Let us assume that the importer must pay €100,000 when the shipment arrives in the United States. If current spot euro/dollar exchange rate is €1.25 = $1 and the payment was made today, the importer would have to pay $80,000. Let us further assume that the importer expects that the dollar will depreciate. In addition, he is short of the $80,000 but expects a cash inflow over the next three months. If the dollar depreciates to €1.1 = $1 in 90 days' time, he would have to pay $90,909 (€100,000/1.1) even though the shipment still costs €100,000.

The importer can reduce the exchange risk by purchasing a forward contract whereby he can buy euros for dollars in 90 days. It is likely that the exchange rate on the forward contract will be different from the current spot exchange rate because its value reflects market expectations regarding the value of the euro/dollar exchange rate in the next three months. If the current 90-day forward exchange rate is, say, €1.2 = $1, the market expects the value of the dollar to fall. The importer enters into a 90-day forward contract where he buys €100,000 at a cost of $83,333 (100,000/1.2). Even though this amount is slightly higher than the amount he would have to pay if the payment were made today ($80,000), the importer is better off not only because he does not have the available cash but also because the forward contract protected him from a higher potential loss because of the depreciation of the dollar (in the absence of a forward contract he would have to pay $90,909). Using foreign exchange market terminology, when the forward exchange rate is higher than the spot rate (i.e., the market expects the dollar to depreciate), there is a forward premium. If, on the other hand, the forward exchange rate is lower than the spot rate (i.e., the market expects the dollar to appreciate), then there is a forward discount. As a general rule, the currency of the country with lower interest rates trades is at a forward premium while the currency of the country with higher interest rates trades is at a forward discount. All major financial newspapers publish forward exchange rates daily.

The spot exchange rate we have dealt with so far is also known as the nominal exchange rate. The nominal exchange rate can be either a bilateral exchange rate (i.e., the exchange rate between two countries) or an effective exchange rate.[5] The effective exchange rate as a measure takes into account the fact that the dollar (or any currency) does not fluctuate evenly against all currencies. For example, the dollar may rise against the euro but fall against the yen and pound sterling. Consequently, in order to see how the dollar performs in general, and not against specific currencies, we need to construct an exchange rate that is a weighted average of the bilateral rates and is expressed as an index relative to a base year. The weights are chosen to reflect the dollar's relationship with other currencies on the basis of trading volume.

The nominal exchange rate, whether bilateral or effective, however, does not give us any information regarding the international competitive position of a country, that is what is the purchasing power of a currency in other countries. Consequently, we must adjust the nominal exchange rate to reflect the differences between the inflation rates or general price levels among countries, that is we need to measure the rate at which American goods exchange for goods from other countries. This rate is called the real exchange rate[6] and is defined as $R = e \times P(\text{home})/P(\text{foreign})$, where R is the real exchange rate, e is the bilateral or effective exchange rate, $P(\text{home})$ is the price level in the home country, and $P(\text{foreign})$ is the price level abroad (or in a specific foreign country). Exhibit 4.6 shows the dollar's nominal and real effective exchange rates against major trading partners from 1998 to 2005.

We can see from Exhibit 4.6 that the dollar appreciated against its major trading partners (including the euro) from 1999 to 2001, thereby making American exports more expensive. A depreciating effective exchange rate does not necessarily imply that American goods have become more competitive in international markets. This will depend not only on the changes in the exchange rate but also on the relative price levels between the United States and its major trading partners, that is, we need to calculate the real exchange rate. The last column in Exhibit 4.6 shows the real exchange rate

Exhibit 4.6

Dollar Nominal and Real Effective Exchange Rates (end of year)

Year	Nominal (1973 = 100)	Real (1973 = 100)
1998	95.41	95.46
1999	96.21	97.82
2000	104.65	108.04
2001	109.51	113.76
2002	101.47	105.63
2003	86.21	90.18
2004	80.11	85.07
2005	85.83	92.85

Source: Federal Reserve, http://www.federalreserve.gov/releases/H10/Summary.

between the US dollar and its major trading partners as calculated by the Federal Reserve.

A rise in the real exchange rate indicates a real appreciation, that is a loss in competitiveness as more foreign currencies will now be exchanged for each $1 worth of American goods outside the United States. This is due to the fact that while the dollar's nominal effective rate appreciated by 4.64 percent between 2000 and 2001, its real effective exchange rate appreciated by 5.3 percent during the same period. This is because the price level in the United States was higher than that abroad and the loss in competitiveness was much higher than the dollar's nominal appreciation against its major trading partners.

On the other hand, a fall in the real effective exchange rate indicates a real depreciation, that is a gain in competitiveness as less foreign currency units can now be exchanged for each $1 worth of American goods in international markets. For example, the dollar's nominal effective exchange rate depreciated by 7.34 percent between 2001 and 2002 and, at the same time, the dollar's real effective rate fell by 7.14 percent during the same period. This indicates that a possible loss in competitiveness through higher domestic inflation has been, more or less, offset by a depreciation in the dollar's effective exchange rate.

Demand and Supply of Foreign Exchange

The exchange rate is a price. In a free market, exchange rates are set by the forces of demand and supply—the demand for US dollars (from the standpoint of the United States) or the demand for euros (from the standpoint of Europe) and the supply of US dollars or the supply of euros. But what exactly is meant by the demand for and the supply of US dollars or euros?

From the standpoint of Europe (the United States), the quantity of euros (US dollars) demanded is the amount that people would buy in a specific time period (e.g., a day) and at a specific price if there were willing sellers. The quantity of euros (US dollars) supplied in the foreign exchange market is the amount that people would sell in a specific time period and at a specific price if there were willing buyers. However, what factors determine the quantities of euros or US dollars demanded and supplied?

For example, if Americans wish to buy European goods, services, or assets, European residents would require payment in euros; American buyers must, therefore, acquire (demand) euros in exchange for dollars. This is the basis of the demand curve for euros. On the other hand, purchases of American goods, services, or assets by European residents form the basis of the supply curve of euros; American suppliers require payment in dollars and, consequently, Europeans must acquire them in exchange for (a supply of) euros.

Exhibit 4.7

Demand, Supply, and Equilibrium in the Foreign Exchange Market

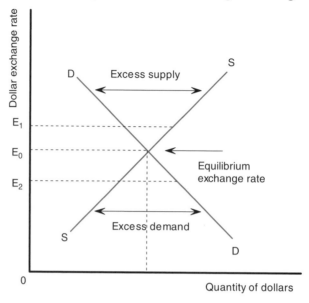

Exhibit 4.7 is a graphical representation of a model of forces at work in the foreign exchange market for euros. The demand curve for dollars, labeled DD, shows a negative relationship between the foreign exchange of the dollar and the quantity of dollars demanded, other things being equal. As the exchange rate (value) of the dollar falls from E_1 to E_0 or from E_0 to E_2, the prices of American goods, services, and assets also fall in the European market. Consequently, the demand for American goods in Europe will increase and this will lead to an increase in the quantity of dollars demanded. In other words, a low exchange rate will encourage American exports to Europe. Alternatively, if the dollar exchange rate increases from E_2 to E_0 or from E_0 to E_1, the prices of American goods, services, and assets will also increase in the European market leading, other things being equal, to a fall in the demand for American goods and a fall in the quantity of dollars demanded. A high exchange rate will discourage American exports to Europe. The demand for dollars (or any other currency) is closely associated with the credit items in the balance of payments.

The supply curve of dollars, labeled SS, shows a positive relationship between the exchange rate (value) of the dollar and the quantity of dollars supplied, other things being equal. A fall in the value of the dollar from E_1 to E_0 or from E_0 to E_2 causes a rise in the price of European goods, services, and assets in the United States and, consequently, a fall in the demand for them. As a result, the quantity of dollars supplied falls, as Americans now require fewer euros for imports from Europe. Alternatively, a rise in the value of the dollar from E_2 to E_0 or from E_0 to E_1 makes European goods, services, and assets in the United States cheaper and, therefore, increases the demand for them. Consequently, the quantity of dollars supplied increases, as Americans now require more euros for imports from Europe. In other words, a high (low) exchange rate encourages (discourages) imports and, as a result, the supply of dollars in the foreign exchange market increases (decreases). The supply of dollars (or any other currency) is closely associated with the debit items in the balance of payments.

The equilibrium exchange rate is determined by the intersection of the demand and supply curves. The forces at work are identical to those of any market. At all other possible exchange rates there can be no equilibrium. An exchange rate below equilibrium, E_2, means that the quantity of dollars demanded exceeds the quantity supplied, that is there is an excess demand for dollars. A cheap dollar (i.e., below equilibrium) makes American goods, services, and assets more attractive in Europe and increases the demand for dollars by European residents. At the same time, Americans demand less European goods, services, and assets and the quantity of dollars supplied falls. This excess demand for dollars prevailing in the market causes the exchange rate to rise toward equilibrium at E_0.

On the other hand, an exchange rate above equilibrium, E_1, signifies an excess supply of dollars as quantity supplied exceeds quantity demanded. A strong dollar (i.e., above equilibrium) reduces the price of European imports and increases the demand for them. At the same time, American exports to Europe become more expensive and, as a result, the demand for dollars falls as Europeans demand less. This excess supply can be eliminated by a fall in the exchange rate toward equilibrium at E_0. In reality, equilibrium is achieved very rapidly. Exchange rates are continuously adjusted by foreign exchange dealers as customers all over the world demand and supply currencies.

As is the case with all relevant market models, demand and supply curves are constructed according to the "ceteris paribus" assumption (i.e., all other factors remaining constant). Consequently, any change in the various demand and/or supply determinants (as explained below) will shift the demand and/or supply curves and alter the equilibrium positions.

Exchange Rate Determination

The forces influencing the demand and supply of the dollar (or any other currency) include relative national incomes, relative national price levels, interest rates, and expectations about the future value of a currency. A change in some or all of these factors can cause the demand curve and/or the supply curve of a currency to shift.[7]

Relative National Incomes. Any student who has taken an introductory course in macroeconomics should know that the demand for a country's imports is directly related to the country's income. From the standpoint of the United States, when income falls, as a result of a recession, the demand for imports declines. Consequently, as Americans demand less imports, the supply of dollars falls (i.e., the supply curve of dollars shifts to the left). If we assume that there is a constant demand for dollars, the leftward shift will bring about an appreciation of the dollar. Alternatively, when income increases as a result of an economic boom, the demand for imports increases. Hence, the supply of dollars increases as more dollars are needed to buy foreign currency (i.e., the supply curve of dollars shifts to the right). Other things being equal, the rightward shift will cause the dollar to depreciate.

In the reverse situation, incomes in the rest of the world have a direct effect on US exports. When incomes abroad rise, there is an increased demand for US goods. Hence, the demand for dollars increases as foreign residents supply more foreign currency in exchange for dollars. The demand curve for dollars shifts to the right. If we assume that there is a constant supply of dollars, the rightward shift will cause the dollar to appreciate. Alternatively, if incomes in the rest of the world fall, the demand for dollars falls and the resulting leftward shift of the demand curve, other things being equal, causes the dollar to depreciate. The above analysis could also explain a change in tastes toward American goods.

Relative Price Levels. The demand for imports in the United States and foreign demand for US exports will also depend on the price levels prevailing in the United States and abroad. If inflation is higher in the United States, exporting becomes more difficult as foreign goods become comparatively cheaper. At the same time, foreign firms will increase their market share in the US markets. As a result, exports will fall and imports will increase. The fall in exports will cause the demand curve for dollars to shift leftward whereas the rise in imports will bring about a rightward shift of the dollar supply curve. The dollar will depreciate. The size of the depreciation will depend on the relative magnitude of the shifts, that is if exports fall more then imports increase and vice versa. The dollar will depreciate relatively more if the demand effect dominates (i.e., the shift of the demand curve is larger than the supply curve shift). The opposite will hold true if inflation is lower in the United States; exports will rise and imports will fall. The demand curve for dollars will shift rightward while the supply curve of dollars shifts to the left and the dollar appreciates.

Interest Rates. Capital markets today are global. Massive amounts of money travel with the speed of light in search of the highest returns. If the United States provides higher yields than comparable securities in, say, Europe, investors will sell their assets denominated in euros and will buy dollar assets. To do this, they need to sell euros and buy dollars. The demand curve for dollars will increase (i.e., shift rightward) and, other things being equal, the dollar will appreciate. At the same time, the supply curve of dollars may shift leftward as fewer Americans buy foreign assets. Conversely, if European interest rates are higher than US interest rates, the opposite would hold true: the demand for dollars will fall whereas the supply of dollars will increase and the dollar will depreciate. It should be emphasized that in the short run capital movements in search of higher interest rates will exert a much greater influence on exchange rates than will trade flows.

Expectations. Expectations about changes in the future value of a currency also exert a significant influence on exchange rates. Market fundamentals—trade flows, inflation, interest rates, the government's fiscal and monetary policies—prompt investors and foreign exchange dealers to form expectations about the future value of the dollar (or any other relevant currency). For example, if markets are doubtful as to the ability of the US government to control inflation, they will expect the dollar to depreciate. As a result, investors and foreign exchange dealers will sell dollars and the expected depreciation will actually take place.[8]

Foreign exchange speculations—demand for a currency for possible gains is—based on expectations. For example, if Americans believe that the euro will appreciate relative to the dollar at a future date, they will increase their holdings of euros today so that they can gain from a possible appreciation by exchanging euros for dollars. As a result, expectations about a future appreciation cause the current exchange rate to rise. The supply curve of dollars will shift rightward and the dollar will depreciate. Similarly, if European investors expect an appreciation of the dollar, they will demand more dollars today for possible future gains. The demand curve for dollars shifts rightward and the dollar appreciates.[9]

In the absence of restrictions on capital movements, the high degree of capital mobility among major industrialized countries ensures that expected returns on comparable assets will tend to be equalized as exchange rates adjust whenever funds shift in search of higher interest rates. This is known as the interest parity condition whereby, in conditions of perfect capital mobility, the interest rate on the home currency minus the expected depreciation rate of the home currency is equal to the foreign interest rate.[10] What the interest rate parity condition implies is that the exchange rate of the country with lower interest rates will be expected to appreciate. Conversely, if interest rates in one country are higher, markets expect the exchange rate to depreciate. The latter implication provides a powerful link between expected exchange rates and differences in inflation rates. In other words, higher inflation rates lead to higher interest rates and an expected depreciation of the home currency.

Exhibit 4.8 summarizes the above discussion. Graphs (a) and (b) show what happens in the foreign exchange market when the demand curve for dollars shifts rightward and leftward, respectively, while the supply curve

Exhibit 4.8

Changes in the Foreign Exchange Market

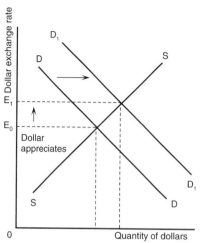

(a) Increase in demand—increase in exports; lower US inflation; US interest rates higher than foreign interest rates; expected appreciation of the dollar

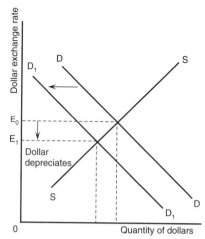

(b) Decrease in demand—decrease in exports; higher US inflation; US interest rates lower than foreign interest rates

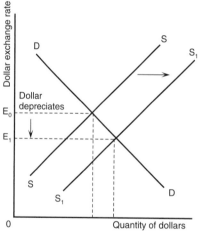

(c) Increase in supply—US incomes increase; increase in imports, higher US inflation; US interest rates lower than foreign interest rates; expected depreciation of the dollar

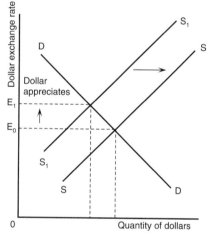

(d) Decrease in supply—US incomes fall; decrease in imports; lower US inflation; US interest rates higher than foreign interest rates

remains constant. Similarly, graphs (c) and (d) illustrate the case of a rightward and leftward shift in the supply curve of dollars while the demand curve remains constant. It should be emphasized that, as in any other market, it is highly likely that both curves will shift in response to external disturbances. For example, while an increase in the demand curve for dollars may cause the dollar to appreciate, a simultaneous increase in the supply curve of dollars may offset the demand effect depending on the relative magnitudes of the shifts.

Purchasing Power Parity

Economists tend to believe that factors affecting exchange rates differ significantly in the short, medium, and long runs. Exchange rate volatility in the short run is largely due to capital movements as funds are shifted internationally in search of higher interest rates. The medium-term determinants of exchange rates are largely affected by trade flows. This section examines the determinants of the long-run trends in exchange rates. A key economic "fundamental" variable that seems to explain long-term trends in exchange rates is differences in national price levels.[11]

The purchasing power parity (PPP) theory holds that exchange rates between two currencies adjust to reflect differences in the price levels between the two countries. This means that the exchange rate between two countries should equal the ratio of the two countries' price level of a fixed basket of goods and services. When a country's domestic price level is increasing (i.e., a country experiences inflation), that country's exchange rate must depreciate in order to return to PPP.

The PPP theory is based on the "law of one price." In the absence of transportation costs, exchange rates should adjust so that the same product costs the same whether it is measured in dollars, euros, yen, or any other currency. For example, if the euro/dollar exchange rate is €1 = $1, a specific product selling for $1000 in the United States should cost €1000 in Europe. If the product's price were lower in the United States, consumers in Europe would prefer buying the product in the United States. As a result, the value of the dollar will rise as Europeans sell euros and buy dollars. This process of a "product arbitrage" will continue until the product sells for the same price in both countries. Different versions of the PPP theory have existed throughout the modern history of international economics. Basically, two versions of PPP are used:

- Absolute PPP, which is based on the law of one price and refers to the price levels between two countries. For example, the euro/dollar exchange rate equals the US price level divided by the European price level, that is €/$ = P(US)/P(Europe).
- Relative PPP, whereby changes in exchange rates reflect differences in relative price levels, that is inflation rates. According to relative PPP theory, the rate of depreciation (or appreciation) equals the difference in inflation rates between the two countries. For example, if the inflation rate is 2 percent in the United States and 5 percent in Europe, the euro is expected to depreciate by 3 percent.

Absolute PPP and the "law of one price" do not hold well in practice because of the presence of significant barriers to trade (tariffs, quotas, etc.), transportation costs, and other transaction costs. In addition, the law of one price and absolute PPP refer only to traded goods; physical assets (houses, land) and a large number of services are not traded between countries. In general, the relative PPP theory seems to be a rather good determinant of exchange rates in the long run, but not in the short run. However, a relationship consistent with PPP is clear: the currencies of high-inflation countries tend to depreciate while low-inflation countries tend to have appreciating currencies. Empirical evidence between currencies shows a tendency for PPP to hold in the long run (a period between 5 and 10 years) with, however, large deviations from PPP in the short run.[12]

Exchange Rate Regimes

Exchange rate variability has given rise to a vast international literature on the relative merits of different exchange rate systems. Three basic exchange rate regimes have operated during the twentieth century: fixed exchange rates, flexible exchange rates, and managed exchange rates.

Fixed Exchange Rates

A fixed exchange rate is pegged at a certain level by the national monetary authorities and can only be changed by a government decision. Of course, this does not imply that the exchange rate will never be different from a market-determined exchange rate. As discussed above, many significant factors cause the exchange rate to change. Consequently, the monetary authorities will have to take offsetting actions by continuous intervention (buying or selling foreign exchange) in order to maintain the exchange rate at the prescribed level.

In practice, fixed exchange rates are normally maintained within bands whereby exchange rates are allowed to move within upper and lower limits. The monetary authorities intervene whenever the exchange rate moves outside the targeted limits. Exhibit 4.9 illustrates the case of maintaining an exchange rate band above the equilibrium exchange rate. In this case, as we know from the previous analysis, there is an excess supply of dollars, that is balance of payments deficit as a result of an appreciation of the dollar. The central parity (midpoint) is E_2 whereas E_1 and E_3 are the lower and upper limits of the band, respectively. In the absence of intervention by the monetary authorities the equilibrium exchange rate (i.e., the rate determined by market forces) is E_0. To prevent the exchange rate from falling and to keep it at least within the lower limit, the monetary authorities must buy dollars equal to AB. The purchase of dollars requires the use of foreign exchange reserves of the currency against which dollars are pegged, say, euros. It becomes obvious that this process will end when the government runs out of foreign exchange reserves. The depletion of reserves creates expectations

Exhibit 4.9

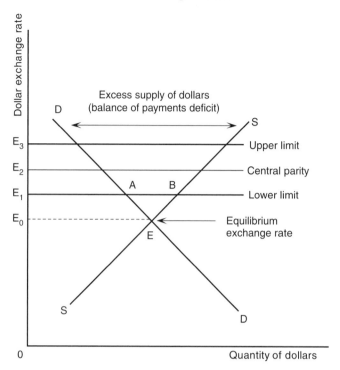

Fixed Exchange Rates

of depreciation and once markets are convinced that the exchange rate cannot be maintained any longer, investors will sell the overvalued currency in anticipation of its depreciation. The opposite holds true in the case of excess demand. The monetary authorities will have to sell dollars in order to keep the dollar from appreciating.[13]

Flexible Exchange Rates

Under a flexible or freely floating exchange rate system the monetary authorities do not intervene in the foreign exchange market. The price of a currency is allowed to rise or fall according to prevailing demand and supply conditions. In other words, the exchange rate adjusts to clear the market and, as a result, balance of payments equilibrium is achieved automatically. Thus, debit items in the current and capital accounts are equal to the corresponding credit items as payments to foreign residents are exactly equal to receipts from foreign residents.[14]

Managed Exchange Rates

An intermediate system, sometimes referred to as a "dirty float," may be, and has been, used whereby the monetary authorities intervene in varying degrees in order to influence the exchange rate in the desired direction by the purchase and sale of foreign currencies. Intervention can be substantial when the monetary authorities consider that market forces (such as large volumes of speculative capital flows) threaten macroeconomic policy goals or when the exchange rate is considerably misaligned. On the other hand, intervention can be limited in smoothing out daily fluctuations mainly caused by capital movements. In other words, a managed float is partially market-determined and partially government-determined.

Fixed or Flexible Exchange Rates?

In the real world the choice between alternative exchange rate systems is less extreme as there are varying degrees of government intervention in the foreign exchange markets. However, before proceeding to a discussion of the relative merits of fixed and flexible exchange rates, it is convenient to discuss the adjustment mechanism to a balance of payments disequilibrium under fixed and flexible exchange rates.

The Adjustment Mechanism

One of the main objectives of macroeconomic policy is the achievement of balance of payments equilibrium in the medium and long run. The most interesting case is the case of a nation with a balance of payments deficit although the opposite arguments hold true for surplus countries.

Assume that the United States runs a current account deficit, which is associated with an excess supply of dollars. Under freely determined exchange rates, the dollar will depreciate, as there will be a greater supply of dollars than demanded. The result of this depreciation will be to stimulate exports and restrict imports, thereby eliminating the deficit and restoring international competitiveness. This process depends on a fall in the price of exports, which increases the demand for dollars, and a corresponding rise in the price of imports that decreases the supply of dollars. This is feasible only if the demand for exports and imports is elastic. This is known as the Marshall–Lerner condition. If demand for imports were inelastic (i.e., less than one), a rise in import prices will place a greater burden on the economy by increasing expenditure on them and will lead to a deterioration rather than an improvement in the balance of payments.

If exchange rates are fixed, the deficit nation, in order to improve the balance of payments position, can resort to expenditure reduction polices by using a restrictive monetary and fiscal policy mix to reduce aggregate demand, which will in turn reduce demand for imports relative to exports (whose demand, of course, depends on foreign incomes). This restrictive policy will also dampen domestic inflationary pressures, which are expected to improve international competitiveness even further. However, the use of expenditure reduction policies solely for the purpose of improving balance of payments disequilibrium results in recession by constraining output and increasing unemployment.

The other alternative for the deficit nation is the use of expenditure switching policies aimed at boosting exports and inducing home residents to buy home-produced goods and services. The most common method is devaluation, whereby the declared fixed exchange rate is lowered or the declared band is revised downward. The word "devaluation" is equivalent to depreciation but is commonly used to describe the lowering of the exchange rate in a fixed exchange rate system. The devaluation mechanism is similar to the depreciation mechanism under flexible exchange rates, that is it brings about a reduction in the price of exports and an increase in the price of imports. For a devaluation to be effective, the Marshall–Lerner condition must hold so that domestic consumers respond to the increased prices of imports and reduce their expenditure on them. The devaluation will also have a positive influence on the domestic economy as it raises domestic aggregate demand, output, and employment. It can, however, create inflationary pressures as increased import prices, especially in oil and raw materials, are transmitted to domestically produced goods.

Another policy measure, not necessarily independent of direct intervention, is the use of interest rates as an instrument of exchange rate management. If, for example, the US monetary authorities wish to stop the dollar from depreciating, the Federal Reserve raises interest rates and dollar-denominated assets become more attractive as they yield higher returns. The demand for dollars increases as European investors transfer funds to the United States. However, higher interest rates have a negative influence on the domestic economy as they dampen domestic demand and output and increase unemployment. Alternatively, lower US interest rates cause a leftward shift of the demand curve for dollars and a depreciation of the dollar.

Advantages and Disadvantages of Fixed and Flexible Exchange Rates

The debate on the relative merits of the two exchange rate systems focuses primarily on the following issues:[15]

- International monetary stability
- Economic policy independence.

International Monetary Stability. It is argued that fixed exchange rates facilitate international trade. Pricing is easier and the cost of foreign exchange transactions is very low. In addition, the (relative) certainty as to the future value of the exchange rate makes future contracts less risky. Since rates are fixed, there is no scope for speculation. All the above factors encourage the growth of international trade, specialization, and economic growth in the countries that have adopted a fixed exchange rate system. However, such advantages can be enjoyed only if there exists credibility regarding the fixing of exchange rates. Expectations of exchange rate changes provoke speculative flows, which force monetary authorities to abandon fixed exchange rates.

In a fixed exchange rate system, the monetary authorities must have adequate foreign exchange reserves in order to maintain the rate within the prescribed limits. If the exchange rate is set at a high level (i.e., the domestic currency is overvalued), there is a current account deficit as exports are now more expensive and foreign demand for them is low. In this case, the monetary authorities must defend the rate by using their foreign exchange reserves (i.e., purchasing the domestic currency in the foreign exchange market). If, on the other hand, the exchange rate is set at a low level (i.e., the domestic currency is undervalued), there is a current account surplus. The monetary authorities in this case must defend the rate by building up foreign exchange reserves (i.e., selling the domestic currency). This means that another country is losing reserves. The continuous gain or loss of foreign exchange reserves will ultimately bring about a change in the fixed exchange rate.

Problems can arise from destabilizing speculation when a country is about to run out of foreign exchange. In this case, markets believe that the monetary authorities are unable to sustain the exchange rate and expectations of a drop in the value of the currency set in. Investors expect a capital loss and they start selling the domestic currency. The supply curve shifts to the right and the authorities will have to use more foreign exchange reserves in order to shift the demand curve to the right. Eventually, they will either abandon the fixed rate or let the exchange rate fall. The cause of the 1997 Asian financial crisis was destabilizing speculation as the Asian Tigers attempted to defend a fixed exchange rate to the US dollar while experiencing balance of payments deficits. However, speculation can also be stabilizing. If the exchange rate falls below the lower limit but markets are convinced that the monetary authorities are committed to that rate and will intervene, investors will buy the domestic currency in anticipation of the intervention so that they can realize capital gains. The purchase of the home currency shifts the demand curve to the right and back to equilibrium.

Advocates of flexible exchange rates argue that exchange rate adjustments are made in an orderly fashion without excessive fluctuations. Any deficits or surpluses are eliminated by appropriate exchange rate adjustments. However, one may ask the question: will free markets set the right exchange rate? Since various factors cause continuous shifts in the demand and supply curves, there is no guarantee that the exchange rate is determined by long-run equilibrium forces. Short-run equilibrium does not imply long-run equilibrium. The market provides incorrect signals and the economy is subjected to abrupt fluctuations as expectations regarding long-run equilibrium shift continuously.

Economic Policy Independence. The main advantage of fixed exchange rates (which can also be considered a disadvantage) is the imposition of discipline on the conduct of macroeconomic policy. Here, the rule is to ensure that a country's inflation rate does not diverge from the average of its main trading partners. Higher inflation will lead to a balance of payments deficit and will require corrective action through expenditure-switching policies. On the other hand, lower inflation will bring about a balance of payments surplus and an expansion of the domestic money supply, thus creating inflationary pressures.

For example, suppose that the home country decides to run an expansionary monetary policy by lowering interest rates in order to stimulate the economy and bring down unemployment. Expansionary monetary policy will bring about an increase in aggregate demand but will also lead to higher domestic inflation. This has negative implications on the country's international competitiveness as exports become more expensive and a current account deficit is likely to emerge. As deficits cannot be sustained in the long run, the government will be forced to conduct a deflationary policy, thereby reducing aggregate demand, output, and employment. The main point here is that the government cannot use the exchange rate as an instrument of monetary policy, that is it cannot let the exchange rate depreciate.

> **Talking to Professor Otmar Issing**
> **Member of the Executive Board, European Central Bank**
>
> "Which factors do you think will affect the medium and long-run performance of the euro against major currencies such as the US dollar, the yen and the pound sterling and how can the euro challenge the dollar's position as a major reserve currency?"
>
> In the long run the *external* performance of the euro—as one would expect for any currency under freely floating exchange rates—should reflect its *internal* stability. Over longer horizons the trend in the nominal exchange rate should make up for inflation differentials between different currency areas. In addition, the real exchange rate may also evolve over time, reflecting differences in the longer-term growth potential and productivity developments.
>
> The primary objective of the European Central Bank is to maintain price stability in the euro area. This is our job and this is also a prerequisite for the euro as a strong and trusted currency internationally. Enhancing the attractiveness of the euro area as a place to invest and do business is the job of European governments. It is then up to the markets to judge the euro area's performance on both counts.

(*Continued*)

Price stability is the precondition for money to properly fulfill its functions as a reliable unit of account, as a trusted medium of exchange, and as a stable store of value. This holds domestically and also with respect to the international role of the euro. As we know from history, however, the international use of currencies tends to evolve only slowly over time. This regards both *private* use, e.g., as invoicing currencies and vehicle currency in the exchange markets and *official* use as foreign exchange reserves. I don't see this as a challenge or competition with the dollar. The ECB has adopted a neutral stance on the international role of the euro, neither fostering nor hindering its development. Private agents and governments will over time determine how the benefits of scale in international currency use balance with the gains from diversification. Further integration of euro area financial markets could make the euro more attractive in this regard. As I see it, the euro as a stable currency can only be positive for the International Monetary System.

Lower interest rates can also have important implications on capital flows through the interest rate parity condition. Since exchange rates are fixed and there is a high degree of capital mobility between countries, home interest rates are closely linked to foreign interest rates. To maintain a fixed exchange rate, the monetary authorities must make sure that home interest rates are more or less equal to foreign interest rates. If the home central bank lowers interest rates in order to stimulate the economy, there will be a capital inflow as lower domestic interest rates induce foreign investors to sell the domestic currency and seek out higher returns elsewhere. To defend the rate of the home currency and prevent it from changing, the home monetary authorities will be forced to raise interest rates. Alternatively, an attempt to increase interest rates in order to dampen domestic inflationary pressures will induce capital inflows and an appreciation of the home currency. In this case, the central bank will be forced to lower interest rates, which may further exacerbate domestic inflation.

Maintaining a fixed exchange rate places limitations on the actions of the monetary authorities in conducting monetary and fiscal policies. A high-inflation country has much to gain by pegging its currency because it provides the necessary discipline to bring inflation down. Although the loss of an independent macroeconomic policy is one of the main arguments of the proponents of flexible exchange rates, it is also one of the main arguments in favor of exchange rates. This analysis will prove useful in Chapter 5 when the European Monetary Union is discussed.

Advocates of flexible exchange rates argue that since the government does not intervene in the foreign exchange market, the need for foreign exchange reserves is limited. Second, the monetary authorities are not forced to conduct monetary and fiscal policies to restore balance of payments disequilibrium since the exchange rate adjusts to equilibrate demand and supply. However, this does not imply that the adjustment process is a "free ride" or that economic activity at home is isolated from the rest of the world. And the case becomes more valid in a globalized economy with high degrees of interdependencies among open economies that are open to international trade. For example, if inflation is higher in the United States than in the rest of the world, the dollar will depreciate, causing the dollar price of imports to rise. By adopting flexible exchange rates the government is free from the balance of payments constraint when pursuing policies for achieving domestic macroeconomic goals such as increased output and employment since the exchange rate will adjust so as to bring about balance of payments equilibrium.

However, changes in exchange rates involve domestic costs such as higher inflation for domestic residents, and in essence this freedom can be interpreted as the right for a country to choose its own inflation. Not to mention the fact that matters are further complicated as domestic macroeconomic policy itself influences the exchange rate. For example, lower interest rates will cause a capital outflow, leading to a depreciation in the exchange rate. Consequently, the government's attempts to stimulate the domestic economy by raising interest rates may cause an even greater depreciation (and higher inflation) as the capital flight has the same effect on the exchange rate as direct intervention in the foreign exchange market through the sale of the domestic currency.

The dilemma between two rather extreme cases can be partially set aside when governments choose an intermediate policy that will incorporate the advantages of both fixed and flexible exchange rates. If national authorities believe that long-run fundamental forces cause exchange rate movements, they may allow the market to determine the equilibrium exchange rate. However, if they believe that the exchange rate is either too high or too low and exchange rate adjustment cannot eliminate balance of payments disequilibrium, they may intervene in the foreign exchange market. For example, if the Federal Reserve considers that the dollar's value against the euro is too low and creates inflationary pressures, the Fed may then intervene in the foreign exchange market by buying dollars (and selling euros). If, at the same time, the European Central Bank considers that the value of euro is too high and undertakes reverse intervention, nothing will change as the two efforts cancel each other out. In order for intervention to be effective, international cooperation is imperative.[16]

The International Monetary System

The international monetary system can be seen as a network effecting international payments through institutions, rules, and regulations. In order to fulfill its role effectively, an international monetary system should possess certain characteristics:

- A time element regarding the elimination of balance of payments disequilibrium among countries, that is countries must be allowed sufficient time to adjust without severe recessions or high inflation but, at the same time, should not be allowed to avoid adjustment at the expense of other countries.
- The choice of the unit of account, that is the agreed measure of the value of currencies.
- International cooperation with respect to adjustment methods, concerted intervention, and reserve assets.
- Promotion of free international trade so that productive resources are optimally allocated.

We can now briefly examine the different systems that have prevailed throughout modern economic history.[17]

The Gold Standard

The gold standard is the only example in history when exchange rates were truly fixed. It was a system whereby the values of currencies were fixed relative to the value of gold, which was used as a unit of account and the main reserve asset. Each country participating in the gold standard fixed the value of its currency relative to gold and maintained gold reserves. The difference between the quantity demanded and supplied of a country's currency was determined by the purchase or sale of gold so that the value of the currency in terms of gold remained fixed. The amount of purchase or sale depended on the balance of payments deficit or surplus, respectively.

A country with a balance of payments surplus would sell its currency (i.e., buy gold) in order to hold the revaluation (appreciation) of its currency. Because the domestic money supply was based on gold, the inflow of gold would increase the money supply and lower interest rates. Lower interest rates would provoke capital outflows while the resulting expansionary monetary policy would increase income and cause domestic inflation, which encouraged imports and discouraged exports. All these forces would work toward the elimination of the balance of payments surplus.

On the other hand, a balance of payments deficit would necessitate the purchase of the home currency (i.e., sale of gold) in order to keep the exchange rate from falling. The resulting money supply contraction would dampen domestic demand and output, decrease imports, and bring about a rise in interest rates. As a result, the balance of payments deficit would be eliminated.

It is apparent that the system provided an automatic method of adjustment so that no management was needed. Since the money supply was directly tied to gold, the government could not pursue an independent monetary policy in order to achieve domestic goals. The gold standard was suspended in 1914, just before World War I. It was reintroduced in the 1920s and finally collapsed following the financial chaos of the Great Depression and World War II.

The Bretton Woods System

Following the collapse of the gold standard, the Great Depression, and the years before and during World War II, massive unemployment and severe recessions induced many countries to resort to protectionism, that is insulating domestic industries from foreign competition while interest rates were used as a purely domestic monetary policy instrument. When the war ended, the Allies met at Bretton Woods, New Hampshire, in 1944 in an attempt to establish a stable international monetary system that would restore international trade. The resulting agreement led to the adoption of fixed, but adjustable, exchange rates based on the free convertibility of the US dollar to gold and the establishment of the International Monetary Fund (IMF).[18] It was clearly an attempt to create a "new order."

The Bretton Woods was essentially an agreement for a return to fixed exchange rates.[19] The agreement also provided for the establishment of the IMF to oversee and manage the new international economic order and tackle two main problems: the financing of temporary balance of payments deficits (or dealing with surpluses) and the correction of fundamental disequilibrium. The Fund provided a stabilization fund from which a country with temporary balance of payments difficulties could obtain short-term loans. The correction of fundamental disequilibrium required structural changes in the domestic economy and for this reason the World Bank was also established for providing long-term financing.

The system was based on mutual agreement about the actions of countries when experiencing balance of payments deficits or surpluses. The United States agreed to buy and sell gold to maintain the $35 per ounce price established in 1933. Currencies were to be freely convertible to other currencies. The monetary authorities of the signatory nations would maintain an exchange rate within a band of ±1 percent of the agreed central parity, along the lines of Exhibit 4.9. If the value of a currency fell below the lower intervention point, the central bank had to purchase the domestic currency by selling foreign exchange reserves. The main reserve asset was gold but, in practice, countries bought or sold dollars. To ensure the adequacy of reserves, a country could obtain a short-term loan from the stabilization fund in order to deal with short-run adjustments.

Adjustment was to be achieved by domestic expenditure-switching policies but provision was made for changes in the exchange rate in cases of fundamental imbalances. The IMF had to authorize a one-time change in the exchange rate by more than 10 percent. A distinction was also made between trade and capital movements. Restrictions on payments of goods were not allowed whereas countries could resort to foreign exchange controls or other policies inhibiting the free inflow or outflow of capital.

There were two basic weaknesses inherent in the Bretton Woods system. First, exchange rate adjustments reflecting fundamental imbalances were not timely and, as a result, deficits became chronic. When devaluations were allowed, exchange rate adjustments were of sizeable proportions. In addition, they could be foreseen with almost perfect certainty and speculators realized large profits when they "attacked" weak currencies by selling them in large amounts. Second, there was a shortage of official reserves and international liquidity. The IMF created the Special Drawing Rights (SDRs), a type of international money, to offset these shortages but the SDRs were never established as an international currency and the US dollar was the main international reserve asset.

While deficit nations were ultimately forced to devalue, surplus nations resisted revaluations in order to avoid recessions. Because the US dollar was fixed in terms of gold, the United States could not devalue the dollar to restore competitiveness and the only way the exchange rate of the dollar against other currencies could change was if surplus countries revalued their currencies. Since such revaluations were stringently resisted, the dollar became overvalued and the United States ran a large balance of payments deficit. The number of dollars held by foreigners grew dramatically in the 1960s and by the early 1970s that number exceeded the amount of gold held by the United States. As a result, the depletion of foreign exchange reserves and the accumulation of foreign debt forced the United States to end its policy of exchanging gold for dollars at $35 per ounce. And that was the death of the Bretton Woods system.[20]

The Present "Nonsystem"

Following the breakdown of the Bretton Woods system, the United States and other industrialized countries switched to managed exchange rates but the system is so diverse that it is sometimes referred to as a "nonsystem." Most industrial countries' exchange rates are allowed to fluctuate although monetary authorities intervene in the foreign exchange market or use interest rates to influence the exchange rate by buying or selling their currencies.

Countries constantly need to distinguish between a temporary balance of payments disequilibrium and fundamental imbalance. Should they decide that it is a temporary phenomenon, they must intervene in the foreign exchange market to stabilize the exchange rate at what they perceive to be an appropriate level. On the other hand, if they consider that a balance of payments imbalance is a fundamental one, they must let the exchange rate be determined by market forces.

Most Western countries' exchange rates are managed although, especially in Europe, fixed (but adjustable) exchange rates have existed since 1979 when a group of European Community countries formed the European Monetary System. Since 1998, 12 member countries of the European Union adopted irreversible fixed exchange rates among their currencies by electing to have one common currency—the euro. Other currencies are fixed relative to the dollar, some others use a crawling-peg system (fixing the exchange rate relative to a hard currency and letting it depreciate gradually), and yet others fix their currencies to a basket of several currencies.

Fundamental disequilibrium cannot be clearly defined and such issues are considered through international cooperation. In 1978 the dollar's free fall was stopped by the concerted intervention of major central banks and in 1985 the Group Five (G5) central banks sold dollars in order to stop the prolonged appreciation of the dollar. In the Louvre Accord in 1987, the G5 (plus Canada) recognized the need for greater stability among the world's major currencies as a prerequisite for trade growth and economic expansion. The Accord established informally acceptable ranges of exchange rate changes taking into account the economic conditions prevailing in each country so that exchange rate levels are both sustainable and appropriate.[21]

Closing Case

The Asian Crisis

The 1997 Asian crisis began when speculators attacked baht, the Thai currency. Thailand, like many Asian economies, had a fixed exchange rate system whereby the baht was fixed relative to the US dollar. The country was running substantial balance of payments deficits and was losing reserves as it was defending the exchange rate against the dollar. As markets realized that the government could not sustain the exchange rate any longer, investors shifted to other hard currencies. The Thai stock market index plunged by 50 percent within a year and banks were in danger of collapse as they had loaned funds using inflated assets as collateral.

The domino effect also hit the other Asian economies as they were experiencing similar problems. Investors fled from the Philippines, Malaysia, and Indonesia, as expectations of a fall in their exchange rates grew stronger. The authorities in these countries were forced to abandon the exchange rate peg and, at the same time, Taiwan and Singapore also abandoned their fixed exchange rates. The United States was also affected by fears of a widespread financial crisis and the Dow Jones plunged 554 points in October 1997. The selling spell spread from Asia to Russia and Brazil.

The governments of the affected countries had to generate recessions, with disastrous consequences in terms of lost output and unemployment, by raising interest rates to stop capital outflows and by resorting to devaluations in order to restore international competitiveness. In doing so, the prices of imports rose and so did domestic inflation. In addition, as these countries had resorted to heavy foreign borrowing, devaluation raised the cost of repaying international debt as its value in terms of domestic currency was also raised.[22]

Source: Compiled by Dr. Spyros Hadjidakis, Associate Professor of Economics and Finance, School of Business, Intercollege, Nicosia, Cyprus.

Question: Was the Asian Crisis resolved? How? Please conduct outside research to support your answer.

Chapter Summary

The balance of payments provides a record of transactions between domestic and foreign residents. While payments within a country are made in the same currency, payments between residents of different countries involve different currencies. The balance of payments accounts are compiled through the use of double-entry bookkeeping with credit and debit entries; credit items include all transactions that give rise to foreign exchange inflows whereas debit items include all transactions causing foreign exchange outflows. The balance of payments is divided into different sections: the current account dealing with trade in goods and services, the capital account dealing with investment flows and transactions in assets, and the official reserves accounts, which equates the overall balance of payments.

The foreign exchange market sets the exchange rates between different currencies. The exchange rate is the price of one nation's currency in terms of another's. The demand for a currency arises from its exports and all credit items in the balance of payments accounts while the supply of a currency arises from its imports and all debit items. In a free market, the equilibrium exchange rate is determined by the interaction of demand and supply. Factors influencing the demand for and the supply of currency are incomes at home and abroad, relative inflation, interest rates, and expectation. In the long run, the PPP theory states that inflation and currency depreciation should balance so that the prices of any given product in different countries are equal.

A flexible exchange rate system is one in which the monetary authorities do not intervene in the foreign exchange market by buying or selling their currencies and let exchange rates be determined in free markets by the laws of demand and supply. A currency appreciates if its value rises whereas a currency depreciates if its value falls.

A fixed exchange rate is pegged at a certain level, or within a band, by the national monetary authorities and can only be changed by a government decision. In such a case the government must continuously intervene in the foreign exchange market in order to maintain the exchange rate at the desired level by buying its currency if it is overvalued and if there is excess supply or by selling its currency if it is undervalued and if there is excess demand. The former case refers to a balance of payments deficit while the latter refers to a balance of payments surplus.

The main argument for fixed exchange rates is that they facilitate trade by providing monetary stability and that they impose discipline on the conduct of macroeconomic policy. The arguments against fixed exchange rates is that the correction of balance of payments deficits depends on the adequacy of foreign exchange reserves and that the country is susceptible to destabilizing speculation when it is about to run out of reserves.

Proponents of flexible exchange rates argue that exchange rate adjustments are made in an orderly fashion without excessive fluctuations since any deficits or surpluses are eliminated by appropriate exchange rate adjustments. They also argue that flexible exchange rates allow independence in the conduct of domestic monetary and fiscal policies, which is, in effect, the reverse of the discipline argument for fixed exchange rates. The argument against flexible exchange rates is that expectations shift as rates change, thus causing exchange rate variability, which is detrimental to international trade and investment flows. The other argument against flexible exchange rates is that the automatic adjustment mechanism allows higher inflation.

The gold standard was a system of fixed exchange rates whereby the value of each currency was fixed in terms of gold. This created problems because countries could not control domestic money supply. The Bretton Woods system replaced the gold standard after World War II. Under this system, exchange rates were fixed in terms of US dollars and the dollar was fixed in terms of gold. The system came to end in 1971 as the dollar became overvalued and the United States was running chronic balance of payments deficits. Since 1971, the world turned into a system of managed exchange rates in which diversity was so great that it is referred to as a nonsystem.

Review and Discussion Questions

1. Explain the difference between autonomous and offsetting (or accommodating) transactions.
2. Since the balance of payments must always balance, how do balance of payments deficits or surpluses emerge?

3. If the price of euro falls from $1.250 to $1.180, is that depreciation or devaluation? Explain the difference.

4. The dollar/euro exchange rate is $1 = €1.17. Ford sells a consignment of cars to Europe for $10 million. Explain how the transaction is effected.

5. How will the dollar/euro exchange rate be affected if American consumers consider that it is fashionable to own a BMW car?

6. An independent American fashion importer decides to import Armani clothing from Italy. The Italian exporter quoted a price of €20, 000 for the consignment but the American firm had planned on spending no more than $13,000. (a) If the exchange rate is $1 = €1.2 can he afford to pay for the consignment? (b) What should the exchange rate be for the importer to import Armani clothing?

7. The following are indirect quotations of the dollar against the Swiss franc, the Japanese yen, and the British pound:

$1 = SF1.4814 − 1.4828
$1 = ¥124.26 − 124.37
$1 = £0.6419 − 0.6428

   (a) Calculate the midpoints in each rate and the direct quotation of each of the above rates.
   (b) Calculate the cross rates between (i) the Swiss franc and the Japanese yen, (ii) the Swiss franc and the euro, and (iii) the Japanese yen and the euro.

8. Do you agree with the view that a country is in a better position if it experiences a balance of payments deficit rather that a surplus?

9. Assume that the United States decides to adopt a fixed exchange rate system and pegs the dollar in relation to the euro. Trace out the possible effects on the US economy if (a) inflation is higher in the United States that in Europe, (b) the markets expect the dollar to depreciate.

Endnotes

1. For a comprehensive guide to balance of payments accounting, see International Monetary Fund, *Balance of Payments Manual*, 5th edn (Washington DC: IMF, 1993).
2. For an explanation of the revised accounting format used by the United States, see Bach, C. L. (1999), "US. International Transactions, Revised Estimates for 1982–1998," *Survey of Current Business*, July.
3. Several web sites offer daily exchange rates, cross rates as well as historical data including exchange rate converters some which are:
   Federal Reserve Bank of New York (www.ny.frb.org)
   Bloomberg (www.bloomberg.com)
   CNN (http://money.cnn/markets/currencies)
   OANDA (www.oanda.com)
   Exchange Rates (www.x-rates.com).

4. For more detailed discussion of the forward as well as the spot exchange rate market, see Connix, R. G. F., *Foreign Exchange Today*, 3rd edn (London: Woodhead-Faulkner, 1990), Chapters 7 and 8; Walmsley, J., *The Foreign Exchange Market and Money Markets Guide* (New York: John Wiley and Sons, 1992); Batiz-Rivera, F. and Rivera-Batiz, L., *International Finance and Open Economy Macroeconomics* (New York: Prentice Hall, 1994), Chapters 1, 5 and 6 and Levich, R. M., *International Financial Markets: Prices and Policies* (Boston: Irwin McGraw Hill, 1998), Chapters 3–8.

5. Different indexes can be used in the calculation of effective exchange rates. For a full account, see Rosensweig, J. A. (1987), "Constructing and Using Exchange Rate Indexes," *Economic Review of Federal Reserve Bank of Atlanta*, Summer.

6. For a recent review of real exchange rates, see Devereux, M. B. (1997), "Real Exchange Rates and Macroeconomics: Evidence and Theory," *Canadian Journal of Economics*, Vol. 30, November and Hau, H. (2002), "Real Exchange Rate Volatility and Economic Openness: Theory and Evidence," *Journal of Money, Credit and Banking*, Vol. 34(3), August.

7. There are different, but not competing, theoretical approaches to exchange rate determination depending on the time horizon examined. Traditional exchange rate theories mainly focus on the long run and fundamental determinants (such as trade flows and the price level) whereas more modern theories examine short-run determinants such as interest-rate differentials, capital flows and expectations.

8. For an account of the effect of capital flows on exchange rates, see Gibson, H. D., *International Finance: Exchange Rates and Financial Flows in the International System* (London: Longman, 1996), Chapters 2 and 3. See also the references cited below.

9. The asset-market approach to exchange rate determination, whereby exchange rates are determined in the asset markets, is treated in Salvatore (2001), *op. cit.*, Chapter 15 and Krugman, P. and Obstfeld, M, *International Economics: Theory and Policy*, 5th edn (New York: Addison-Wesley, 2000), Chapter 13. For a literature survey on the asset approach, see Frankel, J. and Rose, A. K., "An Empirical Characterization of Nominal Exchange Rates," in Grossman, G. and Rogoff, K, *Handbook of International Economics*, Vol. III (New York: North-Holland, 1995).

10. A full treatment of the interest parity condition makes use of both spot and forward exchange rates with or without coverage against exchange rate risk. For a presentation of theory and evidence, see Pigott, C. A. (1993–1994), "International Interest Rate Convergence: A Survey of the Issues and Evidence," in *Federal Reserve Bank of New York Quarterly Review*, Vol. 18, No 4, Winter and Martson, R. C., *International Financial Integration: A Study of Interest Differentials Between the Major Industrial Economies* (New York: Cambridge University Press, 1995).

11. For the long-run determinants of exchange rates, see Batiz-Rivera, F. and Rivera-Batiz, L., *op. cit.*, Chapter 13 and Salvatore, D. (2001), *International Economics*, 7th edn (New York: John Wiley & Sons, 1994), Chapters 16 and 17.

12. For empirical evidence on the PPP, see Rogoff, K. (1996), "The Purchasing Power Parity Puzzle," *Journal of Economic Literature*, Vol. 34, June; Dornbusch, R., "Purchasing Power Parity," *The New Palgrave Dictionary of Money and Finance*, Vol. 3 (New York: Stockton Press, 1992). In addition, the *Economist* magazine publishes every year the "Hamburger Index," a simple version of PPP where it compares the price of a Big Mac hamburger around the world.

13. Official intervention is treated in Mussa, M. (1981), *The Role of Official Intervention*, Occasional Paper No 6, Group of Thirty, New York; Sarno, L. and Taylor M. P. (2001), "Official Intervention in the Foreign Exchange Market: Is It Effective and, If So, Dow Does it Work?" *Journal of Economic Literature*, Vol. 39, September; Dominguez, K. M. and Frankel, J. A. (1993), *Does Foreign Exchange Market Intervention Work?* Institute for International Economics, Washington DC.

14. The most enthusiastic supporter of flexible exchange rates is the economist Milton Friedman. For a presentation of his case in favor of flexible exchange rates, see Friedman, M.,

"The Case for Flexible Exchange Rates," *Essays in Positive Economics* (Chicago: University of Chicago Press, 1953).

15. For the pioneering work on the relative merits of fixed and flexible exchange rates, also known as the Mundell-Fleming model, see Mundell, R. *International Economics* (New York: Macmillan, 1968) (especially Chapters 16 and 18) and Fleming, M. J. (1962), "Domestic Financial Policies Under Fixed and Floating Exchange Rates," *IMF Staff Papers*, March. For a more recent debate over fixed and flexible exchange rates, see Artus, J. R. and Young, J. H. (1979), "Fixed and Flexible Exchange Rates: A Renewal of the Debate," *IMF Staff Papers*, December; Goldstein, M. (1980), "Have Flexible Exchange Rates Handicapped Macroeconomic Policy?" *Special Papers in International Finance*, No 14, Princeton University Press, June; Bergsten, F. C. (ed.) (1991), *International Adjustment and Financing: The Lessons of 1985–1991*, Institute for International Economics, Washington DC; Edwards, S. (1996), *The Determinants of the Choice Between Fixed and Flexible Exchange Rate Regimes*, NBER Working Paper No 5756, September.

16. For a discussion and evaluation of managed floating, see Artus, J. R. and Crocket D. (1978), "Floating Exchange Rates and the Need for Surveillance," *Essays in International Finance*, No 127, Princeton University Press, May; Argy, V. (1982), "Exchange Rate Management in Theory and Practice," *Princeton Studies in International Finance*, October; Kenen, P. B. (ed.) (1994), *Managing the World Economy*, Institute for International Economics, Washington D. C.; International Monetary Fund (1999), *International Exchange Rate Arrangements and Currency Convertibility: Developments and Issues* (Washington DC: IMF).

17. For a brief but thorough treatment of the gold standard and the Bretton Woods system, see Krugman, P. and Obstfeld, M. (2000), *op. cit.*, Chapter 18 and Salvatore (2001), *op. cit.*, Chapter 21.

18. For more information on the IMF and the signatory countries, see the IMF's web site www.imf.org.

19. The Bretton Woods is discussed in more detail in Solomon, R., *The International Monetary System, 1945–1976* (New York: Harper and Row, 1977) and Bordo, M. and Eichengreen, B. eds, *Retrospective on the Bretton Woods International Monetary System* (Chicago: University of Chicago Press, 1992).

20. Robert Triffin predicted the dollar crisis in his classical work Triffin, R., *Gold and the Dollar Crisis* (New Haven: Yale University Press, 1960).

21. For proposed reforms to the current system, see Krugman, P. (1991), "Target Zones and Exchange Rate Dynamics," *Quarterly Journal of Economics*, August; Frankel, J. A., Goldstein, M. and Masson, P. R. (1991), "Characteristics of a Successful Exchange Rate System," *IMF Occasional Paper*, No 82, July; Frankel, J. A. (1996), "Recent Exchange Rate Experience and Proposals for Reform," *American Economic Review*, May and Eichengreen, B. (1999), *Towards a New Financial Architecture*, Institute for International Economics, Washington DC.

22. For a treatment of global financial crises, see Basurto, G. and Atish Ghosh (2001), "The Interest Rate-Exchange Rate nexus in Currency Crises," *IMF Staff Papers*, Vol. 47, Special Issue. For a treatment of the 1997 Asian crisis, see Salvatore, D. (1999), "Could the Financial Crisis in East Asia Have Been Predicted?" *Journal of Policy Modelling*, May.

5

International Economic Integration

Objectives

Through this chapter, the student will be exposed to:

- Explain globalization
- Understand economic integration
- Distinguish between different forms of economic integration
- Become familiar with the main features of the European Union
- Understand Economic and Monetary Union
- Become familiar with economic integration in different parts of the world.

Opening Case

An Increase in Globalization: So??!!

During the past decade we have witnessed an increasingly rapid tendency toward globalization in the world economy. Rapid globalization has occurred in national tastes, in international trade and investments, and in labor markets, and this has sharply increased international competitiveness among industrial countries and between industrial countries and emerging Asian economies.

Convergence of Tastes. The tremendous improvement in telecommunications and transportation has lead to a strong cross-fertilization of cultures and convergence of tastes around the world. Tastes in the United States affect tastes around the world and tastes abroad strongly influence tastes in the United States. Coca-cola has 40 percent of the US market and an incredible 33 percent of the world's soft drink market, and today you can buy a McDonald's hamburger in most major cities of the world. As tastes become global, firms are responding more and more with truly global products. For example, in 1990, Gillette introduced its new Sensor Razor at the same time in most nations of the world and used the same advertisement (except for language) in 19 countries in Europe and North America. By 1999 (when Gillette introduced its Match3 Razor), over 200 million Sensor razors and 4 billion cartridges had been sold. In 1994, Ford spent more than $6 billion to create its "global car" conceived and produced in the United States and Europe and sold under the name of Ford Contour and Mercury Mystique in the United States and Mondeo in the rest of the world. The list of global products is likely to grow rapidly in the future and we are likely to move closer and closer to a truly global supermarket.

In his 1983 article "The Globalization of Markets" in the *Harvard Business Review*, Theodore Levitt asserted that consumers from New York to Frankfurt to Tokyo want similar products and that success for producers in the future would require more and more standardized products and pricing around the world. In fact, in country after country, we are seeing the emergence of a middle-class consumer lifestyle based on a taste for comfort, convenience, and speed. In the food business, this means packaged, fast-to-prepare, and ready-to-eat products. Market researchers have discovered that similarities in lifestyles among middle-class people all over the world are much greater than we once thought and are growing with rising incomes and educational levels. Many small national differences in taste do, of course, remain; for example, Nestle markets more than 200 blends of Nescafe to cater to differences in tastes in different markets. But the converging trend in tastes around the world is unmistakable and is likely to lead to more and more global products. This is true not only for foods and inexpensive consumer products but also for automobiles, portable computers, phones, and many other durable products.

Globalization in Production. Globalization has also occurred in the production of goods and services with the rapid rise of global corporations. These are companies that are run by an international team of managers, have research and production facilities in many countries, use parts and components from the cheapest source around the world, and sell their products, finance their operation, and are owned by stockholders throughout the world. In fact, more and more corporations operate today in the belief that their very survival requires that they become one of a handful of global corporations in their sector. This is true in automobiles, steel, aircraft, computers, telecommunications, consumer electronics, chemicals, drugs, and many other products. Nestle, the largest Swiss Company and the world's second largest food company, has production facilities in 59 countries, and America's Gillette in 22. Ford has component factories in 26 different industrial sites around the world and assembly plants in 6 countries, and employs more people abroad (201,000) than in the United States (188,000).

One important form that globalization in production often takes in today's corporation is in the foreign "sourcing" of inputs. There is practically no major product today that does not have some foreign inputs. Foreign sourcing is often not a matter of choice for corporations to earn higher profits, but simply a requirement for them to remain competitive. Firms not looking abroad for cheaper inputs face loss of competitiveness in world markets and even in the domestic market. This is the reason that $625 of the $860 total cost of producing an IBM PC was incurred for parts and components manufactured by IBM outside the United States or purchased from foreign producers during the mid-1980s. It is also the reason that 13 of the 33 major parts and components going into the production of the Boeing 777 were made outside the United States. Such low-cost offshore purchase of inputs is likely to continue to expand rapidly in the future and is being fostered by joint ventures, licensing arrangements, and other nonequity collaborative arrangements. Indeed, this represents one of the most dynamic aspects of the global business environment of today.

Foreign sourcing can be regarded as manufacturing's new international economies of scale in today's global economy. Just as companies were forced to rationalize operations within each country in the 1980s, they now face the challenge of integrating their operations for their entire system of manufacturing around the world to take advantage of the new international economies of scale. What is important is for the firm to focus on those components that are indispensable to the company's competitive position over subsequent product generations and "outsource" other components for which outside suppliers have a distinctive production advantage. Indeed, globalization in production has proceeded so far that it is now difficult to determine the nationality of many products. For example, should a Honda Accord produced in Ohio be considered American? What about a Chrysler minivan produced in Canada (especially now that Chrysler has been acquired by Mercedes-Benz)? Is a Kentucky Toyota or Mazda that uses nearly 50 percent of imported Japanese parts American? It is clearly becoming more and more difficult to define what is American and opinions differ widely. One could legitimately even ask if this question is relevant in a world growing more and more interdependent and globalized. Today, the ideal corporation is strongly decentralized to allow local units to develop products that fit into local cultures, and yet at its very core is very centralized to coordinate activities around the globe.

Globalization in Labor Markets. Globalization also strongly affects labor markets around the world. Work, previously done in the United States and other industrial countries, is now often done much more cheaply in developing countries. And this is the case not only for low-skilled assembly-line jobs but also for jobs requiring high computer and engineering skills. Most Americans have only now come to fully realize that there is a truly competitive labor force in the world today willing and able to do their job at a much lower cost. If anything, this trend is likely to accelerate in the future.

Even service industries are not immune to global job competition. For example, more than 3500 workers on the island of Jamaica, connected to the United States by satellite dishes, make airline reservations, process tickets, answer calls to toll-free numbers, and do data entry for US airlines at a much lower cost than could be done in the United States. Nor are highly skilled and professional people spared from global competition. A few years ago, Texas Instruments set up an impressive software programming operation in Bangalore, a city of 4 million people in southern India. Other American multinationals soon followed. Motorola, IBM, AT&T, and many other high-tech firms are now doing even a great deal of basic research abroad. American workers are beginning to raise strong objections to the transfer of skilled jobs abroad, as the fall 1995 strike against Boeing demonstrated. Of course, many European and Japanese firms are setting up production and research facilities in the United States and employing many American professionals. In the future, more and more work will simply be done in places best equipped to do the job most economically. By restricting the flow of work abroad to protect jobs in the United States a company risks losing international competitiveness or ends up moving all of its operations abroad.[1]

Question: Do you anticipate this trend of globalization to continue? At what cost? At whose cost? What do you believe the United States' and other industrial nations' position will be?

Source: Salvatore, D. (1998) "Globalization and International Competitiveness," in Denning, J.H. (ed). Globalization, Trade and Foreign Direct Investment, New York, Pergamon Press.

The Changing World Context

The world has undergone significant changes since the end of World War II. At that time, most countries, and especially Europe, were divided by superpower-dominated blocs and the economies were recovering from the devastating effects of war. International trade and capital flows were hindered by trade barriers and capital controls. Economic policies were dominated by myopic domestic considerations and the international element of these policies was often set aside.

The present economic context is different in many ways. The decade of the 1970s was dominated by the two energy crises. Industrial economies were faced with a new "enemy": stagflation—a combination of high inflation and unemployment. Developing countries were increasingly becoming more dependent on foreign borrowing and centrally planned economies were unable to secure economic growth.

The world witnessed a radical transformation during the 1980s and 1990s. The greatest economic experiment of the twentieth century was the movement from communism to a market economy, which began in Mikhail Gorbachev's Russia in the mid-1980s, spread in Eastern Europe at the beginning of the 1990s, and in China later on during the same decade.[2] Although the transition to a free market has led to disappointing outcomes, most countries of Eastern Europe have concentrated on integrating their economies with Europe and on becoming part of the European Union (EU).[3]

The distinction between the industrial countries and the developing countries of Latin America, Africa, the Middle East, and Asia—often referred to as less-developed countries (LDCs)—was blurred as several countries were industrializing fast and moved to the ranks of middle-income countries. These countries are now called newly industrialized countries (NICs). The International Monetary Fund (IMF) dropped the term "industrial countries" and replaced it with "advanced countries," which include the high-income countries (Western European countries, the United States, Canada, Japan, Australia, and New Zealand) and Hong Kong, Korea, Singapore, Taiwan, and Israel.

Meanwhile, the oil-exporting countries were accumulating foreign exchange reserves and experiencing huge current account surpluses from the second oil crisis while industrial and oil-importing countries saw their current account deficits mounting to unprecedented levels. The Organization of Petroleum Exporting Countries (OPEC) surpluses were invested in the financial centers of Europe, America, and Asia, a fact that allowed banks to increase their lending to the developing countries. Foreign borrowing was one of the main factors for their rapid industrialization and also the source of serious problems as foreign debt mounted and the current account deficits could no longer be financed. Many developing countries, especially in Latin America, defaulted on their debt, as they could no longer service it. This initiated a series of "bank runs" in the industrial countries with negative repercussions in the financial markets. The low-income developing countries in Africa and south Asia had to rely on foreign aid to finance their deficits.

The advanced countries also experienced a shift in economic policies and performance as the emergence of political leaders changed dramatically the philosophy of economic policy. Ronald Reagan in the United States and Margaret Thatcher in the United Kingdom made a dramatic impact on their economies as they sought to fight inflation and slow growth by reducing the role of the government and trade unions and through tax cuts, deregulation, and strict monetary and fiscal policies. The wave of socialism in Europe led by Francois Mitterrand in France and Felipe Gonzalez in Spain sought to reduce inflation and unemployment and to secure economic growth through structural reforms and nationalization of industries, and by attracting foreign investment. Helmut Kohl in Germany managed to contain inflation and consolidate the economic and monetary cooperation in Europe through the European Monetary System (EMS) initiated by his predecessor, Helmut Schmit, and the French President Valery Giscard d'Estaing. His greatest political achievement was the unification of Germany in 1990 although the adverse economic consequences of the unification are still haunting Germany. Japan developed an impressive current account surplus and became a major investor in Europe and the United States although the situation was reversed in the 1990s when Japan entered into a major economic and political crisis.[4]

In the 1990s there was a remarkable shift toward the market economy in advanced and developing countries alike. Governments privatized state-owned enterprises, markets were liberalized and deregulated, trade barriers were lowered, and the forces of demand and supply replaced central planning. Globalization, through the increased level of trade and capital movements, was intensified. This increased international integration brought into the foreground the interdependence among countries, and national governments realized that this interdependence could no longer be ignored. Regional arrangements, the most important of which are the EU, the North American Free Trade Agreement (NAFTA), and the Asia Pacific Economic Cooperation (APEC), were intensified. Another fact that demonstrated changing perceptions regarding interdependence was the resolve shown on the completion of the negotiations in December 1993 on the General Agreement on Tariffs and Trade (GATT)—also known as the Uruguay Round—and its replacement by the World Trade Organization (WTO) in January 1995.

Globalization and Economic Activity

There has been much discussion on globalization—the name given to the closer integration of all nations through the increased level of trade and capital flows.[5] It also refers to labor movement, technology transfer across international borders, as well as cultural and political issues that are beyond the scope of this chapter. Globalization is the result of technological process mainly in the areas of information technology, telecommunications, energy, transport, and biotechnology as well as a shift in economic policies. Since World War II, there has been an increasing tendency in the removal of trade and investment barriers. Globalization is not a new phenomenon. The world has been through a process of globalization before, as early as the sixteenth century and, more recently, at the beginning of the twentieth century[6] before trade and investment barriers were erected following World War I and the Great Depression.

The rationale for a market economy is increased efficiency through competition and specialization of factors of production. Global markets present greater opportunities for countries to have access to more funds, know-how, cheaper imports, and larger export markets. But it is also true that the benefits from this increased efficiency are not equally shared. All countries did not share the remarkable income growth during the second half of the twentieth century equally. The gap between the rich and the poor countries has grown. Gross domestic product (GDP) per capita in rich countries increased sixfold during the century while that of poor countries increased less than threefold.[7] At the same time, not all developing countries followed the globalization process at the same pace. Countries that followed outward-oriented policies and export-led growth, such as those of East Asia, were able to integrate into the global economy more rapidly and experience remarkable growth. Conversely, many countries in Latin America and Africa pursued inward-oriented and import-substitution policies with disastrous results: stagnation, high inflation, and poverty.

One significant aspect of globalization is the growth of trade. Traditionally, attention has focused on trade in goods (as services, to a certain extent, are considered nontraded items) as a mechanism for the integration of international economic activity and a significant transmission mechanism of economic disturbances or shocks among national economies. As Exhibit 5.1 shows, world trade continued to grow faster than world output following a dramatic rise in living standards, albeit not equally, a substantial reduction in transportation costs, a continuous improvement in technology, and a progressive reduction in trade barriers. There now exist "world products." Large firms in a globalized economy have subsidiaries in many countries and compete in global markets rather than in segmented national markets. The nationality of goods and services is not easily identifiable as many goods are assembled from parts made in several countries. Small and medium enterprises are increasingly taking into account the global opportunities and constraints of their investment decisions. This increased integration of the international economy has necessitated the development of trade policies. The WTO provides a venue for trade agreements and resolves trade disputes.

From the perspective of developing countries, the removal of trade barriers is seen as serving the interests of advanced countries that continue to subsidize sectors such as agriculture and textiles and thus make it difficult for developing countries to exploit their comparative advantage in these sectors. The United States and the EU have a system of preferential trade agreements

Exhibit 5.1

World Merchandise Exports, Production, and GDP (Index, 1995 = 100)

	1996	1997	1998	1999	2000	2001	2002	2003	2004
World merchandise exports									
Value									
Total merchandise	104	108	107	111	125	120	126	146	178
Agricultural products	103	102	97	93	94	94	100	116	133
Mining products	114	117	93	107	159	144	144	176	234
Manufactures	104	108	111	114	126	121	128	147	177
Volume									
Total merchandise	105	116	121	127	140	139	144	151	165
Agricultural products	104	110	112	113	117	119	124	128	132
Mining products	103	111	114	114	119	118	119	124	131
Manufactures	105	117	122	129	145	143	149	157	172
World merchandise production (volume)									
Total merchandise	104	109	111	115	121	119	122	127	132
Agriculture	104	107	109	112	114	116	118	121	124
Mining	103	106	107	106	110	110	110	114	118
Manufacturing	103	109	112	116	123	121	125	129	134
World real GDP	103	107	109	112	117	118	120	123	127

Source: World Trade Organization website, Statistics, www.wto.org.

with developing countries whereby developing countries are given access to US and European markets. However, as mentioned above, as world markets are opened to advanced countries, they do not fully reciprocate and still attempt to protect certain sectors such as agriculture and textiles, which are of particular importance to developing countries. Developing countries as a whole increased their share in world trade from 19 percent in 1971 to 29 percent in 1999 although there is significant variation among regions, with the NICs doing well and Africa performing poorly. The most significant rise has been the export of manufactured goods while the share of primary commodities (food and raw materials) in world exports has declined.[8]

International trade theory tells us that free trade allows each country to benefit by exploiting its comparative advantage. While it is true that free trade hurts certain sectors as they lose market shares from low-cost competitors, in the long run total benefits generally outweigh losses. However, since those who are worse off are not usually compensated, there will always be outcries against the removal of trade barriers unless ways can be found for all to benefit.

The protest marches in Seattle, Washington, Prague, and Genoa clearly show a hostile response to globalization. Many demonstrators saw globalization as threatening their own jobs from low-cost competition. Others protested against the unfairness of globalization toward developing countries as advanced countries still protect their markets while, at the same time, asking developing countries to open their markets to them. The problem becomes more acute for poor developing countries where unemployment is high and capital scarce. The removal of trade barriers can exacerbate the situation, as the loss of jobs can be rapid and the required investment may be too low to allow them to exploit their comparative advantage. It can be argued that the migration of factors of production from low- to high-productivity sectors will increase incomes. It can be also argued, however, that unemployment in low-productivity sectors will reduce incomes. Unless measures are taken to help these countries increase their incomes and to enable them to exploit their comparative advantage, the backlash against globalization will continue.

Globalization particularly influences financial markets as billions of dollars of capital flow from one country to another. Exhibit 5.2 shows what is often associated with globalization: increased capital flows to developing countries during the 1990s and before the global financial crisis that started in East Asia in 1997 and then spread to Russia and Brazil. The composition of capital flows changed after the crisis. Foreign direct investment became the most significant category while portfolio investment was highly volatile.

While the EU has greatly contributed to financial integration among advanced countries through decreased exchange rate volatility and reduced interest rate spreads, financial integration among developing countries developed at a much slower pace.[9] The 1997–1999 financial crisis in the emerging markets, which turned into a global financial crisis, demonstrated that gains from globalization are not without costs—costs arising from the volatility of capital movements. Capital market liberalization in the emerging markets during the 1980s and 1990s created optimism and led to massive capital inflows. However, investors' sentiments became volatile as they realized that these economies could not sustain a fixed exchange rate. Such a sentiment led to massive capital outflows from these markets as global investors sought to take advantage of high returns and to diversify their portfolios. Developing countries were unable to manage this volatility. Trying to prevent their exchange rates from depreciating, all foreign exchange reserves were used up and the IMF provided more than $150 billion bailout packages. Many banks became extremely weak as recession increased the number of outperforming loans.

Exhibit 5.2

Net Capital Flows[1] In Emerging Markets (Billions of $ US dollars)

	1997	1998	1999	2000	2001	2002	2003	2004
Total								
Private capital flows, net	195.0	70.5	88.1	46.6	47.8	61.2	120.4	81.6
Private direct investment, net	144.9	155.0	173.4	177.1	191.2	143.5	147.6	166.9
Private portfolio flows, net	63.3	41.9	66.6	16.1	−91.3	−99.6	−11.0	−21.3
Other private capital flows, net	−13.2	−126.4	−151.8	−146.6	−52.0	17.3	−16.2	−64.0
Africa								
Private capital flows, net	12.3	8.3	12.2	5.6	13.5	11.9	14.8	16.6
Private direct investment, net	7.9	6.6	9.0	8.0	23.8	13.1	13.6	14.4
Private portfolio flows, net	7.0	3.7	8.7	−1.7	−8.4	−0.5	−0.1	1.4
Other private capital flows, net	−2.6	−2.0	−5.5	−0.7	−2.0	−0.7	1.3	0.8
Emerging Asia[2]								
Private capital flows, net	37.6	−52.2	8.6	−4.5	9.6	25.4	52.8	79.8
Private direct investment, net	56.5	56.1	66.4	67.4	60.5	53.8	70.0	77.2
Private portfolio flows, net	6.7	8.1	56.1	19.8	−56.9	−59.6	5.5	12.0
Other private capital flows, net	−25.5	−116.4	−113.9	−91.7	6.0	31.2	−22.8	−9.4
Middle East (including Israel)								
Private capital flows, net	7.8	13.3	−0.6	−20.6	−7.9	−23.6	−14.0	−45.5
Private direct investment, net	5.3	5.8	5.3	6.4	7.8	5.8	13.4	8.8
Private portfolio flows, net	−2.7	−2.1	−2.3	−0.3	−7.9	−15.6	−16.7	−33.3
Other private capital flows, net	−5.2	9.6	−3.5	−26.7	−7.8	−13.8	−10.7	−21.0

Exhibit 5.2 *continued*

	1997	1998	1999	2000	2001	2002	2003	2004
Western Hemisphere								
Private capital flows, net	97.4	66.6	37.3	39.6	22.2	1.4	–	−3.3
Private direct investment, net	57.7	61.9	65.8	69.0	70.2	41.7	31.8	38.0
Private portfolio flows, net	29.4	25.8	1.5	1.3	−9.4	−17.1	−1.7	−2.8
Other private capital flows, net	10.4	−21.1	−30.0	−30.6	−38.6	−23.2	−30.1	−38.5
Central and Eastern Europe								
Private capital flows, net	20.2	27.2	36.7	39.1	12.1	55.3	51.5	53.2
Private direct investment, net	11.6	19.2	22.6	23.9	24.2	25.1	14.9	22.7
Private portfolio flows, net	5.4	−1.4	5.7	3.1	0.5	1.5	7.0	9.2
Other private capital flows, net	3.2	9.4	8.4	12.1	−12.6	28.7	29.6	21.2
CIS[3]								
Private capital flows, net	19.6	7.2	−6.1	−12.6	−1.7	−9.2	15.2	−19.2
Private direct investment, net	5.9	5.3	4.3	2.4	4.6	3.9	3.8	5.7
Private portfolio flows, net	17.6	7.7	−3.0	−6.0	−9.2	−8.2	−5.0	−7.9
Other private capital flows, net	−3.9	−5.8	−7.4	−9.0	2.9	−4.8	16.4	−17.1

[1] *Net capital flows comprise net direct investment, net portfolio investment and other long- and short-term net investment flows, including official and private borrowing.*
[2] *Consists of developing Asia and the newly industrialized Asian economies.*
[3] *Commonwealth of Independent States (Armenia, Azerbaijan, Belarus, Georgia, Kazakhstan, Kyrgyz Republic, Moldova, Mongolia, Russia, Tajikistan, Turkmenistan, Ukraine, Uzbekistan)*
Source: IMF, hhttp://www.imf.org/external/pubs/ft/weo/2004/02/data /1_3.pdfInternational Institutions.

A characteristic common to all emerging markets was a weak banking and financial system. There were loose supervision and prudential standards, no clear-cut capital requirements, and inadequate provisions for bad loans. It is therefore argued that countries with weak financial systems should maintain restrictions on private capital flows, allowing them more flexibility in stabilizing their currencies, until they have in place well-regulated financial institutions and good macroeconomic management.[10]

Increased trade and capital flows as a result of globalization necessitate the presence of international institutions in order to regulate these flows. There are three such international institutions: the WTO responsible for international trade agreements and for resolving trade disputes; the IMF, which supports the world's financial stability by providing financial assistance to developing and transition economies in times of crisis; and the World Bank whose primary scope is the promotion of economic development by providing long-term loans to poor countries.[11]

The World Trade Organization

The WTO is the successor to the GATT, which was signed in 1947 in Geneva by 23 countries and was designed to provide an international forum for encouraging free trade between member states by regulating and reducing tariffs on traded goods and by providing a common mechanism for resolving trade disputes.[12] GATT played a major role in liberalizing trade and contributed greatly to the dramatic expansion of world trade during the second half of the twentieth century.

The fundamental principle of GATT was indiscriminate trade, in the sense that member nations opened up their markets equally to one another. The most-favored nation clause meant that an agreement on tariff reductions was automatically extended to every other GATT member. The only exception was made to cases of economic integration, i.e., that is countries that were members of regional trade arrangements such as customs union and common markets, such as the European Economic Community (EEC, now EU), were allowed to make special concessions to each other. Also, an escape clause allowed signatory countries to change existing agreements in case of excessive losses of domestic sectors as a direct result of trade concessions. In 1965 GATT introduced the nonreciprocity principle because of which developing countries were allowed preferential trade treatment whereby they could benefit from tariff reductions without being obliged to grant equivalent trade concessions to developed countries. GATT favored trade protection through tariffs and sought to remove import quotas and other quantitative and nontariff trade barriers.

Apart from holding negotiations on specific trade problems involving specific commodities, GATT also held several rounds of major trade conferences regarding tariff reductions and other major trade issues. Exhibit 5.3 shows that eight such rounds were held from 1947 to 1993, the last of which is known as the Uruguay Round whereby tariffs on industrial goods were reduced, on average, by 35 percent, agricultural subsidies were lowered, new

Exhibit 5.3

GATT Trade Rounds, 1947–1993

Year	Location	Participants	Issue	Tariff cut (%)
1947	Geneva	23	Tariffs	21
1949	Annecy	13	Tariffs	2
1951	Torquay	38	Tariffs	3
1956	Geneva	26	Tariffs	4
1960–1961	Geneva (Dillon Round)	26	Tariffs	2
1964–1967	Geneva (Kennedy Round)	62	Tariffs and antidumping	35
1973–1979	Geneva (Tokyo Round)	102	Tariffs, nontariff barriers, multilateral agreements	33
1986–1993	Geneva (Uruguay Round)	123	Tariffs, nontariff barriers, agriculture, textiles, services, intellectual property, trade disputes, establishment of the WTO	34

Source: World Trade Organization, Rounds of Negotiations, WTO website, www.wto.org.

agreements were made on trade in services (General Agreement on Trade in Services—GATS) and intellectual property rights (Trade-Related Aspects of Intellectual Property Rights—TRAPS). The Uruguay Round also established a new global organization, the WTO, to regulate international trade. GATT's principles and trade agreements were adopted by the WTO.[13]

The WTO was established on January 1, 1995, with 104 countries as signatories. Today, the WTO has 144 members including China, which joined in 2001. The organization monitors the member countries' compliance with all prior GATT agreements including those of the Uruguay Round and is responsible for negotiating new trade arrangements. The WTO is empowered to:

- set up and enforce rules regarding international trade
- encourage further trade liberalization

- resolve trade disputes
- ensure transparency in decision making
- cooperate with all major international institutions
- assist developing countries in benefiting fully from international trade.

Since the inception of the WTO, open access to markets has increased. This is due to three main factors: (1) the fact that the WTO focuses on all goods, services, and intellectual property, in contrast to GATT, which focused mainly on goods with the exception of textiles and agriculture; (2) the strengthening of the mechanisms for reviewing trade policies and resolving trade disputes; and (3) the fact that the number of signatory countries has increased significantly and the combined share of international trade under the WTO exceeds 90 percent of the total.

Despite this progress toward trade liberalization, there are several outstanding problems such as agricultural subsidies, trade in agricultural products and textiles, labor[14] and environmental standards, and the formation of regional trade blocks in Europe, North America, and Asia, which, while facilitating intra-region trade, may lead to less free trade worldwide. In the late 1990s the WTO was associated with globalization and came under strong criticism regarding labor and environmental standards. In December 1999 a WTO trade conference—the "Millennium Round"—was held in Seattle and provoked massive demonstrations from environmental, labor, and human rights organizations. Environmental and labor groups claimed that free trade harms the interests of low-skilled workers and leads to environmental damage in trying to serve the interests of large multinational corporations.[15] Since Seattle, three more ministerial conferences were held: Doha, September 9–13, 2001; Cancun, September 10–14, 2003; Hong Kong, December 13–18, 2005. Details of the meetings and topics discussed can be found on WTO's official website (www.wto.org).

The International Monetary Fund and the World Bank

In the previous chapter it was mentioned that the IMF was established in order to manage the Bretton Woods system of fixed exchange rates by providing finance to temporary balance of payments deficits. The role of the IMF in the present international monetary system is quite different. The IMF examines the economies of all its member states on a regular basis. When a country runs into serious financial difficulties as a result of balance of payments deficits, it can turn to the Fund, which provides short-term financing on the condition that the country will follow a stabilization program whose main elements include:

- Contractionary monetary policy—interest rate increases and restrictions on public-sector credit.
- Contractionary fiscal policy—a reduction in the government budget deficit through a combination of tax rises and cuts in government spending.
- Currency devaluation.
- Contractionary income policy—wage increases below the rate of inflation and reduction of transfer payments.
- Economic liberalization—privatization of state-owned enterprises and reduction or elimination of controls.

The purpose of these policies is to reduce the level of aggregate demand, which are, without doubt, deflationary. As a result, exports become more competitive, imports are curbed, the current account improves, and debt is reduced but at the cost of lost output and employment. The IMF came under heavy criticism for its handling of the 1977–1999 financial crisis. Critics argued that the Fund set strict conditions on debtor nations, requiring them to reduce government budgets and raise interest rates—a recipe that accelerates economic recession—instead of recommending more relaxed monetary and fiscal policies that will help boost the economy. The IMF, on the other hand, started from the premise that the financial crisis was due to lack of business confidence. Stabilization of the exchange rate would restore confidence while higher interest rates would again attract capital inflows. At the same time, a strict fiscal policy would reduce aggregate demand and GDP but would also decrease imports and a fall in the demand for foreign exchange that would eventually reduce the balance of payments deficit and stabilize the exchange rate. On the other hand, it was also argued that high interest rates can bring about capital inflows only if investors believe that borrowers are in a position to repay loans. The exacerbation of recession will increase the risks of debt default and the end result will be capital outflows rather than inflows, which is what actually happened.

The criticism of the IMF focuses on the fact that stabilization programs are excessively strict, aiming only at curbing demand without taking into account other structural problems, and thus impose large adjustment costs in terms of lost output and employment. In addition, help packages are imposed rather than negotiated and are relatively small in magnitude and their duration is too short to cure the long-run structural problems of developing countries.[16]

The World Bank was established in 1945 along with the IMF. It has established goals for improving education, reducing child mortality, and achieving other indicators of economic development and improved standards of living through loans, policy advice, and technical assistance. It is supported by 184 member nations who are also its shareholders and have decision-making powers. The World Bank provides two main types of loans:

1. Investment loans, accounting for approximately 80 percent of total lending, for a wide range of activities (dams, irrigation, health, water and sanitation, communication, transport facilities, natural resource management, etc.) designed to provide the necessary infrastructure to encourage private capital inflows and secure sustainable development.

2. Adjustment loans, accounting for approximately 20 percent of total lending, are not project-related but are designed to support structural reforms in a specific sector or the economy as a whole, which may involve elements of institutional changes leading to sustainable and equitable growth such as reforms in agriculture, trade, financial and social policy, and public-sector resource management. These loans are "supply side" programs and are aimed at increasing the aggregate supply of the economy, thereby reducing the price level and increasing output. However, such policies can become effective only if radical adjustments are made to institutions as well as to labor and capital markets.

The World Bank Group is made up of five institutions each one of which has specific functions: (1) the International Bank for Reconstruction and Development (IBRD), which provides investment and adjustment loans to middle-income and poorer countries; (2) the International Development Association (IDA), which makes "soft" loans to poorer countries on better terms than the IBRD; (3) the International Finance Corporation (IFC) whose main function is to promote private-sector investment in developing countries; (4) the Multilateral Investment Guarantee Agency (MIGA), which promotes foreign direct investment to developing countries by providing guarantees (political risk insurance) to investors; and (5) the International Center for Settlement of Investment Disputes (ICSID) whose primary function is to provide arbitration on disputes between foreign investors and host countries. The term "World Bank" loosely refers to the IBRD and the IDA.[17]

Economic Integration

The concept of "economic integration" has been growing in significance for the past 50 years and was established by economists who investigated the early attempts of European countries to combine separate economies into larger economic regions.[18] More specifically, economic integration—also called "regional integration"—refers to the discriminate reduction or elimination of trade barriers among participating nations. This also implies the establishment of some form of cooperation and coordination among participants, which will depend on the degree of economic integration that ranges from free-trade areas to an economic and monetary union. Specifically:

1. A free-trade area refers to a group of countries where all trade barriers among members are removed but each participating country retains trade barriers to third countries. Examples include the European Free Trade Association (EFTA), the NAFTA, and the Latin American free-trade area, the Southern Common Market (MERCOSUR).[19]
2. A customs union is similar to the free-trade area and in addition participating countries pursue common external trade relations whereby they set common external tariffs on imports from nonparticipating nations. The most famous example is the EEC—now EU.
3. A common market embodies a customs union and also allows free factor mobility (capital, labor, technology) among participants. The EU achieved a common market status in 1993 with the establishment of the Single Market.
4. An economic union implies not only a common market but also the coordination and unification of economic polices so as to ensure effective free factor mobility.
5. An economic and monetary union embodies an economic union plus a monetary union, which refers to irrevocable fixed exchange rates and full convertibility of member states' currencies or one currency circulating in all member states. Such a union implies a common monetary policy and a very high degree of integration of fiscal and other economic policies. The EU achieved this status on January 1, 2002, with the circulation of the euro as the common European currency. The United States and the unification of West and East Germany are example of a complete economic and monetary union whereby participating countries become one nation.

The relative benefits of economic integration are treated in the academic literature in terms of customs unions and free-trade areas but the analysis implicitly extends to other forms of regional integration. The theory of customs unions is based on the pioneering work of Viner, Meade, and Johnson.[20] The static economic effects of the formation of customs union are measured in terms of trade creation and trade diversion. Trade creation refers to the benefits from free trade within the customs union as member countries concentrate on economic activities for which they are particularly suited and, as a result, domestic production in a member state is replaced by lower-cost imports from another member state. This brings about enhanced efficiency through specialization and increased competition between producers in different member countries and a subsequent widening of consumer choice, increased output as the increased market size allows the achievement of economies of scale, and improved bargaining power by acting as a single unit in international trade negotiations. The above-mentioned welfare gains are also shared by nonmembers, as there are spillover effects since part of the increase in income takes the form of increased imports from outside the customs union.

On the other hand, trade diversion refers to a situation where trade between members of a customs union increases at the expense of imports from nonmembers. In this case, a product that can be supplied at a lower cost from outside the customs union is replaced by a higher-cost product from another member country as a result of the preferential treatment given to members. The net result is a move away from economic efficiency. Nevertheless, while trade diversion itself reduces welfare, a trade-diverting customs union leads to both trade creation and trade diversion. The net effect will depend on the relative magnitude of these two opposing forces.[21] If one goes beyond the customs union level, there can be further possible benefits such as coordination of macroeconomic policies, increased factor mobility within the union, and higher possibilities for the attainment of macroeconomic objectives such as lower inflation, increased output and employment, and external balance.

However, it should be emphasized that benefits from the formation of customs union are possible gains and there is no guarantee that they will actually be achieved. The degree of success will depend on the nature and composition of the union and it is possible that, if certain conditions are not met, economic integration will have negative effects.

For practical reasons, a customs union is more likely to lead to trade creation and increased welfare if a number of conditions prevail:

1. The degree of substitutability between domestic and imported goods—countries whose products are competitive are more likely to penetrate other members' markets rather than countries whose products are complementary. For example, a customs union between industrial nations is more likely to increase welfare rather than one between industrial and agricultural nations.
2. Complete lack of trade barriers—removal of tariffs will have a smaller effect in terms of lower prices and increased availability of traded goods if other nontariff barriers such as high transportation cost are not also removed.
3. Economies of scale—if the number of countries is more and their size large, it will permit the exploitation of unutilized economies of scale through specialization and will therefore reduce production costs.

4. Geographical proximity—the closer the member states are geographically the lower are the transportation costs.
5. Preunion trade barriers—the higher the preunion trade barriers the higher the probability that the formation of a customs union will lead to trade creation.
6. Preunion economic relationships—the closer the economic relationships among prospective members the higher the probability of the formation of a successful customs union.

During the 1990s there has been a new wave of economic integration alongside the globalization trend. The EU completed the single-market program, was joined by three new members (Austria, Finland, and Sweden), proceeded toward economic and monetary union with the adoption of the euro as a single currency, and accepted ten new members on May 1, 2004. The United States became increasingly involved with regional integration through the NAFTA, which became operational in 1994.

This wave of regional integration was not restricted to industrial countries. Existing regional arrangements between developing countries were strengthened and new ones formed. Examples include the Association of South East Asian Nations (ASEAN), the Central American Common Market (CACM), the Caribbean Common Market (CARICOM), the MERCO-SUR, the Common Market for Eastern and Southern Africa (COMESA), the Southern African Development Community (SADC), and others. Economic integration among transition economies has not gained momentum since almost all Eastern European countries have signed treaties with the EU and have already started negotiations to become members of the EU. The newly independent states of the former Soviet Union are struggling to restructure their economies and the only step toward a regional arrangement has been the formation of the Commonwealth of Independent States (CIS).

The EU is by far the most successful attempt at economic integration and has become a standard textbook case study. Consequently, a more detailed analysis of the functioning of the EU seems justified.

Economic Integration in Europe: The European Union

Background Information

Belgium, France, West Germany, Italy, Luxembourg, and the Netherlands formed the EU, then called European Economic Community, on January 1 1958 after the signing of the Treaty of Rome in March 1957. The origins of the European Community can be traced in the prevailing economic and political conditions in the aftermath of World War II. The economies of European nations were devastated by war, Germany was divided into military occupation zones, and Europe was bearing the burden of the cold war between the two rival blocks.

The six founding members of the EEC started negotiations to establish institutional structures for increased economic cooperation between the countries of Western Europe, which led to the Treaties that founded the European Coal and Steel Community (ECSC) in 1951, the European Atomic Energy Community (Euratom), and the EEC in 1957. The ECSC had been established in order to control the pooled coal and iron and steel resources of the six founding members. By promoting free trade in coal and steel between members and by protecting against nonmembers, the ECSC succeeded in revitalizing these industries. The Euratom was set up by the same six countries in order to promote growth in nuclear industries and the peaceful use of atomic energy. The formation of the EEC absorbed the two communities that preceded it.[22]

Economic integration was motivated by political and economic considerations as it ultimately involves a reduction in sovereign power and a simultaneous increase of a supranational authority. Consequently, there are different approaches to integration. Three main approaches have emerged. Federalists favored the setting up of a supranational federal authority that will take precedence over sovereign national powers. Functionalists adopted a more pragmatic approach than federalists and favored economic cooperation as a starting point for the attainment of political integration since they considered that national governments do not easily give up sovereignty over political areas such as security, defense, and foreign policy. Jean Monnet, one of the founding fathers of the European Community, was a strong supporter of functionalism. Consequently, market integration will inevitably lead to political integration. Another group within the functionalists, the neo-functionalists, favored a mixed system where supranational institutions and national governments initially share responsibilities and gradually national sovereign powers are transferred to the supranational state. Nationalists were opposed to a new political order and reluctant to transfer any national sovereign powers. They were prepared to participate in European organizations but regarded European economic integration as an intergovernmental cooperation between sovereign heads of state.

Although the goal of both federalists and functionalists is common, an important difference between these two approaches is the means toward achieving this aim. Functionalists favor a gradual approach to integration whereas federalists prefer a "shock treatment" where integration is attained by immediate constitutional and institutional changes. Nationalists, on the other hand, consider that a supranational authority can only develop if emerging benefits are overwhelming and cannot be secured by intergovernmental cooperation. These disputes have influenced the development of the EU. The structure of Community institutions reflects the lack of consensus and possesses a mixture of supranational and intergovernmental characteristics.[23]

The Rome Treaty set out to raise living standards and achieve closer relations between member states; these objectives were to be attained by economic integration well beyond the degree of cooperation required for membership of a customs union. Article 2 of the Rome Treaty stated that the objective is "to establish a common market, to promote throughout the Community a harmonious development of economic activities, a continuous and balanced expansion, an increase in stability, an accelerated raising of the standard of living and closer relationships between the states belonging to it."[24] This effectively meant that all restrictions on the free movement of goods, capital, and labor were to be eliminated. The removal of tariff barriers on industrial trade between members and the imposition of a common external tariff on imports from nonmembers was seen as the first step in the creation of an economic union with the harmonization of national economic policies of member countries. The original "Six" became "Nine" when the United Kingdom, Denmark, and Ireland joined in 1973, and "Twelve" after Greece joined in 1981, and Spain and Portugal in 1986. In January 1995 the "Twelve" became "Fifteen" with the accession of Austria, Finland, and Sweden.[25]

The institutional structure is made up of the Council of Ministers representing the member states, the Commission designated by the Treaty of Rome as an executive body and the proposer of legislation and a directly elected European Parliament with 518 members. The Court of Justice ensures that the law is observed and has the power to rule on the constitutionality of the decisions of the Commission and the Council of Ministers. The European Central Bank (ECB), discussed below, is empowered to conduct the common monetary policy of the EU.[26]

In 1986 the EU amended the Treaty of Rome with the Single European Act, which provided for the removal of all remaining barriers to the free flow of goods, services, and factors of production.[27] This was a major development as it created a single European market by 1993. The Treaty on European Union (the Maastricht Treaty) also amended the Treaty of Rome but also incorporated the previous treaties. According to the Maastricht Treaty, the EU is a structure based on three pillars: (a) the European Community, (b) common foreign and security policy, and (c) cooperation in justice and home affairs. The Treaty of Amsterdam in 1997 consolidated each of the above pillars.

The Single Market

The Single Market is the core of the EU. The central objective of the Rome Treaty was the integration of the economies of member states with the purpose of creating the conditions for greater economic efficiency so that more goods and services can be produced at a lower cost through increased competition and productivity. In a single market there is free movement of factors of production. The demand for, and availability of, these factors varies between countries and the resulting variation in prices provides incentives for factors to move between countries.

To achieve the benefits of a single market, the Single European Act includes a commitment to: (a) free movements of goods and services whereby all customs duties, quantitative restrictions on imports and exports, and restrictions on the provision of services by citizens of member states across national borders are eliminated; (b) free movement of people whereby all obstacles to people's right to move between member countries for the purpose of employments and the right of establishment of self-employed persons are abolished; (c) free movement of capital whereby restrictions on the movement of capital between member states are prohibited.

To make a reality of these freedoms and to enable market forces to operate freely, the Community has developed a framework of rules regarding the removal of capital controls, the facilitation of labor mobility, the liberalization of road transport, the harmonization of technical standards, and a reduction in customs formalities. Important changes were introduced such as the mutual recognition of national norms under which products and services sold in one member country may be sold freely throughout the Community, legislation securing harmonization of policies in order to avoid discrimination through technical standards, a faster decision-making process through majority voting thus restricting the blocking of a decision by a single member state, and an increased role of the European Parliament. Most of the legal framework for integrating the market for goods, services, labor, and capital was completed in December 1992. A major study, the Cecchini Report, estimated that the development of the single market would lead to acceleration of economic growth and increased prosperity for all European citizens.[28] The Report was also subject to criticism because it presented a favorable view of the benefits while it underestimated the costs of economic integration.[29] Nevertheless, the truth remains that integration of national economies into a single market also involves painful structural adjustments in the face of increased competition. The Community, through the Community Support Framework and the establishment of the Cohesion Fund, has provided financial resources to facilitate the adjustment process and improve the competitive position of the less developed regions.

Economic and Monetary Union

Historical Background

The principle of the Economic and Monetary Union (EMU) became formally a Community target at the Hague Summit in 1969 where the EEC leaders agreed to proceed gradually toward economic and monetary union. However, important differences emerged regarding the manner in which EMU was to be achieved. A group of countries (Belgium, France, Italy, and Luxembourg), called the "monetarists," supported the view that monetary discipline was the first step toward EMU by keeping exchange rate fluctuations between the currencies of member countries within narrow limits and rendering policy cooperation and economic convergence inevitable. Another group of countries (Germany and the Netherlands), called the "economists," argued that the coordination of economic policies and economic convergence should be achieved first before moving toward EMU. The Werner Report in 1970, taking into account these differences, recommended establishment of EMU in stages by 1980.[30] The first step toward that end was taken in 1972 by establishing an adjustable-peg exchange rate system, the "Snake," whereby participating currencies were allowed a ±2.25 percent margin of fluctuation against the central US dollar rate. However, the 1973 oil crisis and the free fluctuation of the dollar affected European currencies and the goal of achieving EMU by 1980 was abandoned.

A new initiative, the EMS, was launched on March 13, 1979, with the aim of stabilizing exchange rates and promoting closer monetary cooperation leading to a zone of monetary stability. The basic feature of the EMS was fixed exchange rates between the participating currencies and floating exchange rates between participating and nonparticipating currencies.[31] The institutional arrangements included three central features: (1) fixed exchange rates; (2) a new unit of account, the European Currency Unit (ECU) whose value was determined in terms of a basket of currencies weighted according to their relative strengths; (3) borrowing facilities for member countries facing balance of payments problems. The system provided for fixed exchange rates with compulsory intervention limits of ±2.25 percent around the ECU central parity (or ±6 percent in the case of weaker currencies). National governments would take all the necessary steps, such as adjusting domestic interest rates, to keep their currencies within the prescribed limits. However, the system was flexible as it allowed realignments by mutual agreement (i.e., adjustment of central parities) if economic conditions caused a currency to become fundamentally overvalued or undervalued.[32]

The German mark assumed a central role as the currency with the best inflation performance. The remaining members used the fixed exchange rate against the German mark as a means of increasing their own anti-inflationary credibility. Germany pursued a monetary policy defined by the Bundesbank, the German central bank, while the monetary policies of other EMS participants followed that of Germany by limiting money supply growth so that inflation rates were in line with the German inflation rate. The EMS did help stabilize exchange rates despite numerous realignments. In the period between January 1987 and September 1992 there were no realignments.

The stability signified the system's evolution into an instrument of economic policy as participating countries sought economic convergence with low inflation rates.

Strains in the EMS began at the beginning of the 1990s following the German unification. Inflationary pressures in Germany forced the Bundesbank to raise interest rates and this created instability in the system as the other participating countries had to raise their own interest rates in order to keep their exchange rates within the prescribed bands. The instability was reinforced by currency speculation, which reached a peak in September 1992 as markets realized that certain participating currencies could not maintain high interest rates and eventually would have to devalue. The pound sterling and the Italian lira came under heavy pressure and the two currencies were forced to leave the exchange rate mechanism (ERM) as they were no longer able to maintain the prescribed margins. In the following months other currencies also came under attack such as the Spanish peseta, the Danish krone, the Irish punt, and the Portuguese escudo. These currencies remained in the ERM but were devalued in contrast to the French franc, which, although it came under strong speculative attack, resisted devaluation following massive intervention. In August 1993 the EMS countries decided to widen the permitted fluctuation margins to ±15 percent and this gave countries more room to gear monetary policy toward domestic conditions and allowed them to reduce their interest rates below Germany's rate.

The Single Market Act of 1986, which created the single European market in 1992, made the creation of the Economic and Monetary Union (EMU) a Community objective and obliged member countries to work toward economic convergence for the achievement of EMU. The President of the European Commission, Jacques Delors, and the governors of the Community central banks presented the "Delors Report" in April 1989, a decisive step for full unification and the signing of a new treaty.[33] The Delors Report defined EMU as a currency zone where the conduct of economic policy is the result of collective effort for achieving common objectives and set three prerequisites:

1. Total and irreversible convertibility of the currencies of member states
2. Complete removal of restrictions on capital movements and the integration of financial markets
3. The irrevocable fixing of parity rates.

The Report underlined that the fulfillment of the above three preconditions will bring about perfect substitutability of the currencies of member states and full convergence of interest rates. This way, the road was open for the adoption of a common currency, a development that the Report considered desirable but not necessary. Also, the report mentioned the need for a single monetary policy under the auspices of a "federal" System of Central Banks (SCB) whose Board would be appointed by the Council of Ministers and would be independent from national governments.

The Report included a list of four basic parameters that were considered a necessary condition for the achievement of economic growth. These were:

1. The Single Market with complete liberalization in the movement of goods, services, and factors of production
2. The existence of an effective competition policy and other market strengthening measures
3. The existence of common policies aimed at structural changes and regional development
4. The coordination of macroeconomic policies with special emphasis on fiscal policy.

The European Union Treaty (the Maastricht Treaty), which amended the Rome Treaty, was signed on February 7, 1992, and came into force on November 1, 1993 (European Commission, 1992). At a later stage, the Amsterdam Treaty, which was signed on October 2, 1997, and came into force on May 1, 1999, amended both the European Union and the Rome Treaties.

The Treaty adopted the proposals of the Delors Report and decided on the strategy and implementation schedule of the EMU. The strategy was a gradual implementation (the European Commission was against a "two-speed" Europe), that is, in stages as economic convergence and economic policy coordination progressed. The timetable and content of each stage are set out in Articles 105–109 of the Treaty and are described below:[34]

There was a three-stage process to EMU. In Stage 1 (1990–1993), all member state currencies were to join the ERM of the EMS on equal terms. Periodic exchange rate realignments were possible. The 1992–1993 exchange rate crisis described above set Stage 1 behind schedule as some countries did not join at all or were forced to leave the ERM. All member countries were to lift all restrictions on capital movements and improve economic policy coordination. Toward this end, member states would submit Convergence Programs containing specific targets regarding inflation rates and budget deficits.

Stage 2 (1994–1998) began in 1994 with the establishment of the European Monetary Institute (EMI). Monetary policy remained in the hands of national central banks and the EMI defined the framework within which the ECB was to operate in Stage 3. Stage 2 also made provisions so that governments would no longer resort to central bank lending in order to finance budget deficits.

Exhibit 5.4

Official Currency Conversion Rates of the Euro (national currency units/euro)

Country	Currency	Conversion rate
Austria	Schilling	13.7603
Belgium	Belgian franc	40.3399
Finland	Markka	5.94573
France	French franc	6.55957
Germany	Deutsche mark	1.95583
Greece*	Drachma	340.750
Ireland	Punt	0.787564
Italy	Italian lira	1936.27
Luxembourg	Luxembourg franc	40.3399
The Netherlands	Guilder	2.20371
Portugal	Escudo	200.482
Spain	Peseta	166.386

Except Greece, which joined the euro zone on January 1, 2001
Source: European Central Bank (1998), Press Release, 31 December.

Stage 3 began in 1998 with the introduction of the common currency (the euro), the irrevocable locking of exchange rates (Exhibit 5.4), and the formulation of a common monetary policy according to the provisions of the Treaty by the European System of Central Banks (ESCB) and the ECB. The Exchange Rate Mechanism II (ERM II) was also set up to ensure a smooth transition to the common currency and to reinforce the convergence efforts not only of those countries that did not join the euro zone but also of candidate countries. The 12 countries that fulfilled the Maastricht criteria (see below) and were qualified to join the single currency in 1999 were Austria, Belgium, Finland, France, Germany, Greece (in January 2001), Ireland, Italy, Luxembourg, the Netherlands, Portugal, and Spain. Sweden did not fulfill the convergence criteria since the Swedish currency had remained outside the ERM II and also because its legislation was not compatible with the European Union Treaty and the ESCB Statute. Denmark and the United Kingdom decided not to take part in Stage 3 and remained outside the euro zone. On January 1, 2002, the euro was introduced in note and coin form. A period of six months was given for national currencies to withdraw from circulation and as from July 1, 2002, only the euro is a legal tender in EMU member countries.

Benefits and Costs of EMU. Technically, the single market does not require a common currency but many economists argue that the existence of a common currency is desirable. The relevant economic theory examining whether a region benefits from the existence of a common currency is the theory of optimum currency areas.[35] A region is considered an optimum currency area when the markets of goods, services, capital, and labor within a group of countries are unified to such an extent that it would render the existence of a common currency more effective than several national currencies. Obviously, regions of the same nation sharing a common currency are optimum currency areas. This theory gave rise to an extensive international academic literature where the evaluation of EMU is made under the light of the theory of optimum currency areas. As a general conclusion, the possibility that the benefits from EMU will exceed costs is dependent on four factors: (a) the degree of country interdependence; (b) the degree of capital and labor mobility; (c) the degree of convergence of the economies of the member states so that exogenous disturbances will have a symmetrical effect on all members, and (d) the degree of price and wage flexibility.

The higher the degree of the first two factors, the closer the convergence of the economies, and the greater the flexibility of prices and wages, the higher the possibility that EMU will be successful. This conclusion explains the special emphasis given to the convergence criteria by the European Commission. The benefits from the adoption of a common currency are significant. According to a Commission study, the savings from the elimination of transaction costs amount to 13–19 billion euros (or 0.3–0.4 percent of the EU GDP).[36] The same study estimates that production in the EU will increase by 5 percent of the EU GDP as a result of increased investor confidence because of the absence of exchange rate risk. An additional benefit is the saving of approximately 160 billion euros of foreign exchange reserves. A more recent study estimated that exchange rate variability during the 1995–1996 period caused the loss of 1.5 million jobs and slowed EU GDP growth by 2 percent.[37]

Long-run benefits include the increased convergence of the economies of the member states, increased competition, and downward convergence of interest rates, which results in higher investment levels in a stable environment and an efficient allocation of resources. The main costs associated with the EMU are the loss of the exchange rate and monetary policy as an instrument of national sovereign economic policy and the restricted effectiveness of fiscal and income policies.

According to the theory of optimum currency areas, participating countries are affected symmetrically by exogenous disturbances, as long as there is perfect capital and labor mobility. If an external disturbance is asymmetrical, capital and labor mobility will tend to offset the disturbance. For example, if Greece and Italy are affected asymmetrically by an exogenous shock so that Greece experiences recession and Italy an economic boom, then wages will fall in Greece so that lower prices and production costs will restore competitiveness and will increase in Italy. In addition, unemployed labor will migrate to Italy so that equilibrium can be achieved through the convergence of wages and production costs.

Problems arise when there is no downward price and wage flexibility or when capital and labor mobility is low. In this case, equilibrium can be achieved only through a higher price level (inflation) and a subsequent loss of competitiveness in Italy and a simultaneous competitiveness gain in Greece. However, if Italy is not willing to suffer the consequences of inflation and Greece the consequences of recession, equilibrium can be attained by a change in the exchange rate without the negative effects of recession. If the two countries are members of a monetary union, the use of the exchange rate instrument is no longer an option. The only solution for Greece is to suffer the consequences of long-term recession, unemployment, and chronic current account deficits. Consequently, if the members of a monetary union are affected asymmetrically by an exogenous disturbance and there is no sufficient price and wage flexibility, then it is preferable to retain their interdependence rather than become members of a monetary union.

The European monetary union has the ability to reduce disturbances originating from policy intervention and to mitigate the effects from asymmetrical exogenous shocks. The fact that the ECB follows a policy often called "one size fits all" cannot be interpreted as a weakness of the common currency because the long-term success of the euro depends on the appropriate integration of member countries, which, as the above discussion implies, should behave as one economy in the long run.[38] In general, monetary integration requires high factor mobility and symmetrical effects from exogenous disturbances. Countries fulfilling these conditions will certainly benefit from participation in a monetary union. If, however, there are differences with regard to economic structures, levels of economic development, preferences, and economic policy instruments, at least some participating members will suffer short-term adjustment costs.

The Maastricht Convergence Criteria. A successful transition to a monetary union requires a high degree of convergence among member countries with respect to a low rate of inflation, sound fiscal finance, and exchange rate stability. On the basis of the above preconditions, member countries wishing to adopt the common currency must fulfill four convergence criteria set out in the European Union Treaty (Maastricht Treaty).[39] These are the following:

- *Inflation*—According to Article 109 (j) and Article 1 of the Protocol Agreement, a high degree of price stability is required. Such a development is evident from a rate of inflation close to that of the three best-performing member states in terms of price stability. The inflation rate in the previous year must be at most 1.5 percent above those in the three member states with the lowest inflation as measured by the consumer price index (CPI), taking into account the difference in national definitions. The index used for comparison purposes is the harmonized index of consumer prices (HICP) constructed by the Commission's Statistical Service (EUROSTAT), the EMI, and the ECB. The low inflation criterion makes it evident that the member state is ready for a smooth transition to the new common currency system together with the remaining member states that have achieved price stability.

- *Fiscal discipline*—Article 109 (j) requires fiscal discipline position without excessive budget deficits. Article 104 defines the excessive deficit procedure. The European Commission will prepare a report if a member state does not fulfill the requirements of fiscal discipline, which are (a) the ratio of planned or actual government deficit to GDP should not be greater than a reference value of 3 percent and (b) the ratio of government debt to GDP should not exceed a reference value of 60 percent. The fiscal discipline criterion aims at the convergence of the fiscal policies of member states. Such a convergence will limit tensions within EMU because it precludes an expansionary monetary policy as a means to offset the effects of excessive budget deficits.

- *Exchange rate stability*—Article 109 (j) requires the observance of normal fluctuation margins of the ERM of the EMS (later replaced by ERM II) without realignments or severe tensions for at least two years. A member country should not devalue its currency's bilateral central rate against any other member country's currency on its own initiative for the same period (two years). It should be recalled that the fluctuation margins widened from ±2.25 percent to ±15 percent in August 1993 following the 1992–1993 exchange rate crisis. These wider margins remain for member countries outside the euro zone (i.e., the United Kingdom, Sweden, and Denmark) as well as for candidate countries. The exchange rate stability criterion reflects the smooth transition to the common currency following a period of successfully maintaining fixed exchange rates. It also aims at limiting the ability of a member country to use the exchange rate as a "last devaluation" instrument in order to achieve a competitive advantage before adopting the common currency.

- *Long-term interest rates*—Article 109 (j) requires the durability of convergence achieved by member states, being reflected in long-term interest rates. The criterion on the convergence of interest rates defines that nominal long-term interest rates in the previous year should not exceed the average of those of the three member states with the lowest rates by more than 2 percent. Interest rates are measured on the basis of long-term government bonds or comparable securities after taking into account differences in national definitions. The interest rate criterion reflects the fact that money markets take into consideration the credibility and low credit risk of the member country. A high-inflation country is expected to maintain higher interest rates on its long-term debt. This tendency toward higher expected inflation puts at risk the viability of fixed exchange rates and the other member countries must suffer the consequences of higher interest rates required to maintain their currencies within the prescribed margins.

The Growth and Stability Pact. The Maastricht Treaty requires that member countries consider their economic policies as a matter of common interest, take all necessary measures for the coordination of their policies, and avoid excessive budget deficits. Fiscal discipline aims at low interest rates by giving more room to the formulation of monetary policy and by convincing money markets about their credibility so that long-term interest rates remain at low levels. Also, fiscal discipline reduces the servicing of the government debt and allows national governments to restructure their expenditures toward long-term growth and full employment.

These considerations led the European Council to adopt the Growth and Stability Pact (GSP). The resolution of the European Council in Amsterdam defined the obligations of the member countries, the European Commission, and the European Council for the implementation of the GSP.[40] Specifically, member countries should avoid excessive deficits in order to strengthen the conditions for price stability, long-term growth, and increase in employment. Fiscal discipline is expected to allow member countries to deal with normal business cycle fluctuations and, at the same time, confine budget deficits within the reference value of 3 percent of GDP.

The Maastricht Treaty has defined the procedures for avoiding excessive budget deficits in the convergence criteria but Germany insisted on stricter procedures within the framework of the GSP. Following the adoption of the GSP, the European Council adopted two important resolutions. The first referred to the monitoring of fiscal developments and coordination of economic policies while the second referred to the implementation of excessive budget procedures. Member states should aim at budget deficits below the 3 percent reference value so that in case of recession the member country can conduct an expansionary fiscal policy and still remain within the 3 percent guideline. Nations that violated the fiscal indicator would be subject to heavy fines.[41] Germany's concern focused on the fact that many countries with a long history of high budget deficits would resort to their "old bad habits" after fulfilling the convergence criteria and joining the euro zone. It is an irony that in January 2002 the European Commission issued a warning to Germany (and Portugal) regarding excessive budget deficits.

Monetary Policy. Monetary integration is a gradual process during which a member country conducts its own monetary policy but with increasing restrictions. The primary goal of a monetary policy is the establishment of credibility: the attainment of objectives coupled with low inflation will create favorable expectations that the value of the currency will not be lowered because of inflation. This reduces the risk of generating inflationary pressures originating from inflationary expectations.

The Community, since its inception, defined the objectives of the economic policy of member countries. Article 104 of the Rome Treaty declared that each member state should formulate the appropriate economic policy for achieving balance of payments equilibrium, maintaining a lasting confidence in the national currency, and, at the same time, should take all steps necessary for attaining a high level of employment and a stable price level. In the same Treaty, Article 105 asked for the coordination of economic and monetary policies so as to facilitate the achievement of the Community's objectives. The Maastricht Treaty retained these provisions and also has an entire chapter on economic policy according to which every member country should consider its economic policy as an issue of common interest.

The Maastricht Treaty created an economic policy framework based on close coordination of the policies of member states, the single market, and the definition of common objectives according to the principles of free market and free competition. This economic policy framework reveals the importance given to inflation: the primary objective of Community monetary and exchange rate policy is price stability. Reference to a sound fiscal policy without excessive budget deficits precludes a stabilization policy through fiscal means. Consequently, it is implied that in the long run there is no choice between different inflation—unemployment combinations and the objective of price stability does not affect employment. Community policy for achieving high employment levels is aimed at the microeconomic level through measures for promoting investment and training of the labor force.

Monetary policy is, therefore, essentially a technical matter conducted by experts within a framework of guidelines with complete absence of political intervention. This necessitates an institutional structure where monetary authorities (central banks) are independent, though accountable for their actions. Monetary policy is formulated by the ESCB, which consists of the national central banks and the ECB, a supranational institution entirely independent from national governments and EU institutions. For example, the Council of Ministers or the European Commission is not in a position to demand interest rate cuts in order to boost the economy. The ultimate objective is to minimize the effects of inflationary expectations on economic decisions.

The European Union Treaty sets price stability as a primary objective in the entire euro zone and not separately in each country. The strategy with respect to monetary policy is based on the quantitative definition of price stability and on two pillars. The Governing Council of the ECB defines price stability as the annual increase of the HICP at a rate of less than

Interview with Professor Otmar Issing
Member of the Executive Board, European Central Bank

Convergence of macroeconomic policies has been remarkable since the inception of the European Monetary System. Can you give a more accurate definition of convergence and how can greater convergence be achieved given the imminent enlargement of the European Union and the regional disparities still existing among member states?

Indeed, looking back to the 1970s the progress that has been made in Europe is remarkable. Convergence has been a very long process and there have been also a number of setbacks along the way. Let me only mention the EMS crisis of 1992–1993, when rigidity in nominal exchange rate relations in the end proved to be premature in view of underlying fundamental adjustment needs in the wake of German unification.

The convergence momentum was not lost but rather quickly reestablished. This had to do with the experience and understanding in Europe that there were no viable alternatives to a path of continued fiscal consolidation and monetary stability. The principle of sound public finances and the objective of price stability safeguarded by an independent central bank were firmly enshrined in the Maastricht Treaty. These two "cornerstones" of the treaty provide the basis for the macroeconomic convergence both the in the run-up to and inside the Monetary Union.

The notion of "sustainable convergence" was given operational content by the well-known convergence criteria, including the 3 percent ceiling for the deficit-to-GDP ratio, the 60 percent reference value for the public debt ratio as well as provisions regarding the convergence of inflation rates and exchange rate stability. The criteria were aimed at ensuring that candidate countries had shown sufficient ability to sustain sound macroeconomic policies before joining in order to reduce the risk of tensions inside Monetary Union. The same criteria will also be applied in judging sustainable convergence of any accession countries' application to join Monetary Union after they have become members of the European Union.

The Treaty—together with the Stability and Growth Pact—provides a framework aimed at ensuring sufficient convergence and co-ordination of national economic policies. However, this framework does not—and should not—mean that economic policies should be fully harmonized or that economic developments will be the same across the euro area. Inside Monetary Union greater flexibility is needed to address divergences at the national/regional level and to deal with so-called asymmetric shocks. This calls for structural reforms aimed at enhancing the capacity of (labour, product, and financial) markets to adjust. However, also the example of the United States shows that inside a unified currency areas a significant degree of divergence in regional economic developments is still to be expected in the presence of differences in local economic structures.

2 percent in the entire euro zone. The ECB allows a margin for price increases not attributable to inflationary factors such as improved quality of goods and services, although, at the same time, it does not consider deflation (a sustained decrease in prices) compatible with price stability, which must be achieved in the medium term so as to allow short-term deviations attributable to exogenous disturbances.

The first pillar puts an emphasis on the broad definition of the money supply (M3) and includes a reference value (currently 4.5 percent) for annual money supply growth, which is used in analyzing monetary and credit developments. The second pillar consists of an analysis of a wide range of economic variables such as labor cost, fiscal indicators, economic activity indicators, exchange rates, term structure of interest rates, and economic developments in the euro zone and in the rest of the world. Monetary management aims at influencing the rate of credit expansion by controlling the cost or the supply of credit. The ESCB has a wide range of monetary policy instruments, a detailed description of which is beyond the scope of this chapter.[42] The Eurosystem consists of the ECB located in Frankfurt and the ESCB, which includes all the national central banks. The Governing Council comprises the governors of the participating central banks and members of the Executive Board. It is responsible for the formulation of monetary policy and for establishing the guidelines for its implementation. The president of the ECB chairs the Governing Council. The Executive Board is responsible for the implementation of monetary policy and gives instructions to the participating national central banks. The Board comprises the President and Vice-President of the ECB and four other members. A third body, the General Council, provides a forum for discussion between the national central banks of participating countries and nonparticipants. It has no role in formulating or implementing monetary policy but serves as a link between EMU members and other European Union member countries and also responsible for fixing exchange rates of new entrants.[43]

Economic Integration in North America—NAFTA

The North American Free Trade Agreement (NAFTA) was signed in December 1992 and came into force on January 1, 1994, between the United States, Canada, and Mexico. It incorporates a previous bilateral free-trade agreement between the United States and Canada and extends to Mexico the obligation to liberalize trade and investment. Trade barriers between the United States and Canada were abolished in 1999 while those between Mexico and the two countries will be abolished in 2009.

In general, tariff barriers and most nontariff barriers on textiles, clothing, cars, vehicle parts and telecommunications equipment, and agricultural products will be abolished over a period of 10 to 15 years. In addition, banks and insurance companies will be allowed total access to all three markets. Other goals include the opening up of the North American advertising market and loosening the rules on the movement of corporate executives and some professionals. The free-trade area could gradually spread to 34 other countries in the western hemisphere, an idea expressed by George Bush when the Unites States launched the Enterprise for the Americas Initiative (EAI). He hoped for the establishment of what is now referred to as the Free Trade Areas of the Americas (FTAA), which was formed in 1998 and is still under negotiation.

The NAFTA is in reality a loose regional arrangement (i.e., it is a free-trade area and not a common market) and it does not involve any surrender of sovereignty. There is no free movement of people, and national energy and transport industries are still heavily protected. To an extent, NAFTA reflects a structural adjustment of the United States economy in order to face increased competition. Empirical evidence shows that Mexico is a net beneficiary in terms of real income and real wage gains while gains for the United States and Canada, in terms of the above variables, are marginal.[44] However, other gains for the United States are substantial and are discussed in the reverse case at the end of the chapter.

Economic Integration among Developing Countries

Developing countries form regional arrangements in an attempt to help growth and achieve fundamental structural changes. Such a regional arrangement would create a market large enough to support large-scale production and would eventually bring about a reduction in production costs through economies of scale that would enable international competition without protection. The idea was appealing in theory but not very successful in practice because the formation of such regional arrangements lacked binding commitments to free trade. In addition, the distribution of benefits was unequal and the achievement of economies of scale led to concentration of industries in a few industrial centers. As a result, most attempts during the 1960s and 1970s led to small groups with minimal bilateral agreements.

The adoption of outward-looking policies during the 1980s and 1990s following economic reforms toward trade and financial liberalization, the wave of globalization, and the fall of communism brought a new momentum to regionalism whereby many such arrangements were strengthened and new ones formed. The following sections give a brief account of the most important regional arrangements in Asia, Africa, Latin America, and the Middle East.[45]

Economic Integration in Asia

Economic integration is a less prominent issue in Asia given the existence of such large countries as India and China. The best-known regional integration scheme is the Association of South East Asian Nations (ASEAN) followed by the South Asian Association for Regional Cooperation (SAARC) and Asian Pacific Economic Cooperation (APEC).

Association of South East Asian Nations

This association comprises ten nations: Brunei, Cambodia, Indonesia, Laos, Malaysia, Myanmar, the Philippines, Singapore, Thailand, and Vietnam. ASEAN was founded in 1967 by seven of these countries. Brunei joined in 1984, Vietnam in 1996, Laos in 1997, and Myanmar in the same year. It originated back in the 1960s from the desire to have closer political and security cooperation in the region. The most important elements of economic cooperation are trade liberalization, industrial development, banking and finance, and investment. Trade liberalization was intensified in 1992 with the establishment of the ASEAN Free Trade Area (AFTA) over a period of ten years. Also, various schemes of industrial cooperation were established during the 1970s and 1980s and there was cooperation in the fields of tourism, services, and intellectual property. Although AFTA will not lead to complete free trade and its trade liberalization process has been modest, it has grown into an important regional arrangement.

South Asian Association for Regional Cooperation

The SAARC was set up in 1985 with seven members: Bangladesh, Bhutan, India, Maldives, Nepal, Pakistan, and Sri Lanka. This arrangement mostly involves functional cooperation in the areas of agriculture, poverty alleviation, transport, and telecommunications. Trade and economic cooperation was initiated through the South Asian Preferential Trading Arrangement (SAPTA) with the aim of encouraging the removal of tariff and nontariff barriers and of working toward the creation of a free-trade area (SAFTA) by 2005. The SAARC has no institutional arrangements and its goals are very modest, the main reason being divergent views among members and territorial conflicts especially between India and Pakistan.

Asian Pacific Economic Cooperation

The APEC is not so much an institution as a forum for discussing the economic issues affecting its members. It was established in 1989 by ASEAN and Australia, Canada, Japan, New Zealand, South Korea, and the United States. China, Hong Kong, and Taiwan joined in 1991 and Peru, Russia, and Vietnam in 1998. The medium-term objective is the creation of a free-trade and investment zone among these countries by 2010. The economic potential of APEC is huge and if it is successful it will truly promote trade and investment liberalization as it accounts for about 60 percent of the world's GDP.

Economic Integration in Africa

Regional integration in Africa became an objective after the establishment of the Organization for African Unity (OAU) in 1963. The idea of the economic integration of all African nations has its origin in the OAU even though its activities are largely political. A unique characteristic of economic integration in Africa is a multitude of partly overlapping regional arrangements. The Treaty of the African Economic Community (AEC) of 1991 foresees an African economic and monetary union over a period of 35 years, the first stage being the consolidation of existing arrangements. The OAU, together with the United Nations Economic Commission for Africa (UNECA), has been trying to rationalize and harmonize regional arrangements but with little progress because existing arrangements are weak and there is low political commitment. The most important regional arrangements in terms of aggregate GDP are the Economic Community of West African States (ECOWAS), the COMESA, the SADC, and the Southern African Customs Union (SACU).

Economic Community of West African States
The ECOWAS is part of the first integration wave in Africa inspired by the success of European integration. It was set up in 1975 with Nigeria as the main driving force and has 16 member states: Benin, Burkina Faso, Cape Verde, Cote d' Ivoire, Gambia, Ghana, Guinea, Guinea-Bissau, Liberia, Mali, Mauritania, Niger, Nigeria, Senegal, Sierra Leone, and Tongo. It was set out to first achieve a customs union and then to establish a common market along the lines of the EU. The ECOWAS progressed little toward trade liberalization as the schedule was modified and postponed several times. The only significant progress has been on labor mobility and functional cooperation in the fields of telecommunications and transport infrastructure. Failure to progress was mainly due to the unequal size of its members, with Nigeria being the largest, richest, and most influential member. Another reason is the lack of political commitment, as members did not implement agreed measures.

Common Market for Eastern and Southern Africa
The COMESA was established in 1993 and has 21 members: Angola, Burundi, Comoros, Djibouti, the Democratic Republic of Congo (joined in 1995), Egypt (joined in 1998), Eritrea, Ethiopia, Kenya, Madagascar, Malawi, Mauritius, Namibia, Rwanda, Seychelles (joined in 1997), Sudan,

Swaziland, Tanzania, Uganda, Zambia, and Zimbabwe. It succeeded the Preferential Area for Eastern and Southern Africa (PTA) and was an ambitious plan to create not only a customs union but also an economic and monetary union. Extreme divergences among members in terms of GDP, population, culture, and political systems have not allowed much progress toward the ultimate objective. The only progress achieved has been toward trade liberalization whereby most members apply tariff preferences between 60 percent and 90 percent. Also, there had been some progress toward the establishment of a Common External Tariff by 2006 but this progress is limited to unilateral trade liberalization.

Southern African Development Community

The SADC was founded in 1992 and succeeded the Southern African Development Coordination Conference (SADCC). It has 14 members: Angola, Botswana, Lesotho, Malawi, Mauritius (joined in 1995), Mozambique, Namibia, Seychelles (joined in 1997), South Africa (joined in 1994), Swaziland, Tanzania, the Democratic Republic of Congo, Zambia, and Zimbabwe. SADC's objectives are in the direction of regional economic integration. However, the majority of the SADC member states are also members of COMESA, a substantial overlap that has created tensions and rivalry between the two regional arrangements and has delayed the accomplishment of the declared objectives. SADC is one of the best-known regional organizations in Africa. South Africa's membership has contributed to its success in becoming a prominent political and security forum and in promoting and coordinating functional cooperation in transport and food security.

Southern African Customs Union

The SACU was established in 1969 between Botswana, Lesotho, Swaziland, and the Republic of South Africa and was later joined by Namibia. It is a customs union with a reasonably free movement of labor and capital and a common external tariff. It is an integrated economic area and an area of monetary stability, with all the benefits deriving from membership in a customs union. The only significant strain within the union is the planned free-trade area between South Africa and the EU because the remaining members are concerned about the loss of revenue from the common external tariff and about the increased competition in the South African market from cheaper EU products.

Economic Integration in Latin America and the Caribbean

Regional arrangements in Latin America have been quite volatile since the experience of the 1960s and 1970s was different from that of the 1980s.

The Latin American Free Trade Association (LAFTA) was established in 1960 by Mexico and by most of the South American countries except for Guyana and Surinam, which aimed at accelerating the process of integration and at establishing a common market. In 1980 the Latin American Integration Association (LAIA) superseded LAFTA. The Managua Treaty of 1960 established the Central American Common Market (CACM) between Costa Rica, El Salvador, Guatemala, Honduras, and Nicaragua, which was dissolved in 1960 and revived in 1990. During the 1980s Mexico joined the NAFTA and the more developed nations of LAIA formed the most successful regional arrangement, the Southern Common Market (MERCOSUR). The Caribbean Community (CARICOM) is the only regional arrangement in the Caribbean.

Southern Common Market

Southern Common Market (MERCOSUR) was formed by Argentina, Brazil, Paraguay, and Uruguay in 1991. It became a customs union in 1995 and Bolivia and Chile joined it in 1996 as associate members. It is considered a success story as it bought together the two main economic powers, Argentina and Brazil, against a background of political changes and economic policy reform. Its main objectives are free movement of factors of production, coordination of macroeconomic policies, and functional cooperation. Progress in trade liberalization was satisfactory as it chose to eliminate trade barriers on all goods rather than enter into product-by-product negotiations. The common external tariff rates range between 0 percent and 20 percent. Discussions on trade and investment liberalization between MERCOSUR and EU started in November 1999 and there is a commitment toward monetary and fiscal harmonization among the member countries.

Caribbean Community

The CARICOM was formed between Antigua, Barbados, Belize, Dominica, Grenada, Guyana, Jamaica, Montserrat, St. Kitts-Nevis, St. Lucia, St. Vincent and the Grenadines, Suriname, and Trinidad and Tobago in 1973. CARICOM operated along the lines of the European Free Trade Area (EFTA) and replaced the Caribbean Free Trade Association (CARIFTA), which was established in 1966. Its main objectives are economic integration, functional cooperation, and the coordination of foreign policies. Progress toward trade liberalization has been slow and the establishment of a common external tariff has been postponed several times as it was difficult to reconcile between the interests of the more developed and the less developed member states. However, there has been progress with regard to functional cooperation in the areas of education and science and toward the coordination of foreign policies such as the signing of preferential trade agreements with Venezuela, Colombia, and the Dominican Republic, the establishment of formal relations with the revived CACM in 1992, and the establishment of the Association of Caribbean States.

Economic Integration in the Middle East

The Middle East has had less success with economic integration than has any other part of the world. There are several arrangements but some extend beyond the geographical area of the Middle East since there are Arab nations in parts of Africa. There have been several attempts at regional integration. The Arab League (AL) was created in 1945 in order to promote close links among Arab states and to promote political, economic, social, and military cooperation. The AL has 22 members extending from the Gulf to Mauritania and Morocco. A second step was taken in 1957 with the establishment of the Council of Arab Economic Unity (CAEU) whose aim is to promote economic integration of all AL states. In 1965 Egypt, Iraq, Jordan, and Yemen set up the Arab Common Market to promote economic cooperation and integration but practically it never got off the ground. In 1981 the Gulf Cooperation Council (GCC) was established between Bahrain, Kuwait, Oman, Qatar, Saudi Arabia, and the United Arab Emirates whose goal is to form a common market. Some progress has been made in the area of economic integration by abolishing tariffs and other restrictions on mutual trade and there is a relative freedom on labor mobility but a common external tariff has not yet been established.

Closing Case

What about NAFTA?

The implementation of NAFTA benefits the United States by increasing competition in product and resource markets as well as by lowering the prices of many commodities to US consumers. In fact, between 1994 and 1999, two-way trade between the United States and Mexico more than doubled. Because the size of the US economy is more than 20 times that of Mexico, the US gains from NAFTA as a proportion of its GDP were much smaller than Mexico's. Furthermore, because wages in the United States were more than six times the wages in Mexico, NAFTA was expected to lead to a loss of 150,000 unskilled jobs, but an increase of 325,000 skilled jobs, for an overall net increase in employment of 175,000 in the United States. In fact, the 1999 estimates put the net gain in US employment as a result of NAFTA at between 90,000 and 160,000. Low-wage areas of the United States (such as Alabama and Arkansas) suffered while high-wage areas gained, but because of the 15-year phase-in period and about $3 billion assistance to displaced workers, the harm to workers in low-income areas in the United States was minimized.[46]

Source: Salvatore, D. (2001), International Economics, Chapter 10, 7th Edition, John Wiley & Sons, New York.

Question: What are the pros and cons of the NAFTA in terms of economic integration? Do all three countries benefit equally from it? Discuss with examples.

Chapter Summary

Since the end of World War II, the world has undergone significant changes. The decade of the 1970s was dominated by the two energy crises. Industrial economies were faced with a new "enemy": stagflation—a combination of high inflation and unemployment. Developing countries were increasingly becoming more dependent on foreign borrowing and centrally planned economies were unable to secure economic growth. Furthermore, the world witnessed a radical transformation during the past two decades. The greatest economic experiment of the twentieth century was the movement from communism to a market economy, which began in Mikhail Gorbachev's Russia in the mid-1980s, and then spread to Eastern Europe at the beginning of the 1990s and to China later on during the same decade.[47] Although the transition to a free market has led to disappointing outcomes, most Eastern Europe countries have concentrated on integrating their economies with Europe and on becoming part of the EU.

All these events led to the world becoming more and more global in nature and to defining globalization as a closer economic integration among nations through increased trade and capital flows. It also refers to labor movement and technology transfer across international borders as well as cultural and political issues, which are beyond the scope of this chapter. Globalization is the result of technological processes occurring mainly in the areas of information technology, telecommunications, energy, transport, and biotechnology as well as a shift in economic policies.

In this chapter a number of international organizations, such as the WTO, the IMF, and the World Bank, were presented and their role in terms of globalization and economic integration issues described.

In the course of all these developments, economic integration, also called "regional integration," which refers to the discriminate reduction or elimination of trade barriers among participating nations, came into being. This also implies the establishment of some form of cooperation and coordination among participants, which will depend on the degree of economic integration that ranges from free-trade areas to an economic and monetary union.

Developing countries form regional arrangements in an attempt to help growth and achieve fundamental structural changes. Such a regional arrangement would create a market large enough to support large-scale production and eventually bring about a reduction in production costs through economies of scale that would enable international competition without protection. The idea was appealing in theory but not very successful in practice because the formation of such regional arrangements lacked binding commitments to free trade. In addition, the distribution of benefits was unequal and the achievement of economies of scale led to the concentration of industries in a few industrial centers. As a result, most attempts during the 1960s and 1970s led to small groups with minimal bilateral agreements. The adoption of outward-looking policies during the 1980s and 1990s following economic reforms toward trade and financial liberalization, the wave of globalization, and the fall of communism brought a new momentum to regionalism whereby many such arrangements were strengthened and new ones formed.

Review and Discussion Questions

1. What are the causes of globalization?
2. Do you agree with the view that globalization leads to increased poverty? Yes. No. Why?
3. What is the difference between a free-trade area and a customs union?
4. Distinguish between trade creation and trade diversion.
5. What are the costs and benefits of economic and monetary union?
6. What does an optimum currency area mean?
7. What is the significance of the Maastricht convergence criteria?
8. Do you agree with the "movement" of economic integration? What is its future? Will the number of countries adopting economic integration increase or decrease in light of globalization?

Endnotes

1. Salvatore, D., "Globalization and International Competitiveness," in Denning, J. H. (ed.), *Globalization, Trade and Foreign Direct Investment* (New York: Pergamon Press, 1998).
2. The twelve states of the former Soviet Union comprising the Commonwealth of Independent States (CIS) are Armenia, Azerbaijan, Belarus, Georgia, Kazakhstan, Kyrgyzstan, Moldova, Russia, Tajikistan, Turkmenistan, Ukraine, and Uzbekistan. The Central and Eastern European states (CEE) comprising the three Baltic states of the former Soviet Union and the other states in this geographical area are Albania, Bulgaria, Croatia, Czech Republic, Estonia, F.Y.R. Macedonia, Hungary, Latvia, Lithuania, Poland, Romania. Slovak Republic, and Slovenia.

3. The first group of candidate countries recommended by the European Commission on October 9, 2002 to join the European Union on January 1, 2004 are Cyprus, Malta, the Czech Republic, Estonia, Hungary, Latvia, Lithuania, Poland, the Slovak Republic and Slovenia.

4. For an excellent account of the different capitalist, socialist and market socialist economic systems around the world, see Gregory, P. R. and Stewart, R. C., *Comparative Economic Systems* (Boston: Houghton Mifflin Company, 1999).

5. For a critical definition of globalization, see Hirst, P. and Thompson, G., *Globalization in Question* (Cambridge: Polity Press, 1996).

6. For a historical account of globalization, see Bairoch, P. and Kozul-Wright, R. (1996), "Globalization Myths: Some Historical Reflections on Integration, Industrialization and Growth in the World Economy," in *UNCTAD Discussion Paper*, No 113, March; Bordo, M. D., Eichengreen, B. and Irwin, D. A. (1999), "Is Globalization Today Really Different than Globalization a Hundred Years Ago?" in *National Bureau of Economic Research*, Working Paper 7195, Cambridge, Massachusetts, June.

7. International Monetary Fund website, www.img.org.

8. Ibid. (2000), *World Economic Outlook: Direction of Trade*, IMF, Washington DC, May.

9. For an account of the capital market integration in developed and developing countries, see Mussa, M. and Goldstein, M., "The Integration of World Capital Markets," *Changing Capital Markets: Implications for Monetary Policy* (Kansas City, Missouri: Federal Reserve Bank of Kansas City, 1993).

10. For an account of capital liberalization in developing countries, see Fry, J. M. (1993), *Money, Banking and Economic Development*, John Hopkins University Press, Baltimore and McKinnon, R. C. (1991), *The Order of Economic Liberalization: Financial Control in the Transition to a Market Economy*, John Hopkins University Press, Baltimore.

11. Students are encouraged to visit the websites of the WTO at www.wto.org, IMF at www.imf.org and World Bank at www.worldbank.org for a wealth of information regarding up-to-date news, statistics, legal texts and discussion papers on a variety of issues.

12. For an overview on the role of GATT, see Jackson, J. H., *The World Trading System*, (Cambridge MA: MIT Press, 1989).

13. For an account of the Uruguay Round as well as gains and losses to specific countries and regions, see Martin, W. and Winters, A. L., *The Uruguay Round* (Washington DC: The World Bank, 1995).

14. The labor standard argument stems from the fact that advanced countries are asking for an equalization in the working conditions between developed and developing countries so that the latter will not compete unfairly by denying workers acceptable wages and working conditions. The US President Bill Clinton asked at the Seattle meeting that labor and environmental standards should be included into the WTO agreements and countries breaking these rules should bear the consequences. Developing countries strongly opposed and the attempt failed.

15. Trade and the environmental issues are discussed in Bhagwati, J. N. and Hudec, R. E. (1996), eds, *Fair Trade and Harmonization: Prerequisites for Free Trade?*, Economic Analysis, Vol. 1, MIT Press, Cambridge MA; Uimonen, P. and Whalley, J. (1997), *Environmental Issues in the New World Trading System*, St. Martin's Press, New York.

16. For a critical approach on IMF's stabilization programs, see Feldstein, M. (1998), "Refocusing the IMF" *Foreign Affairs*, Vol. 77, No 2, March–April. For the effects of stabilization programs on developing countries, see Killick, T., *IMF Programs in Developing Countries: Design and Impact* (London: Routledge, 1995); Evers, B. and Nixxon, F. (1997), "International Institutions and Global Poverty" *Developments in Economics*, Vol. 13, Causeway Press.

17. For a detailed account of World Bank institutions, types of loans and eligibility, see the World Bank website, www.worldbank.org.

18. Pioneering works on economic integration include Viner, J. (1950), *The Customs Union Issue*, Carnegie Endowment for International Peace, New York; Timbergen, J. (1954), *International Economic Integration*, Elsevier, London; Balassa, B. (1961), *The Theory of Economic Integration* (London: Allen & Unwin). For a survey of the earlier literature on economic integration, see Maclup, F. (1977), *A History of Thought on Economic Integration* (Basingstoke: Macmillan, 1977).

19. Sometimes, reference is made to *preferential trade arrangements* (PTA), as the loosest form of economic integration, which implies that trade barriers are not yet fully eliminated between participating nations. A PTA is usually considered as an interim arrangement towards a free-trade area.

20. Viner, J. (1950), *The Customs Union Issue*, Carnegie Endowment for International Peace, New York; Meade, J. (1955), *The Theory of Customs Unions*, North Holland, Amsterdam; Johnson, H. G. (1958), "The Gains from Freer Trade with Europe: An Estimate" in *Manchester School of Economics and Social Studies*, September. For a more recent account on the theory of customs unions, see Moore, L. (2001), "The Economic Analysis of Preferential Trading Areas" in Artis, M. and Nixson, F., eds, *The Economics of the European Union* (Oxford: Oxford University Press); El-Agraa, A. M. (2001), "The Theory of Economic Integration" *The European Union: Economics and Policies*, Financial Times-Prentice Hall, Essex.

21. Empirical evidence shows small net static welfare gains. For a review of the evidence, see El-Agraa, E. M. (2001), "Measuring the Impact of Economic Integration" *The European Union: Economics and Policies*, Financial Times-Prentice Hall, Essex.

22. Another major scheme of regional integration in Europe was the European Free Trade Association (EFTA) formed in 1960 by the UK, Austria, Denmark, Norway, Portugal Sweden, Switzerland (and Liechtenstein) and Finland (which became an associate member in 1961). The EFTA achieved free trade in industrial products only although there were some relatively insignificant provisions on non-manufactures. The creation of EFTA, following the initiative of the UK, reflected the different political approaches to integration and was composed of those states that preferred limited arrangements and national sovereignty. However, as more EFTA members also became members of the European Community and European Union, EFTA membership is now limited to Iceland, Norway and Switzerland. For details are provided in EFTA's website www.efta.int.

23. For a detailed account of the different approaches to economic integration, see McCormick, J., *Understanding the European Union: A Concise Introduction* (London: Macmillan, 2005).

24. European Commission (1973), *Treaties Establishing the European Communities*, Office for Official Publications of the European Communities, Luxembourg.

25. For the origins of the European Union, see European Commission (1990), *European Unification: The Origins and Growth of the European Community*, Office for Official Publications of the European Communities, Luxembourg.

26. For a detailed description of the institutions of the European Union, see Nugent, N., *The Government and Politics of the European Union* (Basingstoke: Macmillan, 1999).

27. European Commission (1985), *Completing the Internal Market: White Paper from the Commission to the European Council*, Office for Official Publications of the European Communities, Luxembourg.

28. The Report estimated an overall gain of 5.3 percent of the 1988 European Union's GDP from the Single Market. For a full account, see Cecchini, P. (1988), *The European Challenge: 1992, The Benefits of a Single Market*, Wildwood House, Aldershot. See also European Commission (1988), "The Economics of 1992," *European Economy*, No 35, Directorate General of Economic and Financial Affairs, Luxembourg. For a more recent study of the effectiveness of the Single Market, see European Commission (1996), "Economic Evaluation of the Internal Market: Reports and Studies," *European Economy*, No 4, Directorate General of Economic and Financial Affairs, Luxembourg.

29. For a critical analysis of the Cecchini Report, see Davies, E., Kay, J. and Smales, C., 1992, *Myths and Realities* (London: London Business School, 1989) and Grahl, J. and Teague, P., (1992), *The Big Market* (London: Lawrence & Wishart, 1990).

30. European Community (1970), "Report to the Council and the Commission on The Realization By Stages of Economic and Monetary Union in the Community," *EC Bulletin*, No 11, Supplement, Luxembourg.

31. Initially, the participating currencies were the Belgian/Luxembourg franc, the Danish krone, the French franc, the Dutch guilder, the German mark, the Irish pound and the Italian lira. The Spanish peseta joined in 1989, the pound sterling in 1990 and the Portuguese escudo in 1992.

32. For a detailed description of the EMS, see Ludlow, P., *The Making of the European Monetary System* (London: Butterworth, 1982); Giavazzi, F., Micossi, S. and Miller, M. (1988), eds, *The European Monetary System*, Cambridge University Press; Hadjidakis, S. (1988), *The Implications of European Monetary System Membership on the Conduct of National Monetary Policies*, PhD Thesis, University of Reading; Gros, D. and Thygesen, N., *European Monetary Integration* (New York: Longman, 1998).

33. European Commission (1989), *Report on Economic and Monetary Union in the European Community* (the Delors Report), Committee for the Study of Economic and Monetary Union, EC Publications Office, Luxembourg.

34. European Commission (1992), *Treaty of the European Union*, Office for Official Publication of the European Communities, Luxembourg.

35. The theory of optimum currency areas was developed in the 1960s by Mundell, R. A. (1961), "A Theory of Optimum Currency Areas," *American Economic Review*, No 4, September and McKinnon, R. (1963) "Optimum Currency Areas" in *American Economic Review*, No 1, March.

36. European Commission (1990), "One Market One Money," *European Economy*, No 44, Directorate General for Economic and Financial Affairs, December.

37. European Commission (1998), *The Euro*, Directorate General II, Economic and Financial Affairs, February, Luxembourg.

38. For an analysis of these issues, see Kenen, P. (1995), *Economic and Monetary Union in Europe: Moving Beyond Maastricht* (Cambridge: Cambridge University Press, 1995).

39. European Commission (1992), *Treaty of the European Union*, Office for the Official Publications of the European Communities, Luxembourg. For a report on the convergence progress of countries outside the euro zone, see and European Central Bank (2000 and 2002), *ECB Convergence Report*, ECB, Frankfurt.

40. For a detailed description of the GSP, see European Community (1997), "The Growth and Stability Pact," *Official Journal of the European Communities*, No 326 C, August.

41. For an account of the resolution regarding the monitoring of fiscal developments and the coordination of economic policies, see European Commission (1997), "European Council Resolution No 1466," *Official Journal of the European Commission*, No 209 L, August. For a description of the excessive budget deficit procedures, see European Commission (1997), "European Council Resolution No 1467," *Official Journal of the European Commission*, No 209 L, August.

42. Monetary management and the instruments of monetary policy are described in European Central Bank (2000), "Monetary Policy Transmission in the Euro Area," *Monthly Bulletin*, July, ECB, Frankfurt; European Central Bank (2000), "The Two Pillars of the ECB's Monetary Policy Strategy," *Monthly Bulletin*, November, ECB, Frankfurt.

43. Institutional arrangements are discussed in European Central Bank (1999), "The Institutional Framework of the European System of Central Banks," *Monthly Bulletin*, July, ECB, Frankfurt.

44. Brown, D. K., Deardorff, A. V. and Stern, R. (1992), "A North American Free Trade Agreement: Analytical Issues and a Computational Assessment" *World Economy*, No 15, January; Hufbauer, G. and Schott, J. J. (1993), *NAFTA: An Assessment*, Institute for

International Economics, Washington DC, February; Klein, L. and Salvatore, D. (1995), "Welfare Effects of the North American Free Trade Agreement" in *Journal of Policy Modelling*, April.

45. This analysis draws heavily from World Trade Organization, *Regionalism and the World Trading System* (Geneva: WTO, 1995); World Bank, *A Symposium on Regionalism and Development*, (New York: The World Bank, 1998), May and UNCTAD (1996), *Handbook of Economic Integration and Cooperation Groupings of Developing Countries*, Vol. 1, Geneva.

46. As cited in Salvatore, D., *International Economics*, 7th edn (New York: John Wiley & Sons, 2001), Chapter 10.

47. The twelve states of the former Soviet Union comprising the Commonwealth of Independent States (CIS) are Armenia, Azerbaijan, Belarus, Georgia, Kazakhstan, Kyrgyzstan, Moldova, Russia, Tajikistan, Turkmenistan, Ukraine and Uzbekistan. The Central and Eastern European states (CEE) comprising the three Baltic states of the former Soviet Union and the other states in this geographical area are Albania, Bulgaria, Croatia, Czech Republic, Estonia, F.Y.R. Macedonia, Hungary, Latvia, Lithuania, Poland, Romania. Slovak Republic, Slovenia.

6

Government, Law, and Political Risk in International Business

Objectives

Through this chapter, the student will be exposed to:

- The political aspects of conducting international business
- The political risks involved in international business
- The strategies of minimizing the risks
- The legal aspects of conducting international business
- The role of government in international business
- The various aspects of corruption, including bribery.

Opening Case

Mario Monti

Mario Monti—judge, jury, and executioner all rolled into one. That is how many bosses of American multinationals view the courtly Italian who heads the European Union's (EU) Competition Commission. Europe's antitrust chief rocked the industrial world in the summer of 2001 when he shot down the proposed $42 billion merger between General Electric Co. and Honeywell International Inc. But that could just be a warm-up act for Monti, who now has his sights set on another American behemoth, Microsoft. Born in Varese, Italy, in 1943, he earned a degree in economics and management from Bocconi University in 1965. Appointed professor of monetary theory in 1971, he rose to become rector and president. He studied economics at Yale University in 1968–1969. He helped draft Italy's first law on competition and was a key player in banking reform. He served as EU's Commissioner for Internal Market (1995–1999) and has been Commissioner for Competition since 1999.

But to put an American slant on Monti's moves is far too simple. Yes, the formal, soft-spoken Italian arguably wields more brute influence than any elected politician in Europe. But here's the twist: Monti is the closest thing in Europe to a free-market zealot. He praises the "greater dynamism" of the United States, and he' is busy using his formidable power to push Europe along the same path.

In truth, Monti wreaks far more havoc in the Old World than in the New with his push for reform. Just ask German Chancellor **Schroeder** during 2002. In late February of 2002, Monti pushed the chancellor to dismantle VW's takeover defenses—a move the Chancellor vows to resist. Days later, Monti and his fellow commissioners used the EU's national governments, which are bucking Brussels' mandates to cut state subsidies. And in 2001 when he found DaimlerChrysler guilty of price manipulations, he fined the car company $65 million.

Monti's case is piled high with paradox. The 59-year-old Italian, for decades an economics professor at Milan's Bocconi University, favors free enterprise. But he pushes for it by using the biggest of big governments, a Brussels bureaucracy that operates largely by decree. He regularly dispatches investigative hit squads to make dawn raids on companies he's investigating for overcharging consumers, from cell-phone giant Vodafone Group PLC to Coca-Cola Co. Search warrants? A signature from Monti will suffice.

What's more, Monti has never held elected office and claims disdain for partisan jostling. Yet he finds himself at the heart of two vital political dramas. One involves nothing less than establishing a central government in Europe. In the other, he's working to make Europe's role as a referee for global antitrust equal to that of the United States. Both jobs require political smarts and a knack for deal making. Yet, the upright Monti, who associates negotiations with the sly nods and winks of politics in his native Italy, runs the other way. "It's his reluctance to negotiate that gives him such a scary reputation," says Alec Burnside, a partner at the Brussels office of Linklaters & Alliance, a London law firm. A leading Italian chief executive officer (CEO) adds: "He acts like a high priest." Monti's political greenness, and some priestly inflexibility, may have gotten him into trouble in the GE case. The result was a rift between the US Justice Department and Monti's European team.

Washington's Worries and Monti's Defense

Washington DC's complaint: Monti favors competitors over consumers.

Monti: That's a false dichotomy. More competition is good for consumers.

Washington DC: While Washington must prepare every antitrust case for court, Monti can rule by fiat, with few checks and balances.

Monti: The Competition Commissioner has to convince other commissioners and member states. And the European court has teeth, though it takes up cases years after the decision.

Washington DC: Monti's staff is packed with zealous career regulators who have never worked in the private sector.

Monti: Yes, but they're smart, they're pros, and—with the exception of GE-Honeywell—they've worked harmoniously with Washington.

Washington DC: Monti wants to hijack global antitrust, establishing European standards.

Monti: Nonsense. The heritage of antitrust is American, and despite occasional differences, Europe is moving toward the US norms.

Washington DC: Monti is antibusiness.

Monti: Preposterous. From his university post in Milan, he was long a leading advocate of free markets in an Italian economy dominated by the state. He has served on the boards of leading companies, from Fiat to Generali.

Washington DC: Monti ignores economic analysis, tending to fall for worst-case scenarios.

Monti: Why would an economist ignore economics? True, the analysis came out differently in GE-Honeywell, but in 98 percent of the cases, Washington and Brussels agree.

More than two decades ago, Monti as a young free-market economist traveled to London for a private audience with Margaret Thatcher. Now, until his terms ends in 2004, he has a chance to extend a Thatcher-like jolt to all of Europe. And there is a speculation that Monti will return home to Italian politics? Get serious! After this high-voltage tour in Europe's capital, for Mario Monti even the top job in Italy would probably feel like a demotion.

Question: What is Mario Monti's role in terms of politics and government's involvement in international business? What would be your assessment of Monti's negotiating skills?

Source: Business Week; March 25, 2002, pp. 48, 50.

Introduction

As has already been stated in the opening chapters of this book, international companies, by definition, operate across national boundaries, doing business in more than one country. Managers in international companies, therefore, are faced with different political and regulatory systems; thus, these managers are invited to become familiar and understand how these systems might have an impact on the companies' operations. The political environment provides both opportunities and drawbacks, and with the uncertainties of today, for example war in Iraq, the transition in Afghanistan, the ongoing turmoil in the Middle East, the future status of the EU—ten countries joined the EU in 2004 and Rumania, Bulgaria and Turkey are waiting to join—the United Kingdom's status within the EU, these opportunities decrease in numbers, and the obstacles increase.

Managers who work in domestic companies relate to a political system that is relatively familiar and well understood by them. However, international managers may face a number of unfamiliar, unfriendly, political environments. The international company may even find itself in the midst of discriminatory practices in certain countries around the world. Managers in these companies must assess the possibility of discrimination and decide how they will deal with risks associated with foreign political systems.

The Political Environment

Proactive international firms maintain an up-to-date profile of the political and economic environment of the countries in which they maintain operations (or have plans for future investment).

What Are Political Risks?

Political risks are the actions by groups of people or governments that have the potential to affect the immediate and/or long-term viability of a firm. This definition encompasses a large number of events—all the way from a revolution that results in confiscation of a firm's operations down to small changes in the tax code. Another definition we offer is the financial risk that a country's government will suddenly change its policies. Some of the things we will discuss directly involve legal issues (such as a law that does not permit exports to a certain country).

Many of the factors involved in determining political risk are difficult to predict or anticipate, even for an expert in international politics. For example, many experts believed that Iraq would not invade Kuwait in 1990 and therefore did not consider the potential negative effects on business operations in the country. Although the Middle East is generally viewed by many as relatively risky, there are some forms of risk inherent in most areas and countries. For example, the EU severely restricts Japanese auto imports, and the United States has a history of tight control over foreign investments in the banking and airline industries. Many of these restrictions appear to be politically motivated.

Since even experts have trouble making political predictions, it would be difficult for managers to anticipate all the political risks affecting their many international operations. Nevertheless, because of the potentially catastrophic effects of political events, management needs to do at least two things: (1) investigate political risk before entering a new market, and (2) continually monitor political events that may affect ongoing operations.[1] Some firms, for example, maintain and consult up-to-date descriptions of the political environment in an effort to predict the negative and positive effects on their operations.

Types of Political Risk[2]

Let us take a look at the two basic general types of risk:

1. *Systematic Risk*: A risk that influences a large number of assets. An example is political events. It is virtually impossible to protect yourself against this type of risk.
2. *Unsystematic Risk*: Sometimes referred to as "specific risk." It is risk that affects a very small number of assets. An example is news that affects a specific stock such as a sudden strike by employees.

Now that we have determined the fundamental types of risk let us look at more specific types of risk, particularly when we talk about stocks and bonds:

- *Credit or Default Risk*: This is the risk that a company or individual will be unable to pay the contractual interest or principal on its debt obligations. This type of risk is of particular concern to investors who hold bonds within their portfolio. Government bonds, especially those issued by the US Federal Government, have the least amount of default risk and the least amount of returns while corporate bonds tend to have the highest amount of default risk but also the higher interest rates. Bonds with lower chances of default are considered to be "investment grade," and bonds with higher chances are considered to be junk bonds. Bond-rating services, such as Moody's, allow investors to determine which bonds are investment-grade and which bonds are "junk."
- *Country Risk*: This refers to the risk that a country will not be able to honor its financial commitments. When a country defaults it can harm

the performance of all other financial instruments in that country as well as other countries it has relations with. Country risk applies to stocks, bonds, mutual funds, options, and futures that are issued within a particular country. This type of risk is most often seen in emerging markets or countries that have a severe deficit.

- *Foreign Exchange Risk*: When investing in foreign countries, firms must consider the fact that currency exchange rates can change the price of the asset as well. Foreign exchange risk applies to all financial instruments that are in a currency other than your domestic currency. As an example, if you are a resident of the United States and invest in some Japanese stock in Japanese yen, even if the share value appreciates, you may lose money if the Japanese yen depreciates in relation to the US dollar.
- *Interest Rate Risk*: A rise in interest rates during the term or debt securities hurts the performance of stocks and bonds.
- *Political Risk*: This represents the financial risk that a country's government will suddenly change its policies. This is a major reason that Second and Third World countries lack foreign investment.
- *Market Risk*: This is the most familiar of all risks. It is the day-to-day fluctuations in a stock's price. It is also referred to as volatility (i.e., a highly volatile market means that prices have huge swings in very short periods of time). Market risk applies mainly to stocks and options. As a whole, stocks tend to perform well during a bull market and poorly during a bear market—volatility is not so much a cause but an effect of certain market forces. Volatility is a measure of risk because it refers to the behavior, or "temperament," of your investment rather than the reason for this behavior. Because market movement is the reason why people can make money from stocks, volatility is essential for returns, and the more unstable the investment the more chance it can go dramatically either way.

As you can see, there are several types of risk that a smart investor should consider and pay careful attention to. Deciding your potential return while respecting the risk is the age-old decision that investors must make.

In offering a further detailed analysis of political risk, we present a system that divides types of threats or risks into three main categories. These include risks due to (1) the political/economic environment, (2) the prevailing domestic economic conditions, and (3) external economic relations.

Political/Economic Environment Risk

First, there are many types of political/economic variables that could present a risk to conducting business. For example, the stability of the government and the political system in a prospective country is an important source of uncertainty. In recent years, we have seen the effects of dramatic and some-times violent changes in political systems on the operations of multinational corporations (MNCs) in many countries (e.g., Afghanistan, Iraq, the Middle East in general, the former Soviet Union, Nigeria, South Africa).

Perhaps the most important risk faced by companies in such situations is nationalization. If a government nationalizes an industry or company and then compensates the MNC that is affected, then that action is called expropriation.[3]

Expropriation is the seizure of businesses with little, if any, compensation to the owners. Such seizures of foreign enterprises by developing countries were very common in the old days. Expropriation is more likely to occur in countries that are poor, with a relatively unstable political system, and might be suspicious of MNCs. When nationalization discriminates against foreign firms by offering little or no compensation for loss of property, this action is called confiscation. Although expropriation and confiscation have started to become a rare phenomenon, especially after the 1990s, MNCs should be aware of the risks associated with these events, especially since their effects are substantial. However, there are many other political/economic events that could occur. With the recent wave of nationalism occurring all over the world, today civil war and terrorism represent a greater business risk for an MNC than they have for some time. Clearly, what has happened in former Yugoslavia is an example of this risk. What has happened in Afghanistan, the ongoing situation in Iraq, the ongoing civil conflicts in Somalia and Angola, the ongoing political unrest in the Middle East, North Korea, and so on are just a few examples of events that create a high risk for investment by an MNC.

Exhibits 6.1 and 6.2 show the level of attacks and terrorism, respectively, around the world, as an indication of the political risk involved in MNCs' strategic plans to invest in countries where terrorism is high, and an MNC must take this into consideration before making any move for foreign invest-ment in a country and/or region where, for example, anti-American and/or anti-Western sentiments are very high.

Domestic Economic Conditions

Domestic conditions in the host country, such as the ability of a country to purchase a company's products (which depends on factors like per capita income and growth rate) and the presence of infrastructure (such as roads, airports, and other transportation systems), can add to or reduce the amount of risk a company faces in a foreign location. Usually, good infrastructure support reduces risk and thereby facilitates entry and expansion of business.

Other domestic risk factors include the passing of legal regulations regard-ing environmental pollution. The enforcement of such laws could restrict

Exhibit 6.1

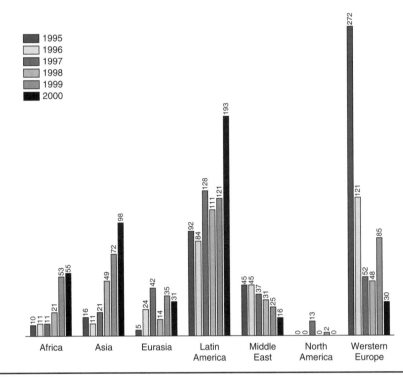

Total International Attacks by Region, 1995–2000

Legend:
- 1995
- 1996
- 1997
- 1998
- 1999
- 2000

Africa: 10, 11, 11, 21, 53, 55
Asia: 16, 11, 21, 49, 72, 98
Eurasia: 5, 24, 42, 14, 35, 31
Latin America: 92, 84, 128, 111, 121, 193
Middle East: 45, 45, 37, 31, 25, 16
North America: 0, 0, 13, 0, 2, 0
Werstern Europe: 272, 121, 52, 48, 85, 30

Source: CIA Fact Book, 2003.

how an MNC may operate in a foreign country. In turn, this almost always increases the operational costs of the company.

For example, in Germany, as in the United States, and other industrialized countries, there are many very restrictive environmental laws that affect the production and disposal of industrial wastes. In many developing countries, such as Bangladesh, Nepal, and Ethiopia, environmental laws are almost nonexistent. Partly this is because these countries are struggling to improve economic conditions and often wish to do as little as possible to discourage foreign investment. Consequently, these countries may become places for industrialized countries to dump their unwanted waste. To deal with this issue, over 50 countries signed the so-called agreement of the Basel Convention, which refers to the international transport of hazardous wastes. This agreement states that there must be a written consent for the movement of toxic waste and permission should be received from all countries through which it passes. The exporting country cannot move the waste until it receives written permission, obtains insurance coverage against damage, and enacts domestic laws making it a crime to violate the agreement.

Exhibit 6.2

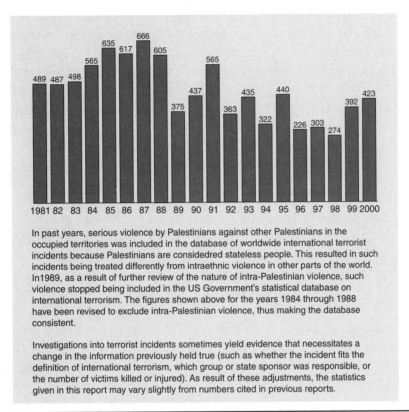

Total International Terrorist Attacks, 1981–2000

In past years, serious violence by Palestinians against other Palestinians in the occupied territories was included in the database of worldwide international terrorist incidents because Palestinians are considedred stateless people. This resulted in such incidents being treated differently from intraethnic violence in other parts of the world. In1989, as a result of further review of the nature of intra-Palestinian violence, such violence stopped being included in the US Government's statistical database on international terrorism. The figures shown above for the years 1984 through 1988 have been revised to exclude intra-Palestinian violence, thus making the database consistent.

Investigations into terrorist incidents sometimes yield evidence that necessitates a change in the information previously held true (such as whether the incident fits the definition of international terrorism, which group or state sponsor was responsible, or the number of victims killed or injured). As result of these adjustments, the statistics given in this report may vary slightly from numbers cited in previous reports.

Source: CIA Factbook, 2003.

Despite all these, many countries are increasingly concerned about the effect of industry on their environment. Several events that have taken place in the last 15–20 years, such as the toxic release at Bhopal, India, the meltdown of the Chernobyl nuclear plant in the Ukraine, and the Exxon-Valdez oil spill off Alaska, have increased the awareness of environmental issues. In some countries like Germany, there are even major political parties organized around environmental issues. Thus, there are direct and indirect forms of risk associated with this factor. Clearly, these affect the business decisions of MNCs. For instance, a consumer products company may build its plant in Mexico rather than in the United States (its intended market) because pollution control regulations in the United States require expensive equipment. Similarly, a chemical company may manufacture in Indonesia rather than in Germany to avoid extensive industry restrictions. These examples raise ethical and other issues, such as whether an MNC should capitalize on weaker restrictions in certain countries.

External Economic Relations as Risk Factors

There are also a large number of factors that deal with how a country relates economically to another country. Furthermore, although some of the earlier factors that we considered are quite rare (civil war), virtually every country restricts its external economic relations in several ways. For example, many countries have restrictions on imports, usually in the form of tariffs. A tariff would increase the price of a foreign product or service relative to the domestic counterpart. So through the use of import taxes a country can partially restrict imports and provide protection for domestic industry. This presents a risk for the foreign MNC.

Tariffs are not the only way imports can be restricted. One nation may wish to limit imports in order to force other countries to open their markets. The United States, for example, restricts the number of automobiles that Japan may import in order to pressurize Japan into purchasing more US-made components. The EU also limits the import of Japanese autos to a very low percentage of the total autos sold in the EU. Finally, a country may restrict imports when they are perceived to be a threat to the health or safety of its citizens. For example, foreign producers of food must receive the approval of the Food and Drug Administration (FDA) regarding their hygiene standards before exporting their products to the United States. Back in 1996, some British cattle were affected by "mad cow" disease—an affliction that produced many nervous system symptoms and eventually death. Although the British argued that the disease did not affect humans or the harvesting of the beef, many countries (including other EU members) temporarily banned the import of British beef. British farmers incurred great losses as a result of this ban, and eventually they destroyed nearly half of the cows in Britain.

The Legal Environment

A domestic firm must follow the laws and customs of its home country. An international business faces a more complex task: It must obey the laws not only of its home country but also of all the host countries in which it operates. The laws of both the home and the host countries can affect directly and indirectly the international companies and the way they conduct their business. These laws determine the markets the firms serve, the cost of goods and/or services they offer, the price they charge, and costs for labor, raw materials, and technology.

Different laws and practices are found among countries of the world. In most Western cultures the law functions within the framework of society whereas in theocratic cultures the law is a function of both societal and spiritual guidance. Hebrew and Islamic laws are the result of what God dictates, of what the scripture says, and of any prophetic practices.

In addition to understanding the politics and laws of both home and host countries, the international manager must consider the overall international political and legal environment. International law plays an important role in the conduct of international business. Although there is no body to enforce international law, certain treaties and agreements are respected by a number of countries and influence international business operations. The World Trade Organization (WTO) is such an international agency that defines internationally acceptable economic practices for its member countries. There are many other agreements that provide some legal regulation of international commerce, including the EU, North American Free Trade Agreement (NAFTA), and others. Similarly, the United Nations (UN) and its many allied organizations (such as the International Labor Organization, World Bank, and the International Monetary Fund) provide the legal and regulatory context within which global business operates. Many feel that the invocation of international legal principles by the UN after the Iraqi invasion of Kuwait in 1990 signaled a major change in the appreciation and adherence of many countries to international law.

Resolving International Disputes

The presence of an agreement to oversee trade does not mean that there will be no conflict between countries. There is considerable trade and legal disagreement among countries. Resolving any disputes across borders is very complex. Partly, this is because a trade conflict might be treated differently by international and domestic laws. The United States, for example, has been castigated by some other countries for trying to restrict exports to nations in conflict with the United States, like Cuba or Iraq. Those other countries claim that US action is in violation of WTO regulations, whereas the US officials point to domestic laws and constraints that force their hand. An important question in situations like this is where should the issue be resolved? Which court or country has or should have jurisdiction in circumstances like this?

Source of Jurisdiction

An instance where the issue of the source of jurisdiction came to the fore happened in 1984 when one of the most deadly industrial accidents in history unfolded near Bhopal, India. Union Carbide India, Limited (UCIL), an Indian corporation, operated a chemical plant near Bhopal. An accident, allegedly resulting from negligence of the operators, was disastrous. Winds blew a lethal gas into the densely populated city, and the death toll was staggering. Over 2100 people lost their lives and nearly 200,000 other people suffered injuries—some of which were very debilitating. It is important to note that UCIL was incorporated under Indian laws, and its stock was traded publicly on the Bombay Stock Exchange. A majority of its stock (50.9%) was owned by Union Carbide Corporation (UCC), a US company; 22 percent of the stock was owned by the Indian government; and the remaining 27 percent by private Indian investors.

Immediately after the accident, American lawyers traveled to India and signed up many Indian clients. (All of those affected, including all the plant employees, were Indian.) Within four days of the accident, the first of over 100 legal actions was filed in the US District Court. To justify the filing of these suits in US courts, the argument was made that the US parent corporation (UCC) controlled the subsidiary (UCIL). Union Carbide countered by claiming that they no longer had operational control over this or the other seven UCIL plants in India. UCC's participation via employees and plant operation was terminated at least a year before the accident. They claimed, therefore, that Indian courts were the correct forum to hear the case. It is probably true that all parties (UCC, the US lawyers, and the victims' families) were aware that damage awards would be substantially higher in US courts than in India. In addition, the fact the lawyers would get one third of the awards as their fees also probably accounted for this situation. As it turned out, the US Circuit Court of Appeals ruled in 1987 that India was in fact the appropriate forum to hear the case, provided that UCC submit to the jurisdiction of Indian courts and agree to satisfy any judgment reached against them in those courts. Eventually, Union Carbide (US) reached an agreement with the Indian Supreme Court to pay $480 million to the victims, a relatively small amount by US standards.[4]

Although this situation raises questions about whether parent companies are responsible for the activity of their foreign subsidiaries, the point here is that it is difficult to decide which country's courts and laws apply in any one situation. Often this confusion may be the result of political issues surrounding the legal ones.

The Political Environment

Proactive international firms maintain an up-to-date profile of the political and economic environment of the countries in which they maintain operations or have plans for future investment. In the early 1990s, the formerly rigid ideological systems of capitalism, communism, and socialism underwent profound changes, and the lines of demarcation between those systems have increasingly blurred. It is now best to measure such systems along a continuum of economic systems—from those that operate primarily according to market forces (such as the United States) to those that use central planning for resource allocation (such as the People's Republic of China). Near the center of the continuum lie the industrialized Western European countries and Japan. Less developed countries in Africa, Asia, and Latin America are continuing to develop their market mechanisms and economic systems to improve their economic health. More detailed information on these regions will be provided, Chapters 13 to 16.

An important aspect of the political environment is the phenomenon of ethnicity—a driving force behind political instability around the world. In fact, many uprisings and conflicts that are thought to be political are actually expressions of differences among ethnic groupings. Often, religious disputes lie at the heart of these differences. Uprisings based on religion operate in conjunction with ethnic differences (as probably was the case in former Yugoslavia) and separate from them (as in Northern Ireland). Many terrorist activities are also based on religious differences, as in the Middle East. Managers must understand the ethnic and religious composition of the host country in order to anticipate problems of general instability as well as those of an operational nature—such as effects on your workforce, on production and access to raw materials, and your market. For example, in Pakistan one must understand the differences between Punjabi and Sindi. In Malaysia it is essential to recognize the special economic relationship between Chinese and Malay. In the Philippines it is important to understand the significant and lead financial role played by the Filipino Chinese. In Cyprus, it is important to understand the differences and similarities between the Greek and Turkish Cypriots.

The Legal Environment

Closely related to the political system, the legal system is another dimension of the external environment that influences business. Managers must be aware of the legal systems in the countries in which they operate; the nature of the legal profession, both domestic and international; and the legal relationship that exists between countries. Legal systems differ in terms of the nature of the system—common law, civil law, and theocratic law—and the degree of independence of the judiciary from the political process. Also, some of the totalitarian countries, for example China, Libya, that are going through a transition to democracy and to a free-market economy do not have a legal system in place that deals with business transactions in a global market context.

Legal systems usually fall into one of three categories: common law, civil law, and theocratic law.

Common Law
The United States and the United Kingdom are examples of countries with a common law system. Common law is based on tradition, precedent, and custom and usage. The courts fulfill an important role by interpreting the law according to these characteristics. Because common law in the modern

setting originated in the United Kingdom, its former and current colonies, such as Hong Kong, also have common law systems.[5]

Civil Law

A civil law system, also called a codified legal system, is based on a detailed set of laws organized into a legal code. Rules for conducting business trans-actions are a part of the code. Over 70 countries, including Germany, France, and Japan operate on a civil law basis.

One important difference between common law and civil law systems is apparent in the roles of judges and lawyers. In a common law system the judge serves as a neutral referee, ruling on various motions by the opposing parties' lawyers. These lawyers are responsible for developing their clients' cases and choosing which evidence to submit on their clients' behalf. In a civil law system, the judge takes on many of the tasks of the lawyers, determining, for example, the scope of evidence to be collected and presented to the court. Common law is based on the court's interpretation of events, whereas civil law is based on how the law is applied to facts. An example of an area in which the two systems differ in practice is contracts. In a common law country, contacts tend to be detailed, with all contingencies spelled out. In a civil law country, contracts tend to be shorter and less specific because many of the issues that a common law contract would cover are already included in the civil code. Thus, when entering into contracts abroad, it is important for the manager to understand which type of legal system will establish the contract. Civil law also tends to be less adversarial than common law because judges rely on detailed legal codes rather than on precedent when deciding cases. This is one reason why British and US law firms encounter so much resistance when they enter civil law countries. They are used to the competitive, adversarial approach that the common law system engenders.[6]

Theocratic Law

This law is based on the officially established rules governing the faith and practice of a particular religion. A country that applies religious law to civil and criminal conduct is called a theocracy.[7] In Iran, for example, a group of mullahs, or holy men, determine the legality or illegality through their interpretation of the Koran, the holy book of Islam. Religious laws can create interesting problems for firms. Consider the teaching of the Muslim holy book, the Koran, which denounces charging interest on loans as an unfair exploitation of the poor. Muslim firms and financial institutions have had to develop alternative financing arrangements to acquire and finance capital. Muslim businesses often rely on leasing arrangements, rather than borrowing money, to obtain long-term assets. In Iran, banks often charge up-front fees that act as a substitute for loan interest payments, and owners of bank deposits receive shares of the bank's profits rather than interest payments. Pakistani banks are in the process of adopting similar policies—often referred to as Islamic banking—because Pakistan's Supreme Court issued a ruling in 1999 declaring all interest-bearing transactions to be contrary to Islamic law. The ruling gave the government, bankers, and investors two years to revise laws,[8] rewrite existing loans, and eliminate interest payments. Family-owned firms are often influential in countries where legal systems are based on the Koran because members of an owner's extended family may be the best available source of capital, given the costs of circumventing the prohibition on interest.[9,10]

Differences in laws and regulations from country to country are numerous and complex. These and other issues in the regulatory environment that concern multinational firms are discussed briefly here.

Countries often impose protectionist policies, such as tariffs, quotas, and other trade restrictions, to give preference to their own products and industries. The Japanese have come under much criticism for protectionism, which they use to limit imports of foreign goods while they continue exporting consumer goods (e.g., cars, electronics) on a large scale. The American auto industry continues to ask the US government for protection from Japanese car imports. In fact, as the economic recession dragged on in the early 1990s, Americans began to lay much of the blame on the Japanese and their protectionist policies. In 1992, as General Motors proceeded with its retrenchment strategy of closing down 21 auto plants in North America, those workers who were losing their jobs started a wave of anti-Japanese sentiment. Their anger was fueled by Japanese leaders publicly criticizing American workers and pointing out the inefficiencies of US car manufacturing. Calls to "buy American," however, were thwarted by the difficulty of identifying cars that were truly American-made; the intricate web of car-manufacturing alliances between Japanese and American companies often makes it difficult to distinguish the maker.

A country's tax system influences the attractiveness of investing in that country and affects the relative level of profitability for an MNC. Foreign tax credits, holidays, exemptions, depreciation allowances, and taxation of corporate profits are additional considerations the foreign investor must examine before acting. Many countries have signed tax treaties (or conventions) that define terms such as income, source, and residency, and spell out what constitutes taxable activities.

The level of government involvement in the economic and regulatory environment varies a great deal among countries and has a varying impact on management practices. In Canada, the government has a significant involvement in the economy. It has a powerful role in many industries, including transportation, petrochemicals, fishing, steel, textiles, and building materials—forming partly owned or wholly owned enterprises. Wholly owned businesses are called Crown Corporations (Petro Canada, Ontario Hydro Corporation, Marystown Shipyard, etc.), many of which are as large as the major private companies. The government's role in the Canadian economy, then, is one of both control and competition.[11] Government policies, subsidies, and regulations directly affect the manager's planning process, as do other major factors in the Canadian legal environment, such as the high proportion of unionized workers (30%). In Quebec, the law requiring official bilingualism imposes considerable operating constraints and expenses. For a foreign subsidiary, this regulation forces managers to speak both English and French, and to incur the costs of language training for employees, translators, the administration of bilingual paperwork, and so on.[12]

Evaluating country risks is a crucial exercise when choosing sites for international business, particularly if investment is to be undertaken. Certain risks can be managed through insurance, hedging, and other types of financial planning, but other risks cannot be controlled through such financial mechanisms. Each corporation confronts a unique set of country risks. For corporations that are searching for foreign suppliers and customers, as well as those that are evaluating investment opportunities, the analysis of country risks has attained a new importance and a new complexity. More careful differentiation among countries and business sectors is now required. For example, instead of viewing Southeast Asia as a group of tigers that have been involved in an economic miracle and in subsequent downfall, it is now necessary to carefully analyze the situation that each individual country faces.

Managers should prepare themselves accordingly with an analysis of interest rates and stock prices, the country's balance of payments, projections of probable macroeconomic policies, and fiscal and current account deficits. It is important to examine alternative potential scenarios and projections, and assign probabilities to each scenario in order to determine the risks and rewards connected with particular business opportunities. Pricewaterhouse-Coopers has developed an index that indicates how one may quantify the impact of country risks in terms of equivalent tax rates and rates of return.

The events of September 11 and the subsequent conflicts have added another dimension to country risk. How to preserve the personal security of employees has gained new prominence in corporate strategies. Here, significant differences exist among countries, as some appear to be experiencing a heightened antipathy toward foreigners. Specific plans for protection and exit must be based on an analysis of each country.

The relative significance of various country risks differs from one corporation to another, depending on features such as the type of business activity, experience in managing a certain risk, and financial strength. Hence, each corporation has to develop its unique country risk strategies. In the context of globalization, the New Economy, and the changing role of governments, the analysis and management of country risks is now of paramount importance.

Government Issues and Corruption

As Peter Eigen, Chairman of Transparency International, stated: "Politicians and public officials from the world's leading industrial countries are ignoring the rot in their own backyards and the criminal bribe-paying activities of multinational firms headquartered in their countries."[13]

There is no doubt that the government's role in international business, trade, investment, and so on is of utmost significance. However, corruption in governments throughout the world used to be considered a fact of life: undesirable, but not especially harmful. Now that attitude has changed. High levels of corruption are no longer regarded as inevitable. Consensus now exists that corrupt behavior reduces economic growth and can destabilize governments. Corruption erodes respect for the law and deters honest people from entering public service. It results in over-invoicing and substandard work by contractors and reduces tax revenues. Corruption also undercuts environmental regulations and building code regulations, discourages foreign direct investment in developing countries, and facilitates other crimes, such as drug trafficking.

Corruption—broadly defined as "the abuse of public or private office for personal gain"[14]—takes many different forms, from routine bribery or petty abuse to the amassing of spectacular personal wealth through embezzlement or other dishonest means.

The international community is adamant that corruption must be stopped. It is demanding that the governments of poorer countries eradicate corruption within their countries if they want to be considered eligible to receive Western aid.[15] Yet there is a deep hypocrisy in the international community's approach, at the heart of which are the taxpayer-backed export credit agencies of industrialized countries.

Bribery—Business as Usual. Between 1994 and 2001 the US government received reports of 400 international cases worth US$200 billion signed between governments and businesses worldwide that purportedly involved bribery.[16] Between May 2001 and April 2002 alone, the US government learned of 60 contracts worth a total of US$35 billion that had been affected by bribery.[17] Some 70 percent of the allegations that the US government received in 2000–2001 involved companies from countries that had signed the Organization for Economic Cooperation and Development's (OECD's) 1997 anti-bribery Convention.[18]

Corruption scandals in the 1990s (in France, Brazil, Japan, Pakistan, and elsewhere) demonstrated that corruption is widespread, even in democracies. In recent years, government leaders and nongovernmental organizations have developed a variety of strategies to expose corruption and counter its effects.

Transparency International, a global organization with 80 chapters, builds anticorruption coalitions with governments, business people, and representatives of civil society. The World Bank and the International Monetary Fund focus on introducing reforms in developing countries to address the demand side of bribery. In cases where a country has high levels of corruption and a government that is not instituting reforms, international financial institutions may reduce or eliminate aid. In 1996 the UN General Assembly approved a code of conduct for public officials and called on member states to make the bribing of public officials a crime. Corruption reform programs have been successful in exposing government bribery by conducting national surveys and by publishing "report cards" that detail specific instances of corruption. "Big Mac Indexes," which reveal suspicious cost differences in a country for similar commodities, such as a school lunch or a bottle of aspirin, can be especially effective.

As an example, Transparency International/Argentina conducted a Big Mac survey, which revealed that a school lunch in Buenos Aires cost the equivalent of $5. A comparable lunch in Mendoza, which had been implementing anticorruption measures, cost the equivalent of 80 cents. Within days of publication of the survey's results, the cost of a school lunch in Buenos Aires was more than halved.[19]

World Bank research, meanwhile, shows that one third (35 percent) of foreign companies operating in the countries of the former Soviet Union pay kickbacks to obtain government contracts, of which US and European companies are among the worst offenders. Despite US anticorruption legislation,[20] 42 percent of US companies reported paying bribes in these countries, compared to 29 percent of French firms, 21 percent of German firms, and 14 percent of British ones.[21] In those countries with particularly high levels of corruption, meanwhile, over 50 percent of multinationals admitted to paying public procurement kickbacks.[22]

A total of 40,838 people were surveyed in 47 countries in the Voice of the People survey, a general household survey conducted by Gallup International in July 2002. The survey included a series of questions on behalf of Transparency International, specifically the TI Global Corruption Barometer survey (Exhibit 6.3). In addition, 1315 adults were surveyed in the Palestinian Authority by the Palestinian Center for Policy and Survey Research in April 2003, the results of which are not included in the overall totals. About 30,487 people were polled in 44 of the countries on the following question. They were asked: If you had a magic wand and you could eliminate

Exhibit 6.3

The Transparency International Global Corruption Barometer 2003

Country	Business licensing %	Courts %	Customs %	Education system %	Political parties %	Utilities (phone etc.) %	Medical services %	Immigration/passports %	Police %	Private sector %	Tax revenue %	Other %
Argentina	3.6	19.2	3.2	4.3	58.2	0.5	0.9	0.2	3.1	0.6	3.4	2.7
Austria	7.5	8.4	2.7	2.7	35.7	3.9	5.7	6.9	10.8	2.7	12.0	0.9
Bolivia	18.2	7.7	10.8	2.4	34.8	2.2	1.2	1.2	16.0	0.9	3.7	0.9
Bosnia and Herzegovina	14.5	17.0	4.2	6.6	24.2	2.4	20.4	0.3	4.8	1.7	3.5	0.3
Bulgaria	9.9	19.8	16.5	4.8	20.2	3.3	14.3	0.9	4.1	1.8	2.7	1.7
Cameroon	3.8	31.0	6.5	11.1	10.4	1.2	11.2	2.1	13.7	3.2	4.3	1.4
Canada	3.2	8.3	1.8	6.5	39.7	2.3	9.7	8.8	5.7	4.4	5.7	3.8
Colombia	2.4	3.4	3.4	8.8	38.0	8.1	8.8	1.0	8.5	1.4	12.9	3.4
Costa Rica	4.3	8.6	14.0	3.2	29.0	1.1	2.2	12.9	5.4	4.3	15.1	0
Croatia	12.9	21.6	0.4	2.8	18.6	4.2	22.5	1.9	4.9	3.4	2.5	4.2
Denmark	4.0	16.3	1.8	2.2	36.1	2.2	11.5	4.8	7.7	6.2	3.3	4.0
Dominican Republic	2.0	12.1	6.1	8.1	25.3	13.1	0	2.0	4.0	0	8.1	19.2
Finland	9.5	27.7	0.7	1.3	38.0	1.6	6.1	3.6	4.2	3.1	3.9	0.3
Georgia	4.8	18.1	8.2	6.0	12.4	4.5	19.7	0.9	13.4	0.4	6.0	5.7

(Continued)

Exhibit 6.3 *continued*

Germany	4.9	8.6	0.8	3.1	39.2	3.9	9.9	7.8	2.9	7.2	10.5	1.2
Guatemala	3.0	8.0	14.0	12.0	27.0	6.0	4.0	8.0	10.0	6.0	2.0	0
Hong Kong	1.7	8.9	5.4	3.9	15.4	4.8	3.3	1.3	35.4	12.1	5.0	2.8
India	2.0	3.8	1.8	24.9	41.2	4.4	4.0	0.5	12.8	1.4	2.1	1.2
Indonesia	5.8	32.8	3.2	8.7	16.3	11.1	1.8	0.4	10.2	2.8	6.4	0.7
Ireland	3.9	8.8	0.8	3.7	38.3	0.8	13.4	5.1	10.3	2.7	10.7	1.4
Israel	2.5	14.8	1.0	10.2	33.4	9.6	8.4	3.3	7.1	1.7	5.6	2.3
Italy	10.4	18.0	1.1	4.4	29.0	4.4	15.0	4.0	3.8	1.3	7.2	1.5
Japan	8.7	3.7	1.4	3.8	51.9	4.0	7.3	0.2	9.6	1.2	2.8	5.4
Korea (South)	19.1	10.3	3.0	15.7	27.9	6.2	3.7	0.1	5.0	2.9	6.0	0.1
Luxembourg	9.8	18.1	1.6	4.9	15.6	5.3	9.3	7.9	5.8	4.9	12.6	4.2
Macedonia	8.5	15.4	17.9	9.4	28.2	2.7	8.5	0.9	2.8	0.6	3.3	1.8
Malaysia	6.8	8.5	8.0	5.0	24.6	0.8	1.3	4.0	32.0	3.5	3.6	1.9
Mexico	2.9	6.6	3.3	8.7	19.9	9.0	3.5	1.4	36.5	0.8	6.1	1.1
Netherlands	4.0	10.0	1.0	0.6	27.1	0.8	6.7	11.5	7.7	26.3	3.5	0.8
Nigeria	4.3	4.8	3.0	12.6	27.0	7.4	3.4	1.1	32.1	0.7	2.5	1.2
Norway	12.5	12.3	2.8	1.4	19.7	1.6	4.9	17.2	6.0	17.2	3.0	1.4

Palestinian Authority	7.4	8.6	3.2	16.4	10.4	4.7	4.6	2.4	23.8	1.5	3.8	8.5
Panama	3.0	15.0	6.0	2.0	35.0	10.0	3.0	3.0	11.0	2.0	2.0	8.0
Peru	2.6	35.0	3.1	2.3	15.9	10.0	2.0	3.1	10.0	2.3	9.7	4.1
Poland	5.8	15.4	2.2	5.0	27.2	3.5	21.6	0.7	11.1	1.8	4.5	1.2
Portugal	9.2	14.8	1.4	4.2	18.7	4.6	18.7	6.2	6.7	0.7	14.5	0.2
Romania	15.1	20.2	2.7	2.9	24.3	1.6	12.6	1.2	6.4	1.9	9.3	1.7
Russian Federation	5.3	10.9	1.1	8.8	24.5	8.3	15.3	2.0	17.9	0.4	4.2	1.3
South Africa	2.1	3.9	0.2	14.4	21.1	5.5	11.3	6.0	23.8	3.5	5.1	3.1
Spain	4.7	26.6	2.3	3.8	34.8	0.9	3.4	11.3	1.6	2.3	6.8	1.6
Sweden	8.2	16.2	2.4	1.7	19.3	2.9	12.8	11.6	9.7	7.5	6.3	1.4
Switzerland	5.8	9.8	1.3	4.9	23.0	4.1	13.6	11.5	6.2	6.0	10.2	3.6
Turkey	7.1	6.6	3.4	11.7	42.5	5.1	7.3	0.8	6.2	1.5	4.8	3.0
UK	2.7	8.6	1.7	4.0	41.2	1.1	10.5	8.8	11.8	3.6	4.8	1.3
USA	3.4	9.1	1.1	8.6	39.1	1.6	10.1	8.3	7.2	4.4	3.8	3.2
Overall total	**7.0**	**13.7**	**4.2**	**7.5**	**29.7**	**4.1**	**8.4**	**3.3**	**11.5**	**3.1**	**5.2**	**2.2**

* Data was missing for this and other questions from Gallup International data for Pakistan, China, and Brazil.
Source: http://www.transparency.org/surveys/barometer/barometer2003.html.

corruption from one of the following institutions, what would your first choice be?

According to this survey it is evident that the political parties are the ones with the highest percentage of corruption, followed by the justice system: courts and the police. These are the three areas that are very vital for conducting international business and have political and legal implications. The MNCs need to be aware of these issues, which also raise ethical and moral issues. Furthermore, as depicted in Exhibit 6.4, when asked about the future, more people expected corruption to increase rather

Exhibit 6.4

Colombians and Indonesians are most Optimistic that Corruption will Fall					
Country	Increase a lot (%)	Increase a little (%)	Stay the same (%)	Decrease a little (%)	Decrease a lot (%)	Don't know/no response (%)
The optimists					
Colombia	14.0	10.0	11.7	28.3	32.0	4.0
Croatia	7.8	10.8	30.2	34.6	9.2	7.4
Indonesia	10.0	7.8	25.9	41.0	13.7	1.6
Ireland	9.8	17.0	27.2	27.4	14.8	3.8
Palestinian Authority*					
The uncertain					
Costa Rica	32.3	9.1	16.2	24.2	15.2	3.0
Nigeria	27.9	16.6	8.2	18.0	20.6	8.6
The pessimists					
Cameroon	39.4	15.1	13.3	15.3	4.7	12.1
Georgia	34.6	20.6	11.5	9.2	1.3	22.8
India	55.8	18.5	13.6	6.7	1.2	4.1
Israel	19.0	39.5	23.0	7.4	1.6	9.6
The Netherlands	21.5	37.9	20.0	4.5	0.0	16.2
Norway	6.7	43.5	29.2	10.5	1.6	8.5
South Africa	36.1	14.7	13.5	19.3	10.8	5.6
Turkey	37.2	19.4	14.7	9.0	3.0	16.7
Overall total (%)	19.4	21.3	26.3	14.8	4.5	10.8

* The results from the Palestinian Authority are not included in the overall totals.

Exhibit 6.5

The Transparency International Bribe Payers Index 2002

Rank	Country	Score
1	Australia	8.5
2	Sweden	8.4
3	Switzerland	8.4
4	Austria	8.2
5	Canada	8.1
6	Netherlands	7.8
7	Belgium	7.8
8	United Kingdom	6.9
9	Singapore	6.3
10	Germany	6.3
11	Spain	5.8
12	France	5.5
13	United States	5.3
14	Japan	5.3
15	Malaysia	4.3
16	Hong Kong	4.3
17	Italy	4.1
18	South Korea	3.9
19	Taiwan	3.8
20	People's Republic of China	3.5
21	Russia	3.2
22	Domestic companies	1.9

Source: Transparency International, www.transparency.org.

than fall over the next three years. Three out of ten said that it would increase and one in five said that it would fall. One in four respondents expected the level of corruption to stay the same. In Colombia and Indonesia, the most optimistic people in the survey, a majority expected corruption levels to decrease. A clear majority of Cameroonians, Georgians, Indians, Israelis, Dutch, Norwegians, South Africans, and Turks expected corruption to increase in their countries.

Furthermore, Transparency International publishes the Transparency International Bribe Payers Index (Exhibit 6.5), which focuses on the supply side of corruption by ranking countries according to how many bribes are offered by their international businesses.

Eight hundred and thirty-five business experts in 15 leading emerging market countries were asked: In the business sectors with which you are most familiar, please indicate how likely companies from the following countries are to pay or offer bribes to win or retain business in this country?

A perfect score, indicating zero perceived propensity to pay bribes, is 10.0, and thus the ranking starts with companies from countries that are seen to have a low propensity for foreign bribe paying. All the survey data indicated that domestically owned companies in the 15 countries surveyed have a very high propensity to pay bribes—higher than that of foreign firms.

Russian, Chinese, Taiwanese, and South Korean companies are widely seen to be using bribes in developing countries. Furthermore, companies from Italy, Hong Kong, Malaysia, United States, Japan, France, and Spain have a high propensity to bribe overseas too. The construction and arms industries are the top sectors involved in bribery.

In Russia, President Putin is leading the Kremlin's biggest crackdown on corruption since the Soviet Union's collapse. A high-profile probe of suspect bureaucrats—as seen in the charges pending against Railways Minister Nikolai Aksyonenko for illegally spending Ministry funds—is making headlines. But a second less-sensational effort is the heart of this campaign: the drive to limit the myriad opportunities for bribery and pilferage that plague business and government.[23] Putin's rewrite of the Unified Energy System (Russia's electricity monopoly) restructuring plan is just one example of this so-called structural approach. Another is a new package of reforms, enacted on December 17, 2001, that aims to cut down on courtroom bribes by increasing judges' woeful salaries fivefold. The new law also bans the intervention of state prosecutors in private litigation between contending business parties.[24]

In conclusion, a skillful international manager cannot develop a suitable strategic plan or consider an investment abroad without first assessing the environment—political, legal, governmental—in which the company will operate and the risks involved. This assessment should result not so much in a comparison of countries as in a comparison of the relative risk and the projected return on investment among these countries. Similarly, for ongoing operations, both the subsidiary manager and headquarters management must continually monitor the environment for potentially unsettling events or undesirable changes that may require the redirection of certain subsidiaries or the entire company.

Clearly, the international manager must assess and manage a number of different kinds of risk in the global environment. When you consider, for example, the effects of the Asian economic crisis of the late 1990s on MNCs, the ability to effectively practice risk management will determine the success of international firms now and in the future.

As we have already seen in Chapter 2, the managerial functions and the daily operations of the firm are also affected by a subtle, but powerful, environmental factor in the host country—that of culture.

Closing Case

The Legal Aspects of a Joint Venture

What follows is a situation where we will negotiate a strategic alliance. For the sake of simplicity let's create a hypothetical equity joint venture (JV) between two partners of different nationalities and with roughly equal bargaining positions. The vehicle we shall use for this collaboration is a new business equity in which both partners take equity positions. We shall assume that the two partners have already agreed to go ahead with the alliance and have widely considered the strategic and financial implications of doing so. Their agreement currently exists in outline form only, possibly as a Memorandum of Understanding (MOU) or based on an oral understanding and a handshake. The partners have agreed to put into place a contract to cover the details of the alliance, and this contract is to be negotiated and drafted with the assistance of lawyers.

In establishing the JV, key clauses that set out the scope of the agreement and the partners' obligations to each other are to be negotiated. Major establishment issues to be considered include initial discussions, setting up the JV, the parties and framework of contract, performance clauses, restrictions on the partners, and liability. Here we will explore the negotiation process itself by considering the identity and role of negotiators and the interaction between managers and their lawyers. The intention here is to raise international managers' awareness of some of the salient issues and concerns that arise during the course of alliance negotiations.

Although lawyers play an important role in negotiating and drafting alliance agreements, no clear dividing line exists between so-called legal and business issues, and the commercial managers will often need to be involved in making decisions on the legalities mentioned here. For this reason, commercial managers may wish to consider some of their alternatives in advance so they know where they stand on the issues to be covered in the agreement and decide which proposals (partner restrictions, transfer of shares, etc.) they wish to put forward for negotiation. Negotiations normally involve at least two participants per partner—one commercial representative and one lawyer. Some companies prefer to have more representatives from different business areas, and often the lawyer will have at least one junior colleague involved. The more complex the JV, the more negotiators are likely to be involved. If more than two partners are entering into the alliance, negotiations become more complex, with representatives and lawyers of each partner needing to agree over the terms of the contract. If the JV is between companies from three different countries, for example Chile, the United States, and France, you can imagine how complex the negotiation process is from the legal, political, and cultural standpoint.

Source: Compiled by the author, April 2004.

The Challenge: What are the legal implications of the international JV?

Chapter Summary

This chapter has addressed a plethora of issues ranging from political, economic, and legal aspects of conducting international business. The political aspects of international business were discussed within the context of the government's role and the political risk undertaken by MNCs in pursuing entry into a foreign market. Various economic conditions were also described as a result of the political situation in a country. The political risk and the strategies for minimizing it were also discussed and references to terrorism and attacks in general were also presented as obstacles to foreign direct investment.

Review and Discussion Questions

1. How should the international managers deal with the foreign political environments?
2. What is political risk? How should international managers minimize the political risk?
3. How does the political environment affect the economy?
4. How does the legal environment affect international business? How should the international managers address the various legal challenges in different countries?
5. What ways are there in resolving international disputes?
6. What are the differences between Common, Civil, and Theocratic Law? How do international managers deal with these different types of laws?
7. What is corruption and how does it affect international business?
8. What is bribery and how is it being addressed by international agencies?

Endnotes

1. Howell, L. D. and Chaddick, B., "Models of Political Risk for Foreign Investment and Trade," *Columbia Journal of World Business*, Fall 1994.
2. Rugman, A. M. and Verbeke, A., *Global Corporate Strategy and Trade Policy* (New York: Routledge, 1990); D. B. Yoffie, "How an Industry Builds Political Advantage," *Harvard Business Review* (May–June 1988): 82–89.
3. Daniels, J. D., Radebaugh, L. H. and Sullivan, D. P., *International Business. Environments and Operations*, 10th edn (Pearson: Prentice Hall), 2004, p. 671.

4. McFarlin, D. B. and Sweeney, P. D., *International Management. Trends, Challenges and Opportunities* (Southwestern, Thompson Publishing, 1998), pp. 555–556.

5. Griffin, R. W. and Pustay, M. W., *International Business*, 4th edn (Pearson: Prentice Hall, 2005), p. 59.

6. Ibid., p. 60.

7. Ibid.

8. "Court Ruling on Islamic Banking Poses a Challenge for Pakistan Interests," *Financial Times* (January 4, 2000), p. 2.

9. "Court Orders Islamabad to Ban Interest," *Financial Times* (December 24/25, 1999), p. 4.

10. "Pakistani Court Rules That Interest Is Illegal," *Houston Chronicle* (December 24, 1999), p. 2C.

11. Robbins, S. P. and Stuart-Koze, R., *Management* (Prentice Hall: Canada, 1990), pp. 4–11.

12. Ibid.

13. Transparency International, *Transparency International releases new Bribe Payers Index (BPI) 2002*, press release (May 14, 2002).

14. Asian Development Bank, *Anti-Corruption Policy: Description and Answers to Frequently Asked Questions* (Manila, 1999), p. 5.

15. The US has introduced a "Millennium Challenge Account," for instance, which will give aid only to countries that prove that they are fighting corruption and introducing market-friendly policies. The UK government has also announced a new source of funding for development, the International Finance Facility, which will be accompanied by "tough conditionality (insisting) on corruption-free regimes that pursue stable, equitable and sustainable economic growth." *See* Brown, G., "An assault on poverty is vital too," *The Guardian* (February 13, 2003), p. 22.

16. "The Short Arm of the Law," *The Economist* (February 28, 2002).

17. Control Risks Group, *Facing Up to Corruption—Survey Results 2002* (London, 2002), p. 5.

18. US Government, "Third Annual Report to Congress: Implementation of the OECD Anti-bribery Convention," 29 June 2001. www.usinfo.state.gov/topical/econ/group8/summit01062905.html. The OECD Convention on Combating Bribery of Foreign Public Officials in International Business Transactions was signed by all 30 OECD countries as well as four non-OECD countries (Argentina, Brazil, Bulgaria and Chile) in 1997 came into effect in February 1999 after six of the major OECD countries ratified it. The Convention now has 35 signatory countries (Slovenia signed in late 2001), of which 34 have ratified it.

19. Progress Against Corruption. Efforts accelerate to make governments more transparent and accountable. Maidment, F. (ed.) Annual Editions, *International Business, 03/04* (McGraw-Hill/Dushkin), 12th edn, pp. 89–90.

20. The 1977 Foreign Corrupt Practices Act (FCPA) criminalizes the payment of brides to foreign government officials and political parties by US businesses. It requires companies to keep accurate and detailed accounts reflecting all transactions. But it specifically excludes facilitation payments.

21. Hellman, J., Jones, G. and Kaufmann, D., "Are Foreign Investors and Multinationals Engaging in Corrupt Practices in Transition Economies?" *Transition* (May–July 2000), pp. 5–6.

22. Ibid., p. 4.

23. Starobin, P. and Belton, C., "Cleanup Time in Russia," *Business Week online* (January 14, 2002).

24. Ibid.

7

Global Strategic Planning

Objectives

Through this chapter, the student will be exposed to:

- Understand the definition and importance of the global strategic planning process (GSPP)
- The significance of foreign markets in relation to the GSPP
- Understand the strategic formulation process
- Draft objectives and strategies within a global framework.

Opening Case

Diebold

For most of its 142-year history, Diebold, Inc., never worried much about global strategy. As a premier name in bank vaults and then automated teller machines (ATMs) and security systems the North Canton (Ohio)-based company focused on US financial institutions, content to let partners hawk what they could abroad. But in 1998, with the US ATM market saturated, Diebold decided it had to be more ambitious.

Since then, Diebold has taken off. Sales of security devices, software, and services surged 38 percent last year, to $1.74 billion, led by a 146 percent jump in overseas sales, to $729 million. The momentum has continued this year. With ATM factories in Asia, Latin America, and Europe, international sales have gone from 22 percent of the total to 40 percent in just two years, and will soon overtake North America.

The ventures overseas have taken Diebold to whole new directions. In China where it now has half of the fast-growing ATM market, it is also helping the giant International Commercial Bank of China design its self-service branches and data network. In Brazil, Diebold owns and manages a network of 5000 ATMs, as well as surveillance cameras, for a state-owned bank. In Colombia, it's handling bill collection for a power utility. In Taiwan, where most consumers still prefer to pay bills in cash, Diebold is about to introduce ATMs that both accept and count stacks of up to 100 currency notes and weed out counterfeits. And in South Africa, its ATMs for the techno-illiterate scan fingerprints for identification.

Diebold didn't plunge willy-nilly into overseas markets. "We tend to put a high emphasis on analyzing the daylights out of things before we go in," says Michael J. Hillock, Diebold's international operations president. In the 1980s, wary of doing it alone, it used foreign electronics giant Philips to distribute its ATMs, before forging a manufacturing and sales joint venture with IBM. By 1998, though, it needed faster overseas growth to lift its bottom line. And Diebold figured it knew enough to assert more control over foreign operations. So, Diebold bought IBM's stake, snapped up the ATM units of France's Groupe Bull and Holland's Getronics, gained majority ownership of its China ATM manufacturing venture, and bought Brazilian partner Procomp Amazonia Industria Electronica, a top Latin American electronics company.

Diebold found it could serve much broader needs in emerging markets than in the United States. Across Latin America, consumers use banks to pay everything from utility bills to taxes. So Diebold ATMs handle these services, 24 hours a day. In Argentina, where filing taxes is a nightmare, citizens can now fill out returns on a PC, store them on disk, and have their disks scanned on one of 5000 special Diebold terminals, most of them at banks. Red Link, which owns the biggest network for the tax service, gave Diebold the job because "they are extremely flexible and can adapt technology to solve any problem," says Commercial Manager Armando Avagnina. Diebold is also landing new contracts across Latin America to manage bank ATM networks.

The $240 million acquisition of Brazil's Procom also gave Diebold an entree into an entirely new line: It landed a huge contract to supply electronic voting machines for Brazil's presidential election last year. Now Diebold is getting into the voting machine business in the United States. Globalization, it seems, can even unveil new opportunities in the home country.

Question: What is Diebold's international challenge? What is your opinion of Diebold's international strategy?

Source: Business Week, August 20, 2001, Issue 3746, p. 138.

Introduction

Beyond the standard steps in a traditional business plan, strategic planning is geared especially to the objective of being competitive. The degree to which an individual, an enterprise, a nation, or a region can produce goods and services that meet the tests of global marketplace while maintaining or increasing real income is even more dependent on operational processes, not just products and markets. Of growing importance to products and markets are the questions of how the product is made; how it is taken to the market; how it is received, sold, and serviced in the market; and how it changes in relation to the changing environment.

How the manager as an individual, the firm as an organization, the industry as a sector, the state as an economic policymaker, and the region as an economic actor factor into these processes are crucial aspects of strategic planning for competitiveness. Planning per se means looking for threats, opportunities, strengths, and weaknesses, and devising strategies to exploit or counter particular aspects of the overall environment. It is future-oriented but sensitive to the past. It is a process within which decisions are designed before they are taken and evaluated so as to increase the probability of a successful outcome.

Overview on Global Strategic Planning

Global planning necessitates an awareness that decisions taken by managers, firms, industries, nations, and regions are done so in a cross-cultural environment.

Competitiveness is now a global fact of business life, and all companies must think internationally and plan globally. Even if the company in question markets its products only domestically, its strategic planning must take into consideration the nature of its industry worldwide, the policies of its national government on international issues, its overall regional environment, and even global trade and financial issues among others. The company's external environmental considerations (e.g., national trade balance) and internal environment (e.g., labor–management relations in the firm) must be factored into the process of planning. How these external and internal aspects affect its competitiveness is core to strategic planning and, therefore, is more than acquiring a competitive advantage. It is strategy to come with competition, to achieve competitiveness.

Much of the literature on achieving competitiveness has focused on structural aspects of the business environment, which should be taken into consideration by corporate strategic planners. It is almost uniformly accepted that the radius of competition for all companies is global, whether or not one accepts Kenichi Ohmae's "borderless world" concept.[1] The myth of "bigness equals advantage" has been discarded in favor of organizational responsiveness to changing markets. Acquisitions, takeovers, and diversification have all been reexamined in terms of their conventional wisdom; strategic planning as a process has been key to these developments.

Furthermore, it is essential in the approach taken here to keep the focus of strategic planning itself on processes as a guide to looking at the global political economy. The collected works of strategic analysts such as Porter,[2] Hammer,[3] Lorange,[4] can be presented under the general concept of "re-engineering." But it is crucial to understand that re-engineering as a tenet of strategic planning is not quite the same as the more limited notion of cost-effectiveness and accountability typically achieved by downsizing.

Re-engineering insists on a broad review of a company's (with our levels of analysis approach one could also say a nation's or region's) business processes and then evaluating them in relation to the changing conditions and demands of the global environment. Constantly redesigning and reevaluating the operating processes in a firm or industry or nation can facilitate competitiveness in markets worldwide.

Over time, management theorists have been frequently caught in self-contradictions. Yesterday big was beautiful; today small is sensitive. Once control equated with excellence, now chaos is the core of creativity. (For a long time, one management school argued that competitive advantage could best be attained by a company adjusting to its own unique situation, only to be then confronted by a school advocating the universal principle of the experience curve.) With some theorists the stress is on generic strategies of a given industry, while with others the emphasis is on each enterprise taking an independent strategy to success. The levels of analysis quagmire continues with those who argue that globalization has made national economic policies obsolete on the one hand and those who counter that the same process of globalization has led to association of like national types into regional groupings, in a sense revitalizing national identity. Of special interest to the process of global strategic planning is the debate on the issue of "managerial universalism," or the notion that there is one set of management principles applicable to firms of any national origin or in any national setting. Opposed to this notion is the theory that specific countries should conform to their cultural traditions, perhaps collectivist in one case and individualist in another.

Whether the strategic planner is re-engineering the operational processes in response to conditions internal to the firm or external to the firm, there is increasingly a consensus that overcoming borders and boundaries and creating mechanisms for cooperation and synergy are a necessity for achieving competitiveness. Forming teams from among the divisional structures within the enterprise, forming alliances with suppliers and customers, and forming venture partnerships in other markets all point to innovative operating processes at work. Strategic planning by firms in a global environment also denotes the necessity of understanding the interrelatedness of processes that allow border crossing inside and outside the enterprise. Monitoring change in the global environment and then adjusting internal operating processes to meet the challenge can in turn lead to new products and markets. This continual interplay of understanding operating processes internal and external to the firm in relation to one another forms the process of global strategic planning.

One need not succumb to the optimism of Peter Drucker,[5] who believes that global strategic management will lead to improved international relations because the mutual self-interests of global managers will force national political leaders to their point of view, in order to understand the principle of "universal localism" espoused by Akio Morita, the retired Chairman of Sony Corporation.

It is worth spending some time on Sony Corporation and Akio Morita, the man behind Sony's success. Akio Morita is a man who created one of the first global corporations. He saw long before his contemporaries that a shrinking world could present enormous opportunities for a company that could think beyond its own borders, both physically and psychologically. And he pursued that strategy with his relentless brand of energy in every market, particularly the United States. It wasn't a coincidence that some years ago Sony was rated the No. 1 brand name by American consumers, ahead of Coca-Cola and General Electric. Sony's globalization began in the United States, where Morita moved his entire family in 1963.[6] In that way he would understand Americans and their market, customs, and regulations, thereby increasing the chance of his company's success. It was a brilliant decision. From that year on, Sony began its journey to a successful global presence. Morita expanded his vision. Now it was "Think globally, act locally," that is have a common value system that transcends national objectives: serve international customers, shareholders and employees, regardless of the origin of the company.

Global strategic planning should point to processes achieving that objective. What is the global political economy within which these processes take place, and what in particular should we analyze and evaluate in that environment from a strategic planning perspective? These questions will be answered then.

Global Political Economy: Foreign Direct Investment, Trade, Financial Flow, and Technology Transfer.

Total foreign investment fell worldwide in 2003 for the third consecutive year, driven mainly by a slump in the industrialized world, but Africa and the Asia Pacific region enjoyed healthy rises in outside spending, according to a major UN report.[7] The report released by the UN Conference on Trade and Development (UNCTAD) argues that the outlook for the year ahead is promising, thanks to better economic growth, increasing corporate profits, higher stock prices, and more mergers and acquisitions (M&A). Foreign investment is also increasingly being targeted at services, especially the business, financial, telecommunications, and leisure industries, and away from manufacturing and primary industries. The annual report shows that foreign direct investment (FDI) inflows dropped 18 percent to $560 billion in 2001 from $679 billion in 2002—well below the $1.4 trillion mark reached in 2000.

The slow and irregular pace of economic recovery in the developed world—which dominates the overall FDI totals—was the biggest reason for the slide, with the United States (down 30 percent to its lowest levels since 1992) and the European Union (EU) (down 21 percent) both suffering. FDI inflows into Central and Eastern Europe also slumped, but the report's authors at UNCTAD forecast that the trend will turn around given that many of the region's nations joined the EU on May 1.

The picture in the developing world was more mixed, with Africa and the Asia Pacific—led by China—gaining overall, but Latin America and the Caribbean enduring another fall. The changes were unequal even within continents, with many of Africa's most impoverished countries unable to attract nearly as much FDI as their neighbors (Exhibit 7.1).

African states rich in natural resources, such as Morocco, Angola, Equatorial Guinea, Nigeria, and Sudan, attracted the bulk of the increased FDI to the continent—a total of $15 billion—whereas 24 countries received less than $100 million each.

Professor Jeffrey Sachs, Special Adviser to Secretary-General Kofi Annan on the Millennium Development Goals (MDGs), a set of eight, time-bound targets for reducing poverty and hunger and improving overall living standards, told a press briefing in September 22, 2004 that the outlook for the globe's poorest states remains bleak.

"Many of the poorest countries are simply being bypassed by globalization, and the promises of the rich countries are not being fulfilled," he said, adding that FDI is so important because it is one of the strongest engines for growth in the developing world. Professor Sachs said the solution was not to try to halt the forces of globalization but to make them fairer, and to pressurize affluent nations to meet their pledges.

> We need more globalization that reaches the poor countries, and more successful globalization, not less. The kind of globalization that the poorest countries are feeling is brain drain. They're not seeing the inflow of foreign investment.[8]

Exhibit 7.1

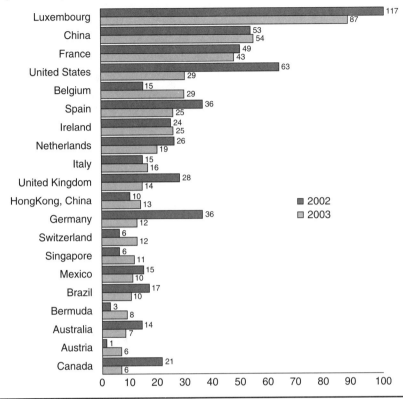

Top 20 Recipients of FDI Inflows, 2002 and 2003 (Billions of Dollars)

Source: UNCTAD, World Investment Report 2004.

FDI Inflows Down[9]

The UNCTAD notes that FDI flows to different regions and countries were uneven. Worldwide, 111 countries experienced a rise in FDI inflows and 82 a decline. Flows to developing countries as a group rose by 9 percent (from $158 billion in 2002 to $172 billion in 2003), but they varied by region. Africa recorded 28 percent more inflows in 2003 ($15 billion, up from $12 billion in 2002), driven mainly by natural resource projects. There was an increase in flows to 36 countries and a decline to 17. FDI flows to the Asia Pacific region reached $107 billion, up from $95 billion in 2002, with 36 countries receiving higher flows than in 2002 and 21 receiving lower inflows. Latin America and the Caribbean, however, experienced a fourth consecutive year of decline. But the decline was marginal—from $51 billion in 2002 to $50 billion. Of 40 countries in the region, 19 received lower inflows. The share of developing countries in global FDI inflows rose by 8 percentage points, to 31 percent in 2003.

After a record year in 2002, when inflows reached $31 billion, FDI flows to countries of Central and Eastern Europe (CEE) fell sharply in 2003, to $21 billion. FDI inflows were higher for 10 countries in the region and lower for 9. Inflows into the "accession-eight"—the Czech Republic, Estonia, Hungary, Latvia, Lithuania, Poland, Slovenia, and Slovakia—declined from $23 billion to $11 billion. FDI inflows to the Russian Federation also plunged, from $3.5 billion in 2002 to $1.1 billion in 2003. FDI flows to developed countries fell by 25 percent (from $490 billion in 2002 to $367 billion in 2003). Inflows in 2003 represented one third of the $1.1 trillion peak in 2000. FDI flows to the United States fell to $30 billion, the country's lowest level since 1992 and only a tenth of their peak in 2000–2001. Members of the EU, notably Germany and the United Kingdom, also recorded much lower inflows than in 2002, as did Japan. In all, FDI inflows were lower for 16 countries in the region and higher for 10.

FDI Outflows Up[10]

Unlike inflows, FDI outflows from developed countries rose in 2003, albeit marginally. The United States was again the main investor country (having lost this position to Luxembourg in 2002), with a 32 percent increase in outflows in 2003 (Exhibit 7.2). Outflows from the EU were down by 4 percent, even though outflows from France and the United Kingdom rose by 16 percent and 57 percent, respectively. Outflows from Germany declined by 70 percent, as parent company loans to their foreign affiliates fell. Japan's outflows continued to fall (−11 percent), mainly in the services sector, having also declined in 2002.

While uneven performance characterized outward FDI by developed countries, the world's 100 largest transnational corporations (TNCs) showed signs of resumed growth in terms of sales and employment in 2002, the latest year for which complete data on the companies are available. Nine of the top 10 among the 100 largest TNCs in the world ranked by foreign assets are based in three countries (France, the United Kingdom, and the United States). General Electric heads the list (Exhibit 7.3). Firms from developing countries too are increasingly becoming outward investors.

It is important to mention here that the most recent entrants to outward FDI are China, India, Brazil, and Mexico. Some examples of such international expansionary activities by businesses from emerging markets include the following:

- Lenovo, the largest manufacturer of PCs in China, acquired IBM's PC unit in December 2004, for US$1.2 billion.
- Haier, a household appliances Chinese company, has established manufacturing plants in South Carolina, USA.

Exhibit 7.2

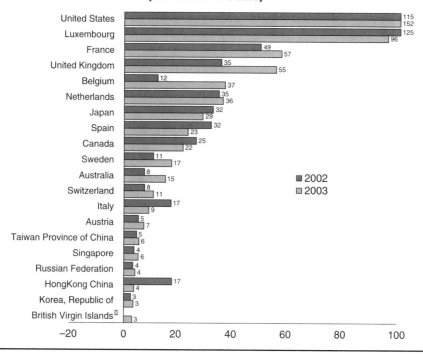

Top 20 Economies for Outward FDI, 2002, 2003
(Billions of Dollars)

Source: UNCTAD, World Investment Report 2004.

- TCL, the leading electronics business in China, recently bought the television arm of France's Thomson SA as well as the handset operations of France's Alcatel, SA.
- In 2004, AmBev (Companhia de Bebidas das Americas, a Brazilian company) merged with Interbrew to form InBev, the world's largest brewer in terms of volume.
- Ranbaxy, an Indian pharmaceutical company and leading manufacturer of generic drugs in the world, has expanded into Japan with further plans to buy its US rival.
- China Minmetals has proposed to buy Noranda, a leading Canadian mining and metals company, for US$5.74 billion.
- Cemex, a Mexican cement giant, recently took over its main American competitor, Southdown, and made it the largest cement producer in the United States.

Dynamic Growth of Services FDI[11]

What is being seen, however, is a dramatic shift toward the services sector. Indeed, today the services sector accounts for about 60 percent (Exhibit 7.4)

Exhibit 7.3

The World's Top Ten Nonfinancial TNCs, Ranked by Foreign Assets, 2002 (Millions of Dollars and Number of Employees)

Rank	Corporation	Home economy	Industry	Foreign			TNI %
				Assets	Sales	Employment	
1	General Electric	United States	Electrical and electronic equip-ment	229,001	45,403	150,000	40.6
2	Vodafone Group PIC	United Kingdom	Tele-communi-cations	207,622	33,631	56,667	84.5
3	Ford Motor Company	United States	Motor vehicles	165,024	54,472	188,453	47.7
4	British Petroleum Company PIC	United Kingdom	Petroleum expLitef./distr.	126,109	145,982	97,400	81.3
5	General Motors	United States	Motor vehicles	107,926	48,071	101,000	27.9
6	Royal Dutch/Shell Group	United Kingdom/The Nether-lands	Petroleum expLitef./distr.	94,402	114,294	65,000	62.4
7	Toyota Motor Corporation	Japan	Motor vehicles	79,433	72,820	85,057	45.7
8	Total Fina EF	France	Petroleum expLitef./distr.	79,032	77,461	68,554	74.9
9	France Telecom	France	Tele-communi-cations	73,454	18,187	102,016	49.6
10	ExxonMobil Corporation	United States	Petroleum expLitef./distr.	60,802	141,274	56,000	65.1

Source: UNCTAD, World Investment Report 2004.
"TNI" is the abbreviation for "Transnationality Index." The Transnationlity Index is calculated as the average of the following three ratios: foreign assets to total assets, foreign sales to total sales and foreign employment to total employment.

of the global inward FDI stock (equivalent to an estimated $4.4 trillion), compared to less than 50 percent a decade earlier. This share will increase,

Exhibit 7.4

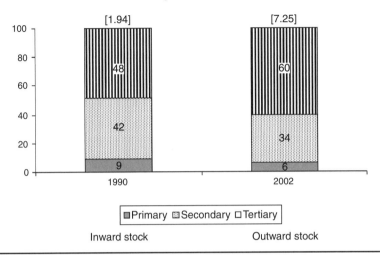

Global Inward FDI Stock, by Sector, 1990 and 2002, Percent

Primary ▪ Secondary ▤ Tertiary ☐

Inward stock   Outward stock

Note: Figures in brackets represent total values in trillions of dollars.
Source: UNCTAD, World Investment Report 2004.

as some two thirds of FDI flows are now (during 2001–2002) in services, valued at an average of $500 billion.

The shift of FDI toward services has gone hand-in-hand with a change in the industry mix of services FDI. While services FDI has traditionally concentrated on trade and finance, since 1990 FDI in several other service industries has shown dynamic growth. Notable among them are electricity, telecommunications, water services, and various business services. Thus, between 1990 and 2002, the value of total inward FDI stock in electricity, gas, and water rose from an estimated $10 billion to $144 trillion (mainly due to a large increase in FDI in electric power generation and distribution). The equivalent value in telecommunications, storage, and transport rose from an estimated $29 billion to $476 billion and in business activities from $126 billion to $1.1 trillion. Rapid growth in demand for these services, the increasing recognition of their importance for the efficiency and productivity of industries in all sectors, and policy liberalization in many countries have played an important part in the growth of FDI in these services. As a result, the combined share of these three groups in total inward FDI stock rose from 17 percent in 1990 to 41 percent in 2002, while that of trade and finance—still dominant in services FDI—fell from 25 percent and 40 percent, respectively, in 1990 to 18 percent and 29 percent in 2002. Two of the world's top ten TNCs are from the telecommunications industry (Exhibit 7.3).

What drives the shift of FDI toward services? Partly, it reflects the ascendancy of services in economies more generally[12] and the nontradable nature of services (i.e., most services need to be produced when and where they are consumed). Because of the latter, the principal way to bring services to foreign markets is through FDI. In addition, countries have liberalized their services FDI regimes, including through the privatization of state-owned utilities. Finally, service firms invest more and more abroad as they seek new clients and exploit their own ownership advantages, frequently spurred on by competitive pressures.

FDI Prospects

Prospects for global FDI are expected to be positive in both the short term (2004–2005) and the medium term (2006–2007). The extent and the speed of the FDI recovery, however, will vary by region and industry. Despite the FDI recovery, competition for FDI is expected to remain fierce in the years to come. The stage for the expected FDI recovery is set by the acceleration of global gross domestic product (GDP) growth, the relatively low levels of interest rates in major capital exporting economies, and the increase in domestic investment and industrial output. Corporate profits of TNCs are also rising, as are stock valuations. All groups surveyed by UNCTAD agreed that investment confidence is returning and that global FDI flows are likely to increase during the period 2004–2007.

Services are expected to be the sector most attractive to FDI, particularly in tourism, telecommunications, and IT. Prospects for manufacturing are also expected to be good, although they might vary by industry. Electronics, automobiles, and machinery are expected to perform better.

The primary sector is expected to see a moderate FDI recovery. Asia and Central and Eastern Europe are viewed as the most attractive regions for FDI, while relatively weaker FDI recovery is expected in Western Europe and Africa in 2006–2007—and in Latin America in 2006–2007. The top FDI recipients for 2006–2007 are likely to be China and India in Asia; South Africa and Egypt in Africa; Brazil and Mexico in Latin America; the Caribbean, Poland, and Russia in Central and Eastern Europe; and the United States and the United Kingdom among the industrialized countries. The United States, the United Kingdom, France, Germany, and Japan will continue to be the main sources of FDI, but newcomers such as China and South Africa will also be on the list of top FDI providers.

Mergers and acquisitions are expected to resume their popularity in developed economies, while greenfield investments will be preferred in developing countries. The surge in offshoring worldwide indicates that lower labor cost countries will benefit most from FDI, in activities such as production, logistics and support, and sales and marketing. Infrastructure and skill-dependent investments will also expand in certain countries. Policy competition for FDI is getting fierce. Most host countries are expected to intensify their efforts in investment targeting, in addition to offering more generous investment incentives and further liberalization. These generally positive trends may be counterbalanced by a number of risk factors, including oil price volatility, the rise of new protectionism impeding trade and outward FDI, regional conflicts, and increased threats from terrorism. Also on the downside, some major developed and developing countries continue to struggle with structural impediments to economic growth and FDI flows. Overall, the positive factors will outweigh the negative ones, although the recovery will be modest when compared to the 1999–2000 FDI boom driven by massive M&A deals.

Prospects for Major Host and Home Countries

Top Destinations for FDI

The largest recipients of FDI flows in each region are expected to be the most likely destinations of FDI in the future too, with some important exceptions. In Asia for instance, India was ranked right behind China, even though it is yet to become a major FDI recipient in the region (Exhibit 7.5). Thailand's third place is also somewhat surprising considering that there are several countries in Asia that have received more FDI than Thailand in the past.

In Africa, South Africa and Nigeria are the only sub-Saharan countries in the list of the top five destinations for the continent as a whole. The

Exhibit 7.5

Bright Spots for FDI as Ranked by FDI Experts, 2004–2005

Region/ country	Africa	Asia and the Pacific	Latin America and the Caribbean	Central and Eastern Europe	Developed economies
Top 1	South Africa	China	Brazil	Poland	United States
Top 2	Egypt	India	Mexico	Russian Federation	United Kingdom
Top 3	Morocco Nigeria	Thailand	Argentina	Hungary Czech Republic	Canada
Top 4	–	Vietnam Republic of Korea	Chile	–	Germany
Top 5	Algeria	–	Venezuela	Romania	Japan

Source: UNCTAD, www.unctad.org/fdiprospects.

other three top destinations are Egypt, Morocco, and Algeria. The responses suggest that a country's natural resources, rather than its level of economic or political stability, determine the likeliness of receiving increased FDI in the future in the region.

In Latin America and the Caribbean, the traditional FDI powerhouses—Brazil, Mexico, Argentina, and Chile—are on top of the list, with Venezuela in fifth place. Brazil leads the way by a huge margin.

In the CEE region, Poland is placed on top (ahead of the Russian Federation) because of its accession to the EU. The high rankings of Hungary and the Czech Republic can also be attributed in part to EU accession. The rankings, however, point to the emergence of a more complex picture than just a mere accession versus nonaccession divide in CEE countries. For example, Romania, a nonaccession country, ranks among the top five in the region. These results could revive discussions on the applicability of the "flying geese" model used to describe industrial restructuring in Southeast Asia to the CEE countries (UNCTAD, 2003). The accession countries continue to receive FDI with an increasing share of upgraded and high value-added investments, while investments based mainly on low labor costs are gradually shifting to other countries in the region, including Romania, where accession-driven pressure on prices and wages has not yet set in.

In the case of developed countries, Canada and Japan were designated as the most attractive destinations by respondents, which is somewhat surprising, especially since Japan has only relatively recently begun to seek FDI actively. Japan's high ranking might be explained by the renewed trust of investors and the country's economic recovery after years of stagnation. These results, however, should be interpreted with caution. They do not mean that the respondents expect the countries in top places to receive the largest FDI flows in absolute terms. Rather, the results point to the business opportunities for firms in their respective industries, even if their scale of operations in those developing countries is smaller.

Leading Sources of FDI

For the first time, a developing country, China, has made the list of the expected top five home countries worldwide in terms of geographical coverage (2004–2005), replacing Japan, which traditionally has been a significant home country (Exhibit 7.5).[13] Many developing countries rank China second after the United States as an expected country of origin for FDI. This may be because so far Chinese TNC ventures abroad have raised expectations on the part of developing country IPAs as to the likelihood of attracting additional Chinese investment. The phenomenon is particularly significant because it underscores China's growing importance as regards FDI, not only as a host but also as a home country. However, in terms of the value of individual FDI projects, Chinese investment is still smaller than that of traditional home countries.

The Role of the Transnational Corporations

Transnational corporations are envisioned as engines of growth partly because of their role in providing capital and training, stimulating trade, and generating and transmitting technology and innovation. Thus crucial to any global strategic planning approach is the awareness of the linkage FDI provides among trade, financial, and technological flows. The significance of strategic planning by managers is heightened by the assumption that FDI to some degree determines the flow of trade, capital, and technology.

If in fact TNCs determine to some extent international patterns of trade flows, the transfer of technology across national borders, and the international allocation of finance, have national economic policies of both home and host countries become less effective in proportion to the role of the TNCs? With an acknowledged growth in the volume of international trade occurring within TNCs in the form of intrafirm trade across national borders, can national policies in such areas as immigration and exchange rates continue to be effective with respect to achieving desired volumes of imports and exports? International production as an economic stimulant has led to increased attention to factors that influence FDI, such as host country geopolitical position, human and material resources, and values (e.g., work ethic). Foreign production plays a role in the growth and direction of regional economic groupings such as NAFTA and the EU. The distribution of foreign production by TNCs seems to affect international labor migrations. But it is equally clear that TNCs have a demonstrable impact on qualitative aspects of development. Social, cultural, and political characteristics are affected by FDI in the host country. Positive and negative effects can be seen in changing lifestyles, consumption patterns, labor force composition, health, safety and environment cost, and management practices in the cross-border transfer of business culture by TNCs. Labor unions are another area of impact to be assessed as a result of the growing role of TNCs. To what extent will TNCs allow unions to represent workers in intrafirm decision processes? To what extent might labor unite internationally to achieve leverage against the power of TNCs?

The sometimes contradictory considerations of the need to reap the rewards of participating in the international division of labor on the one hand and of controlling the adverse effects of worldwide competition on the other have resulted in increased attention being paid to the problem of achieving balanced restructuring of companies and nations alike. The next chapter will present the view that there is an almost universal reassessment of the relative roles of state and market, but the process is especially significant in the emerging markets. The necessity of the efficient use and allocation of resources in a global environment beset by debt, diminished private credit, and reluctant multilateral development funding points to the ever-increasing role played by foreign private investment as a source of capital.

Thus FDI can be seen as instrumental in human and material resource development, and trade development. Strategic planners must be able to monitor the impact of the corporation crossing borders on the host country in all aspects of human resource development. Linkages between government, industry, and education in this process are vital. Management skills, job training and retraining, and employment enhancement, as opposed to simple employment creation, are factors to be considered in the strategic planning process. An understanding of the human and material resource base of the recipient of FDI will add to the understanding of technology transfer and its impact on host country economic development.

Since export orientation is a key element in most developing countries' strategies for economic development, FDI and its relationship to trade should be understood. Corporations crossing national borders with innovative production techniques and market linkages will impact trade in terms of foreign exchange earnings. Domestic producers will also be affected by the diffusion of marketing information and methods.

The macroeconomic picture of FDI provides important pointers for the strategic planning process. Regionalization of the global political economy, already established by the international trade patterns of previous decades, is now reinforced in the trends of FDI. It is to this aspect of the framework for global strategic planning that attention has been drawn.

There is a growing bias to regional affiliation as a result of the Triad— North America, European Economic Area, and Japan—domination. If just five developing countries account for over half of the total flow of FDI into the developing world, how can others join the process? Once again, one must look at the linkages of FDI to trade, financial flow, and technology transfer to understand the current preference for these five: Brazil, China, Hong Kong, Mexico, and Singapore. The message is clear: participate in regional integration. There is a message delivered to developed nations as well. If TNCs target regions rather than individual countries as FDI sites, then national governments should form their FDI policies in the regional context. This logic is important for foreign investor strategic planners as well as for those who formulate regional and national policies to attract investment.

Strategic planners in donor and recipient countries should heed warnings. If governments such as Germany and Italy hold constant their taxes as a percent of GDP, while maintaining current levels of spending, public-sector debt would rise 400 percent and 700 percent by the year 2030. When governments borrow, they divert savings from productive investments. The

2 trillion dollar need in China for the next decade must be viewed with some consternation against a possible 10 trillion dollar level of borrowing if current government policies are not reversed.

Further integration of the global capital market is one hedge against this rise. Debt-ridden governments are all being forced to pay bigger risk premiums. The prices of financial instruments with similar risks should converge across markets. The continuing liberalization of financial markets, the trend toward securitization and tradability of financial assets, and more effective management of risks and returns through the use of derivatives are all indicators of erasing barriers between domestic financial markets.

The trend toward services in FDI is evident at the global regime level as well as at the level of the TNC. The Uruguay Round of General Agreement on Tariffs and Trade (GATT) placed services high on the agenda of policy-makers worldwide. In the General Agreement on Trade in Services (GATS), a comprehensive framework for the liberalization of investment and trade in services is envisioned. Aside from the success or failure of the agreement, the recognition that global competitiveness is correlated with access to modern producer services is moving countries in the same direction. Strategic planners at all levels and on both sides (donor and recipient) must share a heightened awareness that FDI in services will be crucial for development in emerging markets, again particularly for the transitional economies. Corporate strategists, national policymakers, and regional actors must assess the costs and benefits of liberalizing FDI, trade, and supplier movement in services. What are the structures and how to implement them? Can strategic planners steer a course between regional protectionism and liberalized FDI/free trade? Answers to the question rest not only on sound fiscal policy and resultant national financial stability, but also on the knowledge of markets and resultant success of FDI.

Though continued economic reform will be the sine qua non for sustained economic growth in the developing economies, trade and FDI can act to insure those measures and their institutionalization in the transitional economies. In the first instance, however, it is necessary to underline the importance of understanding that trade and FDI are not zero-sum games. Strategic planners must view the existing structure of trade and investment or core—periphery relations potential in human and material resources and value systems of market targets in the context of mutual enrichment.

It is concluded here with a rejoinder to the claims that free trade and liberalized FDI will lead to mass unemployment and wage inequality as a result of mass migration by TNCs to areas of cheap land and labor. This is no truer than the claims of some in developing countries that being a target of advanced industrial systems will serve to widen the income gap and deplete their resource base. In the 1950s and 1960s, the developing world argued that trade with the developed countries was a threat to their own industrial development. The "victims" of that era have now been transformed into the "villains" of the contemporary era. The advanced industrial nations now worry about competition from the less-developed nations rather than about their economic development. The irony is that developing world growth rates mean less poverty for them and more business opportunities for the developed world. Each of the emerging markets to be viewed offers specialized opportunity matches (buyer—supplier, joint venture) for potential investors and traders in terms of their individualized core—periphery relations, human and material resources, and value systems.

The strategic planning process in companies, countries, and regions from donor and recipient perspectives must systematically address these components in relation to one another. Strategic planners have no choice but to concentrate on (and capitalize on) the opportunities of this reciprocal process. Increased transactions by TNCs and further integration of world markets have spawned both "forward" and "reverse" linkages. Developing world market targets now constitute not only export markets but also competition for the developed world. Re-engineering to take advantage of this global demand—supply relationship between developed and developing nations is a direct challenge for global strategic planners.

The Strategic Planner in a Global Multicultural Environment

Moving into the twenty-first century, managers around the world will be faced with additional challenges. They will be expected to find more and better ways of better managing resources: human, financial, physical, and informational. As Elashmawi and Harris put it, "some organizations will attempt to survive these new challenges by staying on the leading edge of product development and technology, or by introducing more automation and robotics. Other institutions invest in helping their people to work smarter, so as to better meet customer needs."[14] The latter seems to be the most appropriate multicultural management strategy, for the private and/or nonprofit sectors. For global competitiveness and success, organizations of today need the multicultural manager who must possess the necessary cultural sensitivity and skills to enable their organizations to adapt to the foreign countries' overall environment.

These multicultural managers should be able to do the following:

- Think beyond local perceptions, and transform stereotypes into positive views of people.
- Prepare for new mind shifts while eliminating old mindsets.

- Re-create cultural assumptions, norms, and practices based on new insights and experiences.
- Reprogram their mental maps and constructs.
- Adapt readily to new and unusual circumstances and lifestyles.
- Welcome and facilitate transitional experiences.
- Acquire multicultural competencies and skills, including foreign languages.
- Create cultural synergy whenever and wherever feasible.
- Operate effectively in multinational/multicultural environments.
- Envision transnational opportunities and enterprises.
- Create optimistic and doable scenarios for future.

Furthermore, multicultural managers are (as adapted from Simons, Vazquez, and Harris, 1993):[15]

- Students of worldwide human relations and values.
- Open and flexible in dealing with diversity in people.
- Comfortable with those from different disciplines, fields, backgrounds, races, and genders.
- Facilitators of newcomers, strangers, minorities, and immigrants to the workplace.
- Collaborators in joint ventures, consortia, or coalitions.
- Planned change agents and futurists.

The multicultural strategic planner will have to become familiar with the value systems across cultures. This will assist the organization operating in a country's market to implement its strategies with the minimal resistance to change (new strategies to be implemented). The strategic planner will prepare the ground for strategy implementation for his/her organization in the foreign culture, by becoming familiar with the cultural values of the people involved in the strategic planning process and more importantly during the implementation stage. As an illustration, Exhibit 7.6 compares certain contrasting values of American, Japanese, and Arab cultures. The value of freedom is listed as the top one—freedom to choose your own destiny—whether it leads to success or failure. In contrast, the Japanese culture finds a higher value in belonging. In this culture, one must belong to and support a group to survive. Belonging to a group is more important to Japanese culture than individualism. Arab culture is less concerned with individualism or belonging to a group. In contrast, it concentrates on maintaining family security and relying on Allah for destiny. This individual destiny is based most of the time on the person's family background and position.

The importance the American culture places on independence and individual freedom of choice obviously leads to the idea that everyone is equal

Exhibit 7.6

Cultural Contrasts in Value

Americans	Japanese	Arabs
1. Freedom	1. Belonging	1. Family security
2. Independence	2. Group harmony	2. Family harmony
3. Self-reliance	3. Collectiveness	3. Parental guidance
4. Equality	4. Age/seniority	4. Age
5. Individualism	5. Group consensus	5. Authority
6. Competition	6. Cooperation	6. Compromise
7. Efficiency	7. Quality	7. Devotion
8. Time	8. Patience	8. Very patient
9. Directness	9. Indirectness	9. Indirectness
10. Openness	10. Go-between	10. Hospitality
11. Aggressiveness	11. Interpersonal	11. Friendship
12. Informality	12. Hierarchy	12. Formal/admiration
13. Future-orientation	13. Continuation	13. Past and present
14. Risk-taking	14. Conservative	14. Religious belief
15. Creativity	15. Information	15. Tradition
16. Self-accomplishment	16. Group achievement	16. Social recognition
17. Winning	17. Success	17. Reputation
18. Money	18. Relationship	18. Friendship
19. Material possessions	19. Harmony with nature	19. Belonging
20. Privacy	20. Networking	20. Family network

Source: Farid Elashmawi and Philip R. Harris, Multicultural Management 2000, Gulf Publishing Company, 1998, p. 72.

regardless of age, social status, or authority. Japanese and Arab cultures, however, place more value on age and seniority. The Japanese will always give way to the feelings of the group; the Arabs on the other hand show respect to authority and value seniority and status.

The phrase "time is money" is commonly accepted as a framework in the American culture, for the desire to finish a task in the shortest amount of time with the greatest possible profit. The Japanese on the other hand value high quality over immediate gain, and they patiently wait for the best possible result. The Arabs also value quality more than fast results but the trust in the business relationship is the most important value.

The American culture encourages individual achievement and results orientation. Thus, the Americans value directness and openness when dealing with others; consequently, individuals are encouraged to finish tasks faster. Because of these values of directness and equality, Americans tend to be informal when speaking and writing, often using first names. The

Japanese, on the other hand, prefer to follow an indirect, harmonious style while dealing with others. Go-betweens help to accelerate the process, and a harmonious relationship is more important than confrontation. The Arab culture avoids confrontation as well, but the Arabs prefer to negotiate directly in the spirit of hospitality and friendship until a compromise is reached.

Americans are future-oriented, which explains why Americans take risks. Americans accomplish tasks fast and that brings the future closer. The Japanese, however, view time as a continuum, and are long-term-oriented. As a result of that and the fact that they value quality relationships, the Japanese tend to be conservative and patient. In contrast, the Arabs believe that the present is a continuation of the past and that whatever happens in the future is due to fate and the will of Allah (Inshallah).

Individual achievement is an important value in American culture. When someone accomplishes something based on individual effort, he/she expects and receives recognition for being a creative person or the one who developed the best idea. The Japanese, because they value the group, seek information in order to help the entire group succeed. For the Arabs, preserving tradition is more important than the individual. Arabs measure success by social recognition, status, honor, and reputation.[16]

According to Harris and Moran "global leaders are required to meet, socialize, and negotiate with foreign business people and government officials on a regular basis."[17] In other words, the global strategic planner should be able to communicate and work with people who have grown up and who have been socialized in a different cultural environment. For the global strategic planner to be effective, he or she must be aware of the many beliefs and values that underlie his/her country's business practices, management techniques, and strategies. The awareness of such values is critical for the global strategic planner who wishes to transfer technology to another culture or who wishes to collaborate with people who have different values and assumptions. It is interesting to note that the same authors offer a framework of strategic collaborations within a multicultural context by stating: "To create opportunities for collaboration, global leaders must learn not only the customs, courtesies, and business protocols of their counterparts from other countries but they must also understand the national character, management philosophies, and mindsets of the people."[18]

This is what one executive from an international company from Belarus stated in an interview about global strategic planning and culture:

> Being in a transport and logistics business we have to interact with people from different countries all over the world. Some of them are very pleasant, some extremely short-tempered, some enjoy making fast decisions, some get

easily hurt, and so on and so forth. So, in order to be accepted as a partner, set our rules of the game where appropriate, and most importantly not to offend our potential business partners, we have to know and understand the culture of different countries, and adjust our strategy accordingly. Thus, both culture and international strategy are very important in the strategic planning process.

Mikhail Podolinski, Karat-Expeditsiya, Belarus

Closing Case

Going Globally and Acting Locally: The Case of Matsushita 30

In 1918, Konosuke Matsushita founded the Matsushita firm, which has become the world's largest consumer electronics firm. From that time until his death in 1989, he impressed the world with his leadership in manufacturing high-quality, high-volume, and low-priced products, and in his caring and loyal approach to employees. Matsushita spent more than 30 years expanding around the world, unstoppable like a bulldozer, but at the same time careful, making few mistakes. Matsushita currently has more than 150 production and R&D bases in 38 countries. Global brands such as Panasonic and National were part of revenues in 1994, with 20 percent in video equipment; 13 percent in home appliances; 12 percent in electronic components; and the rest in entertainment, audio equipment, and kitchen products. Around the world, the workday starts with workers singing the company song about how their work is in noble pursuit of everyone's future welfare.

Yoichi Morishita, current president, has continued Matsushita's success in going global, transplanting high-level manufacturing skills into mini-Matsushitas—factories producing a variety of products in Europe, the Middle East, America, Latin America, and Africa. But though experts are going global, Matsushita has also had to work hard to localize all aspects of its businesses, including the procurement of local management; the company was quick to recognize the difficulties in operating in various cultures, political and economic systems, languages, currencies, voltages, and so on. It has encouraged its overseas plants to develop products and marketing plans so as to tailor the home appliances and electronic devices to the needs of local customers, such as designing the cooking controls on microwave ovens differently in Europe to accommodate cooking and food preferences of, for example, both the British and the Germans.

In addition to localizing product design, manufacturing, and marketing strategies, Matsushita adapted to different cultures and work habits from

Kuala Lumpur, Malaysia, to Beijing. The US company cafeterias in Malaysia, for example, provide different ethnic foods for the diverse employees, which includes Muslim Malays, ethnic Chinese, and Indians. Special prayer rooms are set aside for Muslim prayer sessions, allowing two sessions per shift.

Matsushita's founder also founded the company's policy to be a good corporate citizen in every country when he said: "When you go abroad don't eat another person's pie." When Matsushita took over a National Semiconductor plant at Puyallup, Washington, in the United States, for example, Matsushita brought in its no-layoff policy and guaranteed a job for every employee who wanted to stay, even keeping people at their existing salaries when they were assigned to lesser positions. Both sides had to get used to some differences, though, since the company asked for more efficient practices: The Japanese, for instance, had to get used to the fact that, at five 0' clock, the Americans go home, whereas in Japan, they stay until the work is finished. In China the company is working on encouraging teamwork, which the Chinese lack. In addition, Matsushita is trying to accommodate employees' needs by providing them with housing and a preschool for their children. In Malaysia, where Matsushita employs 23,500 people in its 13 new subsidiaries, the company diligently follows its policy of trying to keep the expatriate headcount down and train local managers—only 230 employees there are Japanese.

Much of Matsushita's success is apparently attributable to its "go global, act local" practices and policies, some of which are listed here:

- Be a good corporate citizen in every country, respecting cultures, customs, and languages.
- Give overseas operations your best manufacturing technology.
- Keep expatriate headcount down and groom local managers to take over.
- Let plants set their own rules, fine-tuning manufacturing processes to match the skills of workers.
- Develop local R&D to tailor products to markets.
- Encourage competition among overseas outposts and with plants back home.

Question: From the case above try to see what Matsushita's global strategy has been in different countries. What was the basis of the company's success in other countries? In the United States?

Source: B. Schlender, "Matsushita Shows How to Go Global," *Fortune*, July 11, 1994; and "Matsushita: Value-Added Management for Global Partnerships," *Business Week*, July 12, 1993.

Chapter Summary

Chapter 7 introduced a level of analysis approach in developing a framework for global strategic planning. At the global level, relationships among FDI, trade, financial flow, and technology transfer have been discussed in the context of interaction between developed and developing countries. The utility of a management perspective of "re-engineering" was presented as key to the strategic planning process in a global political economy.

The FDI characteristics and trends have also been discussed with a plethora of statistical information. Basic analytic factors of core—periphery relations in markets, regions, human and material resources, and value systems were outlined in terms of their significance for strategic planning that involved processes that moved across borders and cultures. The importance to strategic planners of knowing not only where one is going and from where one is coming but also of how to get there was underlined.

Furthermore, the chapter presents the attributes of the global strategic planner who must develop certain skills to become sensitive to other cultures and be able to lead his/her organization to a successful "journey" abroad.

Review and Discussion Questions

1. What are some of the major incentives for advanced industrial nations to invest in less developed countries? What are the reasons for the so-called third and fourth world countries attracting foreign direct investment? What are some of the problems developed and developing nations might face in this process?
2. Protectionism is an explicit threat in the process of the regionalization of the global political economy. What steps can be taken in the strategic planning process to avoid this obstacle.
3. Select one company from the manufacturing sector and one company from the service sector in the United States. Discuss how each might strategically analyze the core—periphery, human and material resources, and value system factors in a specific emerging market such as Russia or China.
4. Discuss the FDI increase in the service sector. To what would you attribute this increase?
5. Discuss the changes taking place in some major industries (e.g., automobiles, computers, banking) from the perspective of management "re-engineering."

6. What are some of the principal lessons to be learned from this approach to the strategic planning process?
7. What are the characteristics of the global strategic planner?
8. What is the importance of understanding culture in the strategic planning process? Discuss with examples.

Endnotes

1. Ohmae, K., "Managing in a Borderless World," *Harvard Business Review* 67 (May–June, 1989): 152–161.
2. Porter, M., *Competitive Advantage of Nations* (Free Press, 1990).
3. Hammer, R. M., "Dramatic Winds of Change," *Price Waterhouse Review* 33 (1989): 23–27.
4. Lorange, P., "Human Resource Management in Multinational Cooperative Ventures," *Human Resources Management* 25 (Winter 1986): 133–148.
5. Drucker, P. F., *Managing for the Future: The 1990s and Beyond* (T.T. Books/Dutton, 1992).
6. See www.time.com/time/time100/builder/profile/morita.html.
7. *UN Conference on Trade and Development* (UNCTAD), "World Investment Report 2004: The Shift Towards Services."
8. *UN News Service*, "Foreign investment keeps falling but outlook healthier" (September 22, 2004).
9. Ibid., "The World Investment Report 2004...."
10. Ibid., "The World Investment Report 2004...."
11. Ibid., "The World Investment Report 2004...."
12. By 2001, this sector accounted, on average, for 72 percent of GDP in developed countries, 52 percent in developing, and 57 percent in CEE countries.
13. For a comprehensive analysis of China's outward FDI, see UNCTAD's e-brief: China: an emerging outward investor, December 4, 2003, available at: http://r0.unctad.org/en/subsites/dite/.
14. Elashmawi, F. and Harris, P. R., *Multicultural Management 2000*, Gulf Publishing Company, 1998.
15. Simons, G. F. et al., *Cultural Diversity—Fresh Visions & Break throughs for Revitalizing the Workplace* (Princeton, NJ: Peterson's/Pacesetter Books, 1996).
16. *Op. cit*, Elashmawi and Harris (1998).
17. Harris, P. R. and Moran, R. T. *Managing Cultural Differences*, 5th edn (Gulf Publishing Company, 2000).
18. *Op. cit.*, Harris and Moran, 2000.

8

Entering the International Market

George Baourakis and Marios I. Katsioloudes,
Spyros Hadjidakis

Objectives

Through this chapter, the student will be exposed to:

- The alternative options available to enter a foreign market
- The pros and cons of every market entry method
- The restrictions and opportunities that arise when considering a particular market entry method
- The practical limitations imposed by the existing foreign marketing channels and logistical issues.

Opening Case

The AMSUPP–NIPPONSUPP Story

An American multinational company, "AMSUPP," had a very strong market position in an industrial supplies business in all major countries except Japan. There they had set up a joint venture with the leading Japanese company in the industry, "NIPPONSUPP." The venture gave AMSUPP a 45 percent ownership in return for technology transfer as well as capital investment. In discussing global coverage and global market share, the AMSUPP managers included Japan in their calculations. With Japan, AMSUPP's global market participation looked very complete. Japan's inclusion was particularly important and AMSUPP's managers identified the country as the most globally strategic country, even more than the United States. Unfortunately, the way in which the venture was set up and the way in which the AMSUPP managers operated really negated the possibility of genuine participation by AMSUPP.

First, AMSUPP owned a share only of the manufacturing subsidiary of NIPPONSUPP and not a share of the parent company, which was responsible for marketing and sales. AMSUPP, therefore, had no legal right to access NIPPONSUPP's markets and customers. Second, while NIPPONSUPP had sent marketing representatives to the United States to learn from AMSUPP about the American market, AMSUPP had not done the same in Japan. Many American companies have found that in joint ventures with Japanese companies, the latter have gained far more access to their American partners' knowledge than have the former to their Japanese partners' knowledge. In effect, AMSUPP did not participate in the Japanese market in any strategic sense: They merely had a financial investment and not a very profitable one either. When the AMSUPP managers understood their problem and tried to change it, they found that they were in the proverbial position of riding a tiger: they could not get off for fear of being eaten.

In this case, if AMSUPP ended the joint venture, they would lose all their business in Japan. Worse, they had created the tiger themselves by setting up NIPPONSUPP with the best technology. That, combined with NIPPONSUPP's manufacturing skills, resulted in NIPPONSUPP's products being of higher quality than AMSUPP's. AMSUPP now had to maintain the relationship in order to prevent NIPPONSUPP from becoming a fearsome global competitor.

Question: What are the issues in this joint venture? What is your reaction to the following statement: Joint ventures and alliances help much more in strengthening the core strategy and the internationalization strategy than the globalization strategy.

Source: The case was compiled by the author.

Concerns and Issues of Going International

Business strategy, marketing strategy, and managerial considerations are the determining factors a company examines when it decides to enter a new foreign market. Most companies are established with the ambition to serve a particular market/consumer need within a given national market. However, as the activities of some of these companies expand and if their products appear to have a very strong appeal to a certain market segment or they are substantially differentiated from their competing products or services, these companies are faced with a situation where they are asked to serve some customers abroad and deliver their products or services to a foreign and distant market. In this way most companies develop a gradual consideration about the way they should treat their chances of expanding their activities through a more carefully designed and managed foreign market entry.

A relatively smaller number of business ventures, though, usually related to high technological applications or other very specialized fields are launched at an international level from the moment of their conception. In this case, all alternative market entry modes are assessed in combination with the considered business model and the overall business and marketing strategy pursued.

Motivation

Increasing international trade liberalization along with the gradual declining of barriers to trade and investment has created a business environment where almost every firm is likely to be subject to international competition. As a result the nature of international business has changed and many international firms have developed a home market on a broad multicountry regional basis, instead of a single national market.

Consistent objectives that could constitute parts of a global marketing strategy may refer to increasing sales volumes through expansion in similar market segments whereby the company would be serving the same consumer need across multiple countries, improving profit margins by taking advantage of relative competitive cost structures and attractive demand levels in foreign markets. Increased global competition through the expansion of many global firms throughout the world is a frequent factor that leads companies to counterattack by similar moves in other markets. Another frequent phenomenon is that a company follows its clients when they expand abroad, especially in the case of service provision, while some of the latter greatly value the possibility of maintaining their preferred provider even at an international level. A stagnant national market, or an attempt to reduce the dependency and the associated risk from the national market, is another cause leading to international expansion.[1]

Concerns, Risks, and Issues

International marketers have to make a multitude of decisions regarding the entry mode, which may include the target product/market, the goals of the target markets, the mode of entry, the time of entry, a marketing mix plan, and a control system to check the performance in the entered markets.

A broad initial distinction should be made between the option just to export and distribute certain products or services (foreign entry ventures made for market access reasons) in a foreign market (while production is maintained in the home market) and the option to develop a production basis in the foreign market (resource-orientated, or foreign production-related market entry) along with marketing activities.

Alternative methods for foreign market entry:

1. Production in home market
    - Indirect export
        - Trading company
        - Export management company
        - Piggyback
    - Direct Export
        - Foreign distributor
        - Agent
        - Marketing subsidiary
2. Foreign production sources
    - Contract manufacture
    - Licensing
    - Assembly
    - Joint venture
    - Full ownership

Although several options will probably be available when a company is considering or designing a foreign market entry, choices and compromises will have to be made between the desired or necessary levels of control, capital investment, and expected profitability[2] (Exhibit 8.1).

Some entry modes, such as exporting and licensing, are associated with low levels of control over operations and marketing, but are also associated with lower levels of risk. In contrast, other entry modes such as joint ventures and full ownership of facilities involve more control, but entail additional risk.

Most classifications of decision criteria for mode of entry list the following criteria:

- Market size and growth
- Risk

Exhibit 8.1

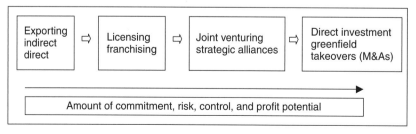

Foreign Market Entry Strategies

- Government regulations
- Competitive environment
- Local infrastructure
- Company objectives
- Need for control
- Internal resources
- Assets and capabilities
- Flexibility.

To choose between the optimal levels of the aforementioned factors the firm has to consider all the elements of the external environment[3] that it will encounter once it enters the foreign market, in combination with the internal environment that characterizes the firms' operations, skills, and competencies.

Most past studies on the foreign market entry strategies of multinational firms have mainly concentrated on the factors and the conditions behind the use of each entry mode and four main schools of thought have been formulated to explain the choice of entry mode. Some studies have adopted one of two theoretical approaches. One is the transaction cost analysis (TCA) approach, which prescribes international activities according to the economic rationale that firms will minimize all costs associated with the entire value-added chain (from production to consumption of goods), thereby considering the entire foreign market entry as one transaction. This approach stresses the importance of firm-specific variables and has been used to explain how firms enter and operate in foreign markets.[4] According to this school of thought, organizations will internalize those activities that can be performed at a lower cost but will subcontract all other activities to external providers. A similar approach was proposed by Dunning[5] who with his eclectic framework (or location-specific factors or contingency theory) proposes that three types of factors affect international business activities: host country-specific factors, ownership-specific factors, and (most importantly) internalization factors. The host country-specific factors include country risks and location familiarity, while ownership and internalization factors focus on the industry-specific and firm-specific variables. The agency or bargaining power theory[6] views entry mode choice as an outcome of negotiations between the firm and the government or local firms of the host country. In the agency theory the principles (new entrants) are highly motivated to collect data about their agents (entry modes in foreign markets) in the target market. The relationship between the two parties is described as if a contract is to be made between them, in which one party delegates work to another.

The Scandinavian "stages" model of entry suggests a gradual involvement pattern of entry into successive foreign markets, coupled with a progressive deepening of commitment to each market. Increasing commitment is particularly important for some other researchers who closely associate the stages models with the notion of "psychic distance," which attempts to conceptualize and, to some degree, measure the cultural distance between countries and markets 2003.[7] Resource commitment and the level of risk to be accepted are the central explanatory factors in this theory. Therefore, the higher the risk in the target market, the fewer the resource commitment-related entry modes that would be deployed in that market. Also, the more experience the organization has, the higher the tendency to use resource commitment-related entry modes.

In explaining foreign market servicing policies, the role of nonproduction activities must be made explicit. The location of research activities is widely debated, especially in relation to spatial agglomeration. There is also an extensive literature on the entry aspects of marketing and distribution, much of it in a transactions cost framework.

International Business Research: Determining International Business Research Objectives

Marketing research is of utmost importance for attaining the necessary information that will allow correct decision making and avoid costly mistakes of either poor strategies or lost opportunities. It is therefore inconceivable to proceed toward a foreign market entry mode decision without first having an adequate marketing plan, which in turn will have assessed all relative information of the potential target market environments along with the internal business environment of the firm.

Decision making for the appropriate marketing mix that will subsequently allow the firm to build a competitive position within the targeted foreign market will have long-lasting consequences for the firm. Selection of a certain customer segment and the type of products and services provided to them will result in specific resource commitments, thus requiring a sufficient period of time so that investments yield adequate returns.

Therefore, careful market segmentation and selection constitutes the cornerstone of effective business and marketing planning allowing for an optimal market entry choice. The starting point of any marketing research would require analysis of the market environment factors prevailing in each country/national market (factors such as economic development, institutions, consumer attitude, response to alternative test ideas on either competitive products or potential product mix bundles of pricing, distribution, advertising, sales promotion, sales force competition).

Literature on factors affecting the choice of foreign market entry has suggested that physical and cultural distance certainly has an effect on foreign market entry mode choice 1994.[8] Research on country attractiveness can be assessed with the systematic analysis of factors such as market size, market growth rate, government regulations, price controls, nontariff barriers, local culture, economic and political stability, inflation, and trade balance. The level of (potential) competitive strength in each of these markets might be assessed by measuring factors such as the (expected) market share, product fit, contribution margin, market support, quality of the existing distribution system, and the possible advertising against competition.

Existing competition in each country definitely requires thorough analysis. In order to develop a competition-monitoring system, multiple facts have to be collected concerning overall company statistics (sales and market share profits, balance sheet, capital expenditures, number of employees, production capacity, research and development capability), marketing operations (types of products, service and warranty granted, prices and pricing strategy, advertising strategy and budget allocated on advertising, type and size of sales force, distribution strategy, especially potential entry strategies, delivery schedules, and geographic sales territory), future intentions (new product developments, current test markets, scheduled plant capacity expansions, planned capital expenditures, planned entry into new markets/countries), and competitive (reactive) behavior (pricing behavior, reaction to competitive moves, past and expected).[9]

Important additional ways to estimate potential demand and market attractiveness/potential should be considered in the form of visiting major trade fairs, where all major firms active in the given sector participate, allowing for a fast overview of the competitive activities. Another option would be to establish contact with a liaison office in major activity centers (such as Brussels or Geneva), or to establish an integrated business intelligence system that would incorporate data from specialized data banks and intelligence firms such as "ICAP" or "Euromonitor," or other organizations.

With the increase of economic integration among many regional country groups (e.g., European Union (EU), Association of South East Asian Nations (ASEAN)) it has become imperative to monitor the regulatory environment that might either encourage or try to prevent certain business forms that will have major impacts on the type of market entry favored in each particular case.

Distribution and Sales Channel Identification

Especially in the case of an export marketing type of foreign market entry, firms are concerned about the degree of market coverage that agents, distributors, or export management companies (EMCs) claim they can achieve. Market coverage and degree of market penetration are key factors for successful marketing performance in the foreign market. Trading companies and agents active in distribution channels tend to operate in different market segments; thus the firm that wishes to serve a particular customer base while aiming to achieve high levels of market coverage and market penetration should carefully select its foreign distribution partner, so as to create favorable conditions for an optimal long-run return on investment.

Foreign Market Entry Strategies

Export Marketing

Most firms usually operate within their national market boundaries until they start considering their international expansion either through replying to an unsolicited request to serve a foreign customer or by systematically researching and designing their international marketing activities. Export and import activities lead the international economic development course of the modern era, especially as technology has made transportation and communications much more efficient than ever before.

International trade was boosted in the second half of the twentieth century and some initiatives such as the General Agreement on Tariffs and Trade (GATT), and the subsequent World Trade Organization (WTO), aimed to liberalize world trade mainly through reducing various types of trade barriers (tariffs, duties, and non-tariff barriers to entry) so as to further stimulate international economic growth and development. Additional political initiatives have been undertaken by many countries around the world with similar objectives, in the form of free trade areas, customs unions, common markets, and economic unions.

Imposing market protection measures through various types of barriers to entering a specific market has been part of the economic policy of many national governments for a long time. Tariffs and duties are the two main market protection instruments used in such policies, while nontariff trade barriers of various types are also frequently practiced with results equal or similar to those obtained with market protection.[10] In a single-column tariff system the rate of duty imposed remains the same for all countries, while in the two-column tariff system a "special" (reduced) rate is applicable to all countries that qualify for it besides the "normal" rate imposed for most countries. They are taxed through a system of mutually signed conventions for a "normal trade relations, NTR" (formerly Most Favored Nation) status within the WTO. A quite complex international system with multiple code numbers and different tariff rates has existed for long, as national custom duties and tariffs where imposed, when goods were imported in a country, based on a national codification system. The Harmonized Tariff System (HTS) has been adopted by most trading nations, allowing for the same codification of goods and services for both exports and imports in various markets. A preferential tariff rate was the mode adopted often by bilateral government agreements in the past, so as to apply reduced duty rates for the export of many products in certain countries. Along with the aforementioned efforts to facilitate international economic transactions, all signatory countries at GATT and WTO are no longer allowed to apply preferential tariffs. Instead NTR is the effective norm and much emphasis is also placed on monitoring that normal rates are applied on real (market) transaction values, as multinational corporations (MNCs) and international firms are sometimes tempted to increase (or decrease) the nominal value of the international transaction, so as to gain various accounting or economic benefits, even to avoid the imposition of duties. Nontariff (hidden) trade barriers include several administrative measures that are a deterrent or obstacle to foreign trade. Such trade barriers are the quotas, which essentially serve maximum limits to the allowed quantity or value of a product or service that is allowed to enter a certain market. The imposition of a quota is a very strict measure to control imports, because it establishes a quantitative ceiling regarding the amount a producer can export to a certain market, regardless of the other parameters of the product or service offered, thus being much more effective than a tariff or a duty imposed. Another barrier might be imposed by a government in the form of discriminatory procurement policies, which are rules that usually favor or give priorities under certain circumstances to national providers. Customs procedures might also act as a trade barrier in certain cases, especially when they establish complex, lengthy, and costly procedures that discourage exports to the particular market. In a very similar way discriminatory exchange rate policies are imposed as a form of an arbitrary monetary policy and certainly have a negative effect on export attempts. For various other reasons (safety, local traditions, convenience, special local conditions, etc.), governments may also adopt other restrictive administrative and technical regulations that effectively act as a barrier to international trade and exports to a certain market.

Customs duties fall into two main categories, namely ad valorem duties that are expressed as a percentage of the value of the goods or specific duties that are expressed as a specific currency amount, per measurement unit of the concerned good. Sometimes a combination of both types of duties (the so-called compound or mixed duties) is imposed.

When a dumping phenomenon occurs (i.e., when producers offer their goods at unfair price levels or below production cost level), governments may intervene to charge antidumping duties that act as a surcharge that is covering the difference created by the dumping margin. To offset the export subsidies that some governments introduce to stimulate exports, host governments impose countervailing duties. In the agricultural sector, variable import levies are often imposed, so as to balance the competitive price levels of the domestic products with the international prices that exist in the international market. Exporters should also be alert for temporary surcharges that are imposed to provide additional protection in case this is deemed necessary.

The type of export requirements prevailing is of utmost importance for selecting the export foreign market entry mode for every firm in each target market, so as to bring the total transaction cost to an optimal level. The same factor is equally important for financing of exports and the required methods of payment. The letter of credit (by which the necessary trustworthiness of the importer buyer is guaranteed by his bank) is the most widely used method as a form of payment in export activities. Other methods of export finance are the documentary collection method where a bill of exchange is used as the basis of the transaction, the cash in advance method that is applicable in cases of increased risk as regards the payout of the amount due for the export of goods, the sale on open account that is the most usual method applied in the case of transactions between branches or subsidiaries of the same firm, or in all other cases of repeated transactions between mutually trustworthy firms, and finally the sales on consignment basis, which is a common method applied in free trade zones and for certain product categories such as agricultural products and goods that may be transported and gradually released for the final sale without an initial tangible obligation until the sale is accepted.

Export Market Entry Modes

Even when a firm limits its international activities to export marketing, it still faces several options with variable levels of commitment, investments, control, and risk. Direct export entry modes are chosen whenever a relatively high volume of exports is projected and therefore a higher level of investment is needed. The various indirect forms of export offer more flexibility, requiring less commitment, thereby being suitable for relatively limited export volumes.

Indirect Exports

International trading companies have a dominant position in some countries and regions, like Mitsui and Mitsubishi in Japan and others in Europe, with extensive market coverage, penetration, distribution networks, and marketing skills (firms such as Mitsui and Mitsubishi that are characterized by extensive Cross-shareholding, are named "Sogoshosha" in Japanese), thus being very attractive trading partners. Having a large and powerful company as a foreign trading partner might have some drawbacks (stemming from limited control) like the limited importance within the range of products it distributes leading to underperformance and nonoptimal exploitation of its full marketing potential 1997.[11] Under a special legislation in the United States, some American giant firms like General Electric, Citicorp, and

General Motors attempted to establish export trading companies, through collective efforts with other firms of the same industry and with the same characteristics as the Japanese "Sogoshosha" mentioned above, in order to take advantage of economies of scale in building expertise and skills to serve international markets.

A similar type of indirect export activity with cooperation in exporting has been established through the Webb-Pomerene associations in the United States. Large exporting corporations had been formed in the past to take advantage of economies of scale in exporting and to avoid duplicating efforts, especially in cases where new products were about to be launched in the global marketplace and cooperation made sense for the export market despite the fact that participating firms were considered competitors in the domestic market.

Export management companies (EMCs) undertake the full export department operations of a firm on its behalf, but without charging an equally high amount, as they simultaneously perform the same function for several firms. The advantage of using one of these firms is the fact that exporting firms exert a high degree of control at a fraction of the cost. Many small and medium-sized enterprises may find an ideal export partner using one of the hundreds of existing EMCs, to gain export market expertise, to achieve low-cost transportation and efficient customs clearance, and, most often, foreign credit responsibility as well. It should however be emphasized that although EMCs are a very convenient export support option for small and medium-sized firms, when the export volume increases considerably, they might not be the optimal solution anymore. The exporting firm should be aware that EMCs, knowing that they could lose part of their activities due to their good performance, might be tempted to hold back to a nonoptimal level of export marketing effort (mainly on market research issues). Piggyback is the practice undertaken when a manufacturer uses the sales force and distribution network of another firm, in order to market its products. Piggyback exporting is most frequently used as a method of achieving an excellent level of marketing support without considerable effort and investments, so as to build a sales and distribution network in a foreign market. The carrier is usually the larger firm that has already established either its own export facilities or a distribution network and is willing to undertake similar exporting and distribution activities on behalf of another firm, either in order to complement the range of its products and services so as to give better services to its clientele or simply to increase the level of usage of its existing distribution capacity in order to reduce its average costs by receiving additional fees from the riding firm. Thus the rider, which is using the ability of the other firm to "carry" its products in a foreign market, might find that this alternative method has similar advantages as EMCs and the aforementioned types of indirect exporting have, with a still limited range of product lines served, often achieving an even better level of control, while keeping both investments and cost at a low level. Recently, the piggyback method has been adopted with encouraging results by not only medium-sized firms, but also large firms such as Whirlpool when it agreed with Sony to become its appliance distributor in Japan.

Direct exporting is favored as an export market entry mode when the firm depends on its foreign market operations at a higher level and either wishes or needs to commit more resources in these operations (assume a higher level of risk), which requires a relatively higher level of control as well. When the firm is undertaking the whole export procedure on its own it has to begin from the preparation of an export plan, much in the way it prepares its domestic marketing plan, where all marketing mix elements have to be considered and carefully handled to provide effective solutions to all the necessary activities according to the objectives of the firm. Such an export plan should be prepared for every target market irrespective of the fact that its components might differ considerably, due to the particular conditions existing in each of these foreign markets.

The most significant part of such an export plan is the selection of the level and the type of physical presence in the foreign market. If both the size of the target market and the expected export volume justifies exporting activities then firms should consider establishing their own marketing subsidiaries that will only undertake the necessary local marketing operations and delegate or subcontract the physical distribution part to other distributors. Otherwise, firms must develop their own distribution networks when more control is needed or when volumes are high enough. Alternatively, choosing a foreign distributor might be preferable in order to keep investment needs low, at least till a distributor that could qualify for geographic coverage, adequacy of sales staff, nonrivalry with other product lines he carries, effectiveness to deliver with accuracy, and, finally, overall reliability can be found.

Whenever the size of the firm and the target market are relatively small, a local agent or sales representative might be the more suitable solution. These persons could either be working exclusively for one firm or might be representing more than one firm in the local market. Local agents or representatives usually operate on a commission basis and besides being intermediaries for the initial sale of goods, they should provide additional services whenever necessary.

There are several other forms of key export participants that act on behalf of the client such as foreign purchasing agents, export brokers, and export merchants, while some other intermediaries, such as freight forwarders, clearly operate on the basis of assigned responsibilities by the exporter. Foreign purchasing agents act on behalf of foreign importers. They are remunerated according to various terms (commission or fee basis) and their role is to seek a manufacturer that fulfills the quality and price requirements of the importing firm. Export brokers usually operate in the commodities markets and their role is to bring together local and foreign sellers, without assuming any financial or other responsibility. Export merchants or jobbers operate on an ad hoc basis, trying to fill gaps with needs existing in certain markets, by locating the goods that might essentially fulfill those needs in the international market. Freight forwarders specialize in transportation services and customs clearance while sometimes they undertake additional services such as packing and freight insurance. Their role is to optimize the entire freight process on behalf of the exporter.

Selection of the appropriate form of entry in a foreign market heavily depends not only on economic factors such as existing infrastructure, distribution networks, market institutions but also on social and cultural parameters. The issue has received the attention of researchers. Armstrong and Sweeney[12] addressed and analyzed the issue of cultural differences between Western and Eastern cultures stating that the prime distinction between Chinese (and other Asian societies) and North American cultures (also Australian and others) lies within the collective orientation of the Chinese and the individualistic orientation of the North Americans. Other scholars[13] have attempted to clarify issues related to a sort of "cultural distance paradox" concerning the relationship between national cultural distance and entry mode choice, due to conflicting research results. Some scholars find cultural distance associated with choosing wholly owned modes; others find cultural distance linked to a preference for joint ventures. It should in any case be clear that culture and mode of entry have a significant effect on the perception of ethical problems and it is therefore recommended that firms intending to enter international markets should first develop a good understanding of the ethical values of the host country, industry, and organization, before developing a strategy for market entry into that country. In general, though, firms select more cooperative modes of entry in low investment risk markets, but select wholly owned modes of entry in high investment risk markets.

Contractual Entry Modes

Licensing

This form of foreign market entry is based on a contractual relationship where the licensor is the firm that possesses an asset in the form of a patent (or the know-how to produce a product or provide a service) and the licensee is a firm in the host country that is willing to exchange the use of the foreign firm's technology in the host market with a certain remuneration (generally the payment of royalties). Licensing can be a very effective way for the internationalization of the activities of small and medium enterprises that might have developed very good products and technologies that could serve clients in the international market but lack the resources for an autonomous international expansion. It can serve equally well through large (and sometimes already international) firms that operate in multiple markets and have gained considerable experience with a given product/technology but consider licensing as an option whenever the risk associated with an additional foreign market entry outweighs the benefits of a direct investment entry choice. Bradley[14] has summarized the pros and cons (for the licensor) of licensing foreign entry modes:

Advantages

- Appealing to small companies that lack resources due to low risk and capital commitment, while maintaining improved delivery and service levels in local markets.
- Fast market access and more importantly the ability to circumvent barriers to foreign entry that have been imposed through quotas, high tariffs, or limited licensing to local firms.
- Adequate marketing information and control through access to low-cost information about local market performance and competitive reactions, as soon as the licensed product enters the local market.
- Ability to take advantage of the possession of a patented product that is subject to rapid technological changes while it is otherwise unprofitable to simultaneously exploit along multiple markets.

Disadvantages

- Potential creation of future competitors, through disclosure of accumulated knowledge and experience when the license contract ceases.
- Licensee may not be committed to this particular product line, and thus possible marketing underperformance may not be controlled.
- Passive interaction with local market, leading to limited market learning.
- Limited flexibility to apply sophisticated technology and marketing advances at a later stage.
- Limited profit potential in case the product is more successful than initially thought.
- Policing the implementation of the licensing agreement is either inefficient or very expensive.

Although licensing could be a very efficient form of technology transfer, it is imperative that the license agreement receives utmost attention. Two types of license agreement could be made. One is the type concerning an existing technology/product while another more difficult one is the making of provisions for technology sharing as it evolves during the lifetime of the agreement.

A typical license agreement package might consist of the following elements:

- Patents, designs, trademarks, copyrights
- Product and processes specifications
- Quality control procedures
- Manufacturing blueprints and manuals
- Product manuals and other supporting material
- Programs and material for technical and commercial staff training
- Minimum performance clauses
- Clear arrangements for a fixed minimum royalty or a percentage commission (royalty ranging between 1 and 20 percent, but 3–5 percent in most cases) based on the actual sales figures realized, or a combination of both.

In addition to the above, the licensor firm should also have worked well in advance for the following:

- Adequate patent or trademark protection (preferably by submitting application to international patent organizations such as the European Patent Office)
- Preparation of thorough profitability analysis (through market share projections)
- Careful selection of prospective licensees (participation in international trade fairs, sector conventions, organized foreign trade missions, and the use of various databases and services provided by national authorities)
- Careful consideration of alternative solutions and clauses for all contract parameters (technology package, use conditions, compensation, and provisions for the settlement of disputes)

A key point for an effective control of the licensee is to develop a system under which critical components are patented and provided by the licensor. In this way a higher level of profitability, combined with more control on quality and performance, may be achieved for the licensor.

Franchising

Although franchising cannot be characterized as a novel way to conduct business, it is growing at such a pace that it tends to revolutionize international business expansion in many sectors 1992.[15] The reasoning behind assuming a franchise operation is very similar to the one justifying licensing. The difference lies rather on the type of operations, with services being the favored area to develop a franchise type of activity. The firm that has developed the know-how about the provision of a certain service is thus called the franchisor, while the franchisee is the firm that agrees to use the trademark, brand name, and other product- or service-related technology against an agreed remuneration in the form of royalties. As franchising often concerns retailing, quite often there are some hundreds or thousands of franchisees in a certain local market, in which case a master franchising firm might be presented as a type of "franchise wholesaler" that intervenes between the owner of the trademark and the know-how and the retailing entrepreneur of the firm that is serving consumers. Master franchising is based on granting the foreign franchisee exclusive territorial right to a particular region or country. The master franchisee in the foreign country then assumes the role of franchisor, and he or she may choose either to operate all outlets or to engage in sub franchisees. In the latter case, each sub franchisee would generally pay the royalty fees via the master franchisee, who then keeps a certain percentage (usually 50 percent) and remits the rest to the franchise headquarters. Franchising has proved to be a very efficient form of international expansion, especially for various restaurant and fast food chains (McDonald's, KFC), hotels (Holliday Inn), and other retailers in clothing and apparel (Benetton), petrol stations, personal care products (Bodyshop), furniture (IKEA), and various other activities.

Advantages

- Rapid entry and expansion in the foreign market without any major risk assumption or capital investment requirements.
- High franchisee motivation to achieve objectives, boosting profits as they are closely tied to their own efforts.
- Effective adaptation to local market conditions based on excellence due to affiliation of local knowledge of the franchisee.
- Efficient trademark or brand name promotion, along with increased ability to invest in R&D through the collection of royalties by numerous franchisees.

Disadvantages

- Revenues may not be adequate, due to the usually low level of royalties that are established to attract more franchisees.
- Absence of a master franchisee in a certain country might cause entry delay.
- Limited control over the franchisees' operations, difficulty in supervising performance and high-quality standards.
- Cultural problems (sweatshops, fair-trade, and sustainability issues) might affect the image of the whole chain.

Franchising is well suited to serve as a market entry mode in activities with a relatively high human resource and service component and that need to be delivered in geographically dispersed local outlets. The willingness and availability of many people to undertake limited entrepreneurial risks and duties, combined with the financial and institutional support from the firms themselves, governments and banks, has stimulated the rapid growth of franchising.

An alternative form of entering a foreign market is through a management contract, where the international firm undertakes the responsibility to manage a production or service-providing facility in the foreign market against a certain fee, according to the provisions of the management contract agreed. This form of foreign market entry is suitable in cases where managerial experience and expertise is the only or the most important asset missing (such is the case often in many hotel chains around the world) from the local entrepreneurial initiative.[16]

Foreign Manufacturing

International firms engage in contract production or contract manufacturing either within a framework of allocating low-cost production facilities in many countries around the globe (depending mostly on the local labor market conditions prevailing at that period of time) or because this is the only market access possible due to government limitations and other local conditions. Global firms such as Nike and IKEA subcontract various local manufacturers in multiple countries to produce according to technical specifications that have been developed by their own design and R&D departments. Nike also coordinates logistics and concentrates on core marketing activities in the global market. In any case this type of market entry mode as the term denotes focuses primarily on production and not marketing (at least when target countries are considered). The international firm makes a distinction between favorable production conditions that may occur in certain countries and market opportunities that may or may not coexist with a favorable production environment in the same country.

Advantages

- Labor cost advantages
- Savings via taxation, lower energy costs, raw materials, and overheads
- Lower political and economic risk
- Quicker access to markets not only for production but also for marketing purposes.

Disadvantages

- Risk of future competition from contract manufacturer becoming a future competitor by enhancing technology and marketing skills

- Backlash from the company's home market employees and labor unions due to the loss of employment in the home country
- Environmental protection and labor and fair trade issues posing a challenge for the social responsibility profile of the international firm, thereby negatively affecting the image of the company publicly (sweatshops, resource exploitation, environmental degradation)
- Issues of quality and production standards (strict codes of ethical and total quality conduct should be imposed on subcontractors).

Local assembly is a different option of foreign manufacturing, related usually to the last stages of the production chain, which are often labor-intensive. Local assembly thus is arranged with an independent local firm, with a contractual agreement aiming to reduce the total production cost by locating assembly facilities close to a low labor cost markets (many global car manufacturers such as DaimlerChrysler, Ford, Toyota, Mitsubishi, and others adopt this approach, establishing local assembly units in Eastern European or South American countries).

Investment Entry Modes

Firms that consider investing in a foreign market usually base themselves on some experience they already have with either production or marketing transactions they have developed in the course of some years. Examples of international firms investing abroad abound, regardless of whether we refer to direct investments through mergers, acquisitions, greenfield investments, equity participations, or broader agreements to form a strategic alliance. All types of investments in a foreign market may have a greater implication than the other market entry modes discussed in the preceding section of this chapter, thus needing more consideration, careful planning, and a higher level of resource allocation.

Portfolio Investments by Multinational Corporations

In order to maintain a balanced investment portfolio, MNCs regularly invest in foreign firms by acquiring a relatively small percentage of their equity capital. Within the framework of a corporate strategy they systematically monitor opportunities and conditions in foreign markets and evaluate their equity participation in the most promising foreign firms. In case the equity participation in the foreign firm is significant (above 3–5 percent depending on the individual company), the investor might also participate in the managing board, thus acquiring valuable knowledge of the local market conditions. Otherwise, even a very limited equity participation gives access to the standard information that any investor receives and therefore an investor must decide on the effort and resources that should be devoted to following a particular market and firm. Thus, MNCs are always alert about the option of proceeding to a more direct way for entering a foreign market through one of the following foreign market entry modes.

Foreign Direct Investment

Early literature on foreign market entry focused on the choice between exporting and foreign direct investment (FDI). The cost-based view of this decision suggested that the firm must possess a certain advantage that would overcome the cost of "foreignness." Superior technological and marketing skills had been identified as such "compensating" factors. This could contribute to a successful foreign entry. A similar approach suggested by other researchers was "core competencies," which were identified as the firm-specific advantages that constitute the most important success factors for FDIs. Another approach is the "sequential modes of internationalization," where it is suggested that firms embark from an exporting phase before switching first to market access and then to cost-reducing FDI. Another research approach has been the one that envisaged the firm as an internalized bundle of resources that can be allocated between product groups, and between national markets.[17] Foreign market entry involves two interdependent decisions on location and mode of control but FDI is (by definition) foreign-located and administratively controlled.

A basic distinction can be made between two types of FDI: the horizontal FDI where the firm expands by entering a foreign market, increasing the volume of its operations while at the same time maintaining the same activities, and the vertical FDI that denotes the simultaneous vertical integration in either upstream or downstream operations, along with the foreign market entry.

Although the decision to proceed in any type of investment is up to the investor, almost all governments would welcome an FDI, and most adopt suitable legislation and regulation to facilitate and attract the highest possible amount of FDI in the host country. The logic behind this approach is the highly appreciated transfer of technology that typically accompanies this type of investment. Technology transfer is particularly important to less-developed countries (LDCs) not only because this is usually the only way they can increase their immediate economic growth but also because it may support local medium- and long-run R&D programs, with appropriate technology that can constitute the troublesome missing factor endowment.

Joint Ventures

Although cooperative joint ventures between two or more firms are the most frequent type of international joint venture (IJV), in cases where governments impose restrictions as to the maximum allowed level of control to a firm in the host market, a (minority) equity joint venture becomes the most appropriate alternative solution.

Recent literature on IJVs summarizes the conditions conducive to IJVs as the possession of complementary assets, opportunities for collusion, and barriers to full integration—economic, financial, legal, or political. Hennart,[18] having studied and empirically analyzed a large sample of IJVs between US and Japanese firms, concluded that IJVs are formed when firms need to combine with other firms' intermediate inputs that are subject to high market transaction costs, while the necessary conducive conditions exist when firms expand to operations beyond their main industry activities and expertise, when tacit knowledge is present and necessary for the success of the venture and when they seek access to resources held by local firms.

In addition to the aforementioned factors, IJV literature has also focused particularly on partner selection, management strategy, and the measurement of performance.[19] The performance of IJVs is the subject of much debate. An international joint venture termination does not necessarily indicate failure; on the contrary it might precisely indicate that planned objectives have been achieved. Similarly, the restructuring of joint ventures and alliances may indicate the exploitation of the flexibility of the organizational form, rather than a response to underperformance-related entry mode to performance, and examines the role of repeated ties between partners as contributing to success—an interesting attempt to encompass "cultural" variables. To summarize the above, literature has identified several factors that play a role in determining firms' foreign market entry decisions, most of which relate to location costs, internalization factors, financial variables, cultural factors such as trust and psychic distance, market structure and competitive strategy, adaptation costs (to the local environment), and the cost of doing business abroad.

Advantages

- Higher rate of return and more control over the operations
- Creation of synergy, through complementing assets and resources or sharing costs and risks
- Quick access to distribution network
- Contact with local suppliers and government officials.

Disadvantages

- Lack of full control
- Susceptibility to mistrust and culturally related conflicts
- Conflicts arising over matters such as strategies, resource allocation, transfer pricing, and ownership of critical assets like technologies and brand names.

The drivers behind successful international joint ventures are the following:[20]

- Pick the right partner
- Establish clear objectives from the beginning especially as to the scope of the agreed activities, the duration of the venture, and the potential overlap with activities and/or interests of the constituting firms
- Bridge cultural gaps, transparency, establishment of ethical codes, and effective communication lines
- Gain top managerial commitment and respect
- Use incremental approach.

Wholly-owned Subsidiaries

Wholly owned and fully controlled entry modes especially branches and subsidiaries represent the highest level of resource commitment in the target market. Literally, these two entry modes are used by organizations (parent organizations) that are globally oriented and their competitive position in one country is significantly affected by their position in another one and vice versa.[21] When a firm is considering establishing a wholly owned subsidiary (WOS), it might choose between either merging or acquiring an existing firm, or proceed to a greenfield investment.

Mergers and Acquisitions

Acquisition refers to the purchase of sufficient stock of an already existing firm in order to gain control, whereas in a merger two or more firms might form a new company, by pooling resources and assets and sharing equity of the new firm according to the valuation of the resources each contributed.

Mergers and acquisitions (M&A) are usually discussed versus greenfield ventures as part of an analysis of the organization of the multinational firm. Takeovers seem to predominate as a form of entry in most advanced economies, while particular attention has been paid to the costs of adaptation and cultural integration that are encountered in the case of mergers. Some empirical studies for M&A against IJVs[22] indicated that US firms favor acquisitions, followed by joint ventures and start-ups, whereas Japanese organizations prefer joint ventures to acquisitions and start-ups, while MNCs from both countries avoid start-ups in general.

Advantages

- Quick foreign market access, sometimes even the only available way to access the market if there is either a government restriction or the market structure does not leave room for a new entrant
- Acquisitions of assets, in the form of qualified personnel, management skills, clientele, providers, and possibly existing long-term contracts.

Disadvantage

- Adaptation difficulties, delays, and increased cost in case of incompatible assets, resources, and tangible (location, infrastructure) and intangible (business culture) elements of the acquired firm.

Greenfield Operations

A Greenfield investment entails building a subsidiary from scratch and usually targets local production and marketing in the host market as well. Real estate and other resources are purchased locally and employees are hired and trained using the investor's management, technology, know-how, and capital.

Advantages

- Greater control, flexibility, and higher profits
- Strong commitment to the local market on the part of companies
- Ability of the investor to manage and control marketing, production, and sourcing decisions.

Disadvantages

- Higher risks due to full ownership
- Development of a foreign presence without the support of a third party, which may cause delay and increase sunk costs
- Risk of nationalization (in comparison to case of joint venturing with a local firm)
- Issues of cultural and economic sovereignty of the host country.

Although the term greenfield investment is used when there is no other firm existing in the host market, what often happens in reality is that we have the phenomenon of so-called Brownfield investments, a term denoting a hybrid mode of entry based on an acquisition (to ensure quick entry and immediate access to local resources) and also when the acquired company requires such a deep restructuring (usually the case in emerging markets) that the new operation resembles a greenfield investment.[23] This type of foreign market entry might be characterized in the case of the German car manufacturer VW AG when it invested in Czech (then Czechoslovakian) Skoda.

Strategic Alliances

International strategic alliances can take various different forms such as simple licensing agreements between two partners, market (access)-based alliances, operations and logistics alliances, operations (shared production)-based alliances; their most distinct characteristic is that they are made so as to pursue a common goal. The logic behind strategic alliances relates to building market position, or in other words, if it is worth entering a relatively long-lasting alliance when as a firm you have to defend, to catch up, to remain, or to restructure. The need to form an alliance instead of agreeing to cooperate along a more trivial basis relies on the very nature of the pursued goal, which is often susceptible to frequent amendments while its core reason for existence is long-lasting. The rapid technological changes (telecommunications, Internet, transportations, etc.) have increased the need for interfirm cooperation on a more permanent basis while maintaining the attractive features of an alliance. That is why alliances have significantly replaced more traditional forms of foreign market entry such as M&As during the last decade.

Successful international alliances share some characteristics that denote a balance between interests, control, risks, and potential profits:

- Allies should have the same market power; alliances between strong and weak partners seldom work.
- All allies maintain their autonomy and a high degree of flexibility.
- The participation on ownership should be equal so as to ensure equally shared benefits, while all allies should equally maintain an ongoing contribution.

Other factors that play an important role in the success of the alliance are as follows:

- Commitment and support of the top partners' organizations
- Strong alliance managers who are the key
- Alliances between partners that are related in terms of products, technologies, and markets
- Similar cultures, asset sizes, and venturing experience
- A shared vision on goals and mutual benefits with mutual organizational learning
- Horizontal hierarchy between the relationship decision-making and communication lines between the same-level employees of the engaged organizations, instead of a vertical hierarchy.

Forming an alliance bears a certain resemblance to the relationships existing in the Japanese Keiretsu system. More and more firms, especially in the United States, seem to be trying to learn how to collaborate within an alliance, in order to achieve common goals usually related to technology development, soft infrastructures, and networking solutions.

International Logistics and Transportation Issues Related to Foreign Market Entry

Modern supply chain structures and management are discussed more extensively in the next chapter, as part of the marketing mix that the international firm is going to design and implement in order to operate in any given market. It should, however, be noted that most firms heavily invest and depend on distribution systems and supply chain networks in order to increase both effectiveness and the value component of the products or services they offer in the market. Another reason for this is to decrease the cost by improving efficiency of the system. Significant investments and application of innovative technological solutions have contributed to better communications within the supply chain, improved customer service within shorter time periods, higher delivery precision (Just In Time Systems), to name but a few improvements within distribution networks.[24]

Upon forming an international partnership, or making a contractual agreement, firms should in one way or another be subject to significant resource commitment. The importance of selecting the foreign partner and the foreign firm that is going to be delivering to clients in the host country cannot be emphasized often enough. The contact with the final client is made through the distributor and the venture cannot get any better than the level of quality and performance of the distributor.

When a firm is considering selecting a foreign distributor it is in most cases simultaneously selecting a market segment, due to the fact that supply chains tend to develop in a selective if not exclusive way. The main issues that need to be considered are as follows:

- Market coverage, clients, and penetration of the distribution system not only in the host country but also in connection with global distribution systems
- The level of infrastructure and IT integration for modern logistical applications
- Key infrastructure (e.g., "hot" or "cool" network infrastructure is often of utmost importance for foreign expansion in the food and drink sector, just like the number of stores for other merchandise)
- Personnel quality and competence.

Existence or absence of the necessary or desired distribution firms in any foreign market may have significant implications on the mode of market entry selected. If, for instance, the product or service needs to be delivered under special conditions or the service content is high and the firm in the home market has very high standards or unique expertise in those accompanying services, then more controlled forms of market entry should be preferred (e.g., direct investment through acquisition or greenfield operation) over rather more standardized forms of entry (export). Much in the same way, contractual forms of foreign market entry (e.g., licensing) would be greatly affected by the skills of the licensor to effectively manage and monitor the quality performance of the licensees and by the learning and adaptation skills of the latter to develop a high level of quality in the distribution of the designed good.

Closing Case

Koc Holding: Arcelik White Goods

In February 1997, the top management of Arcelik, the major appliance subsidiary of Koc Holding, Turkey's largest industrial conglomerate, assembled in Cologne, Germany, for the biannual Domotechnica, the world's largest major appliances trade show. The team was led by Hasan Subasi, president of Koc Holding's durables business unit, and by Mehmet Ali Berkman, general manager of the Arcelik white goods—major kitchen appliances—operation, which accounted for two-thirds of the durables business unit's turnover.

The Arcelik stand was in a prime location in Building 14; nearby were the booths of Bosch, Siemens, and Whirlpool. The Arcelik stand displayed 236 products carrying the Beko brand name (most Arcelik products sold outside Turkey carried the Beko brand name), 35 percent of them refrigerators and freezers, 25 percent washing machines, 20 percent ovens, and 15 percent dishwashers. Several innovative products were on display including washing machines that were more water- and energy-efficient than were competitive products, as well as refrigerators made from materials that were 80 percent recyclable and incorporated special insulation panels for greater operational efficiency. In 1996, Arcelik's Beko brand had received a Green Dove award from the EU for the attention to the environment in design and production.

The trade show exhibit, costing $1 million to organize, reflected Arcelik's determination to become a major player in the global white goods industry. There was, however, still debate in the company regarding how much emphasis to place on international sales; which geographical markets to concentrate on; and on whether to focus on supplying appliances on an original equipment manufacturer (OEM) basis, building the company's own Beko brand, or both (an OEM sells products to other manufacturers, distributors, or retailers; these products typically carry brand names specified by the purchasing companies).

In between hosting visitors to their Domotechnica booth in Cologne, Arcelik's managers continued to discuss informally whether or not they were placing the correct emphasis on international markets, and whether their brand-building and market selection strategies were appropriate. Some of the comments at the booth included:

"In 1996, we showed we could hold our own in the Turkish market against the top brands in the world. In fact, our market share in refrigerators actually increased. This means we can now push our international exports more aggressively.

Wait a minute. Capacity is tight. If the Turkish market continues to grow at the current rate, we will need most of our planned capacity for 1997 to meet domestic demand. And we know that we make at least twice as much unit margin if we sell an appliance in Turkey than if we export it.

The current rate of economic growth is not sustainable. The government, in anticipation of a general election, is pumping money into the economy. The economy will probably slow down, may be even go into recession in 1997. I don't think we will have a capacity problem.

We've got to emphasize building Beko brand worldwide. We will never make big money on OEM business, whether we are making to order for other manufacturers—who are in fact, our competitors—or for retail chains. Special orders add to complexity costs in our plans and we lose our R&D edge when we simply follow the customers' blueprints. Occasionally, you can build time deliveries but, more often than not, OEM orders are one-shot deals through which the customer is trying to exert leverage on his or her other suppliers or cover against a strike threat.

I am not so sure. Selling OEM production is more profitable than selling the equivalent number of Beko branded units. Marketing costs per unit are lower and we don't have to invest in full advertising support through our national distributors.

You don't understand. We are making products of outstanding quality these days. Because Turkey's reputation for quality manufacturers is not well-established, we've had to work doubly hard to achieve recognition. We shouldn't be wasting any more time doing OEM production of lower-priced, simple models when we have the quality to take on the best in the world at the premium end of the white goods market."

Sources: Adapted from John A. Quelch, Cases in Strategic Marketing Management. Business Strategies in Muslim Countries, Prentice Hall, 2001.

Question: What strategy would you suggest the managers of Arcelik ought to pursue? Why?

Chapter Summary

Gradual trade liberalization with decreasing protectionism, along with rapid technology changes that affect all types of economic activities, stimulates an environment of more international transactions. Firms are becoming subject to more intense international competition and their home markets have become regional instead of just national, while customer segmentation has become international or even global, leading to increased probabilities that the firm will consider entering a foreign market either in order to defend its home market position or in order to achieve the much-needed room for growth.

The firm will be motivated to enter a foreign market initially by responding to unsolicited request for its products or services and gradually, as it builds more experience and understanding of the international environment, it will consider the various alternative ways to systematically exploit foreign market opportunities.

Various existing forms of foreign market entry strategies move along a continuum consisting of choice factors such as control, risk, investment intensity, and potential profitability, starting from an export activity and continuing with licensing (franchising, foreign manufacturing, contract production) and various forms of FDI (portfolio investments, JVs, M&A, and greenfield investments), and concluding with strategic alliances options.

Apparently, exporting presents a low level of commitment and as the required resource commitments are minimal, the risk of bearing a potential loss is minimal as well. Various forms of licensing make it possible to exploit marketing opportunities through franchising agreements or produce very attractive terms through contract manufacturing agreements while keeping resource commitments and the risks assumed at a low level.

Proceeding to an FDI should be considered on the basis of more market research, planning, and careful selection efforts, as stakes are higher due to the long-lasting character of the venture and the amount of resources that need to be committed. Portfolio investments are a routine option for MNCs that allow minimal exposure to the target markets, with limited organizational implication and higher flexibility. JVs through either a merger or an acquisition have been repeatedly practiced in thousands of occasions worldwide, as a means to exploit certain market opportunities by joining forces, complementing competencies, and sharing risks. Greenfield investments are favored when a no-buy alternative is available and more control is needed, due to either technological concerns or market structure limitations.

Strategic alliances are currently gaining in popularity, partly due to the intrinsic characteristics of the agreement (namely maintaining independency while pooling forces together to achieve a common goal) and partly due to market globalization conditions that require access to resources and networking structures of a much larger scale and scope than ever before.

Review and Discussion Questions

1. Which is the most appropriate foreign market entry mode for a small and medium enterprise? For a relatively big and well-established firm?
2. Do you expect increased M&A investments to follow the EU expansion with 11 more countries joining this economic union?
3. What is the easiest way to enter any foreign market? What is the hardest way to exit from a market? Can you describe the risks, difficulties, and potential losses when exiting a market after having established a fully owned subsidary? Consider different types of firms and industries.
4. Do you think a professional football club firm (e.g., Real Madrid) could expand its activities (beyond participating in international competition) and enter foreign markets? What would be the most applicable market entry mode to do so? Why?
5. Which is the single country that will probably be targeted for potential entry by most firms of all other countries? What would be the most favored types of foreign market entry in that specific country? Why?
6. Should governments of LDCs welcome contract manufacturing type of market entry modes when they know that these are attractive because of low labor cost conditions? What would be the safeguard clauses that you could suggest so that the host country would indeed be better off by such a relationship?

Endnotes

1. Philip Kotler, Marketing Management, Analysis Planning Implementation and Control. Prentice Hall International, Inc., 1997.
2. Franklin R. Root, *Foreign Market Entry Strategies*, AMACOM, 1982.
3. James D. Goodnow and James E. Hansz, "Environmental determinants of overseas market entry strategies," *Journal of Business Studies*, 1972, 3, 33–50.
4. David K. Tse, Yigang Pan, and Kevin Y. Au, "How MNCs choose entry modes and form alliances: The China experience". *Journal of International Business Studies*, 1997, Vol. 28(4), pp. 779–805.
5. J. H. Dunning, "The Eclectic Paradigm of International Production: A Restatement and some Possible Extensions," *Journal of International Business Studies*, 1988, Vol. 19, pp. 1–31.
6. E. Williamson, "Corporate Finance and Corporate Governance," *Journal of Finance*, 1988, Vol. 43(3), pp. 567–591.
7. Mansour Lotayif, "A theoretical model for matching entry modes with defensive marketing strategies," *Journal of American Academy of Business*, Vol. 2(2), pp. 460–466.
8. Franklin Root, *Entry Strategies for International Markets*, Heath & Company, Washington, DC., 1994
9. Jean-Pierre Jeannet and H. David Hennessey, *Global Marketing Strategies* (5th edn). Houghton Mifflin Company, 2001.
10. Warren J. Keegan and Mark C. Green, *Global Marketing* (3rd edn). Prentice Hall, 2003.

11. Vern Terpstra and Ravi Sarathy. *International Marketing* (7th edn). The Dryden Press, 1997.

12. Robert W. Armstrong and Jill Sweeney. "Industry type, culture, mode of entry and perceptions of international marketing ethics problems: A cross-culture comparison," *Journal of Business Ethics*, 1994, Vol. 13(10), p. 775.

13. Keith D. Brouthers and Lance Eliot Brouthers "Explaining the national cultural distance paradox," *Journal of International Business Studies* 2001, Vol. 32(1), pp. 177–189.

14. Frank Bradley, *International Marketing Strategy*. Prentice Hall, 1991.

15. Chan, Peng S. and Robert T. Justis, "Franchising in the EC: 1992 and Beyond," *Journal of Small Business Management*, 1992, Vol. 30(1), p. 83.

16. Dahringer, L. D. and Mühlbacher, H. *International Marketing; A Global Perspective*. Addison-Wesley Publishing Company, 1991.

17. Peter J. Buckley and Marc C. Casson, "Analyzing foreign market entry strategies: Extending the internalization approach," *Journal of International Business Studies*, 1998, Vol. 29(3), pp. 539–561.

18. Jean-François Hennart, "The transaction cost theory of Joint Ventures. An empirical study of Japanese subsidiaries in the US," *Management Science*, 1991, Vol. 37(4).

19. Jafor Chowdhury, "Performance of international joint ventures and wholly owned foreign subsidiaries: A comparative perspective," *Management International Review*, 1992, Vol. 32(2), p. 115.

20. Masaaki Kotabe and Kristiaan Helsen, *Global Marketing Management*, 2nd edn., John Wiley & Sons, Inc., 2001.

21. Michael E. Porter, Competitive Strategy: Techniques for Analyzing Industries and Competitors (New York: Free Press, 1980) & Competitive Advantage (New York: Free Press, 1985).

22. Somkiat Mansumitrchai, Michael S. Minor, and Sameer Prasad, "Comparing the entry mode strategies of large U.S. and Japanese firms, 1987–1993," *International Journal of Commerce & Management*, 1999, Vol. 9(3/4), pp. 1–18.

23. Klaus E. Meyer and Saul Estrin. "Brownfield entry in emerging markets," *Journal of International Business Studies*, 2001, Vol. 32(3), pp. 575–584.

24. G. Baourakis and M. Stroe. "The optimization of the distribution system in the context of supply chain management development," in Pardalos P. (ed.), *Financial engineering, E-commerce & Supply Chain Management*, Kluwer, 2002, pp. 321–334.

9

International Marketing

George Baourakis and Marios I. Katsioloudes,
Spyros Hadjidakis

Objectives

Through this chapter, the student will be exposed to identify the major dimensions and implications of international marketing in the current increasingly globalized business environment.

Listed below are the five main objectives of this chapter:

1. To realize the need to introduce a global dimension to the marketing concept
2. To analyze the deviations of international marketing and the necessary adaptations to standard marketing methods and practices
3. To present the additional dimensions to the marketing mix elements on issues that need to be addressed when marketing is applied on a global scale
4. To describe major trends that are shaping the future of international marketing
5. To discuss the implications for marketing processes of economic and social development worldwide (which are of particular interest to the marketer).

Opening Case

"Nike," an Innovative Marketing Vision "Born in the USA," Caters to "Athletes" Worldwide

Nike's impressive history dates back to 1957 when its founders, Bill Bowerman and Phil Knight, met at the University of Oregon. Phil Knight (who is still Chairman of the Board of Nike) participated as a runner at the university track team that was coached by Bowerman. Bill Bowerman's quest was for light, durable racing shoes for his runners while Knight's dream was to pursue a professional career without having to abandon his favorite sport. In search for a suitable marketing strategy that could combine their aims, they established a company that later became Nike. Bowerman was not just the person who helped initiate the jogging craze in the 1960s; he also designed an innovative shoe for it. Bowerman was inspired for that shoe (known as the "waffle") by his wife's waffle iron and thus by pouring rubber on the surface of a shoe he created a running shoe sole with unique features of strength, lightweightness, and elasticity.

Back in 1963, Phil Knight was still teaching accounting classes at Portland State University, when he traveled to Japan to subcontract Tiger Company for the manufacturing of running shoes that would be subsequently marketed by "Blue Ribbon Sports" through a small running specialty shoe store in Oregon. They became successful and upon exceeding $1 million in sales in 1971, Knight devised the Nike name and the Swoosh trademark with the help of Caroline Davidson who was a student in advertising, and for $35.00 she created the famous SWOOSH ✔ graphic design that has since then become the worldwide emblem of Nike, representing the wing of the Greek Goddess Nike. Nike is the Greek name of the ancient Greek winged Goddess of Victory. Knight and Davidson visualized the wings of the ancient goddess as a symbol of the victory that could be embraced by the world's greatest athletes, with the same appeal as that of the Greek Goddess, as she was the inspiration for the brave warriors on ancient battlefields.

Sports Marketing/Advertisement Revolution by Nike

Nike established a policy of endorsing top athletes from almost the very beginning by persuading Steve Prefontaine, one of the first distance runners, to wear a Nike shoe. Nike has continued endorsing its brands to influential athletes, coaches, teams, colleges, and sports leagues and has thoroughly and actively sponsored sporting events and clinics (Exhibit 9.1).

Not only was Nike endorsing athletes in all sports, the company also started to advertise to everyone. And that is where "Just Do It" was derived from. In 1988, by introducing the "Just Do It" motto, Nike launched its most successful advertisement campaign ever. The motto is still being used in campaigns and it successfully communicates the affiliation of the brand with popular culture. This highly successful campaign skyrocketed Nike's sales. Then, in 1990, Nike established a new approach to improve communication

Exhibit 9.1

Air Jordan I

Air Jordan I

In 1985, Nike signed a contract with Michael Jordan (when he entered as a rookie in the NBA) and launched the new Air Jordan shoes. With the Air Jordan, Nike also became the market leader in basketball shoes and immediately started expanding the brand in other product lines by addressing the general public, with huge success.

with the public by opening its first "Nike Town," with a goal to get people more involved in the "Nike experience."

Vision and Global Strategy

Visualizing an expansion and operation in multiple market segments, Nike has formulated a broad mission statement: "To maximize profits to shareholders through products and services that enrich people's lives." Its strategic objectives thus are to "provide an environment that encourages people to maximize their contribution to Nike, identify *focused consumer segment opportunities*, provide *quality and innovative services* and products internally and externally, establish and *nurture relevant emotional ties* with consumer segments, and maximize profits." Success for Nike depends upon its skills in design research and development and in production and marketing, but in addition Nike is filing application for patents on inventions, designs, and improvements. NIKE® and the Swoosh Design® trademarks are considered as most valuable assets.

Nike Constantly Strives for Innovation

The 1990s marked the decade when Nike first marketed the shoe with a see-through air pocket, designed to give more comfort and appeal to younger buyers, and continued to innovate the running shoe by introducing the "Air Huarache," with lacelles technology. Nike nowadays introduces entirely new series of products, each one designed with the improved features of functionality, physical endurance, and/or aesthetic appearance. The new "Nike Goddess" line targeting the women's segment worldwide and the ACG outdoor clothing, equipment, and apparel are indispensable elements of Nike's marketing strategy to expand in new market segments besides athletes and youngsters. It is noteworthy that when it comes to the definition of an athlete, Nike defines an athlete as "any person with two feet." By focusing on high manufacturing quality and innovative design, Nike expanded its product lines by producing and selling posters, school supplies, and electronic media devices (CDs and mp3 players together with Philips).

Innovative Communication

A more recent tactic of Nike in the field of advertisement is the so-called guerilla marketing, by which Nike uses nonconventional means to communicate with its target audience, through alternative media and not through the conventional approach of officially sponsoring the big sport events, like the Olympics and the World Football Cup.

Innovation through Integration Logistics and Supply Chain Management

Nike was among the first to implement the method of preorder inventory that allowed retailers better control over their provisions. It was a revolutionary business decision of the time, but soon became standard practice among major businesses. Nowadays Nike uses the "futures" ordering online program, which allows retailers to order five to six months in advance of delivery with the guarantee that 90 percent of their order will be delivered within a set time period at a fixed price. The system is also used to network some 47,000 retailers worldwide, with independent distributors, licensees, and subsidiaries in 140 countries, branch offices in 42 counties, 19 distribution centers (DCs) in Europe, Asia, Australia, and Canada, and manufacturers in 28 countries.[1]

Nike Activities in Southeast Asia: Ethical Dilemmas and Social Responsibility Policies

Asian sourcing is of crucial importance not only for Nike but also for all firms that market products with an increased element of labor cost, in order to maintain low manufacturing costs. Nike, though, has in recent years received severe criticism regarding its manufacturing policies in less developed countries because of its "sweatshops," where young workers receive low wages and work long hours in unpleasant and unhealthy conditions, whereas they should normally be attending school and living in decent conditions. The initial reaction of Nike was to downplay the whole issue by adopting a defensive stance of doing nothing illegal since these operations where subcontracted to local agents and as such Nike had neither the legal responsibility nor adequate control over these operations. Nike, after all, was doing nothing more than following practices common to every other company including its competitors. But as public perception regarding this issue continued to have a negative effect on its image, Nike adopted a more radical approach and accepted the social responsibility of not only monitoring but also improving the working conditions for all those employed in the respective manufacturing facilities worldwide. To achieve this, it developed a code of conduct that had to be applied by its contractors and, most importantly, along with other companies in the sector, established a new institution, initially named the Apparel Industry Partnership and subsequently the Fair Labor Association (FLA—http://www.fairlabor.org/), which is a nonprofit organization combining the efforts of industry, nongovernmental organizations (NGOs), colleges, and universities to promote adherence to international labor standards and to improve working conditions worldwide. Moreover, Nike has developed a full social responsibility policy by establishing, monitoring, and reporting rules and practices on environmental, community, diversity, workers, and other stakeholder issues (http://www.nike.com/nikebiz/).

Question: What were the challenges faced by Nike and how did the company overcome them in marketing their products in the global arena?

The Global Environment

Global Marketing

The role of marketing in any social organization system is to effectively respond to consumer needs and wishes, by providing the optimal choices between certain combinations of production alternatives based on limited resources. If the task seems enormous in any national market environment, one can easily appreciate the scope of the endeavor when it is put to action on a global scale. International marketing deals with the set of methodological tools that have been developed to unlock the numerous and complex problems associated with multiple alternative choices available when a company goes international.

International trade has, in fact, been a common practice that has developed along with the rise of some of the most sophisticated civilizations such as the ones located in the eastern Mediterranean basin, during the first millennium BC. Local producers, traders, and city states have been competing since then, even in remote markets, emphasizing the superiority of their merchandise in terms of unique traits, promising a higher level of customer satisfaction.

As enterprises and organizations strive to continuously improve effectiveness and efficiency in order to maintain their competitiveness, they seek opportunities in remote geographic locations or other market segments in order to achieve a vital growth pace.

The volume of international trading, whether financial or economic, is increasing with technological improvements and the progress of suitable institution building. Large companies (such as Coca-Cola, McDonald's, and Daimler-Chrysler) are coordinating their strategic marketing and production operations on a global scale. Nevertheless, "The Globalization of Markets" appeared as a notion through the article of Prof. Theodore Levitt in a 1983 edition of *Harvard Business Review*. In the article Prof. Levitt contended that a certain level of homogeneity appeared in markets throughout the world, thus requiring a similar marketing approach.[2]

Until recently, international marketing used to be the term that characterized all marketing-related activities when they were performed at the level of simple export or import transactions, or when multinational companies needed to adjust to the local environment conditions they were facing in each distinct market environment. But since the introduction of the concept of globalization, a more sophisticated marketing approach has dominated marketing executive thought. In contrast to the traditional approach where marketers had to assess competition in terms of their domestic environment (think locally), these very same competition forces are still exerted locally, but at such a scale that it tends to take global dimensions, thus guiding marketers toward a global market assessment approach (to think globally).

Although the underlying concept of increasing global homogenization is standardization, a blind application of the latter has proven to be a wrong approach in many global campaigns. An example of a well-known failure is "Parker" pen, which, during the 1980s, aimed to apply the same advertising campaign in all the markets it operated in.[3]

In contrast to the early international marketing approaches, most companies that operate in multiple countries nowadays recognize the need to "think globally" but "act locally," without neglecting any opportunities to homogenize as many elements of their marketing mix as possible, according to the constraints and requirements of the local market environment.

By the term "act locally," we refer to the need to adapt the marketing mix elements to the requirements of the local environment whereas by "think globally," we imply a process of standardization, used as method to improve efficiency when a product is marketed in multiple environments.

We should emphasize that global marketing is not a modern term used to replace the term international marketing that has been in use for decades. Global marketing should be considered as a different and distinct subset of international marketing.

In order to clarify the scope of global marketing, it is worthwhile to distinguish the different scope of marketing methods when applied in different parts of the market, whether that is a particular geographic location or some other functional type of criteria.

When marketing is applied within a single market, which is ordinarily the firm's domestic market, then it is referred to as domestic marketing. This is the classical case of marketing research, marketing planning, and marketing management with the usual methods of analyzing the market environment and serving consumers according to their preferences on each of the elements of the marketing mix offered by the business.

When a firm exceeds its domestic market and begins to export abroad, it has to embark on modified marketing activities, related to the specific market environment of those areas. Thus the term "export" marketing is used to describe activities such as market assessment and selection, as well as the appropriate product modification/adaptation that would be necessary so that the product fulfills the local customer needs at an optimal level. Special procedures like shipping, customs clearance, and export documentation are also a usual element of the typical export marketing activity.

When a company gets more involved in marketing activities at the various local environments where it is operating, a marketer is expected to apply the methods of international marketing, namely to collaborate with local sales subsidiaries in order to develop entire marketing strategies for each of the foreign markets it operates in.

With the development of multinational corporations, which extend their operations in multiple domestic environments simultaneously by mobilizing resources at all these environments, another more appropriate type of marketing, the multinational marketing approach, has been adopted. Within this framework a multi-domestic strategy is applied in order to maximize the level of adaptation to local competitive forces, with completely tailor-made marketing strategies.

In an attempt to use resources more efficiently, multinational firms sometimes tend to combine strategies within regions that have a high level of similarity, such as the European Union (EU), thus applying a pan-regional type of marketing.

Global marketing strategy is a strategy that international companies develop within a framework of taking advantage of existing economies of scale, as they tend to serve large parts of the entire global market that shows certain commonalities. With a global marketing strategy, a company aims to develop one general strategy that can be applied throughout the world, with some minor adaptation to local market requirements whenever this might be considered necessary.

International Market Assessment

The international market evaluation process does not concern only the factors residing in the respective market environments. Instead, each firm establishing such an evaluation process should begin from an evaluation of the internal firm environment by analyzing the firm's objectives and its inventory of available or accessible resources that will constitute the basis for suitable opportunity exploitation in international markets.

In order to develop an appreciation for the opportunities existing in world markets, it is essential to develop a method that would allow for an accurate non-misleading assessment of the existing potential in these markets.

The Global Marketing Environment

In order to analyze the global environment in a meaningful way so as to allow a marketer to proceed in decision making within an international marketing strategy framework, one has to start by unveiling the complexity of the global marketing environment. The first possible distinction can be made on the type of economic system in one country, where distinctions are made between market capitalism, a centrally planned socialistic system, or a centrally planned capitalistic/market socialism system. In all these economic systems, markets and central planning coexist up to a certain level. Thus, it all comes down to which of the two elements has the primary command of the economy and, more specifically, which parts of the economy are governed by one of these sets of rules.

The second distinctive parameter that characterizes a country is the stage of economic development. The criterion used in this case is the average income of that country's population. The World Bank[4] is currently using such a four-level classification system. The low-income countries have a total population of 2283 million, but are sharing only 3 percent of the world gross national product (GNP), with an average GNP per capita of $355 in the year 2000. The next category of lower middle-income countries is almost equally populous with 2283 million people, contributing 10 percent to the world GNP, with an average per capita GNP at the level of $1303. The upper middle-income countries comprise 449 million people contributing 7 percent to the world GNP, with an average per capita GNP of $4476. Finally, the top segment of the high-income countries comprises 983 million people contributing 80 percent to the world GNP, with an average per capita GNP at the level of $24,693.

Besides the previous two broad types of criteria to distinguish between global market environments, there have been many attempts to classify countries, and various authors, analysts, and institutions have used different criteria as a basis for their classifications.

To name a few, Dichter[5] has used the size and development of the middle class in a country to distinguish between the almost classless society, contented countries, the affluent countries, countries in transition, and revolutionary countries/primitive countries.

Rostow[6] has used the element of economic growth to classify countries in the categories of: traditional society, development of preconditions for takeoff, the take off, the drive to maturity, and the age of high-mass consumption.

United Nations (UN) is largely using classifications of developed market, developing market, and centrally planned nations. However, alternative methods have been used such as in the case of Liander et al., who grouped countries according to their geographic locations in the areas of Western Europe, Latin America, the Middle East and North Africa, the Far East and Ssub-Saharan Africa.

Kotler[7] used the type of industrial structure and the level of national income as criteria. He distinguishes between subsistence economies; raw-material-exporting economies; industrial economies; very low family incomes/economies; mostly low family incomes/economies; very low, very high family incomes/economies; low, medium, high family incomes/economies; mostly medium family incomes/economies.

Another classification approach has been attempted by Sethi,[8] Goodnow and Hansz,[9] and others,[10] who have used different multiple variables (e.g., aggregate production and transportation, personal consumption, trade, health, and education, political stability indicators, market opportunity variables, economic development, cultural unity, legal barriers, physiographic barriers, geocultural distance, and performance) to distinguish certain clusters of countries.

The National Marketing Environment

Decisions and Environments of International Marketing

Some of the most typical elements of any of the targeted national environments that should be reviewed in such an evaluation process concern the following.

National Market Environmental Dimensions[11]

- Market characteristics such as the technology, investments and stock of capital goods, the stage of development, the stage of product life cycle, saturation levels, buyer behavior characteristics, social/cultural factors and the physical environment, volume, and variety of goods
- Marketing institutions, namely distribution systems, communications media, marketing services (advertising, research, size of trading area, transport systems, etc.)
- Industry conditions, competitive size, and practices of technical development
- Legal environment (laws, regulations, codes, tariffs, taxes, etc.)

Exhibit 9.2

The National Marketing Environment

- Resources, manpower (availability, skill, potential, cost), finance (availability, cost)
- Financial environment such as balance of payments, foreign exchange rate, regulations
- Political environment, current government policies and attitudes, long-range political environment
- Demographic environment, total population, population density, annual percentage rate of increase in population, percentage of population of working age, literacy (percentage of literate population aged 15 and over), agricultural population as a percentage of total population, urbanization (percentage of population in cities with over 20,000 people), primacy (population of the primary city as a percentage of the total population of the four largest cities)
- Social environment, ethnographic density (number of distinct ethnographic groups that comprise 1 percent of the total population), religious homogeneity and identification, racial homogeneity and identification, linguistic homogeneity, social units, structure, behavior patterns, and values

While analyzing the elements of each country's national environment a marketer should be looking for distinctions according to unique characteristics/differentiating influences so that he/she is able to form groups with differentiated attitudes; on the other hand, a marketer should look for similar characteristics/unifying influences so as to segment markets according to essential characteristics and to avoid unnecessary or costly separations.

A typical element that contributes to understanding social behavior in any society is its class structure and social mobility. In most societies it is possible to distinguish between persons of different levels of social status and power and this is coded under the term "class." Even in communist societies, which describe themselves as "classless societies," it is possible to make distinctions between those who belong to the elite party at the top, such as professionals, artists, scientists, and managers, and the workers at the bottom. What is of importance to the marketer is to identify differences in the consumption patterns of each class. Such noticeable differences exist in housing and home furnishings for instance. Members of each class generally live in different types of homes and purchase different kinds of home furnishings, although their income differences might not often be significant. These class differences apply in many consumption categories. The types of food consumed, clothing worn, and the entertainment pursued vary among classes.

Besides identifying the existing class structure, the international marketer should also devote his/her attention to the degree of social mobility. Some societies tend to be characterized by high mobility and persons that have been born and raised in the middle class could move to other higher classes

via education and occupational achievements. In other societies, class structure is less fluid; a person's inherited class determines the educational and
occupational opportunities he or she might have. Consumption patterns are
thus much more likely to be different across social classes in the socially
rigid countries than in those with higher mobility.

The degree of social mobility is generally highest in Western counties, such
as the United States, where the "land of endless opportunity" motto denotes
the opportunity for lower-class individuals to move upward in society. The
degree of social mobility is important to the marketer since in socially mobile
societies, people's social status is often measured at least to some extent by
where they live, what they wear, what kind of car they drive, etc. Depending
on the degree of social mobility in each society, the same product might
require a different marketing strategy to succeed in different markets.

Another important dimension of class structure, however, is the relative
size and number of distinct classes within a society. The following figure
illustrates different societies in terms of the relative sizes of different social
classes (the top rectangle shows the size of the upper class relative to middle
and lower classes for each society in the figure). Ernest Dichter believes that
upper classes seem to be more similar to each other than they are to the rest
of their own society.[12] Lower classes tend to be more culture bound; i.e.,
they are less aware of other cultures and their corresponding "lifestyles."
Their consumption and behavior patterns therefore are more distinct from
those of other classes as regards their clothing, eating, housing, and leisure
attitudes. Middle classes are more apt to do cultural "borrowing" when there
is some social mobility from lower to middle class and within the middle
classes. The international marketer is more likely to address the higher and
middle classes in a foreign market with a standardization approach, while
adaptation is more likely to be needed to the extent that lower classes would
be targeted (Exhibit 9.3).

Exhibit 9.3

The Social—Cultural Environment for International Marketing

Country Risk Assessment

Country risk analysis has its roots in the origin of cross-border lending, which, in turn, evolved along with a similar type of trade that developed between city states in the eastern Mediterranean in the fourth century BC. During the period of colonization, there had been several incidents of failure to meet the terms of loans granted to colonial powers such as Spain, Portugal, England as well as colonies in the Americas of the nineteenth century.[13] As a result, losses were suffered due to insufficient information regarding the debtor's actual financial position, or other factors affecting his ability or willingness to repay the debts.

In the current international economic environment, the political and socioeconomic categories are the two main classifications of risk-associated factors, resulting usually in some kind of financial damage or instability. Political stability is broadly considered as a risk reduction element, while social and political unrest often result in abrupt or even violent regime changes and constitute a factor that increases uncertainty, thus increasing risk. Civil wars, revolutions, and army invasions are the most characteristic cases of political unrest and certainly imply major social and economic effects.

As for the economic content of country risk we can identify three different dimensions of it: political, economic, and financial risk. To further analyze the nature of these risks, we refer to sovereign risk as the ability and willingness to repay debt, transfer risk (which might occur in the event of restrictions) to remit funds across borders that might in turn be attributed to structural economic changes, balance of payments, or external asset or liability management causes. Additional distinctions of country risk elements are duration risk, which denotes the risk associated with the length of the repayment period, and the longer the period the more likely it is that the assets might be exposed to greater market- or country-specific risks. Counterparty risk refers to the type of entity that is contracted, and distinguishes between sovereign governments, which enjoy a higher level of creditworthiness, semi-government agencies and organizations, and private sector enterprises. Industry risk is related to the trends, expectations, relevant competitive position, stage of development, and actual events in each specific industry. Finally, the product and contract-related risk is related to the specific terms and conditions of the contract.

Nowadays, country risk analysis relies on intelligence in the form of aggregated comparative indices, or regional or industry reports, which are regularly provided by many specialized services such as Business Environment Risk Intelligence (BERI) S.A., Control Risk Information Services (CRIS), Economist Intelligence Unit (EIU), Institutional Investor, Moody's Investor Services, Political Risk Services: International Country Risk Guide (ICRG),

Political Risk Services: Coplin-O'Leary Rating System, and Standard and Poor's Rating Group.

The ICRG, being one of the foremost providers of country risk intelligence, compiles monthly data on a variety of political, financial, and economic risk factors to calculate risk indices in each of these categories as well as a composite risk index. Five financial, 13 thirteen political, and 6 six economic factors are used for the compilation of the index.

Some other sources of specialized and thorough international market analysis are provided by the following:[14]

- BMI International News reports on political and economic conditions in 21 emerging market countries such as Chile, China, Egypt, Hungary, Iran, Mexico, Russia, Turkey, and Vietnam, in four global regions (Asia, emerging Europe, Latin America, the Middle East, and Africa) and offers forecasts for their performance.
- Interfax International News provides cross-national and country-specific political, economic, financial, and business news, coupled with in-depth analysis. Interfax is the leading source of political, economic, and financial information from the emerging markets of Central Eastern and European countries (CEECs), China, Russia, the Commonwealth of Independent States (CIS), and the Baltic states.
- PRS Group Country Reports provide basic information on a country, including its political, economic, demographic, and social structures. Reports also cover geographical details, territorial and maritime disputes, power structures, and the business climate.
- PRS Group International Country Risk Guide provides a detailed country-by-country breakdown for more than 130 countries on the comparative risks of operating in, investing in, or lending to particular countries.

The US government and its various agencies also produce intelligence reports, such as the following:

- Country Commercial Guides, which cover 146 countries and contain information on the business and economic situation of foreign countries and the political climate.
- BISNIS Reports (Business Information Service for the Newly Independent States), which provides country and industry reports on prospects for US businesses in Russia and the NIS—Armenia, Azerbaijan, Belarus, Georgia, Kazakhstan, Kyrgyz Republic, Moldova, Russia, Tajikistan, Turkmenistan, Ukraine, and Uzbekistan.

Within the process of market assessment for each country that might be a potential target market, it is essential for the marketer to look beyond general economic risks and concentrate on risks that might affect the marketing strategy of the firm.

Such marketing-associated risks are related to market access, country infrastructure, and logistics. A company wishing to assess the marketing environment should gather intelligence and make its own analysis on issues such as industry analysis and trends, market potential and risk, market entry strategies, potential expansion, customer and product analysis.

Market Information

Scanning the Global Marketplace for Opportunity

Elements of a Marketing Information System

When a firm expands its operations beyond the domestic market, it has to develop a system to retrieve, process, and analyze the necessary information that it will use for information-based decision making within the framework of an integrated marketing strategy. The process and methods presented in the previous two sections will assist the firm in forming a basic evaluation of the global environment, through analysis of the existing international opportunities as well as the competitive forces it will have to handle in order to decide whether to "go international" or remain in the domestic market.

The market and risk assessment intelligence will also be necessary in the same context, allowing for classification and comparison between countries or regions, because due to the limited resources that are available to a firm, it will always have to make a choice of which markets to enter. This part of intelligence should allow for the determination of the political context, prospects of economic growth, the stage of economic cycle, purchasing power, related industry growth trends, and government policies and regulations.

Additional information concerning the size of the market, potential trade barriers, transport and logistics costs, local competition, government policies and political stability will be used in order to decide how to enter each market. Competition needs to be analyzed in terms of competitors' strengths and weaknesses, tactics, strategies, existing relative market shares, new product launches, pricing policies and cost positions, and image and brand perceptions.

The final group of necessary information elements concerns decision making related to the management of the marketing mix elements, namely information on customer profiles, distribution channels, promotional practices, and consumer behavior. As for the product element itself, the analysis will focus on the profile of the targeted users, either individual consumers or industrial buyers, with data concerning their demographic characteristics, growth rates of the segment, customer response to promotional campaigns, the launch of new products, price responsiveness, switching behavior, and other cultural differences. As for the other elements of the marketing mix, data should be collected on the structure, evolution, and performance of distribution channels, the relative pricing policies, price elasticity, types of advertising and promotional campaigns, service offered, and the functioning effectiveness of logistics networks.[15]

How to Reach the Necessary Information Sources

Relevant sources of information exist in abundance nowadays for the international marketer who needs to be very selective, based on his specific project information needs. The web offers a myriad of information sources on the Internet that can be used for an initial evaluation of the most generic type of data. Besides that, there are many specialized market research companies with various services in the form of access to online databases and ready or tailor-made reports. Some of those sources are provided by:

- Edimax Market Newsletters, which contain information on the following four regions: Africa and the Middle East, Asia Pacific, Europe, and Latin America. The reports contain information on changing market trends in different sectors such as communications, insurance, health care, and consumer durables, along with analytical reports on macro- and microeconomic activities.
- Euromonitor Reports, with market-related analysis and background statistics for 185 countries. Topics include consumer segmentation and spending patterns, eating and drinking habits, media use, economic indicators, and industry performance. Over 6000 documents are covered from Euromonitor's Consumer Lifestyle and World Marketing Data & Statistics series.

Additional information sources can be found, for instance, in the reports of various US government agencies, such as the following:

- International Market Insight Reports, which cover 189 countries with export market reports designed for US companies interested in doing business in foreign countries.
- Industry Sector Analysis (ISA) Reports, which analyze a specific industry within a country and cover 73 countries.
- GAIN Reports, which focus on the agricultural markets within a country. They provide information on agricultural production, trading

forecasts, foreign legislation and regulations, and trade policies affecting US trade.

- Central and Eastern Europe BIS Reports, which focus on financing, marketing, and changing business conditions and regulations in the 15 CEECs.

Marketing Information Systems

Information technology has contributed significantly to the options available today to the marketer. A marketing information system (MIS) may be designed to incorporate data from specific applications such as electronic point of sales (POS), electronic data interchange, intranet, and efficient consumer response systems, all of which are designed so as to primarily assist in managing various parts of the business activities, while at the same time providing data for the improvement of marketing decision making. Data regarding the volume and replenishment speed of stocks, the volume of sales on specific product items, the peak sales periods, especially when combined with pricing or promotional data, can contribute significantly to the design of an effective marketing mix program. Most international firms maintain some kind of an international MIS that collects data in electronic online form through the network of their agents, distributors, sales representatives, shippers, wholesalers, and retailers regarding the inventory, and sales figures per product, time period, and geographic location as well as many other significant marketing mix elements.

Formal International Marketing Research Programs

Having scanned the global marketplace and identified the most interesting market segments that could possibly define a target market, the international firm should assess whether it should pursue the potential opportunities or reject them due to possible incompatibilities with the firms' international global marketing strategy.

Thus in order to acquire detailed and precise information on the expected costs and benefits of the specific project, such as entering a new market/segment, or introducing a new product line, a firm has to develop a tailor-made marketing research program that will allow it to objectively assess the opportunity presented.

The basic method for designing an international marketing research plan does not differ too much from that for a similar research plan that is intended for a single market. Essential parts of the research would be to identify the research problem(s), then process the available secondary or desk research data that was aforementioned in the preceding paragraphs in order to accumulate much of the information needed in the most cost-effective way, followed by a primary data and survey research section. Primary data collection is usually an indispensable part of marketing research as most often some of the research data predetermined to be essential for the purpose of the study are not readily available through published statistics, reports, and studies. Depending on the type of product, or service concerned, there are different methods of primary data collection such as survey research, personal interviews, consumer panels, observation, focus group research, sampling, and finally various technology-based methods such as POS data, Internet surveys, and television viewership determined through specially designed electronic devices.

As for the last part of any research plan, which is data analysis and presentation, the applied techniques do not necessarily differ in the case of international marketing when compared to conventional data analysis techniques. They depend on the type of research question rather than the scope of research as a whole. Nevertheless, some data analysis techniques have proved to be more useful and, thus, are commonly applied in international marketing research. Such techniques are comparative analysis, which is applied for market potential and marketing performance comparisons between countries and market segments for the company or product; cluster analysis, which is used to identify within-group similarities and between-group differences; market estimation by analogy, which is used to draw an analogy (when very detailed data are not available or are difficult to get) for the market potential; and demand pattern analysis, which is used to estimate consumer or industrial demand as it correlates with the growth level of certain industries or the general level of development.[16]

However, what makes a real deference in international marketing research is the almost constant incompatibility of statistics and secondary data for similar subjects among countries and systems, along with culturally related perceptions that need to be taken into consideration in the design of an effective research plan. Often it is imperative that many modifications (concerning, for instance, the phrasing of questions or the meaningful structure of evaluation scales) be made according to the national research plans when a survey is to be run in multiple countries.

International Marketing Strategy and Management

Cross-national Marketing Planning and Strategy Development

Strategy and planning are two terms that, although they are often used interchangeably, are two distinct concepts. Strategy formation is more about choices rather than plans of action or overall effectiveness optimization, while planning is about selecting the optimal way to pursue the given objectives or an efficiency optimization process regarding the strategic choices that have proceeded. Nevertheless, to the extent that firms regularly devote their resources to strategy formation and development on a long-term basis, the process itself is subject to a planning framework. In this sense, we often refer to the term strategic planning as denoting the long-range planned process of strategic decision making.

Strategic decision-making takes places at various levels by different types of entities. Large national, multinational, or global corporations, which are active in various industries/sectors in many different countries, formulate their portfolio or corporate strategy by deciding in which sectors, industries, and market segments they should compete.

As far as marketing managers are concerned, the strategic decision-making they have to make at a corporate level relates mostly to the selection of the appropriate market to compete in or market entry strategies. Licensing agreements, along with contract manufacturing and franchising, are some comparatively limited committing forms of engagement to a market, whereas other market entry strategies like direct investment or joint venture imply more resource commitments, thus increasing the level of potential risk. The most extensive form of participation in a foreign market is via ownership or equity stake, also known as a greenfield investment, or alternatively, through a merger and acquisition (M&A) of an existing firm. In fact, firms develop various additional types of international partnerships, in the form of collaborative agreements, strategic alliances, or strategic partnerships, in order to jointly exploit opportunities appearing in the market, while limiting costs and risks. It is common for global firms to choose the most suitable of the aforementioned forms of market entry strategies or a combination of them, according to the specific conditions existing in each country. Sometimes they might opt to just set up an exporting operation, avoiding a higher commitment in that market.

Other types of collaborative strategies are the ones existing in Japan and Korea and referred to as the Keiretsu and Chaebol systems, respectively. Such systems are vast conglomerates of related and unrelated activities sharing as common characteristics the mutual support through cross stock ownership, with large stock shares owned by a bank or a family and managerial coordination through cross executive participation in management boards. This strategy aims to defend the competitive position and market share.

An additional international marketing strategy is related to the choice of market expansion. Companies might expand in new markets either by diversifying their activities and products by serving different market segments or by expanding in more countries to increase their competencies and market share by concentrating in the same global segment across countries. Different combinations between the concentration and diversification are also possible; country diversification and market segment concentration, for instance, is the classic example of a global company focusing on serving one consumer need but across multiple countries, thus concentrating on one global segment to attain expertise combined with a competitive cost structure.

Once these decisions are made, the need arises for deciding and designing an appropriate competitive business strategy for each of the business activities that the firm engages in for every market segment. Choices at this level may be based on Porter's model[17] that distinguishes between three generic business strategies, namely cost leadership, differentiation, and focus. Each strategy aims to create and attain a competitive advantage for the firm in the respective markets it chooses to enter.[18] The choice can be based on a SWOT type analysis that considers market opportunities and threats in combination with strengths and weaknesses of the firm when compared to those of competitors.

A combination of the approaches mentioned in the two preceding paragraphs can be drawn with a reference to the three respective strategies followed in global marketing. Thus, a standardized global marketing strategy may be followed when the firm has identified one homogenous global segment for the same product or need and can attain a competitive advantage while keeping costs at a low level. Concentrated global market concerns small market niches and a firm chooses to follow this strategy when it can offer superior quality and service to a small market segment. In contrast, a differentiated global marketing strategy is to be followed when a firm wishes to develop broad market coverage with different marketing mix combinations for each of the different types of markets it operates in.

International marketers also frequently engage in additional corporate planning processes, which might refer to the broadly applied models of the Boston Consulting Group approach (BCG), the General Electric/McKinsey (GE) approach, the Profit Impact of Market Strategy (PIMS) approach, or even scenario planning. These are the main traditional corporate planning models but since they concentrate more on elements like profitability, market growth, market shares, and other operational or market environment elements, international marketing is not a major input in these processes.

Beyond the initial phase of strategic decision-making that has been referred to till this point here (market segment commitment, country selection, mode of entry, and marketing strategy), international marketing planning also has an operational and controlling part.

Such marketing operational plans might refer to the medium-term period (2 to −4 years), to the short-term period (1 year), or even to quarterly action plans, which are essentially controlling plans. Such plans of international firms contain targets and milestones that should be met at all control levels (head, regional, and local offices), referring to all marketing mix elements (sort of products developed, segment selection, positioning, pricing, sales and distribution channel objectives). These plans, through the imposition of objectives and targets, enable marketing executives to evaluate the implemented strategy and, whenever necessary, to undertake action so as to improve or amend the less effective parts of it.

The International Marketing Mix: Product, Promotion, Pricing, and Placing Strategies

The task of designing an effective international marketing mix should incorporate the decisions made in the previous stages of the international marketing strategy. The decisions concerning issues of market segmentation, market entry, generic marketing strategy, as well as other objectives and policies that the firm should pursue in different geographic locations, comprise the basis for the formation of an appropriate international marketing mix (Exhibit 9.4).

Exhibit 9.4

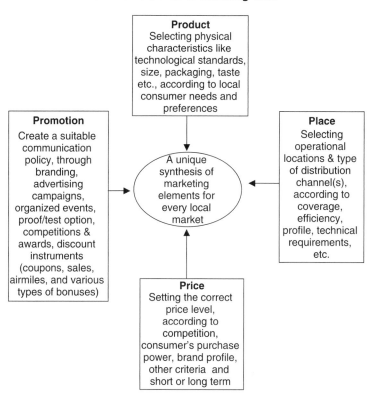

The International Marketing Mix

Product
Selecting physical characteristics like technological standards, size, packaging, taste etc., according to local consumer needs and preferences

Promotion
Create a suitable communication policy, through branding, advertising campaigns, organized events, proof/test option, competitions & awards, discount instruments (coupons, sales, airmiles, and various types of bonuses)

A unique synthesis of marketing elements for every local market

Place
Selecting operational locations & type of distribution channel(s), according to coverage, efficiency, profile, technical requirements, etc.

Price
Setting the correct price level, according to competition, consumer's purchase power, brand profile, other criteria and short or long term

Product

The definition of what is a product for any given market segment is very crucial in order to decide on elements that make up the total product besides the core product. These include the brand name, image, product standards, packaging, labeling, warranty, installation, after-sales service, and credit.

The choice between product adaptation and (global) standardization is central not only to the design of the total product but also to every other aspect of the marketing mix elements. The core concept of marketing is, after all, to optimize customer satisfaction by offering solutions to problems corresponding to needs and wants. Thus, researching and analyzing customer preferences and corresponding by developing suitable products directly implies the need to adapt the global firms' product to local needs. Nevertheless, as has previously been explained in the introduction of this chapter, the higher the level of adaptation the higher the cost. On the other hand, the more global the standardization tends to be, the more cost-effective the entire marketing operation of the firm is (Exhibit 9.5).

Another product strategy is product extension in combination with communication adaptation, which aims to keep cost low while increasing the effectiveness of communication through adaptation to local conditions, which is often preferred due to cultural differences. The reverse combination, namely of product adaptation, i.e., communication extension, is effective when the core product has to be adapted due to certain conditions imposed

Exhibit 9.5

Standardization and Branding

The World's 10 Most Valuable Brands		
RANK	BRAND	2003 BRAND VALUE BILLIONS
1	COCA-COLA	$70.45
2	MICROSOFT	65.17
3	IBM	51.77
4	GE	42.34
5	INTEL	31.11
6	NOKIA	29.44
7	DISNEY	28.04
8	McDONALD'S	24.70
9	MARLBORO	22.18
10	MERCEDES	21.37

Data: Interbrand Corp., J.P.Morgan Chase & Co., Citigroup, Morgan Stanley

The list is produced annually from Business week based on multiple criteria that are used in order to estimate the market value of global brands.

Standardization is not only an element of cost consideration, but it is preferred as an approach in terms of branding as it is usually one of the highest appreciated assets of the firm. The brand name conveys most of the communication content that the firm wants to emit and it is closely related to the total image of the company. For that reason, and in order to achieve advertisement effectiveness, international companies prefer to maintain the same brands along with the same product in all markets, when they follow the *Product & communication extension strategy (dual extension)*, especially when they aspire to establish global brands[1].

by the local market environment (for physical, legal, or cultural factors), while this is not deemed necessary for the communication element. The final choice is for a dual-adaptation strategy, with both product and communication being adapted to local market conditions, which was often implemented by multinational corporations (Exhibit 9.6).

Exhibit 9.6

Dual Adaptation Strategy

In the automotive sector, **General Motors** along with its subsidiaries and with participation in various other local manufacturers, has crafted an extensive network of production facilities in 16 countries which share most of the know-how and technology in order to provide service to 80 different countries, but are nevertheless adapted to the local market conditions.

Factory Location, Country	Badge (Brand name)
Eisenach, Germany	Vauxhall/Opel corsa
Zaragoza, Spain	Vauxhall/Opel corsa
Azambuja, Portugal	Opel corsa
Sao Caetano do sul, Brazil	Chevrolet Corsa
Ramos, Mexico	Chevrolet Chevy (Corsa)
Shangai, China	Buick Sail
Bogota, Colombia	Chevrolet Corsa
Quito, Equator	Chevrolet Corsa
Valencia, Venezuela	Chevrolet Corsa
Rosario, Argentina	Chevrolet Corsa
Port Elizabeth, South Africa	Corsa
Halol, India	Corsa
Australia	Holden Barina
Cairo, Egypt	Corsa

A **Vauxhall** brand model made for the United Kingdom

A German **Corsa** version

A **Corsa** model destined for Brazil

A **Holden Barina** version in Australia

Besides the aforementioned strategies that relate to the existing product lines of the mother company, and having first introduced those products in the domestic market, international companies also follow the innovation strategy when they introduce new product lines through product invention and through new product line development. This product strategy is necessary when differences may not be compromised between existing and newly targeted market segments.

Price

Setting the price at an appropriate level is not a simple task when marketing a product in any market. When the task is applied to the international market, however, it becomes a crucial element testing the limits of all other areas of marketing efforts. There are two limiting ranges of the international price of a product. Cost is the determining factor for the lower limit (price floor) and prices of comparable products for the upper limit (price ceiling). The question boils down to what is the right price within the aforementioned range.

If the global market was indeed a homogeneous one, then one global price should also prevail. But since there are myriad factors differentiating between the conditions prevailing in international markets, price differences tend to reflect at least a certain analogy of these differences. The factors that need to be considered when deciding international pricing strategies can be distinguished as those existing in the internal company environment (i.e., fixed/variable, production and marketing costs, market share, positioning, profitability) as well as those factors concerning the product (i.e., stage of the product life cycle, product attributes) and those characterizing the local markets (i.e., consumer's ability to pay, adaptation needs, distribution channels, barriers to trade), and the external market environment (i.e., competition, government regulations, exchange rates, inflation). Besides these factors, decision making regarding price relates to a number of managerial (i.e., transfer pricing, foreign currencies, gray markets, export price escalation) and financial issues/alternative options (bank, government or countertrading financing, customer vs. supplier arranged financing) as well.[19]

In accordance with overall international strategies, and after considering the aforementioned factors, there are alternative pricing strategies. The market skimming pricing strategy is applied when a company deliberately wishes to limit its market segment, by imposing a very high price level, thus immediately distinguishing from mass market segments and mass producers/competitors. Companies pursuing a differentiation strategy by offering luxury goods and targeting the elite global market segment often apply such pricing strategies.

A sort of opposite pricing strategy is the penetration pricing strategy, which is in essence an attempt to penetrate a foreign market through offering a price that is often set lower than the cost and at a level that can be afforded by the consumer of the targeted market segment. Although no company can survive by offering below-cost prices for long, this pricing strategy is often necessary in order to create an initial customer base that will allow continuation, adequate market growth, higher volumes, and economies of scale, thereby leading gradually to improved profitability through lower production costs.

Choosing between extending national policies and adapting to local conditions applies to the pricing issue just like it applies to the global strategies adopted for products by global firms. Extension or ethnocentric pricing is the strategy that sets the price per unit at the same level in all markets where the firm is operating, disregarding local condition, which is, of course, a simple approach but might (as it often does) give fertile ground to competitors to respond with similar-quality products offered at lower prices. In order to respond to local conditions and better coordinate marketing strategies, international firms often follow the adaptation/polycentric pricing strategy by assigning the responsibility for price setting to their local subsidiaries. When a firm considers issues such as the fact that price should reflect the product's quality, that it should be in line with local competition, or that it should distinguish between market segments, then the geocentric pricing strategy is more likely to be implemented for the more efficient conformance to local market objectives and requirements.

Place

The international marketing strategy and management decisions related to the appropriate placement of products within the local distribution channels worldwide have to be taken into consideration along with the overall international marketing strategy objectives. In order to reach each national market there are multiple alternatives, starting from the domestic market where it is possible to select between export management companies, export agents, and exports directly undertaken through the establishment of an internal department. Some companies even choose to export through the Internet, employing different types of distribution systems in foreign markets that consist of multiple levels of import intermediaries (agents), wholesalers, industrial buyers, and retailers.

Because of the rapid changes occurring in social and business structures worldwide and because entering into a distribution agreement resembles a marriage or a long-term commitment, the international marketer has to decide upon the most effective distribution system that will remain effective in the competitive environment in the future. On the basis of objectives of the predetermined international marketing strategy, the marketer will have to choose between a selective distribution system where he would have to carefully select one or more distributors that will be able to meet some strict selection criteria (such as support expertise and service) and an intensive distribution system that aims to take advantage of all possible distribution options in order to achieve the broadest possible coverage of the market.[20]

At the retail level, distribution channels offer many alternatives, which evolve under different concepts, regarding the service and options offered. Alternatives range between department stores, specialty retailers, supermarkets, convenience stores, discount stores, hypermarkets, supercenters, category killers, factory outlet stores, and even networks of automatic vending machines. Other options that are becoming increasingly popular include the possibility of operating through a fully owned chain of stores or through independent stores under a franchise agreement. Many firms are increasingly using the Internet to develop e-commerce options such as retailing (selling directly to final consumers). Examples include amazon.com or online auction systems such as ebay.com, or even the so-called business-to-business (B2B) industrial distribution networks. Piggyback marketing is another practice used especially in emerging markets that do not have many developed distribution networks. In this scenario, companies make use of an existing distribution system, which they contract to market their own product lines as well as their initial assortment.

When distribution concerns perishable products, the entire system becomes more challenging. Supply chain management and inventory management (such as just-in-time) practices have been developed to improve the effectiveness and efficiency of distribution systems, having as a main objective the cost reduction through less time and volume of inventory needed in the supply chain and more accuracy/lower returns due to faults. In the perishable products market the same cost-cutting objectives combined with value increase objectives in the form of supplying fresher products, within reduced lead delivery time.

Because of the advances in technology, physical distribution, logistics management, and transportation, alternative solutions are rapidly changing, thus allowing a higher level of efficiency for innovative distribution networks, but the international firm that is about to enter in a new market and select a distribution partner should be alert and monitor the continuously changing options that may drastically affect its competitive position.

Promotion

Various forms of communication are indispensable elements for the success of the international marketing strategy. Advertising, public relations, sales promotion, personal selling, and various new forms of marketing communication through the new media are usually studied within the promotion element of the company's marketing mix.

Once more, as in all other marketing mix elements, the debate of adaptation versus standardization becomes relevant, this time regarding the appropriate design and composition of the promotional mix.[21]

Effective communication is the essence in all promotion elements. In a communication system, it is the international firm that acts as a sender (source) that transmits a signal (information) considered important in relation to the total product offered to a final receiver (customer) through advertisement, personal contact, and other means. At the same time, the communication channels should allow feedback information to flow backward, from the customer toward the firm. The objective of the first direction of communication transmission is usually described with the use of the term AIDA derived from the initials of the words attention, interest, desire, and action. The term AIDA refers to the process of attracting the attention of the target public so as to motivate them into the desired direction of action (endorsing the product). The reverse direction of communication (i.e., from consumer to the company) is also vital, not only for the evaluation of the effectiveness of the communication process itself, but even more for the adaptation of the marketing mix, whenever this might be considered necessary (Exhibit 9.7).

Nevertheless, global advertising and marketing agencies thrive in the global marketplace, focusing on serving the global accounts (large promotional campaigns of global firms with high budgets) and managing the promotional mix on behalf of their clients. Global advertising agencies can take advantage of economies of scale to use rare creative resources in combination with media networks, which can secure global coverage. Despite the fact that local advertising agencies restrict their operations only to advertising and not to additional services, they are better suited when it comes to following a persuasive rather than an informative approach as they can better associate with the local culture.

Moreover, an effective international promotional mix will have to decide whether it is appropriate to follow a pull or a push promotional strategy. A pull strategy is the one that the company pursues when the company wants to communicate effectively with the end consumer, who in turn reacts with increased demand, actually pulling the distribution channels to operate from the end point toward the source. The opposite promotional strategy is characterized as the push strategy, where the company commits its resources to strengthen the function of the distribution channel so that its increased effectiveness will finally reach the end consumer. When it comes to industrial or durable products, or products with a high technological content, then personal selling and good sales personnel performance are essential for the effectiveness of the campaign. Thus, a push strategy is preferred, as it empowers the distribution channels to work in this direction.

Exhibit 9.7

Communication Transmission

Promotion and advertising campaigns for **Joanne Rowling's** *Harry Potter* book series have been translated in 35 languages and embraced all types of modern communication media, targeting not only child audiences worldwide, but carefully selected adult consumer segments as well.

International promotion

To design an effective common international promotion campaign, a marketer has to assume that he would be addressing the messages to a homogeneous audience, but since this is rarely the case, the formation of a promotional campaign will have to take all possible differentiating factors into consideration. To mention some of these factors, we might, refer to legal restrictions that might, for instance, forbid the use of television advertisement for certain consumer products such as tobacco, children's toys, or the use of nudity. These restrictions, though, are usually imposed because of national *values*, *norms*, *traditions*, and other *cultural characteristics* of the *local society*. Even more common factors are language, literacy, sub-cultural differences, all of which call for distinct treatment.

Additional means of promotion that are available to the international marketer are direct mail, catalogs, tele-shopping, sponsoring, indirect endorsement through placement in motion pictures or television shows, and advertisement hosted on web sites on the Internet, each of which can play an important promotional role provided that it adequately covers the targeted market segment at a cost-effective ratio.

Cross-cultural Consumer Marketing

The most cumbersome decision element is to understand, evaluate, and modify the international marketing mix (through the entire process of market research, assessment, marketing strategy, formation planning, management, and control), to make up for cultural differences existing among people all around the globe.

Because culture pervades all aspects of marketing, which are numerous, and because of extensive coverage of this issue in previous sections of the book, we can briefly identify the impact of cultural differences in international marketing.

Consumer behavior, the study of which is the cornerstone of marketing, differs across countries and cultures with different basic human perceptions about time and space, the concept of the self and others, innate human nature, the way one interacts with others based on social factors such as "power distance," "masculinity/femininity," uncertainty avoidance, interaction clashes, and self-reliance versus dependence. Very essential for marketing management is also the cultural relativity of management theories and cultural differences concerning attitudes toward action, the way people deal with desires and feelings, and how they cope with rules. Differences also exist regarding the position of one culture against other cultures (the issue of cultural borrowing). Studying these differences and identifying to what extent people in the examined segments differ is of crucial importance for successful market segmentation and distinction between homogeneous and heterogeneous groups. Identifying similarities is equally important.

Designing an international market research plan should not be complete without considering the equivalence of research methods across cultures. The use of personal interviews and the construction of measurement scales are just some of the most frequently used methodological tools.

The most powerful methodological tool that contributes to decision making regarding appropriate international marketing is the distinction between global strategies and locally customized strategies.[22]

Other culture-associated factors also play an important role in the composition of the international marketing mix. We might for instance refer to the extent to which groups of countries or consumers share the same cultural traits, or to the differences in the utility derived from product attributes or the consumers' perception regarding the brand or the country of origin, as a factor that shapes brand image. We can also refer to the bargaining rituals and price-related perceptions that affect pricing decisions and finally the importance of personal contacts and the channel style and service as important parameters for the distribution channel choices.[23]

Industrial Marketing

Business marketing, otherwise known as industrial marketing, is used as a term to distinguish it from consumer marketing. Both of these areas of marketing are discussed and analyzed with a common body of knowledge, principles, and theoretical and methodological tools. However, since they are applied to different buyers and markets, they should also be handled differently. What is certainly different is the nature of markets, demand functions, behavior of individuals/institutions/buyers and sellers, market environment influences, and the appropriate marketing strategies and marketing mix composition that should be applied.

The nature of transactions is different as well, because industrial or business buyers do not derive a personal utility from the products they purchase. Instead, they do so in order to respond to a derived demand. In other words, business/industrial products are destined to be used further downstream in order to satisfy consumer needs at a later stage. Thus, collaboration or partnership between the initial supplier and the in-between firm, before their combined "synthesized" product reaches the consumer level, is an essential and vital requirement and method to improve the outcome.

An additional critical concept is the value chain, in which all "actors" at all intermediate stages should coordinate and optimize their performance so that the outcome will have a certain value to the consumer. To focus on, analyze, and understand primary customer (consumer) needs is an essential function for all partners in the chain; it motivates, disciplines, and streamlines employees and executives to a certain target.

The concept of supply chain management addresses all issues that influence the effective and efficient function of the chains, at all stages and involving all decision makers.[24]

The element of timely generation of intelligence, and process and response to that, is of critical importance and, if handled effectively, could give a competitive advantage. Reducing the necessary time for market needs assessment, product design, production, distribution, and new product introduction is a factor of utmost importance.

The role of telecommunications, transportation, and Internet technology also plays a crucial role at this point, with global online communications drastically improving the physical infrastructure basis that allows more efficient development of industrial marketing transaction at an international basis.

Industrial International Marketing Applications

The market for industrial products is international to a much higher level in comparison with the consumer product markets. Culture and personal influences are much less relevant in industrial marketing as they appear only in some parts of the transaction/buying and (personal) process and not in the formation and expression of needs and preferences as in the case for consumer products. The role of persons is thus restricted so as to maintain effective communication between the two transaction parties regarding the content of the product transacted, and not to influence it.

The initial stages in the value chain of many industries like the automobile, the electronics, the computer appliances, and many other industries are virtually global, with most of the parts standardized, produced, and traded all over the world.

Nevertheless, some parts of the international industrial marketing mix require particular attention from the international marketer. The process of responding to international calls for tenders to supply products, whole projects or long-term services to international firms, or governments, or other institutions is a very distinctive approach that differentiates industrial marketing communication and sales process from the consumer marketing approach. Because of the significance of these activities and the level of resources involved, special technical, legal, and communication expertise are required in these circumstances.

Another point where attention must be focused with regard to international industrial marketing relates to the different methods of pricing. Cost estimation methods like activity-based costing, which is a method used to improve measurement of every distinctive activity, or total cost of ownership, which attempts to reveal all types of hidden (sometimes) costs that are associated with the entire process that a product or a service is involved in, are very crucial for selection on the correct basis.

Vertical Coordination in the Retailing Sector

Responding to changing demographics, consumer attitudes, declining average household size, convenience preferences, and health risk concerns, retailers are replacing the simple transactional model of relationships (most vital information was lost with the completion of each transaction in the spot market), building up long-term relationships with key suppliers in order to utilize all the available information through a continuation of the information flow, parallel to the existing product flows, in order to offer improved services (quality management) in a more efficient way.

Retailers were pursuing a differentiation marketing strategy for decades through innovation and other modifications of the marketing mix (higher value-added products, new products, new product lines, better services), in order to secure adequate profit margins, but this has changed as the return on investment (ROI) principle was adopted in the early 1990s. With ROI, the focus is not on efficient management of Stock Keeping Units (SKUs), but rather on the performance of the product section as a whole. Following this approach, consideration is given to the self-space and expenses made by each subcategory for every product, thus reducing assortment to more realistic levels (where consumer choices become more evident), while there is adequate variety, but most importantly, cost remains a central consideration.

Efficient consumer response (ECR) is a term used for a similar approach, described as the responsive, consumer-driven system, in which distributors and suppliers work together as business allies to maximize consumer satisfaction while cost efficiency remains an equally important parameter as well. Accurate information and high-quality products flow through a paperless system between manufacturing line and checkout counter. ECR is split up into four activities: efficient replenishment, efficient assortment, efficient promotion, and efficient product introduction.

Logistics is also a critically important success factor for the development of multilateral supply chain collaboration, so as to achieve continuous transportation under controlled conditions, accurate delivery according to the program that has been agreed with the retailer, at the regional distribution centers (DCs), and flexibility to increase or reduce pace of delivery according to actual conditions.

Value-added logistics is a process that integrates processing steps, thus adding value to the product. An effort is made to reorganize some activities that take place in the logistical process in such a way so as to make activities occur simultaneously with others, or at a different location, while at the same time decreasing costs.

Chain Marketing

From the marketing perspective, ECR comprises several methods and systems that are developed to meet consumer needs more effectively. Information is collected for the few actors in the segment, e.g., by means of a client card. So, marketing can cater for individual clients and adapt effectively to the consumers' shopping pattern.

Transparency has become a very important element of the marketing and communication efforts of large retailers. Thus, information systems have to be able to convey critical information (usually related to food safety) or just purely descriptive information related to the origin and the methods applied for the production of each item.

Chain marketing refers to the marketing of products that takes into consideration the interaction of the links in the chain too. Such an approach is essential in order to optimize operations throughout the production, processing, and distribution steps in the chain.

Integrated management and marketing information systems facilitate the development of internal (between all the partners in the chain) and external (customer) communication, with a twofold scope, which is used internally in order to improve management effectiveness and produce products and services that satisfy consumers and externally to improve promotion techniques and communication with customers.

Chain inversion is the reorientation of information and actions flow, from the market to the production process, in order to make market information influential and productive throughout all relevant stages of the production chain and to improve the match between actual market demand and production. Decisions about the product assortment, promotion, and introduction to market are thus primarily based on demand.

Continuous information flow throughout the chain is about conveying market information in relevant forms at all relevant places in the chain to advance the timely delivery (just-in-time) of adequate products at the proper places. For this purpose, specific online communication systems are used for the management of logistic and production systems.

Pricing policy and methods can be developed within a chain, not only based on cost (cost+margin) but also in a dynamic way that takes into account the conditions created by competition. With regard to pricing policies, *activity based cost accounting and economic value added* (EVA) principles have replaced the historic cost accounting practices. According to the new approach, cost should account for all the product elements that the consumer actually chooses, including services. Accordingly, prices should be based on consumer preferences rather than on internal expense handling.

Supply Chain Strategy and Management

Retailers, pursuing improved performance in every product section, have introduced the principle of category management, aiming to offer high-quality products that are unique and attractive to consumers at a competing price level. Category management sets return on investment (ROI) as its driving principle regarding decisions that have to be made on the assortment, the space on the shelves, and the other elements of the marketing mix. When suppliers wish to gain the status of a "preferred supplier" they would have to be able to offer appropriate marketing and management services in close collaboration with the retailer, sometimes even by accepting the challenge to undertake a significant management task of that particular section in the supermarket.[25]

Chain management refers to continuous monitoring and control regarding the planning and execution of activities. All partners should evaluate the execution of activities in conformance with the planning, in order to improve the functioning of the chain. Chain management is dedicated to management covering all links as well as to management of individual links from a chain perspective.[26]

The application of modern (chain) management tools, such as operational planning methods, budgeting techniques, and review methods, along with integrated information systems, is considered essential for the effective and efficient management of the chain. Such information systems are the systems that interlink POS data with stock control in external DCs (distribution centers) and identification systems locating products in various stages in the chain.

Another important chain management method is resource sharing, which refers to the joint use of internal and external resources by partners in the chain in order to achieve the common goals. Such examples of sharing resources are knowledge bases about consumer behavior, laboratory facilities, and financial resources.

International Marketing Implementation in Challenging Areas of the Global Economy

Marketing in the Developing World

What differentiate international marketing in the developing world are the dramatic market environment conditions that characterize the developing world—low gross domestic product (GDP) per capita, poverty, high unemployment, different types of societal structures, perceptions, behaviors, and consumption patterns, to name a few.

The UN world development reports indicate that the number of people residing in developing countries (mostly in East Asia, Pacific and South Asia, sub-Saharan Africa, the Middle East, North Africa, Central Eastern Europe, Central Asia, Latin America, and the Caribbean) live on less than $1 a day. In 1999 this number was 1.2 billion and in 2005 the proportion of people living in extreme poverty comprised 23 percent of the total population. As a direct consequence, hunger and malnutrition still pose a major challenge to many developing countries; especially since malnutrition starts a vicious cycle of ill health, lower learning capacity, and poor physical growth.

Social structures differ in terms of social status, gender relations, and functions and also due to different demographic developments, with much wider pyramids (i.e., a higher percentage of younger ages represented in the total population).

The very different levels of economic development and environmental differences on all dimensions of the environment constitute the prevailing market conditions in developing countries, and determine the character of consumers' and industrial users' needs. Infrastructure (or rather its absence in most cases) is also an essential factor that differentiates market conditions in developing countries. Absence of a wired telephone network, for instance, in large parts of the developing world thus makes the wireless mobile phone technology more appealing. But the marketer should realize the different communication and product mix design needed when a mobile phone is presented to a customer in a third world country that does not have access to an alternative product, in comparison to the approach that is usually followed to promote purchase of mobile phones among customers of the developed world (who have access to wired telephone network services).

Product adaptation strategies are thus essential in most cases, at least when international firms target large customer segments in these markets, while consideration should also be paid to the other marketing mix elements (price, place, promotion) regarding the need to adapt in order to suit local needs, or to standardize to reducing cost, which is also an essential need for large consumer segments in these markets. A fragmented and multi-level distribution channel is often the prevailing distribution network structure in developing countries, requiring therefore suitable modification to the international distribution strategy of the firm.[27]

Marketing in the Newly Emerging and Former Eastern Bloc Economies

The Central and Eastern European countries as an emerging market region are of great importance for the international marketer, because of the unique combination of different economic, cultural, institutional, and structural elements. Cultural differences mainly due to the centrally planned character of the society have contributed to a distinct consumer attitude, which when coupled with the difficulties of a transition phase toward new economic and institutional structures reveal the complete profile of the conditions prevailing in the region.

This group of countries consists of a huge potential market since it is inhabited by 430 million people and, although currently the average disposable income of the greatest market segment in the region is way below the respective level of a comparable Western European region, because of their rapid growth countries of the group have received increasing attention from international companies, which are always eager for interesting opportunities to expand their operations. Global companies see the region as an important source of growth and often follow an ambitious marketing strategy, hoping to establish a leadership position and concur significant market shares by entering at an early stage.

Although the challenges they face are significant due to the absence of reliable institutions (including adequate distribution network alternatives), international firms occasionally follow a penetration pricing strategy, hoping that gradually their high market shares will be translated to increased profitability as soon as the conditions improve, once the transition is completed and free, and once stabilized and effective market conditions prevail in most market sectors. One attractive opportunity is in engaging in local production, assembly, or processing activities since wage rates are much lower than the ones in the neighboring regions. Joint ventures are also a common practice especially when foreign firms are not allowed to have full control, or they are not willing to undertake a high risk on their own.[28]

The most critical element of successful market entry in the region is finding or creating a functional distribution network. Centrally planned distribution networks, which were operating in these markets during the communist era, have become almost obsolete. Reaming network consists of small shops with no clear status of ownership in many occasions and owners or personnel that lack the necessary entrepreneurial willingness and skills to engage in a process of improvements and investments. Thus, international firms that invest and enter in the region not only have to provide funding for the development of the necessary distribution infrastructure but also have to support the human resource development, so as to develop the skills necessary for effective local management and support of the operations. One should remember that this is not an easy task, because the concept of a market economy is completely unfamiliar to most of the local people, and it is not unusual for personnel to be unable to function according to the expected standards of the foreign firm.

During a recent interview, Professor Gert van Dijk*, director general of the National Co-operative Council in the Netherlands, was asked to describe the international marketing strategies of internationalized Dutch Co-operative businesses, the major markets in which they seek opportunities, and their entry modes.

---

* Dr. van Dijk is director general of the Netherlands Council for Co-operatives and professor of co-operative theory at the department of marketing of the Wageningen University. He is also a professor of entrepreneurship at The Netherlands Business School—Nyenrode University.

The two leading Dutch Co-operative enterprises, namely Friesland Coberco Dairy Foods (FCDF)[†] and Campina[‡], are both active in the dairy sector and they rank among the top 20 companies of the sector worldwide, with a broad international activity.

The FCDF operates in a wider and more diverse geographical region and its marketing strategy emphasizes the strengthening of its key drive brands. FCDF has been established in the international markets since decades, through exporting the excess domestic production of standardized dairy products (also supported by the favorable EU export subsidy regime), but in more recent years the management realized that it could only gain a competitive advantage by building an effective marketing strategy based on strong brands. High margins, sustained growth, and profitability could only be built on differentiated branded products that were perceived by consumers to have an added value. For this reason Friesland currently concentrates its research innovation, advertising, and promotion spending on a portfolio of 21 key drive brands (out of which seven are international brands) that contribute comparatively more than the rest on growth and profitability. This strategy is purely market-driven and aims to continue introducing innovative concepts according to the changing wishes of customers and consumers. In contrast to the aforementioned differentiation strategy, the company purchases the raw material from local or nearby producers such as New Zealand for the Far East market instead of exporting from its own member production. Through foreign direct investments (FDIs) and acquisitions, Friesland has built a strong position in the Netherlands and Germany, as well as in Southeast Asia and West Africa, and it has gradually acquired a strong position in the rapidly expanding dairy markets of Central Europe. In the future, Friesland will concentrate on selected markets where it can maintain a considerable market share with branded products, through considerable investments in innovation and marketing support. Nevertheless, because of the high degree of adaptation of local and regional brands in these markets, Friesland is rather cautious about any changes that could threat its well-established market position.

On the other hand, Campina during the same period followed a parallel development, growing through a series of M&A into a significant international firm; it concentrates primarily in the European market, considers its

---

[†] Friesland Coberco Dairy Foods (ranked 13th worldwide in 2001) is a multinational company that develops, produces, and sells a wide range of branded dairy products and fruit-based drinks for the consumer market, professional users, and food producers. The company operates from 94 branches worldwide, in more than 100 countries, having production operations in 17 countries, while it focuses mostly in Western Europe, West Africa, and Southeast Asia.

[‡] Campina in Europe is among the largest providers of liquid milk, yoghurts, desserts, and cheese, while globally (ranking 16th worldwide in 2001) Campina is one of the main players in the field of dairy ingredients for the worldwide food and pharmaceutical industries. It mainly operates in the Netherlands, Belgium, Germany, the United Kingdom, Spain, Poland, and Russia.

operations in the Netherlands, Germany, and Belgium as its base, it now defines its home market as between London and Moscow and attempts to introduce the Campina, as well as a few German brands, gradually in most of its markets. Its brand portfolio consists also of local brands, but the concept is to use the Campina brand in the many market segments that have homogeneous characteristics throughout the region. Growth is pursued primarily in emerging market regions like the CEECs (in Russia, Campina already marks a strong growth and defines the top segments there) where an opportunity for profitability growth is also pursued through significant investments in product and communication innovation, especially in value-added product categories like desserts and functional type of food products. At the same time, Campina extended its co-operative structure toward foreign producers of milk.

Closing Case

"The Greenery": How Dutch Fresh Vegetable Growers Develop their International Marketing Organization

Developing Marketing Competencies through the Establishment of the Greenery: The Background that led to the Establishment of the Greenery

- Dutch horticultural auctions had dominated the market for almost a century, before reaching the crisis situation of the 1990s. Auctions had been a very effective marketing mechanism for over one century, but changes in market conditions forced fruit and vegetable farmers to change their institutional arrangements, by merging into one strong co-operative in order to create the Greenery that would be taking over the marketing operations. Its major objective was to effectively apply all necessary marketing strategies and methods.

The most evident and important problems that led the auctions to reevaluate their strategy had to do with the following:

- (Structurally) low prices because of the increasing concentration of the retailers and wholesalers, which decreased the number of buyers and increased their bargaining power.
- Dissatisfaction among retailers, which in turn was attributed to insufficient orientation to consumer preferences and inefficiencies in logistics.

First Period of the Greenery

When the Greenery was founded in 1996 as a 100 percent subsidiary of the VTN (the nine co-operative auctions that had merged), it set five goals in its first five-year business plan:

1. To reduce costs
2. To increase scale of operation
3. To add more value
4. To enhance market orientation
5. To improve coordination in the production and distribution chain.

This huge restructuring effort, accompanied with some administrative and managerial problems, resulted in a sharp decrease in the total number of members. When VTN/Greenery was established in 1996 the members (members of the former auctions) were close to 10,000, while by 1998 this number was reduced to 7300. Currently it has reduced to approximately 3200.[29]

For a period of approximately 100 years, the institution that marketed fresh fruit and vegetables in the Netherlands had been the auction. Auctions were the ideal institutions when the situation was characterized by the presence of many suppliers and many buyers. Along with changes in the technological and economic environment, the decisive change that led to the gradual abandoning of the auction has been the concentration of the retailers (CR4 is 72 percent in the Netherlands). The grower's response to these changes was the adoption of direct negotiation mechanisms, instead of the traditional auctions. To show the magnitude of the change in supply chain structure, we can refer to the market share of auctions in 1990. At that time 92 percent of all greenhouse vegetables, 78 percent of all fruits, and 50 percent and of all open field vegetables were sold through the auctions (Exhibit 9.8).

Within the new structure only a few auctions are operating and their market share has dropped dramatically. Apart from the Greenery, some smaller producer organizations are more and more willing to negotiate directly with the (few) big buyers (Exhibit 9.9).

In the new structure, the Greenery has completely replaced the auction system with direct negotiation between growers and wholesalers/retailers. The Greenery is offering its mediation services in these negotiations, acting as the trustworthy party where negotiators can refer to all the aspects of quality, and services and cost structure, and provide market information about consumer demand and the international markets were it spreads its activities.

Exhibit 9.8

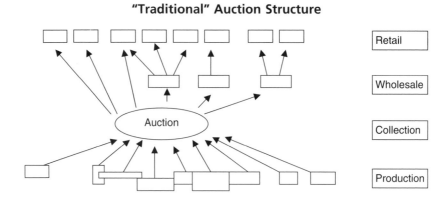

"Traditional" Auction Structure

Retail

Wholesale

Collection

Production

Exhibit 9.9

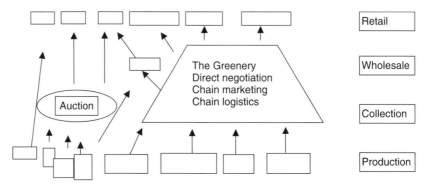

Vertical Co-ordination with Supply-chain"Partnership"

Retail

Wholesale

Collection

Production

The Later Phase

In relation to the five strategic goals, several functional changes were introduced. The Greenery was formed right from the beginning with the purpose of following an offensive marketing strategy.[30] This strategy is based on high quality, extended market research, brand promotion, product innovation, and differentiation. These elements were considered important in order to achieve a close relationship with major retailers, and the Greenery was aiming at becoming a preferred supplier to them. In order to achieve this, the Greenery focuses on responding more effectively to consumer demands on behalf of and in close collaboration with the retailer. On the basis of extensive research on consumers' preferences the Greenery undertakes the responsibility of optimizing the range of produce on sale at each store, the produce selection, presentation, pricing, logistics, promotional policy, as well as of improving store staff skills. These actions are all in line with the category management approach, the objective of which is to maximize performance of and returns on the product group, based on consumer wishes and preferences as a starting point.

A pilot project that the Greenery applied based on the aforementioned principles and methods, in collaboration with the second largest Dutch retailing chain on the tomatoes product group, was established three years ago and proved to be very successful. Both category turnover and profitability have been raised and consumers' reaction was confirmed by increased consumption and spending on the category.

One of the indispensable elements of such a marketing strategy is wholesale and value-added processing. The Greenery realized that in order to establish close relationships with large retail chains it would have to be able to supply most of the total assortment of the fruit and vegetable section, on a year-round basis. On the basis of this conclusion they reached the decision of buying two major wholesaling firms in the Netherlands (the Van Dijk Delft Group and the Fresh Produce Division of Perkins Food Plc), which were both importers and exporters with major retailers in the United Kingdom and Germany as their clients. With this significant acquisition, the Greenery gained expertise; it thus acquired a competitive advantage to provide superior marketing services not only to the domestic market, but also to the strategically important export markets of Western Europe, the United States, and Japan.

Alternative price determination mechanisms were introduced, next to the typical auction (which had already started to fade). Contract mediation was set up as an internal agency to mediate between growers and wholesalers. This method has the advantage of better communication regarding the introduction of new varieties with distinct characteristics and allows growers to receive better market demand information. This method is applicable especially for large buyers as it allows growers to group their produce in order to meet the size of the demanded quantity. Another price determination mechanism that was introduced was "unilaterally setting a price, and inviting buyers to make a bid for specified quantities."

Another significant change is related to quality control that has now been extended to the production, processing, and transportation stages, while in a typical auction, quality control was restricted only to a final control of the product, when it was reaching the auction. The Greenery requires its members to follow regulations on environmental impact, food safety, and working conditions.

Finally logistics is another area where the Greenery brought some changes as well. Since retailers and wholesalers have been going through a concentration process, but the size of growers has significantly increased as well, it is now possible to ship the product directly from the greenhouse to a central DC of a retail chain. But this was only possible with the introduction of contract mediation (avoiding the need to go through the auction). Besides cost, another benefit is the reduction of transportation time, resulting from less movement of the product, thus quality is improved (especially in some highly perishable products).

Chapter Summary

This chapter introduced the concepts and issues related to the selection, design, and management of international marketing strategies and global marketing strategies.

An initial distinction was made between the content and the scope of the two aforementioned terms. The term global marketing, although it appears more frequently nowadays in the literature and in practice, is in fact a section of the international marketing concept that includes other forms of foreign marketing such as export marketing and multinational marketing. Beginning with the analysis approach of the international market environment, reference has been made to the methods of market assessment, which proceeds with a distinction of the most significant elements of each national market environment and then attempts to make a comparison between them in order to reach a meaningful classification, before concluding with an actual assessment of the attractiveness or lack of each international market segment selected. Different factors that generate risk for international marketing operations were presented in the following section, and accompanied with a reference to the methods to organize, collect, process, and use information and market research data, in order to complete the section referring to the international market environment evaluation.

The chapter continued with a second section that presented the methods of international marketing planning and strategy formulation. The choice between following a standardized one or one adaptive to local conditions approach is the central point of consideration at this stage. The same problem also pertains to the rest of the marketing mix elements, as they have been discussed here. The product element is subject to an adaptation consideration, to the extent that it becomes imperative due to local physical, institutional, or consumer-related reasons, or, alternatively, a product standardization decision might be more appropriate when cost effectiveness precedes importance. Alternative pricing strategies and options were discussed, focusing on the main practices followed in the form of price skimming and penetration pricing according to the limitation in the international markets considered. Placement and distribution channel issues and options are an indispensable part of marketing mix analysis. Selective and intensive distribution are the two alternative directions that might conform to the overall marketing strategy of the international firm. The promotion mix elements were also discussed here, with a description of the choice between an adaptive or a standardized communication approach, along with the options for the implementation of a pull or push type of advertising campaign.

The section continues with a description of trends and methods applied in industrial marketing relationships, by discussing supply chain management, category management, and some of the multiple current practices developed to improve effectiveness in this particular field of international management. The final element in this section of the chapter presents the impact of cultural differences in international marketing. Culture is an element intrinsic to all aspects of human and social behavior and decision making, while it is also the most intricate part for an effective marketing strategy and management application. Nevertheless, it should not be ignored in any stage of analysis and decision making, but effort should be made to distinguish between the intrinsic cultural elements that are subject to short-run changes and those that have been formed as a consequence of the prevailing social and economic conditions.

The chapter concludes with a presentation of the main points that need to be considered by an international marketer who is confronted with the task of formulating or operating a marketing strategy for areas that hold a special interest for international firms such as the developing and emerging countries. Countries in both areas of interest present their own particularities, and marketing strategies should always consider these differences when they approach aims to be standardized or adaptive toward local market needs and requirements.

Review and Discussion Questions

1. In the Opening Case, would you say that Nike is a multinational corporation or a global company? What is its main marketing strategy?
2. Which are the principal areas of concern to the marketer when a company embarks its operations in the international market, in comparison to a single country marketing approach?
3. Could you identify the types of companies that pursue various forms of international marketing and those companies that pursue global marketing practices?
4. In the Reverse Perspective Situation: "The Greenery," how would you describe the marketing strategy applied by the Greenery in terms of its effectiveness in expanding to international markets?
5. Which are the types of firms and products that might use a global marketing strategy approach in the near future to improve their competitive position?

6. What is the most favorable marketing strategy approach between adaptation and standardization for the developing countries (think of both the foreign company's and the local citizens' point of view)? Can you distinguish between different types of products?
7. Would you say that international cultural pluralism is an asset or a liability to the international marketer?

Endnotes

1. NIKE Inc., Annual Report, 2001, http://www.NIKE.com/main.html
2. Theodore Levitt. "Globalization of Markets," *Harvard Business Review*, May–June 1983, pp.11–17.
3. Jean-Claude Usunier. *Marketing Across Cultures* (2nd edn). Prentice Hall Inc., 1996.
4. World Development Indicators 2002, World Bank, Washington, DC, 2000, http://www.worldbank.org/data/.
5. Ernest Dichter, "The world Customer," *Harvard Business Review*, 40, no. 4 (July–August 1962), pp. 113–123.
6. W. W. Rostow, *The Stages of Economic Growth*. New York: Cambridge University Press, 1960.
7. Philip Kotler, *Marketing Management, Analysis Planning Implementation and Control*. Prentice Hall International, Inc., 1997.
8. Sethi, S. Prakash "Comparative Cluster Analysis for World Markets." *Journal of Marketing Research*, August 1971.
9. Goodnow, James D. and Hansz, James E. "Environmental determinants of overseas market entry strategies," *Journal of Business Studies*, (1972), 3, 33–50.
10. Elias G. Rizkallah, *"Multiple Product: Multiple Market Allocations—A Portfolio Approach,"* a paper presented at the Academy of International Business Annual Meeting in New Orleans, October 24, 1980, pp. 8 and 9.
11. Bertil Liander, Vern Terpstra, M. Y. Yoshimo, and Aziz A. Sherbini, *Comparative Analysis for International Marketing* (Boston: Allyn & Bacon, 1967).
12. Ernest Dichter, "The world customer" *Harvard Business Review*, 40 no 4 (July–august 1962) pp. 113–23.
13. Ronald L. Solberg. *Country Risk Analysis, a Handbook*. Routledge, 1992.
14. Edward W. Cundiff, Marye Tharp Hilger. *Marketing in The International Environment*. Prentice Hall, 1984.
15. Subhash C. Jain. *International Marketing Management* (3rd edition). PWS-Kent Publishing Company, 1990.
16. Warren J. Keegan, Mark C. Green. *Global Marketing* (3rd edition). Prentice Hall, 2003.
17. Michael E. Porter, *Competitive Strategy: Techniques for Analyzing Industries and Competitors* (New York: Free Press, 1980) & *Competitive Advantage* (New York: Free Press, 1985).
18. Frank Bradley. *International Marketing Strategy*. Prentice Hall, 1991.
19. Jean-Pierre Jeannet, H. David Hennessey. *Global Marketing Strategies* (5th edition). Houghton Mifflin Company, 2001.
20. Vern Terpstra, Ravi Sarathy. *International Marketing* (7th edition). The Dryden Press, 1997.
21. L. D. Dahringer, H. Mühlbacher. *International Marketing: A Global Perspective*. Addison-Wesley Publishing Company, 1991.
22. Leon G. Schiffman, Leslie Lazar Kanuk. Consumer Behavior (5th edition). Prentice Hall International Inc., 1994.
23. Jean-Claude Usunier. *Marketing Across Cultures* (2nd edition). Prentice Hall Inc., 1996.

24. G. Baourakis, M. Stroe. "The optimization of the distribution system in the context of supply chain management development," in: Pardalos P. (ed.), *Financial engineering, E-commerce & Supply Chain Management*, Kluwer, 2002.

25. G. J. Verra. *Category Management: A Matter of Joint Optimization*. Nyenrode University Press, 1998.

26. Michel D. Hutt, Thomas W. Speh. *Business Marketing Management: A Strategic View of Industrial and Organizational Markets* (6th edition). The Dryden Press, 1998.

27. Joanna Kinsey. *Marketing in Developing Countries*. Macmillan Education, 1988.

28. L. D. Dahringer, H. Mühlbacher. *International Marketing; A Global Perspective*. Addison-Wesley Publishing Company, 1991.

29. Jos Bijman. *Essays on Agricultural Co-operatives: Governance Structure in Fruit and Vegetables Chains*. Erasmus Research Institute of Management, 2002.

30. The Greenery, Annual report, 2001, http://www.thegreenery.com/sites/GreeneryInternet/index.htm.

International Accounting, Finance, and Taxation

John L. Haverty and Marios I. Katsioloudes, Spyros Hadjidakis

Objectives

Through this chapter, the student will be exposed to:

- Changes occurring in global financial markets resulting in increasing cross-border flows of capital
- The causes and consequences of international diversity of financial accounting
- International efforts to harmonize worldwide financial accounting diversity
- International consolidation of financial statements
- Foreign currency translation issues and procedures
- International auditing
- International financial statement analysis
- International taxation
- International transfer pricing.

Opening Case

International Accounting Diversity

Chris Baker is a junior portfolio analyst at Chartright, a portfolio manager for several major mutual funds. Susan Santelli, the portfolio manager, just informed Chris that one of the funds she managed, the International Horizon Fund, was considering to include one company from the People's Republic of China in its portfolio. She asked Chris to investigate Chinese airlines, since airlines were under-represented in this particular international portfolio. She felt that with the People's Republic of China's recent accession to the World Trade Organization and their selection as host for the 2008 Olympics, a Chinese airline stock would represent a good growth opportunity for her portfolio. Chris started researching two Chinese airlines traded on the New York Stock Exchange, China Eastern Airlines and China Southern Airlines. Since Chris's knowledge of Chinese companies was very limited he tried to find some simple performance measures to establish trends. Chris looked on some websites and downloaded some annual reports. He did find some background information about China Eastern Airlines.

China Eastern Airlines Corporation Limited is a state-owned, People's Republic of China company. It provides passenger, cargo, and mail services worldwide, operating out of the People's Republic of China. In addition, China Eastern Airlines provides ticket handling services and airport ground support services for airlines operating to and from Hong Qiao International and Pudong International Airports in Shanghai, People's Republic of China. The company is one of the three largest carriers in the People's Republic of China and is the primary air carrier serving Shanghai, China's eastern gateway.

China Eastern Airlines Corporation Limited was established in the People's Republic of China in 1995 as a joint stock company, as part of the restructuring of a state-owned enterprise. In January 1997, the company received government approval to issue abroad-listed shares (H-shares) not to exceed 15 percent of the authorized shares. In February 1997, the company completed its initial public offering on the Stock Exchange of Hong Kong and the New York Stock Exchange.

In 1998, China Eastern Airlines Limited reported its first loss after four years of profitable operations. This loss was attributed largely to the decline in air traffic as a result of the Asian Financial Crisis in 1998. The Company issued financial statements in accordance with People's Republic of China's Accounting Standards for Enterprises and the Accounting Regulations for the Stock Limited Companies. The statements were audited in accordance with the independent Auditing Standards of Certified Public Accountants in the People's Republic of China (PRC GAAP). The Annual Report also included financial statements in accordance with International Accounting Standards (IAS GAAP). The statements were audited by PricewaterhouseCoopers in accordance with Statements of Auditing Standards issued by the Hong Kong Society of Accountants.

He started to take a look at China Eastern Airlines' annual report and was searching for net income. This is where his confusion started. Chris went back to Susan and reported: "I found two different income statements with two different profit figures reported. The statements were in English, but they were in the Chinese currency, RMB yuan. One of the statements wasn't even called an income statement but was called the profit and loss account. I'm not sure why there are two income statements here, and I am certainly not sure which one to use. I was trying to calculate some ratios and compare them to some airlines in other countries, and I am really not sure where to begin. Can I trust these things?" Susan suppressed a chuckle and said cryptically, "Welcome to the wild, wonderful world of international accounting."

Question: Which financial statement should Chris use? Can Chris calculate ratios from these statements and compare them to other airlines?

Introduction

Accounting exists to provide information useful for making business and other economic decisions. In a very real sense, accounting generates the information that matches people with money to people with ideas, so those ideas can get developed. International accounting exists then to support business and economic decisions that cross borders, matching people with money in one country to people with ideas in another country. It is a field that is characterized by complexity and broadness. The complexity arises because accounting is different in every nation of the world. The broadness is inherent in accounting, which includes measurement techniques, disclosure requirements, techniques of auditing and assuring that the information provided is reasonably accurate, and tax considerations. In each of these components of accounting, every nation in the world has its own unique way of doing business.

This chapter first discusses the environment of global capital markets, including the crucial role of accounting information in the growth and development of these markets. Then international accounting is addressed in some detail, including the causes and consequences of accounting diversity, the recent international accounting harmonization movement, and some selected issues in preparing and using international financial statements. The chapter concludes with a brief discussion of some international tax planning issues.

The Environment of Global Financial Markets

Just as more and more goods and services are moving across borders as globalization increases, more and more capital is moving across borders as well. Companies can raise capital either internally, through their own operations, or externally, through transactions in various financial markets. External financial markets can be considered short-term, less than a year, or long-term. Short-term financial markets are often called money markets. Long-term financial markets are called capital markets, and include the equity market, sales of rights of ownership in the company, the debt market that includes borrowing from other firms, and the bank market. Multinational companies that used to raise equity capital solely from sources within their own borders now look to other countries for potential shareholders. Coca-Cola Company, for example, lists its stock on the German Exchange in Frankfurt and the Swiss Exchange in Zurich. Companies that used to borrow from sources within their borders now look to lenders outside their borders. Coca-Cola's 2004 annual report lists $663 million in long-term debt denominated in euros. Companies that obtained loans from local banks now seek banking relationships far from their national home. Coca-Cola shows $296 million in short-term borrowing related to its international subsidiaries. With an increasing cross-border flow of capital, including equity, debt, and bank loans, the need for information that is useful in a cross-border context arises, and international accounting is evolving to meet that challenge.

The Rise of Cross-border Financing

Companies engage in cross-border financing for a variety of reasons, some financial and some nonfinancial. Financial reasons include the fact that a company might be able to obtain cheaper financing outside its own borders, lowering its overall cost of capital. In addition, a company might find it convenient to obtain external financing wherever it has significant operations. Nonfinancial reasons to engage in cross-border financing might include a general desire to be a world-class company maintaining financial relationships in many countries. A company might have a desire to broaden its shareholder base to include citizens and other institutions from many countries in addition to its home base. A company might find it politically expedient to maintain financial relationships inside a particular country in order to obtain additional business contacts both inside and outside of a foreign government, or simply to stay on the good side of a local government. In any case, cross-border financial activity is increasing right along with the cross-border movement of goods and services.

International Money Markets

International short-term money markets are often called eurocurrency markets. A eurocurrency is not to be confused with the euro, the European common currency, but is rather any foreign currency-denominated deposit or account at a financial institution outside the country of the currency's issuance. Strangely, neither the currency nor the country of deposit needs to be European to be called eurocurrency. For example, US dollars deposited in a bank in either London or Singapore would be eurodollars. Japanese yen on deposit in Germany would be termed euroyen. Activity in this market is largely due to a lack of regulation or government interference in these markets. There are a wide variety of interest rates applicable in these markets depending on the particular international financial center involved, such as London, New York, Singapore, or Hong Kong. The most significant interest rate in these markets is LIBOR, the London interbank offer rate. LIBOR is set at 11:00AM London time on each business day by the British Bankers Association. Only very large players operate in this market, but a large number of international short-term loans are set in terms of LIBOR.

Global Equity Markets

Equity markets facilitate the transfer of shares of ownership of a firm by providing a mechanism through which firms can sell shares in the ownership of a company to investors hoping for rewards in the form of dividends or an increase in the market price of their investment. The market also provides liquidity to investors, enabling them to turn their investments into cash with relative ease. The existence of this liquidity makes investors more willing to assume the risks of ownership.

The sheer number and size of equity markets around the world is growing as more companies see the benefits of equity financing. In addition, the various national equity markets are becoming more international themselves, aggressively seeking foreign issuers as a means of increasing their volume. In addition to self-serving reasons, these national equity markets want to provide their citizens and customers with additional investment opportunities, even if these opportunities exist outside the exchange's national borders. Similar to the terminology involving eurocurrencies, euroequities are shares of stock sold outside the boundaries of the issuing company's home country. Exhibit 10.1 lists most of the more significant national equity exchanges throughout the world, and also shows the total number of equity listings on each exchange and breaks down the total into domestic and foreign listings on that exchange.

The role of accounting is crucial in any equity market. The basis of any exchange or investment is trust, and trust is increased by the provision of timely, understandable, and accurate financial information about the investments. One role of accounting is to provide such information to investors and

Exhibit 10.1

Number of Domestic and Foreign Equity Issuers Listed by Exchange

Exchange	Total	Domestic Companies	Foreign Companies
Americas			
American SE	575	502	73
Bermuda SE	58	21	37
Buenoe Aires SE	107	103	4
Colombia SE	106	106	0
Lima SE	224	192	32
Mexican Exchange	326	151	175
Nasdaq	3,229	2,889	340
NYSE	2,293	1,834	459
Santiago SE	240	239	1
Sao Paulo SE	388	386	2
TSX Group	3,604	3,572	32
Total region	11,150		
Europe – Africa – Middle East			
Athens Exchange	341	339	2
Borsa Italiana	278	269	9
Budapest SE	47	46	1
Copenhagen SE	183	176	7
Deutsche Börse	819	660	159
Euronext	1,333	999	334
Irish SE	65	53	12
Istanbul SE	297	297	0
JSE South Africa	389	368	21
Ljubijana SE	140	140	0
London SE	2,837	2,486	351
Luxembourg SE	234	42	192
Malta SE	13	13	0
OMX Helsinki SE	137	134	3
OMX Stockholm SE	276	256	20
Oslo Bore	88	166	22
Swiss Exchange	409	282	127
Tehran SE	402	402	0
Tel Aviv SE	578	573	5
Warsaw SE	230	225	5
Wiener Börse	120	99	21
Total region	9,316		

Exhibit 10.1 *continued*

Exchange	Total	Domestic Companies	Foreign Companies
Asia-Pacific			
Australian SE	1,583	1,515	68
BSE, The SE Mumbai	4,730	4,730	0
Bursa Malaysia	959	955	4
Colombo SE	242	242	0
Hong Kong Exchange	1,096	1,086	10
Jakarta SE	331	331	0
Korea Exchange	683	683	0
National Stock Exchange India	957	957	0
New Zealand Exchange	200	158	42
Osaka SE	1,090	1,090	0
Philippine SE	235	233	2
Shanghai SE	837	837	0
Shenzhen SE	536	536	0
Singapore Exchange	633	608	25
Taiwan SE Corp.	702	697	5
Thailand SE	463	463	0
Tokyo SE	2,306	2,276	30
Total region	17,583		
WFE TOTAL	38,049		

Source: World Federation of Exchanges Website, www.worldexchanges.org, Table 1–3, February 2006.

potential investors. Accounting information is the oil that keeps the market mechanism running smoothly. If equity markets were restricted to domestic participants, the information could be presented using domestic rules and formats. As international participants enter the equity markets, however, their information needs change, and accounting must provide information that is useful to participants with differing cultures, languages, and ways of doing business. As international equity investment increases, the various national accounting establishments must somehow provide information useful to international participants.

Global Debt Markets

A company may also raise capital by borrowing money from some lender without giving up any ownership rights, but rather incurring the burden of periodic interest payments and the repayment of the principal at some future date. There are an almost infinite variety of borrowing arrangements possible, but three of the most frequent arrangements are called foreign bonds, eurobonds, or global bonds. Foreign bonds are sold outside the borrower's country but are denominated in the currency of the country of issue. Eurobonds are sold in countries other than the one in whose currency the bond is denominated. For example, a US company floating a bond in euros to be sold in Europe would be selling a foreign bond. If the bond were denominated in US dollars but sold in Europe, it would be called a eurobond. A relatively new form of bond is called a global bond which is sold in many financial markets and is registered in each national market. This debt is often traded publicly on the various national exchanges. There is also a great deal of this type of financial activity internationally, as evidenced in Exhibit 10.2, which lists the various national exchanges, and additionally shows the total number of bond issuers on the exchange as well as the number of foreign companies issuing bonds on each exchange.

The issuance of debt requires information about the future cash flows of the debtor so that the lender can assess the probability of receiving the promised cash flows and the principal at the conclusion of the debt. Accounting provides this information, and as the debt crosses borders, the information must be useful to lenders of a different nationality.

Exhibit 10.2

Number of Domestic and Foreign Equity Issuers by Exchange

Exchange	2004			
	Total	Domestic private sector	Domestic public sector	Foreign
Americas				
American SE	13	12	1	0
Bermuda SE	4	2	0	2
Buenos Aires SE	120	93	26	1
Colombia SE	228	194	30	4
Lima SE	60	56	1	3
Mexican Exchange	115	97	18	0
NYSE	NA	NA	NA	NA
Santiago SE	121	119	2	0
Sao Paulo SE	60	60	0	0
TSX Group	83	0	83	0

Exhibit 10.2 *continued*

| | 2004 | | | |
Exchange	Total	Domestic private sector	Domestic public sector	Foreign
Europe – Africa – Middle East				
Athens Exchange	13	12	1	0
Borsa Italiana	57	38	4	15
Budapest SE	13	12	1	0
Copenhagen SE	87	52	3	32
Deutsche Börse	698	148	39	511
Euronext	695	369	61	265
Irish SE	1,070	158	5	907
Istanbul SE	2	0	2	0
Ljubijana SE	27	24	3	0
London SE	1,594	943	57	594
Luxembourg SE	3,377	185	2	3,190
Malta SE	65	21	44	0
OMX Helsinki SE	107	104	1	2
OMX Stockholm SE	97	79	11	7
Osio Bors	202	125	70	7
Swiss Exchange	415	123	27	265
Tel Aviv SE	87	86	1	0
Warsaw SE	7	5	1	1
Wiener Börse	208	136	7	65
Asia-Pacific				
Australian SE	50	31	4	15
BSE, The SE Mumbai	1,100	125	975	0
Bursa Malaysia	60	60	0	0
Colombo SE	13	12	1	0
Hong Kong Exchanges	52	17	6	29
Korea Exchange	728	655	71	2
National Stock Exchange India	148	88	59	1
New Zealand Exchange	43	40	1	2
Osaka SE	58	56	2	0
Philippine SE	0	0	0	0
Shanghai SE	17	16	1	0
Shenzhen SE	20	0	20	0
Taiwan SE Corp.	16	9	4	3
Thailand SE	15	15	0	0
Tokyo SE	151	147	2	2

NA: Not Available
Source: World Federation of Exchanges Website, www.world-exchanges.org, Table 1–3, February 2006.

Global Bank Markets

A third source of capital involves borrowing from banks subject to an almost infinite variety of credit and banking arrangements. Traditionally, bankers relied more on personal knowledge of the management of the firm with whom it had a relationship. This knowledge was often obtained through personal or family contacts, or perhaps a seat on its board of directors. This personal information often mitigated the need for formal financial reporting, since the banker often could obtain much inside information through personal contacts. With international expansion, the traditional personal banking relationships often become more difficult, and the need for accounting information increases. The expansion of international banking is shown in Exhibit 10.3 which shows the international assets held by banks throughout the world from 2000 through 2004.

Exhibit 10.3 shows the major international banking actors as well as the trend in international banking over that period. In all countries listed, with the exception of Austria, international banking activity seems to be increasing.

Exhibit 10.3

International Positions (assets) By Nationality of Ownership of Reporting Banks (In Billions of US $)

	Q4 2000	Q4 2001	Q4 2002	Q4 2003	Q4 2004
ALL COUNTRIES	11652.1	12223.9	14451.1	18140.3	22168.9
Reporting countries	11216.7	11888.3	14122.8	17801.2	21794.9
Australia	50.1	90.3	109.8	161	176.4
Austria	172.1	87.7	107.2	139.9	165.3
Belgium	399.1	424	556	794.4	975.9
Bermuda	–	1.5	12	15.3	13.7
Brazil	–	–	22.4	41.7	44.6
Canada	287.9	307.7	323.2	382.3	397.6
Chile	–	–	6.1	5.4	9.6
Denmark	100.3	96.4	114.8	164.8	211.2
Finland	44.4	63	57.4	58.2	66.9
France	976.9	1153.9	1299.6	1792.7	2524.8
Germany	2259.1	2439.9	2716.7	3425.5	3903
Greece	–	–	–	61.9	64.9
Guernsey	–	–	–	–	–
Hong Kong SAR	96.7	26.3	93.1	122	123.1
India	–	23.9	25.9	32	43.6
Ireland	61.6	71.6	191.4	257.1	379.1
Isle of Man	–	–	–	–	–

Exhibit 10.3 *continued*

	Q4 2000	Q4 2001	Q4 2002	Q4 2003	Q4 2004
Italy	412	393.2	440.2	501	598.1
Japan	1638.7	1513.7	1568.8	1687.5	1874
Jersey	–	–	–	–	–
Luxembourg	30.3	38	46.4	58.3	63.7
Mexico	–	–	–	4.7	5.8
Netherlands	580.9	728.6	935.6	1184.1	1561.8
Norway	24	22.1	26.4	33.8	25.9
Panama	–	–	6.3	6.1	7.2
Portugal	69.5	86.6	109.7	151.4	171
Spain	210	202.5	233.8	292.9	459.2
Sweden	130.8	138.9	188.6	223.2	280.5
Switzerland	1239.1	1253.1	1650	2291.9	2615
Taiwan China	82.7	97.6	97.9	122.2	138.6
Turkey	45.3	55.7	56.4	71.7	88.1
United Kingdom	831.1	1016.1	1450.4	1731.2	2121.9
United States	1338.4	1398.8	1508.9	1714.3	2177
Unallocated	121.3	134.3	144	182.4	288.4

Source: Bank for International Settlements Webpage, www.bis.org, International Banking Statistics, Table 8, February 2006.

Some Trends

Of the three sources of capital listed above (equity, debt, and banks), the equity market requires the most amount of financial information in order to maintain the level of confidence necessary for an active and efficient equity market. The debt market and banks normally require less information since they are not assuming the risks of ownership and the market participants are traditionally closer to the inner workings of a company. The debt market and banks do, however, require some financial information, and the need for this information increases as international debt and banking activity increase. A major trend worldwide is the rise of a global equity culture, necessitating the need for accounting information appropriate to international participants in the equity markets.

This growing worldwide equity culture was fueled by a number of factors. The collapse of the Soviet Union represented a philosophical collapse that was even larger than the political collapse. Communism was discredited as an economic system, and even in countries that did not have a communist system, the viability of state ownership and control of an enterprise was questioned, and government after government at least partially privatized large state-owned enterprises, selling shares of stock to individuals through a variety of privatization initiatives. These privatizations led to a notion that equity was, in fact, a viable way for a company to raise capital. This philosophical sea-change was accompanied by a technological sea-change: the information revolution. Information transmission became cheap, reliable, and fast, and an investor in New York can watch market activity in Hong Kong, and an investor in Beijing can visit the London Stock Exchange by Internet. This inexpensive information transmission made it easier for capital to cross borders since investors could obtain information from anywhere in the world quite easily. The combined effects of these changes gave rise to a global equity culture: investors throughout the world were becoming comfortable with the notion of equity investment. At the same time, companies in search of capital felt they could raise money quite easily from investors within their own borders and even outside their own political borders. It became easier for someone with a good idea to match up with someone with money available for investment. This matching is dependent, however, on information useful to investors wherever they may be, and accounting must evolve to provide that information internationally just as it has done domestically for so many years.

The Environment of International Financial Accounting

International financial accounting is characterized by what appears to be an almost hopeless amount of diversity: accounting is different in every country on earth. This diversity is not as hopeless as it appears, however. It becomes reasonable and understandable when the causes of the diversity are explored, and clusters of similarity emerge. In addition, there is an active and very successful international movement to harmonize accounting standards worldwide to facilitate the cross-border flow of capital.

International Financial Accounting Diversity

One challenging aspect of international business is the fact that no two countries have exactly the same accounting standards or procedures. What this means is that a financial statement such as a balance sheet or an income statement prepared in the United States is prepared under a different set of rules than a balance sheet prepared in some other country, such as the United Kingdom. Even though these balance sheets might look the same on the surface, comparisons between the two might be fraught with peril. For example, US accounting procedures require that the value of plant and equipment on a balance sheet be shown at historical cost of the asset. The UK accounting procedures, however, permit plant and equipment to be revalued to current value. Therefore, $1,000,000 in plant and equipment on a US balance sheet would represent the original cost of an asset that was purchased perhaps twenty years ago. The same amount on a UK balance sheet, however, would represent the current value of that asset.

In order to properly evaluate an investment in another country, an investor must somehow translate the financial statements prepared under a foreign set of accounting standards into financial statements in accordance with the accounting standards of the investor's home country. This unfortunate situation is a considerable barrier to the cross-border flow of capital.

Causes of International Financial Accounting Diversity

The unfortunate fact that financial accounting is different in every country on earth arose for very good reasons. Accounting in any society does not exist in a vacuum, but is rather shaped and molded by the very forces that shape the unique culture of a particular country. Accounting is a social system and the exact structure and processes of such a system are determined by the larger system of which it is a part. The role of accounting is to provide information to users, and the types of users and the needs of those users are determined by the larger economic and social systems operative in a particular country. Scholars[1] list six classes of variables that shape the accounting system of a particular country. These are (1) the source of external financing, (2) the legal system, (3) political and economic ties with other countries, (4) levels of inflation, (5) the size and complexity of business enterprises, sophistication of management and the financial community and general levels of education, and (6) culture.

External funding for a business usually comes from three sources: the owners (equity financing), lenders (debt financing), or the government. The accounting system serves as a mechanism to provide information to the providers of capital, whether they are equity providers, debt providers, or government finance providers. Therefore, the accounting system of a particular country will evolve to serve the information needs of the various providers of capital. In certain economies, equity providers dominate, in others debt providers dominate. In some economies, the government is the dominant external capital provider. Whichever class of external equity provider is dominant in a particular country, the needs of that class will shape the accounting system.

In many nations, especially the United States and Great Britain, equity investors are the dominant external capital providers. In these types of economies, equity investors expect a large amount of information from a country's accounting system. Providers of equity capital are often not close to the management of the firm, and need highly detailed information about the firm in order to make their investment decisions with at least some degree of rationality. Often the only information they have about a firm is through publicly disclosed accounting information. Therefore, to induce equity investors to invest, an accounting system would be designed to provide as much information as possible to a widely diverse set of equity owners.

In countries such as Germany and Japan, there is not a long tradition of equity ownership, and the dominant means of obtaining external capital is borrowing. In such a scenario, the banks or the large lenders might have a more direct access to the management of a firm and would not need a large amount of public information. This access could be through membership on the Board of Directors or through family connections. In economies such as these, the accounting system would not be designed to serve any large diverse group of equity owners, but would rather provide information privately through personal contacts. Much less public information would be available to the public at large in such a scenario.

Where the government is the most significant capital provider, the accounting system would evolve to serve the needs of the government to facilitate governmental control or at least to provide uniformity to facilitate large-scale government planning. China is perhaps the best current example of this type of economy (the collapse of the former Soviet Union removed many other examples). In this type of economy, we would expect a great deal of standardization since the main user of the financial statements provided by a firm would be government central planners. Since the government has the power to obtain substantial information from a firm in such an economy, there would be little reason to make a substantial amount of information available to the public.

The legal system of a particular nation has a great influence on the nature of a country's accounting system. There are two main types of legal traditions, code law and common law. The legal system of a code law country takes the form of a series of "thou shalts," which specifies a minimum standard of behavior and expects citizens to comply with the letter of the law. In a code law country, such as France or Germany, the accounting law evolves based on a similar philosophy: the accounting principles are part of the law of that country, are administered by the government of that country, and are highly detailed, prescriptive, and procedural. In code law countries, professional judgment is often discouraged in favor of detailed prescriptions. The legal system of a common law country takes the form of a series of "thou shalt nots" establishing a set of legal limits. It is up to the individual to use reasonable judgment to stay within these limits. The law evolves by a series of cases that test these limits. In common law countries, such as the United States and the United Kingdom, accounting is usually separate from the national law and is often maintained by the accountants themselves. There is often a great deal of room for professional judgment inherent in the accounting system of a common law country. Accounting evolves by becoming generally accepted in practice.

Political and economic ties, both historic and current, also influence a nation's accounting system. The former British colonies such as the United States, Canada, and Australia imported their original accounting systems from Great Britain. Wartime allies such as Germany and Japan developed similar accounting systems. After World War II, the United States imposed an accounting system on Japan. Soviet model accounting systems were utilized in the former Warsaw Pact nations. China imported a Soviet model accounting system from her Communist neighbor. Current economic ties also influence the development of a nation's accounting system. Countries that are large trading partners tend to develop similar accounting systems as a result of their frequent business contacts. For example, the North American Free Trade Agreement (NAFTA) countries—Canada, Mexico, and the United States—maintain fairly similar accounting systems.

The level of inflation experienced by a country influences its accounting system. The hyperinflation experienced in Germany after World War I influenced the economic psyche of Germany so deeply that the Germans will most likely never have any accounting principle that even hints of inflation. They are probably the strongest adherents of the historical cost principle that assumes the unit of monetary measurement used to measure financial results is reasonably stable. Certain other countries, such as Mexico and many South American countries, have a different philosophical approach to inflation and have decided to accept it as a fact of life. They have developed systems of inflation-adjusted accounting that attempt to present financial results that take inflation into consideration. The United States experimented with inflation-adjusted accounting in the early 1980s and abandoned it when inflation subsided a bit, and it was judged that the additional costs of inflation-adjusted accounting were not justified by the benefits obtained by the users.

The accounting system of a nation is also influenced by a series of internal factors: the size and complexity of business enterprises, the sophistication of management and the financial community, and general levels of education. In a complex economy, these factors generally work in tandem. If business enterprises are relatively simple, then a simple accounting system is needed. If the management and the financial community are relatively unsophisticated, only a relatively unsophisticated accounting system is needed. If the general level of education is low, a complex accounting system is not likely to be developed. Thus, if economic development is relatively low, only a relatively unsophisticated system is likely to be developed. A country with a low level of economic development may, however, choose to import an accounting system from some outside party. For example, some relatively unsophisticated nations have chosen to adopt the United States' generally accepted accounting principles as their own in lieu of taking the effort to develop a set of accounting principles on their own.

Some Manifestations of International Financial Accounting Diversity

This financial accounting diversity among nations can be manifested in two ways: (1) differences among clusters of nations having similar accounting practices and (2) differences in handling specific accounting issues among countries. On a large scale, the diversity does not result in a completely unmanageable set of differences among nations, but rather a set of clusters of nations having somewhat similar accounting practices within each cluster, and some differences between each of the clusters. One such set of three such clusters[2] is shown in Exhibit 10.4.

Exhibit 10.4

Accounting Clusters

Fair Presentation/Full Disclosure Model

Australia	Kenya	South Africa
Bangladesh	Malaysia	Taiwan
Canada	Netherlands	Thailand
Denmark	New Zealand	United Kingdom
India	Nigeria	United States
Indonesia	Pakistan	Venezuela
Ireland	Philippines	Zimbabwe
	Singapore	

Legal Compliance Model

Algeria	Germany	Portugal
Austria	Greece	South Korea
Belgium	Italy	Spain
Cameroon	Japan	Sweden
Cote d'Ivorie	Luxembourg	Switzerland
Egypt	Morocco	Turkey
Finland	Norway	Zaire
France		

Inflation-adjusted Model

Argentina	Israel	Peru
Brazil	Mexico	Uruguay
Chile		

Source: Gernon and Meek,[2] p. 12.

The authors of this clustering advise caution in its interpretation and use. Accounting in each country is constantly under revision and, as will be discussed later, the differences between countries are fading as a result of increased globalization and efforts of various national and international accounting bodies. Keeping that caution in mind, some comments about each cluster can be made. The first accounting model called the fair presentation/full disclosure model originated in Great Britain and spread throughout the British colonies. This model is found in common law countries in which there is a vibrant capital market. The second model called the legal compliance model originated in code law countries such as France and Germany, and spread throughout their colonial systems. This model is designed to satisfy the government as opposed to external investors, since these countries did not have a long tradition of equity financing. Since the banks in these countries had extensive personal and family contacts with the firms, extensive disclosure was not needed. In addition, much of the wealth was concentrated in powerful family groups, so accounting was designed to be very conservative to minimize the value of the firm and the inheritance taxes as ownership was passed from generation to generation. The third accounting model was called the inflation-adjusted model and is composed largely of Latin American countries who have experienced substantial inflation and have chosen to develop mechanisms to deal with it.

In addition to the general accounting models or clusters discussed above, there are a large number of specific accounting issues that vary among nations and are worth illustrating. Some of these are definitional differences, translation of foreign currencies, income measurement, asset valuation, treatment of acquisitions, and issues involving research and development.

Assets and liabilities may often have the same name from country to country, but the actual definition for measurement purposes may be quite different. For example, what is defined as "cash and cash equivalents" in the United States might have a very different definition in some other country. Some countries might permit a bank overdraft or some short-term borrowing to be netted against cash rather than being shown as a separate liability. Notions of short term and long term might vary from country to country. Recognition of liabilities is equally complex, and there might be many different ways to handle a contingency such as a pending lawsuit.

Rules and traditions governing income measurement might vary from country to country. The stock market usually rewards smooth income patterns from year to year, and the accounting regulations of various nations provide different degrees of flexibility in the reporting of income through the use of provisions and reserves. Some nations permit certain transactions to avoid the income statement altogether, allowing a direct reduction of owners' equity instead of showing it as a reduction of income and then reducing owners' equity.

The valuation of assets varies from country to country. In the United States, assets are valued at their historical cost. This principle assumes there is no inflation, and an asset such as land that was purchased in 1950 for $10,000 is still on the books today at $10,000 despite years of market price inflation. Some nations permit revaluation of assets to their current value, some nations require revaluation to their current value, and some nations attempt to restate their financial statements via a general price-level adjustment.

Countries also have different ways of treating acquisitions. When an acquisition is made for a price that is greater than the book value of the acquired firm, the acquisition results in the creation of an intangible asset called goodwill that represents the difference between the price and the book value of the acquired firm. The handling of this intangible asset is a source of great international diversity. Some countries recognize it as an asset, and allocate a portion of the asset to expense each year over an arbitrary period such as forty years, eventually reducing the value of that intangible asset to zero. For a large acquisition, this results in a significant deduction from income each year until the intangible asset reaches zero. Some countries recognize this asset, but permit a direct deduction from owners' equity and avoid the income statement altogether. Some countries require a periodic review of the intangible asset and require an estimate of its "future value" and may require a write-off as the goodwill is considered "impaired."

Handling of research and development expenditures varies from country to country. In the United States, research and development expenditures are always considered an expense and are immediately deducted from net income in the period in which they are incurred. Other countries distinguish between research and development and choose to directly expense anything classified as research, but permit capitalization of an expenditure defined as "development." The development costs are shown as an asset on the balance sheet and are reduced and expensed over the useful life of the development process.

Sadly, this discussion touches only on some of the differences involved from country to country. The reader is advised to consult an international accounting textbook to explore these differences in greater detail. On the positive side, there are efforts within many countries as well as international efforts to lessen these differences.

Consequences of International Financial Accounting Diversity

Despite the many differences from country to country measured above, capital still manages to move across borders, so perhaps the accounting diversity noted above is merely a "bump in the road" to a truly global financial system.

The global financial system would most likely be better off without these bumps. If the accounting information flowed smoothly, perhaps the costs and risks of investing internationally might be lowered. Individual investors might make better-informed decisions with access to information, without having to translate the accounting rules of one country into the accounting rules of another country to compare investments. Likewise, companies seeking investment funds might be better able to find funds across borders if they did not have to incur the expense of presenting financial information under a different accounting regime to attract investors living in a different country.

Harmonization of Financial Accounting Diversity

Despite the forces favoring international diversity of accounting systems, there are also a number of strong forces favoring harmonization of the various national accounting systems. Some of these forces include the explosive growth in cross-border financing, improvements in communication technology, formation of cross-national economic blocs such as the EU and NAFTA, and efforts by the United Nations. As a consequence, attempts have been made to encourage accounting harmonization at the international level as well as at the local level of various nations.

Internationally, a milestone in the march toward accounting harmonization was the formation of the International Accounting Standards Commission (IASC) in 1973. The IASC was formed as an independent, private sector body whose objective was to facilitate the cross-border flow of capital by making financial statements more comparable, even though they were prepared under various sets of national accounting standards. Membership in the IASC included professional accounting bodies of various nations. Immediately after its founding in 1973, the IASC chose the politically expedient strategy of permitting a wide variation in permitted accounting methods. Disclosure of the accounting method was emphasized instead of forcing compliance with a particular model. Major international players such as the United States, Japan, and various European nations were not forced to change their domestic standards to be in compliance with an emerging set of international accounting standards created by the IASC. This strategy insured at least passive international support for IASC's efforts from the world's major financial powers. As the years progressed, however, the IASC gradually reduced the number of permitted alternative accounting methods.

In April 2001, the IASC was restructured and renamed the International Accounting Standards Board (IASB). Its objectives include (1) developing a set of high quality, understandable, and enforceable global accounting standards, (2) promoting the use and rigorous application of these standards, and

(3) bringing about convergence of national accounting standards and International Accounting Standards.[3] Standards issued by the IASB are designated International Financial Reporting Standards (IFRS). As of September 2006, there were five such standards issued. Standards originally issued by the IASC are known as International Accounting Standards (IASs). As of September 2006, there were 41 of these standards with 31 still being effective. The IASB has no authority to enforce compliance with these standards, but many national accounting standard-setting bodies have permitted or encouraged the use of IFRS as alternatives or supplements to their own national accounting standards. Belgium, France, and Italy, for example, passed laws in 1998 allowing IFRS to be used for domestic financial reporting. At the time of writing, the IOSCO has recommended that its members should allow multinational issuers to use IFRS in their cross-border offerings and listings. In addition, the EU now (after January 1, 2005) requires IFRS for all EU-listed companies. Australia has adopted IFRS as its national standard as of the same date. New Zealand will require IFRS from 2007. The IASB notes that over 90 countries claim they will be following IFRS in 2005.[4]

Harmonization efforts also occur at the local level of various nations. The very existence of IFRS and its persuasive promotion on the part of the IASB have influenced the development of various national accounting standards. Accounting bodies of various nations, even if they have not adopted IFRS, sometimes model their own national standards or at least modify their own standards with international standards in mind. The United States, for example, has not adopted IFRS for domestic reporting, but has stated that it will formulate accounting policy with due regard to international considerations. The Norwalk Agreement,[5] signed by the United States' standard-setting body, the Financial Accounting Standards Board (FASB), and the IASB pledged to use their best efforts to make their existing financial reporting standards fully compatible and to coordinate their future work programs. The United States permits foreign companies raising capital in the United States to use either their own domestic accounting standards or IFRS as long as there is a note reconciling net income and net assets to US GAAP. The United States has pledged to review this reconciliation requirement in the near future.

Other Players in Financial Accounting Harmonization

In addition to the IASB, the following are the other significant players[6] in the accounting harmonization movement:

1. Commission of the European Union (EU)
2. International Organization of Securities Commissions (IOSCO)
3. International Federation of Accountants (IFAC)

4. United Nations Intergovernmental Working Group of Experts on International Standards of Accounting and Reporting (ISAR), part of the United Nations Conference on Trade and Development (UNCTAD).

The EU was set up after World War II, and is now composed of 15 European member states and is preparing for the accession of 13 eastern and southern European countries. The member countries are Belgium, Denmark, Germany, Greece, Spain, France, Ireland, Italy, Luxembourg, the Netherlands, Austria, Portugal, Finland, Sweden, and the United Kingdom. The members of the EU delegate sovereignty to common institutions representing the interests of the EU as a whole on questions of joint interests. Harmonization of accounting standards among its members is one such area, and the EU has been a significant player in accounting harmonization via its Directives. Directives of the EU become law of the member states through a complex process of ratification. The Directives are binding on member states, but implementation is left to individual states and can be a lengthy process. The Fourth, Seventh, and Eighth Directives bear on accounting directly. The Fourth Directive establishes some basic rules for which statements must be presented, some format guidelines, and certain disclosure rules. The most significant aspect of the Fourth Directive is philosophical, the establishment of the "true and fair" rule, which is much like the rule in the United States in which financial statements must "fairly present" financial statements. This requirement goes beyond simply complying with applicable laws and regulations. The Seventh Directive requires consolidated financial statements as opposed to simply presenting the financial statement of a parent company. Issues involving consolidation will be discussed subsequently in this chapter. The Eighth Directive involves uniform requirements for auditors in the EU member states.

The IOSCO is composed of over 170 various national securities regulatory organizations, whose objectives are as follows:

- To cooperate together to promote high quality standards of regulation in order to maintain just, efficient, and sound markets.
- To exchange information on their respective experiences in order to promote the development of domestic markets.
- To unite their efforts to establish standards and an effective surveillance of international securities transactions.
- To provide mutual assistance to promote the integrity of markets by a rigorous application of the standards and by effective enforcement against offenses.[7]

IOSCO has worked extensively on accounting standards, and a milestone in the movement toward accounting harmonization occurred when IOSCO endorsed IASB's accounting standards.

The IFAC is an organization of national professional accountancy organizations that represents accountants employed in various aspects of the accounting profession. At the time of writing, IFAC had 163 member bodies in 120 countries and claimed to represent 2.5 million accountants.[8] The IFAC strives to develop the accounting profession and to harmonize its standards worldwide to enable accountants to provide services of consistently high quality in the public interest. Perhaps its most noteworthy achievement is the development and promotion of sets of high quality technical, professional, and ethical publications and guidance, including a set of international auditing standards.

The United Nations maintains some involvement in accounting harmonization via its Intergovernmental Working Group of Experts on ISAR. The ISAR attempts to insure that the financial statements of businesses will contain reliable, comparable, and transparent financial information, which is needed for the efficient functioning of stock markets, banks, and foreign direct investment. The ISAR also attempts to improve disclosures on corporate governance by enterprises in developing countries and countries with economies in transition. The ISAR accomplishes its objectives through an integrated program of research, intergovernmental consensus building, and technical cooperation.[9]

International Financial Reporting

This section discusses some issues that arise in the preparation and use of international financial statements. Two issues that arise in the preparation of international financial statements are consolidation and foreign currency translation. Multinationals must somehow aggregate the individual financial statements of their subsidiaries. Most likely, the multinational has a subsidiary in each country in which it has substantial operations. This consolidation is made even more problematic since each subsidiary may be maintaining its own accounts in its local currency. This creates a need for foreign currency translation: converting a set of financial statements prepared in one currency to a second currency. International auditing is then discussed, and the section concludes with some issues involved in the use of international financial statements.

International Consolidations

The Coca-Cola Company operates in over 200 countries worldwide, most likely, and each country has at least one reporting entity and these entities must be somehow combined to form a single consolidated set of financial statements, which are disclosed publicly.

Simply stated, consolidation involves "adding" up the accounts of two separate financial statements, eliminating the effects of any transactions between the two entities, and producing a single set of financial statements as if the two companies were a single entity. Consider the balance sheets of two affiliated companies, Parent Company and Child Company found in Exhibit 10.5.

Exhibit 10.5

An Example of Balance Sheet Consolidation

Parent Company Balance Sheet December 31, 2005		Child Company Balance Sheet December 31, 2005	
Cash	$20,000	Cash	$2,000
Receivables	30,000	Receivables	3,000
Inventory	50,000	Inventory	5,000
Plant and Equipment	200,000	Plant and Equipment	20,000
Total Assets	$300,000	Total Assets	$30,000
Payables	$50,000	Payables	$5,000
Equity	250,000	Equity	25,000
Total Liabilities and Equity	$300,000	Total Liabilities and Equity	$30,0000

Note 1. Parent Company owes the subsidiary $1,000.

Parent and Child Company
Consolidated Balance Sheet
December 31, 2003

Cash	$22,000	
Receivables	32,000	a.
Inventory	55,000	
Plant and Equipment	220,000	
Total Assets	$329,000	
Payables	$54,000	b.
Equity	275,000	
Total Liabilities and Equity	$329,000	

a. $30,000 + 3,000 - 1,000 = 32,000$
b. $50,000 + 5,000 - 1,000 = 54,000$

In order to produce a single balance sheet for the consolidated entity, Parent and Child Company, it is necessary to add up the balance sheet items while eliminating the effects of any inter-company transactions. As an example of an inter-company transaction, Parent Company owes the subsidiary $1000 as in Note 1 on Exhibit 10.5. This would be reflected as a payable (liability) on the books of the Parent Company and as a receivable (asset) on the books of the Child Company. In order to report the financial position of the combined entity, however, the inter-company payable of $1000 on the books of the Parent Company does not represent a payable for the consolidated entity. The entire entity of Parent and Child Company does not owe that $1000 to anyone outside the entity. Likewise, the entire entity of Parent and Child Company does not have the right to collect that $1000 from anyone outside the Parent and Child entity. Thus, when consolidating these two companies, the inter-company payable and the offsetting inter-company receivable must be eliminated. The consolidated balance sheet of Parent and Child Company is shown at the bottom of Exhibit 10.5.

The same logic applies to inter-company transactions that affect the income statement. Assume Child Company sold merchandise to Parent Company for $1500 that cost Child $1000 to manufacture. Parent Company then sold it for $3000. Consider the income statements of the Parent and Child Companies shown in Exhibit 10.6.

In order to produce a single income statement for the consolidated entity, Parent and Child Company, it is necessary to add up the income statement items while eliminating the effects of any inter-company transactions. As an example of an inter-company transaction, the inter-company sale described above is repeated as Note 2 on Exhibit 10.6. The inter-company sale of $1500 from Child Company to Parent Company represents revenue of $1500 to Child Company, but it does not represent revenue to the combined Parent and Child entity since it was not sold to a customer outside the entity. Likewise the $1500 represents an expense to the unconsolidated Parent Company, but it does not represent a $1500 expense to the combined entity since the expense was not yet used up by the combined entity. The $1500 inter-company revenue and the offsetting $1500 inter-company expense must be eliminated. The consolidated income statement of Parent and Child Company is shown at the bottom of Exhibit 10.6.

In addition to the two simple inter-company transactions described in Exhibits 10.5 and 10.6, there are a variety of more complex inter-company transactions that can also occur: for example, inter-company lending, inter-company rental or leasing, inter-company dividends, and inter-company purchases and sales of assets, services, or merchandise. The mechanics of these inter-company transactions can be quite complex, but the logic of eliminating them is similar to the logic in the Parent and Child Company examples.

Exhibit 10.6

An Example of Income Statement Consolidation

Parent Company Income Statement Year Ended December 31, 2005		Child Company Income Statement Year Ended December 31, 2005	
Revenues	$100,000	Revenues	$10,000
Expenses	80,000	Expenses	8,000
Net Income	$20,000	Net Income	$2,000

Note 2. Child Company sold merchandise to Parent for $1500. The merchandise cost Child company $1000 to manufacture and Parent sold it for $3,000.

Parent and Child Company
Consolidated Income Statement
Year Ended December 31, 2005

Revenues	$108,500	a.
Expenses	86,500	b.
Total Assets	$22,000	

a. $100,000 + 10,000 - 1,500 = 108,000$
b. $80,000 + 8,000 - 1,500 = 86,500$

Consolidations, which are facts of life in multinational corporations, become even more complex when we consider the possibility of an unconsolidated subsidiary that is under the effective control of a parent company. The possible existence of an unconsolidated subsidiary that is controlled by a parent company makes the financial statements of the company open to a large degree of manipulation. If a parent controls the subsidiary, the parent can direct the subsidiary to engage in inter-company transactions designed for the benefit of the parent. For example, the parent company could force the subsidiary to purchase, rent, or lease assets from it at a hugely inflated price. Risky accounts receivable might be relegated to the subsidiary; obsolete inventory might be forced on the subsidiary. Thus, a situation in which the parent has control over the subsidiary and the subsidiary is unconsolidated leaves open the possibility of a lot of nefarious transactions designed to make the parent company look more attractive to investors.

The decision as to when a parent has control over a subsidiary is not always clear, however. If a parent owns 100 percent of a subsidiary, the subsidiary should clearly be consolidated because the parent has control. Control could be exercised with less than 100 percent ownership; even with 50 percent ownership, a parent would have voting control. Effective control might, however, be reached with considerably less than 50 percent ownership depending on the structure of the remaining ownership. It is possible to have effective control of a subsidiary with only 5 percent ownership if the remaining ownership is diffused and/or very passive. Different nations have different rules of consolidation, and a knowledgeable international investor would be advised to look at the consolidation rules quite closely. This is another example of accounting diversity, and it is insidious because the consolidation rules are sometimes not evident.

Foreign Currency Translation

In addition to dealing with consolidation issues, the fact that the Coca-Cola Company operates in over 200 countries, many having different forms of currency, necessitates that Coca-Cola somehow translates the financial statements produced by those subsidiaries and combine them into one consolidated financial statement denominated in US dollars. This is a very complex issue when we ask ourselves which exchange rate we should use to translate the statement. The following are some possibilities:

- Current exchange rate—the exchange rate for the current date.
- Historical exchange rate—the exchange rate in place when a particular transaction occurred.
- Average exchange rate—the average rate over a particular period of time.

There is certainly merit in using each of the above rates in particular circumstances. The current exchange rate might be appropriate to translate the value of current assets or current liabilities that are readily convertible to cash. The historic exchange rate might be appropriate to translate the historical cost of a long-term asset such as a plant and equipment. Average exchange rates might be appropriate to translate certain income statement items such as sales or cost of goods sold, assuming the transactions for these items occurred evenly throughout the period over which the average is taken.

Which exchange rate to use has been the subject of much controversy in accounting among both academics and professionals over the last two decades, and no perfect solution has emerged. The situation is made even more complex by the fact that whenever anything other than a single exchange rate is used to translate a set of financial statements, a translation gain or loss is generated, which is sometimes quite volatile and often outside the control of a manager. The volatility of this gain or loss might affect the valuation of the firm by the stock markets, and management often advocated translation methods that minimized reported translation gains or losses, sometimes at the expense of theoretical soundness. As a result, a number of methods using different exchange rates to translate different portions of the financial statements arose worldwide. Saudagaran[10] lists four of the more popular methods worldwide: the current rate method, the current/noncurrent method, the monetary/nonmonetary method, and the temporal method. These methods are outlined in Exhibit 10.7.

Exhibit 10.7 shows which exchange rate is used to translate a particular income statement or balance sheet item under each of the four translation methods.

The current rate method translates all balance sheet items (except owners' equity) at the current exchange rate. Common stock and additional

Exhibit 10.7

Exchange Rates Employed in Different Translation Methods for Specific Balance Sheet Items

	Current	Current/ noncurrent	Monetary/ Nonmonetary	Temporal
Cash	C	C	C	C
Accounts receivable	C	C	C	C
Inventories				
Cost	C	C	H	H
Market	C	C	H	C
Investments				
Cost	C	H	H	H
Market	C	H	H	C
Fixed assets	C	H	H	H
Other assets	C	H	H	H
Accounts payable	C	C	C	C
Long-term debt	C	H	C	C
Common stock, paid-in-capital	H	H	H	H
Retained earnings	B	B	B	B
Revenues	A	A	A	A
Cost of goods sold	A	A	H	H
Depreciation expense	A	H	H	H
Amortization expense	A	H	H	H

Note: A = Average rate; B = Residual, balancing figure representing a composite of successive current rates; C = Current rate; H = Historical rate.
Source: Saudagaran,[10] (2004), p. 65.

paid-in-capital accounts are carried at the historical exchange rate that was in place when the stock was issued. All income statement items are translated at the average exchange rate for the period. The year-end shareholders' equity includes a translation adjustment, which is a plug to make the balance sheet balance. Under this method there is no foreign exchange translation adjustment on the income statement.

The current/noncurrent method involves translating all current assets and current liabilities at the current exchange rate. Noncurrent assets and noncurrent liabilities are translated at the historical exchange rate in place when the asset or liability was acquired. Income statement items are translated at average exchange rates, except those associated with a noncurrent asset or liability. These are translated at the rate corresponding to the associated asset or liability.

The monetary/nonmonetary method is similar to the current/noncurrent method except that the classification is based on similarity of the asset rather than its maturity date. Items considered monetary are translated at the current exchange rate, and assets considered nonmonetary are translated at the appropriate historic exchange rate.

The temporal method translates monetary items (cash, receivables, and payables) at the current exchange rate. Nonmonetary items (inventories and fixed assets) are translated at the current rate if they are carried on the books at current value, or at the historical rate if they are carried at the original cost. Income statement items are mostly translated at average rates.

All four methods have been used by various countries at one time or another as no perfect method has emerged. In the United States today, a wide range of latitude is given by the currently governing set of principles, Statement of Financial Accounting Standards, SFAS 52.[11] The SFAS 52 introduces the notion of the functional currency of a subsidiary, and offers three choices of functional currency: the local currency, the US dollar, or a third currency. The SFAS 52 introduces certain parameters to govern this choice. When the local currency is the functional currency, the current rate method is used to translate the financial statements into US dollars. If the local currency is a third currency, a two-step approach is used. The statements are first translated into the local currency using the temporal method and then translated into the US dollar using the current rate method.

Internationally, a variety of methods exist and the reader of a financial statement must investigate which method is being used in a particular country at a particular point in time. The international standard concerning currency translation, IAS 21, "The Effects of Changes in Foreign Exchange Rates," is very similar to the US standard concerning currency translation, SFAS 52, with some differences in terminology, and one important difference.[12] The IAS 21 provides special procedures to translate the financial statements of a subsidiary in a highly inflationary economy. Subsidiaries in such an economy must first restate their financial statements to the current price level and then translate the statements using procedures outlined in IAS 21.

Auditing in an International Environment

Auditing is the process by which specialized accounting professionals (auditors) examine and verify the adequacy of a company's financial and control systems and the accuracy of its financial records.[13] Auditing plays a key role in any financial market, since an investor must somehow have faith that a set of financial statements produced by a company are reliable. Just as accounting standards are different from country to country, auditing standards are also different from country to country. In addition, the numbers, training, and status of auditors are different from one country to the next. An audit from a qualified accountant gives investors faith in an investment, but as one moves across borders investors must make a longer leap of faith, since the methods and qualifications of auditors vary from country to country. This difficulty is being attacked on two fronts, however. Multinationals themselves have developed mechanisms to increase investors' faith in auditing across borders, and various international organizations have made significant inroads in harmonizing the auditing profession across borders.

Multinationals themselves have an interest in maintaining high quality auditing across borders. Since the consolidated financial statements of a multinational such as Coca-Cola are audited by a single firm, Ernst & Young, LLP, that auditing firm must somehow satisfy itself that enough of Coca-Cola's subsidiaries have been audited by reputable auditors so they can issue an opinion. They do this either by auditing a subsidiary with a branch office of Ernst & Young or by engaging a local firm to do the audit and review that auditor's work. The 2004 audit opinion of Coca-Cola states, "We conducted our audits in accordance with auditing standards of the Public Company Oversight Board (United States)." Since auditing standards are different from country to country, Ernst & Young must insure that any local auditors used should perform this audit in accordance with the United States' generally accepted auditing standards.

In addition to the procedures employed by a multinational company and its auditors, several international organizations, notably the IFAC, IOSCO, and the EU, are working to promote the harmonization of auditing standards worldwide.

The IFAC publishes a set of International Standards on Auditing (ISA) that are to be applied in the audits of financial statements and are intended for international acceptance. In addition, IFAC is active in the standardization of the education of accountants internationally by issuing a series of

International Education Standards that are intended to establish the essential elements on which education and training for all accountants should be founded. The IOSCO has worked with IFAC in both the development and promotion of IFAC's auditing standards worldwide, recognizing that high-quality audit standards are a crucial aspect of vibrant and trusted securities markets worldwide. Within the European Community, the Eighth Directive sets the qualification and education standards for auditors.

International Financial Statement Analysis

When a user in one country examines a financial statement produced in another country, there are many barriers to be overcome. In addition to the fact that there is an almost endless diversity among the accounting and auditing rules and procedures from nation to nation, there are also some additional subtle differences in language and format.

Language differences are obvious when an English-speaking user is confronted with a Spanish financial statement produced by a Mexican company, but there are even some subtle language differences that occur between nations that speak ostensibly the same language, such as the United States and the United Kingdom. A brief listing of some of those subtle language differences is contained in Exhibit 10.8. For example, receivables in the United States are known as debtors in the United Kingdom. An income statement in the United States would be known as a profit and loss account in the United Kingdom.

In addition to the language differences shown above, UK balance sheets tend to be presented in a different format from a US balance sheet. A balance sheet of a UK multinational Cadbury Schweppes is presented in Exhibit 10.9.

The reader can examine Exhibit 10.9 and see some of the language differences. In addition to those differences, a drastic difference in format should

Exhibit 10.8

Some Differences in Terminology between the United States and the United Kingdom

United States terminology	United Kingdom terminology
Receivables	Debtors
Inventory	Stock
Payables	Creditors
Reserves	Provisions
Retained Earnings	Profit and Loss Account
Income Statement	Profit and Loss Account
Sales	Turnover
Consolidated	Group

Exhibit 10.9

Cadbury-Schweppes
Balance Sheet
Balance Sheets at 2 January 2005 (Note 1)

Notes		Group 2004 £m	Group 2003 (restated) £m	Company 2004 £m	Company 2003 (restated) £m
	Fixed Assets				
10	Intangible assets and goodwill	5,485	5,827	–	–
11	Tangible fixed assets	1,613	1,633	115	146
12	Investments in associates	324	313	9	9
12	Investments	11	15	5,699	6,177
		7,433	7,788	5,823	6,332
	Current Assets				
13	Stocks	708	672	–	–
14	Debtors				
	– Due within one year	1,182	1,221	141	161
	– Due after one year	67	81	22	44
19a	Investments	145	242	–	–
19a	Cash at bank and in hand	201	191	–	–
		2,303	2,407	163	205
	Current Liabilities				
	Creditors: amounts falling due within one year				
19a	– Borrowings	(630)	(1,069)	(2,589)	(2,813)
15	– Other	(1,881)	(1,977)	(367)	(403)
	Net Current Liabilities	(208)	(639)	(2,793)	(3,011)
	Total Assets less Current Liabilities	7,225	7,149	3,030	3,321
	Non-Current Liabilities				
	Creditors: amounts falling due after more than one year				
19a	– Borrowings	(3,586)	(3,575)	(899)	(987)
15	– Other	(211)	(123)	(5)	–
16	Provisions for liabilities and charges	(340)	(428)	–	(12)
		(4,137)	(4,126)	(904)	(999)
	Net Assets	3,088	3,023	2,126	2,322

(continued)

Exhibit 10.9 *continued*

Balance Sheets at 2 January 2005 (Note 1)

Notes		Group 2004 £m	Group 2003 (*restated*) £m	Company 2004 £m	Company 2003 (*restated*) £m
	Capital and Reserves				
21	Called up share capital	259	258	259	258
21	Share premium account	1,098	1,071	1,098	1,071
21	Revaluation reserve	59	59	1	1
21	Other reserves	(46)	(80)	624	1,015
21	Profit and loss account	1,489	1,472	144	(23)
	Shareholders' Funds	2,859	2,780	2,126	2,322
	Minority Interests				
22	Equity minority interests	21	18	–	–
22	Non-equity minority interests	208	225	–	–
		229	243	–	–
	Total Capital Employed	3,088	3,023	2,126	2,322

On behalf of the Board Directors: John Sunderland and Ken Hanna, 11 March 2005.

be noted. A US balance sheet typically uses the format of the basic accounting equation:

$$\text{Assets} = \text{liabilities} + \text{owners' equity} \tag{10.1}$$

A UK balance sheet uses the format

$$\text{Net assets} = \text{total capital employed} \tag{10.2}$$

Equation (10.1) is equivalent to Equation (10.2) knowing that net assets = assets — liabilities and total capital employed = owners equity. In the United States, assets are listed in order of decreasing liquidity, that is cash, accounts receivable, and so on. In the United Kingdom, fixed assets are listed first. This difference in format is not simply between the United States and the United Kingdom. Users of financial statements are likely to see this difference in format in a number of nations that were influenced by the United Kingdom such as many of its former colonies. The UK format is also likely to be adopted by countries trying to raise funds in an exchange influenced by the United Kingdom such as the Hong Kong Stock Exchange. The IASB accepts both formats.

Both preparers and users of international financial statements must somehow cope with this international accounting diversity. Gernon and others[14] note several ways in which preparers of financial statements deal with this diversity: (1) do nothing; (2) prepare a convenience translation; (3) prepare convenience statements; (4) restate on a limited basis; (5) prepare secondary financial statements.

A corporation might decide to do nothing about the problem. For example, a Mexican company might simply prepare financial statements in the Mexican peso, in Spanish, and under Mexican accounting procedures. This company might not have the need to raise capital or borrow money outside Mexico, and perceive little benefit from incurring the expense of translating their financial statements.

A corporation might prepare what is called a convenience translation. This involves translating the statement into the foreign user's language and retains the home country's accounting principles and currency unit. The Cadbury-Schweppes balance sheet shown in Exhibit 10.9 is an example of a convenience translation.

A convenience statement translates the statement into the foreign user's language and retains the home country's accounting principles, but expresses the monetary amounts in the reader's home currency. These are usually translated at the year-end exchange rate, and ignore the issue of any translation gains or losses.

A multinational might reconcile certain balance sheet and/or income statements from the preparer's accounting principles to the user's home accounting principles and explain any major differences. Exhibit 10.10 shows an example of such a limited restatement. Cadbury-Schweppes reconciles profit per UK accounting principles to profit per US accounting principles. Some countries might require a statement in a home country's accounting principles to be accompanied by a reconciliation such as Exhibit 10.10 for certain items on the financial statements. At the time of writing, it was noted that for years 2005 and thereafter Cadbury-Schweppes would prepare its financial statements using IFRS rather than the UK GAAP. In the United States, the Securities and Exchange Commission (SEC) requires reconciliation of net income, earnings per share, and net assets from foreign GAAP to US GAAP. This requirement stands even if the foreign GAAP is IFRS.

Finally, a multinational might prepare a complete set of financial statements under its home accounting principles and publish another complete set of financial statements (known as secondary financial statements) under some other nation's accounting principles. Sometimes a multinational might choose to publish its own financial statements and publish a set of secondary financial statements under US accounting principles if it wants to raise capital or create visibility in the United States. A frequent practice today is for a multinational to prepare a set of financial statements under their own

Exhibit 10.10

Cadbury-Schweppes
Reconciliation of Profit per UK GAAP to Profit
to US GAAP

31 Summary of differences between UK and US Generally Accepted Accounting Principles Accounting Differences

The financial statements are prepared in accordance with generally accounting principles applicable in the UK ("UK GAAP"), which difer in certain significant respects from those applicable in the US ("US GAAP"). The following is a summary of the adjustments to consolidated profit for the financial year and consolidated shareholders' funds that would have been required in applying the significant differences between UK and US GAAP.

Effects on profit of differences between UK abd US generally accepted accounting principles

Notes		2004 £m	2003 £m	2002 £m
	Profit for the Financial Year from continuing operations, net of tax (per UK GAAP)	431	366	548
	US GAAP adjustments:			
31(a), (b)	Goodwill/intangible amortisation	106	93	53
31(c)	Business combinations	–	(21)	–
31(n)	Restructuring	(24)	34	(1)
31(d)	Interest capitalised	7	6	6
31(d)	Depreciation of capitalised interest	(3)	(2)	(2)
31(i)	Retirement benefits	(26)	(33)	10
31(m)	Disposal gain adjustments	–	–	7
31(e)	Derivatives – Impact of transition adjustment	(1)	–	1
31(e)	Derivatives	16	(93)	(9)
31(j), (k)	Employee share arrangements	(11)	(12)	4
31(o)	Deconsolidation of variable interest entity	17	–	–
	Taxation on above adjustments	(2)	47	(4)
31(f)	Deferred taxation	(26)	(12)	(48)
	Profit for the Financial Year per US GAAP	484	373	565

home-country's accounting principles, and then prepare a secondary set of financial statements under IASB accounting standards due to the increasing worldwide acceptance of IASB accounting standards.

In any case, it is up to the user of the financial statement to know which currency and, even more importantly, whose set of accounting principles was used to construct a financial statement they wish to analyze. Users have a number of choices as well. The user could choose not to invest in a foreign company. The user might learn about the accounting and business practices of a foreign company, or the user might depend on a broker or some expert to provide advice. In any case, the user must tread carefully.

International Taxation and International Transfer Prices

Differences in taxation practices from country to country exert a huge influence on both the strategies and the tactics of multinationals. Every nation sets its own tax policy in line with its own national goals and traditions. This section discusses the international tax situation and concludes with a look at international transfer prices used by multinationals to both cope with and take advantage of international tax diversity.

International Diversity of Tax Systems and Tax Rates

Just as multinationals are forced to cope with a staggering diversity in accounting customs and regulations, there is a corresponding diversity in tax systems and rates in virtually every country on earth. A nation's tax policy is set by the government, and the tax law of a particular country is a product of the economic and social goals and circumstances of that country. A multinational must file a tax return in every country in which it operates, based on a profit calculated according to the laws and regulations of that country. A country-by-country examination of tax systems is certainly beyond the scope of this chapter, but some basic philosophical differences among the various national tax systems can be noted. Gernon and others[15] note two different national philosophies of taxation: the territorial principle and the worldwide principle. The territorial principle implies that income earned outside a home country's territory is not taxable. This is, in fact, a kind of governmental subsidy to encourage a home country's businesses to sell their products outside their borders. The worldwide principle implies that a country has the right to collect taxes on income earned outside the home country by a company domiciled in the home country. The worldwide principle results in double taxation, since income earned outside a country is taxed by the foreign tax authorities and then taxed by the home tax authorities.

In addition to philosophical differences, there is also a wide variation in the effective tax rates from country to country. A flavor of the diversity is captured in Exhibit 10.11, which lists effective tax rates in a variety of developed countries.

Exhibit 10.11

International Tax Rates

Country	Central government corporate income tax rate
Australia	30
Austria	25
Belgium	33
Canada	21
Czech Republic	26
Denmark	30
Finland	26
France	33.33
Germany	25
Greece	n.a.
Hungary	16
Iceland	18
Ireland	12.5
Italy	33
Japan	30
Korea	25
Luxembourg	22
Mexico	30
Netherlands	31.5
New Zealand	33
Norway	23.75
Poland	n.a.
Portugal	25
Slovak Republic	19
Spain	35
Sweden	28
Switzerland	8.5
Turkey	30
United Kingdom	30
United States	35

n.a. – Not available
Source: Organization for Economic Cooperation and Development (OECD) website www.oecd.org, Table II.1, Corporate Income Tax Rate, accessed February 2006.

The desire of multinationals to minimize the taxes they pay worldwide undoubtedly enters into decision-making in a significant fashion. Multinationals produce the product in one location and sell it in another, resulting in an ability to choose the tax jurisdictions in which they perform various operations. The different tax rates shown in Exhibit 10.11 provide the opportunity for worldwide tax minimization, which can be perfectly legal, but sometimes skirts the edge of legality.

Tax Minimization Strategies

Multinationals have a variety of tools to escape double taxation and minimize the worldwide taxes they have to pay. Some of them include tax credits, tax treaties, and use of tax incentives tax havens.

A tax credit is a mechanism to mitigate the effects of a worldwide taxation philosophy on multinationals. A tax credit enables a multinational to reduce its home country tax paid by the amount of any taxes paid to foreign governments. Tax credits are generally used to offset the effect of double taxation, but sometimes are limited.

A tax treaty is between nations, and establishes which items of income will and will not be taxed by each local taxing authority that is a party to the treaty. Tax treaties are becoming quite common, and a list of countries with which the United States has tax treaties is shown in Exhibit 10.12.

A tax haven is a country with low or perhaps even no income tax. Tax havens are sometimes used by multinationals to shift income from a high-tax country to a low-tax country. For example, consider a company with three subsidiaries: subsidiary A and subsidiary B in high tax jurisdictions, and subsidiary C in a tax haven. Subsidiary A might sell the product to Subsidiary C at a low price. Subsidiary C might then sell the product at a high price to Subsidiary B. This series of sales puts a large amount of profit in Subsidiary C, while subsidiaries A and B report low profits in their high-tax jurisdictions. If the taxing authorities do not have sufficient interest or capability to investigate this situation, taxes would be minimized for this company. Depending on the laws of each of these jurisdictions, this strategy might be perfectly legal. The OECD has been active in identification of tax havens and pressuring them to avoid practices considered harmful to the world economy. Through the efforts of the OECD, real tax havens are becoming fewer and fewer, but they still can be an effective mechanism to minimize worldwide taxes.

International Transfer Pricing

A final method for reducing worldwide taxes is through judicious use of transfer prices. A transfer price is the price charged between organizational

Exhibit 10.12

United States Tax Treaty Countries

Australia	Iceland	Philippines
Austria	India	Poland
Barbados	Indonesia	Portugal
Belgium	Ireland	Romania
Canada	Israel	Russia
China	Italy	Slovak Republic
Commonwealth of	Jamaica	Slovenia
Independent	Japan	South Africa
States	Kazakstan	Spain
Cyprus	Korea, Republic of	Sweden
Czech Republic	Latvia	Switzerland
Denmark	Lithuania	Thailand
Egypt	Luxembourg	Trinidad and
Estonia	Mexico	Tobago
Finland	Morocco	Tunisia
France	Netherlands	Turkey
Germany	New Zealand	Ukraine
Greece	Norway	United Kingdom
Hungary	Pakistan	Venezuela

The US–USSR income tax treaty applies to Armenia, Azerbaijan, Belarus, Georgia, Kyrgystan, Moldava, Tajikistan, Turkmenistan, and Uzbekistan.
Source: US Department of the Treasury, Internal Revenue Service, Publication 901, US Tax Treaties, rev. May 2004, p. 48.

units of the same company. Internationally, the transfer price is the price paid for the transfer of goods and/or services between two subsidiaries of the same multinational corporation. These transfer prices can occur for both goods and services. Many multinationals produce a product in one country and sell it in a second country, or charge a subsidiary for some type of service the multinational may provide. Thus transfer prices occur even if no actual goods cross borders. For example, McDonald's in the United Kingdom pays a transfer price for royalties. United Parcel Company in Germany pays a transfer price to lease airplanes from United Parcel in the United States. Since there are different tax rates from one country to another, the issue of transfer prices gives multinationals an incentive to shift taxable profit to low tax rate jurisdictions using transfer prices as a mechanism.

A simple example should explain this. A multinational corporation has three subsidiaries, one in the United Kingdom, one in Ireland, and one in the United States. A product is manufactured in the UK subsidiary for $100, it is then sold to a subsidiary in Ireland which adds $10 in costs, and then it is sold to the US subsidiary which adds an additional $10 in costs and sells it to a US customer for $200. The UK tax rate is 30 percent, the Irish tax rate is 16 percent, and the US tax rate is 35 percent. Two transfer pricing scenarios are considered (scenario A and scenario B).

In transfer pricing scenario A shown in Exhibit 10.13 the transfer price between the United Kingdom and Ireland is $120. Since it cost the United Kingdom $100 to manufacture the product, the UK taxable profit and tax rate are $20 and 30 percent respectively, resulting in an Irish tax paid of $6. The Irish subsidiary pays the $120 transfer price, adds $10 in costs, and sells it to the US subsidiary for $160, resulting in Irish taxable profit of $30. With an Irish tax rate of 16 percent, Irish tax paid would be $4.80. The US subsidiary buys the product from Ireland for $160, adds $10 in additional costs, and sells it to a US customer for $200. This results in US taxable profit of $30 and with a 35 percent US tax rate; United States tax paid would be $10.50. Total pre-tax profit across all three subsidiaries would be $80.00, total tax paid to the three tax authorities would be $21.30, and total after tax profit to the multinational as a whole would be $58.70.

Scenario A

This multinational could increase its worldwide after-tax profit simply by establishing different transfer prices that would shift profits to a lower tax jurisdiction. Scenario B, illustrated in Exhibit 10.14, changes the United Kingdom–Ireland transfer price from $120 to $110 and the Ireland–United States transfer price from $160 to $185. All other data are unchanged from scenario A.

The new transfer prices allocate more of the profit to the Irish subsidiary, which has the lowest tax jurisdiction. A simple change in the two transfer prices after tax profit on this transaction increases from $58.70 to $64.85.

Exhibit 10.13

Transfer Pricing Example, Scenario A		
United Kingdom	Ireland	United States
Manufactured for $100	Adds $10 in costs	Adds $10 in costs
Sold to Irish subsidiary for $120	Sold to US subsidiary for $160	Sold to US customer for $200
UK taxable profit $20	Ireland taxable profit $30	US taxable profit $30
UK tax rate 30%	Ireland tax rate 16%	US tax rate 35%
UK tax paid $6	Ireland tax paid $4.80	US tax paid $10.50

Total pre-tax profit = $200 − $100 − $10 − $10 = $80

Total tax paid = $6 + $4.80 + $10.50 = $21.30

Total after-tax profit = $80 − $21.30 = $58.70

Exhibit 10.14

Transfer Pricing Example, Scenario B

United Kingdom	Ireland	United States
Manufactured for $100	Adds $10 in costs	Adds $10 in costs
Sold to Irish subsidiary for $110	Sold to US subsidiary for $185	Sold to US customer for $200
UK taxable profit $10	Ireland taxable profit $65	US taxable profit $5
UK tax rate 30%	Ireland tax rate 16%	US tax rate 35%
UK tax paid $3	Ireland tax paid $10.40	US tax paid $1.75

$$\text{Total pre-tax profit} = \$200 - \$100 - \$10 - \$10 = \$80$$
$$\text{Total tax paid} = \$3 + \$10.40 + \$1.75 = \$15.15$$
$$\text{Total after-tax profit} = \$80 - \$15.15 = \$64.85$$

This is a substantial increase in after-tax profits simply due to transfer pricing sleight-of-hand.

Scenarios A and B illustrate how important tax planning is to a multinational. This profit differential per transaction is multiplied many times over, and a multinational ignores tax consequences in its strategic and tactical decisions at its peril.

The example is of course greatly oversimplified, and ignores tariffs and a host of other considerations such as tariffs and currency controls that governments might take to discourage this behavior. In order to explore the complexity of international transfer pricing, it is necessary to look at the winners and losers in this simplified example as the multinational shifts from scenario A transfer prices to scenario B transfer prices.

The multinational itself is the winner as it shifts its reported profits to a low tax jurisdiction. The Irish government is a winner in this situation as it increases Irish taxes it receives. The Irish government might also benefit from increased employment and economic activity at the Irish subsidiary. The local management of the Irish subsidiary might also benefit in this scenario since reported profit for Ireland would be higher and that might influence the manager's compensation. The US and the UK governments are losers in this situation as their tax revenue decreases. Management of the UK and the US subsidiaries might also be losers in this situation since their compensation might suffer with lower reported income. The losing governments in this situation would be expected to exert pressure to ensure a "fair" allocation of the reported profit to their countries, and have developed laws that attempt to ensure a "fair" allocation among countries. Enforcement of these laws varies from country to country, but the laws do allow the countries to investigate transfer pricing practices and call them into question if they feel the transfer pricing practices are abusive.

If the transfer price approximates a market price, generally taxing authorities will not question a transfer price. More often than not, however, market prices are not readily available in an internal transfer price situation. The various national tax authorities have a number of mechanisms to determine the acceptability of a transfer price, in the absence of a competitive market, mostly based on an examination of costs and some reasonable markup.[16] Increasingly, multinationals are able to negotiate advanced pricing agreements with governments to reduce the uncertainty in transfer pricing enforcement.

It must be added that worldwide tax minimization, though it is a very important consideration, is not the only factor that influences a multinational's transfer pricing policy. Sometimes multinationals accept payment of taxes in a country as evidence of good citizenship, or as a means to gain favors in other areas from a government. Sometimes multinationals prefer to let subsidiary managers negotiate transfer prices with other affiliated subsidiaries as if they were at arms length, and then strictly evaluate the management of the subsidiary on subsidiary financial performance.

Closing Case

China Eastern Airlines

China Eastern Airlines, like several other People's Republic of China companies, is attempting to raise needed capital in international financial markets to finance its economic restructuring and opening to the outside world. China inherited an accounting system similar to the Soviet Union that supported central planning and the tight control that the central government had over all industry. As China opened itself and restructured, it changed its accounting system, but did not adopt IAS due to what the Chinese government felt were very special circumstances. In an attempt to raise capital outside China, Chinese companies do sometimes prepare secondary financial statements under International Accounting Standards, to encourage investment from outside markets. These standards are quite different from Chinese standards, resulting in significant variations in reported accounting numbers from one set of standards to another. Since China Eastern Airlines also raises capital on the New York Stock Exchange, it is required to report a limited restatement of net income per Chinese standards to net income per IAS, to net income per US standards. This extra information is sometimes found in a footnote to the IAS financial statements, but is always found in the company's filing with the US SEC.

The effects of this multiple reporting are discussed in the following excerpt from the Asian Wall Street Journal:

One of the main drivers for the move toward better standards in Asia is the desire by investors to be able to measure corporate results across a wide range of countries. As it is now, standards vary so much that it is often like comparing apples and oranges. However, Asian governments and regulators are choosing among different competing standards: one pushed by Europe, the other dominant in the US, and local standards. Which one gets adopted could have a big impact on the balance sheets and profits of companies around the region.

Singapore and Hong Kong are well on their way toward adopting International Accounting Standards, or IAS, the accounting method being promoted by the EU as the best global standard.

Some Chinese companies look better under international standards, for example take China Eastern Airlines which has a US listing and reports under American Generally Accepted Accounting Principles, or GAAP, and IAS. For its most recent interim results, the company reported a loss under local rules and a profit under IAS.

According to Nigel Reid, a partner at Ernst & Young's Hong Kong office, China Eastern's earnings do not look as healthy under Chinese standards in part because the companies there have to allow for faster depreciation on the value of their assets than under the other accounting standards. If your main asset is airlines, that is a big hit.[17]

Question: Why is China Eastern Airlines listed on the New York Stock Exchange? Why does China Eastern Airlines show two income statements in its annual report?

Chapter Summary

Accounting exists to provide information to users of financial statements so they can make better decisions. Accounting information helps those with financial resources make decisions about the use of these financial resources, and direct them to those with good ideas. As globalization increases the movement of goods and services across political and cultural borders, the movement of financial resources across borders is increasing as well. Borrowing and lending across borders is growing. Cross-border stock ownership is growing at an even faster pace, as companies seek equity capital in foreign countries as well as in their home country. There is a growing culture of equity ownership throughout the world as developing countries experience economic expansion, and more developed countries seek to privatize many economic entities that were owned by the state. These trends require accounting information that is useful as it crosses political, cultural and geographic boundaries.

Just as cultural, political, linguistic and economic factors that differ from one country to another, make cross-border transactions difficult, accounting information can sometimes add to this difficulty. No two countries on earth have exactly the same set of accounting rules to produce financial statements. These differences were caused by good reasons, notably 1) differing sources of external financing, 2) differing legal systems, 3) various political and economic ties, 4) varying levels of inflation, 5) varying levels of economic development, and 6) cultural differences.

There are strong forces at work, however, to mitigate the effects of this accounting diversity, notable the work of the International Accounting Standards Board (IASB). This is an independent, international body that has put together a set of accounting standards known as International Financial Reporting Standards (IFRS), which are becoming widely accepted throughout the world as an alternative or sometimes even a substitute for a nation's own domestic accounting rules. The European Union, as of 2005, has mandated that all companies listed on a stock exchange use IFRS. IFRS are becoming acceptable in many other countries throughout the world as well, and many national accounting bodies throughout the world have publicly stated their intention to converge with IFRS in the near future.

In addition to the accounting diversity problem and the resulting worldwide movement toward convergence, there are several other accounting issues multinational organizations must face. Multinationals must aggregate the financial statements of their various subsidiaries throughout the world to produce a single consolidated set of financial statements, including issues arising from the use of different currencies. Multinationals must also deal with different tax laws and rates in different countries, and often attempt to minimize their total worldwide tax liability. This situation becomes even more complex when a one subsidiary of a company buys or sells a product or service to another subsidiary of the same company in a different tax jurisdiction. Companies often manipulate these internal transactions, using transfer prices, to shift profits from a high tax jurisdiction to a low-tax jurisdiction. Countries, depending on their own particular circumstances often develop complex legal mechanisms to insure that their particular country receives a "fair" portion of the tax revenue.

Review and Discussion Questions

1. What is meant by "cross-border financing?" Is it increasing or decreasing?
2. What are eurocurrencies, eurobonds, and euroequities?
3. What does it mean to say there is a "growing worldwide equity culture?"
4. What causes accounting to be different from country to country?
5. What difficulties does international financial accounting diversity cause?

6. What efforts are being undertaken worldwide to address accounting diversity?

7. What are International Financial Reporting Standards?

8. What is a consolidated financial statement and why is it useful to investors?

9. What are the four different methods used to translate financial statements from one currency to another?

10. Explain the differences among the following: convenience translations, convenience statements, limited restatements, and secondary financial statements.

11. Explain how a multinational can make use of transfer prices to minimize its worldwide taxation payments?

Endnotes

1. Gernon, Helen and Gary Meek (2001). *Accounting: An International Perspective* 5th edn, New York: Irwin McGraw-Hill, pp. 3–8.

2. Gernon, Helen and Gary Meek, *op. cit.*, p. 12.

3. *International Accounting Standards Board* (2002) IASB Constitution (2000) as amended on 5 March 2002, www.iasc.org.uk/cmt/0001 accessed May 8, 2002.

4. *International Accounting Standards Board* website, www.iasb.org.uk, accessed February 9, 2006.

5. *Financial Accounting Standards Board (FASB)* website, www.fasb.org/news/memorandum.pdf, accessed February 9, 2006.

6. Choi, F. D., Frost, C. and G. Meek. (2001). *International Accounting*, 4th edn. Upper Saddle River, NJ: Pearson Education, Inc., pp. 308–19.

7. *International Organization of Securities Commissions (IOSCO)* (2006).www.iosco.org/about, accessed February 9, 2006.

8. *International Federation of Accountants (IFAC)* (2006). www.ifac.org/about accessed 9 February, 2006.

9. *United Nations Intergovernmental Working Group of Experts on International Standards of Accounting and Reporting (ISAR)* (2006). www.unctad.org/isar/accessed 9 February 2006.

10. Saudagaran, S. M. (2004). *International Accounting: A User's Perspective*, 2nd edn. Mason, Ohio: Thomson-Southwestern, pp. 65–7.

11. Financial Accounting Standards Board (1981). *Statement of Financial Accounting Standards No. 52, Foreign Currency Translation.* Stamford, Conn.: FASB.

12. Saudagaran, S. M., *op. cit.*, 76.

13. Choi, F. D., C. Frost, and G. Meek. *op. cit.*, p. 1.

14. Gernon, Helen and Gary Meek, *op. cit.*, p. 56.

15. Ibid., p. 167.

16. Saudagaran, S. M., *op. cit.*, p. 207.

17. McBride, Sarah (2002). "Asia Speeds Up Accounting Reforms," *The Asian Wall Street Journal*, March 1–3, p. 1.

11

International Operations Management

Harry Kogetsidis and Marios I. Katsioloudes,
Spyros Hadjidakis

Objectives

Through this chapter, the student will be exposed to:

- What is production and operations?
- What is operations management?
- What do operations managers do?
- How is operations management done in the international arena?
- How has good management of operations helped a small airline company become one of the most successful companies in its industry in the world?
- How can forecasting help in international operations management?
- How can project management help in international operations management?

Opening Case

Simulating patient arrivals and service rates at the Luton & Dunstable Hospital

The outpatients department of the Luton & Dunstable Hospital, based 30 miles north of London in the southeast of England, is visited by dozens of patients every day. A patient visiting the hospital first checks in at reception and is then directed to the doctor who is on duty on that day. The doctor examines patients on a first-come first-served basis. Obviously, there are a number of doctors on duty every day in order to deal with the large number of patients visiting this busy hospital. When the consultation with the doctor is over, the patient checks out at reception in order to make sure that all the relevant forms have been filled in properly in accordance to the British National Health Service regulations.

A team of analysts have studied the various operations that take place at the outpatients department of this hospital and have produced a simulation model that can be used to represent the system. Simulation is a modeling approach, which attempts to imitate the dynamic operations of a real-world system. It is used as a means to undertake experiments that would not be possible or easy to conduct in the real-world system. Managers responsible for operations can therefore use simulation in order to assess the demands on resources created by variable patterns of arrivals and service rates, such as those experienced in hospital outpatient departments. Simulation is an area with a large number of applications, from assisting health care planners in the evaluation of different options for the prevention of the HIV virus[1] to providing support to the British Ministry of Defense on issues such as equipment procurement, force structure, and operational tactics/strategy.[2]

Exhibit 11.1 shows a simulation model developed to imitate the operations that take place at the outpatients department of the Luton & Dunstable Hospital.

Exhibit 11.1

A Simulation Model for the Luton & Dunstable Hospital's Outpatients Department

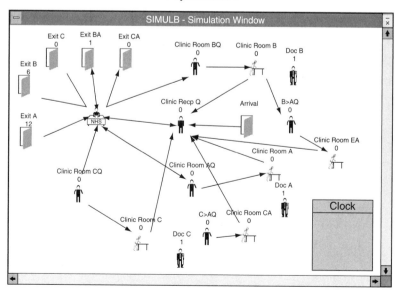

As it can be seen in the above model, patients enter the system at Arrival, where they join a waiting line (Clinic Reception Queue). They are then checked in and routed by the Receptionist to either Doctor A or Doctor B or Doctor C. Some patients seen by Doctor B or Doctor C are then seen by Doctor A (the senior doctor). Those patients are accompanied to Doctor A by Doctor B or Doctor C. When their clinical consultation is over, patients must check out at reception, something that affects the waiting line at reception for patients checking in.

Question: What are the activities that take place at the outpatients department of the Luton & Dunstable Hospital? Who are the people who carry out these activities? How would good modeling of the operations that take place at the outpatients department help management allocate the right number of resources to this department?

Sources: Brian Lehaney, Steve Clarke and Harry Kogetsidis (1998). Simulating hospital patient flows. *Journal of the Royal Society for the Promotion of Health*, vol. 118, no. 4, 213–216.

Production and Operations

All organizations, from small family companies to large multinational enterprises, exist in order to achieve some purpose. That purpose is usually the creation of goods or services that would be beneficial to society and would be consumed by customers. Consider, for example, an American company that produces electrical appliances. Its products would have been designed in such a way to meet certain safety standards and customer demands. They should also follow current trends in the market and take into account the particular characteristics of the market they will serve. Consider another example of a trendy restaurant based in the south of Spain. Its products would again aim to meet customer demands and keep customers happy at all times. The friendly and relaxed atmosphere that exists in the restaurant would help customers enjoy a nice evening out over some good food and wine. Consider a third example of a medical doctor in Holland, who keeps her own medical practice in a busy street in Amsterdam. That doctor would use her medical expertise in order to offer her services to the people of Amsterdam.

In all the examples given above, we can identify a large number of operations that take place on a daily basis. Thus, the delivery and installation of an electrical appliance, the preparation of a meal, as well as the medical consultation offered by the doctor to one of her patients are all typical examples of operations.

Operations can be defined as processes that transform resources (inputs) into goods or services (outputs). Examples of the resources that are typical inputs in such transformation processes include raw materials, machinery, and labor.

Operations take place both in organizations producing goods and organizations offering services. However, in organizations that do not create physical products, the production function may be less obvious as the end result cannot be seen in the form of a tangible product. For example, the service that a patient would receive by his doctor in Amsterdam does not result in the production of a tangible product, although we could perhaps consider the written prescription produced by the doctor as such. Similarly, we could think of product manufacturers who, in addition to offering their customers with a physical product, also provide them with an intangible service (e.g., the repair service provided by the manufacturer of a washing machine, covered by a warranty). Sometimes there might even be confusion as to whether an organization is a goods or a service provider—for example, restaurants like Pizza Hut and McDonald's are regarded as services, even if they produce tangible goods, such as pizzas and burgers.

Operations are performed in organizations in both the private sector and the public sector. In that respect, we expect to see a large number of operations taking place in a large private clinic in Milan, Italy (a profit organization), as well as in the British Red Cross based in London, United Kingdom (a not-for-profit organization).

What is Operations Management?

The creation of goods and services requires changing resources into goods or services. Operations management includes all those mechanisms responsible for transforming inputs into outputs, that is changing resources into goods or services. In other words, operations management involves the management of systems or processes that create goods or services to be consumed by the public.

The results from the transformations of inputs into outputs do not necessarily have to be goods or services for external customers, as each functional area or department of an organization also needs to carry out its own operations, which would produce goods or services for other functional areas or departments (e.g., the finance office of a college preparing the payroll for the employees—an operation that affects all the departments of the college).

As all organizations involve some sort of output-generating transformations, the management of these transformations is a crucial area for any organization. This makes the operational function one of the most important functions in an organization, regardless of its type, size, industry, or country of operation.

Operations management is one of the four basic functions in an organization. Apart from operations management, these basic organizational functions—also known as line functions—include demand management, money management, and design management. In very small start-up companies, the four line functions are indistinct and overlapping with a few people sharing all responsibilities (see Exhibit 11.2). As the organization grows, the line functions often form the basis for the first departments and a functional organization structure, such as the one shown in exhibit 11.3, emerges.[3]

In Exhibits 11.2 and 11.3, the various functions perform different but related activities, which are necessary for the operation of the organization.

Exhibit 11.4, shows the historical development of operations management. Although the field of operations management is relatively young, its development has been influenced by a number of key events that took place in the twentieth century. In the 1910s, for example, Frederick W. Taylor and his colleagues were among the first to systematically seek the best way to produce. In the late 1950s and early 1960s, scholars began to deal specifically with operations management, as opposed to industrial engineering or operations research. They noted the commonality of problems faced by all production systems and emphasized the importance of viewing production operations as a system. They also stressed the useful application of waiting-line theory, simulation, and linear programming, which are now standard topics in the field.[4]

Exhibit 11.2

Line Management Functions: Start-up Company

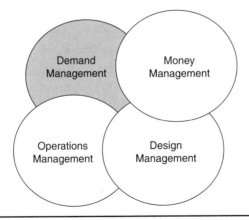

Source: Edward M. Knod and Richard J. Schonberger (2001), Operations Management: Meeting Customers' Demands. McGraw-Hill, p. 10.

Exhibit 11.3

Line and Staff Functional Activities

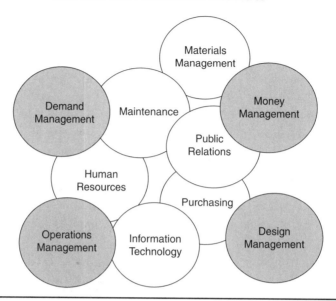

Source: Edward M. Knod and Richard J. Schonberger (2001), Operations Management: Meeting Customers' Demands. McGraw-Hill, p. 10.

Exhibit 11.4

Historical Development of Operations Management

Year	Concept	Tool	Originator
1910s	Principles of scientific management	Formalized time-study and work-study concepts	Frederick W. Taylor (US)
	Industrial psychology	Motion study	Frank and Lillian Gilbreth (US)
	Moving assembly line	Activity scheduling chart	Henry Ford and Henry Gantt (US)
	Economic lot size	EOQ applied to inventory control	F.W. Harris (US)
1930s	Quality control	Sampling inspection and statistical tables for quality control	Walter Shewhart, H.F. Dodge and H.G. Romig (US)

Exhibit 11.4 *continued*

Year	Concept	Tool	Originator
	Hawthorne studies of worker motivation	Activity sampling for work analysis	Elton Mayo (US) and L.H.C. Tippett (UK)
1940s	Multidisciplinary team approaches to complex system problems	Simplex method of linear programming	Operations research groups (UK) and George B. Dantzig (US)
1950s–1960s	Extensive development of operations research tools	Simulation, waiting-line theory, decision theory, mathematical programming, project scheduling techniques of PERT and CPM	Many researchers in the US and Western Europe
1970s	Widespread use of computers in business	Shop scheduling, inventory control, forecasting, project management, MRP	Led by computer manufacturers, in particular IBM; Joseph Orlicky and Oliver Wight were the major MRP innovators (US)
	Service quality and productivity	Mass production in the service Sector	McDonald's restaurants
1980s	Manufacturing strategy paradigm	Manufacturing as a competitive weapon	Harvard Business School faculty (US)
	JIT, TQC, and factory automation	KANBAN, Poka-yokes, CIM, FMS, CAD/CAM, robots, etc.	Tai-Ichi Ohno of Toyota Motors (Japan), W.E. Deming and J.M. Juran (US) and engineering disciplines (US, Germany, and Japan)

(Continued)

Exhibit 11.4 *continued*

Year	Concept	Tool	Originator
	Synchronous manufacturing	Bottleneck analysis, OPT, theory of constraints	Eliyahu M. Goldratt (Israel)
1990s	Total quality management	Baldrige quality award, ISO 9000, quality function development, value and concurrent engineering, continuous improvement paradigm	National Institute of Standards and Technology, American Society of Quality Control (US), and International Organization for Standardization (Europe)
	Business process re-engineering	Radical change paradigm	Michael Hammer and major consulting firms (US)
	Electronic enterprise	Internet, World Wide Web	US government, Netscape Communiation Corporation and Microsoft Corporation
	Supply chain management	SAP/R3, client/server software	SAP (Germany), Oracle (US)
2000s	e-Commerce	Internet, World Wide Web	Amazon, eBay, America Online, Yahoo

Source: Richard B. Chase, Nicholas J. Aquilano and F. Roberts Jacobs (2001), Operations Management for Competitive Advantage. McGraw-Hill, P. 15.

What Do Operations Managers Do?

The job of an operations manager, as well as the exact responsibilities that he or she has, vary from organization to organization, largely because of the type of operations that the organization performs. For example, being responsible for the operations of a General Motors assembly plant in the United States would involve overseeing a completely different type of operations than being in charge of operations at Barclays Bank in the United Kingdom.

Operations managers, like all other managers, must be able to perform the four basic management functions of planning, organizing, leading, and controlling. Planning is about defining goals, establishing strategy, and developing plans to coordinate activities. Organizing is about determining what tasks are to be done and by whom, and how the organization is structured. Leading includes motivating employees, directing the activities of others, selecting the most effective communication channel, and resolving conflicts. Controlling is the process of monitoring performance, comparing it with goals, and correcting any significant deviations.[5]

Operations managers must follow the mission and overall strategy that their organization has. Based on these, operations managers can then produce plans for the operations function of the organization. These plans should be subject to periodic review and revision and are expected to change whenever the overall strategy of the organization changes as a result of changes in the external environment. For example, a growth strategy involving the expansion of a company to a new market would require an increase in the number of operations that the various departments of that organization will have to perform.

Changes in the overall strategy that an organization follows usually have an effect on the structure of the organization and would inevitably change the way in which a number of operations are performed. An example of this would be the changes that many British universities have implemented to their academic structures since 1995, in response to the fact that students in higher education are choosing to move away from some subject areas, such as those within the sciences, and toward the more creative industries, such as design and media.

Apart from their good technical skills in areas such as forecasting and project management, operations managers should also have good communication skills and the ability to resolve conflicts—something that can very easily occur in the area of operations. Operations managers should also have a good knowledge of the various theories of motivation and maintain a highly motivated workforce.

The controlling function is particularly important in operations, as any omissions or mistakes made during an operation will inevitably affect the quality of the product, whether this is a good or a service. Operations managers can perform either concurrent control—through direct supervision, something that could stop problems before they become too costly for the organization—or feedback control, which would enable them to provide feedback to their employees and would certainly be a more realistic option in bigger organizations performing a large number of operations.

Apart from performing the four basic functions of planning, organizing, leading, and controlling, operations managers also have to make decisions. Depending on their style of management, operations managers may involve their staff in the decision-making process, in an effort to offer a better product to consumers. For example, the manager responsible for operations at a busy department store based in Oxford Street in London, United Kingdom, might have regular meetings with all his staff and discuss their ideas as to how the store could provide a better service to their customers.

Within the management function, management decisions can be divided into two categories: strategic decisions and operational (also known as tactical) decisions. Strategic decisions concern the development of long-term plans (normally covering five-year periods), which aim to place the organization in terms of its environment. Operational decisions concern the development of short-term plans (less than one year), which specify how the organization's objectives will be achieved.

The decision-making strategy used in operations management, that is how the operations manager tackles certain problems, will be greatly influenced by the need to achieve given objectives. Those objectives may have been determined for the operations manager by others, or jointly, or largely by the operations manager himself or herself. How the operations manager tackles certain problems must also reflect what is possible. That, in turn, may be influenced by the type of the organization and the nature of the operations that need to be performed. The magnitude of these two constraints will largely determine the scope that the operations manager has to exercise choice, that is his/her 'freedom of movement'.[6]

One of the main responsibilities of the operations manager is the efficient transformation of resources into goods or services. And the efficient production of goods or services requires effective application of operations management methods and tools. It is important here to distinguish between being effective and being efficient. Being effective means to do the right thing (i.e., produce the right product), whereas being efficient means to do the thing right using the minimum resources. In a local post office, for example, being efficient means using the minimum number of employees behind the counter, whereas being effective would include minimizing the waiting time for customers.

Although efficiency and effectiveness are different terms, they are interrelated and closely connected. For instance, it would be easier for an organization to be effective if it ignored efficiency. Hewlett-Packard, for example, could produce more sophisticated and longer-lasting toner cartridges for its laser printers if it disregarded labor and material input costs. Similarly, some government agencies are regularly criticized on the grounds that they are reasonably effective but extremely inefficient. That is, they accomplish their goals but do so at a very high cost. On the other hand, organizations can be efficient but not effective, simply by doing the wrong things well. A number of institutions of higher education, for example, have become highly efficient in processing students. Through the use of computer-assisted learning, distance-learning programs or a heavy reliance on part-time faculty, administrators may have significantly cut the cost of educating each student. Yet some of these institutions have been criticized for failing to educate students properly.[7] Although high efficiency is normally associated with high effectiveness, operations managers must find a balance between the two and never sacrifice the one at the expense of the other.

The more efficiently the resources are transformed into goods or services, the more productive the organization becomes and the more value is added to the good or service provided. Operations managers must ensure that the organization achieves productive use of what they have, that is it obtains maximum effect from their resources and minimizes their loss, under-utilization, or waste. Productivity can be defined as the ratio of outputs (goods or services) divided by the inputs (resources such as labor or materials). This can be expressed as follows:

$$\text{Productivity} = \frac{\text{Output}}{\text{Input}} \qquad (11.1)$$

Consider, for example, the case of a Burger King restaurant in New York. That restaurant employs four staff in the kitchen and prepares an average number of 154 burgers per hour. Its labor productivity will be as follows:

$$\text{Productivity} = \frac{154}{4} = 38.5 \text{ burgers/hour}$$

Operations managers can improve productivity in two ways: either by reducing inputs and keeping output the same (e.g., using three rather than four staff in the kitchen and keeping the same output would increase productivity to 51.3 burgers per hour), or by increasing output and keeping input constant (e.g., continuing with four staff in the kitchen but increasing output to 205 burgers per hour would also increase productivity to 51.3 burgers per hour).

Productivity is closely related to performance. See, for example, Mukherjee et al.'s paper which discusses a framework for measuring the efficiency of banking services and relates it to performance.[8] Performance describes how the organization does in terms of time, cost, quality, and flexibility. When there are gaps between the actual and the desired levels of performance, operations managers need to make improvements in order to close these gaps. By adopting modern Japanese management practices, many Western organizations have improved the performance of their operations—including reducing space, lowering inventory levels, and achieving faster throughput times—which, in turn, has lead to better financial results such as improved cash flows. Key performance indicators (KPIs), such as customer service time, cost, or quality, provide feedback to the operations manager as to how well the operations function is performing.[9]

Operations Management in the International Arena

It has been argued that the world has become a "global village"—a term often used to refer to the production and marketing of goods and services worldwide. The world indeed feels smaller today than before. Fifty years ago it was very expensive and time-consuming for people to travel abroad, something that also had an effect on companies which were considering crossing the boundaries of their home country. Today, it is much easier and faster for people to move from one country to another—something that also applies to managers who conduct business internationally.

Advances in computer technology and particularly the World Wide Web (WWW) with its main applications—e-mail and the Internet—have also had an important effect on organizations, particularly on how they perform their operations. Before the days of the Internet, people would have to visit their bank in order to carry out some basic transactions, such as money transfer from a current to a savings account or payment of bills. Today, customers can perform these operations themselves on the Internet without having to talk to a personal banker. In the same way, customers can buy their theater tickets, book a summer holiday, or do their weekly shopping on the Internet and pay for these products electronically. All this has a significant effect on the way an organization is performing its operations.

As it was explained in previous chapters, globalization is the term used to describe the fact that people around the globe are more connected to each other than ever before; information and money flow more quickly than ever; goods and services produced in one part of the world are increasingly available in all parts of the world; and international communication is commonplace. Globalization has two main components: the globalization of markets and the globalization of production. They both affect the way in which organizations perform their operations and the jobs of operations managers. The globalization of production, for example, refers to the tendency among firms to source goods and services from locations around the globe to take advantage of national differences in the cost of the production. Boeing, for instance, has contracted more than half of its work outside the

United States, a savings of $600 million per year. The company claims that it is impossible to export planes without sending a significant number of jobs overseas. When a foreign nation now agrees to buy planes from Boeing, it typically does so on condition that some work will be done in that country.[10]

It is impossible to ignore the impact that the emerging global marketplace and free trade are having on organizations and their operations. The North American Free Trade Agreement (NAFTA) and the General Agreement on Tariffs and Trade (GATT), for example, are designed to reduce or eliminate tariffs and other trade restrictions. They are increasing the opportunities for countries to focus on areas of trade and commerce where they have a relative advantage. For example, before these agreements, Chrysler's Jeep assembly plant shipped unassembled Jeeps to some countries. The jeeps would be assembled there because these countries had laws that limited the amount of foreign content on imported products. Now, the jeeps can be assembled in the United States and shipped abroad, thus adding jobs for Chrysler's workers. Under NAFTA and GATT, it would be increasingly common for finished products to have components from many different countries. Global sourcing and production of goods and services will become more common.[11]

Operations management is a dynamic field, which is adapting to the new era of globalization and a changing global economy. In this new environment, operations managers are faced with the following challenges:

1. *Global focus*. The vast decline in communication and transportation costs has made markets global. But at the same time, resources in the form of materials, talent, and labor have also become global. Operations managers are responding with innovations that generate and move ideas, parts, and finished goods rapidly, wherever and whenever needed.

2. *Just-in-time performance*. Vast financial resources are committed to inventory, making it costly. Inventory also impedes response to rapid changes in the marketplace. Operations managers are viciously cutting inventories at every level, from raw materials to finished goods.

3. *Supply-chain partnering*. Shorter product life cycles, as well as rapid changes in material and process technology, require more participation by suppliers. Suppliers usually supply over half of the value of products. Consequently, operations managers are building long-term partnerships with critical players in the supply chain.

4. *Rapid product development*. Rapid international communication of news, entertainment, and life styles is dramatically chopping away at the life span of products. Operations managers are responding with technology and alliances (partners) that are faster and management that is more effective.

5. *Mass customization*. Once we begin to consider the world as a market-place, then the individual differences become quite obvious. Cultural differences compounded by individual differences, in a world where consumers are increasingly aware of options, place substantial pressure on firms to respond. Operations managers are responding with production processes that are flexible enough to cater to the individual whims of consumers. The goal is to produce individual products, whenever and wherever needed.

6. *Empowered employees*. Knowledge explosion and a more technical workplace have combined to require more competence at the workplace. Operations managers are responding by moving more decision-making to the individual worker.

7. *Environmentally sensitive production*. The operations manager's continuing battle to improve productivity is increasingly concerned with designing products and processes that are environmentally friendly.[12]

The next section presents the case of a European organization that performs its operations in such a way as to get maximum advantage of the new era of globalization.

Operations Management at Easyjet Airlines

Easyjet is a British low-cost airline based in the southeast of England. Easyjet was created in the mid-1990 by Stelios Hadji-Ioannou, a young Greek entrepreneur who until then had nothing to do with the airline industry. Stelios took his idea from Southwest Airlines—an American low-cost airline flying more than 70 million passengers a year to 60 cities in the United States. He thought that creating an airline that could offer low fares to customers would become a successful venture in Europe. Obviously, to keep fares down, he had to keep costs down. One way to achieve this was by bringing new ideas into how the company would perform its international operations.

Easyjet's first routes were between London and Scotland (Edinburgh and Glasgow). The company is based at Luton airport, a much smaller and cheaper alternative than Heathrow airport. To keep costs down, the company does not use travel agents but offers its services directly to customers. Customers can obtain information and book their tickets by calling the company's phone center using a national number. Their call is then transferred at the company's expense to its phone center in England. Depending on where the call is coming from, it is answered by a specific bilingual reservation agent who greets the customer and carries out all the conversation in the language of the country that the call has come from (unless, of course, the customer initiates the conversation in English). The agent then explains the company's policies and clarifies that all tickets are for instant purchase only and cannot be reserved. The customer then pays for the ticket using his or her credit card. Once the ticket is issued, changing the date of travel incurs a penalty fee as well as paying the difference in case the new ticket is more expensive than the old one.

Easyjet has put a lot of effort in producing a website that would represent the company's philosophy—that is, be easy to use. Selling tickets on the Internet has now become Easyjet's much preferred option, as the company aims to gradually decrease its reservation agents' involvement in selling tickets on the phone and increase their customer service duties—that is, dealing with customer complaints or any other issues of concern to customers. To encourage customers to buy their tickets on the Internet, the company offers a discount on all seats that are purchased electronically.

The way that Easyjet performs its operations has helped the company keep its costs down and offer huge savings to customers. Although the company faced strong competition from British Airways, as well as from other low-cost airlines that have followed Easyjet's model, it is today one of the most successful low-cost airlines in Europe offering 222 routes across 67 key European airports. The way in which this company is performing its international operations has helped it survive in a very competitive environment and at difficult times for the airline industry.

Operations Management Applications

Organizations that engage in international business face much greater competition and far greater challenges than those operating within their national boundaries. Good management of international operations requires managers with good analytical skills and a good grasp of quantitative methods. Such methods can help operations managers in their decision-making and problem-solving. Two of the most important areas that operations managers are particularly involved in are forecasting and project management. These areas are discussed in the next two sections.

Forecasting

Forecasting is concerned with making predictions about what is going to happen in the future. Predicting the future is an important activity that operations managers frequently have to carry out, as it can help them make better decisions and control some of the uncertainty that the future holds. This is particularly the case when companies perform operations across national borders.

Regardless of industry or whether the company is a manufacturer, a wholesaler, a retailer, or a service provider, effective demand forecasting helps organizations identify market opportunities, enhance channel relationships, increase customer satisfaction, reduce inventory investment, eliminate product obsolescence, improve distribution operations, schedule more efficient production, and anticipate future financial and capital requirements.[13]

Forecasting is an integral part of the decision-making activities of operations management. The need for forecasting is increasing as management attempts to decrease the dependence on chance and becomes more scientific in dealing with its environment. The following are some of the areas affecting the management of operations in an organization in which forecasting plays an important role:

1. *Scheduling.* Efficient use of resources requires the scheduling of production, transportation, cash, personnel, and so on. Forecasts of the level of demand for the product, material labor, financing, or service are an essential input to such scheduling.
2. *Acquiring resources.* The lead time for acquiring raw materials, hiring personnel, or buying machinery and equipment can vary from a few days to several years. Forecasting is required to determine future resource requirements.
3. *Determining resource requirements.* All organizations must determine what resources they want to have in the long-term. Such decisions depend on market opportunities, environmental factors and the internal development of financial, human, product and technological resources. These determinations require good forecasts and managers who can interpret the predictions and make appropriate decisions.[14]

Forecasting is often confused with planning. Planning concerns what the world should look like, while forecasting is about what it will look like. Exhibit 11.5 provides a summary of these relationships. Planners can use forecasting methods to predict the outcomes for alternative plans. If the forecasted outcomes are not satisfactory, they can revise the plans and obtain new forecasts, and then repeat the process until the forecasted outcomes are satisfactory. They can then implement and monitor the actual outcomes to use in planning the next period. Although this process might seem obvious, in practice many organizations revise their forecasts and not their plans, believing that changing the forecasts will change behavior.[15]

Forecasting can be used in operations management for both short-term and long-term decisions. For example, predicting the demand for a particular product over the next six months would be a short-term prediction, whereas predicting the rate of unemployment and how this could affect the demand for labor over the next five years would be a long-term prediction. The

Exhibit 11.5

Framework for Forecasting and Planning

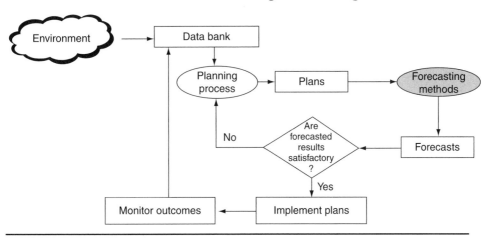

Source: *J. Scott Armstrong (2001), Principle of Forecasting—A Handbook for Researchers and Practitioners. Kluwer Academic Publishers, p. 3.*

period over which a forecast will be made is known as the time horizon of the forecast. Depending on their time horizon, forecasts can be:

- Short term (up to one year ahead)
- Medium term (from one to three years ahead)
- Long term (for more than three years ahead).

A large number of forecasting methods exist today and the advent of computers has greatly facilitated their acceptance by management. The further development of forecasting methods and their practical application has enabled not only forecasting experts but also managers to understand and use these methods.[16]

The main classification of forecasting methods is between statistical and judgmental. Statistical forecasting methods are based on measurement. In other words, they concern data that either exist or can be obtained through experimentation. These methods vary from a simple extension of the past into the future to more complicated and elaborate procedures. The advent of computers has greatly facilitated the acceptance of statistical methods in business. Judgmental forecasting methods, on the other hand, are based on personal judgment and/or expert opinion. Because these methods do not use any numerical data, they are highly subjective. Generally speaking, judgmental forecasting methods are used more for longer-term forecasts, whereas statistical forecasting methods are used more for intermediate and shorter-term forecasts.

When we forecast we should always keep in mind that the future is by definition unpredictable. No forecasting method can therefore guarantee that it will produce perfectly accurate forecasts. Even the most accurate forecasts will never be 100% accurate. A good forecast is therefore one that will be close enough to what will actually happen.

The results of a classic competition (known as the M-competition) regarding the accuracy of a large number of forecasting methods when applied to 1001 different time series data sets across different industries showed that simple forecasting approaches, such as exponential smoothing, produced accurate results. Regression methods, on the other hand, were not found to be as robust.[17] Although no reasonable forecaster would identify the best method from the various forecasting competitions and adopt that method for his or her specific forecasting problem, competitions on the accuracy of different forecasting methods have been helpful at improving the actual practice of forecasting in industry.[18,19]

The following example illustrates how the method of exponential smoothing—a simple numerical approach to forecasting—can be used to help managers make better decisions regarding the operations of their organization.

Example 1

A small Japanese manufacturer of electrical appliances exports its products to a number of European destinations. The operations manager of the company wants to predict the number of component parts needed for the production of a particular model. The following data have been collected over a six-week period:

Week	Parts
1	130
2	70
3	140
4	150
5	90
6	180

Exponential smoothing is a time series forecasting method that smoothes out random fluctuations of data. It provides a procedure for continually revising a forecast in light of more recent experience. The method is based on the following equations:

$$F_{t+1} = \alpha Y_t + (1 - \alpha)F_t \qquad (11.2)$$

or

$$F_{t+1} = F_t + \alpha(Y_t - F_t) \qquad (11.3)$$

where F_{t+1} is the forecast value of the dependent variable for period $t+1$; F_t is the forecast value of the dependent variable for period t; Y_t is the actual value of the dependent variable for period t; and α is the value of the smoothing constant.

As it can be seen from the above equations, exponential smoothing is an average forecasting approach that requires only three pieces of data: the forecast for the most recent time period (F_t), the actual value for that time period (Y_t) and the value of the smoothing constant. The smoothing constant is a weighting factor (its value lies between 0 and 1) that reflects the weight given to the most recent data values (the larger the value given to α the more strongly the model reacts to most recent data).

The value of the smoothing constant also determines the degree of smoothing and how responsive the model is to fluctuations in the data. As it can be seen from Equation (11.3), exponential smoothing is simply the old forecast (F_t) adjusted by α times the error ($Y_t - F_t$) in the old forecast. That means that when the value of α is close to 0, the new forecast will be very similar to the old. On the other hand, when the value of α is close to 1, the new forecast will include a substantial adjustment for any error that occurred in the preceding forecast.

Application of Equation (11.3) with a smoothing constant value of $\alpha = 0.3$ will produce the following forecasts:

$$F_2 = 130 + 0.3(130 - 130) = 130$$

$$F_3 = 130 + 0.3(70 - 130) = 112$$

$$F_4 = 112 + 0.3(140 - 112) = 120.4$$

$$F_5 = 120.4 + 0.3(150 - 120.4) = 129.28$$

$$F_6 = 129.28 + 0.3(90 - 129.28) = 117.5$$

$$F_7 = 117.5 + 0.3(180 - 117.50) = 136.25$$

Note that as the forecast value for week 1 did not exist, we took it to be the same as the actual value for that period (i.e., we assumed a perfect forecast).

An exponential smoothing model with a different value of α will obviously produce different forecasts. For example, a smoothing constant value of $\alpha = 0.8$ will produce the following forecasts:

$$F_2 = 130 + 0.8(130 - 130) = 130$$

$$F_3 = 130 + 0.8(70 - 130) = 82$$

$$F_4 = 82 + 0.8(140 - 82) = 128.4$$

$$F_5 = 128.4 + 0.8(150 - 128.4) = 145.68$$

$$F_6 = 145.68 + 0.8(90 - 145.68) = 101.14$$

$$F_7 = 101.14 + 0.8(180 - 101.14) = 164.23$$

As it can be seen from the above example, the operations manager can try out a number of different forecasting models on some historical data, in order to see how each of these models would have worked had it been used in the past. The accuracy of these forecasting models can be measured by a number of simple tests. A popular test for measuring forecast accuracy is the mean absolute percentage error (MAPE) test, which is based on the following equation:

$$\text{MAPE} = \frac{\sum |e_t/Y_t|}{n} \times 100 \tag{11.4}$$

where Y_t is the actual value of the dependent variable for period t; e_t is the forecast error for period t (i.e., $e_t = Y_t - F_t$); and n is the number of forecast errors. $Y_t \neq 0$.

The MAPE values for the forecasts produced by the two exponential smoothing models can be produced as follows:

Model 1 ($\alpha = 0.3$):

(t)	(Y_t)	(F_t)	(e_t)	$|e_t/Y_t|$
1	130	130.00	–	–
2	70	130.00	−60.00	0.86
3	140	112.00	28.00	0.20
4	150	120.40	29.60	0.20
5	90	129.28	−39.28	0.44
6	180	117.50	62.50	0.35
7	130	136.25	–	–

$$\text{MAPE} = \frac{\sum |e_t/Y_t|}{n} \times 100 = \frac{2.05}{5} \times 100 = 41\%$$

Model 2 ($\alpha = 0.8$):

(t)	(Y_t)	(F_t)	(e_t)	$|e_t/Y_t|$
1	130	130.00	–	–
2	70	130.00	−60.00	0.86
3	140	82.00	58.00	0.41
4	150	128.40	21.60	0.14
5	90	145.68	−55.68	0.62
6	180	101.14	78.86	0.44
7		164.23	–	–

$$\text{MAPE} = \frac{\sum |e_t/Y_t|}{n} \times 100 = \frac{2.47}{5} \times 100 = 49.4\%$$

The first exponential smoothing model has therefore produced more accurate forecasts than the second, as it has a lower average forecast error. Based on this and on the assumption that the future will not be dramatically different from the past, the operations manager of the company could use an exponential smoothing forecasting model with a low value of α in order to predict the number of component parts that will be required in the future.

Different forecasting models would obviously produce different forecasts. For a good discussion of the various forecasting methods, both statistical and judgmental, refer to Hanke et al.[20]

Project Management

Much of the business world is becoming project oriented.[21] The success of an organization is very much dependent on projects being completed on time and within budget, something which becomes more crucial when organizations engage in international business. Project management is concerned with planning, scheduling, and controlling projects that consist of numerous tasks or activities performed by a variety of departments or individuals and using different resources.

There are examples of several techniques which can be used to plan, schedule, and control projects. The two most well known ones are the Project Evaluation and Review Technique (PERT) and the Critical Path Method (CPM). The two techniques were developed independently in the late 1950s and their main difference was that time estimates were assumed to be probabilistic for PERT and deterministic for CPM. In other words, PERT was designed to handle the uncertainties that existed in predicting the time necessary to compare various project activities, while CPM assumed that both time and costs were known with certainty. Operations managers today tend to use a combination of the best features of PERT and CPM and this has resulted in a new PERT/CPM technique. The PERT/CPM technique is a descriptive tool, which determines the completion time of a project and identifies those activities that are critical for its on-time completion. With this information, operations managers can work toward completing the project on time and within the budget.[22]

The PERT/CPM technique uses simple networks in order to represent the activities that take place in a project, as well as how these activities interrelate. A PERT/CPM network is made up of activities and events. An activity is a task or job that consumes time and resources and is shown as a line on the network. An event is a project milestone, which occurs at one point in time and does not consume time or resources. Events are shown as nodes on the network.

Consider the following example involving the opening of a new restaurant in France.

Example 2

An Italian fast-food chain wants to open a new restaurant in Cannes in the South of France. The operations manager has compiled a list of activities that need to take place, together with an estimate of the expected time that each activity would take. All the activities, their preceding activities, and their expected durations (in weeks) are shown in the table below:

Activity	Description	Preceding Activity	Duration
A	Find location	–	12
B	Recruit staff	–	6
C	Make alterations	A	6
D	Order new equipment	A	2
E	Install equipment	D	5
F	Train staff	B	3
G	Open restaurant	C, E, F	1

The operations manager wants to produce a network in order to represent the activities of this project and then estimate the project's expected completion time.

The resulting network is shown in Exhibit 11.6.

Exhibit 11.6

PERT/CPM Network for Example 2

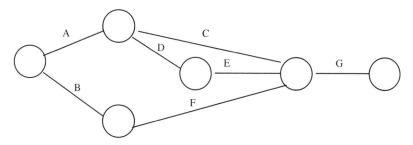

Once a PERT/CPM network has been drawn and the expected times of the activities have been determined, it is possible to determine the minimum completion time of the project and to schedule each activity.

To identify the completion time of the project, we should look for the path with the longest completion time. That path is called the critical path through the network. Obviously, more than one critical path may exist on a network.

The operations manager of the restaurant can identify three paths on his network. These paths together with their expected completion times are as follows:

- Path 1: ACG, expected completion time = 19 weeks
- Path 2: ADEG, expected completion time = 20 weeks
- Path 3: BFG, expected completion time = 10 weeks

As path 2 has the longest completion time, it is the network's critical path. In other words, activities A, D, E, and G are all critical activities—that is they cannot be delayed if the project is to be completed on time. The expected completion time of the project is 20 weeks.

All the activities which are critical for the project's on-time completion (i.e., the ones on the critical path) have a slack time of zero. The slack time that exists on the non-critical activities will determine how long each of these activities can be delayed without delaying the overall completion time of the project. (For a good discussion of the concept of slack in project management, refer to Tormos and Lova.[23])

Once the expected duration of a project has been determined, it may be necessary or desirable to shorten its completion time. The completion time of a project can usually be shortened by allocating additional resources. However, these additional resources usually imply extra costs.

To reduce the completion time of a project, we need to shorten a number of its activities. When we do this, however, we need to remember that:

1. Not all the activities on the network can be shortened.
2. The activities to be shortened must be on the critical path.

The process of shortening the completion time of a project is known as project crashing. The duration figures in the above example give the normal time for each activity of the project. Each activity also has its crash time, which is the least possible time it can take to complete that activity. Similarly, the cost of an activity under normal circumstances is the activity's normal cost and the cost of an activity under crash circumstances is its crash cost. Now consider the following example involving the expansion of a small factory.

Example 3

A small American manufacturer of leather products is expanding its factory. The operations manager who is responsible for this project has identified a total of ten activities and has produced time and cost estimates for each of them. He has produced two different sets of estimated times and costs — one for completing the project under normal circumstances and one for completing it under crash circumstances. This information is shown in the table below (activity durations are shown in weeks):

Activity	Normal Time	Crash Time	Normal Cost ($)	Crash Cost ($)
A	4	3	3000	3300
B	3	2	2100	2450
C	6	3	7200	9300
D	5	5	2200	2200
E	7	5	3400	3900
F	5	2	2800	3400
G	5	4	3000	3650
H	8	6	6000	7500
I	4	3	1600	1750
J	2	2	800	800

There is a bonus of $600 if the project duration can be reduced by one week, an extra bonus of $600 if the project duration can be reduced by a second week, and another extra bonus of $600 if the project duration can be

Exhibit 11.7

PERT/CPM Network for Example 3

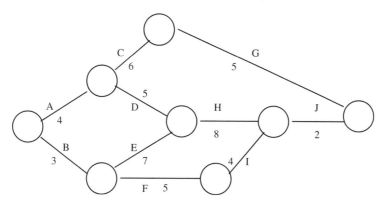

reduced by a third week. Should the operations manager go for the bonus
A PERT/CPM network for this project is shown in Exhibit 11.7.

There are four possible paths on this network with the following expected
completion times:

1. Path 1: ACG, expected completion time = 15 weeks
2. Path 2: ADHJ, expected completion time = 19 weeks
3. Path 3: BEHJ, expected completion time = 20 weeks
4. Path 4: BFIJ, expected completion time = 14 weeks

The critical path is therefore made up of activities B, E, H, and J
and the expected duration of the project under normal circumstances is
twenty weeks.

To start the project crashing process, the operations manager should first
determine the maximum time reduction and the crash cost per week for all
the activities. The maximum time reduction is the maximum time that an
activity can be reduced by and the crash cost per week is the additional cost
per week resulting from reducing the duration of an activity by one week.
These can be found using the following equations:

$$\text{Maximum time reduction} = \text{normal time} - \text{crash time} \qquad (11.5)$$

$$\text{Crash cost/week} = \frac{\text{Crash cost} - \text{normal cost}}{\text{Normal time} - \text{crash time}} \qquad (11.6)$$

Application of the above equations will produce the following results:

Activity	Normal Time	Crash Time	Normal Cost ($)	Crash Cost ($)	Maximum Time Reduction	Crash Cost/Week
A	4	3	3000	3300	1	300
B	3	2	2100	2450	1	350
C	6	3	7200	9300	3	700
D	5	5	2200	2200	0	–
E	7	5	3400	3900	2	250
F	5	2	2800	3400	3	200
G	5	4	3000	3650	1	650
H	8	6	6000	7500	2	750
I	4	3	1600	1750	1	150
J	2	2	800	800	0	–

The activities to be shortened must be on the critical path. This means that the operations manager should start the crashing process by concentrating on the four activities on the critical path. The activity with the lowest crash cost/week should be selected, provided that its maximum time reduction figure is not zero.

Activity E has the lowest crash cost/week and a maximum time reduction of two weeks. This is therefore the activity that should be crashed first. Its normal time now becomes six weeks while its maximum time reduction figure decreases to one week.

Having reduced the expected duration of the project by one week (from twenty to nineteen weeks), we have an extra cost of $250. As the bonus of $600 exceeds this cost, the operations manager should go for the bonus.

To reduce the expected duration of the project by a second week, the operations manager needs to go through the same process again. Note, however, that there are now two critical paths. The original one (BEHJ) and a new one made up of activities A, D, H, and J. Two activities should then be crashed, one on each path (unless the crash cost/week figure indicates that one activity which is common in both paths would be more economical to crash). Thus, the activities to be crashed should be activity E from the original critical path and activity A from the new one.

Having reduced the expected duration of the project by a second week (from twenty to eighteen weeks), we have an extra cost of $550 ($250 + $300). Again, as the bonus of $600 exceeds this cost, the operations manager should go for the bonus.

Finally, to reduce the expected duration of the project by a third week, activity H (a common activity in both paths) should be chosen. This implies an additional cost of $750. This time, however, the operations manager should not go for the bonus, as a bonus of $600 for reducing the expected duration of the project to seventeen weeks would not justify the additional cost of the reduction.

The operations manager should therefore use extra resources in order to reduce the project's expected completion time from twenty to eighteen weeks and receive a total bonus of $1200. Reducing the project's duration further to seventeen weeks would not be economical to do, as the extra cost required for this reduction would exceed the bonus.

For further discussion of the concepts of project management, refer to L.V. Tavares.[24]

Closing Case

Hazel

Hazel had worked for the same Fortune 500 company for almost fifteen years. Although the company had gone through some tough times, things were starting to turn around. Customer orders were up, and quality and productivity had improved dramatically from what they had been only a few years earlier due to a companywide quality improvement program. So it came as a real shock to Hazel and about 400 of her co-workers when they were suddenly terminated following the new CEO's decision to downsize the company.

After recovering from the initial shock, Hazel tried to find employment elsewhere. Despite her efforts, after eight months of searching, she was no closer to finding a job than the day she started. Her funds were being depleted and she was getting more discouraged. There was one bright spot, though: She was able to bring in a little money by mowing lawns for her neighbors. She got involved quite by chance when she heard one neighbor remark that now that his children were on their own, nobody was around to cut the grass. Almost jokingly, Hazel asked him how much he would be willing to pay. Soon Hazel was mowing the lawns of five neighbors. Other neighbors wanted her to work on their lawns, but she did not feel that she could spare any more time from her job search.

However, as the rejection letters began to pile up, Hazel knew she had to make an important decision in her life. On a rainy Tuesday morning, she decided to go into business for herself—taking care of neighborhood lawns. She was relieved to give up the job of stress hunting, and she was excited about the prospects of being her own boss. But she was also fearful of being completely on her own. Nevertheless, Hazel was determined to make a go of it.

At first, business was a bit slow, but once people realized Hazel was available, many asked her to take care of their lawns. Some people were simply glad to turn the work over to her; others switched from professional lawn care services. By the end of her first year in business, Hazel knew she could earn a living this way. She also performed other services such as fertilizing lawns, weeding gardens, and trimming shrubbery. Business became so good that Hazel hired two part-time workers to assist her and, even then, she believed she could expand further if she wanted to.

Question: Hazel is the operations manager of her business. Among her responsibilities are forecasting and project management. What kind of things would need to be predicted? What type of activities would need project management? In what ways are Hazel's customers most likely to judge the quality of her lawn care services? What are some of the trade-offs that Hazel would need to consider with regard to working for a company instead of for herself and to expanding her new business?

Sources: William J. Stevenson. Production/Operations Management. Richard D. Irwin Publications, 1996, pp. 35–36.

Chapter Summary

Operations management includes all the mechanisms responsible for transforming inputs into outputs, that is changing resources into goods or services. In other words, operations management involves the management of systems or processes that create goods or services to be consumed by the public.

Advances in computer technology and particularly the World Wide Web (WWW) with its main applications have had an important effect on organizations and particularly on how they perform their operations.

The new era of globalization and the emerging global marketplace bring new opportunities as well as threats to all organizations conducting business across national boundaries. Operations management is a dynamic field, which needs to be adapted to the new era of globalization and the changing global economy.

Organizations that engage in international business face much greater competition and far greater challenges than those operating within their national boundaries. Good management of international operations requires managers with good skills in planning, organizing, leading, and controlling. It also requires managers with good project management skills, a good grasp of the principles of forecasting, and the ability to make good decisions regarding their organization's operations.

Review and Discussion Questions

1. What is operations management? Why is good management of operations important for a company that engages in international business?
2. List and discuss a number of typical operations that would take place in a car assembly plant and in the sales department of a large travel agency specializing in organizing cruises to the Mediterranean. Would the management of these operations require similar management skills?
3. Discuss how a company that engages in international business can be both effective and efficient in managing its operations.
4. If the operations manager of a large multinational enterprise had to choose between being effective and being efficient in managing the organization's operations, which would be more important and why?
5. How does the management of operations of a company that performs international business relate to its mission and strategy? How does it relate to its structure?
6. Discuss how advances in information technology can affect the operations of a company that engages in international business. Provide examples to illustrate your answer.
7. Discuss how globalization and the emerging global marketplace have affected the way in which a company would carry out its operations. Provide examples to illustrate your answer.

Problems

1. The operations manager of a large chain of fast food restaurants wants to use a simple forecasting approach to predict the demand for a new product based on its sales in four restaurants over an introductory three-week period. The following data have been collected.

Day	Sales	Day	Sales
1	448	12	618
2	420	13	714
3	388	14	729
4	472	15	620
5	522	16	645
6	678	17	689
7	514	18	640
8	555	19	726
9	407	20	778
10	448	21	698
11	592		

Formulate an appropriate exponential smoothing forecasting model and use it to produce forecasts for periods 2–22. Then measure the accuracy of your forecasts using the mean absolute percentage error test. Advise the operations manager on how he or she can improve the accuracy of his or her forecasts.

2. The operations manager of an offshore company based in Cyprus is in charge of the installation of a new computer system in the main office of the company in Limassol. The project consists of nine activities and their expected durations (in weeks) and costs are as follows:

Activity	Preceding Activity	Normal Time	Crash Time	Normal Cost ($)	Crash Cost ($)
A	–	5	4	1500	2000
B	–	3	2	2000	2500
C	A	7	5	2500	3000
D	A	6	4	2500	3500
E	B	7	5	4000	4400
F	D, E	3	3	3500	3800
G	D, E	10	8	4500	5000
H	C, F	8	6	4000	4500
I	G, H	4	2	4500	5000

What is the expected completion time of this project? If there is a saving of $1000 if the project duration can be reduced by one week, then advise the operations manager on his or her options.

Endnotes

1. Vieira, I. T., Harper, P. R., Shahani, A.K. and de Senna, V. (2003) "Mother-to-child transmission of HIV: a simulation-based approach for the evaluation of intervention strategies." *Journal of the Operational Research Society*, 54, 713–722.
2. Taylor, B. and Lane, A. (2004) "Development of a novel family of military campaign simulation models." *Journal of the Operational Research Society*, 55, 333–339.
3. Knod, E. M. and Schonberger, R. J. (2001), *Operations Management: Meeting Customers' Demands* (7th edition). McGraw-Hill.
4. Chase, R. B., Aquilano, N. J. and Jacobs, F. R. (2001), *Operations Management for Competitive Advantage* (9th edition). McGraw-Hill.
5. Robbins, S. P. and Decenzo, D. A. (2005), *Fundamentals of Management* (5th edition). Prentice Hall.
6. Wild, R. (1995), *Production and Operations Management* (5th edition). Cassell Educational Ltd.

7. Robbins, S. P. and Decenzo, D. A. (IBID).

8. Mukherjee, A., Nath, P. and Pal, M. (2003) "Resource, service quality and performance triad: a framework for measuring efficiency of banking services." *Journal of the Operational Research Society*, 54, 723–735.

9. Brown, S., Blackmon, K., Cousins, P. and Maylor, H. (2001), *Operations Management—Policy, Practice and Performance Improvement*. Butterworth-Heinemann.

10. Heizer, J. and Render, B. (2004), *Operations Management* (7th edition). Pearson/Prentice Hall.

11. Vonderembse, M. A. and White, G. P. (1996), *Operations Management–Concepts, Methods, and Strategies* (3rd edition). West Publishing Company.

12. Heizer, J. and Render, B. (IBID)

13. Moon M. A., Mentzer J. T. and Smith C. D. (2003). *Conducting a sales forecasting audit. International Journal of Forecasting*, 19, 5–25.

14. Makridakis S., Wheelwright S. C. and Hyndman R. J. (1998), *Forecasting Methods and Applications* (3rd edition). John Wiley.

15. Armstrong J. S. (2001), *Principles of Forecasting—A Handbook for Researchers and Practitioners*. Kluwer Academic Publishers.

16. Makridakis S., Wheelwright S. and McGee V. (1983), *Forecasting: Methods and Applications* (2nd edition). John Wiley.

17. Makridakis S., Andersen A., Carbone R., Fildes R., Hibon M., Lewandowski R., Newton J., Parzen E., and Winkler R. (1982). "The accuracy of extrapolation (time series) methods: results of a forecasting competition." *Journal of Forecasting*, 1, 111–153.

18. Fildes R., and Lusk E. J. (1984). "The choice of a forecasting model." *Omega*, 12, 427–435.

19. Fildes R., and Ord, K. (2002). "Forecasting competitions—their role in improving forecasting practice and research." In Clements M., and Hendry D. (eds), *A Companion to Economic Forecasting*. Oxford: Blackwell.

20. Hanke J. E., Wichern D. W. and Reitsch A. G. *Business Forecasting* (8th edition). Prentice Hall, 2005.

21. Williams T. (2003). "Learning from projects." *Journal of the Operational Research Society*, 54, 443–451.

22. Dennis T. L., and Dennis L. B. *Management Science*. West Publishing Company, 1991.

23. Tormos P., and Lova A. (2001). "Tools for resource-constraint project scheduling and control: forward and backward slack analysis." *Journal of the Operational Research Society*, 52, 779–788.

24. Tavares L. V. *Advanced Models for Project Management*. Kluwer Academic Press, 1999.

12

Strategic Human Resource Management of International Assignments

Marie-France Waxin and Marios I. Katsioloudes,
Spyros Hadjidakis

Objectives

Throughout this chapter, the student will be exposed to:

- The different approaches to staffing foreign operations
- The reasons for using international assignments: position filling, sharing and transferring knowledge, developing employees, and controlling and coordination of international activities
- The different categories of international personnel: parent country, host country, and third country nationals, impatriates
- The different types of international assignment for parent country nationals: expatriates, short-term assignees, international commuters and frequent flyers, global managers, and high potentials.
- The different steps of the strategic management of international assignments: strategic planning and job analysis, recruitment, selection, preparation to transfer, cross-cultural adjustment and organizational support, performance appraisal, compensation, repatriation, and retention.

Opening Case

The Letter

Imagine that you are Stephen Grant, marketing manager in a large international company in London, United Kingdom. The following are some personal facts.

- You are married to a financial analyst who works in a bank located in the same city.
- You have two children—a boy, aged 10, and a girl, aged 8.
- You and your family are actively engaged in a variety of volunteer activities sponsored by your church, which include environmental activities and providing food for the needy.
- You and your spouse enjoy sports activities together—you jog, play tennis, and golf on regular basis. You also enjoy cultural events together, such as concerts and plays.

You have just received the following letter from your employer.

Dear Stephen,

We are pleased to inform you that you have been selected as a candidate for an overseas position in our subsidiary in Kenya. Please contact M. Santerre, our international human resources manager, as soon as possible to discuss this opportunity further.

Best regards
Graham White, International Marketing.

Question: Individually, consider this situation and how you would react to it.

Identify your major concerns as well as reasons why you would want to accept or decline such an offer.

Source: Compiled by Marie-France Waxin.[1]

International managers constitute valuable resources that organizations do not always use to the best of their potential. Further, senior managers assigned to positions in foreign subsidiaries do not always live up to their bosses' expectations. When they succeed in their international assignments, they often leave the organization upon returning to their country of origin. Organizations can reverse this trend by encouraging managers' international mobility, through better planning of assignments, better recruitment and selection practices for international assignments, better pre-departure preparation, better performance management, and better management of the return of their international managers.

The following challenges are associated with the strategic management of international assignments:

- Assigning the right kind of international manager to the right position, at the right time
- Designing international HR practices for balancing generic and local needs on the one hand, and control, coordination, and autonomy needs on the other
- Establishing balance between global competitiveness and reactiveness to the local environment's peculiarities
- Identifying the needs for international personnel with a high degree of precision
- Strategic management of international assignments and of international personnel at the lowest cost: what type of international employee must be chosen, and to fulfill which position? Which type of contract must be drafted?

In the following sections, we will first look at the different approaches to international staffing, the reasons for using international assignments, and the different types of international employees. Then, we will propose a model for the strategic management of international assignments. Finally, we will look at the role played by women in the global arena.

The Different Approaches to International Staffing

The international HRM (iHRM) literature uses four terms to describe MNE approaches to managing and staffing their subsidiaries. These terms come from Perlmutter[2] who identified among international executives three different attitudes—ethnocentric, polycentric, and geocentric—toward building a multinational enterprise. The distinctions are based on top management assumptions upon which functional and geographical decisions about key products are made. Perlmutter's distinction between these three different approaches was later refined by Heenan and Perlmutter,[3] who added a fourth attitude: regiocentric. To describe these four attitudes, the authors use the concepts of complexity of organization, authority and decision-making, evaluation and control, rewards and punishments, communication processes, geographical identification, basic HRM strategy and state of internationalization (Exhibit 12.1). These distinctions, now widely accepted, have been used in various scholarly books on international human resource management. Heenan and Perlmutter's[3] attitudes are presented in Exhibit 12.1. We will see how these four attitudes influence the degree of utilization of the different categories of international personnel.

Exhibit 12.1

The Four Approaches to International Staffing

	Ethnocentrism	Polycentrism	Regiocentrism	Geocentrism
Complexity of organization	Complex in home country, simple in subsidiaries	Varied and independent	Highly interdependent on a regional basis	Increasingly complex and highly interdependent on a worldwide basis
Authority and decision-making	High in headquarters (HQ)	Relatively low in headquarters	High regional HQ and/or high collaboration among subsidiaries	Collaboration of HQ and subsidiaries around the world
Evaluation and control	Home standards applied for persons and performance	Determined locally	Determined regionally	Standards which are universal and local
Rewards and punishments; incentives	High in HQ; low in subsidiaries	Wide variation; big or small rewards for subsidiary performance	Rewards for contribution to regional objectives	Rewards to international and local executives for reaching local and worldwide objectives
Communication and information flow	High volume of orders, commands, advice to subsidiaries	Little to and from headquarters; little among subsidiaries	Little to and from corporate HQ, but may be high to and from regional HQ and among countries	Both ways and among subsidiaries around the world

Exhibit 12.1 *continued*

	Ethnocentrism	Polycentrism	Regiocentrism	Geocentrism
Geographical identifica- tion	Nationality of owner	Nationality of host country	Regional company	Truly worldwide company, but identifying with national interests
Basic HRM strategy	People of home country developed for key positions everywhere in the world	People of local nationality developed for key positions in their own country	Regional people developed for key positions anywhere in the region	Best people everywhere in the world developed for key positions everywhere in the world
State of international- ization	Early	Middle	Middle	Late

Source: Heenan and Perlmutter.[3]

Ethnocentric Approach. Strategic decisions are made at headquarters, and foreign subsidiaries have little autonomy. Key jobs at both domestic and foreign operations are held by headquarters management personnel and subsidiaries are managed by expatriates from the home country. Head office managers see expatriation as a way to accelerate the progression of their career, since the competence development of expatriates is preferred to that of local managers.

Polycentric Approach. In this case, expatriation is no longer at the center of the international development strategy. The MNC treats each subsidiary as a distinct national entity and empowers it with some decision-making autonomy. Subsidiaries are usually managed by local nationals (HCNs), who are seldom promoted to positions at headquarters. With this approach, the MNC avoids the difficulties associated with expatriation and cross-cultural adjustment. The control exercised by the head office is weak, and the diversity of the situations in which the subsidiaries find themselves complicates the process of integrating the organization's international activities.

Geocentric Approach. With this approach, the MNC designs its strategy from an international standpoint right from the beginning. The organization favors ability and experience over nationality. Parent country nationals (PCNs), third country nationals (TCNs), and host country nationals (HCNs) are thus equally mobile internationally. In order to be successful, this approach to staffing without regard to nationality must be accompanied by a worldwide, integrated business strategy.

Regiocentric Approach. The MNC that favors a regiocentric approach adopts uniform practices for all managers within the same geographical zone. Like the MNC that functions with a geocentric approach, it utilizes a wider pool of managers but in a limited, regional way. Personnel may move outside of their countries, but only within their particular geographic region. For instance, European managers are mobile solely within Europe. Regional managers may not be promoted to headquarters positions but they enjoy considerable regional autonomy in decision-making (see Exhibit 12.1).

Functions of International Assignments

Why use international employees? Reasons vary from one multinational organization to the other, but an analysis of the literature suggests that international employees fulfill five major roles. The first three roles are tactical in nature: fulfilling a need for a certain type of personnel that is not available in the host country, sharing and transferring information, and developing the capacities and level of implication of managers within the organization. The other two roles are strategic in nature: controlling and coordinating activities.

Fulfilling a Specific Need for Personnel and Know-how

The first role of international assignments is to fulfill the insufficient technical and managerial competencies in certain countries where the market structure is often characterized by a shortage of engineers, senior technicians, and trained managers.

Sharing and Transferring Knowledge

Another reason for using international assignments is to share and exchange information. A multinational organization can send an expatriate employee in order to better understand a subsidiary's activities in a particular context, to share knowledge regarding a new type of equipment or a specific tool, or to communicate elements of its organizational culture, processes, or competencies. Expatriation allows for a rapid and efficient transfer of know-how. The need for such an assignment can arise, for instance, when setting up an activity that does not exist in the host country. Expatriation then plays a role in the training of the local personnel, until the subsidiaries enter a growing phase, who then replace the expatriate employees in management and supervision positions. It is important to note that the knowledge transfer does not only flow from the head office to the subsidiaries, but also between the subsidiaries and from the subsidiaries toward the head office. According to Black et al.,[4] there are two unique aspects to expatriation with regard to information exchange. First, the duration of the assignments, between one and five years, allows the collection and transfer of complex information. Secondly, the information exchange takes place not only during the expatriation, but also afterward. The organization can benefit from the expatriate's acquired knowledge concerning the foreign subsidiaries and integrate that knowledge in the strategic planning and decision-making processes.

The Development of Managers and their Implication Toward the Organization

International assignments constitute a proven method for developing global managers. Most senior managers have extensive international experience. When the expatriate's role comprises supervision functions, expatriation can play a prominent role in developing managerial competencies and in fostering loyalty toward the organization. Indeed, expatriation allows junior managers or high-potential employees to face new situations, to develop new competencies, especially when it comes to acting autonomously and taking risks, thus facilitating the development of abilities required for becoming a senior manager. The managers' various international experiences help in developing a global understanding of the organization. Moreover, international transfers develop the individual's commitment toward the organization, his orher feeling of belonging and his loyalty. Organizations that use expatriation to improve their managers' competencies, either formally or not, associate expatriation with promotions. Organizations that use expatriation to improve their managers' abilities associate international assignments more or less formally with a promotion. This practice gets the message through to expatriates that their international experience will be valued as an asset.

Control of Activities. From an organizational standpoint, managers are generally expatriated in the early phase of the internalization process, in order to control the subsidiaries' activities. In an international context, the transfer of managers constitutes an informal control mechanism, which can complement or replace more formal control measures such as the elaboration of norms and procedures common to all subsidiaries. Expatriate employees are also used to reduce the uncertainty stemming from the environment (political risk, cultural distance, legal environment, competition), which is also a form of control. As these uncertainty factors increase in importance, the role of the expatriate becomes increasingly managerial in nature. Similarly, the higher the interdependence between the head office and the subsidiaries and the more complex the activities, the more the expatriates' function will be control oriented.

Coordination of Activities. Expatriates as well as impatriates play an essential part in the coordination of subsidiaries' activities. Through complex dialectic processes (local/global, individual/collective), international assignments are aimed at reinforcing the integration of individual and organizational dynamics which contribute to the cohesion of the firm. International assignments indeed allow for the creation and development of international networks that reinforce the integration of activities. According to Janssens and Brett,[5] the coordination of a global organization relies on three elements: centralization (decision-making by a core of senior managers), formalization (decision-making following established rules and procedures), and socialization (decision-making following shared norms and values).

The various functions of international assignments demand different types of international employees, with different profiles. For instance, if the main purpose of an assignment is managerial development, the organization will select a junior manager or a high-potential employee. If, on the other hand, the main purpose of an assignment is to control a subsidiary's activities, the organization will select an experienced manager who is familiar with the head office's values and managerial procedures. Finally, it must be noted that the five functions of international assignments are not mutually exclusive and can be combined.

Types of International Personnel

In this section, we will look at the main categories of international employees, discuss their respective advantages and disadvantages, and present the various types of assignments for employees from the organization's country of origin.

The Different Categories of International Personnel

In the literature, four categories of international personnel have been identified, based on their country of origin and the location of their assignment. These categories are parent PCNs, HCNs, TCNs, and impatriates.

The PCNs are employees from the multinational's head-office (expatriate employees). For instance, a Japanese manager working in a Japanese multinational's French subsidiary is an expatriate, or a PCN.

The HCNs are employees from the host country (the subsidiary's). For instance, a French manager working in a Japanese multinational's French subsidiary is an HCN.

The TCNs are employees from countries other than that of the multinational's head office and that of the subsidiary. For instance, a Belgian manager working in a Japanese multinational's French subsidiary is a TCN. An example of a multinational using these three types of international employees is Honda: working in Honda's subsidiary in Dubai are one Japanese manager, an expatriate from Honda JAPAN, the international head office, one French expatriate from the European head office, and 35 HCNs (Indians and Philippinos).

"Impatriates" (as opposed to expatriates) are HCNs sent to the head office. The reasons most frequently cited to justify hiring HCNs for transfer at the head office have to do with competence development of managers, knowledge transfer, and subsidiary integration. Moreover, generating a flow of impatriates toward the head office is an excellent way to trigger the process of socializing NPHs. Through impatriation, HCNs develop a sense of belonging to the global organization. The reasons for using impatriation determine the selection criteria for future impatriates. When the main goal is knowledge transfer and subsidiary integration, for example, communication skills in the multinational's official language as well as in the subsidiary's language are important criteria. Finally, it is worth noting that the duration of impatriations is generally shorter than that of expatriations. Many organizations use impatriates in order to reduce, in the end, the number of expatriates.

When a specific position needs to be filled, how should organizations choose between the different categories of international employees? Usually, the choice is partly determined by three elements: the general staffing policy on key positions in headquarters and subsidiaries (ethnocentrism, polycentrism, geocentrism, and regiocentrism), the constraints imposed by the host governments on hiring policies, and staff availabilities. Beyond these considerations, the advantages and disadvantages associated with PCNs, HCNs, and TCNs, presented below, are considered.

Six criteria seem relevant to discuss the respective advantages and disadvantages of these three categories of international employees.

1. Cost
2. Knowledge of the organization (products, organizational culture)
3. Cultural proximity
4. Knowledge of the local environment
5. Attitude of the foreign government
6. Promotability of local employees.

With regard to costs for the organization, hiring a PCN always costs more than hiring an HCN. On average, an expatriate's salary is two to two and a half times that of a local employee or of a TCN. These costs increase if the expatriate fails in his assignment. The high cost of expatriation sometimes leads the organization to opt for other solutions, such as short-term assignments.

The PCNs, however, present two advantages compared to the other categories of international managers. First, their technical and managerial competencies have been put to test in their previous positions, in the parent country, and have been recognized by the head office. Secondly, they possess extensive knowledge of the organization: its products, its managers, and the organizational culture. These two characteristics allow for efficient communication with the head office.

As far as cultural proximity and knowledge of the local environment are concerned, HCNs are obviously at an advantage. All things being equal, a local employee who speaks the local language, understands the political system and, often enough, is a member of the local elite, should prove to be more efficient than a foreign manager. For local personnel, cultural adjustment is not an issue. Training HCNs also seems simpler, from a short-term point of view, than selecting high-potential employees from the organization's country of origin and spending resources in order for them to adjust to the host country. Well-trained local managers thus constitute first-rate candidates for organizations. On the other hand, local managers are not familiar with the organization and with its culture. In addition, local managers might be too deeply involved in the local community and have a hard time understanding the parent company's global strategy, and few of them might truly identify with the organization and its goals.

Local governments sometimes exert explicit or implicit pressure on multi-national companies so that they develop and promote local managers to key positions in order to "nationalize" the management or foreign subsidiaries. Local legislation concerning working visas partly determines the subsidiary's capacity to hire TCNs. In some countries, such as Canada, companies may hire TCNs only if they can prove that available "local" candidates were not suitable for the position.

Finally, the constitution of a pool of international managers takes place at the expense of the recruitment and promotion of local managers and vice versa. Third country nationals can be closer to the country of origin's culture than HCNs, but they hinder local managers' chances to get promoted. The choice to hire TCNs must thus be made taking all these considerations into account.

Selection between the three classic categories of managers will be influenced, beyond the vast differences in terms of advantages and disadvantages of each, by the degree of internationalization of the company, its internationalization strategy, its iHRM approach, its international assignment policy, and the specific needs of its subsidiaries. The more the head office wishes to impose its nationalistic views (ethnocentric approach), the more it resorts to expatriation, and the more the head office wishes to expose its geocentric side without trying to impose the control methods used at the head-office, the more it will select based on competence rather than nationality.

Exhibit 12.2 summarizes the advantages and disadvantages of the various categories of international managers.

The Different Types of International Assignment for PCNs

Within organizations, many types of assignments can be found for PCNs. The duration of assignments distinguishes between expatriations and different kinds of short-term assignments. In addition, the role of international assignments in an employee's career distinguishes between global managers, expatriates, and international junior managers.

Long-term Assignments, or Expatriations. An expatriation is an assignment abroad, for a duration of one to five years, but generally three. The employee and his family are relocated to the host country. At the end of his initial contract, if the employee wishes to remain with the subsidiary, it will be under a local contract. According to Harris,[6] expatriations are mostly used for strategic missions, and meet the needs of the control function (a function that was mentioned by 62 percent of companies using expatriate employees), knowledge transfer function (74%), and professional development function (60%). Expatriations, however, are costly for companies. The main difficulties related to expatriate management concern dual career couples, lack of candidates for assignments in less-attractive areas and repatriation. Organizations' first concern is, however, the high cost associated with expatriations. In order to avoid those costs and the difficulties associated with managing expatriates, more and more companies reduce the number of expatriate employees, propose shorter-term assignments, localize their

Exhibit 12.2

The Advantages and Disadvantages of the Various Categories of International Managers

Type of international manager	Advantages	Disadvantages
Parent country nationals (PCNs)	• Control over the subsidiaries • Share a common culture and educational background • Facilitate communication and coordination with corporate headquarters	• Lack of knowledge regarding country's economic development, culture, legal system, and political process • Very expensive to both relocate and maintain (expatriates—people working and residing in their non-native countries) • Legal restrictions imposed by many countries as to the number of foreign employees that can be employed
Host country nationals (HCNs)	• Understand and know local laws, culture, and economic conditions • Cost is much lower • Opportunity for development and source of motivation • Legal regulation of employment	• Cultural difficulties hindering recruitment and training activities • Lack of knowledge concerning the organization, its products, and its services • Communication problems with the head office • May not be as familiar with the business culture and practices • Control and coordination of headquarters may be impeded
Third country nationals (TCNs)	• Costs are lower than those of PCNs • Knowledge of the organization, of its practices, of its management policies • Culture close to that of the head office	• Legal restrictions imposed by many countries as to the number of foreign employees that can be employed • Hinders local employees' chances to get promoted • Lack of loyalty towards the organization

expatriates, offer less generous compensation packages, and hire more local employees.

Avaya's strategies to reduce the number of career expatriates

Avaya Inc., a provider of communication systems in Basking Ridge, New Jersey, with 15,000 employees, keeps its number of expatriates low (currently at 15, down from 90 two years ago) by using three strategies:

First, Avaya started sending more employees on short-term assignments in 2002. The short-term assignment, generally six months long, is treated more like a business trip. The employee stays in a hotel or company apartment and is reimbursed for meals and trips to home every other month, eliminating the need to pay pricey housing allowances and costs related to moving the employee's family. The company is now tightening its policies for short-term assignments. "We want to treat employees on a fair and equitable basis . . . rather than basing it on each person's negotiating power or each manager's willingness to say yes or no".

Second, Avaya controls costs by hiring third country nationals. Avaya currently has 365 foreign nationals, about twice as many as it had two and a half years ago. By hiring foreign nationals, the company saves because benefits such as tax assistance, education for dependents and housing allowances are offered only for a limited time. Also, foreign nationals aren't paid a cost-of-living adjustment, a hardship allowance or an expatriate premium. Foreign nationals also typically don't need as much time to acclimate because they don't face the cultural barriers that an American might. There's no language problem and that person is also in tune with the business style of the region.

And third, Avaya started localizing some of the expats. Once expatriates are localized, Avaya phases out housing and schooling allowances after a year, pays employees in the local currency, switches them to local health benefits and doesn't have to pay income tax in both countries. For an expatriate who earns a salary of $100,000, the dual income taxes alone cost $140,000.

Source: Leslie Gross Klaff.[7]

Short-term Assignments (1–12 months). Employees sent on short-term assignments stay in the host country between one and twelve months. Technically, the employee might be hired by the subsidiary, and receive a mobility bonus. The employee's family may go along but, in practice, this rarely happens. Career management takes place at the head office and performance evaluation is often shared between the head office and the host country. According to Harris,[6] short-term assignments can be used to compensate for the lack of mobility of dual-career couples. This type of assignment is used mainly for knowledge transfer (69%) and for managerial development (39%). Short-term assignments may prove stressful for employees. Indeed, it becomes difficult to maintain a proper balance between work and private life, because of the long work hours in the host country and because of the distance between the employee and his social and family environments. Organizations have a hard time establishing consistent policies and practices, and managing taxation and compensation issues.

In addition, Harris[6] identifies two other sub-categories of short-term assignment: the "international commuters" and the "frequent flyers." "International commuters" travel between their country of origin and the host country once or twice per week, while their family remains in the country of origin. "Frequent flyers" travel frequently for business, for periods of thirty-one days or less, while remaining based in the country of origin. Usually, business trip and per diem policies apply to those trips. According to Harris,[6] "international commuters" and "frequent flyers" are used to carry out operational assignments, but are also adequate for control and knowledge transfer functions, as well as replacement of local competencies and coordination. These assignments often lead to problems with work/family balance and excessive fatigue among employees. In addition, the impact of cultural differences is often underestimated in these assignments and cross-cultural training is generally nonexistent. Finally, organizations often lack consistent policies regarding these assignments.

According to Harris,[6] organizations are not monitoring these alternatives to long-term expatriation closely enough, often having little idea of their number, how much they cost them, and how cost-effective they might be.

Global Managers. As opposed to the expatriate manager, who spends between one and five years abroad and then returns to the head office, the global manager strings together multiple expatriations for the duration of his or her career. Global managers have an international career, have shown their ability to survive and work efficiently in various cultures, have great communication skills, and an open mind. The international life style is a true motivation for them, and the management of their career is centralized at the head office.[7]

International Junior Managers. International junior managers are sent abroad to develop their managerial abilities. They are young managers, mostly high-potential employees.

In conclusion, organizations use global managers and expatriates for strategic assignments, short-term assignments for tactical missions, commuters and frequent flyers for operational missions, and international junior managers for managerial development. These distinctions between the various types of international assignments for PCNs give organizations the flexibility to react to the different problems they encounter at the lowest possible cost. In expatriation policies, specific sections can be found concerning the different types of contracts.

Strategic Management of International Assignments

Many companies are sending employees and managers abroad to implement their global strategies and to control or coordinate their far-flung subsidiaries.[9] But sending managers abroad is very expensive. Black and Gregersen[10] showed that expatriates cost two to three times what they would in an equivalent position back home. Moreover, between 10 and 20 percent of the expatriates come back before the end of their contract because they could not adjust to the job or to the country. Among those who stay in their position abroad, one-third do not perform up to their supervisor's expectations.[10] International managers constitute a crucial and competitive resource for multinationals, a resource that needs to be managed and developed. Value created by international assignments depends on the way they are planned and managed. Basing themselves on the literature and on interviews with international HR managers, Waxin et al.[11] propose a model for the strategic management of international assignments. This model comprises eight steps: (1) strategic planning and job analysis, (2) recruitment, (3) selection, (4) preparation for the transfer, (5) adjustment and organizational support, (6) evaluation and performance management, (7) Compensation and (8) repatriation and retention (Exhibit 12.3).

Exhibit 12.3

A Model for the Strategic Management of International Assignments

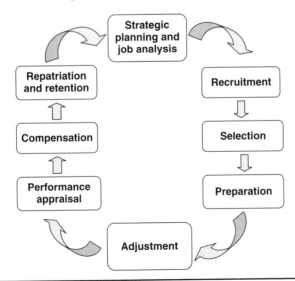

Source: Waxin et al.[11]

Strategic Planning and Job Analysis

According to Waxin et al.,[11] the first step for each international assignment consists of (1) the goals, (2) the job description, (3) the job specification and (4) the ownership for the responsibility of managing the full expatriation/repatriation cycle.

Firstly, the goals of each international assignment must be specified, and their strategic value must be determined with regard to the organization's strategic objectives. What are the assignment's goals? (increase the organizational performance, train local employees, transfer the head office's organizational culture toward a subsidiary, solve a technical problem, launch a new product, etc.). Which of these objectives are directly linked with the organization's strategic objectives? Dowling and Welch[12] distinguish between hard, soft and contextual job goals. Hard goals are objective, quantifiable, and can be directly measured (e.g., return on investment, or market share). Soft goals tend to be relationship- or trait–based, like leadership style or interpersonal skills. Contextual goals attempt to take into consideration factors that result from the situation in which performance occurs, like arbitrary transfer pricing or other financial tools for transactions between subsidiaries to minimize foreign risk exposure. Job goals will be translated later on into performance appraisal criteria so specificity and measurability are essential. However, there are considerable differences in the way the goal-setting process is handled in different countries. Tahvanainen[13] found that in Sweden and Germany, for example, it is normal for managers to participate in the setting of job goals, whereas setting job goals is the priority of senior managers in the USA.

The job analysis, which comprises of the job description and the competency profile, must then be carried out. The *job description* contains general information on the position, the goals to be met, a list of tasks in order of importance, the particular conditions, the context of the position, the duration of the contract, the date of review, and the date of approval. In the context of an international assignment, the job's context must be described in great detail; the main characteristics of the subsidiary's organizational culture must be identified, as well as those of the host country. Harvey[14] suggests that job analysis must generate criteria that adequately capture the nature of international work as opposed to the domestic context, in order to provide valid appraisal information.

The *job specification* states the required knowledge, abilities (know-how) and experience, and personal characteristics for the job. The profile must be objective and realistic. In order for such a profile to be drawn, the competencies required to complete each task of the job description must be identified and weighed. In the context of an international assignment, it is important to include in the profile cultural competencies and personal characteristics, such as a social orientation, cultural flexibility, stress resistance, and so on that are required.[15] Ideally, the job specification will be used again as a basis for the choice of the evaluation criteria.

Finally, ownership for the responsibility of the management of the full expatriation/repatriation cycle must be determined. Will the expatriate refer to their home- or host-country HR manager during their assignment? This is where collaboration between home and host HR and line management is essential. Confusion will only make communication between the expatriate and HR more difficult, and will make the expatriate feel less supported.

This first step helps determine the ideal type of international manager for the position (PCN, TCN, HCN, other type of international employee). The objectives of the position, the job description and specification, and the details about the management of the expatriation/repatriation processes should be explained to the candidate by the end of the selection process. In any case, the expatriate should know the exact purposes of his assignment before the beginning of his assignment.

Recruitment of International Employees

The main objectives of international recruitment are (1) elaborating ways and techniques which will allow the organization to attract a sufficient number of motivated and qualified international candidates, (2) identifying candidates susceptible to filling foreign positions at the lowest possible cost, and (3) increasing the pool of international candidates at the lowest possible cost, anticipating for the organization's future needs in personnel. The major decisions at this step regard the sources and the methods of recruitment.

Recruitment Sources. The first decision to be made is whether to recruit internally or externally. In spite of the external recruitment possibility, it is well documented that the majority of firms depend almost exclusively on internal recruitment for foreign positions, especially for their expatriate's positions. This preferred recruitment option can be found even in local markets where there is plenty of skilled labor. Why is there not a greater emphasis on external recruitment? The answer has to do with the strategic value of the international assignment. Internal recruitment is justified if the strategic purpose of the assignment is coordination or control of operations. However, in the case of learning units, for example when the subsidiary acquires and develops new resources that may be later exported to other parts of the organization, recruiting from the external market can be more appropriate.

Recruitment Methods. The second decision to be made regards the choice of the recruitment methods. The major internal recruitment methods for international positions are (international) job posting and utilization of internal databases. To enable the company to identify suitable *internal* expatriates candidates, HR departments need to build global databases that include data on potential candidates, their work experience, performance, skills, availability, and their preferences regarding a potential international assignment: where he or she would be interested in working, in what capacity, and on what sort of projects.[16] For example, Tetra pack developed their "Management Planning and Development" centralized database which contains the profile of over thousands high potential employees and which is updated once a year. This database is consultable by the HR directors' community and can be used to support the expatriates' recruitment process.[8]

The Danone Group's Career recruitment site, for internal and external recruitment

The Danone Group has opted for daily posting all vacant positions on the Danone Career website, which is accessible from the outside as well as from inside the company. To apply, candidates must find positions that correspond to their profile. The site is the fastest and most efficient way to obtain information regarding vacant positions within the Group, from anywhere in the world. To apply for a position, candidates must:

1 Conduct a search, specifying their level of experience (student seeking an internship, junior (1–2 years of experience), senior (2 years + of experience), or director/executive), their field of specialization and the geographical area where they wish to work.
2 Select a job offer within the search results
3 Study the job descriptions and apply.

After having filled out his or her personal information on a form, the candidate can attach his or her CV and cover letter. Within 72 hours of applying, the candidate will get a receipt notification.

The English language is preferred throughout the recruitment process. The Group searches for candidates with an international profile, and proficiency in English is highly valued. The candidate may, however, use the language of his or her choice in the free-text fields or in the attached documents.

The progressive opening of the Careers website to foreigners will help facilitate the internationalization of the recruitment process. Fifteen countries currently use the website, and the international development continues.

Source: Danone.fr

When suitable candidates cannot be found internally, companies turn to the external market. External recruitment methods for international positions include using the Internet, launching campaigns in international media, using the services of recruitment agencies and/or international head-hunters, and establishing relationships with learning institutions.

Selection of International Employees

The main objectives of the selection process are (1) enabling the company and the employee to determine whether the candidate possesses the competencies and motivation to successfully accomplish his or her international assignment, (2) minimizing the risk of assignment failure and the related costs, and (3) assigning candidates to suitable positions, thus maximizing the organization's and the candidate's benefit. Because of the specificity and implications of the task the expatriate will have to perform, multinational companies should ensure that they have an appropriate selection process for international assignments. We will now take a closer look at the selection criteria, the choice of the evaluators and the selection methods.

Selection Criteria. In theory, the choice of selection criteria for international employees is based on an analysis of the characteristics of the multinational, those of the subsidiary, the host country, and the position to fill.[11]

Depending on the results of this analysis, the ideal candidate's profile varies from one international assignment to the other (Exhibit 12.4).[17]

Given the considerable diversity of potential positions and host countries, it is not possible to draw a list of key competencies for expatriates.[18] Unfortunately, organizations tend, when selecting expatriates, not to look far beyond technical expertise and previous performance in the country of origin. However, in the context of an international assignment, criteria related to the cross-cultural competencies and individual characteristics of the candidate, such as social orientation, will to communicate, good stress resistance, and open-mindedness, should be considered.[15] Studies show that individuals who seek challenges, new experiences, and who enjoy learning are more likely to approach an international assignment in a positive and creative way, and are also more likely to succeed as expatriates. If the job analysis has been done properly, the selection criteria will be based on the international assignment's competency profile.

Choice of Evaluators. Black et al.[4] recommend forming an expatriate selection team which includes managers from the country of origin and managers from the host country, as well as a representative from the iHRM department. Harris and Brewster[16] note, however, that most of the time, the iHRM specialist's role is limited to that of an advisor, while the actual decision is taken by the managers alone. Marchon[8] states that when the expatriation is requested by a subsidiary, the selection process is more transparent: the subsidiary, responsible for the selection, will make a final selection among

Exhibit 12.4

Determinants of the Selection Criteria for International Employees

Multinational's characteristics
Stage of internationalization
Industrial sector
Business strategy
HRM orientation
iHRM policies
Organizational culture

Selection criteria
- Type of international manager
- Education
- Experience
- Professional competencies
- Personal characteristics
- Cultural competencies

Subsidiary's characteristics
Legal form/ownership mode
Localization

Host country's characteristics
National culture
Labor laws and regulations

Position's characteristics
Function of the international assignment
Job description and specification
Contract duration
Hardness of communication

Source: Waxin et al.[11]

several candidates it has chosen. However, when the expatriation is deemed necessary by the head office, the subsidiary's role is often limited to approving or rejecting the final choice of the candidate.

Selection Methods. Several methods are available, like interviews, psychological tests, assessment centers, work simulations or role plays, references, biographical and background data and so on.

According to Linehan et al.,[19] the interview is the most used and is still regarded as the most effective method to select overseas assignees. It provides a forum to understand the expectations and motivations of the candidate and to inform him/her about the job.

The use of formal testing like psychological or relational tests is very limited in the practice but according to Harvey[20] they are becoming used more frequently. Finn and Morley[21] cite that cultural awareness and adaptability tests are almost never used because they are expensive, difficult to construct and interpret, and their reliability is questioned. Forster and Johnsen[22] mention that in an international context there are some enormous problems with both suitability and comparability of tests for different national groups and cultures. Finally, the same authors note that the introduction of these tests encounters resistance from the selectors because this could undermine their power and prestige in terms of decision-making.

Assessment centers are considered costly and time-consuming, but they regroup all the methods of evaluation in a single place within a few days. They allow the assessment of the communication skills and the adaptability of the candidates as well as their strategic competencies.

References, and biographical and background data are principally used to ensure that the applicant has the necessary technical expertise to do the job, and are so less decisive in the selection of an expatriate, even if they can be useful to spot a particular candidate. According to the authors in iHRM, the best thing to assess a candidate correctly is the use of several different techniques and sources of data.

Expatriates selection process in a global fast-food multinational company

Tricon Restaurants International, based in Dallas, Texas, is the franchiser for over 10,000 overseas Kentucky Fried Chicken, Pizza Hut, and Taco Bell Restaurants. The company has 100 expatriates; 20 are Americans working overseas.

Tricon has established a very formal selection process to staff its overseas positions.

Selection Criteria. Rather than choosing candidates who are merely excited about overseas assignment and who have the technical skills to perform the job, Tricon is taking a closer look at whether the candidates have the necessary personality characteristics, such as their empathy, their ability to adapt to different situations, their ability to interact with others (sociability), and the family support needed to succeed in overseas assignments.

Selection Methods:

(1) To select candidates for overseas assignments, Tricon interviews candidates about the positions, the country's culture, and its marketplace.

(2) If there is any doubt whether the candidate can make the adjustment, a consulting firm is hired to further assess whether the candidate has the personality needed to succeed in an overseas assignment.

(3) If candidates pass the interview, a 360-degree feedback survey, which asks peers and their managers about their strengths and weaknesses, is used to evaluate their skills.

(4) If the evaluation is positive, candidates and their families are sent overseas for a one-week look-see trip. During the visit, local managers evaluate the candidate while the family evaluates the community. The family spends time touring local schools and potential housing locations, and meeting with other expatriates in the country who help them understand the local culture and environment.

(continued)

(5) If the local managers find the candidate acceptable, the candidate, with input from family, can accept or reject the position.

Source: Based on C. Patton.[23]

Harris and Brewster[16] propose a typology of selection methods for international managers, which comprises four categories, placing the various selection methods on two axes: open/closed procedure and formal/informal procedure.

First, the selection process can be open or closed. In an open system, all vacancies are advertised and anyone with appropriate qualification and experience may apply. All the candidates are interviewed with greater or lesser degrees of formalized testing. Selection decisions are taken by consensus amongst selectors. In contrast, in a closed system, selectors at corporate headquarter choose or nominate through line managers the "suitable" candidates. These candidates are informed only once agreement about acceptability has been reached between headquarter personnel and the line manager. The selection interview consists of a negotiation about the terms and conditions of the assignment.

Then, the selection process can be formal or informal. In formal systems, vacancies are advertised internally, selection criteria are made explicit and are business focused, and directly related to the job description and job specification. Psychometric testing is likely to be used, and selectors need to agree among themselves about candidate match. In informal systems, there is a lack of specificity between competencies and job description, criteria are often not specified. Selectors assume that personality characteristics are already known, and give a great importance to networking, reputation, and team fit. There is an increasing likelihood that individual preferences of selectors can predominate (Exhibit 12.5).

In practice, however, the majority of organizations operate predominantly closed and informal selection systems, which are not that different from the systems used for domestic assignments. Stahl[24] states that 81 percent of the 116 expatriates sampled in his study were recruited through an opaque selection system, on the basis of nonstructured interviews. Only 19 percent of the candidates went through a structured interview. None of the candidates had had to pass a test, and in no case, at any moment during the selection process, was the life-partner taken into account (Exhibit 12.6).

Closed and informal selection systems present at least three major disadvantages.[16] First, they limit the degree to which interpersonal and intercultural skills are taken into account when selecting international managers. Secondly, they restrict the pool of potential candidates to the candidates who are appreciated by the selectors. This is particularly

Exhibit 12.5

Typology of Expatriates Selection Processes

	Formal	Informal
Open	• Clearly defined criteria • Clearly defined measures • Training for selectors • Open advertising of vacancy (Internal/external) • Panel discussions	• Less defined criteria • Less defined measures • Limited training for selectors • No panel discussions • Open advertising of vacancy • Recommendations
Closed	• Clearly defined criteria • Clearly defined measures • Training for selectors • Panel discussions • Nominations only (networking/reputation)	• Selectors' individual preferences determine criteria and measures • No panel discussions • Nominations only (networking/reputation)

Source: Harris and Brewster.[16]

Exhibit 12.6

The Expatriates Selection Methods

N = 116 expatriates

Unstructured Interview	Structured Interview	Psychological Tests	Assessment Center	Inclusion of Partner
81%	19%	0%	0%	0%

Source: Stahl.[24]

problematic for women, given the fact that between 80 and 95 percent of international managers are men. Within such an imbalanced selection context, it is all the more important to ensure that an open/formal selection system prevents potential discriminatory biases on the part of selectors. An open formal selection system forces the selectors to continually question their assumptions about women's or other minorities' suitability and their acceptability in international management positions. Thirdly, they prevent the organization from managing international assignments strategically. The role of the HR manager is limited to dealing with the financial, physical,

> ### The expatriates selection processes in five Swiss multinational companies
> ### (Credit Suisse, Nestle, Holcim, Tetra Pak, Novartis)
>
> In each case the task of the selection falls to the host company, either through the line manager or through the HR., with sometimes a possible involvement of a central department. These persons have generally no particular international experience and therefore do not emphasize the cultural dimension throughout experience and therefore do not emphasize the cultural dimension throughout the selection process. The selection criteria mainly used by these five companies are based on technical and professional competencies, when the literature recommends relying firstly on crosscultural skills, without of course forgetting the professional skills. For all five companies, the selection methods employed to evaluate the competencies of the candidates are the references, the background of the employee and an interview. The informal selection procedure mainly leans on the personal contacts and the network of the selectors. An interview is normally used to confirm the selection choice. None of the companies uses any kind of formal testing to assess the cross cultural or relational skills of the candidate. However, three out of the five companies say they are willing to improve their selection processes in the near future by introducing some more structured selection tools in the selection process.
>
> *Source: Marchon*[8].

and social aspects of international selection, instead of having an input into which kind of international manager is needed and what kind of assignment could be optimal for that international manager.

In conclusion, although the researchers are unanimous about the significance of an effective selection system, there is a big gap between their suggestions and the organizations' practices. As we will see, the work accomplished during the selection is also useful for determining the preparation needed by the selected candidate.

Preparation to Transfer

When an appropriate candidate has been selected for an international assignment, he or she must get prepared to face the challenges of the new position. The purpose of the preparation step is to provide the expatriates with all the necessary elements that will help them succeed during the international assignment by facilitating their adjustment in the host country and allowing them to work efficiently throughout the duration of their contract. The options company can use include organizing preliminary visits, providing practical assistance to the international employees, providing language and cross-cultural training.

Preliminary Visits or Look-see Visits. This is a trip to the host country offered to the assignee so that he or she can assess by himself the situation he or she will have to face. This option is sometimes used at the end of the selection process so that the candidate can confirm his or her acceptance of the position. During this trip the expatriate will finalize the contract and settle some issues like finding an accommodation or a school for the children. The expatriate will also get an idea about the new work environment. Usually, a preliminary visit includes the spouse, sometimes the children.

Practical Assistance. This aspect of the preparation is to make *everything ready for the transfer* of the expatriate and his family in order to facilitate the settling in. This consists in arranging for the visas, for the transportation, finding a new accommodation for the family, new schools for the children, if it has not been done during the look-see trip, and so on. Many multinationals now use the services of relocation specialists to provide this practical assistance. Informing the expatriate on how the transfer will occur and how life in the host country will be will reduce the stress related to the uncertainty of the foreign assignment and facilitate the adjustment in the new environment. The organization should give adequate notice of the new posting given the professional and personal arrangements that the employee will need to make before he leaves his home organization and country.

Language Training. The assignee is taught the language of the region where he or she will be sent. According to Ashamalla,[25] language ability facilitates the adjustment in the local environment and enhances effectiveness in dealing with foreign counterparts groups including government officials, bankers, labor organizations, suppliers, and customers. The rigor of the training should depend on the relational aspect of the expatriate's job.

Cross-cultural Training. The objective of cross-cultural training is to teach members of one culture to interact effectively with members of another culture, and to predispose them to a rapid adjustment to their new positions.[26] Brislin,[27] a cross-cultural psychologist, identifies three methods of cross-cultural training: cognitive, affective, and behavioral. The cognitive method corresponds to a diffusion of information, using conferences or nonparticipative sessions, in a foreign cultural environment. The affective method aims at provoking individual reactions so the subject can learn to deal with critical cultural incidents. The behavioral method aims at improving participants' capacity to adapt to their communication style and to establish positive relationships with members of another culture. Management science researchers have used Brislin's model and have added to it the situational (hardness of the culture and hardness of the communication, function and role of the manager, planned duration of expatriation) and individual variables (personal learning objectives, degree of active participation). Tung[28] suggests that the training method should be chosen according to the type of assignment and should be contingent to two determinant factors: the degree of similarity between the culture of origin and the host culture (which is a synonym of cultural distance) and the degree of interpersonal interaction between the manager and the host country's inhabitants, which would be linked, according to Black et al.,[4] to the role and function of the manager. In conclusion, the different models of cross-cultural training and their content are built around three fundamental variables: the cultural distance between the country of origin and the host country, the manager's level of integration with his environment, and the duration of the overseas assignment (Exhibit 12.7).

Gertsen[30] proposes a typology of training methods encompassing four categories. First, she identifies two kinds of training: conventional training, where the information is transmitted through a unidirectional communication, as is the case in schools and universities, and experimental training, where the trainer gets the trainees to participate by simulating real-life situations. Then, she identifies two possible orientations: either the training focuses on the notion of culture in general and aims at sensitizing participants to the notion of culture, or it focuses on one specific culture and aims at making participants more competent in that particular culture. According to Gertsen,[30] the combination of these two dimensions reveals four types of

Exhibit 12.7

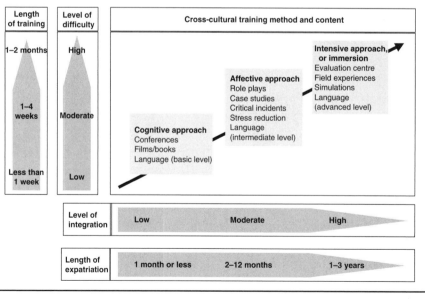

Source: Adapted from Mendenhall, Dunbar and Oddou.[29]

Exhibit 12.8

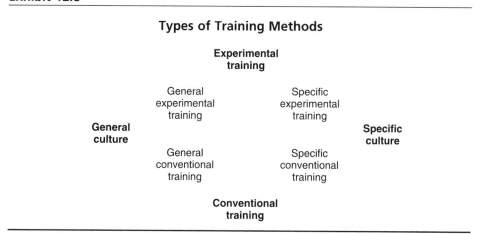

Types of Training Methods

**Experimental
training**

General
experimental
training

Specific
experimental
training

**General
culture**

**Specific
culture**

General
conventional
training

Specific
conventional
training

**Conventional
training**

Source: Gertsen's typology of cross-cultural training.[30]

training, as represented in Exhibit 12.8. In our research, we use these four types of training.

Pre-departure Cross-cultural Training Effectiveness

Studies in the fields of cross-cultural psychology and management demonstrate the beneficial impact of cross-cultural training on expatriates' cross-cultural adjustment.[31] Their findings can be summarized in three conclusions: cross-cultural training is associated with (1) feelings of well-being and self-confidence, (2) development of appropriate behaviors in the context of the foreign culture, and (3) improvement of the relationships with host country's inhabitants. In 2005, Waxin and Panaccio[32] studied the impact of the four types of pre-departure cross-cultural training identified by Gertsen[30] on the three facets of cross-cultural adjustment (work adjustment, interaction adjustment, and general adjustment) for French, German, Scandinavian, and Korean expatriates working in India. In summary, the findings of their research confirm the view expressed by researchers over the last twenty years that pre-move cultural training has a positive effect on adaptation to international assignments. The authors further contribute to the literature in three different ways. First, their study shows that experimental types of training are the most effective ones. Secondly, their results show that the larger the cultural distance between the country of origin and the host country, the more pronounced are the effects of cross-cultural training. Thirdly, the authors show that efficacy of inter-cultural training is clearly influenced by the magnitude of expatriate's prior international experience. Cross-cultural training's effectiveness is indeed stronger for managers with less international experience.

Pre-departure preparation thus appears to be an important factor for adjustment. However, in most multinationals, cross-cultural preparation for expatriates is superficial, incomplete or simply nonexistent.[32] The fact that decision-makers often have no international experience might, among other reasons, explain this state of affairs (see Box below).

Pre-departure preparation at Novartis, Switzerland

Before formally accepting the overseas position, expatriates at Novartis are offered a look-see trip to the host country.

English courses may be offered to the expatriate if needed, English being the official language of the company. Furthermore, if it is considered as essential that the assignee and his spouse have basic knowledge of the host country language, the company can pay for such a language tuition.

Novartis invites then the assignee and the spouse to a pre-assignment briefing to coordinate the arrangements for the transfer, to explain the compensation package and to answer any question about the host country.

Moreover, a cross cultural training is offered, consisting of a country briefing and a course about managing in the host country, communication and negotiation skills useful for the country of assignment. This training is provided by a native of the host country. Even if it lasts only 2 days, this preparation allows a better adjustment and expatriates are globally satisfied with it. A pre assignment check list is also given to the expatriate in order for him/her not to forget any important issue before leaving.

Source: Marchon.[8]

As an alternative to pre-departure training, cross-cultural training in the host country could also be envisaged.[33] Mendenhall and Stahl[34] mention in-country real-time training as one of the three new tendencies that are emerging for HR managers who work in the international HR area, alongside with global mindset training and CD-ROM/Internet-based training. Further, corporations should provide cross-cultural training to expatriates' spouses, since a lack of adjustment on their part could have negative repercussions on the adjustment of the expatriate himself. Finally, Harris[35] notes that corporations would benefit from using their former expatriates as trainers for the new expatriates. Indeed, usage of the newly acquired competencies of expatriates is often neglected, and cross-cultural training constitutes an area where those competencies could easily be put to contribution.

Adjustment of the Expatriate Manager: Organization Support upon Arrival and during the Assignment

Once the expatriate lands in the location of assignment, he or she needs further support from the company to adjust as quickly and smoothly as possible in the new job and in the new environment. Also, since the expatriate is supposed to come back to the home country after the realization of his mission, the company must also keep links with the expatriate so that the employee does not suffer from the out-of-sight, out-of-mind syndrome. Furthermore, maybe even more than the expatriate, the spouse needs also support. First, we will define the notion of adjustment and present the adjustment model and the expatriates' adjustment factors. We will then see how the organization can support the expatriate employee, upon arrival and throughout the assignment.

The Process of Cross-cultural Adjustment

Expatriates' adjustment to their new role and environment is of great significance, both to the organization and to the managers themselves. From the organization's perspective, expatriates' degree of adjustment partially predicts performance and completion of the mission.[36] From the managers' perspective, adjustment is a factor of job satisfaction and psychological well-being.[37] As a result, there has been a burgeoning academic and practical interest in understanding and measuring the adjustment process and its antecedents. Black[38] defined intercultural adjustment as "the degree of an individual's psychological comfort with various aspects of a host country."

The first conceptions of expatriate adjustment correspond to socio-affective conceptions of the cross-cultural adjustment process, which has been conceived for the last decades as following a U-shaped curve over time.[39] The curve's shape corresponds to the various stages which the individual goes through. Black and Mendenhall[40] summarize the curve's four steps in the following manner:

1. The first stage of expatriate adjustment is referred to as the "honeymoon" period. During that stage, the employee is fascinated, excited, and smitten with the host country's culture. At this stage, the employee has only superficial contacts with his or her environment.
2. The second stage, characterized by disillusionment and frustration, is that of the culture shock. The expatriate cannot understand the behavior of the people that surround him/her and realizes that his or

her own behavior does not produce the expected consequences. During this stage, the expatriate doubts his or her own ability to face this new situation and temporarily adopts a negative attitude toward his or her new environment. This stage, which corresponds to the bottom part of the U-shaped curve, takes place approximately six months after the arrival in the host country. If the crisis lasts too long, the remainder of the adjustment process can be jeopardized.

3. The third stage is characterized by a gradual adjustment to the new context. During this stage, the expatriate becomes increasingly efficient.

4. The fourth stage, "mastery," is characterized by a regular improvement in the individual's ability to function efficiently in the new culture (Exhibit 12.9).

Black and Mendenhall[40] presented a critical review of the 18 studies based on the U-shaped curve theory. The results of these studies are difficult to interpret, and the U-shaped curve model remains imperfectly validated. In these studies, adjustment was measured through concepts operationalized in different ways, such as morale, psychological mood, favorable opinion of HCNs, satisfaction, comfort, and difficulties experienced in the new environment. Results of the various studies highlight the existence of individual differences, which suggest that different forms of adjustment may exist, with curves that are not always U-shaped. Some expatriates do not experience a culture shock while some international managers who are considered very

Exhibit 12.9

The U-shaped Curve Model

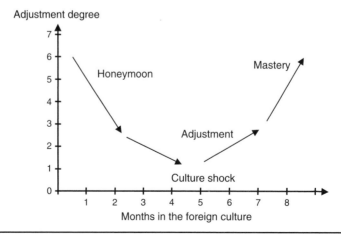

Source: Black and Mendenhall.[40]

efficient in their jobs suffer from profound culture shock. The U-shaped curve theory and the concept of culture shock hide the multi-dimensional character of the adjustment process.

Black[38] conceptualized and demonstrated that intercultural adjustment contains three related but conceptually distinct facets: work adjustment, which concerns responsibilities and performance, interaction adjustment, which concerns relationships with nationals of the host country, and general adjustment, which concerns adjustment to host country's living conditions, such as housing, food, leisure activities, and medical services. This typology has been validated by the works of Black and Stephens[41] and Black and Gregersen,[42] and is currently used in numerous studies. While they do correlate, work, interaction, and general adjustment do not follow the same curves. Studies show that the adjustment facets, despite having some common elements, are explained by distinct factors.

The Integrated Cross-cultural Adjustment Model

Black et al.[43] introduced the concept of "anticipation" in the cross-cultural adjustment model. These authors underline the importance of the anticipated adjustment phase, which takes place before the adjustment phase in the host country. Among the components of this anticipated adjustment phase, the previous international experience and the cross-cultural training or the preparation for the expatriation play a major part in explaining adjustment in the host country. Indeed, they allow the individual to build more realistic expectations toward his or her future work context, which reduces the occurrence and the magnitude of "surprises" while facilitating adjustment.[44]

Most studies on expatriate adjustment following that of Black et al.[43] use their model, (Exhibit 12.10) studying in great detail the impact of the different variables on the cross-cultural adjustment process.[45]

Waxin (2006b) focuses on the in-country adjustment process. She studied the impact of culture of origin on the three facets of expatriates' adjustment (work, interaction and general) and their antecedents.[46, 47] Her research model integrates organizational, individual, and contextual variables and introduces culture of origin as a direct and a moderator variable. She used self-administered questionnaire data from French, German, Korean, and Scandinavian expatriated managers in India, and multiple regressions with moderator variable. The results establish that culture of origin has a direct effect on the three facets of expatriate adjustment and a moderator effect on their antecedents. In the following text, we briefly comment on the major factors of adjustment. The summary of her research findings is presented in Exhibit 12.11.

Exhibit 12.10

Cross-cultural Adjustment Model

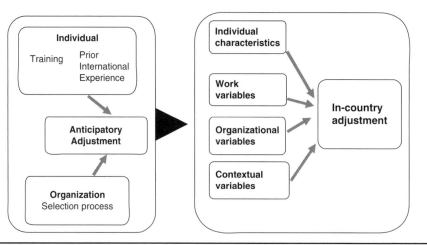

Source: Black et al.[43]

Exhibit 12.11

The Integrative Model of Cross-cultural Adjustment

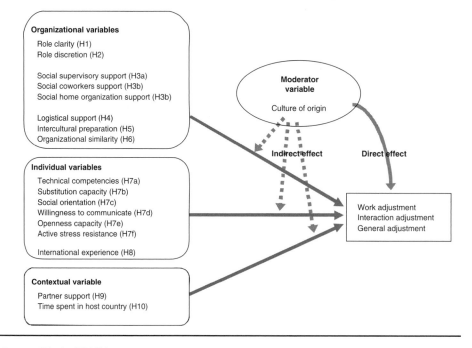

Source: Waxin (2006b).

There are three major categories of variables influencing expatriates' adjustment following expatriation: organizational, individual, and contextual variables.

Organizational antecedents of expatriate's adjustment comprise two job-related variables (role clarity and role discretion), three social support factors (supervisory, coworker(s), and home-country organizational support), logistical support, expatriation training, and organizational culture similarity.

- *Job-related Factors*. Job-related factors of adjustment encompass role clarity and role autonomy. Ideally, before the departure of the expatriate, his or her supervisors in the home and host countries should agree on the precise definition of the role of the expatriate and on the degree of autonomy he or she will have in this position.
- *Organizational Social Support*. This encompasses supervisory, coworkers, and home-country organizational social support. Social support provides expatriates with information about what is acceptable and unacceptable in the new work context. Organizational social support has been shown to reduce the time to proficiency of expatriates and to be positively related to the three facets of adjustment.
- *Logistical Support*. Organizational logistical support can include a career assistance service for the spouse or a relocation service, which helps to reinstall the transferee's family. If these services do not directly help the individual to adapt to his new post, they at least help to diminish the fear of the unknown.
- *Intercultural Training*. Much of the literature suggests that training enhances expatriates adjustment.[32, 48]
- *Organizational Similarity*. Perceived dissimilarity between home-country and host-country organizations is a source of uncertainty and stress and thus relate negatively to expats adjustment.

Individual antecedents of expatriates' interaction adjustment are the six dimensions of expatriates' adjustability and prior international experience.

- *Adjustability*. Based on the works of Mendenhall and Oddou[49] and Black[50], recent studies[15, 51] have identified six dimensions of the expatriate's adjustability, each one being measured by a battery of items. The dimensions are confidence in their own technical competencies, social orientation, willingness to communicate, substitution capacity, cultural openness, and stress resistance. All these adjustability dimensions are positively correlated to adjustment.
- *Prior International Experience*. Theoretical discussions have, for a long time, included previous international experience as relevant for the

adjustment process. Theoretically and intuitively, it makes sense to assume that international experience allows a quicker and more complete adjustment. Waxin (2006b) found that prior international experience was positively correlated with adjustment.

Finally, contextual antecedents encompass partner's social support, time spent in the host country, and culture of origin.

- *Partner's Social Support.* Partner's social support is viewed in the literature as an important influence on the worker abroad. Partner's social support reduces the stress generated by the new work environment and thus facilitates expatriates' adjustment.
- *Length of Time Spent in Host Country.* Adjustment is a time-related process. Individuals need time to get accustomed to their new environment and learn the host country culture and appropriate and acceptable behaviors. Time spent in the host country is positively related to expatriates's adjustment.
- *Culture of Origin.* Research suggests that the more different the host culture is from the home culture, the more demanding the adjustment will be. This phenomenon is known variously as the effect of cultural distance or culture. There is a further point arising out of the cultural differences literature. Different cultures may be more or less effective as expatriates in certain countries. Waxin (2004, 2006b) contributes to the literature in two different ways. First, she showed that expatriates' adjustment degree varies significantly according to their culture of origin. This is termed the direct effect of country of origin on the adjustment degree. Secondly, she showed that the antecedents of adjustment vary according to the specificities of expatriate's culture of origin. This is termed the moderator effect of culture of origin.

The results of this research have important implications for the management of expatriates, especially in the fields of recruitment, intercultural training, and support management policies. As far as expatriate recruitment is concerned, technical expertise and domestic track record are by far the dominant selection criteria. Our results show that different facets of adjustability are crucial to the adjustment process. Crucially, knowledge that culture of origin/cultural distance is a significant predictor of adjustment suggests that organizations may need to revise their international staffing policies. If culture of origin is critical then selecting TCNs for whom the country of assignment is not that different culturally from their own may be a sensible policy. Cross-cultural training appears to be an important factor of adjustment, especially when it comes to interaction and general adjustment. The training must be in accordance with the hardness of the culture of the host country. The more different that culture is from that of the country of origin, the more important and necessary is the use of cross-cultural training programs. Finally, managers might use the results of this study to facilitate the adjustment of expatriates to their new position abroad. Antecedents of adjustment are not the same across the national groups of expatriates. Our results suggest that management may be well advised to implement policies and practices to provide effective support and encouragement to expatriates, which take account of cultural and personal needs.

Support on place at the point of arrival. The first support the expatriate will need after arrival on location should focus on resolving the immediate living problems, as where to register to the local authorities, where to go shopping, and how do the phone system works.

- The company could grant the expatriates leave for the first critical days, or at least allow him/her flexitime during the first week.
- Providing help to the expatriate to fix his or her administrative and practical duties will allow him or her to quickly concentrate on the job-related issues of the assignment. The company can also resort to an external provider to counsel the expatriate during the first days of his or her assignment.
- Moreover, to assist the expatriate in his or her early adjustment, the company should also provide him/her with local information about the social events happening in the region and the different social clubs.
- Furthermore, the support on arrival should also take into account the work environment. The expatriate should be properly introduced to his colleagues and the employees he will work with. Selmer[52] notes that a job overlap is not always possible and is relatively expensive, but very helpful. The predecessor could also assume the role of a temporary personal coach of the successor.
- Finally, continuing an on-site cross-cultural training during the early stages of the assignment will also prove useful to accelerate the expatriate's adjustment process.

Ongoing Support. Hippler[53] (in Linehan et al.[19], p. 180) writes that in the ideal case the on-arrival support with regard to social integration has proven successful to an extent that the expatriate needs no further formal assistance, social support being normal.

- The host company should design a local coach to whom the expatriate can turn whenever he or she experiences sudden difficulties.
- The home company could also formally or informally appoint the expatriate with a sponsor/mentor based in the home organization,

responsible of informing the expatriate about the important issues and changes. The contact should be via regular e-mails and phone calls while the expatriate is in the host location, and the expatriate should meet with the mentor in the home office when possible. The sponsor/mentor will also play an important role at the repatriation step. A mentor can also keep the expatriate "visible" by communicating an expatriate's accomplishments across the organization via articles in company newsletters or reports on the Intranet. In any case, the expatriates should do his or her best to keep formal and informal contacts with former collaborators in the home organization.

- The home company should also stay in contact with the expatriate throughout the assignment, to keep him/her updated about the changes in the domestic operations, the evolution of the organizational policies, the ongoing projects, and the staffing changes. Multiple means of communication are available: visits of head offices managers, homecoming of the expatriate, telephone communications, video conferences, e-mails, letters, company newsletters, and so on.

- Finally, the expatriate should keep in touch not only with his or her home company, but also with his or her family and friends,[19] because being separated from relatives and friends is one of the worst aspects mentioned by the expatriates about their international assignment.

According to Katz and Seifer[54] (p. 42), in-post support systems should be established and coordinated between repatriated staff, senior expatriated staff, and new expatriates. However, the practices in the organizations do not correspond to the suggestions in the literature. The establishment of mentorship programs in the home company is not much developed. Marchon[8] studies expatriation practices in five Swiss multinationals. He found that only one company, Holcim, organizes formal contacts between expatriates and the HR department of the home country, twice a year. Otherwise, the relations an expatriate could have with his or her former subsidiary are generally left to the initiative of the employee.

Support for the Family. The spouse is the most likeliest person to suffer as a consequence of an international assignment, especially if he or she gave up his or her work to follow the assignee and is not reemployed in the new location.

So the company should help the spouse to develop his or her personal network. For example, the company could bring the spouses of expatriates together or encourage the spouses of other employees to take an interest in the newly relocated spouse and provide him/her with information about the neighborhood, the local activities, and serve as a source of new friendship.

- *Language courses* should be provided for the spouses during the assignment, since they will have frequent contacts with the local population when accomplishing the basic tasks of household, going shopping, or dealing with the school. Shaffer and Harrison (Bauer and Taylor[55], p. 136) established that language skills is the factor that most influence the ability of the spouse to rebuild a personal sense of identity and, as a result, achieve greater adjustment.
- The organization should also provide a support for the spouses who want to work in the country of assignment, for example by providing a briefing about the local employment conditions and the way to apply. If no job is found, the spouse could be given the opportunity to continue education.
- Finally, the children's adjustment and education are critical issues in the mind of most expatriated parents. The company must make sure that the children will be able to attend a school providing a good teaching. In many areas, only private, international, or even boarding schools can be considered and the company should take the costs in charge.

Performance Appraisal

The evaluation serves several purposes: development, evaluation of the employee's contribution, give grounds to administrative decisions regarding, for instance, compensation and promotions. Individual performance management involves a formal process of goal setting, performance appraisal, and feedback. When designing a performance appraisal system, at least four elements should be taken into account: the objectives of the organization, the staffing perspective, the internationalization strategies, and the particularities of the local context. The difficulties and specificities of performance appraisal in an international context come from the possible conflict between global and subsidiary objectives, the problem of noncomparability of data between subsidiaries, the volatility of the international market, and the variable levels of market maturity. Further, it is important to reconcile the tension between the need for universal appraisal standards with specific objectives in local units, and to recognize that more time may be needed to achieve results in markets which enjoy little supporting infrastructure from the parent company.[56] The principal challenges related to the performance evaluation of the expatriates are the determination of the evaluation criteria, the choice of the evaluators, and the delivery of timely and culturally sensitive feedback.

The Evaluation Criteria. The criteria must be relevant to the context of the assignment. Black et al.[4] (p. 166) mention that, in the case of an expatriate, the criteria which are seen as factors of success in the home country may make no sense in a foreign setting. The real factors of success of an international assignment can be totally different from the ones in the parent company. For example, for an expatriation in China, developing good relationships with the local government, diffusing a good image of the company, and establishing good working relationships with the suppliers may be much better for the long-term success of the firm than the immediate maximal profits. To determine the proper evaluation criteria, the evaluators should refer to the job description and specification, where the important goals and tasks of the position are defined. Hard, soft, and contextual goals tend to be translated into performance appraisal criteria. Dowling and Welch[12] mention that financial results for any subsidiary do not always reflect accurately its contribution to the achievements of the whole corporation and that, therefore, these should not be used as a primary input in performance appraisal. Janssens and Brett[5] mention that performance appraisal of subsidiary managers against hard criteria is often complemented by frequent visits by headquarter staff and meetings with executives from the parent company. Soft criteria are used to complement the hard ones and take into account arrears that are difficult to quantify like leadership or communication skills. However, in an international context, the evaluation of these soft criteria is somewhat subjective and more complicated due to cultural biases. An appraisal system using multiple hard, soft, and contextual criteria is strongly recommended in the relevant literature. Lindholm et al.[57] mention that European firms are more likely to pay close attention on long-term goals rather that the short-term measures used by US companies. In part, this reflects the growing use of international assignments for developmental purposes in European MNEs and the greater integration of expatriation into the overall career development process in European firms.[58]

The Evaluators. As in any evaluation, the raters must have the competencies and the experience necessary to assess correctly the performance of the expatriate, be given regular opportunities to directly observe the performance, and be motivated to do so.

Theoretically, the evaluators can be a manager from the home country organization or from the regional headquarter, the immediate superior of the expatriate in the host country if there is one, peer managers, clients, and the expatriate himself. Black et al.[4] (p. 175) suggest that a team of organization members should be involved in the performance appraisal of global managers: the team coordinator should be a senior HRM manager and would have to collect and analyze the feedback from the other team members: the expatriate's on-site superior, peer managers, subordinates, clients, and the expatriate himself. The authors suggest to rely on several rater's evaluations to avoid possible biases.

Several studies have focused on the expatriates' evaluation practices in MNE, in US and in Europe. In practice, the local supervisor is the most likely possibility to assess the expatriate performance. Gregersen et al.[59] surveyed HR directors in 58 US multinationals. They report that in the USA the most common rater is the expatriate's immediate supervisor, either from the host country (74%) or from the home country (39%). Moreover, they found that 81 percent of the firms used more than one rater when assessing expatriate performance. The immediate supervisor (in either the home or the host country), the expatriate as self-rater, and the HR manager (either home or host country based) were commonly used as multiple evaluators of expatriate performance. Half of the expatriate group (51%) were on performance-based bonus systems linked to the outcome of the evaluation. The majority of the firms reported annual appraisal practices.

Suutari and Brewster[60] studied the management practices among 170 Finnish expatriates. In Finnish MNE, most commonly, the expats' evaluation is carried out by a foreign supervisor (36%) or by a Finnish supervisor (22%), but other forms like evaluation by the managing directors or area/country managers, who were not direct supervisors of the expatriates, were also common. Of these firms, 76 percent used the same standardized appraisal forms for the expatriate appraisal.

Finally, Marchon[8] studied the evaluation practices in five Swiss multinationals. In all the five studied multinationals (Tetra Pak, Holcim, Novartis, Credit Suisse, and Nestlé), the work of the expatriate is evaluated by the direct supervisor in the host country. At Tetra Pak, Credit Suisse, and Novartis, any assignee is evaluated by his or her direct supervisor, who sets the objectives, assesses the performance, as it is the case for any other employee. At Holcim, the expatriates are also evaluated by the direct local supervisor but using a standardized form developed by the headquarters for the assessment of international assignees. Surprisingly, only one company, Nestlé, has put into place a process by which the home company receives the evaluation of the expatriate's work. The evaluation system is standardized within the group, and is the same for the expatriate and the local employees, but in the case of the expatriate, a report on his performance is sent once a year to his or her home company. In none of the five organizations, a formal team is created for the evaluation of the expatriates.

The performance Feedback. Provision of timely and regular feedback is an important element of an appraisal system in terms of meeting and revising goals, and in motivating work effort. Most of the expatriates are evaluated once a year and sometimes by a geographically distant evaluator, which makes it difficult for them to get timely and regular feedback on anything else than hard criteria. Another difficulty is that sometimes the evaluator is not from the same culture, and that giving feedback must be done in a culturally sensitive manner. People from different cultures give and take appraisal feedback in very different ways. At Pepsi-Cola International, instant feedback is one of the five elements of their standardized performance appraisal system, along with coaching, accountability-based performance appraisals, development feedback, and HR plan.[56] The common system provides guidelines for each of these practices but allow for cultural adaptation of these practices. For example, the instant feedback practice is based on the principle that any idea about any employee's performance is raised appropriately and discussed in a sensitive manner. The "how it is done" is locally adjusted to the different cultures. In Asian cultures, feedback can be tough and direct but never given in public; Indian employees expect some great extent of specificity and precision, Latins can argue very strongly in case of disagreement. Pepsi-Cola International managed to balance the imperative of standardization with the other imperative of cultural sensitivity.

Compensation of International Employees

The objectives of an effective compensation system are to attract and retain quality people for global assignments and to motivate them to an acceptable and ever-improving standard of performance.

Total pay packages have four components: the base salary, taxes, benefits, and allowances. Three standard methods are regularly utilized by multinational companies to determine the base salary of their international employees: the balance sheet (or home based) approach, the local market (or host based) approach and the international approach. Then, different kinds of allowances are meant to compensate particular troubles related to the relocation. Finally, taxes and benefits have to be fixed.

1. Three methods to determine the base salary
   a. *Balance Sheet Approach.* This is the most commonly used approach. It entails developing a total compensation package that equalizes the purchasing power of the expatriate with that of employees in similar positions in the home country and provides incentives to offset the inconveniences of the relocation. The employee starts with a set of costs for taxes, housing, goods and services, and saving (reserve) in the home country. In the host country, these costs are higher. The company must then make up for the difference between costs in the home and costs in the host country. On top of this, the company must provide a premium/incentive for the employee to go through the trouble of the relocation. This approach is particularly recommended when expatriates come back home directly after their assignment and works well when expatriates originate from the same home country.
   b. *Host-based Approach.* The host-based approach calculates the base salary relating to the host-country standards. Typical

allowances will also be added in order to create a fair compensation package. This method reduces the inequality between expatriates coming from different locations and working in the same area, as well as the inequity between local employees and expatriates. But such system is only effective if the country of destination have relatively high wages, because it is easier to convince individuals to accept pay scales that are greater than what they would have otherwise. This approach is principally used by companies which have little need for expatriation.

    c. *International Approach*. The international approach tries to create an equitable system among all international employees. This method begins with a common point of reference for expatriates who receive equivalent pay and benefits regardless of their country of destination. This approach is more easily applicable when the international employees are career internationalists and move from one foreign assignment to another. This approach is often more costly and is used by companies needing as small number of global managers.

2. Tax equalization allowances

Tax equalization allowances are necessary because of the countries' different taxation systems. Under most tax equalization programs, the company withholds the amount of tax to be paid in the home country and pays all of the supplementary taxes accrued in the host country.

3. Benefits

Most of the difficulties encountered at this place relate to the transportability of the pension plans and the heath care coverage. Here are examples of the questions raised: If an expatriate contributing to the home country pension plan is transferred abroad, should he take a new pension plan in the host country or should he continue contributing to the home country plan? How can the company ensure that the expatriate will have equal health care coverage than their colleagues back home?

4. Allowances

Finally, all kinds of allowances are offered to make the expatriate assignment less unattractive. The allowances can be offered in nature or in cash. They can be paid in a lump sum or throughout the assignment as a part of the monthly compensation. The amount usually depends on the employee's position, family size, and area of destination.

- Cost of living allowances are payments that offset the differences in expenditures on day-to-day necessities between the host country and the parent country.
- Housing allowances ensure that the expatriate can maintain the same home country housing standard.
- Education allowances cover the educational costs of the children of the expatriate, when they have to be placed in private home country language schools.
- Relocation allowances usually cover the costs of the moving.
- Home-leave allowance consists in air fare between the countries of assignment and origin for the expatriate and his or her family.

Repatriation and Retention

The repatriation is the activity of bringing the expatriate back to the home organization. Although it is now widely recognized by managers and academics that repatriation needs careful managing, this step is generally neglected. In this section, we will examine the different problems faced by repatriates, then we will discuss some retention issues and finally we will see how organizations could build an effective repatriation system.

Potential Problems Faced by the Expatriates

Although the expatriate and his or her family reintegrate their culture of origin, a several-year experience in a foreign culture makes the rehabilitation difficult. After living abroad for years, the expatriate and his or her family have changed, the home country and the home organization also.

So, when returning home, the expatriate and the whole family may face a "reverse culture shock." If nothing is undertaken to minimize its impact, the employee will suffer from maladjustment, which could lead to job under-performance and job dissatisfaction. The other problems associated with re-entry into the home organization include loss of status, loss of autonomy, loss of career direction, loss of income, and a feeling that their international experience is undervalued by the company.[61] Interestingly, concern over re-entry was cited as a significant reason affecting expatriate performance in European MNEs.[62] For many European MNEs, this problem has become more acute in recent years because expansion of foreign operations has often taken place at the same time as rationalization of domestic operations, and fewer unfilled positions are available to returning expatriates in most companies.[61]

The family may also face important challenges during the repatriation. The spouse may encounter difficulties to reintegrate into the domestic employment market, especially if he or she has not worked during the assignment. The children may come back to a country where they have been out of touch with the latest events and fashion styles, and may have difficulties to adjust to a new educational system.

Moreover, after years abroad, expatriates return to an organization that may have undergone significant changes in strategy, structure, information and assessment systems, and in formal and informal processes. If the communication during the assignment was insufficient, the expatriate may feel a loss of connection with the home office, which can enhance an impression of isolation and encourage the repatriate to leave the company. In the next paragraphs, we will examine how to build an effective repatriation system.

Building an Effective Repatriation Process

The company must anticipate the repatriation problems and plan actions to facilitate the reintegration of its international employees and their family. Most of the methods used to facilitate the adjustment process before the transfer can also be used for the repatriation process. In the next paragraphs, we will examine the steps of an effective repatriation process, which starts during the assignment and extends after the coming back home. The authors in the field recommend generally three steps in the preparation of the repatriation process.

1. *Determination of Ownership for the Repatriation Activities.* Normally, this should have been clarified before the departure. Black et al.[4] propose the creation of a repatriation team, consisting of an HR department representative and the expatriate's supervisor in the home country, or his sponsor/mentor. The role of this team is to initiate the preparation for the return and to take responsibility for identifying an appropriate return position for the expatriate. Collaboration between home and host HR and line management is essential when it comes to the managing of the international assignments. Confusion will make communication between the expatriate and the HR more difficult, and will make the expatriate feel less supported.

2. *Pre-return Preparation.* The repatriation should be planned much before the effective home-coming, and should ideally start at least six months before the end of the international assignment.[63]

   • The company should give the expatriate sufficient time between the warning of the repatriation and the effective transfer to allow the expatriate and his or her family to make anticipatory adjustment before returning to the home country. Several information sources should be made available to the expatriate and his or her family to help them develop accurate expectations about the return.

- The company should inquire about the expectations of the expatriate regarding his or her expected return job and his or her career goals and initiate an internal search to find a suitable position. In the ideal case, expectations about re-entry should have been already set up at the end of the selection process. Even if a specific job at the end of the assignment cannot be guaranteed, the assignee should at least know what opportunities are available in the company and how they can be considered for them.
- The organization should appoint an organizational sponsor/mentor, who could be an accurate source of information about the company-related changes. The sponsor should have himself/herself experienced expatriation and have sufficient influence to act as a supporter for the expatriate
- Periodical visits to the home country just prior to the repatriation give the expatriate the opportunity to develop accurate expectations about what is happening in the home country and in the organization.
- The company should also provide pre-return training and orientation. Essential information about the repatriation process can be provided in a workshop/training program, including such matters as housing, financial compensation packages, school system, and so on.
- Finally, the company should provide assistance to the expatriate family to find a suitable accommodation back home.

3. *Post-return adjustment.* Black et al.[4] note that the most pivotal component of successful repatriation for expatriates is the selection of a return job assignment, taking into account the expats' skills, competencies, and the new interests developed during the international assignment. In order to avoid potential problems between the expatriate and his or her colleagues and supervisor, they could also attend training or an orientation program. The company could also organize a collective debriefing about the expats' international experience. Finally, in order to allow the expatriate to make the transition quietly, the organization should leave time for the expatriate, and give him one week off to settle down, or allow him/her to have reduced working hours during the first days.[25]

Exhibit 12.12 rates the effectiveness of different ways to reduce expatriate turnover, from high, medium to low effectiveness. The results are consistent with many past surveys. Survey respondents included both small and large organizations; for 79 percent of the respondents, the company headquarters

Exhibit 12.12

Methods of Reducing Expatriate Turnover and their Effectiveness

Method	High	Medium	Low
Chance to use experience	62%	32%	6%
Recognition	60	34	6
Position choices upon return	59	33	8
Repatriation career support	31	52	17
Response to security issues	26	51	23
Improve performance evaluation	25	51	24
Family repatriation support	22	48	30

Source: GMAC Relocation Services.[64]

was in the United States. In most cases, respondents were senior HR professionals and/or managers of international relocation programs.

Retention. Many expatriates leave their company on return[60] with the consequent loss of investment and expertise. Moreover, the departure of high-potential repatriates is not only a loss for the company, but may give an advantage to competitors that could attract them and take advantage of their international experience.

Lazagrova and Caligiuri[65] (p. 395) note that most activities that ensure high retention after repatriation happen during rather than after the assignment. According to the 1999 Global Relocation Trends Report (cited by Lazagrova and Caligiuri[65] (p. 390), 12 percent of the expatriates leave their company within a year after returning home and 13 percent leave within the following year, for a total of 25 percent of international managers leaving their company within two years after repatriation. Vermond[66] (pp. 31–32) put forward the fact that many companies, between 25 and 33 percent of the respondents in her survey, do not know the rate of assignees leaving the organization within the twelve months. These statistics show that companies have not yet understood the importance of the retention of their expatriates and do not consider expatriation as an investment.

Women in the Global Arena

The number of female expatriates is low in relation to the overall size of the qualified labor pool.[67] However, the proportion of females is increasing clearly and steadily, from only 5 percent in the ORC 1992 survey to 14 percent in the ORC 2002 survey, and even 18 percent in the GMAC-Relocation Survey 2002.

Several recent studies challenge the usual beliefs regarding the low suitability of females for international assignments.

Caligiuri and Tung[68] studied the performance of male and female expatriates in US-based multinationals. They found that females can perform equally as well as males regardless of a country's attitude toward women in managerial positions.

Stroh et al.[69] found that US and Canadian women are interested in and likely to accept international assignments. The authors note that the women in their study tended to believe that their employers were reluctant to propose an international assignment to them, although their supervisors did not think so.

Fishlmayr[70] studied the external and the self-established barriers to Australian females taking international assignments. The author found three major external barriers: HR managers reluctant to select female candidates, culturally tough locations preclude female expatriates, and those selecting expatriates have stereotypes in their minds that influence the decisions. The major self-established barriers were the following: some women have limited willingness, the dual-career couple, and the fact that women are often a barrier to their own careers by behaving according to gender-based roles. The author concludes that women are partly responsible for their underrepresentation.

Mayrhofer and Scullion[71] studied the experiences of male and female expatriates in the German clothing industry in different countries, including the Muslim ones. They found few differences in the experiences of both groups. However, female expatriates put more values on integration of spouse/family issues before and during the assignment than did their male counterparts in their sample.

Finally, Napier and Taylor[72] studied female expatriates from different countries, Japan, China, and Turkey, distinguishing between traditional expatriates, trailers (spouses of males expatriates), and self-selected expatriates. The authors found that the main challenge of these women was gaining credibility with local clients. Accommodating cultural differences and maintaining an active social life and appropriate interpersonal skills were factors of successes in their missions. Being foreign women granted them higher visibility, and so was an advantage in terms of getting access to key local persons.

To conclude, the predictors of success of women expatriates are the same as for their male counterparts. The differences between both genders are the degree of importance granted to the different factors of adjustment/performance, the value placed on intercultural training issues, and the fact that dual career issues are a greater barrier for female mobility as males are more reluctant to follow their spouse overseas.

Companies that are serious in encouraging women to work as expats will develop a distinct competitive advantage: by stimulating and actively supporting female expat careers, the pool of talent for top management positions gets filled with a larger number of qualified individuals. This increases the chance of appointing the right person for the right top job. With more women becoming expats, it can be expected that traditional assumptions and the related questions will gradually disappear.[73]

Closing Case

A Dilemma

In this UAE MNE, top management at HQ believes local markets are very distinct and local management has a high degree of autonomy. International communication, co-ordination and control are low—the most important monitoring mechanisms are the yearly budgets and the financial objectives for foreign subsidiaries. You are Mohammad, the HRM manager at the head office, in Sharjah, UAE.

In the German subsidiary (250 employees), in Munich, Jürgen, the HR Manager fell ill shortly after his assistant Thomas left for personal reasons. The director will not come back before 5 weeks. The German HRM department is totally disorganized.

The German managing director of the subsidiary, who is clueless, ask you to help them: They urgently need to recruit one high potential manager to replace Thomas, the assistant. This person will help the HR manager in all his activities and specifically be responsible for TQM, Career Development and Training activities in the German subsidiary.

Chapter Summary

Throughout this chapter, we have studied five topics related to iHRM.

First, we have examined the four major approaches to staffing foreign operations: ethnocentric, polycentric, geocentric, and regiocentric. Secondly, we have examined the reasons for using international assignments: position filling, sharing and transferring knowledge, developing employees, controlling and coordination of international activities. Thirdly, we have detailed the different categories of international personnel: PCNs, HCNs, and TCNs, and impatriates. We have also presented the different types of international assignment for PCNs: expatriates, short-term assignees, international commuters and frequent flyers, global managers, and high potentials. Fourthly, we presented the different steps of Waxin (2007) model for strategic management of international assignments. The model consists of eight steps: strategic planning and job analysis, recruitment, selection, preparation to transfer, cross-cultural adjustment and organizational support, performance appraisal, compensation, and repatriation and retention. Finally, we have examined the position of women in the global arena today.

Question: What kind of international employee do you prefer to recruit? Briefly describe the job content, job requirements, and job context of this position.

If you employ a PCN employee, how will you prepare him/her for this international assignment?

Source: Marie-France Waxin.[1]

Review and Discussion Questions

1. What are the different approaches to international staffing? Outline their main characteristics.
2. What are the functions of international assignments?
3. What are the reasons for using international assignments?
4. What are the positive and negative aspects of a Parent Country National?
5. Discuss the statement that most expatriate selection decisions are made informally.
6. What are the challenges faced in training expatriate managers?
7. What organizational factors have an impact on expatriate's cross-cultural adjustment?
8. What are the main objectives of a multinational Company's compensation policy?
9. Describe the main differences between the different methods used to determine the expatriate's base salary.
10. What elements would you include in a repatriation program?

Endnotes

1. Waxin, M.-F., Strategic Management of International Assignments, unpublished document, 2006.
2. Perlmutter H., "The tortuous evolution of the multinational corporation". Columbia Journal of World Business, 1969, pp. 9–18.
3. Heenan, D. A. and Perlmutter, H, Multinational Organization Development (Reading, MA: Addison-Wesley, 1979), pp. 18–19.
4. Black J. S., Gregersen H. B. and Mendenhall M. (eds), Global Assignments: Successfully Expatriating and Repatriating International Managers, (San Francisco: Jossey-Bass, 1992).

5. Janssens M. and Brett J. M., "Coordinating global companies: the effects of electronic communication, organizational commitment, and a multi-cultural managerial workforce". Trend in Organizational Behavior, Vol. 1, 1994, pp. 31–46.

6. Harris H. (ed.), "Strategic management of international workers", Innovations in international HR, Vol. 28(1), Winter 2002, pp. 1–5, Organizational resource consellors, London, 2002.

7. Leslie Gross Klaff, "Thinning the ranks of the 'career expats' at Avaya", Workforce Management, October 2004, pp. 84–87.

8. Marchon J. (ed.), 2004, "Expatriation management: Theoretical principles and practices in Swiss-based multinational companies" (Master's thesis, Economics and Social Sciences Faculty, University of Fribourg, Switzerland), 2004.

9. Harris, H. and Holden, L., "Between autonomy and control: expatriate managers and strategic IHRM in SME". Thunderbird International Review, Vol. 43(1), 2001, pp. 77–101.

10. Black, J. S. and Gregersen, H. B., "The right way to manage expats". Harvard Business Review, March–April 1999, pp. 52–60.

11. Waxin, M.-F., Davoine, E. and Barmeyer, C. "Gestion des Resources Humaines Internationales" (Paris: Les Editions de Liaisons, 2007).

12. Dowling Peter J. and Denice E. Welch (eds), International Human Resource Management: Managing People in Multinational Context (London: Thomson Learning, 2004).

13. Tahvanainen, M. (ed.), "Expatriate performance management: The case of Nokia Telecommunications", Acta Universitatis Oeconomicae Helsingiensis A-134, Helsinki School of Economics and Business Administration, Helsinki, 1998.

14. Harvey M., "Focusing the international personnel performance appraisal process". Human Resource Development Quarterly, Vol. 8(1), 1997, pp. 41–62.

15. Waxin, M.-F. "The adjustability of the expatriate manager: Proposal of an improved measurement scale", 20th Workshop on Strategic Human Resource Management, Brussels, April 28–29, 2005.

16. Harris, H. and Brewster, C. "The coffee-machine system: How international selection really works". The International Journal of Human Resource Management, Vol. 10 (3), 1999, pp. 488–500.

17. Harvey, M. and Novicevic, M, "Selecting expatriates for increasingly complex global assignments". Career Development International, Vol. 6(2), 2001, pp. 69–86.

18. Jordan, J. and Cartwright, S, "Selecting expatriate managers: Key traits and competencies". Leadership and Organization Development Journal, Vol. 19(2), 1998, pp. 89–96.

19. Linehan, M., Morley, M. and Walsh, J. (eds): International Human Resource Management and Expatriate Tranfers: Irish Experiences (Dublin: Blackhall, 2002), pp. 108–109.

20. Harvey, M, "The selection of managers for foreign assignments: A planning perspective". Columbia Journal of World Business, Vol. 31(4), 1996, pp. 102–118.

21. Finn, L. and Morley, M. (2002) in Linehan, M., Morley, M. and Walsh, J. (eds), "International Human Resource Management and Expatriate Transfers". Irish Experiences (Dublin: Blackhall, 2000), p. 102.

22. Forster, N. and Johnsen M, "Expatriate management policies in UK companies new to the international scene". The International Journal of Human Resource Management, Vol. 7(1), 1996, pp. 177–205.

23. Patton C, "Match Game". Human Resource Executive, 2001, pp. 36–41.

24. Stahl, "Between ethnocentrism and assimilation: Challenges and coping strategies of expatriate managers". Academy of Management Proceedings, IM: E1-E6, 2000.

25. Ashamalla, M, "International human resources practices: the challenge of expatriation. Competitiveness review", Vol. 8(2), 1998, pp. 54–65.

26. Mendenhall, M. and Oddou, G, "Toward a comprehensive model of international adjustment: An integration of multiple theoretical perspectives". Academy of Management Review, Vol. 16(2), 1991, pp. 291–317.

27. Brislin, R. W. (ed.). "Orientation programs for cross-cultural preparation", in Marsella A. J., Tharp G., Ciborowski T. J. (eds), Perspectives on Cross-cultural Psychology, pp. 87–304 (Orlando: Acadmic Press, 1979).

28. Tung, R., "Selection and training of personnel for overseas assignments". Columbia Journal of World business, Vol. 16(1), 1981, pp. 68–78.

29. Mendenhall, M., Dunbar E. and Oddou G, "Expatriate selection, training and career pathing: A review and critique". Human Resource Management, Vol. 26(3), 1987, pp. 331–345.

30. Gertsen, M., Intercultural Competence and Expatriates, (Oslo Business School, 1990).

31. Deshpande, S. P. and Viswesvaran C, "Is cross-cultural training of expatriate Managers effective: A meta analysis". International Journal of Intercultural Relations, Vol. 26(3), 1992, pp. 295–310.

32. Waxin, M. F. and Panaccio, A. J, "Cross-cultural training to facilitate expatriate adjustment: It works!" Personnel Review, Special Issue on global human resource management (development), Vol. 34(1), 2005.

33. Selmer, J., "The preference for pre-departure or post-arrival cross-cultural training – An exploratory approach". Journal of Managerial Psychology, Vol. 16(1), 2001, pp. 50–58.

34. Mendenhall, M. E. and Stahl G, "Expatriate training and development: Where do we go from here?" Human Resource Management, Vol. 39(2), 2000, pp. 251–265.

35. Harris J. E, "Moving managers internationally: The care and feeding of expatriates". Human Resources Planning, Vol. 12, 1989, pp. 49–53.

36. Parker, B. and McEvoy, G. M, "Initial examination of a model of intercultural adjustment". International Journal of Intercultural Relations, Vol. 17, 1993, pp. 355–379.

37. Aryee, S. and Stone, R. J, "Work experiences, work adjustment and psychological well being of expatriate employees in Hong Kong". International Journal of Human Resource Management, Vol. 7(1), 1996, pp. 150–164.

38. Black, J. S, "Work-role transition: A study of American expatriate managers in Japan". Journal of International Business Studies, Vol.(19), 1988, pp. 274–291.

39. Adler, N. J. (ed.), International Dimensions of Organizational Behavior. p. 391 (Cincinnati: South-Western, 2002).

40. Black J. S. and Mendenhall M, "The U-curve adjustment hypothesis revisited: A review and theoretical framework". Journal of International Business Studies, Vol. 22, 1991, pp. 225–47.

41. Black, J. S. and Stephens, G. K, "Expatriate adjustment and intent to stay in pacific rim overseas assignments". Journal of Management, Vol. 15, 1989, pp. 529–544.

42. Black, J. S. and Gregersen, H. B, "Antecedents to cross-cultural adjustment for expatriates in Pacific Rim assignments". Human Relations, Vol. 44(5), 1991, pp. 497–515.

43. Black J. S., Mendenhall M. and Oddou G, "Toward a comprehensive model of International adjustment: An integration of multiple theoretical perspectives". Academy of Management Review, Vol. 16(2), 1991, pp. 291–317.

44. Feldman D. C. and Thomas D. C, "From desert shield to desert storm: Life as an expatriate during the Persian Gulf War". Organizational Dynamics, Vol. 20, 1992, pp. 37–47.

45. Bhaskar-Shrinivas, P., Harrison, D. A., Schaffer, M. A. and Luk, D. M, "Input based and time based models of international adjustment: Meta-analytic evidence and theoretical extensions". Academy of Management Journal, Vol. 48(2), 2005, pp. 257–281.

46. Waxin, M. F, "Expatriates' interaction adjustment: The direct and moderator effects of culture of origin". International Journal of Intercultural Relations, Vol. 28(1), February 2004, pp. 61–79.

47. Waxin, M. F. and Chandon, J.-L., "L'adaptation au travail des expatriés: Ses déterminants et l'effet du pays d'origine". Gestion des Ressources Humaines, Vol. 47(1), 2003, pp. 57–71.

48. Eschbach, D. M., Parker, G. E. and Stoeberl, P. A, "American repatriated employees' retrospective assessments of the effects of cross-cultural training on their adaptation

to International assignments". International Journal of Human Resource Management, Vol. 12(2), 2001, pp. 270–87.

49. Mendenhall M. and Oddou G., "The dimensions of expatriate acculturation". Academy of Management Review, Vol. 10(3), 1985, pp. 39–47.

50. Black, J. S, "The relationship of personal characteristics with the adjustment of Japanese expatriate Managers". Management International Review, Vol. 30, 1990, pp. 119–134.

51. Cerdin, J.-L., Chandon, J.-L. and Waxin, M.-F, "The Adaptability of the French expatriates, a confirmatory analysis". EIASM Workshop on International Human Resource Management, Carlos III University, Madrid, September 2000.

52. Selmer, J., "To Train or Not to Train? European Expatriate Managers in China". International Journal of Cross Cultural Management, Vol. 2(1), 2002, pp. 37–51.

53. Hippler, T. in Linehan, M., Morley, M. and Walsh, J. (eds), International Human Resource Management and Expatriate Transfers: Irish Experiences (Dublin, Blackhall, 2002).

54. Katz, J. P. and Seifer, D. M., "It's a different world out there: planning for expatriate success through selection, pre-departure training and on-site socialization". Human Resource Planning, Vol. 19(2), 1996, pp. 32–49.

55. Bauer, T. and Taylor, S., "When managing expatriate adjustment, don't forget the spouse". Academy of Management Executive, Vol. 15(4), 2001, pp. 135–137.

56. Schuler, R. S., Fulkerson, J. R. and Dowling, P. J., "Strategic performance measurement and management in multinational corporations". Human Resource Management, Vol. 30(3), 1991, pp. 365–392.

57. Lindblom, N., Tahvanainen, M. and Bjorkman, I., In Brewster, C. and Harris, H. (eds), International HRM: Contemporary Issues in Europe, Routledge, London, 1999.

58. Scullion, H., "International human resource management". in J. Storey (ed.) Human Resource Management. (London: International Thomson Publishing, 2001).

59. Gregersen, H. B., Hite, J. M. and Black, J. S., "Expatriat performance appraisal in US multinational firms". Journal of International Business Studies, Vol. 27(4), 1996, pp. 711–738.

60. Suutari, V. and Brewster, C., "Expatriate management practices and perceived relevance: Evidence from Finnish expatriates". Personnel Review, Vol. 30(5), 2001, pp. 554–577.

61. Scullion, H. and Brewster, C., "The Management of Expatriates: Messages from Europe". Journal of World Business, Vol. 36(4), 2001, pp. 346–365.

62. Forster, N., "The myth of the international manager". International Journal of Human Resource Management, Vol. 1, 2000, pp. 126–142.

63. Jassawalla, A., Connolly, T. and Slojkowski, L., "Issue of effective repatriation: A model and managerial implications". SAM advanced Management Journal, Vol. 69(2), 2004, pp. 38–46.

64. GMAC Relocation Services, National Foreign Trade Council and the SHRM Global Forum, in Workforce Management Online, August 2004.

65. Lazarova, M. and Caligiuri P., "Retaining repatriates, the role of organizational support practices". Journal of World business, Vol. 36(4), 2001, pp. 389–401.

66. Vermond, K., "Expatriates come home". CMA Management, Vol. 75(7), 2001, pp. 30–33.

67. Linehan, M., Senior Female International Managers. Aldershot: Ashgate Publishing, 1999.
    Scullion, H. and Brewster, C, "The Management of Expatriates: Messages from Europe". Journal of World Business Vol. 36(4), 2001, pp. 346–365.

68. Caligiuri, P. A. and Tung, R. L., "Comparing the success of male and female expatriates from a US-based multinational company". International Journal of Human Resource Management, Vol. 10(5), 1999, pp. 763–82.

69. Stroh, L. K., Varma, A. and Valy-Durbin, S.J., "Why are women let at home: Are they unwilling to go on international assignments?" Journal of World Business, Vol. 35(3), 2000, pp. 241–255.

70. Fischlmayr, I. C., "Female self-perception as barrier to international careers?" International Journal of Human Resource Management, Vol. 13(5), 2002, pp. 773–783.

71. Mayrhofer, W. and Scullion, H., "Female expatriates in international business: emperical evidence from the German clothing industry". International Journal of Human Resource Management, Vol. 13(5), 2002, pp. 815–836.

72. Napier, N. K. and Taylor, S., "Experiences of women Professionals abroad: Comparisons across Japan, China, Turkey". International Journal of Human resource Management, Vol. 13(5), 2002, pp. 837–851.

73. Visser, M., "Women expatriates: What do you do all day?", Reprinted from the XPat Journal, Spring 2005.

13

Doing Business in the Industrialized Countries

Alkis Thrasou and Marios I. Katsioloudes, Spyros Hadjidakis

Objectives

Through this chapter, the student will be exposed to:

- Understand the wider position and role of the industrialized countries in the context of global affairs, changes, and relationships, as well as the historical developments that led to these
- Identify the elements that constitute the business macro-environment and their importance, and be able to distinguish the industrialized countries based on their macro-environmental characteristics
- Comprehend the factors that underlie consumer behavior, and also to differentiate the behavior of consumers in industrialized countries from that of consumers in other countries
- Value the knowledge on consumer behavior in the industrialized countries, and be in a position to utilize it toward achieving business objectives
- Recognize the generic characteristics of the competitive environment of industrialized countries, monitor the parameters of individual competitive environments, and interpret their major elements
- Formulate, plan, and manage strategies that utilize their knowledge of the industrialized countries' competitive environment and consumer needs and behavior
- Structure, organize, and lead businesses in the industrialized countries based on the constrictions imposed and potentialities offered by the economic, cultural, regulatory, and other macro-environmental conditions

- Generally be in a position to not only differentiate the business environment and practice of the industrialized countries vis-à-vis the rest of the world, but also appreciate the uniqueness and distinctiveness of individual countries and areas within them
- Interrelate all the elements, factors, forces, and parameters presented in this chapter, to achieve a comprehensive and spherical perception of the complex conditions under which businesses operate in the industrialized countries.

Opening Case

Harley–Davidson—The Old Years

Harley–Davidson Motorcycle Company was established in 1903 by William Harley, Walter William, and Arthur Davidson, who built their first three motorcycles in a shed in Milwaukee. In 1909, the company introduced its trademark bike: a two cylinder, V-twin engine (the fastest motorcycle at that time), able to reach speeds of 60 mph. However, a few years later the competition was becoming stiffer. During World War I, the demand for US motorcycles grew tremendously overseas. As a result, Harley–Davidson (HD) became a leader in innovative engineering in the 1920s. With the introduction of the front brake and "teardrop" gas tanks, Harley was quickly developing its mystic appearance. The industry, which was thriving after World War I, was diminishing quickly as a result of the Great Depression. As one of only two remaining motorcycle companies, HD survived because of exports and sales to the police and military.

Representative of the World War I motorcycle market, HD prospered from military purchasing during World War II. Over 90,000 cycles were built for the military which elevated their production to record levels and earned them the coveted Army-Navy "E" award for excellence in war-time production. After the war, Harley went from producing military to recreational bikes. Harley developed and introduced the K-model (1952), Sportster ("Superbike," 1957), and Duo-Glide (1958) motorcycles. By 1953, HD was the last remaining major motorcycle manufacturer in the United States.

The HD was taken over by the American Machine and Foundry (AMF) in 1969. AMF put the company up for sale in the late 1970s due to a gross reduction in sales. The reduction in sales was representative of a poor level of quality in the Harley bike compared to their Japanese counterpart. In 1981, thirteen members of the HD management team purchased the company from AMF in a leveraged buyout. But, within the first year, overall demand for motorcycles dropped dramatically and Harley's share of this market also continued to drop. This even-greater reduction in sales for Harley resulted in a large inventory of unsold products. Harley was aware that they would no longer be able to continue their business at their current production level and operating cost. Therefore, production was cut drastically, and more than 1800 of the 4000 employees were let go. In a move to help the floundering US motorcycle industry in 1983, President Ronald Reagan increased tariffs on large Japanese motorcycles from 4.4 to 49.4 percent. But this increase was effective only for 5 years and declined annually.

On December 31, 1985, 4 hours away from bankruptcy, CEO Richard Teerlink convinced Heller Financial of Chicago to accept a restructuring plan and to step in and bail out the company.

Question: What is HD's position in the global economy and more specifically, the industrialized world?

Source: http://stroked.virtualave.net/casestudy.shtml

Introduction—About the Industrialized Countries

The challenge of competing in the business arena of the industrialized countries is unparalleled, and matched only by the satisfaction of proving oneself of being worthy of such challenge. Doing business in the industrialized countries demands the ability to simultaneously handle a multitude of factors and forces, both in the macro- and in the micro-environments, and the wisdom to treat each one with the knowledge that they form the chain that supports an organization—a chain, though, only as strong as its weakest link.

This chapter will investigate and individually present the parameters affecting businesses in the industrialized countries, while retaining a spherical perspective that reveals their most important interrelationships. Strategy and marketing, organizational management and culture, external and internal environments, suppliers and intermediaries, competitors and customers, chance and the unknown are all studied and explained as the interwoven threads that make up the fabric of modern business. The aim of this chapter is not to provide a new perspective on business management theory nor to deepen or elaborate on any individual parts of it. The purpose is to provide a clear and comprehensive picture of the circumstances under which businesses in the most developed economies try to survive and succeed, and also the strategies, relationships, and organizational management approaches they employ in order to achieve their goals.

The various subjects are dealt with in the context of business activity. This necessitates, at a first level, the prioritization of the factors and elements according to their relative weight in relation to business. Secondly, a general assumption that the term "industrialized countries" refers to those which are widely accepted as being the most economically advanced ones, not merely as a matter of wealth and/or economic output, but also as a matter of their corresponding social organization and consumer behavioral complexity and development. At the time of publication of this book, this definition relates to countries such as the USA, Canada, most of the EU countries, Israel, Japan, the so-called "Tiger economies" of Asia, Australia, New Zealand, South Africa, and others. It is also stated that this chapter does not necessarily fully relate to all areas of these countries, as some are characterized by large internal economic and other macro-environmental differences, while it may well relate to specific areas of some countries, which would not be considered as belonging to the groups under study here, for example some of the metropolizes of the former East-European Block.

A Changing World—The Role of the Industrialized Countries

Change in the business environment is the work of events caused by historical forces or streams of related events such as the industrial revolution, the impact of dominant ideologies, the inequality of human circumstances, science and technology, the rise of the nation-states, great leaderships, and change.[1] This first decade of the third millennium finds the world changing at a pace once unimaginable, and organizations struggling to keep up while having a very hard time with longer-term planning. Globalization is shrinking, even eradicating distances and bringing down physical and cultural frontiers. Technological advances, cultural diversity, economic integration, political change, and root-deep human social evolution are forcing the business world to add a new word to its dictionary: globality.[2]

These historical developments that appeared at first to be largely economic and/or socio-political phenomena now fully present themselves as being an interrelated web of forces with complex direct and profound implications on the full spectrum of aspects of our human existence: economic, political, social, technological, cultural, psychological, and even natural. The industrialized countries lie at the heart of these changes as their main originators and the driving force behind the incessant reorganization of our world and our view of it. Some of these countries have in fact led many of the major changes of the past few centuries either through largely cultural forces (e.g., the Renaissance), technological forces (e.g., the industrial revolution), military forces (e.g., the two World Wars), political forces (e.g., the European integration), or a combination of these. Now, the industrialized countries, through their combined power, ability, influence, and weight on the world stage have lured, pulled, or pushed almost every country and nation into the dance of change and integration. A dance choreographed—perhaps for the first time—not by a close set of powerful individuals, but by the spontaneous improvization of the combined elements of investment, technology, information, politics, and militia—a choreography with means but no conscious or visible ends, a choreography for the dance and the dance alone.

Economic and Demographic Forces

The economic and their associated forces (demography, labor, etc.) constitute the driving power behind most social, political, cultural, and general historical developments in human evolution. For modern businesses, the interest in the economic environment relates primarily to factors that affect competition, the consumer purchasing power, and spending patterns.[3] The business manager, nevertheless, of a company operating in a democratic and free-enterprise country—a description largely fitting the industrialized countries—must answer a number of questions of general economic nature to understand the specific effects on his or her business, for example how and when will commodity prices change, what will be the implications, how will the interest rates change, how will consumer purchasing be affected, will stock and prices rise or fall, what will be the repercussions on wage-rates?[4] This section will list and describe the economic factors that mostly affect businesses, with a special emphasis on the ways in which these differ in the industrialized countries.

A New World Economy

The changes mentioned above gave rise to four new realities:[5] (1) an immense increase in the volume of capital movements internationally with the industrialized countries accounting for most, (2) a substantial increase in productivity, (3) the rise of the world economy to become the dominant economic unit. In other words, no company or government alone is powerful enough to determine the economic fate of its corporation or country independently of economic developments in the rest of the world, and (4) the success of the capitalist market system and the largely consequent failure of communism (referring purely to economic comparisons) have reshaped the world economic map and opened new markets and opportunities. This success of capitalism is by large the work of the industrialized countries which also appear to enjoy most of the fruits of change.[6]

Demographic Forces

Population is one of the two main indicators of market potential, the other being income (see p. 445). Population size itself is not usually a sufficient guide to market size, but for some products especially necessary ones, population figures may be a good first indicator for market potential. Industrialized countries include all sizes of population (Exhibit 13.1), but in considering this parameter one does not necessarily have to think in terms of individual countries. Regional economic cooperation and formation of associations, even amongst industrialized countries means that often the question of population relates to groups of countries, with the most notable example being the European Union. Population growth rate helps businesses to predict, among other things, future demand for their product or service. The world correlation between population growth rate and income per capita is negative, with most of the industrialized countries presenting very low to negative growth rates. In fact, only 3 percent of the world's population growth is likely to come from the developed nations. The obvious conclusion is that business in industrialized countries cannot expect any substantial increase of their markets' size as a result of changes in their own population.

Truly understanding population figures, though, involves more than a simple head count. The distribution of population is equally important; therefore, dividing people in a country according to their age group, sex, education, occupation, density, or other characteristics helps businesses understand the population better. The single most noticeable demographic trend in the industrialized countries is the changing age structure. Specifically, as a result of fewer births and increased life expectancy, the average age of the population is rising fast and this is expected to continue over the next fifty years.[7] The consequences on businesses are many and direct with the resulting change in consumer needs/behavior and the changing work-force age structure being first on the list. Population density also affects businesses but there is no clear pattern in relation to the industrialized countries.

Another major change, felt especially in the industrialized countries, is the changing family structure, with smaller families, working father and mother, and little leisure time. This demographic change has a profound impact on consumer behavior and needs, with greater demand for goods and services by the increasingly independent female portion of the population, outsourcing of services traditionally produced within a family, males taking up traditionally female workforce roles and vice versa, and other effects. The industrialized countries are also characterized by very high rates of literacy and overall education levels, affecting both the consumer needs and behavior and the potentialities of the available labor. Furthermore, the great economic development of these countries has attracted large numbers of foreign labor resulting in great cultural and other diversity, again affecting both

Exhibit 13.1

Total population (thousands)

	1994	1995	1996	1997	1998	1999	2000	2001	2002	2003	2004	2005
EU (25 countries)	445336.9	446390.2	447377.8	448318.4	449105.5	449974.7	451080.2	452015.9	452640.8	455049.5	457188.9[(e)]	459485.8[(e)]
EU (15 countries)	370133.8	371187.6	372230.4	373223.6	374066.2	375016.7	376203.9	377653.5	378361.5	380848.6	383047.2[(e)]	385380.8[(e)]
Euro-zone	297899.1	298655.3	299438.2	300198.9	300834.1	301457.6	302389.1	303558.7	304944.2	307060.0	308974.2[(e)]	310923.5[(e)]
Switzerland	6968.6	7019.0	7062.4	7081.3	7096.5	7123.5	7164.4	7204.1	7255.7	7313.9	7364.1	7418.4
United States	259159.0	261687.0	264162.2	266490.1	269106.3	271626.0	275562.7	:	:	:	291685.1	:
Japan	125033.5	125570.0	125503.8	124645.2	126109.7	126056.8	126550.0	:	:	:	:	:
Canada	29076.9	29437.0	29789.0	30110.7	30425.3	:	:	:	:	:	127273.8	:

(:) Not available

(e) Estimated value

Source: http://europa.eu.int/comm/eurostat

the consumer needs and behavior and the competitive and internal environments of businesses.[8] Lastly, urbanization, another demographic characteristic occurring more intensely in industrialized countries (but not only there) affects not only the concentration of populations but also their consumer needs, wants, and behavior.[9]

Income and Purchasing Power

Markets require not only people but people with money. Per capita income figures are averages of income per person and vary widely across countries, with the richest country (Switzerland) having an average of approximately 500 times that of the poorest ones (e.g., Mozambique). The industrialized countries have an income of over eight thousand euros per person.[10,11] Per capita income alone, though, is not enough to understand the potential of the market in relation to a product.

Another factor that needs to be considered is the distribution of income, in other words the degree to which wealth in a country is divided equally among its citizens. This is important information since the average income in a country with uneven distribution can imply, for example, that most of the population can afford certain goods while in reality the concentration of wealth in fact limits the purchasing power only to a small fraction of the population. Although very few countries have a moderately equal distribution of income, the industrialized countries are generally better at it (Exhibit 13.2) and therefore per capita income is more useful for these.[12,13]

Exhibit 13.2

Inequality of Income Distribution (Income Quintile Share Ratio)*										
	1995	1996	1997	1998	1999	2000	2001	2002	2003	2004
EU (25 countries)	:	:	:	:	:	:	4.5[(i,s)]	:	:	:
EU (15 countries)	5.1[(s)]	4.8[(s)]	4.7[(s)]	4.6[(s)]	4.6[(s)]	4.4[(s)]	4.6[(i,s)]	:	:	:
Euro-zone (12 countries)	5.1[(s)]	4.8[(s)]	4.7[(s)]	4.5[(s)]	4.5[(s)]	4.3[(s)]	4.5[(i,s)]	:	:	:

(:) Not available
(i) See explanatory text
(s) Eurostat estimate
* The ratio of total income received by the 20 percent of the population with the highest income (top quintile) to that received by the 20 percent of the population with the lowest income (lowest quintile). Income must be understood as equivalized disposable income.

A third factor that cannot be omitted is purchasing power, which relates to a simple fact: that the same amount of money does not buy the same goods everywhere. Not only because the actual price differs, but also because the needs of people differ from country to country and area to area. Taking into account this factor affects the industrialized countries largely negatively compared to the predictions based on per capita income and income distribution, as naturally prices are usually higher and needs are more, both in number and in complexity.[14,15]

Labor Forces[16]

Labor is a major economic factor and its major determinants are its cost, quality, quantity, composition/diversity, mobility, organization, and regulation. With regard to the industrialized countries, these characteristics are not uniform, though some patterns are easily observed. The cost of labor is undoubtedly on average very high in these countries and largely and naturally also relates to their income per capita. Labor quality again is very high in industrialized countries, both as a result of their high levels of education, but also as a result of their culture and mentality toward work and business. Even within industrialized countries, labor quantity varies from country to country, industry to industry and level to level. Additionally, the prospect of much higher earnings and/or political conditions in their own countries has pushed millions of workers from poorer countries to the industrialized ones. This has provided the latter with cheaper-than-local labor willing to undertake tasks normally avoided by locals and helped the industrialized countries' business to remain cost-effective and competitive. In the United States, over 10 percent of the residing population is foreign-born (US Census Bureau). This phenomenon—in combination with the demographic changes in age structure, the liberalization of women, and the social and cultural freedom found in the industrialized countries—has created a diverse workforce with mixed characteristics in terms of age, skill, gender, race, and religion. Organization of the labor force relates mostly to unionism with strong unions found in all the industrialized countries with different roles and behavior. In Europe, for example, unions identify with political parties, and historically they have played major roles in social and political developments. In the United States, they are less politically positioned and deal more with the immediate needs of workers rather than broad socio-economic issues. Lastly, regulation and legal control of the labor force is more evident in the industrialized countries, where the workers are protected from economic exploitation, unsafe working conditions and anti-social working environments, while securing not only their rights but also their responsibilities.

Nature of the Economy and other Characteristics

The nature of economic activity in a country is another indicator of the kind of market it offers. The industrialized countries may have a strong agricultural sector but it is relatively small compared to manufacturing and services[17] (Exhibit 13.3). In fact, apart from income level, perhaps the most differentiating characteristic of industrialized countries is the proportional size of their services sector, which is continuously growing and it has in fact become a crude way of measuring a county's economic development.

Services are defined as deeds, processes, and performances characterized by time-perishability and intangibility. Exhibit 13.4[18] shows the flow of activity among the principal sectors of the economy. Modern industrialized economies are dominated by employment in the service sector, which represents a natural economic evolution. The industrialized countries, as they continue their development (some use the term "post-industrial" as higher level), measure their standard of living not by the quantity of goods they produce and consume, but by the quality of life as measured by services such

Exhibit 13.3

Persons Employed by Sector*

	1999	2000	2001	2002	2003
Mining and quarrying					
EU (25 countries)	7539	7074	6710	6525[(e)]	:
Manufacturing					
EU (25 countries)	345092	344351	340058	337184[(e)]	:
Electricity, gas, and water supply					
EU (25 countries)	16179	15738	15196	15122[(e,i)]	:
Construction					
EU (25 countries)	117254	117515	117810	121651	:
Wholesale and retail trade, repair of motor vehicles, motorcycles, and personal and household goods					
EU (25 countries)	262774	269510	264675	278700[(e)]	:
Hotels and restaurants					
EU (25 countries)	70463	73857	75160	79863[(e)]	79139.0
Transport, storage, and communication					
EU (25 countries)	107663	104094	105894	113330[(e)]	:[(c)]
Real estate, renting, and business activities					
EU (25 countries)	185818	189647	202153	215366[(e)]	214604.0

(:) *Not available*
(e) *Estimated value*
(i) *See explanatory text*
(c) *Confidential*

* *The number of persons employed is defined as the total number of persons working in the various industries: employees, nonemployees (e.g., family workers, delivery personnel) with the exception of agency workers*

Exhibit 13.4

Interactive Model of an Economy

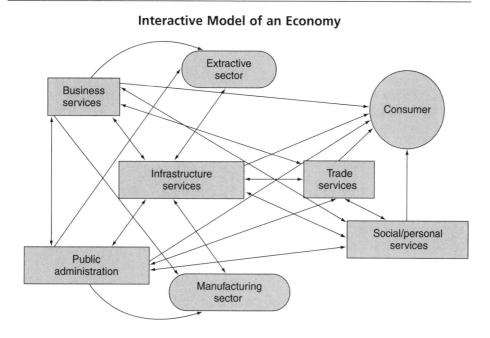

as health, education, and recreation. In modern industrialized countries, the central figure is the professional person and the key resource is information.

Infrastructure refers to the external services and facilities on which business rely to perform their daily operations. External services refer to energy supplies, transportation, communications, and commercial infrastructure. Facilities refer to the presence and quality of financial institutions, advertising agencies, distribution channels, marketing research organizations, and others.[19] The quality of infrastructure is usually directly related to the degree of economic development of a country (and vice versa) and thus the industrialized countries have a high level of infrastructure. Inflation can affect businesses, especially if they are involved in international operations, since high rates complicate cost control and pricing. These problems are relatively minor for the industrialized countries which generally keep their inflation rates low.[20]

The role of government in the economy is a principal factor since it often relates to the degree of freedom and opportunities that businesses are allowed. For example, if a country has strong socialist leanings it may restrict the sectors of the economy where private companies may be engaged.[21] The situation is not the same in all industrialized countries. In the United States, for example, maximum freedom is provided to businesses, both in degree and in nature of activity. In others, usually European industrialized countries, social concerns limit this activity. The reality of the situation, however, is that even where there are limitations, they are moderate. No extreme or dogmatic limitations exist. Furthermore, the trend is toward a greater economic freedom, privatization, and minimization of the role of the government, which also reformed to focus on its regulatory aspect and not on its active participation.[22]

Political, Legal, and Regulatory Forces

Business activities in any country take place within the political and legal environment of governmental institutions, political parties, and organizations through which people and rulers exercise power. These spring from collective ideological beliefs and practical necessities, and affect business in a variety of ways such as stability, sovereignty, taxation, tariffs, conflict resolution methods, employment laws, product liability laws, and many others.[23]

Political Forces

The political environment of all countries is the result of its historical development as it resulted from the interaction of the various macro-environmental forces as well as chance. Perhaps the most obvious, most universal, and at the same time most precious characteristic of industrialized countries' political environment is its stability and law supremacy. These countries, often having passed through considerable political turbulence with catastrophic consequences, have managed to contain political and ideological passions and extremities thus providing the stability to foster economic and social development. Contrary to many of the poorer countries where businesses feel the effects of political risks such as expropriation, disruption of activities, legal insecurity and unreliability, and so on, businesses in industrialized countries can rely on the continuation of their operations within a nurturing environment. An environment that protects property rights (both of the physical means of production and outputs, as in the case of intellectual property rights which guarantee the fruits of continued invention and innovation to the creators), the operation of the market mechanism, and relative justice and equality. These are safeguarded by the same institutions and powers that guarantee the existence of the countries themselves: personal and organizational equality before the law, supremacy of the law, and most importantly a collective acceptance and support to these principles by the populations of the industrialized countries.

Legal and Regulatory Forces

Even the most liberal advocates of free-market economies agree that the system works best with at least some regulation.[24] The need for these has risen largely experientially as a result of the various problems and complications historically associated with business activities. Some of these are: monopolies, damaging natural resource exploitation, destructive competition, externalities, inadequate information, quality-of-life issues, lack of protection of individual rights, and others.[25] Overall, the industrialized countries have enacted business legislation for three reasons: to protect companies from each other, to protect consumers, and to protect the interests of society against unrestrained business behavior.[26]

The main types of laws are presented hereby. Taxation in industrialized countries exists to redistribute income, to encourage consumption of local products rather than imported ones, to discourage investment abroad, and other reasons. Taxation is not a factor that normally differentiates the industrialized countries, and it varies in terms of level, ranging from relatively high in some, especially Western European countries, to zero in tax havens.[27] The three most usual types of taxation in the industrialized countries are income tax, value-added tax (VAT), and tariffs.[28,29] Anti-trust laws are designed to combat restrictive business practices and to encourage competition. In the industrialized countries, these laws are strictly imposed and the business environment is constantly monitored for any activities that prevent, restrict, and distort competition.[30] Civil and criminal product liability laws exist to hold a company and its officers and directors liable when their product causes death, injury, or damage. Amongst the industrialized countries, these laws are predominantly found and most frequently applied in the United States. The EU countries and Japan have been slower to adopt such laws, partly because of their major differences in legal procedures and context compared to the United States and partly (perhaps) because of the general attitudes toward and within the business community where parties are more hesitant to resort to legal action.[31]

Intellectual property protection is of primary concern to industrialized countries not only as a matter of principle and proper business contact, but also as a natural result of the fact that innovation, information, and knowledge are the major competitive advantages of these countries. Consequently, a number of laws and regulations have been developed toward this aim as well as a number of national and international organizations.[32] These protection laws refer to patents, trademarks, trade names, copyrights, trade secrets, and industrial espionage. A distinguishable problem regarding these laws is the difficulty in extending either their adoption or their implementation in other, especially nonindustrialized countries where illegal copying and use of trademarks, music, software, and so on are widespread.[33,34] Employment laws in industrialized countries exist to protect the rights of both the employees and the companies by setting minimum wage limits, securing safe, humane, and nondiscriminating working environments and conditions, and stipulating the rights, obligations, and limits of each side.[35]

These laws are especially strict in the industrialized countries and in fact raise the standard of employment conditions, relationships, and benefits to heights quite unimaginable in most of the less affluent countries of the world. Corrupt practices laws have been introduced to limit the ability of organizations to operate through actions such as bribery and other unethical means. It is worth noting here that many companies in industrialized countries have formal internal regulations that safeguard the ethical, personal, and business behavior of their management, and not just as a matter of abiding by the law, since often internal regulations are actually much stricter than law requirements.[36,37] Anti-boycott laws exist to forbid the compliance to international boycotts that were not sanctioned by the country enacting the law. The most notable example in the industrialized countries is the Anti-Arab Boycott legislation of the United States to prevent American companies from boycotting Israel in their attempt to enter the bigger Arab markets.[38,39]

It is noted that although laws and regulations are powerful champions of proper business conduct, they are not the only ones and they cannot exist without the other forces that support both their creation and implementation. These other forces are the increasing social and ethical concerns of citizens, the purchasing power of the citizens and therefore the markets themselves, the consequent formation and strength of public interest and consumer protection groups and organizations, and finally the right general political environment that allows and nurtures such civil mentalities and behaviors.

International Political/Economic Agreements and Cooperation

Formalized cooperation or associations between industrialized countries and also between industrialized and nonindustrialized countries result in environmental conditions that frequently and substantially affect businesses. The most important example is the European Union (EU), the North American Free Trade Agreement (NAFTA), and the Association of Southeast Asian Nations (ASEAN). The nature of the effect of the above agreements on the business world varies according to their type and degree, ranging from reduced tariffs, quotas, and trade restrictions to the complete elimination of these and to absolute freedom of movement of goods, labor, and capital. Knowledge of these will allow businesses in the industrialized countries to better comprehend the actual extent and nature of their markets, which maybe in fact much bigger than the country they operate in. Equally essential is the information needed in understanding and predicting the competitive environment and its forces, which again are not only larger in number and complexity, but are also dependent on conditions and regulation outside and over and above the ones within a specific country.

The Technological Forces

Technology is perhaps the most dramatic force shaping our destiny and the backbone of social evolution in human history. New technology does not only improve products and services but also often provides better substitutes. Historically, old industries and businesses that fought or ignored new technologies failed.[40] As mentioned previously in this chapter, the industrialized countries are usually the spear of technological change and innovation. Their knowledge, experience, workforce education levels, capital, information and infrastructure, often in combination with high labor and operations costs, intense competition and demanding consumers leave little option but to pursue a strategy of constant innovation and improvement (Exhibit 13.5). This approach builds the pioneering companies that lead technological change and offers a strong competitive advantage, difficult to imitate or counteract. Within this context and always in relation to technology, there are six elements that characterize the current situation:

1. *Fast pace of Technological Change.* This is especially felt in the industrialized countries' business world that is largely to be credited with both its production, and its implementation.[41] Companies operating under these conditions should endlessly scan their environment not only for new technology that relates to their operations, but also for competitors' use of technology.
2. *High Research & Development Budgets.* Another trend of the past few decades is that the cost of technological advancement is rising, especially for some industries, for example the pharmaceutical industry where the development of a new drug may cost hundreds of millions of Euros. In the industrialized countries, one solution is the cooperation between companies to pull resources and expertise together, or the cooperation between the private sector and the government. In Europe, for example, the latter has spawned subsidized programs, such as Eureka and Espirit, while in the United States schemes like Sematech and MCC.[42]
3. *Concentration on Minor Improvements.* Also related to the increased cost of technological innovation, companies often concentrate on minor improvements aiming to improve features, extend current brands rather than gamble on major alterations or even completely new products.[43]

Exhibit 13.5

Gross Domestic Expenditure on R&D (GERD)—As a Percentage of GDP*

	1994	1995	1996	1997	1998	1999	2000	2001	2002	2003	2004	2005
EU (25 countries)	:	1.85(s)	1.83(s)	1.82(s)	1.83(s)	1.87(s)	1.89(s)	1.93(s)	1.93(s)	1.92(s)	1.9(p,s)	:
EU (15 countries)	1.89(s)	1.88(s)	1.87(s)	1.87(s)	1.87(s)	1.92(s)	1.94(s)	1.98(s)	1.98(s)	1.97(s)	1.95(p,s)	:
Euro-zone	1.84(s)	1.84(s)	1.83(s)	1.83(s)	1.84(s)	1.89(s)	1.9(s)	1.91(s)	1.91(s)	1.9(s)	1.89(p,s)	:
Euro-zone (12 countries)	1.9(s)	1.9(s)	1.9(s)	1.9(s)	1.9(s)	1.9(s)	1.9(s)	1.9(s)	1.9(s)	1.9(s)	1.89(p,s)	:
United States	2.4(i)	2.49(i)	2.53(i)	2.56(i)	2.59(b,i)	2.63(i)	2.7(i)	2.71(i)	2.65(i,p)	2.59(i,p)	:	:
Japan	2.58(e)	2.69(e)	2.78(b)	2.84	2.95	2.96	2.99	3.07	3.12	3.15	:	:

(:) Not available
(s) Eurostat estimate
(p) Provisional value
(e) Estimated value
(b) Break in series
(i) See explanatory text
* The four indicators provided are GERD (Gross domestic expenditure on R&D) as a percentage of GDP, percentage of GERD financed by government, and percentage of GERD financed from abroad. "Research and experimental development (R&D) comprise creative work undertaken on a systematic basis in order to increase the stock of knowledge, including knowledge of man, culture and society and the use of this stock of knowledge to devise new applications" (Frascati Manual, 2002 edition, §63). R&D is an activity where there are significant transfers of resources between units, organizations, and sectors and it is important to trace the flow of R&D funds.

4. *Increased Regulation.* As mentioned in Section "Legal and Regulatory Forces" regulations in the industrialized countries are very frequently used to control technological advancements in order to protect the consumers and the general publics from potential harm. This has produced many specialized bodies (usually governmental agencies) to strictly monitor and approve new products, for example the US Federal Food and Drug Administration.[44] This regulatory environment, while improving the living standards of industrialized countries, hinders business activity by increasing costs, delays, and bureaucracy. Furthermore, the companies are often considered legally responsible for harm caused by their products, and liable therefore to fines by the proper authorities and or lawsuits with costly outcomes.

5. *Technological Convergence and Ubiquity of Technology.* This factor relates to a change particularly visible after the invasion of computers in everyday life, and of course even more in the industrialized countries where computers and advanced technology are mostly used. The change is in fact the continuous union of information and communication technologies (Exhibit 13.6[45]), which is quickly spreading to all types of technologies allowing further integration and customization on the one hand, but some confusion and ubiquity on the other concerning the future.[46]

6. *Explosive Growth of the Internet.* The Internet is arguably the single biggest technological change affecting businesses in the industrialized countries. Apart from the communicational abilities and potentialities it offers to businesses, it is also becoming a constantly more favorable channel through which consumers purchase goods and services, and/or are informed about them.[47] The Internet is used primarily in the industrialized countries (Exhibit 13.7) because of the economic ability

Exhibit 13.6

Convergence of Information and Communication Technologies

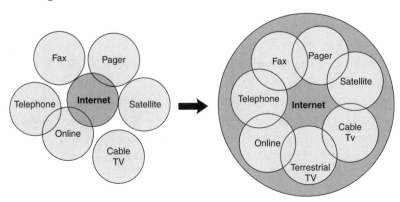

Exhibit 13.7

Level of Internet Access in Households*

	2002	2003	2004	2005
EU (25 countries)	:	:	43	48
EU (15 countries)	39	43	46	53
Euro-zone	36	40	44	50
Japan	49	54	56	:
Canada	51	55	:	:

(:) Not available

* Percentage of households who have Internet access at home. All forms of Internet use are included. The population considered is aged 16–74.

of their people to buy computers, because of their educational level that allows their use, and because of their purchasing power which is of course necessary in order for e-commerce to exist.

The Internet, though, should not be observed in the context of individual countries since its globality is exactly its number one differentiating characteristic both as a technology and as a medium/channel. Businesses in the industrialized countries therefore have probably equally many things to fear and to rejoice about. Looking at the negative side of the situation, they become more vulnerable at home from foreign e-commerce companies. Also, pricing becomes a more straightforward game if consumers can compare prices over the Internet, and this may affect companies offering value through other means than high quality or low price. In the industrialized countries, this is not an infrequent phenomenon. On the bright side of business life, e-commerce allows expansion into previously closed markets, it gives international opportunities to companies of all sizes, and it allows companies that offer better value to their customers an advantage through easier comparison, thus improving the clarity and fairness of competition. Consequently, the Internet does not simply require an adaptation by industrialized countries' businesses, but perhaps a completely new business model (Exhibit 13.8[48]). Even if this is not necessary yet, it will be very soon.

The technological forces will change the shape and environment of businesses, possibly to a degree that now we find difficult to even imagine. Beyond the Internet, rapid advances in biotechnology will revolutionize agriculture and medicine, nanotechnology will be applied in all sectors and all industries, improved and increased number of satellites will improve communication even further, automatic translation phones will allow businesses to communicate with each other and with their customers without the barrier of language, artificial intelligence and embedded learning technology

Exhibit 13.8

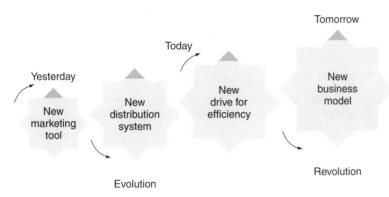

The Evolution of Electronic Commerce

will allow mental functions to machines currently only related to humans, powerful super-computers will allow simulations of environments for testing drugs, training, and other perhaps presently unimaginable purposes. Is this our future? Perhaps not. Most likely, though, yes. All this will happen first in the industrialized countries, and businesses must not only know about them, not only expect them, but also be prepared for them.

The Natural Forces

These include the natural resources and conditions of a country and historically they have had a profound impact on the way people organized their activities and consequently on the formation of their wider macro-environmental situation. Despite their importance nevertheless, their study will be limited in this chapter for two reasons:

1. The industrialized countries are geographically spread across the globe and therefore these forces present no significant pattern or similarities. Consequently there is no set of parameters that might visibly relate the industrialized countries in this context.
2. The effect of the natural forces, although historically significant, is diminishing in importance as a country becomes more economically developed. This is due to the fact that effects of landscape and distances are minimal as a result of the advancements in transportation and communication, weather conditions are again of little significance in view of the ability of modern societies to be protected from the elements, and natural resources do not prescribe economic activity, since agricultureand even manufacturing are losing their importance through the rise of services and information as key economic variables.[49]

Perhaps two natural factors that still bear considerable influence are those of water and energy sources. Water has the dual role of sustaining life and agriculture, and also providing waterways for transportation and outlets to the sea. Obviously, for the industrialized countries prevailing economic activity and alternative means of transportation have reduced waters' importance compared to the past. It still remains, though, a critical force. The second factor, that is the sources of energy, is a primary factor affecting businesses in industrialized countries. Petroleum, coal, natural gas, and renewable sources such as energy provided by water, geothermal activity, the wind, the sun, biomass, and others are increasing in importance and therefore in value as they also become more scarce. In an increasingly globalized economy, nevertheless, industrialized countries do not rely so much on internally found sources as much as on their ability to access and if possible control the sources of other countries.[50,51] It should be noted that although natural forces have partially lost their importance in the industrialized countries, particularly in terms of their ability to stimulate economic activity, they still have some considerable effect on consumer needs, wants, and behavior.

Social and Cultural Forces

The subject of culture and society, their importance and role in business operations and activities, as well as some differentiations across the world have been presented in Chapter 2. Moreover and strictly in relation to the industrialized countries, their effect on consumer behavior, their role in the business environment and management, and their part in differentiating amongst industrialized countries are further investigated throughout the remaining sections of this chapter. What needs to be noted here is the fact that industrialized countries have individually different cultural backgrounds and social behaviors and relationships. Regardless of these differences, however, the form and degree of commonly shared economic and technological development forces a convergence amongst these countries. These increasing similarities affect general social behavior, consumer behavior, and the organizational internal environment. Not surprisingly, convergence begins in the business environment which is usually the first area to shed socio-cultural elements in favor of practically beneficial ones. Another observation is that the slow but real global socio-cultural integration appears to be led by the industrialized countries. This is a rather expected effect of their economic and technological dominance in the world, and also their frequent and conscious use of home-country image as a marketing tool in foreign markets.[52]

From all the aforementioned, it is apparent that the macro-environment of the industrialized countries presents many and significant similarities, often outweighing the differences.

Further characteristics and differentiating factors, largely resulting from the above are studied in the following sections.

Consumer Behavior in the Industrialized Countries

Consumer behavior is defined as the activities people undertake when obtaining, consuming, and disposing of products and services.[53] The aim of this discussion is to note the reasons why consumer behavior knowledge is of utmost importance for doing business in the industrialized countries, and note those ways in which consumer behavior in these countries differs. Starting with the importance of consumer behavior knowledge, the answer rests in the foundation of modern marketing philosophy which recognizes the consumer as being the focus of business activity, and also prescribes that the successful business must be able to attain and use knowledge of the customer to achieve organizational objectives.

As it has already been described in the previous section, the industrialized countries are characterized by economic prosperity, freedom of business activity, high-education levels, technological superiority, upgraded role of knowledge and information, and a socio-cultural environment that supports personal and collective development and expression. The effect of these on behavior is profound in every step of the consumer decision process[54] which distinguishes itself from the reciprocal ones in other countries on a number of factors. Before investigating these factors, though, one has to comprehend the conceptual basis of these differences, and to do that the very personal, internal, psychological motivation that lies behind them must be understood.

One way to achieve this is through the use of Maslow's Theory of Motivation.[55] While the theory bears a number of faults[56] that diminish its reliability as a process of understanding motivation at an individual consumer level, it is an appropriate approach to do so at a collective level. In industrialized countries, while the minority of people are still preoccupied with the first two levels, the majority has moved on to satisfy the higher needs. The combined effect of personal and macro-environmental situation potentially allows the average individual in the industrialized country to be motivated toward higher needs than the individual with a similar personal situation in another country.

The characteristics that differentiate the industrialized countries therefore (economic prosperity, etc.) are the ones that push the average individual motivation level higher in the scale. This does not only result in different motivators, but also in considerably more complex motivational processes, themselves resulting in both quantitative and qualitative upgrades in the decision-making process of the industrialized country consumer.

Differences in the Consumer Decision Process[57–61]

The consumer decision process (Exhibit 13.9)[62] includes the mental and physical steps taken by the consumers from the point of realizing that they want a certain product up to their divestment of it. It is a theoretical model used to understand their behavior and the parameters that affect it, and a practical tool used by businesses to formulate their marketing strategy and mix. Bypassing the theoretical and contextual marketing background already discussed in this book, this chapter concentrates on the specific-to-industrialized-countries' dissimilarities of each step of the model and the factors that lie beneath them.

Step 1—*Need Recognition*. This is triggered by a combination of individual and environmental influences. In the industrialized countries, the

Exhibit 13.9

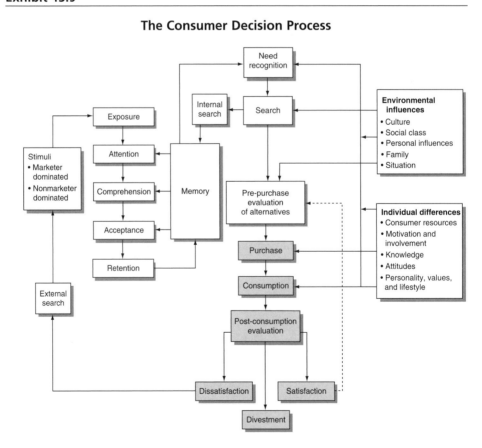

The Consumer Decision Process

majority of consumption relates to the satisfaction of higher needs. Even in consumption of products relating to lower-physiological categories such as food and clothes, the underlying needs aimed to be satisfied are usually of a higher level, such as esteem or aesthetics. Consequently, need recognition, although authentic in the sense that it requires satisfaction of fundamental human requirements, can be artificially directed toward specific products or brands through business/marketing communication, thereby changing tastes and/or preferences. Combining this fact with the macro-environmental factors mentioned earlier, the rate of new need recognition in industrialized countries is very high and often a result of the conscious practices of businesses. These factors include (a) the high average income level that allows not only greater buying power but also different spending patterns to include "less-necessary" products, (b) large number of marketing communication channels with high reach and impact, such as television and magazines, which stimulate if not create need recognition, (c) a general social (perceived) correlation between consumerism and quality of life, and (d) a very much real need for new products that results from their ability to improve life, consequential of the high rates of social and technological changes.

Step 2—*Search for Information*. After the recognition of the need, the consumer will enter the stage of search of information, the intensity of which will depend on his or her perception of urgency and/or value offered by the product. In the industrialized countries, although nonmarketer dominated sources (e.g., friends, family, opinion leaders, media) are extremely important, there is comparatively greater information provision through marketer-dominated channels. The difference is due to (a) the larger number of channels used (media, post, etc.), (b) the potentialities offered by technological advancement (Internet, etc.), (c) the level of education of consumers, which leads to greater demand for information which the businesses pursue to satisfy, and (d) the availability of a many types and brands of products that often largely rely on intense communication to succeed.

Step 3—*Pre-purchase Evaluation of Alternatives*. Here again, a number of significant differentiating characteristics exist in the industrialized countries. First, because of the reasons stated above, the consumers have an easy access to valuable information. This, in combination with the fact that they usually have the education to understand more complicated information, makes it simpler to choose the product and brand most suited for their needs. Secondly, the abundance of marketing channels allows direct comparison of prices, maximizing the value obtained. Finally, the strict regulatory environment and the existence of vigilant consumer-protection organizations provide relative assurance against unsafe and/or fraudulent products, removing a critical parameter from needing to be researched. Another difference of the industrialized countries is the relative value placed on brand names. This value represents not only the trust and appreciation that the individual consumer shows toward a specific brand, but also the value seen in it by the consumers collectively and which is perceived as being partially transferred to the user.

Step 4—*Purchase*. This fourth step refers to five basic questions: whether to buy, when to buy, what to buy, where to buy, and how to pay. In industrialized countries, the differences are often considerable. First of all, because of their higher income, consumers can afford more and better products. Secondly, in industrialized countries, greater competition and more distribution channels offer more options as to the place of purchase. This is further enhanced by easier transportation which increases choice. Place of purchase, though, is not simply a matter of convenience, but also a matter of preference. Personal and social motives play a proportionally greater role in these countries, where consumers place considerable value on the shopping experience itself, thus influencing their choice of place (atmosphere, service, clientele, style, etc.). The Internet and its widespread use have made things more complex as many consumers use it as an alternative place to shop. Another difference is found in the method of payment. Further to cash payments, consumers also make comparatively more frequent use of alternative methods like credit cards, direct debit cards, and so on as well as payments through the Internet. Overall, the purchase stage in the industrialized countries distinguishes itself through more options of products and places, a greater consideration of the shopping experience itself, and the use of technology in the process.

Step 5—*Consumption*. This step answers the questions: when the product is consumed, where, how, and how much of it? The differences in the industrialized countries, considering their macro-environment described earlier, are associated with the fact that comparatively less consumption takes place in relation to immediate practical needs, and more in relation to social and aesthetic ones. Extrapolating on this point, the element of the "consumption experience" is more evident in industrialized countries. Another difference might be considered to be the question of "how much is consumed." However, the answers to consumption-related questions are probably more related to individual countries/areas than industrialized versus nonindustrialized comparisons.

Step 6—*Post-consumption Evaluation*. Although the needs and wants of industrialized countries' consumers differ from other countries', the fundamental question of satisfaction or dissatisfaction is the same. The evaluation is obviously a subjective issue, and the only difference would relate once more to the greater relative weight placed on shopping and product experience, and social and aesthetic factors. Since post-consumption evaluation affects word-of-mouth communication also, it is also possible that nonindustrialized countries are more affected by it, since business-to-consumer communication is on average less intense in these.

Step 7—*Divestment*. Here, substantial distinctions are met in the industrialized countries. First, divestment is often made due to social, not practical reasons. For example, the consumer is very likely to buy new clothes, not because the ones he or she has are old or too few, but because fashion or aesthetic preferences have changed. Secondly, a major social shift toward environmentalism has pushed businesses and governments toward recycling and the use of environmentally friendly materials. Furthermore, the process of disposing of products by consumers has become very environmentally sensitive, and the choice of products is often influenced by their effect during and after divestment.

Time Availability. Concerning all seven steps of the process, there is one crucial factor that has not been mentioned: time. In industrialized countries, people are working long hours and further pursue activities which are not productive in the economic sense of the word. This decreases the time available to spend money, creating a paradox, perhaps found for the first time in this scale: consumers not having the time to exercise their purchasing power. This phenomenon gave rise to time as a vital parameter in consumer behavior with direct and visible repercussions on the business environment. Fast-food, delivery, and drive-through restaurants, super and hyper markets, sourcing out of personal and home tasks such as laundry and gardening, microwaves, and many more are products and services that largely aim at the minimization of time-cost for consumers. Furthermore, new concepts are quickly gaining ground in the industrialized countries, in relation to the time factor, such as polychromic time use. This involves the combination of activities simultaneously, for example eating, watching football and going out at the same time at a sports-pub, or working on your laptop computer while riding the underground. Another concept which is not new, but is ever more used, is the time price, with businesses frequently differentiating themselves by offering the same product as others in less time.

The Individual Determinants of Consumer Behavior[63]

Behavior in general is a result of a combination of factors. Some belong to the wider environment of the consumer, for example culture, social context, family, and some are specific to the individual, for example personality, values, attitudes, lifestyle, and so on. This section presents the latter, while the following one presents the former, both in relation to the industrialized countries. Theories on personality have approached the subject in many ways, which are not within the spectrum of this chapter to present. Regarding values, for example, the essence of the methodologies developed is to describe individuals according to specific traits and characteristics, and then categorize them as being of a specific type on a scale, for example the Rokeach Scale or the Schwartz Scale. Similarly, categorization can be carried out in relation to lifestyle, psychography, and attitudes and general personality, associating consumer behavior characteristics to each category.

Regarding the industrialized countries, even though they are very likely to differ, no specific trend can be observed with regard to personality influence on consumer behavior. Perhaps certain personality types or characteristics are found in certain countries more than in others, but these are differences found even within the industrialized countries. Some similarities between the industrialized countries are however observed. These would include attitudes and values with regards to freedom, individual dignity, the environment, the drive for achievement, and so on, and also a greater relative similarity in lifestyles with common leisure and other activities (although cultural and geographical differences are still predominant differentiating factors, even within the industrialized countries). Another similarity is the consumer knowledge and also understanding of products as a result of high education and marketing communication levels. Overall, although personality as a consumer behavior determinant is extremely important, it does not exhibit any trend to significantly and collectively differentiate the industrialized countries from the rest.

Environmental Determinants of Consumer Behavior[64,65]

Demography

Two characteristics of the industrialized countries are their very low birth rates and their high average life expectancy. The result of these is a changing age structure, with the average age of the population rising fast. Combining this fact with their high income levels, a situation arises where the target markets include a significant proportion of older, often high income and time-affluent consumers. Another impact is the rise of children as a valuable segment through their own moderate purchasing power, and of course their influence on the purchase decisions of their parents. A similar difference of the industrialized countries is also the comparatively high purchasing power of teenagers, especially in some industries such as pop music and magazines, clothing, computer games, and many more.

Cultural and Social Factors

Although each industrialized country has its own culture and social organization, with distinct habits, norms, and behavior, there are commonly shared characteristics. They are not exclusively found in these countries but they do relate to them, either through their commonality or because they are often developed there. Starting with values and beliefs which fundamentally shape culture and society, a number of factors influence consumer behavior including the family, religion, education, peers, media, and early lifetime experiences. Regarding values in the industrialized countries, not only they are different but they are also changing fast.

Family influences are, for example, diminishing due to decreasing time spent by members together. Parents work more, both parents usually work, and children spend more time either in school or in other usually formalized activities. Furthermore, increased divorce rates change both the structure of the family (single-parent) and the perception of family. Finally, the family is becoming more isolated and "nuclear"; in other words, grandparents and other relatives are more rarely in contact with the nucleus family, further changing the perception of the family, and a lack of heritage and continuity. The effect on consumer behavior is direct on everyday life, for example ordering delivery instead of cooking at home, outsourcing normally family duties like babysitting, and so on. It also indirect through a change in the relative degree of influence, that is a shift from family influences to peer and media influences.

Religious influences are also diminishing in effect due to an array of reasons: (a) high education levels increase the probability that people will question the so-called "universal truths and order," (b) freedom of expression in combination with increased cultural diversity gave rise to many alternatives to mainstream religions, (c) liberalization of economic activities resulted in religion(s) becoming a profitable industry and therefore these have been infiltrated by individuals and organizations whose communication disorientates people, and (d) potentially, a questioning of religion's role in modern societies. A shift away from religion has implied a shift away from its corresponding consumer behavior, for example fasting during certain days of the year, according to religion, not happening, with purchases of food made accordingly.

National culture is another factor with diminishing influences in the industrialized countries. This is the result of changes like globalization, diversity, increased and improved knowledge of history, media influences, practicality, and even at times a conscious direction by the national state. In the EU, for example, despite the drive of governments to protect their countries' individual national culture, there is a parallel aim to bring the peoples of Europe closer—the two actions, to some small degree, working against

each other. Another changing factor regarding consumer behavior is education. The influence of education appears, if anything, to be increasing not
only because more people are getting educated and to a higher level, but
also because of the nature of education in the industrialized countries: it is
becoming more liberal in context, it promotes diversity and concentrates on
individual rather than collective national and/or religious values, it provokes
and rewards critical thinking, and it relies more and more on technology
such as the Internetwhich is impossible to control. In many industrialized
countries, there are additional subcultures influencing behavior. These are
based on nationality (e.g., immigrants from other countries), race (Asian,
African, etc.), social class (aristocracy, middle class, working class, cast,
etc.), social stratification, or other factors. Consumer behavior relates to
these in almost every aspect of everyday and business life, from choice
of music, food, and clothes to literature, media, and education. Finally,
reference groups, that is people that significantly influence an individual's
behavior, do so through socialization, self-concept, comparison, conformity,
and role models. The effect of these has not diminished and in view, in
fact, of the falling influence of other factors it is likely that their power has
increased.

Business Social Responsibility and Ethics

Modern businesses largely rely on a simple principle to build their success: the societal marketing concept, that is "the idea that organizations
should determine the needs, wants and interests of target markets and
deliver the desired satisfactions more effectively and efficiently than competitors in a way that maintains or improves the consumer's and society's
well-being."[66] Retaining a realistic perspective on this mentality, it is not
difficult to observe an obvious fact: this concept does not differ at all
from the traditional marketing concept which does not include the phrase
"in a way that maintains or improves the consumer's and society's well-
being." So, where does the ingenuity and philosophical innovation lie? In
the consumers themselves of course. What has necessitated the introduction of this extra phrase in the concept is the change in the demands of
consumers and their overall consumer behavior that requires the businesses
to act in an ethically and socially responsible manner. Businesses in their
turn understand this requirement and deliver accordingly, thus raising the
level of acceptable business responsibility as perceived by consumers, who
raise the bar even higher, to effectively end up with a dynamically self-
improving system. For this reason, in the industrialized countries, the regulatory environment, although much stricter on businesses than elsewhere, is
not the driving force behind social responsibility but simply a catalyst that

Exhibit 13.10

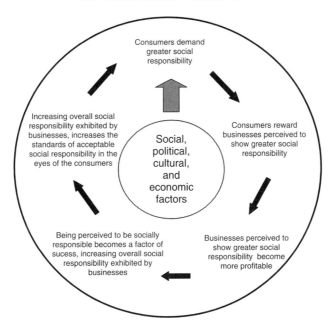

The Cycle of Increasing Business Social Responsibility in the Industrialized Countries

reinforces the conviction of consumers of what to expect from businesses (Exhibit 13.10).

This cycle is not exclusive to the industrialized countries but a number of macro-environmental conditions have contributed to its more effective application. First, there is protection of free competition and therefore little control on consumer behavior. Secondly, there is freedom of expression and therefore companies find it very difficult to build perceptions of being socially responsible without really being so. Thirdly, their strong economies allow the people to be interested in other factors than their immediate personal situation. Fourthly, higher education levels enable people to understand that their own personal situation is dependent on the wider social conditions and if the former is to improve, the latter must do so in parallel. Social responsibility and general business ethics, therefore, have been, are, and will continue to build a better and more transparent relationship between businesses and society.

Communication and Media

What is unquestionable in the industrialized countries is the immense power, control, and influence of marketing communications. This has been the effect of technological advancements enhancing availability and potentialities of communication, the diminishing influence of other factors (see above), improved marketing knowledge, experience and application, and a harsh competitive environment, often demanding extensive reliance on communication for businesses to succeed. This factor is further enhanced by the integration of industries and media to achieve the maximum support to each other, and the maximum impact on consumers. Music, fashion, sports, soft-drinks, movies, and many more apparently independent industries are joining forces, often under common ownership, to become the primary influencers of consumer behavior. For an industrialized world with few concerns about the immediate needs for survival, consumerism appears to have become a point in itself and, through it, consumers find a voice of expression, the way to promote their understanding of a better society, an abstract escape from the predetermined, and the means to build an identity for themselves

Influencing Consumer Behavior[67–79]

Having understood the various parameters that shape consumer behavior in the industrialized countries, the obvious question arising is "how can businesses affect this behavior to their benefit?" The answer is not simple nor can it be presented within the context of this chapter to an adequate degree. Influencing consumer behavior involves first of all understanding it, and that alone includes all the strategic and marketing process used toward this end: environmental and competitive analyses, audits, SWOT analyses, marketing research etc. At this point, the critical points of influencing consumer behavior are listed only to provide a general but comprehensive idea of the foundation of competitive tactics and principles amongst businesses in the industrialized countries.

The severely competitive business environment does not allow large margins of divergence between company supply and consumer demand. This necessitates both the understanding of consumer wants and the ability to satisfy them. Simply meeting customer expectations, however, is often not enough. Businesses have to surpass expectation to meet the prerequisites of quality. Additionally, intense competition means that rarely businesses can truly offer greater value through visibly higher quality, or lower price, or the best combination of these. Consequently, greater value is frequently offered through other means, such as innovation, accompanying products or services, greater customer care, personal attention, convenience, and so on.

Another option available, though, relates to the ability of businesses to create value through the building of appropriate brand image that is perceived as transferable to the consumer. The building of such brand image is often "artificial" in the sense that it relies more on the perception of consumers than reality itself. In an industrialized world dominated by media and other communication channels, perception becomes often a more critical parameter than reality itself. Businesses realize this fact and on average spend a large percentage of their income to shape perception and preferences through advertising and other means of communication with the consumer.

Consequently, consumers are constantly exposed to messages from businesses, thus becoming cognitively saturated with information. This decreases the ability of businesses to influence them, unless extra effort is put into quantitatively or qualitatively increasing the intensity of their communication. Though consumer influences are normally divided into marketer and nonmarketer dominated, with the latter including wider social and cultural factors, this is not completely true. Especially in larger companies, with immense resources and influences, it is sometimes possible to influence the attitudes of people collectively, at a cultural or social level for the benefit of the company alone.

In the industrialized countries, the wider macro-environment and business infrastructure allow the maximization of both the potentialities and their exploitation by businesses. This has placed consumers and businesses in a unique position where not only none is influenced more by the other, but where they coexist in a dynamic equilibrium of influence and dependence. In the industrialized countries, formal regulation and control is no longer the driver of neither the business world nor the society as a whole. It is simply a necessary by-product of the coexistence, even merger of the business with the consumer into a single entity with a life of its own and intra-influences, that balances the wants and abilities of a world led and shaped by these countries.

Other Issues

Small Firms[80–84]

Despite the concentration of existing literature on larger organizations, the economies of the industrialized countries also depend on the small businesses. Small business theory will not be presented here. Nevertheless, as a matter of comprehensively covering the question of doing business in these countries, some special note is hereby made to distinguish the differences relating to small firms. First of all, the trend of the past few years is for smaller companies to be able to compete with larger ones in geographic markets traditionally unreachable to them. Secondly, and largely opposing the above-mentioned force, small firms find it difficult to compete with larger ones, even in their own territory, on account of their limited resources, and the increased costs of marketing communication and product development.

As a consequence, many small firms chose to specialize, focusing on a product or geographic niche market. Another form of reaction is the formation of networks that allows them access to more resources, a greater spectrum of expertise and wider coverage and exposure. Thirdly, small firms, although businesses themselves, are often characterized by aims and goals that are personal as much as they are business related. In other words, the direction, context, and culture of small firms are often based not on purely business criteria, but on a mixture of business rational and the personal aims and values of the owners and/or managers. Fourthly, practically, small firms are usually much simpler not just in structure but with regard to the various managerial processes as well, such as planning, and so on. While management theory and evidence stress that fundamental processes such as strategic planning, environmental analyses and so on are equally important to small as they are to large organizations, either due to lack of will or ability, they are less frequently applied. Lastly, small firms are more sensitive to macro-environmental conditions since they do not have neither the scale of operations that will spread risks, nor the financial capability to withstand long adverse conditions or recessions. At the same time, their small size allows for flexibility, speedy reactions to external changes, and adaptability which largely counteract these disadvantages.

But these differences are not found only in the industrialized countries. Are there any characteristics that differentiate them therefore? The answer is positive. First, the technological infrastructure for the widening of the operations of small companies is clearly better in the industrialized countries. Furthermore, the ability to take advantage of the infrastructure demands a certain level of education and specialization less frequently met outside these countries. Another difference is the protection offered by the regulatory systems that do not allow the control of the markets by the large organizations. This same regulatory system, though, also works against the small companies through the many and strict laws and regulations which are more difficult to be followed by these firms. Finally, small firms in the industrialized countries are not simply a result of economic dimensions. As mentioned earlier, the workforce in these countries has greater demands than its salary from their employer. It wants to satisfy other, higher needs which are often not satisfied. As a result, many employees start a business of their own not because it necessarily makes more financial sense but because that is their only option to find what they are looking for from their work.

Country Uniqueness

The industrialized countries have been treated in this chapter as a collection of environments with many similar characteristics. The primary purpose in fact here was to differentiate them on a number of parameters, factors, and forces, and to outline these differences in comparison to the rest of the world. Facing the danger of creating a misconception, it is imperative to present here the other side of the coin as well.

Almost all the characteristics of a business environment, whether internal, societal, or competitive, and subsequently all management-related issues are directly or indirectly related to culture and locality. In other words, the material of this chapter is a result of a study of trends and patterns that do not relate to all parts, dimensions, environments, and geographic areas of the industrialized countries. Additionally, while the material is presented in an "industrialized vs nonindustrialized countries" fashion, there are usually great similarities between neighboring industrialized and nonindustrialized countries, which may not be found within the industrialized countries themselves. Japanese style of doing business, for example, is likely to bear resemblances to other far-east countries, especially in such areas as communication and wider people management functions. At the same time, these would most likely differ significantly in the United States or Europe. These likenesses and distinctions, nonetheless, do not relate only to geographic regions. For example, there are many similarities between northwest Europe and the United States, which are both industrialized but far apart, as well as between south Europe and Latin America which are industrialized and nonindustrialized respectively, and very far apart at the same time.

What matters therefore is not the degree of resemblance between industrialized countries, but their individual characteristics. Thus, it is necessary for those doing business in the industrialized countries, especially for the first time, to undertake proper environmental analyses on which to base their business strategies and management decisions and, if possible, to make sure that the business is being run by managers who know and understand local culture, values, and behavior. These are prerequisites for all countries, but even more so in the industrialized ones, where the business environment is especially unforgiving.

What follows is a selection of industrialized countries used as examples to demonstrate what business people need to know before entering those countries. More industrialized countries are described in Chapter 15.

Japan

As the world's second largest economy and second largest export market for US goods and services, Japan offers large-scale opportunities and strategic benefits for many foreign firms. As an expensive, highly competitive and highly complex market, Japan remains a challenging place to do business. Foreign firms hoping to succeed in Japan must take a long-term approach to entering the market and building a market presence. Japan remains a highly homogeneous society and business practices are characterized by long-standing, close-knit relations among individuals and firms. Regulatory processes and local business practices in Japan reflect systems designed for indigenous needs with little or no consideration given for potential participation by foreign companies. Even for Japanese business people, it takes time to develop relationships and become an "insider." For the nonJapanese businessperson, the task is formidable, but not impossible.

The Japanese consumer has traditionally been conservative and brand-conscious. However, during the recessionary environment of the past few years, opportunities are emerging for purveyors of "value." More fragmented buying habits are emerging among a new generation of more individualistic consumers. As a result of this, Japan's complex distribution system is now changing dramatically.

The following are some cultural tips.

- Do not expect to make Japan the headquarters for all your Pacific Rim/Asian operations. There are vast differences among cultures in Japan, China, Korea, Malaysia, and so on. Neither is it generally wise to place an executive from any other Asian country in a management position in Japan.
- It is important to view your company's objectives in a global, high-level manner, with an understanding of how all the pieces relate. Be prepared to communicate this big picture to the Japanese, and be ready to answer questions about any and all aspects of the presentation in depth, and in a nonlinear manner. While US executives generally consider it logical to resolve each item one by one, and will "hammer" at a point of disagreement, the Japanese look at the overall picture. The Japanese believe that many issues may be explored (and resolved) simultaneously.
- Emphasize and build on points of agreement with your Japanese counterparts. A persuasive, positive presentation is compatible with Japanese culture, a high-pressure, confrontational approach is not.
- Always give your Japanese contacts time, whether it entails: (a) e-mailing your questions two weeks ahead of your meeting so you know they will be able to answer them comfortably in person; (b) waiting through that may seem an interminable amount of silence for a Japanese executive to respond to a question; or (c) allowing the Japanese negotiating team weeks to reach their consensus. Never impose a US or any other concept of time on Japanese culture.
- Do not be offended by the many personal questions the Japanese may ask you. Expect to be asked about your job, your title, your responsibilities, the number of employees who report to you, and so on. Japanese is a very complex language with many forms of address.

Australia

Geographically, Australia is similar in size to the United States. Despite its small population (approximately 20 million) and vast landmass, the country has well-developed, nationwide air, road, port, and telecommunications infrastructure networks comparable to those in other industrialized countries.

Australians feel a strong impetus to deflate people who put on airs. Referred to as "cutting down the tall poppy," this habit is thought to have grown out of Australia's origin as a British penal colony. Naturally, the Australian prisoners hated their high-class British overseers, and wished to insult them whenever possible. Furthermore, many Australian convicts were Irish, a people already looked down upon by the British at that time. This feeling is still so ingrained that many Australian politicians decline an offer of a British knighthood for fear of alienating their constituents.

The Australian government welcomes foreign investment, and the United States is the country's largest source of foreign capital. Total US investment in Australia, including both direct and portfolio investment, exceeds $54 billion. The federal and state governments vigorously encourage investment by offering incentives to multinational companies to set up regional headquarters for financial and other services, and manufacturing operations. The government touts the benefits of Australia's safe, stable business environment, skilled work force, and lower facility, site, and operating costs in comparison to other regional centers such as Singapore, Hong Kong, and Taiwan.

Australians call themselves Aussies, while New Zealanders refer to themselves as Kiwis (after the Kiwi, their national bird). While there are many similarities between these two peoples, there are differences as well. The following are three ways in which Australia is different from New Zealand.

1. The European colonization of Australia began as a penal colony. New Zealand was never a penal colony.
2. New Zealand declared itself a nuclear free zone and prohibits ships carrying nuclear arms from entering its ports. Since the United States would not confirm which ships carry nuclear weapons, this resulted in a de facto ban on virtually all US military vessels in New Zealand waters, which suspended the ANZUS (Australia/New Zealand/United States) mutual defense treaty.
3. The indigenous people of New Zealand, the Maoris, have not been as marginalized as the Aboriginies of Australia. Maoris still occupy a substantial amount of the country's arable land, and Maori words are in common use. In part, this is because the Maori make up a larger

proportion of New Zealand's population. About 10 percent of New Zealanders are Maori, while only about 1.5 percent of Australians are Aborigines. (Australia will soon have more Asians than Aborigines.)

Switzerland

Switzerland is a small, highly developed, multilingual market located at the crossroads of Europe. Its population of seven and a half million people is diversified, well educated, and affluent. It has a strong and stable economy, low inflation, relatively low unemployment, and a highly qualified workforce, all of which contribute to make the Swiss Confederation a desirable market environment. Per capita income ($32,000) is the highest in Europe and spending power for foreign goods and services is thus extremely high.

Trade and prosperity are synonymous in Switzerland. The country is dependent upon export markets to absorb its production and sustain its wealth, but is also equally dependent upon imports for raw materials and to expand the range of goods and services available in-country.

Switzerland is known for liberal trade and investment policies. Fiscal policy is moderate and cautious. The Swiss franc is one of the world's soundest and most stable currencies. The country is famous for its high standard of banking, ensuring rapid and reliable processing of business transactions.

The Swiss welcome foreign investment and accord it national treatment. Foreign investment is neither actively encouraged nor unduly hampered by barriers. The federal government adopts a relaxed attitude of benevolent noninterference toward foreign investment, confining itself to creating and maintaining the general conditions that are favorable to both Swiss and foreign investors. Such factors include economic and political stability, a firmly established legal system, a reliable infrastructure, and efficient capital markets. The government does not offer large-scale incentives to prospective investors, and those that exist are open to foreign and domestic investors alike. Switzerland is not a member of the European Union, but it has several bilateral agreements with almost all the member countries of the EU.

Switzerland has four distinct cultures which are usually identified by their native languages: French, Italian, German, and Romansch. (Romansch is spoken by less than 1 percent of the Swiss, but its status is accorded and protected as Switzerland's only indigenous language.) Since Switzerland has four native cultures, try to find out the primary language of the people you will do business with. German cultural traditions are quite different from those of the French and Italian.

Age and seniority are important in this country. Avoid sending a young executive alone to Switzerland; he or she will not be taken seriously. Expect to defer to the elderly. Business in Switzerland is serious business, especially among the German-speaking populace. Humor is out of place in business negotiations. Swiss executives dress conservatively, but they are often quite fashionable. Dress as well as you can afford to. Do not forget that this country has the highest standard of living in Europe, so it is an expensive country in which to do business.

Sweden

Sweden which joined the EU in January 1995 is an advanced, industrialized country with a high standard of living. Its population is around nine million people, and foreign trade is vital to Sweden's economy. About 35 percent of Sweden's manufactured goods are exported. Because trade is so important to the economy, Sweden has traditionally maintained a policy favoring trade liberalization. With stable political conditions, a skilled workforce, educated population, well-developed infrastructure, and relatively low corporate tax rates, Sweden is an attractive location for foreign investment. Until the mid-1980s, Sweden's approach to direct investment from abroad was quite restrictive and governed by a complex system of laws and regulations. Foreigners were restricted from acquiring shares of Swedish firms and laws required foreigners to obtain permission to transact business in Sweden. Today, Swedish authorities have implemented reforms to improve the business regulatory environment that will benefit investment inflows. Foreign exchange transactions have been decontrolled; the law requiring foreigners to obtain permission to acquire shares or holdings in Swedish firms has been abolished, and real estate regulations have been changed so that foreigners can now acquire commercial real estate and land for mining in Sweden.

The following are some cultural tips. Rather begin with small talk, Swedes often get right down to business. Be prepared to start your pitch right away. Swedes generally avoid confrontation. They must reach a consensus with all parties before agreeing to a deal. You may find management in favor of your proposal, but opposed by a labor representative. Business lunches and dinners are popular in Sweden. Women are accepted as equals to men and it is not unusual for a business-woman to pick up the check in Sweden, especially if she has an expense account.

The Future

It is tempting to endeavor a preview of the things to come, but this would be to no avail as much as it would be unscientific and irrational. Existing literature on the matter is contradicting, unenlightening, and hardly useful. Some speak of technological wonders beyond our imagination that will change all business parameters in the not-so-long-term future, others speak of a two- or three- or four-speed world that will divide countries distinctly into have and have-nots, other project current globalization trends to assume a uniform future world, others cry over the luck of resources that will sink humanity into regression, and others hope for a future of alternative energy sources and endless prosperity. No one is convincing and no one sounds ridiculous. The absolute truth is that we do not know and we cannot know. What is definite is change itself. A change of increasing pace, a change that is uncontrolled, a change that we are given no option to accept or reject. We live in a world of change, with occasional interruptions of stability. The successful business therefore is not the one to adapt to change, but the one to live with it and for it.

Closing Case

Harley–Davidson—The Good Years

In the summer of 2003, Harley–Davidson reported record second-quarter net income of $202 million, or 66 cents a share, compared with $144 million a year ago. Revenue from sales was $1.2 billion, up 22 percent from a year ago. Harley will probably finish 2003 with its 18th record year in a row and prove once again that it is rightfully considered to be one of the greatest success stories of American business. This was achieved through good relationships, continuous improvement, employee and management involvement, team building or employee training, and empowerment. These are not just words out of a management book for Harley–Davidson. Only by adopting those management techniques and building a solid base between the management and the Unions/employees made it possible for Harley–Davidson to improve its management processes. While management's responsibility is to build relationships with the employees, marketing's responsibility is to build relationship with the potential and existing customers. The realization of the importance of customer feedback led Harley to develop new marketing techniques. But marketing strategies would not be enough if quality and reliability did not improve. Therefore, we can clearly see the impact Harley's improved manufacturing process, which consisted of Just-In-Time inventory, Employee Involvement, and Statistical Operation Control, had on their continuously improving environment.

What really distinguishes Harley–Davidson motorcycle, though, is its perceived concept of existence and purpose. For many, Harley–Davidson motorcycle is more than just a mode of transportation or ordinary product. It is an American icon that is much loved and recognized around the world. So, while the Harley–Davidson Motor Company is dedicated to continuous innovation, it has opted for evolution more than revolution to carefully preserve the elements that make a Harley distinct—the trademark V-twin engine, the teardrop gas tanks and oversized speedometer, among other styling details. "We are constantly improving and modernizing the machine," Ken Schmidt, Harley's director of communications comments, "yet every model retains the classic components. That's what our customers want, and that's also, I believe, what sparks the strong emotional attachments that Harleys generate." Joining the Harley Owners Group (or becoming a HOG member) is not so much about buying a bike as embracing a unique recreational lifestyle. No other "product" can draw thousands of enthusiasts to weekend rallies staged around the country. Or evoke such pride and identification that the owner tattoos the corporate logo on his arm. "There's something going on here that is greater than the sum of its parts," says William G. Davidson, Harley's vice president of styling. Rich Teerlink, Harley-Davidson, Inc.'s president and CEO says, "For us, it's a way of life." It is not surprising to walk through Harley's headquarters and see motorcycle helmets lying on top of file cabinets. Harley people ride their bikes to work and spend vacations touring and attending rallies with fellow Harley riders. 'When a Harley owner explains a great riding experience or rally he's been to, or even a problem he may have had, it's important to be able to say, "I know what you mean," or "How can I help you," says Jeff Bleustein, Harley-Davidson Motor Company president. "A lot of what you see in our product lines—and even the way we run our rallies—are the direct results of input we've received from our customers." Indeed, most weekends you'll find Willie G. at a rally rubbing elbows, hearing stories, fielding questions, and stoking the Harley legend.

This "close-to-the-customer" philosophy, as CEO Teerlink calls it, extends to the dealerships as well. More than just a retail outlet, they are a gathering place where Harley riders come to trade stories and talk with others who share their riding passion. It was not always that way. "Our dealerships, for the most part, used to be glorified garages, with a couple of mechanics in the back and a box of T-shirts out front," recalls Willie G. Six years ago, Harley aggressively put in place a retail strategy to establish a true collection of products, all linked under a common and strong visual identity, and through its dealerships endeavored to create a top-to-bottom presence.

Today, the company promotes the Harley lifestyle experience through "designer store" dealerships that have been either completely remodeled or built from scratch to provide a warm and inviting retail environment. Floor plans and display counters are laid out to draw customers in and surround them with motorcycles, and all one needs is to ride one. Parts, once stored in the back room, are handsomely displayed in user-friendly packaging. There is a separate area for Harley's line of motor clothes, complete with dressing rooms. Many stores also feature customer lounges and rider meeting rooms with Harley–Davidson pinball machines, antique bikes, and rally videos. No detail is ignored and each is designed to enhance the owner's experience and underscore the premium quality of Harley–Davidson products.

Harley–Davidson's merchandising line—which ranges from clothing, tattoo patches, coffee mugs, belt buckles, and infant wear to memorabilia—are also intended to support and amplify the riding experience. Today's Harley customer is as likely to be a factory worker, engineer, housewife, graphic designer or salesperson, and typically family oriented.

Although the company generated more than $1.3 billion in revenues in 1995, it spent less than $2 million in advertising. "We're not dependent on advertising or other traditional marketing techniques as automobile companies or even our competitors are," says Schmidt. "They're selling transportation. We're selling dreams and lifestyle. There's a big difference." Alec Wilkinson writing in *The New Yorker* says, "If you ride a Harley, you are a member of a brotherhood, and if you don't, you are not." For Harley, it is that complex and that simple. All their products spark a feeling, kindle a memory and point to the journey ahead. For Harley management, if it does not, it does not qualify as a genuine Harley.

The three M's to Harley's success (management, marketing, and manufacturing) can be implemented into any company. The key is to understand that all companies are different and the specifics which may have worked for Harley may not work for another. However, the concepts will be the same. If management can grasp the ideals that Harley thrives on, today, any company can learn to compete in this newly developing global economy.

Sources: http://www.cdf.org/cdf/atissue/vol2_1/harley/harley.html, http://www.usatoday.com/money/autos/2003-08-24-harley_x.htm, http://www.cse.ucsc.edu/~callon/hd.html.

Question: What are the lessons other companies can learn from Harley Davidson?

Chapter Summary

Doing business in the industrialized countries is bound by the same philosophy, concepts, and processes met in most other countries, including good knowledge of the macro- and micro-environments, understanding of consumer behavior, needs, and wants, and a management system, attitude, and vision adapted to the situation. What differentiates business activity in the industrialized countries therefore is not the theoretical context, but the variables to be considered within it. These have been presented and discussed throughout this chapter with four main issues clearly transpiring from the study:

1. The "physical/tangible" characteristics of the industrialized countries' environment are different, including greater wealth, very developed

business and technological infrastructure, focus on information, pluralistic marketing channels, and a frequently saturated, harsh competitive environment.

2. The simultaneous cause and result of the above, that is the "abstract/intangible" distinctions, including higher education levels, consumer and employee motivation at qualitatively different levels, more socially sensitive attitudes, and businesses' integral social role.

3. Businesses are people focused - externally, aiming to satisfy customers' needs and wants, and internally, treating their employees as their most valuable asset, and aiming to maximize both the potentialities of human resource and their utilization of it, and finally

4. The industrialized countries' business environment is characterized by constant change which is neither controlled nor significantly affected by any company, industry, or government, and it occurs through the interrelation of a myriad of forces, many unleashed through the liberalization of economies and business activity.

Review and Discussion Questions

1. (a) Which are the forces that compose the business macro-environment?
   (b) How do these differ in the industrialized countries?
2. Describe the main elements that characterize consumer behavior in the industrialized countries and elaborate on the ways businesses adjust their approach to consumers to adapt to these elements.
3. What is the nature of the competitive environment in the industrialized countries, and which are the strategic and tactical options available to businesses operating under these conditions?
4. List and explain the most likely advantages and disadvantages of having to manage a company in an industrialized country (management of the internal environment).
5. Can one assume that knowledge and experience of doing business in one industrialized country can be used at "face value" in another industrialized country? Why?

Endnotes

1. George A. Steiner and John F. Steiner, *Business, Government, and Society – A Managerial Perspective*, 9th edn, McGraw Hill, 2000, pp. 25–26.
2. Donald A. Ball, Wendell H. McCulloch Jr., Paul L. Frantz, J. Michael Geringer and Michael S. Minor, *International Business – The Challenge of Global Competition*, International Edition, McGraw Hill, 2002, pp. 11–14.
3. Philip Kotler, Gary Armstrong, John Saunders and Veronica Wong, *Principles of Marketing*, 3rd European Edition, Pearson Education, 2002, p. 131.

4. George A. Steiner and John F. Steiner, *Business, Government, and Society – A managerial perspective*, 9th edn, McGraw Hill, 2000, pp. 26–28.

5. Warren J. Keegan and Bodo B. Schlegelmilch, *Global Marketing Management – A European Perspective*, Prentice Hall, 2001, pp. 39–41.

6. Ibid., p. 44.

7. Philip Kotler, Gary Armstrong, John Saunders and Veronica Wong, *Principles of Marketing*, 3rd European Edition, Pearson Education, 2002, pp. 124–128.

8. Ibid., pp. 128–131.

9. Vern Terpstra and Ravi Sarathy, *International Marketing*, 8th edn, The Dryden Press, 2000, pp. 78–80.

10. Ibid., p. 74.

11. Ibid., p. 71.

12. Ibid., pp. 67–68.

13. Warren J. Keegan and Bodo B. Schlegelmilch, *Global Marketing Management – A European Perspective*, Prentice Hall, 2001, pp. 48–49.

14. Philip Kotler, Gary Armstrong, John Saunders and Veronica Wong, *Principles of Marketing*, 3rd European Edition, Pearson Education, 2002, pp. 131–132.

15. Warren J. Keegan and Bodo B. Schlegelmilch, *Global Marketing Management* – A European Perspective, Prentice Hall, 2001, pp. 47–50.

16. Vern Terpstra and Ravi Sarathy, *International Marketing*, 8th edn, The Dryden Press, 2000, pp. 68–71.

17. Donald A. Ball, Wendell H. McCulloch Jr., Paul L. Frantz, J. Michael Geringer and Michael S. Minor, *International Business – The Challenge of Global Competition*, International Edition, McGraw-Hill, 2002, pp. 404–430.

18. Vern Terpstra and Ravi Sarathy, *International Marketing*, 8th edn, The Dryden Press, 2000, pp. 75–76.

19. James A. Fitzsimmons and Mona J. Fitzsimmons, *Service Management – Operations, Strategy, and Information Technology*, 3rd edn, McGraw-Hill, 2001, p. 3.

20. Vern Terpstra and Ravi Sarathy, *International Marketing*, 8th edn, The Dryden Press, 2000, pp. 76–78.

21. Ibid.

22. Ibid., p. 82.

23. George A. Steiner and John F. Steiner, Business, *Government, and Society – A managerial Perspective*, 9th edn, McGraw-Hill, 2000, pp. 332–334.

24. Warren J. Keegan and Bodo B. Schlegelmilch, *Global Marketing Management – A European Perspective*, Prentice Hall, 2001, p. 110.

25. Philip Kotler, Gary Armstrong, John Saunders and Veronica Wong, *Principles of Marketing*, 3rd European Edition, Pearson Education, 2002, p. 138.

26. George A. Steiner and John F. Steiner, Business, *Government, and Society – A managerial Perspective*, 9th edn, McGraw-Hill, 2000, pp. 297–299.

27. Philip Kotler, Gary Armstrong, John Saunders and Veronica Wong, *Principles of Marketing*, 3rd European Edition, Pearson Education, 2002, p. 138.

28. Donald A. Ball, Wendell H. McCulloch Jr., Paul L. Frantz, J. Michael Geringer and Michael S. Minor, *International Business – The Challenge of Global Competition*, International Edition, McGraw-Hill, 2002, pp. 379–380.

29. Ibid.

30. Vern Terpstra and Ravi Sarathy, *International Marketing*, 8th edn, The Dryden Press, 2000, pp. 44–45.

31. Warren J. Keegan and Bodo B. Schlegelmilch, *Global Marketing Management – A European Perspective*, Prentice Hall, 2001, pp. 121–122.

32. Donald A. Ball, Wendell H. McCulloch Jr., Paul L. Frantz, J. Michael Geringer and Michael S. Minor, *International Business – The Challenge of Global Competition*, International Edition, McGraw-Hill, 2002, pp. 386–388.

33. Warren J. Keegan and Bodo B. Schlegelmilch, *Global Marketing Management – A European Perspective*, Prentice Hall, 2001, pp. 118–121.

34. Donald A. Ball, Wendell H. McCulloch Jr., Paul L. Frantz, J. Michael Geringer and Michael S. Minor, *International Business – The Challenge of Global Competition*, International Edition, McGraw Hill, 2002, pp. 392–395.

35. Vern Terpstra and Ravi Sarathy, *International Marketing*, 8th edn, The Dryden Press, 2000, pp. 133–135.

36. Donald A. Ball, Wendell H. McCulloch Jr., Paul L. Frantz, J. Michael Geringer and Michael S. Minor, *International Business – The Challenge of Global Competition*, International Edition, McGraw-Hill, 2002, p. 396.

37. Warren J. Keegan and Bodo B. Schlegelmilch, *Global Marketing Management – A European Perspective*, Prentice Hall, 2001, pp. 123–125.

38. Vern Terpstra and Ravi Sarathy, *International Marketing*, 8th edn, The Dryden Press, 2000, p. 130.

39. Donald A. Ball, Wendell H. McCulloch Jr., Paul L. Frantz, J. Michael Geringer and Michael S. Minor, *International Business – The Challenge of Global Competition*, International Edition, McGraw Hill, 2002, pp. 396–397.

40. Vern Terpstra and Ravi Sarathy, *International Marketing*, 8th edn, The Dryden Press, 2000, p. 130.

41. Donald A. Ball, Wendell H. McCulloch Jr., Paul L. Frantz, J. Michael Geringer and Michael S. Minor, *International Business – The Challenge of Global Competition*, International Edition, McGraw-Hill, 2002, pp. 397–398.

42. Philip Kotler, Gary Armstrong, John Saunders and Veronica Wong, *Principles of Marketing*, 3rd European Edition, Pearson Education, 2002, p. 135.

43. Ibid., pp. 136–137.

44. Ibid.

45. Ibid.

46. Ibid.

47. Warren J. Keegan and Bodo B. Schlegelmilch, *Global Marketing Management – A European Perspective*, Prentice Hall, 2001, p. 140.

48. Ibid., p. 139.

49. Ibid., pp. 139–144.

50. Ibid., p. 143.

51. Donald A. Ball, Wendell H. McCulloch Jr., Paul L. Frantz, J. Michael Geringer and Michael S. Minor, *International Business – The Challenge of Global Competition*, International Edition, McGraw-Hill, 2002, Chapter 8.

52. Ibid.

53. Philip Kotler, Gary Armstrong, John Saunders and Veronica Wong, *Principles of Marketing*, 3rd European Edition, Pearson Education, 2002, pp. 132–135.

54. Ibid., 140–145.

55. Roger D. Blackwell, Paul W. Miniard and James F. Engel, *Consumer Behavior*, 9th edn, South-Western, 2001, p. 6.

56. Michael Laroche et al., "Effects of subcultural differences on country and product evaluations," *Journal of Consumer Behaviour*, Vol. 2, 3, pp. 232–247.

57. Philip Kotler, Gary Armstrong, John Saunders and Veronica Wong, *Principles of Marketing*, 3rd European Edition, Pearson Education, 2002, pp. 205–207.

58. Stephen P. Robbins, *Organizational Behavior*, 10th edn, Prentice Hall, 2003, 156–175.

59. Philip Kotler, Gary Armstrong, John Saunders and Veronica Wong, *Principles of Marketing*, 3rd European Edition, Pearson Education, 2002, pp. 214–222.

60. Roger D. Blackwell, Paul W. Miniard and James F. Engel, *Consumer Behavior*, 9th edn, South-Western, 2001, Part II.

61. Gianfranco Walsh et al., "German Consumer Decision-Making Styles," *Journal of Consumer Affairs*, Summer 2001 Vol. 35, 1, p. 73.

62. Roger D. Blackwell, Paul W. Miniard and James F. Engel, *Consumer Behavior*, 9th edn, South-Western, 2001, p. 85.

63. Michael Laroche et al., "Effects of subcultural differences on country and product evaluations," *Journal of Consumer Behaviour*, Vol. 2, 3, 2003, pp. 232–247.

64. Simon Maniyiwa et al., "Determining linkages between consumer choices in a social context and the consumer's values: a means-ends approach," *Journal of Consumer Behaviour*, Vol. 2, 1, 2003, pp. 54–70.

65. Michael Laroche et al., "Effects of subcultural differences on country and product evaluations," *Journal of Consumer Behaviour*, Vol. 2, 3, 2003, pp. 232–247.

66. Philip Kotler, Gary Armstrong, John Saunders and Veronica Wong, *Principles of Marketing*, 3rd European Edition, Pearson Education, 2002, p. 17.

67. Roger D. Blackwell, Paul W. Miniard and James F. Engel, *Consumer Behavior*, 9th Edition, South-Western, 2001, Part V.

68. Courtland L. Bovee and John V. Thill, *Business In Action*, Prentice Hall, 2001, pp. 252–330.

69. Richard Lynch, *European Marketing*, Kogan Page, 1994, pp. 144–219.

70. Karen P. Goncalves, *Services Marketing – A strategic Approach*, Prentice Hall, 1998, pp. 140, 155.

71. James A. Fitzsimmons and Mona J. Fitzsimmons, *Service Management – Operations, Strategy, and Information Technology*, 3rd edn, McGraw-Hill, 2001, pp. 43–83.

72. Richard M. Hodgetts and Fred Luthans, *International Management*, International Edition, McGraw-Hill, 2003, Chapter 9.

73. Christopher H. Lovelock, *Services Marketing*, 3rd Edition, Prentice Hall International Edition, 1996, pp. 184, 204.

74. Vern Terpstra and Ravi Sarathy, *International Marketing*, 8th edn, The Dryden Press, 2000, Chapter 10.

75. Susan Foreman, *Marketing Assets: Branding Communities, Customer Loyalty and Relationships*, Manager Update, autumn 2000, Vol. 12, 1.

76. Philip Kotler, Gary Armstrong, John Saunders and Veronica Wong, *Principles of Marketing*, 3rd European Edition, Pearson Education, 2002, Chapters 11–22.

77. Earl Naumann, Donald W. Jackson Jr. and Mark S. Rosenbaum, "How to Implement a Customer Satisfaction Program," *Business Horizons*, January 2001, Vol. 44, 1, p. 37.

78. Sunil Gupta, Donald R. Lehmann, "What are Your Customers Worth? Not all customers are created equal. You need to know their lifetime value, then compare the cost of acquiring, serving, and keeping them," *Journal of Personal Selling & Sales Management*, Summer 2002, Vol. 22, 3, p. 207(2).

79. Susan K. Foreman, *Customer Satisfaction – Guaranteed*, Manager Update, Spring 2000, Vol. 11, 3.

80. Donald F. Kuratko et al., "Quality practices for a competitive advantage in smaller firms," *Journal of Small Business Management*, 2001, Vol. 39(4), pp. 293–311.

81. Sylvie Chetty, Colin Campbell-Hunt, "Explosive international growth and problems of success amongst small to medium-sized firms," *International Small Business Journal*, February 2003, Vol. 21, 1, p. 5 (23).

82. Anat BarNir, Ken A. Smith, "Interfirm alliances in the small business: the role of social networks," *Journal of Small Business Management*, July 2002, Vol. 40, 3, p. 219 (14).

83. Alkis Thrassou, *Strategic Marketing Management of the Small Consultancy Firm*, Ph.D. Thesis, The University of Leeds, 2002, Chapter 5.

84. Ibid., Chapter 10.

14

Doing Business in the Newly Emerging Economies

Rumen Gechev

Objectives

Through this chapter, the student will be exposed to:

- Characterization of the emerging economies' specifics
- Identification of their comparative advantages in foreign trade, direct, and portfolio investments
- Formulation of the possible investment risk and the mechanisms for its minimization
- Explanation of the business climate differences between the regions of Asia, Europe, Africa, and Latin America
- Analysis of the current trends and the development perspectives in the era of globalization
- Assessment of the interaction of the emerging economies with the world market.

Opening Case

The Case of India

The emerging economies offer a variety of new international business opportunities. India is a fascinating case with its growing potential in the software industry. Today, the country is one of the key suppliers of software products. Some compare the city of Bangalore with the Silicon Valley in California.

This comparison is probably exaggerated, but it really gives an impression about the size and the pace of development of that revolutionary industry. Today, India exports software products for more than $23 billion annually. It is a dramatic increase compared with the $105 million in 1990 or even compared to 1999 ($2.2 billion). The process started in the late 1980s with the American companies Texas Instruments and Verifone and the domestic producers Infosys and Wipro. The Indian government recognized the potential and played an active role in the establishment of Software Technology Parks which were given the preferences of the traditional free trade zones. It eased the capital and technology transfers and created comfortable and simulative environment for various forms of cooperation. All leading computer and software companies have subsidiaries or joint ventures in Bangalore, including IBM, Microsoft, and Motorola. The recently established joint venture JIIT (Japan India Information Technology Company) includes the Japanese corporation CSK which is the largest software and system integrator in Japan and represents a group of 90 companies operating worldwide.

The computerization of virtually all industries and services creates tremendous demand for software products and services and India perfectly utilizes that opportunity. The local professionals are able to produce and deliver the same product whose development in the United States, Japan, or in the EU would cost much more. The trends of transferring services from the highly developed into the emerging economies play a positive role for all stakeholders and help for the better allocation and better utilization of the productive capital. In the case with the software industry, such transfer has a multiplication effect on the host country's economy. It not only boosts the export but helps with the modernization of the rest of the economy and therefore is one of the vehicles for closing the gap between developed and developing countries. In 2006, the Indian software sector produced 4.8 percent of the country's GDP. NASSCOM expects that this sector will produce $60 billion output in the year 2010 (Exhibit 14.1).

Question: To what is India's success attributed? Explain in detail.

Source: Compiled by the author.

Introduction

The emerging economies are the subject of intensive academic research and business analyses. These countries represent the fastest growing sector of the world economy, measured as dynamics of the foreign trade turnover and the net capital inflow. The attractiveness of those economies is the increasing import demand and the improving export potential. The investors from the developed countries look for new opportunities created by the

Exhibit 14.1

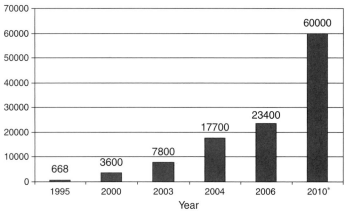

Indian Software Exports in Million US$

Source: NASSCOM–Indian National Association of Software and Services Companies (2006), accessed at http://www.computerwire.com/industries/research/on February 12, 2006.
*Forecast by NASSCOM

market expansion and the opportunities for higher return. We witness rapid globalization of the world market which opens new horizons for better allocation of the capital and the production.

No doubt, such intensified international economic interaction benefits all the participants. However, there are differences among the emerging countries which are determined by their current level of technological development, endowments of resources, degree of economic liberalization, access to the world capital and credit markets, level of indebtedness, and so on. These differences suppose different entry strategies and variety of models for cooperation.

We would like to clarify our methodological approach toward the emerging countries as far as they also belong to the group of developing countries. Some of the emerging economies are also classified as countries of transition from centrally planned toward a market economy. That is why they will be analyzed from different perspectives. Chapter 16 focuses on the developing countries and the countries in transition in Eastern Europe. There, you will find additional aspects, cases, and country analyses which will further broaden your knowledge in that particular field.

We do not share the assumption by some experts that the emerging economies are all developing countries minus the least developed ones. There are some other criteria which have to be applied when defining the scope of the group of emerging economies. Such additional criteria are growth of the economic potential, intensity of interaction with the world marketplace, degree of liberalization, functionality of the market mechanism and attitudes toward the foreign investors. So, the income level cannot be the only and the most reliable criterion for the categorization of a given country as an emerging or nonemerging one.

The discussion on the time horizon of the "emerging" economy is also open-ended. For example, the question if Singapore is still an emerging economy or it used to be such an economy in the 1980s does not have a convincing answer. Another problem is the interrelation between the level and timing of development and the classification "emerging" or "developed" country. Portugal does not count as an emerging economy but Taiwan does; although, from a historical point of view, Taiwan was industrialized earlier than Portugal and has better foreign trade and foreign investment parameters. Such methodological problems create good opportunities for creativity and open discussion.

Business Opportunities in the Financial Markets

Perhaps the financial market is the most volatile but at the same time the most dynamic and the most profitable one. It consists of three submarkets: (i) stock market (corporate shares); (ii) bond market (government and corporate bonds); and (iii) credit market (banks, saving institutions, investment institutions, and agencies). The first two form the capital market. Two determinants, the risk level and the investment return, play a decisive role in the structure of investment. The credit market was the dominant one for the emerging economies in Latin America and Asia till 1990. The second position was for the stock market and the bond market was absent or very weak at this time. The financial crisis since the mid-1990s speeded up the process of development of this bond market which plays a stabilizing role, especially in critical conditions, and also opens more opportunities for the investment diversification.

The structure of the financial market is of extreme importance not only from the point of view of investment interest and the portfolio decisions stock versus bond market, but also because it is a matter of an economic model of development that affects the national and regional economies. The Anglo-Saxon model is based on the priority of the capital markets and especially the stock markets. At the same time, the impressive industrial development of Japan and the other emerging Eastern Asian economies (South Korea, Thailand, Malaysia, Indonesia, India, and China) was based on the credit system, regulated and supported by the government. The importance of the different components of the financial markets could be measured as share of the GDP.

The financial market in the emerging economies is in a process of fast recovery after a series of financial collapses in Latin America and Asia during the 1990s. Fortunately, the world economy shows serious signs of slow economic growth which is gradually increasing. Most experts argue that the average GDP growth for the period 2000–2005 is about 3.2–3.5 percent and the forecast for this growth is to reach 4.5 percent in the period 2004–2006. Most of those countries have been increasing their hard currency reserves which strengthen their import purchasing power.

Another factor is the positive trend of some key macro-economic fundamentals, such as increased propensity to invest and higher investment return; downsized and better-controlled budget deficits; lower inflation; higher employment; stabilization of the balance-of-payments and the net exports; more reliable banking system; sustained inflow of direct investments; further liberalization of the foreign trade and the capital markets.

The degree of confidence is reflected in the spread of the interest rates. The higher the gap between the developed and the emerging economies, measured with the above listed indicators, the higher is the spread. In other words, the spread of interest rates on the securities mirrors the level of investment risk. The investment returns from the security markets in the United States and the other developed countries remain record low for the last few decades. Other things being equal, it moves the demand toward more profitable markets with low enough investment risk. J.P. Morgan's EMBI+ Index (Emerging Markets Bond Index Monitor)[1] showed a yield of 30 percent for 2003![2]

Some of the fundamentals, like the foreign debt, cannot be improved in the short run. Most of the governments of these emerging economies need fresh hard currency inflow to be able to service the debt. They have strong incentives to look for such resources on the world financial markets instead of borrowing from the domestic credit system. The denomination of the government securities in hard currencies is driven by two main factors: (i) unstable and unreliable local currency or (ii) because of the lower debt service cost if the interest rates for hard currency denominated instruments are relatively lower.

Why do the host countries have an interest in massive capital inflow? First, the domestic financial resources are limited and therefore very expensive for the host governments. By offering short- and long-term securities denominated in hard and local currencies, those governments may attract external funds at lower price. The securities denominated in local currencies are offered at higher return rates because of the higher risk for the investors. Secondly, a massive government borrowing could pull the trigger of the crowding-out effect expressed as limiting the investment resources for the private businesses, making them more expensive and limiting the growth in the private sector. Thirdly, the share of the government securities denominated in hard currencies is increasing the expense of the securities denominated in local currencies. It helps the service of the foreign debt at the lowest possible price. Fourthly, if the capital flow is insufficient, the government hard currency borrowing from "national" sources would cause misbalances in the foreign exchange market and problems with the inflation.

The International Monetary Fund's (IMF) statistical data about the period 1990–2001 clearly indicated growing capital market (stock and bonds) in Latin America with emphasis on the stock markets. In 1990, the regional financial market was total $770 billion, including $300 billion in shares and bonds. About ten years later, the financial market was more than doubled and reached $1.8 trillion. Meanwhile, the capital market rose from $300 billion to $1.2 trillion or by 400 percent. At the same time, the bank credits were increased with much lower rate: from $470 billion to $600 billion or by 22 percent.

In Eastern Asia, the share of the financial market in the GDP is still twice as much than in Latin America. It can be viewed as an indicator for the level of development of the market economy in correspondence with the OECD standards. The higher the shares, the better. The Asians pay more attention to the debt market development, especially after the financial turbulences in 1997–1998.

In 2001, the size of the capital markets in the two regions was nearly equal: $1.3 trillion in Eastern Asia and $1.2 trillion in Latin America. South Korea was the leader with $525 billion, Brazil second with $498 billion, and Taiwan took third position with $416 billion. Malaysian and Argentinean capital markets were with similar size of about $200 billion at the beginning of the twenty-first century. The bond markets were better developed in Latin America where they have higher weight in the financial markets, compared with the bank credits and stock capital. Bank credits are still dominant in East Asia, although the size of the Bond market is gradually increasing. The reason is the reluctance of the foreign investors to take the risk after the severe financial turbulences in the region in 1997–1998. The chosen model of economic policy is another factor for the structural differences in the financial markets. Some countries rely more on the traditional credit sources while others emphasize the capital market instruments.

Trade with debt securities is an excellent illustration of the bond market dynamics. Latin America shows a tremendous increase in the trade with such instruments (bonds and treasury bills), from $9.2 billion in 1987 to $66 billion in 1995 and culminating in about $300 billion at the end of 2003. Argentina showed remarkable dynamics in this segment of the financial market in the region, from barely $600 million in 1987 to nearly $95 billion in 2004—an increase of 158 times! Although Tunisia (Africa) is a small economy, it made an increase of 42 times, from $0.1 billion to $4.2 billion for the same period (Exhibit 14.2).

In the region of East Asia, South Korea is the leader with turnover of debt instruments for $65.6 billion and was ranked fourth among all emerging

Exhibit 14.2

International Debt Securities (in Billion US$), 1987–2004

Country/region	December 1987	December 1990	December 1995	December 2000	December 2004	Increase/folds 1987–2004
Singapore	0.9	2.1	1.1	9.2	24.2	27
Tunisia	0.1	0.2	0.8	1.5	4.2	42
South Africa	3.7	1.8	3.3	6	11.3	3
China	4.3	5	12.1	13.7	14.1	3.3
India	1.8	3.1	3.7	4.5	5.9	3.3
Indonesia	1.2	1.5	3.6	2.7	3.9	3.3
Malaysia	6.6	6.4	6.8	14.9	23.4	3.5
South Korea	5.2	4.4	25.9	46.8	65.6	12.6
Turkey	0.7	3.8	12.6	20.8	29.1	42
Argentina	0.6	0.1	18.5	75.4	94.8	158
Brazil	1.8	0.3	16.9	54.1	83.8	47
Chile	0.1	0.1	0.7	7.7	15.1	151

Source: Calculations based on data from the bank of International Settlements (BIS), accessed at: www.bis.org and from OECD: http://www.oecd.org/dataoecd/54/52/31603957.xls on February 10, 2006.

economies after Argentina ($94.8 billion), Brazil ($83.8 billion), and Mexico ($66.6 billion). Russia is a clear leader among the former socialist countries in Eastern Europe. Its international debt securities market reached $66.5 billion in 2004 and continues to grow.

Despite its vulnerability, the capital market, and the debt market in particular, highlights the attractiveness of such investment and the substantial potential for growth if the investment return margin is relatively higher than other alternative investments. The risk acceptability and an appropriate risk premium are other preconditions. Well-established capital market institutionalization, based on reliable legislation, is a must for the development of this market.

What is very important here is that the growing size of the financial markets is based on a combination of internal and external (foreign) sources. We would emphasize the fact that such development makes those countries less dependent on the foreign credit markets. It means that the risk of financial instability transfer from one region of the world economy into another is more limited under these conditions. Certainly, giving more importance to resources on the financial market ease the pressure on the banking system and allows higher independence (sovereignty) in the investment-decision process.

The investment risk includes the possibility of sudden financial collapse and government's insolvency (debt service moratorium), problems with the on-time exit from the troubled markets, and so on. The political factors are traditionally a strong incentive for the investors. Any change or expected change of the political spectrum (leftist, rightist, etc.) affects the risk level. Although the portfolio investments are more risky than the direct investments, it does not mean the portfolio investors do not seek guaranties or exit strategies in case the situation becomes out of control like in the cases of the Asian crisis or the collapse in Mexico in 1994–1995; South Korea and the Philippines (in 1997–1998) and recently when Brazil devaluated its currency in 1999 and when Argentina defaulted on its debt payments in 2002.

There are reliable indicators (indices) offered by leading institutions and consulting agencies like Moody's, Goldman Sachs, and J.P. Morgan. These indices and sub-indices measure the weighted return and the risk in various (short-, mid-, and long-term) portfolio investments. The indices are developed on a country-by-country basis. However, some aggregated indices are available for analysis of the trends on the world market or in some particular region. The indices of J.P. Morgan are based on the return and different maturities (monthly, quarterly, and semi-annually) of the Treasury Bills (TB) because this is the most demanded instrument and usually takes the lion's share of the offered securities.

The debate over the characteristics of the emerging financial markets: integrated versus segmented is still wide-open. We share the understanding of Bekaert and Harvey (2002) that in fact those markets are only partially integrated.[3] The integration process is the result of the overall process of internationalization and globalization of the world economy. There are also some particular factors, including liberalization of the capital outflows and inflows; improvement of the financial instruments for budget financing through the international financial markets; eased transaction mechanism (e-banking); economic cooperation and integration; coordinated macroeconomic policy; increased methodological and finance support from the IMF; and further democratization and increased confidence in the political leadership (especially in Eastern Europe, where the political reforms are irreversible).

The observation on the investment behavior shows some degree of inter-relations between the regional security markets—Latin America, South Asia, Far East, Eastern Europe, and so on. The investors react elsewhere even if the problems arise in one of the regions (contagion effect). They follow the historical experiences that clearly indicate the quick spread of the problems every time the investment risk is increasing for whatever reason. If the economy of Argentina is deteriorating, it affects not only the demand, especially the price on their security instruments, but also the market value of the Brady bonds of Bulgaria and Russia or any other emerging country. It is said that certain securities are marketable if they can be easily converted into cash within a short period (few days). Therefore, the securities issued and traded on the emerging markets are less marketable, that is difficult to convert into cash, which makes their trade much more risky and unpredictable. However, it does not exclude the country-by-country analyses and selection of the most profitable and secured market.

The higher business risk is the main obstacle for the investors on the capital markets. In principle, there are two main techniques of lowering the risk: (i) diversifying the portfolio (spreading the risk) and (ii) hedging the securities (an investment made in order to reduce the risk or adverse price changes in a security, by taking an offsetting position in a related security, such as an option or a short sale). The hedging of a security has different forms and approaches.[4]

K. Dew (2002) argues that there is a difference in the investor's preferences based on the level of the market's maturity.[5] Unlike the investments in the mature markets, the investments in the emerging markets are protected mainly by hedging. The explanation is that even well-diversified investments in securities cannot minimize the risk during sharp deterioration of the capital market conditions. The restructuring of the portfolio is difficult and quite expensive because of the higher transaction costs (converting one type of security into another).

We share the understanding that the liberalization of the financial markets in the emerging economies not necessarily brings stability. Econometric studies have confirmed that such liberalization might be one of the triggers for instability of the banking sector and therefore for the worsening of the parameters of the financial system. Demirguc-Kunt, Ash, and Detragiache (1999) recommended suitable precautions which could assure that the financial liberalization will lead to higher yields and lower investment risks: prudential regulation, permanent bank supervision, control on the security markets, strong creditor rights, reliable accounting practices, and good contract enforcement.[6] The foreign institutional and individual investors are interested in the return, especially the risk level of their investments rather than from the level of liberalization.

Objective analysis leads us to the assumption that the capital markets in the emerging economies are an excellent investment alternative. No question, the interest rates in these countries will remain much higher than in the developed countries. In addition, the volume of issued security instruments is expected to further increase. That means enlargement of the capital markets and what is even more—diversification of the used instruments. M. Goedhart and P. Haden (2003) came to the conclusion that the newly emerged markets are not as risky as some analysts believe.[7] The historical data for more than 15 years support the assumption that a portfolio investment in those markets is less risky than an investment in corporate shares from a given blue chip company in the OECD. If well diversified among different security instruments and among different emerging economies, the risk can be minimized to an acceptable level.

Exhibit 14.3 shows that the statistical data about the flow of net private capital to emerging market economies lead us to few important assumptions: First, the flow illustrates substantial increase in investments in the long run. Those investments in mid-1990s were about $230 billion, compared to an annual average of $16.6 billion in the 1980s. Secondly, although the rising trend is clear, those investments were cyclical: $229 billion in 1996, only 29.4 billion in the year 2000 and rising again to 65 billion in 2003. The explanation for such cycling is in the relatively high-risk component and the numerous financial and economic crises throughout those emerging markets.

Thirdly, there are trend differences between the different regions. The annual average net capital flows in the Western Hemisphere (mainly Latin America and the Caribbean) was increased from $40 billion (1990–1996) to $45.6 billion (1997–2002), while it has decreased in Asia in the same

Exhibit 14.3

Net Private Capital Flows to Emerging Market Economies, 1982–2002

Countries/region	1982–1989	1990–1996	1997–2002
All countries	16.6	142	61
FDI	12	62	156.8
Portfolio	0.6	59	5.2
Others	−1.7	21	−101
Africa	4.2	7.1	9.7
FDI	1.3	2.5	10.9
Portfolio	0.1	1.8	1.1
Others	2.8	2.9	−2.4
Asia	10.3	60.4	0.6
FDI	5	31.7	56.3
Portfolio	1.1	16.5	−0.8
Others	4.2	12.2	−54.9
Middle East and Turkey	1.7	22.5	−11
FDI	0.7	3.5	7.5
Portfolio	0.3	6.3	−10.5
Others	−4.4	12.7	−8.1
Western Hemisphere	1	40	45.6
FDI	0.5	40	45.6
Portfolio	0.1	26.8	10.6
Others	−4.3	−5	−23.8

Source: Deutsche Bundesbank, International Relations Department, J2/J2-2, Frankfurt, February 24, 2003.

periods—from $60.4 billion to record low of $0.6 billion. The decline is even sharper in the Middle East and Turkey, from 22.5 billion to −$11 billion (capital outflow). In fact, the main cause for the fluctuations in the region was the financial collapse in Turkey.

Fourthly, the steadiest FDI growth from annual average $12 billion in the period 1982–89, to $62 billion in the period 1990–96 and culminating to nearly $160 billion in 1997–2002. This obviously stronger foreign investors' interest in equities can be explained with the lower risk, compared to the capital market investments, the growing export potential of the real sector and the stable profitability in the long run. Another explanation is that while the return on portfolio investments in the emerging economies depends on the higher interest rates, compared to the developed countries, the return on direct investments has other determinants. In general, the lower the rates, the stronger the economic expansion and the higher the returns from direct investments.

M. Uribe and V. Yue (2003) found strong correlation (elasticity, maximum 1) between the interest rates level and the aggregated economic activities in Argentina (−0.67), Brazil (−0.51), Ecuador (−0.80), Mexico (−0.58), and Peru (−0.37). This correlation is not as strong in the Philippines (−0.02) and the Southern African Republic (−0.07).[8] The latter is explained by the specifics of the financing mechanisms in those two countries. As a consequence of that correlation, the lower interest rates, other things being equal, boost the growth and the profitability, while the indirect investments in debt instruments, for example, bring better returns only if there is a spread in the interest rates.

Why invest in the capital markets of the emerging economies?

- Higher investment return, based on the higher interest rates than in the developed countries
- Enough variety of government and corporate securities denominated in convertible currencies
- An opportunity to diversify the portfolio among different countries and regions
- Tax preferences in the issuing countries, secured by double taxation treaties.

Foreign Direct Investments

The magnitude and pattern of FDI toward particular country or region differ in correspondence with few crucial factors: (a) level of socio-economic development; (b) endowments with natural resources; (c) functionality of the market institutions and mechanisms; (d) character of the host-country economic policy; (e) stability of the foreign-exchange market; (f) political stability; and (g) legal system and law enforcement.

Some of the factors, like the political stability, determine the volume of investments, while others, like the level of socio-economic development, determine the structure of investments. In analyzing these factors, we see that the investments are in labor-intensive productions in countries with cheap and nonqualified labor and in high-tech productions in countries with highly qualified and experienced labor. Thailand (sport shoes) and Singapore (electronics) are good illustrations of that division.

The market's size is another factor. The smaller emerging economies support investment in productions with relatively low fixed cost because of the limitation of the economies-of-scale effect. In some cases, however, this limitation can be overcome by export-oriented businesses. The sector of electronics requires modern and expensive technologies which mean high fixed cost. It is not a problem for countries like Singapore, Taiwan, or Costa Rica where the production is export-oriented. China has much higher domestic market. Nevertheless its growing consumer electronics sector is also export-oriented.

One cannot expect huge foreign capital inflow if the host country's capital is not incorporated in the development of the host-country economy. The government support and/or participation are of critical importance. For example, Brazil has announced the priorities for the country's industrial development. The policy is oriented toward stimulus for some high-tech industries, like semiconductors, software, biotechnology, capital goods, and pharmaceutical products. The government has mobilized 15 billion Real for 2004 (about $5.2 billion, exchange rate of April 19, 2004) for that program, with most decisive contribution from the National Bank for Economic and Social Development and the government-controlled Banko de Brazil.

A package of almost 30 individual measures (stimuli) was applied in the software industry, including favorable tax exemptions. It will further boost the Brazilian export which reached the record high of $73 billion and brought trade surplus of $24.8 billion—also an unprecedented achievement in the country's economic history.[9] Such policies have double effect on the flow of investment: they mobilize internal public and private resources as well as foreign investments. It is well known that the foreign investors have stronger confidence and are willing to invest more in projects which have multilateral support from different stakeholders in the host country. In that particular case, the World Bank is also an active participant.

One of the notable examples for the decisive role of the legal system quality is the software business. The software industry, thanks to the FDIs, grows much faster in India after the improvement of the intellectual property rights protection. Combined with cheaper and qualified labor that legal factor made the FDI better secured and highly profitable. Today, India is one of the key suppliers of software products on the world marketplace.

United Nations Commission on Trade and Development (UNCTAD) has conducted a survey about the expected FDI developments in the period 2004–2007. The overwhelming majority of experts and CEOs of leading Trans National Corporations (TNC) have expressed high optimism about the possible trends of those investments in the emerging economies. The survey has identified the regional leaders as follows: in Africa (South African Republic, Angola, and Tanzania), in Asia and the Pacific (China, India, and Thailand), in Latin America (Mexico, Brazil, and Chile), and in the countries of transition (Poland, the Czech Republic, Russia, and Romania). We share the understanding that the (a) Greenfield investments will be the dominant one, followed by (b) mergers and acquisitions, (c) licensing, and (d) strategic alliances.

There are regional differences: For Latin America, the preferred entry strategy is expected to be mergers and acquisitions, followed by the greenfield operations. This assumption has emerged from the announced large-scale privatization programs for the public companies in the infrastructure and the extracting industries.

The lion's share of the FDI in Africa will be directed to the service sector, particularly in the production of electricity and water supply. The light industry (nonmetallic products, textile, clothing and food, and beverages) will attract the most foreign investments in the real sector.

The Asian emerging economies will further extend its sectors of consumer electronics, manufacturing, production of transport vehicles, instruments, textile, clothing, and so on. The forecast for more active investments in the sector of business services is very realistic and simply reflect the trends in that field during the last five years. Countries like Taiwan, Singapore, South Korea, and partly China and Malaysia have been focusing on industries with higher value-added, while Thailand, Vietnam, Pakistan, Bangladesh, and the Philippines still specialize in the lower value-added (labor-intensive) productions where they have competitive advantage.

We doubt the assumption of some experts that the main stream of FDI in Latin America will be in the extracting industries. First of all, the price trends for these products continue to be too low; therefore, the low returns cannot stimulate new investments. Second, the main trade partner of Latin America is the EU. Its newly accessed Eastern European countries are probably the main competitors of the Latin American exporters to the EU, because both regions have similar structure of their economies. However, the new EU member states are in privileged trade conditions.

The International Financial Corporation (IFC), which is a private sector lending arm of the World Bank, has a $15 billion portfolio of investments in 140 emerging economies. It now activates its green investment programs, following the recommendations of the summit on the Sustainable development conference in Johannesburg, 2002. About $55 million are assigned for environmental programs: energy saving, more efficient use of nonrenewable natural resources, gas emission reduction, and so on.[10]

All emerging economies rely on the inflow of foreign capital. The FDIs are welcome because they help to keep the technologies and the products at a competitive level. Usually, there are certain criteria for registering an investment as a "foreign investment" before allowing it into a special economic zone or making it eligible for any tax and other incentives. In principle, the requirements are about the size of the investment, the number of newly created jobs, the level of imported technologies and products—compared to the domestic market and the world market yardsticks, possible match with the government prioritized list of sectors and type of productions, the size of the stock owned by foreign companies or individuals measured as percentage from the overall stock of the given company, the source of the investment (excluding the so-called "money laundering"), and so on. The investments in the form of arrangement of external loans for the domestic companies are also considered as foreign investment.

In South Korea, the government counts an investment as a foreign direct investment if its size is at least 50 million Won (about $40,000–45,000, exchange rate in January 2003) or 25 million Won if the number of foreign investors are more than two in the same entrepreneurship. The government has set a list of prioritized 436 business sectors and 97 types of services where the investments would qualify for special incentives. The registration starts at the government's Committee for FDI and finally the Ministry of Finance and Economy (MOFE). The required parameters are even higher for the special Foreign Investment Zones (FIZ): minimum initial investment of $100 million and the newly developed jobs are at least one thousand. In addition, in case of joint venture or portfolio investment, the foreign investment ratio must be at least 50 percent or half of the shares (the equity).

In correspondence with the OECD criteria, applied by the Korean government, the portfolio investors are qualified as foreign direct investors if they control at least 10 percent of the domestic company's shares. It gives them a say in the managerial decision-making. An investment below 10 percent of the shares can also be qualified as direct only if the investment committee assesses it as an important one for the concrete businesses.[11] Otherwise, it is counted as a portfolio investment. The distinction is important, because the regulative regime and the incentives vary accordingly.

We believe that the FDI will continue to grow in absolute and relative values. The most favorable region for such investments in the long run is East and South-East Asia. In 2005, total FDI in Asia were about 110 billion, including $65 billion in China and nearly $6 billion in India. Few industrial sectors in Latin America are capable to attract additional foreign capital.

Brazil is a clear leader in the region with $19 billion in 2005, followed by Mexico, Colombia, and Argentina. Russia is the most attractive place for FDIs, compared to the other former socialist countries from Eastern Europe, which are not EU members yet. FDI in Russia were $17.6 billion in 2005 and the expectations for 2008 are for more than $23 billion. Few factors, among them booming oil/gas sectors, improving current account balance, financial stability, and increased hard currency reserves, explain the favorable investment conditions there. It is unlikely that Africa can change its investment climate in the short run. There is a potential but it cannot be utilized under the current "economic order." The challenge for the countries from that region is how to get out of the vicious circle of external debts.

Why investing in the real sector of the emerging economies?

- Expanding domestic markets that offer increasing investment return
- Elimination of the import restrictions, that is liberalization of the WTO trade rules
- Improving market structure and competitiveness

Harmonization of the business legislation with that in the developed countries

- Qualified, motivated and cheap labor
- Re-allocation of the TNC production facilities at or closer to the raw materials and energy sources
- Tax incentives and government export stimuli
- Utilization of trade preferences when exporting to the developed countries
- Easier access for re-export in the regional markets.

Foreign Trade Potential of the Emerging Economies

The foreign trade turnover mirrors the state of the economy and its export and import potential. The absorption ability of the national and regional markets and their trends of development are important criteria for the size and the patterns of the international business activities. There is a strong interdependence between the development of the export potential, for example, and the direct investments. Such dependence is understandable, because the export opportunities play a decisive role for the return on investments. The Japanese electronic companies invest in China not only because of the growing domestic market but also because of the opportunity to lower the production cost and to have better price competitiveness on the world markets. The same is true for the investments of the European and US car manufacturers in Brazil and Mexico or the US and UK oil corporations in Russia. On the other hand, direct investment inflow strengthens and improves the industrial capacity which further boosts the export.

The emerging economies have amazing developments in their foreign trade potential. Exhibit 14.4 reports that within a period of 23 years (1980–2003) the regional export has jumped as follows: Asia, excluding Japan, from $324 billion to $2106 billion (650%), Latin America from $11 billion to $377 billion (343%), and Africa from $121.5 billion to$172.5 billion (60%). The most significant increase is during the period 1990–2003. The export increase of Africa is very moderate for the same period, just 60 percent—from $121 billion in 1980 to $172.5 billion in 2003. Most recently, the leading exporters are South Africa ($36.5 billion), Nigeria ($20.3 billion), and Libya ($15 billion).

The export of the former socialist countries, including those from the former Soviet Union, has increased more than 2.5 folds—from $157 billion to $400 billion. Russia is a clear leader among them with an annual export of $183 billion in 2004, followed by Poland ($75 billion), Czech Republic ($69 billion), Hungary ($55 billion), and Ukraine ($33 billion). It explains why Eastern Europe is one of the most attractive regions for foreign investments. The growing export potential of this region shows the improving conditions for investments, exports, and re-exports. In fact, FDIs through

Exhibit 14.4

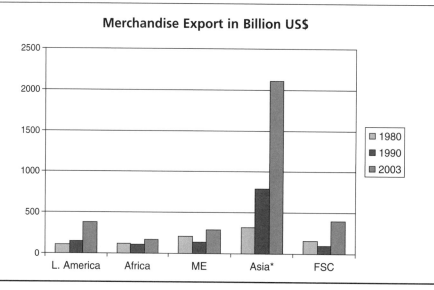

Merchandise Export in Billion US$

* *Excluding Japan*
Source: Calculations based on WTO data, accessed at http://www.wto.org/english/res_e/statis_e/webpub_e.xls on January 7, 2006.

privatization and green field operations are among the decisive factors for the improving competitiveness of these economies on the world marketplace.

Interestingly enough, the export from Middle East in 1990 is less, compared to 1980. It is an excellent example for the disadvantages of the so-called "mono developed economies." As far as the export consists dominantly of crude oil, any change in the oil prices directly reflects the revenue levels. In the period 1978–1981, the oil prices doubled, while at the beginning of the new century it went down. From the first three African exporters, only South Africa has some level of product diversification, including variety of products of the extracting industry, including precious metals, diamonds, minerals, and a limited list of capital goods.

The export structure mirrors the economic capacity of the given country and gives an impression on which are the most appropriate sectors for investments. As we know, there are no bad or good economic sectors. Every sector is good for doing business as long as it generates sustained profitability and enjoys gaining market shares. The main articles of Brazil, which can be counted as an average developed Latin American country, are metal and other basic manufacturing (18%), processed agro-based products (17%), and fresh food (15%). The value of computers, telecommunications equipment, and consumer electronics is only 1 percent of the total export. The only double percentage figure in the Indian export belongs to such group of commodities like textiles (17%), clothing (19%), fresh food (17%), and chemicals (10%). The metals and other basic manufacturing take 9 percent of the export while the computers, telecommunications equipment, and consumer electronics are at the level of 2 percent.

Saudi Arabia is probably the best example of an emerging economy with monoculture structure: the export of mineral products (crude oil) and its derivates represent nearly 97 percent of the export. On the other extreme are countries like Taiwan, which is one of the most prosperous emerging economies. Its annual GDP growth during the last three decades is 8 percent and the GDP per capita is above $16,000 (estimation 1999). The export of electronics, electrical, and machinery equipment embody 52 percent of the total export of $125 billion. In fact, the Taiwanese export is 2.5 times higher than the export of India, $122 billion and $55 billion respectively. The population of Taiwan is only 22.6 million people, while India's population is above one billion. So, the export per capita in India is $52 while in Taiwan it is $5398.[12]

What is a major concern for the emerging countries in general is that with a few exceptions (Singapore, South Korea, Taiwan, Mexico, Brazil and Argentina, and to a certain extent China) the export consists of low value-added commodities. At the same time, the import consists of mainly high-valued commodities which automatically affect the trade balance of those countries. As shown in Exhibit 14.5, the trends of the import closely

Exhibit 14.5

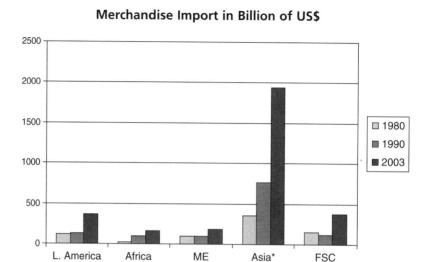

Merchandise Import in Billion of US$

Legend: 1980, 1990, 2003

Categories: L. America, Africa, ME, Asia*, FSC

* *Excluding Japan*
Source: Calculations based on WTO data, accessed at: www.wto.org/english/res_e/statis_e/ webpub_e.xls on January 7, 2006.

follow the trends of the export. In fact, such dependence is not unique for those countries.

Higher export supposes higher import. Also, an increase of the export revenues improves the standard of living which in turn leads to higher demand on imported goods. Theoretically, the balance of unit imported high-valued good or service requires much higher physical volume of low-valued export. The comparative analyses confirm that the value growth of export is still behind the increase of the material production and respectively its realization on the world markets.

The price fluctuations are another reason for that mismatch. Unfortunately, the prices on low processed goods and raw materials show high vulnerability and nonsustainability. The basic trend is toward decrease of the relative prices. However, that situation is gradually improving during the last 10–15 years. Africa had $6.4 billion trade deficit in 1990 and $7.9 billion surplus in 2003. Asia and the Middles East have $66.4 billion and $102 billion surpluses respectively. Latin America used to be below the "red line" with trade deficit of $11.1 billion in 2001. The good news is that the region had positive current account balance in 2003 and 2004, $9.2 billion and $3.0 billion respectively.

For many of those countries, the import structure is a matter of concern. Too many emerging economies continue to rely on the import of consumer goods, including food products, and on expense of the capital goods. Most economists agree that the only instrument for economic restructuring and improvement of the foreign trade efficiency is the import of technologies, equipment, machinery, know-how, licenses, and so on. The less developed emerging economies simply do not have the resources to buy such import nor the markets to realize the final product.

We share the understanding that few measures are to be taken for the enhancement of this situation: debt forgiveness, easier access to modern technologies, substantial FDI, additional export and import (asymmetric) preferences, more justified price policy, downsizing of the subsidies in the developed countries, and an increased financial support.

While the tariff and nontariff barriers for industrial goods were substantially reduced during the last two decades, the import restrictions on agro products, textile, clothing, and other low value-added products, applied by the developed countries, remain relatively high. The average import tariffs on agro products and clothing is about 10–11 percent and about 7 percent on textile products. All three commodity groups have also quota restrictions. In addition, the developed countries spend annually more than $350 billion in subsidies that cause price distortions and directly undermine the competitiveness of the export from the emerging economies. Such unfair policies hamper their export opportunities and limit the economic growth. The consumers in the developed countries are also hurt because they pay higher prices for the same goods.

There are few decisive factors which accelerated the trade augmentation during that period: (a) higher economic growth, (b) liberalization of the economic policy and particularly the import regime, (c) successful bilateral and multilateral trade agreements between the WTO members, (d) trade preferences for the emerging economies, including the status of most favorable nation (MFN), (e) establishment of regional customs unions, (f) enlargement of the aggregate demand in the developed countries, and (g) export-oriented economic policies.

The most impressive boost of merchandise export is in Asia. By WTO (2005) estimations, five out of the first larger exporters in 2004 were from that region, China ($593 billion), South Korea ($254 billion), Taiwan ($183 billion), Singapore ($180 billion), Saudi Arabia ($126 billion), and Malaysia ($127 billion). Mexican export reached $190 billion (third position among the emerging economies) and that of Brazil $97 billion. India demonstrated an increase from $8.6 billion to $76 billion in 2004. However, this volume is rather low if calculated for per capita or as a percentage of the country's GDP. In fact, the structural and the relative analyses of these trends and figures is a must for the different countries.

We would suggest that for the foreign business the most crucial are two criteria: the volume of the export potential and its efficiency. First of all, the same volume of export of similar commodity group made from two different countries may bring different revenues. Why so? First of all, the ratio of production cost (delivery cost) to sale price is different, even for such standard goods like raw materials, textile, or clothing. If we assume that the world market price is the same, the profitability will vary in correspondence with that cost: price ratio. Therefore, the emerging economies are gaining market share because of that comparative advantage in some selected sectors. Those sectors are different in Singapore (electronics, financial services), China (textile, clothing, instruments, consumer electronics), Pakistan (textile, clothing), Brazil (coffee, transport vehicles), Mexico (manufacturing, clothing, food products), and so on.

Growing Potential of the Market of Services

An observation of the basic trends of liberalization for the industrial and service sector shows that the liberalization of the latter is much slower. It is a problem, because the quality and the cost of the various services affects directly or indirectly the productivity of the real sector. The Uruguay Round of the GATT (WTO, since January 1995) was focused on the liberalization of the sector of services. Many of the regional economic groups and international organizations, OECD for example, also work in that direction. As a member of the WTO and OECD (1996), Korea followed that stream.

The financial crisis of 1997–1998 was an additional factor of further liberalization of trade with services. It was proved that the lack of openness of that sector for foreign investments was one of the reasons for the severe negative effects on all emerging economies. Korea substantially reduced the number of fully restricted (radio and TV broadcasting) and partially restricted (processing of nuclear fuel, publishing, telecommunications, domestic banking, and few others) sectors for foreign investments and fully opened its market for services like distribution services, entertainment, and recreational. Partial liberalization was allowed for the financial services, transportation, and communication. In the service sector, 154 business categories were liberalized in the period 1993–2000.[13] This process is further continuing in the new millennium.

By World Bank estimation, the liberalization of the service sector would bring additional $6 trillion revenue for the emerging economies in the period of 2005–2015. It is four times the gain that would result from the liberalization of the trade with goods. It is an important agenda because today more than 45–50 percent of the GDP in those countries is produced in the service sector and this share continues to increase. It is a very profitable sector where the productivity is increasing by impressive rates. Only 19 percent of the employment in India is in the service sector but that sector produced 49 percent of the country's GDP in 2000. It means that the productivity in services is higher than the nation average.

Uganda's service sector produced 40 percent of the GDP in 2000 (WTO report). The growth of that sector today (about 7% annually) is nearly five times higher than the agro production growth and is getting closer to the annual growth of the industrial sector (about 10% annually). The country is becoming a fast developing service center for East Africa offering services where Uganda has comparative advantage: education, health care, inland port and air cargo logistics, distribution, communication technology, publishing, and financial services. The government promotes confidence for the foreign investors in these fields.

An important consideration is that the WTO clearly distinguishes between trade with services and regulation of services. It is a critical clarification because the service sector in general needs appropriate regulation for different reasons, including the phenomena "natural monopoly." So, there is no conflict between the necessity of trade liberalization of services and their regulation. At this stage, the WTO does not require privatization or commercialization of the service companies. Such decisions are left to the government authorities. The most open and profitable sectors for foreign investments are the telecommunications, transportation services, financial services, business consulting, software, and marketing. Less open yet are the port facilities, the energy sector, TV and radio broadcasting, publishing, and some others. However, these restrictions vary for different countries. For example, the services in Thailand and Taiwan are much more liberalized than in India or Korea.

The growth of commercial services trade of the developing countries, including the emerging economies, is above the world average (8 percent). In Latin America, this growth is about 7 percent annually for the period 1990–2004, 6 percent in the Middle East, and an average 12 percent for the developing countries in Asia. In the period 1995—2004, some Asian emerging economies achieved impressive export annual growth: China (14%), South Korea (7%), Singapore (3%), and Turkey (6%). Brazil and Russia show sustained growth in their potential for export of services—about 7 percent for the same period. All selected emerging economies, but Turkey, had trade deficit in services in 2004. Singapore is a leading provider of financial services in the region while Turkey relies mainly on tourist services.

However, these deficits tend to decline. As you see from Exhibit 14.6, the dynamics in import is fading behind the dynamics of export for most of the selected countries. The gap between the exported and the imported services is closing. It is an indicator that the competitiveness of the emerging economies in this particular sector is gradually increasing. Import of services plays a positive role for the dynamics and the structure of the economic growth. The data for 2004 indicates the vulnerability of the tourist and financial services to political and financial instability. The terrorist attacks against the United States in 2001 affected the tourist services around the World and mainly

Exhibit 14.6

Commercial Services in Selected Emerging Economies in 2004 (in Billion US$) and Their Change during 1995–2004 (in %)

	Export Value	Export 1995–2004 (%)	Import Value	Import 1995–2004 (%)
Taiwan	26	6	30	3
Mexico	14	4	20	9
Thailand	19	3	23	2
Turkey	24	6	10	9
Singapore	37	3	36	6
China	62	14	71	13
South Korea	40	7	50	8
India	40	n.a.	41	n.a.
Brazil	11	7	16	2
Russia	20	7	33	6

Source: WTO, 2006, accessed at: http://www.wto.org/english/res_e/statis_e/its2005_e/charts_e/chart_iv02.xls on February 16, 2006.

the neighboring countries. The same factor troubled the number of tourists visiting Turkey. South Korea is still recovering its financial sector after the heavy losses during the Asian crisis at the end of the 1990s.

The share of the "traditional services" transportation and travel (tourism) remain below the share of "other services" (financial, communications, business, medical, educational, etc.) and this gap is increasing. In fact, the absolute value of the traditional services has been increasing substantially during the last few decades. It is the result of the increasing foreign trade turnover and the improvement of the standard of living which in return increases the demand for tourist services.

Exhibit 14.7 simply illustrates the higher dynamics of development of the other services which is based on the structural changes of the world economy and the introduction of new business services. Imagine the revolutionary role of Internet and the e-commerce that change the way we do business and open new horizons for faster, cheaper, and more reliable business interactions. We do expect that the most dynamic and the most profitable business opportunities will be the sectors of telecommunications, e-trade and banking.

Which are the advantages of the foreign trade business in the emerging economies?

- Ongoing liberalization of the trade regime
- Excellent opportunities for re-exporting from the special free trade zones

Exhibit 14.7

World Exports of Commercial Services by Category (Percentage of Total Value)

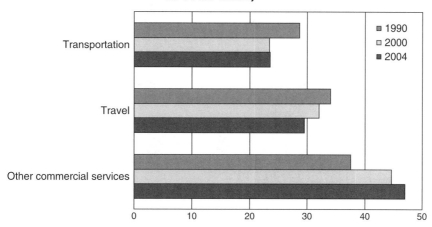

Source: WTO (2005), accessed at www.wto.org/english/res_e/statis_e/its2005_e/charts_e/chart_iv02.xlsWTO, ITC, IMF on February 19, 2006.

- Increasing purchasing power and higher demand of consumer durable and nondurable goods
- Large-scale industrialization and strong demand for capital goods, including the most sophisticated technologies
- Economic restructuring, oriented toward preferable development of the sector of services. It opens opportunities for both import and export of services
- An opportunity for the producers from the developed countries to extend their product's life cycle by entering new markets or new market niches
- Good options to combine the product export with direct investments and production cooperation, including exploitation of sub-contracting systems with local producers. It may reinforce the price competitiveness of the finished product on the host country or on the world market
- Enhanced terms of trade with the developed countries
- Import of healthier, organic agro product.

Closing Case

China: The Future Consumer Superpower

China is the most impressive emerging economy with an annual average GDP growth of nearly 10 percent during the last ten years. High growth results in increasing market potential and aggressive consumer demand. High growth in purchasing power combined with population of 1.3 billion people makes China extremely attractive for FDI and portfolio investments. It is not a surprise that FDI in China are higher than FDI in whole Eastern Europe including Russia and Ukraine.

Leading corporations from all over the world utilize the country's huge domestic market and its enlarging export potential based on cheap production factors, highly qualified and well-motivated labor, and very attractive tax stimuli. Today, China is the largest producer of consumer electronic products, including TV sets, DVDs, digital cameras, electronic games, and PCs.

The Japanese electronic giant Sony began operations in China in 1996. Its annual sales reached $4 billion in 2004 and continue to grow. The combination of Japanese high technology, developed distribution system on the world marketplace, and well-known brand name with the comparative advantages of the Chinese business environment boosts Sony's competitiveness. Many other internationally recognized producers like Siemens (Germany), Philips (the Netherlands), LG (Korea), Samsung (Korea), Hewlett Packard (USA), BenQ of Taiwan, and many others are also present there. These companies were attracted by the $ 14 billion annual sales in consumer electronics. Expectations are even more encouraging—10 percent annual market growth or $22 billion by 2009.

At the same time, high quality and cheap electronics made in China continue to increase its market share on the world marketplace. Most leading corporations in that field transfer their production facilities to China or make new, green field investments in an attempt to utilize as much as possible the country's absolute and comparative advantages in production and foreign trade. For example, Sony announced at the end of 2005 its plans to cut 10,000 jobs of its global workforce by the first quarter of 2008. In addition, the company will close 11 of its 65 plants worldwide. Of course, it does not relate to Sony (China). In fact, the main reason for closing production facilities in other countries is the transfer of production to the territory of China because of the higher investment return and sustained growth of the market potential.

Question: Do you agree with some experts that outsourcing of production (jobs) from the developed toward emerging economies like China favors only the emerging economies?

Sources: Sony chairman. China is key to growth (October 17, 2005) by Elaine Kurtenbach, Associated Press, accessed at www.usatoday.com/tech/news/techpolicy/business/2005-10-17-sony-china_x.htm on march 2, 2006; News& Features (September 26, 2005) by Kenji Hall, accessed at www.business week.com/innovate/content/sep2005/id20050926_379956.htm on March 1, 2006.

Chapter Summary

The emerging markets are increasing their attractiveness for various forms of international businesses. This positive trend is determined by the ongoing process of market liberalization and additional stimuli for the foreign businesses. These stimuli are selective and focused on the host countries' priorities of economic development. Special import incentives, tax exemptions, and cofinancing are applied for the development of production of high value-added goods and services or in the production of goods with substantial import substitution effect or which generate export revenues in hard currencies.

These countries have an increased participation in the world division of labor and the rising volume of trade is accompanied with attempts for more active cooperation in the field of production and export of goods and services. The WTO gives some tariff preferences for the import from the emerging economies. However, further support and better entry opportunities offered by the developed countries may play a more decisive role in the improvement of the terms of trade. Clearly, the volume and the quality of the foreign investments, especially the direct ones, will make it possible to increase their competitiveness in the era of globalization. Every emerging economy, regardless of its stage of development or income level, has its comparative advantages and specific business opportunities. The problem is how to identify these opportunities and how they can be better utilized.

Review and Discussion Questions

1. What is the current role of the emerging economies in the world marketplace?
2. Analyze the basic trends in the development of the emerging economies and identify their advantages and disadvantages, compared to the most developed countries.
3. Compare the advantages and the risks from portfolio investments for the foreign investors and the host country respectively.
4. Explain the different forms of direct investment as an illustration of different entry strategies.
5. Compare the advantages and disadvantages of various forms of business interaction with the different geographic regions: Latin America, sub-Saharan Africa, Europe, Asia, and the Pacific.

6. How is the world business cycle affecting the emerging economies and their net capital flow?

7. Define the main patterns of foreign trade from and to the emerging economies.

8. Is globalization a threat to the emerging economies or does it create new opportunities for them? Support your opinion with arguments and concrete examples.

9. Assess the current WTO rules and suggest possible improvements which may lead to more favorable conditions for the emerging economies.

10. Some US economists and politicians criticize the process of outsourcing of industrial jobs toward the emerging economies, blaming the "irresponsibility" of the corporations' top management. Do you share this understanding or do you disagree with it. What are you pro or con arguments?

11. Explain the business environment specifics of doing business in the former socialist countries.

12. Why is China among the most attractive investment targets?

Endnotes

1. The first EMBI was introduced in 1992 and covered the Brady Bonds (named after the US Secretary of Treasury at that time who proposed this newly invented foreign debt service mechanism). It was later upgraded to EMBI+, indicating the total returns for traded external debt instruments which consist of Eurobonds, Brady Bonds, denominated in convertible currencies, loans, and host country market instruments denominated in US dollars. The EMBI+ is focused on portfolio instruments from the three major Latin American economies (Mexico, Brazil, and Argentina), reflecting the size and liquidity of these external debt markets. The other groups of countries are Bulgaria, Poland, Russia, the Philippines, Morocco, Nigeria, and South Africa. A minimum of $500 million outstanding balances is required for the EMBI+ instruments, accessed at: www2.jpmorgan.com.

2. *The Economist Global Agenda*, April 14, 2004, accessed at: www.economist.com.

3. Bekaert, G. and Harvey, C. "Research in Emerging Market Finance: Looking to the future," *Emerging Markets Review*, 492–498.

4. See at www.investorwords.com/2293/hedge.html.

5. Dew, K. (2002). *Emerging Market Return Correlations*, accessed at: www2.isikun.edu.tr.

6. See in more details: Demirguc-Kunt, Ash, and E. Detragiache (1999). "Financial Liberalization and Financial Fragility," Conference report before the Annual World Bank Conference on Developing Economics in 1998, Editors: Pleskovic, B. and Stigliz, J.

7. Goedhart, M. and Haden, P. *Are emerging markets as risky as you think?*, accessed at: corporatefinance.mckinsey.com.

8. Uribe, M. and Yue, V. *Country spreads and emerging countries: Who drives whom?* Working Paper 10018, NBER, Oct 2003, accessed at: www.nber.org/papers/w10018.

9. Gazeta Mercantil, *Investe Brazil*, DCI 25 March–6 April, 2004.

10. *Investing in Emerging Markets Goes Green*, DevNews Media center, Aug.27, 2002.

11. Korean Trade-Investment Promotion Agency, accessed at: www.invest.go.kr.

12. MF, WTO, national statistics.

13. Jong-Il Kim and June-Dong Kim. Impact of Services Liberalization on Productivity: The Case of Korea, accessed at www.nber.org/~confer/2000/easexi00/kim.pdf.

15

Business Behavior in Europe's Single Market

Christina Ioannou and Marios I. Katsioloudes,
Spyros Hadjidakis

Objectives

Through this chapter, the student will be exposed to:

- Appreciate the economic and political devastation that Europe experienced in the aftermath of World War II and realize that this distraction contained the seeds of co-operation between some Western European states
- Understand how the EU has evolved through time, from its original Community structure to its present arrangement
- Get an idea of the basic institutional design of the EU and the key functions of each of the main institutions
- Become familiar with the EU's policy of enlargement, by looking at successive enlargements over the years
- Recognize national/cultural differences across member states of the Union and appreciate the obstacles that these differences impose on free trade
- Get an idea of how businesses behave in Europe's single market and why they tend to behave in this way
- Realize how the elimination of barriers in the trading of goods has taken place over time
- Measure progress in the field of freeing up the movement of services in the Union and evaluate its significance
- Appreciate that (and to what extent) people/workers can move freely in the EU

- Understand how the freedom of movement of capital has been pursued over the years and value its significance
- Assess the impact of the European Monetary Union (EMU) on business behavior
- Evaluate the importance of adopting a common competition policy in the EU.

Opening Case

Cultural Differences—A Barrier to Free Trade: The Cassis de Dijon Case and the ECJ Decision

The Issue

In the "Cassis de Dijon" case, the European Court of Justice (ECJ) struck down a German import prohibition. The prohibition disallowed the import, sale, and/or marketing of liqueurs in Germany that did not meet minimum German alcohol standards. The ruling gave the European Commission an opportunity to develop the principle of "mutual recognition." Ultimately, the principle implies that any national law with reasonable policy goals, such as environmental conservation, health, and so on, will be tolerated within the regional trading block of Europe.

Description

In February 1979, the ECJ struck down a German prohibition on imports from other EU countries. The prohibition banned the importation of alcoholic beverages that did not meet minimum alcohol content requirements. The case involved Cassis de Dijon, a French liqueur manufactured from black currants. Cassis contains 15–20 percent alcohol and the German standards prescribed 25 percent. Rowe-Zentral AG, a German import/export firm, brought a suit charging that the German regulation on minimum alcohol contents was an illegal non-tariff barrier.

The German government argued the validity of its regulation primarily on health grounds, claiming that the law existed to avoid the proliferation of alcoholic beverages within the German market. It argued that beverages with low alcoholic content induce a tolerance toward alcoholism more than highly alcoholic beverages. Germany also offered a consumer protection justification claiming there was a need to protect consumers from unfair producer and distributor practices. In its final argument, the German government argued that the elimination of the import ban would mean that one country could set the standards for all member states, thus precipitating a lowering of standards throughout the EU.

After the case was brought against the German courts, the ECJ ruled that because Cassis met French standards, it could not be kept out of the German market. The ECJ rejected the German health argument as unconvincing and dismissed the consumer protection justification. After rejecting the German defense claims, the Court spelled out the general principle, which is now the most famous part of the ruling: "There is therefore no valid reason why, provided that they have been lawfully produced and marketed in one of the Member States, alcoholic beverages should not be introduced into any other Member State."

The Court ruled that barriers to trade were allowed only to satisfy mandatory requirements relating to the effectiveness of fiscal supervision, the protection of public health, the fairness of commercial transactions, and the defense of the consumer. When these conditions are threatened and import prohibitions are found to be valid, the EU's Commission would provide minimum standards in the form of a directive. Member states would then be obliged to harmonize their standards to meet the criteria set out in Commission directives.

There were cases before Cassis, which formed new ideas about the integration of standards. The German law had previously been challenged in 1974 in the Dassonville case. It established the legal basis for challenging the validity of domestic standards that create non-tariff barriers. The Dassonville case was identical to Cassis, only the liquor in question was French Anisette. The case was dropped after the German government made an exception for Anisette and allowed it to be imported. But it was the Cassis ruling that was exploited by the Commission in its attempt to foster free trade throughout the EU.

Cassis gained notoriety when a political debate was instigated by the Commission. The Commission extracted the aspects of the ruling that were useful for eliminating non-tariff trade barriers. In the fall of 1979 Etienne Davignon, the internal market commissioner, suggested in front of the EU Parliament that trade policy should take a new direction based on the Cassis ruling.

The Commission's new approach toward liberal trade was to affect the way the member states would harmonize their divergent environmental standards. The principle of "mutual recognition," as set out in the Cassis case, was to replace the policy of "absolute harmonization." Mutual recognition allowed the Commission to issue directives in order to assure a high minimum standard in areas such as environmental protection.

A year and a half after the ruling, the European Commission spelled out the implications for free movement of goods within the EU. The Official Journal of the European Communities states, "Any product imported from another member state must in principle be admitted. . . if it has been lawfully produced, that is, conforms to rules and processes of manufacture that are customarily and traditionally accepted in the exporting country."

Question: Account for the significance of national/cultural differences in blocking the freedom of trade of goods within Europe's single market. How has the ECJ responded to this?

Source: TED Case Studies (1997), in *http://www.american.edu/TED/ cassis.htm*, case number 220, Case Mnemonic: Cassis, case name: Cassis Spirit Trading in the EC.

Introduction: What is Influencing Business Behavior in Europe's Single Market?

As the EU continuously grows, deepens and matures, business behavior is influenced by this constantly changing climate. The increased freedom that nowadays characterizes the movement of goods, services, people, and capital, and which involves a culturally diverse pattern, as all the more countries get involved in this—following the successive enlargements of the Union over the years—impacts upon the ways in which businesses often tend to behave.

In the absence of any regulatory measures, businesses would seek to insulate and protect themselves from any environment of intense competition. In this context, business behavior in Europe's single market, if left uncontrolled, would be characterized by severe competitive pressures, owing to the forces of increased mobility that exist within this enlarged Union, which today includes 25 different nations. Nevertheless, as the ways in which businesses often tend to react to competitive pressures are largely perceived as undesirable for the well-being of the people and the society at large, business behavior has not been left uncontrolled in the EU. Instead, carefully designed competition rules have been laid down to "control the game," and to make sure that this is not conducted at the expense of the people (workers, consumers, and citizens in general).

The aim of this chapter is specifically to account for business behavior in Europe's single market and demonstrate the significance of having a clearly defined competition policy in this framework. The main factors that will be presented and accounted for in this context, as those impacting upon such behavior, are specifically the deepening of the integration process (and the free movement of goods, services, people, and capital that have accompanied this development) as well as the widening of the Union (and the national and cultural diversity that this process of successive enlargements has brought about). The argument that will explicitly emerge from this chapter is that the ways in which businesses behave and the importance of competition rules in the EU, can be demarcated by considering the catalytic role played by the intertwining of the above-mentioned factors of integration deepening and widening.

The Challenges in the European Continent in the Aftermath of World War II

In the aftermath of World War II, the setting was characterized by a devastated Europe that sought the means for reconstruction and development. An economically and politically distressed continent, then, was what determined the order of the day after the War. In the background of this distraction, the Cold War soon emerged between the West and the former Union of Soviet Socialist Republics (USSR). The new threat was primarily an ideological one as, before long, Soviet Communist ideas began to spread in the continent and influence many Eastern European countries. Alarmed by these developments, the United States sought to insulate the Western European nations from the Communist influence of the East, as already events in some countries—such as the 1946 civil war in Greece and the Communist-supported strikes throughout France and Italy in 1947—were seen as very disquieting. Churchill was already talking about an "iron curtain" dividing Europe, and Truman was determined to remain involved not only in events taking place across the Atlantic in the European continent, but also in world affairs in general (the Truman doctrine—March 1947).

The Truman doctrine was soon followed—under the initiative of George Marshall, the US Secretary of State—by the Marshall Plan (June 1947). This was a European Recovery Programme (ERP), the significance of which was not only in its financial aid offer to the Western European countries (of $1.3 billion),[1] but also in the condition that complemented this, namely that the money offered should be used *jointly* by the states for their reconstruction. The aim of this US condition was to create a "safety net" against the perceived Soviet threat, by encouraging and instigating cooperation between Western European states, so that they could come together and stand united against the communist Eastern bloc. The rationale behind this is that the financial incentive would also encourage a more Westernized vision among these ideologically frustrated, war-stricken countries, and they would thus come to form part of the capitalist West and stand united against the Soviets. The end result of this provision was the formation of the Organisation for European Economic Co-operation (OEEC) in April 1948,[2] the purpose of which was to manage the Marshall funds and decide upon their distribution and allocation.

The OEEC laid, in this way, the foundations for cooperation within the European continent. It provided, in other words, the basis for further cooperation between the states involved. The main reason for this was a gradual realization, over time, that the states depended economically upon each other. This had been, in fact (albeit controversially so), the main underling objective of the US Marshall Aid offer: to induce, in other words, this realization that cooperation between the Western states of Europe was to their advantage. A united Western European front essentially meant insulation from the perceived Communist threat.

The First Steps: The Origins of Cooperation in Europe

The Treaty of Paris (1951): The European Coal and Steel Community

The first steps in the direction of creating a united (economically) Western European front that would extend its scope of activity far beyond a recovery program, focusing also upon closer economic cooperation in the process of production, was taken in the early 1950s. The Schuman Plan—suggested in 1950 by Robert Schuman, the French foreign minister, and formulated by Jean Monnet, a French civil servant—proposed cooperation between France and Germany in the production of coal and steel. Based on this proposal, in 1951, the European Coal and Steel Community (ECSC) was formed with the Treaty of Paris.[3] The agreement was between six states, as Germany and France were joined by Italy and the Benelux countries (Belgium, The Netherlands, and Luxembourg), and it involved joint control of the industries of coal and steel in these states. Under the ECSC, production of these two basic commodities, in the member states, was managed together under a body known as the High Authority.

The creation of the ECSC marked the beginning of the European integration process, as this Community gradually evolved to become the Union that today defines cooperation between 25 states of the European continent. The deepening of this process of cooperation is considered stage by stage in the following section.

The Deepening of European Integration: The Evolution of the EU through Treaties

The Treaties of Rome (1957): The EEC and Euratom

In 1957, a decisive step was taken in the direction of deeper co-operation between the six members of the Community, with the signing of the two

Treaties of Rome.[4] The Treaties established the European Atomic Energy Community (Euratom) and the EEC.

The former represented a realization among the members that co-operation should be extended to cover other sectors (other than coal and steel), which were also industrially important, and which were essential resources that, if utilized correctly, could contribute to the affluence of the economy and the society at large. In this capacity, nuclear energy was considered to be a vital resource that was essential for industrial advancement. Pooling energy supplies together was hoped to lead to economic development, growth, and prosperity.

In the Treaty of Rome establishing Euratom, it was stated that a clear objective of the countries was "to create the conditions necessary for the development of a powerful nuclear industry which will provide extensive energy resources, lead to the modernisation of technical processes and contribute, through its many other applications, to the prosperity of their peoples."[5]

Even though the Treaty of Rome establishing Euratom signified a major step in economic cooperation between the members states—by expanding industrial production activities—this was clearly confined to a single field (the atomic energy field). It could be argued that, of the two Rome Treaties, the most important was the one establishing the EEC. This is so because the latter marked, in fact, the establishment of a customs union between the six members, by removing customs duties and quantitative restrictions on trade between them. Moreover, this step was complemented by the adoption of a common commercial policy (CCP), through the introduction of a common external tariff (CET): a tariff, in other words, that was to be imposed upon trade with countries that were outside the Community (non-member states of the EEC).

The Treaty of Rome establishing the EEC also established an institutional structure that was to be responsible for governing the functions of the Community. This was to consist of a Commission, a Council of Ministers, a Parliamentary Assembly and a Court of Justice. This institutional architecture of the Community is discussed in more detail later.

The creation of the EEC was certainly an ambitious step in the deepening of the cooperation process between the countries involved. As specified in the Treaty of Rome establishing the EEC, this move was hoped to *"lay the foundations for an ever closer union among the peoples of Europe."*[6] Indeed, the aspiration was to gradually create a common market, which would progressively and eventually lead to the harmonious development of economic activities within the Union. This was hoped to be accomplished through a steady approximation of the economic policies of the member states.[7] The economic target was nonetheless entwined with a social goal, as the Treaty of Rome establishing the EEC clearly outlined that both economic and social progress were among the fundamental objectives of the Community. Constant improvements in living and working conditions were to be introduced throughout the EEC.

The Single European Act (1986): The Single Market

The adverse economic climate of the early 1970s and early 1980s resulted in a period of stagnation in the process of cooperation between the member states. This period has often been characterized as the "Dark Ages" of the Community. This trend was, however, reversed in the mid-1980s with the signing of the Single European Act (SEA).[8]

The SEA was a step toward the realization of the common market objective that was outlined in the Treaty of Rome establishing the EEC. This revival of the integration process was accompanied by a promise (and goal): to complete the internal market project by 1992. The intention was to remove fragmentation along national lines in various markets, thus enabling businesses to market their products across the various member states at lower costs and with fewer complications. In fact, by 1992, 1000 separate pieces of legislation were adopted, thus opening hitherto closed national markets.[9]

A six-point program that outlined action, and which entailed the implementation of the Act, is clearly outlined by Hitiris:[10]

1. Attainment of a large market without internal frontiers
2. Economic and social cohesion leading to greater convergence
3. A common policy for scientific and technological development
4. Strengthening the European Monetary System
5. Introduction of a European social dimension
6. Coordinated action for protection of the environment.

The basic objective of the single market was to bring economic growth and prosperity through increased cooperation. This was to be achieved through a gradual removal of borders (both physical and administrative) between member states, as well as through the elimination of all forms of technical restrictions, which may arise through legal and regulatory discrepancies and disparities between the members. The ultimate removal of borders, restrictions and any form of protective barriers—technical, regulatory, legal, and bureaucratic—was to eventually enable the free movement of goods, services, people, and capital: the four freedoms of movement. (The four freedoms of movement and their significance in Europe's single market are discussed in Section "The Significance of Europe's Single Market: The Four Freedoms of Movement").

This move toward a common market was also accompanied by a strengthening of the institutional system of the Community. The aim of this was to facilitate the better functioning of the market. The institutional reforms involved a number of issues. The most important of these related to the attempt to speed up the decision-making process by extending the scope of qualified majority voting (QMV) in the Council of Ministers, through the inclusion of a number of single-market issues. In this way, individual national authorities would find it very difficult to block decisions that were concerned with the completion of the single market, as they would not be able to use their veto powers to stop progress on the areas concerned. In these areas where the QMV was extended, the role of the European Parliament (EP) was also strengthened, through an increase in its legislative powers.

Today, the single market represents the core of the Union. It has marked the beginning of the movement toward creating a single European economy. These attempts culminated in 1992 at Maastricht.

The Treaty of Maastricht (1992): The EU

The ambitious goal set in the SEA, to complete the internal market project by 1992, was being pursued with considerable success. One aim that still remained to be addressed and accomplished, however, was that of attaining a monetary union. The Treaty of Maastricht,[11] or Treaty on European Union (TEU), was to large extent intended at fulfilling this promise of adopting a single currency.

The move toward the realization of a EMU was taken with the 1992 Treaty, with the establishment of five economic criteria which member states would have to comply with in order to be able to adopt the single currency. These became known as the Maastricht criteria, and their aim was to set targets for convergence between the national economies of the members. These criteria relate to price stability (inflation), budget deficit, public debt, long-term interest rates, and exchange rate stability. (For a full account of the provisions of the Maastricht criteria, see Chapter 5).

Further to the economic achievements, however, the importance of Maastricht was also in the institutional reforms that it contained and in its provisions for the creation of the EU (hence the name given to the Treaty: Treaty on European Union), under a three-pillar structure. In order to fully appreciate the significance of these reforms, it is important to consider first the broader picture of events taking place at the time. This is so because the momentum for the advancement of the process of integration, in 1992, was in fact given by developments in the wider part of the continent.

The end of the Cold War in the late 1980s and the ensuing collapse of Communism in Central and Eastern Europe had a number of effects. These were the formal reunification of Germany in October 1990 and the absorption of the Eastern part of the country in the "ranks" of the Community,[12] as well as the break-up of the USSR in 1991. In the background of these events, the need arose to deal with the new challenges that were being presented. Dealing with the challenges translated into strengthening the Community and securing the achievements that had so far been made.

Integration moved a lot deeper at Maastricht. From the perspective of institutional reform, the EP was given more powers (legislative powers) in a number of policy areas. But furthermore, from a broader perspective, the scope of the Community was also extended to cover a whole new range of activities. The three-pillar structure that was created with the 1992 Treaty incorporated the EC under the broader framework of the newly established EU. The EC was, under this new arrangement, superseded by the EU, as it now came to constitute merely one out of three pillars—the other two being Common Foreign and Security Policy (CFSP) and Justice and Home Affairs (JHA).

The first pillar of the EU (the EC) involved cooperation on economic and monetary issues, citizenship, as well as on the various common policies pursued at the EU level, such as social, agricultural, environmental and structural policy, among many others. The second pillar (CFSP), on the other hand, involved issues of common defense, and all areas of foreign and security policy in general, whereas the third pillar (JHA) included the policies of asylum, immigration, external border controls, and encompassed also the establishment of a European police (Europol). This three-pillar structure of the Union marked the extension of cooperation between the member states on a broad spectrum of issues. The three-pillar structure of the EU is clearly illustrated in Exhibit 15.1.

This strengthening and deepening of cooperation with the Treaty of Maastricht was clearly an objective that was successfully pursued. In Article 1 of the Treaty, it is clearly stated that "This Treaty marks a new stage in the process of creating an ever closer union among the peoples of Europe, in which the decisions are taken as openly as possible and as closely as possible to the citizen."[13]

The Institutional Design of the EU: How Europe is Governed

The European Commission

The European Commission is the main executive body of the EU and the most independent one. Among its many functions, the most crucial ones are

Exhibit 15.1

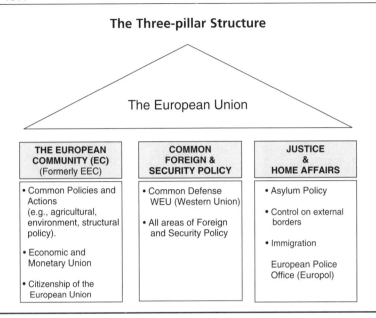

The Three-pillar Structure

Source: George, S., and Bache, I., Politics in the European Union, Oxford University Press, Oxford,
p. 214 (as adapted from EP slides).

to initiate legislation, draft the annual budget, and oversee the implementation of EU legislation in the member states.

The Council of Ministers

The Council of Ministers is the main decision-making body of the EU. Its
main responsibility is to make decisions on the Commission's proposals,
although decision-making processes vary according to the issue being discussed (ranging from unanimity to simple majority to QMV).

The EP

The EP acts as a legislative body within the EU, sharing some co-decision
powers with the Council. It can draft directives and regulations, and is also
authorized to approve the budget.

The ECJ

The ECJ is responsible for deciding whether member states comply with EC
law. It has the power to rule against members brought before it, which are
not in full compliance. Moreover, the ECJ can give an opinion on the correct
interpretation of EU treaties and legislations.

The Court of Auditors

The Court of Auditors is there to oversee the financial affairs of the Union, and make sure that these are carried out lawfully.

Some other important bodies of the EU are the European Economic and Social Committee, the Committee of the Regions and Local Authorities (CoR), the European Ombudsman, the European Central Bank (ECB), and the European Investment Bank.

The Widening of the EU: The Policy of Enlargement

Since its creation in 1951 by six countries (Germany, France, Italy, Belgium, The Netherlands and Luxembourg), the Community—and thereafter the EU—has passed through five successive enlargements.

The First Enlargement (1973)

The first enlargement of the Community took place in 1973 and involved three countries, whose objectives were primarily economic. These were the United Kingdom, Ireland, and Denmark.

The Two Mediterranean Enlargements (1981, 1986)

The Mediterranean enlargements of the Community comprised two waves of enlargement: the first in 1981 involving Greece and the second in 1986 involving Spain and Portugal. The 1981 and 1986 enlargements followed the emergence of these Mediterranean countries from a period of dictatorship. Under these circumstances, they sought membership in the Community in an attempt to consolidate their newly established democracies.

The EFTA Enlargement (1995)

The 1995 enlargement of the EU followed from concerns in three states, which were members of the EFTA, to become part of Europe's single market. This was because they saw potential benefits accruing to them, mainly through investment opportunities. These states were Austria, Finland, and Sweden.

The Eastern Enlargement (2004)

The fifth wave of enlargement in the EU took place in 2004 and involved ten countries from Central and Eastern Europe, as well as two Southern

Mediterranean states. Most of these sought to consolidate their democracies and find support in their transitional phase from Communism. The ten that joined the Union in 2004 were Cyprus, the Czech Republic, Estonia, Hungary, Latvia, Lithuania, Malta, Poland, Slovakia, and Slovenia.

National and Cultural Differences within the EU: The Importance of Diversity

The Evidence

The successive enlargements of the EU have clearly brought about a great degree of diversity in the ranks of the Union. 25 member states are today included in its ranks, which together cover a significant amount of the surface area of the continent. This is depicted in Exhibits 15.2 and 15.3, for the former EU-15 and for the ten new EU entrants of 2004, respectively. It can be seen from the diagram that the EU today stretches over an area of almost four million square kilometers (the five largest countries being France, Spain, Sweden, Germany, and the newcomer Poland).

The various enlargements of the Union have also been characterized by a steady and considerable increase in the population of the EU. This is depicted in Exhibits 15.4 and 15.5, for the former EU-15 and for the new EU entrants of 2004 respectively (as measured on January 1, 2003). It can be

Exhibit 15.2

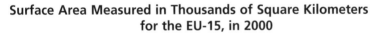

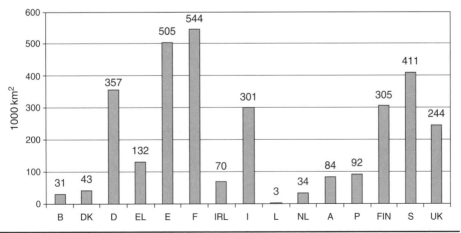

Source: European Commission (2004), Key Facts and Figures about the European Union, Office for the Official Publications of the European Communities, Luxembourg.

Exhibit 15.3

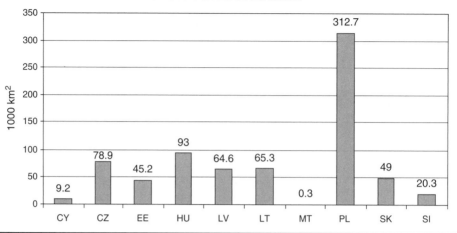

Surface Area Measured in Thousands of Square Kilometers for the Ten 2004 Entrants

Source: European Commission (2004), Key Facts and Figures about the European Union, Office for the Official Publications of the European Communities, Luxembourg.

Exhibit 15.4

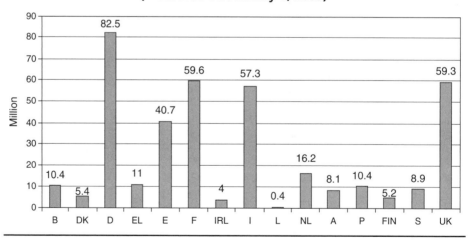

Population Measured in Millions of People for the EU-15 (Measured on January 1, 2003)

Source: European Commission (2004), Key Facts and Figures about the European Union, Office for the Official Publications of the European Communities, Luxembourg.

seen from the diagram that, the EU today has over 400 million inhabitants. This figure represents, in fact, over 6 percent of total world population, whereas the EU's population is the third largest in the world today (after China and India).

Exhibit 15.5

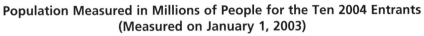

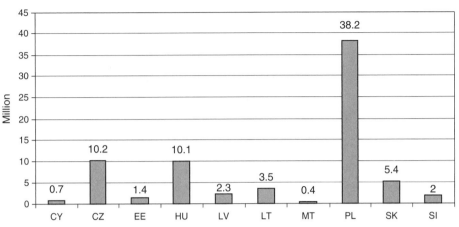

Population Measured in Millions of People for the Ten 2004 Entrants (Measured on January 1, 2003)

Source: European Commission (2004), Key Facts and Figures about the European Union, Office for the Official Publications of the European Communities, Luxembourg.

Clearly, then, national diversity is a major issue in the EU, which involves millions of citizens. People's affinities are primarily with their national roots. Along with national affinities come traditional and cultural ones also, which largely determine people's attitudes toward the EU. As McCormick (2005)[14] neatly remarks:

> As late as the 1960s and 1970s, European states still related to each other as sovereign states with strong and independent national identities. They had their own bodies of law, they pursued their own distinctive sets of policies, and travellers were reminded of the differences between countries when they crossed national borders and had to show their passports. [...] The nation state was dominant, and was both the focus of mass public loyalty and the source of primary political and administrative authority. Italians were clearly Italians, the Dutch were clearly Dutch, and Poles were clearly Poles—at least this is what most Europeans wanted to believe, and were encouraged to believe by circumstances.

The degree of pride of people in being Europeans is considered in Exhibit 15.6. This is based on a Eurobarometer survey carried out in spring 2002 in the 15 member states of the Union at the time, which asked EU citizens the following question: "Would you say you are very proud, fairly proud, not very proud, or not proud at all to be a European?" Even though most of the respondents said that they felt "very of fairly proud," the significance of the survey is that it revealed that a quarter of those who responded said that they felt "not very or not at all proud."

Exhibit 15.6

Degree of Pride in Being European, as a Percentage of the People Surveyed, in the Former EU-15 ("don't knows" are not included)

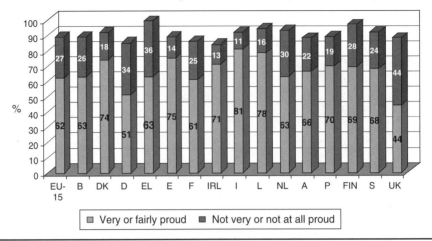

Source: European Commission (2004), Key Facts and Figures about the European Union, Office for the Official Publications of the European Communities, Luxembourg.

Another Eurobarometer survey carried out in spring 2002 demonstrated the degree of public support for EU membership, in the 15 member states of the Union at the time (Exhibit 15.7). Even though this amount varied from one country to another, evidence revealed that approval of membership was at much higher percentage levels than disapproval, in all the members. Support for the EU was, however, weakest in the prosperous countries that joined the EU in the 1995 EFTA enlargement (Austria, Finland, and Sweden) and in the United Kingdom, whereas it proved to be stronger in Luxembourg and Ireland. It is also worth investigating the levels of approval of EU membership in the ten new states of the EU. Exhibit 15.8 is based on a Eurobarometer survey that was carried out in these countries, in spring 2003, and which asked the question of whether EU membership was a good or a bad thing. Once again, approval levels were a lot higher than disapproval level. The highest approval levels were in fact recorded in Cyprus (72%), Lithuania (65%), and Hungary (63%), and the lowest in Estonia (32%), Latvia (37%), and the Czech Republic (47%).

The Impact of National Diversity on Business Behavior

National diversity is a very important factor impacting upon business behavior in Europe's single market. This is so because, in many instances, national

Exhibit 15.7

Approval of EU Membership, as a Percentage of the People Surveyed, in the Former EU-15 ("don't knows" and non-committal answers are not included)

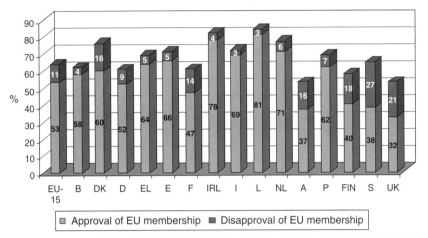

Source: European Commission (2004), Key Facts and Figures about the European Union, Office for the Official Publications of the European Communities, Luxembourg.

Exhibit 15.8

Approval of EU Membership, as a Percentage of the People Surveyed, in the Ten 2004 Entrants ("don't knows" and non-committal answers are not included)

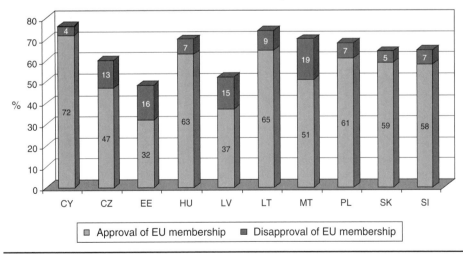

Source: European Commission (2004), Key Facts and Figures about the European Union, Office for the Official Publications of the European Communities, Luxembourg.

ventures are being favored over cross-border businesses. The Cassis de Dijon Opening Case, at the beginning of this chapter, was a clear vindication of such restrictive practices by national governments. The resistance of the German authorities to import the French-produced black-currant liqueur Crème de Cassis, on the grounds that its spirit content was below the minimum set by the German authorities (the West German government to be exact) for fruit liqueurs, was a clear case of discrimination set along national differences.

Fragmentation along national lines is also evident in cases when national governments discriminate against companies from other EU countries. This is demonstrated in Exhibit 15.9, by taking the example of public procurement in the EU. As demonstrated in the diagram, the number of cross-border contracts awarded, following invitations to tender, is at very low levels. In 2001, for instance, there were 93,558 invitations to tender. Following these invitations, 50,841 contract award notices were recorded, out of which only 643 were cross-border awards—a difference of 50,198, which indeed indicates a very noteworthy "gap."

These examples are clear evidence of discrimination by national governments, at the expense of other member states' enterprises. National diversity is thus an important factor that influences the way in which business is conducted in Europe's single market. The key to eliminating such forms of favoritism, or even bias, is not only by raising awareness but also by

Exhibit 15.9

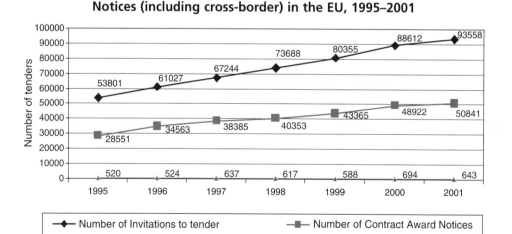

Public Procurement in the EU: Invitations to Tender vs Contract Awards Notices (including cross-border) in the EU, 1995–2001

Source: European Commission (2002), Report from the Commission, Economic Reform: Report on the functioning of Community Product and Capital Markets, Annex 1 to the Report, COM (2002) 743 final, Brussels.

cultivating perceptions, so that they come to realize that when goods and services (as well as people and capital) travel from one EU state to another, they are essentially moving between the Union's borders, rather than being imported from or exported abroad. In other words, there is an in-built notion of perception associated with this, which needs to be taken into consideration in order to effectively overcome problems resulting from national diversity.

The Significance of Europe's Single Market: The Four Freedoms of Movement

Free Movement of Goods

Prior to looking at the steps taken toward freeing up the movement of goods in Europe's single market, it is vital to appreciate first the importance of the goods market in the EU. This can be understood by considering the Union's share of the world's total trade in goods. This is illustrated in Exhibit 15.10, for the year 2001, in the 15 states that made up the EU at the time (EU-15). Total trade in goods, in that year, reached 19.4 percent, only 0.6 percentage points, in other words, below the US' share, and 11.7 percentage points above the level of Japan. This is indeed a comparatively high percentage, which represents the significance of the goods market in the EU.

Exhibit 15.10

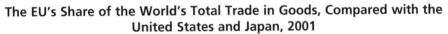

The EU's Share of the World's Total Trade in Goods, Compared with the United States and Japan, 2001

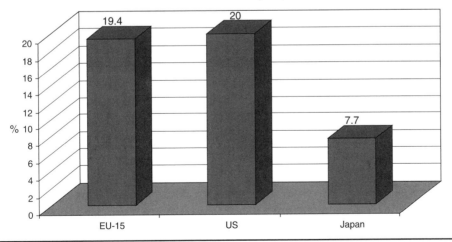

Source: European Commission (2004), Key Facts and Figures about the European Union, Office for the Official Publications of the European Communities, Luxembourg.

The free movement of goods in Europe's single market has been made possible through a gradual reduction of the barriers to trade. The underlying objective of removing these hurdles was to enable businesses to trade their products freely throughout the EU, without having to undergo the inconvenience and bear the costs of a fragmented market. At the same time, on the consumer side, the objective was to make it possible for them to buy goods in any country of the Union, without, once again, incurring any costs. Elimination of trade barriers essentially meant dealing with physical, fiscal, and technical restrictions.

Removing physical barriers to trade signified the abolition of custom checks and checks on borders. Such checks were not only very expensive, but also extremely time-consuming, as goods could be delayed for hours at the borders, before completing heavy loads of paperwork. Red tape had to be removed, for both cost and efficiency requirements.

Elimination of fiscal barriers involved control over direct and indirect forms of taxation. The former relates to personal income tax and corporation tax, and the latter to excise duties and value-added tax (VAT). This is an area where work still needs to be done, but it is, nevertheless, deemed as an important step that needs to be taken for the completion of the single market, especially with regard to indirect taxation. The levels of these taxes are not uniform across member states, and this represents a barrier to free trade as prices are artificially distorted. Equating VAT levels across the countries would also permit a greater degree of price uniformity, thus enabling consumers to compare prices more easily.

As far as technical barriers are concerned, these relate mainly to discrepancies, across member states, in their definitions of various standards, specifications, and regulations. Such barriers involved, for example, health, safety, and quality controls on products, environmental requirements, standards on consumer protection, as well as public procurement practices. Even though the use of these measures was justified with the label of "consumer protection," this ostensible objective was many times overshadowed by wider national and economic concerns. The measures were, in other words, intended, in many cases, as protectionist, as member states' governments sought to insulate their national markets from free enterprise and promote their own products at the expense of those coming from other EU states. The Cassis de Dijon Case was an example of technical barrier to trade, which was devised by the West German government in an attempt to promote its locally produced liqueurs (at the expense of the French-imported Crème de Cassis).

The Principle of Mutual Recognition, which marked the 1979 judgment of the ECJ, started a process of automatic recognition in member states, of goods coming from other countries of the Union, as long as they met standards, specifications, and regulations in their home country. This Principle was gradually complemented by a process of technical harmonization of standards and specifications, which meant steadily bringing these rules into line across the various states of the Union.

The relative progress made in freeing up the movement of goods has resulted in an overall increase in the volume of goods traded between different members of the Union. This is illustrated in Exhibit 15.11, which compares import penetration in the EU between goods coming from other EU countries (intra-EU imports) and those coming from outside the Union (extra-EU imports). It is clear from the exhibit that intra-EU imports have experienced a generally upward trend in the period from 1995 to 2001, and they have also constituted a much higher percentage of GDP than extra-EU imports, throughout the time period examined.

Free Movement of Services

As in the case of the free movement of goods considered earlier, prior to looking at the steps taken toward freeing up the movement of services in Europe's single market, an attempt will first be made to appreciate the importance of the services market in the EU. This is understood by considering the Union's share of the world's total trade in services, as illustrated in Exhibit 15.12, for the year 2001, in the former EU-15. Total trade in

Exhibit 15.11

Import Penetration in the EU: Imports of Goods from other EU Countries and from Outside the EU, as a Percentage of GDP (1995–2001)

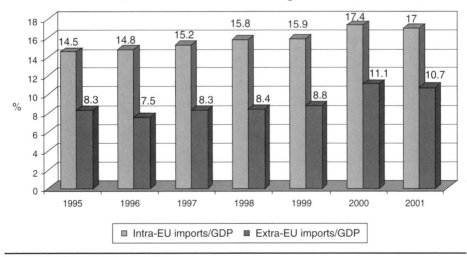

Source: European Commission (2002), Report from the Commission, Economic Reform: Report on the functioning of Community Product and Capital Markets, Annex 1 to the Report, COM(2002)743 final, Brussels.

Exhibit 15.12

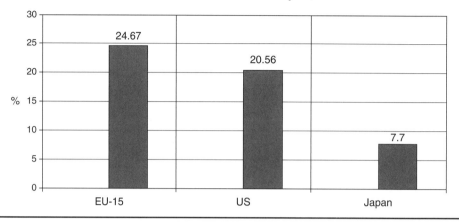

The EU's Share of the World's Total Trade in Services, Compared with the United States and Japan, 2001

Source: European Commission (2004), Key Facts and Figures about the European Union, Office for the Official Publications of the European Communities, Luxembourg.

services, in that year, reached 24.67 percent—a percentage that was comparatively higher than that of the United States (20.56%), by 4.11 percentage points, and a lot higher than Japan's (7.7%), by 16.97 percentage points. This very high percentage clearly represents the significance of the services sector in the EU.

The significance of this sector in the Union can also be valued by looking at the number of people working in each of the three sectors of the economy: primary, secondary, and tertiary sector (or agriculture, industry and services respectively). Exhibit 15.13 shows that this figure is significantly higher in the services sector, as compared to the other two. In 2001, in fact, the number of people working in the services sector amounted to 116.4 millions. This was 2.6 times higher than the amount of people working in the industry sector and, what is more, 16.4 times higher than the amount of people working in agriculture in that year. In addition to this, it can also be noticed that the services sector had experienced an expansion of 13.5 millions in the number of people that it employed, during the period from 1995 to 2001. The equivalent figure in the case of the industry sector, for the same period, was only 0.2 million people, whereas in the case of agriculture, the sector had experienced a contraction of 0.9 million people.

The free movement of services, albeit involving a very significant sector (as demonstrated by the Exhibits 15.12 and 15.13) and despite the fact that it is unquestionably an important objective of the Union, still remains an area in which a great amount of progress needs to be made. Insurance, banking, legal aid, architecture, and many more are examples of sectors in

Exhibit 15.13

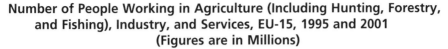

Number of People Working in Agriculture (Including Hunting, Forestry, and Fishing), Industry, and Services, EU-15, 1995 and 2001 (Figures are in Millions)

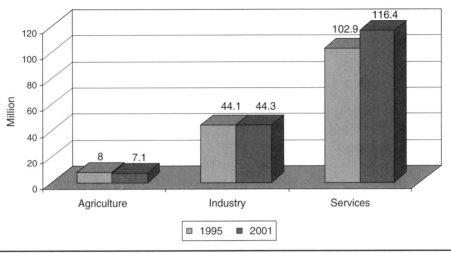

Source: European Commission (2004), Key Facts and Figures about the European Union, Office for the Official Publications of the European Communities, Luxembourg.

which work remains largely unfinished. The idea of achieving a free market is to be able to offer to the consumers the opportunity to enjoy these services in any member state of the Union, regardless of the country of origin of the producer or provider of that service.

The Directive on Services, otherwise known as the Bolkestein Directive,[15] provides for the creation of a single market for the services sector within the EU. In other words, its effectiveness would essentially mark the removal of barriers (both legal and administrative), which today restrict the provisions of services by a company to other members states of the Union. The aim of the Bolkestein Directive is to boost cross-border competition in the areas that it covers. These are construction, car hire, estate agencies, advertising services, hotels and restaurants, as well as advice provided by professionals such as architects, and certain public services, such as social care and environmental services.

The Directive has so far, however, been met with great controversy, as it has been the root for protests within the EU. The main cause of trouble has been its so-called "country of origin principle." This principle effectively stipulates that a company offering its services in another country of the Union would have to operate according to the rules and regulations of its home country (its country of origin, in other words). The result of this was to precipitate fears that companies would eventually respond to this by relocating to countries with lower wages and weaker consumer protection rules and employment rights, as well as lower safety requirements. When relocating in these countries, businesses would be able to take advantage of the cheaper labor force and the looser rules, and use these to price competitors out of the market.[16]

Protests to the "country of origin principle" of the Directive were widespread throughout the EU, escalating in February 2006. Demonstrations were most prevalent in those countries that enjoyed higher standards of living, higher wages, stronger consumer protection rules and employment rights, and higher safety requirements. In this context, workers and trade unions were worried that, if implemented, this principle would lead to a great loss of jobs in these countries, and it thus added, in this way, to the already existing concerns of unemployment (especially acute in France).[17]

Following the wave of protests and demonstrations, the Parliament eventually removed the "country of origin principle." Under the new provisions of the Directive, service providers are to be governed by the rules and regulations of the country in which the service is being provided, rather than the home country. Work, then, is still under way in the services sector and progress still needs to be made. Nevertheless, it is highly unlikely that the Directive will become law before 2009. It must also be stressed, however, that the Directive does not address a number of services sectors, which still remain an area of unfinished business in Europe's single market.

In order to fully grasp the significance of these protests, it is important to get an overall idea of unemployment levels in general that prevail in the Union, so as to appreciate citizens' concerns. The unemployment trend in the former EU-15 is illustrated in Exhibit 15.14 (for the period 1993–2003). Even though this trend is largely a downward one, thus expressing a lowering in the unemployment rate in the period, unemployment still remains at high levels. In 1993, in fact, around 8 percent of the Union's labor force was unemployed.

The rates of unemployment in the ten new members that joined the EU in the 2004 Eastern enlargement, as well as in Bulgaria, Romania, and Turkey (three acceding countries), are also depicted in Exhibit 15.15 (for the year 2003). Countries such as Poland and Slovakia (with 19.3% and 17.6% unemployment rates respectively), and to a lesser extent Lithuania and Latvia (with 13.4% and 10.7% unemployment rates respectively) contributed to a considerable extent to overall unemployment rates, following the 2004 enlargement.

Finally, by considering the rate of unemployment of tertiary education graduates by age group, it also becomes clear why most of the people

Exhibit 15.14

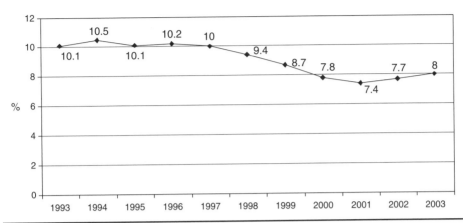

Trend in Unemployment in the EU-15, 1993–2003

Source: European Commission (2004), Key Facts and Figures about the European Union, Office for the Official Publications of the European Communities, Luxembourg.

Exhibit 15.15

Unemployment Rate in the 10 New Members (also including Romania, Bulgaria, and Turkey), 2003

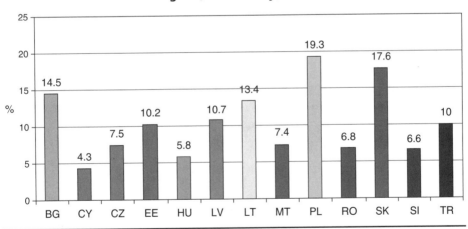

Source: European Commission (2004), Key Facts and Figures about the European Union, Office for the Official Publications of the European Communities, Luxembourg.

protesting against the services Directive were from the younger generation of the working force. Exhibit 15.16 illustrates this trend, clearly indicating that unemployment was comparably and considerably higher among the younger generation in the year 2002.

Exhibit 15.16

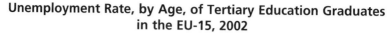

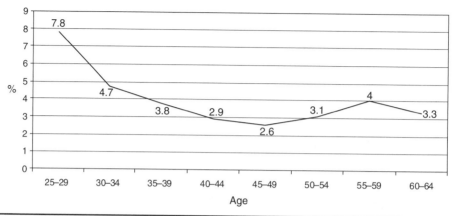

Unemployment Rate, by Age, of Tertiary Education Graduates in the EU-15, 2002

Source: European Commission (2004), Key Facts and Figures about the European Union, Office for the Official Publications of the European Communities, Luxembourg.

Free Movement of People

The free movement of people in the Union essentially marked the removal of internal border checks, so that EU citizens could move in a border-free area. This area came to be known as the "Schengen area," named after the town (in Luxembourg) in which the first agreements were signed in 1985, between Germany, France, and the three Benelux countries. Gradually, the Schengen area was extended to include 13 member states (all of the former EU-15, except from the United Kingdom and Ireland).[18]

The importance of the Schengen Agreement[19] is that it removes checks on travelers-citizens of the EU, when crossing internal borders. Some of the main measures adopted by the Schengen group members are outlined in the Union's official website (Europa website):[20]

- The removal of checks at common borders, replacing them with external border checks
- A common definition of the rules for crossing external borders
- Separation in air terminals and ports of people traveling within the Schengen area from those arriving from countries outside the area
- Harmonization of the rules regarding conditions of entry and visas for short stays
- Coordination between administrations on surveillance of borders (liaison officers, harmonization of instructions, and staff training)
- The definition of the role of carriers in the fight against illegal immigration

- Requirement for all non-EU nationals moving from one country to another to lodge a declaration
- The drawing up of rules for asylum seekers (Dublin Convention)
- The introduction of rights of surveillance and not pursuit
- The strengthening of legal cooperation through a faster extradition system and faster distribution of information about the implementation of criminal judgments
- The creation of the Schengen Information System (SIS).[21]

Further to all these measures, it must also be underlined that the free movement of people has also brought about moves toward the free movement of labor, as EU citizens can now work in any EU country they choose. Further to this, member states recognize a wide variety of each other's professional qualifications and tertiary education diplomas.

The basic principle underlying the recognition, by these states, of each other's diplomas is that "if you are qualified to exercise a profession in your home country, you are qualified to exercise the same profession in any other country."[22] Even though the Union applies this principle to a great extent and has, in fact, set up a system for recognizing diplomas and training qualifications, it must be recognized that there are difficulties involved in fully applying this in practice.

Nevertheless, as shown in Exhibit 15.17, the number of EU citizens working in another EU country has increased in the period from 1997 to 2002,

Exhibit 15.17

Number of EU Citizens (Men and Women Separately) Working in Another EU Country, 1997 and 2002

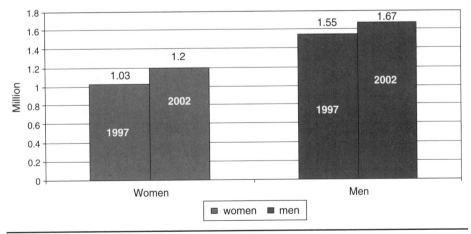

Source: European Commission (2004), Key Facts and Figures about the European Union, Office for the Official Publications of the European Communities, Luxembourg.

in the case of both women and men. As far as women are concerned, the number employed in another EU country has experienced, in that period, an increase of 0.17 million. The equivalent figure in the case of the male working population has been 0.12 million.

Free Movement of Capital

Freeing up capital movement essentially means removing all restrictions on payments between member states. This mainly involves FDI and provisions of financial services. As with regard to this sector, progress has indeed been made in Europe's single market, thus bringing about benefits for companies and private investors, even though fragmentation is still evident.

The composition of FDI going toward EU countries, both from inside and from outside the Union, is depicted in Exhibit 15.18, for the period from 1995 to 2001. It is clear from the exhibit that intra-EU FDI as a percentage of total FDI is much higher throughout the period under examination, indicating that FDI from countries of the EU going toward other EU members makes up a much greater percentage of the overall composition.

As far as the integration of financial services is concerned, more progress could be achieved by the completion of a single market in stocks and shares and the full realization of the movement toward replacing borrowing by the

Exhibit 15.18

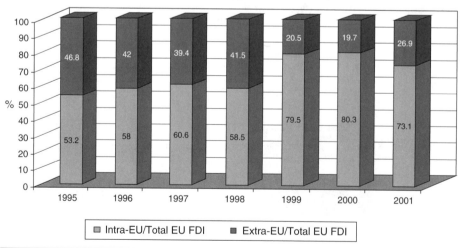

Composition of FDI Going Toward EU Countries (Intra-EU FDI and Extra-EU FDI as a Percentage of Total FDI)

Source: European Commission (2002), Report from the Commission, Economic Reform: Report on the functioning of Community Product and Capital Markets, Annex 1 to the Report, COM (2002) 743 final, Brussels.

issue of shares and bonds by companies. In 2003, these benefits translated into great economic gains. These are summarized by the European Commission (2003)[23] as follows: "More integration of financial services will bring measurable benefits. For example, making it easier for companies to issue shares and bonds as an alternative to borrowing could save 0.3 percent of GDP. The creation of a truly single market in stocks and shares would, overall, add at least 1.1 percent to GDP and increase employment by half a percentage point."

The full integration of financial services markets is also expected to bring benefits to other sectors of the economy. In the long run, macro-economic benefits could accrue, in the form of increases in employment, and growth benefits in general. As far as consumers are concerned, the potentials for them include gains in retail financial markets, such as mortgage, insurance, and pensions.[24]

In the recent White Paper on Financial Services,[25] the European Commission pinpoints its objectives in the financial services policy, which are to be pursued in its five-year plan, from 2005 to 2010. These objectives are specifically to:

- Consolidate dynamically toward an integrated, open, inclusive, competitive, and economically efficient EU financial market
- Remove the remaining economically significant barriers sothat financial services can be provided and capital can circulate freely throughout the EU at the lowest possible cost—with effective levels of prudential and conduct of business regulation, resulting in high levels of financial stability, consumer benefits and consumer protection
- Implement, enforce, and continuously evaluate the existing legislation and to apply rigorously the better regulation agenda to future initiatives
- Enhance supervisory cooperation and convergence in the EU, deepen relations with other global financial marketplaces and strengthen European influence globally.

Finally, on the issue of capital movements, it must also be emphasized that the variation of interest rates across the member states of the Union also leads to a failure to realize the full benefits that can accompany free movement in the capital market. As the European Commission (2002)[26] identifies, "despite the introduction of the euro, consumer interest rates continue to vary widely between Members States, even within the eurozone. Little cross-border activity is reported in retail markets, largely because of regulatory differences and lack of harmonized financial products and of comparable information."

The European Monetary Union: Conducting Business in the Euro-Zone

As already outlined, the major thrust in the realization of the EMU was given with the 1992 Treaty of Maastricht. Nevertheless, the full economic and monetary integration started to be realized in 1999, with the launch of the single currency—the Euro—in eleven member states of the EU.[27] The first eleven members to adopt the Euro were Austria, Belgium, Finland, France, Germany, Ireland, Italy, Luxembourg, The Netherlands, Portugal, and Spain. The eleven became twelve in 2001, when Greece joined them.[28] These are the twelve countries that are today members of the Euro-zone. As far as the United Kingdom, Denmark, and Sweden are concerned, they chose to retain their national currencies, rather than to adopt the euro. As with regard to the ten countries that joined the EU in the 2004 enlargement, these are committed, by the Treaty of Accession, to join the Euro-zone in the next few years.[29]

Meeting economic targets in the Euro-zone is not however a process that only takes place prior to Euro adoption. It is, rather, a process that undergoes continuous assessment in the EMU, as the Commission monitors developments. The Stability and Growth Pact is in fact designed for the exact purpose of controlling the public finances of the member states and setting targets for compliance. These targets constitute the rules of the Pact and it is important for members to adhere to them. If broken, then corrective action and measures are imposed upon the member state(s) that has/have violated them, and these must be implemented. Additional to this, the low-inflation environment in the Euro-zone is safeguarded through the operations and monitoring activities of the ECB.[30] By setting interest rates, the ECB monitors inflation levels and tries to maintain and preserve price stability.

Operating in the Euro-zone has a number of benefits not only for businesses, but also for consumers and travelers. The convenience that the single currency has brought about owes not only to the fact that it is now much easier to compare prices, but also to the fact that changing money is no longer necessary, either when traveling to or when investing in another country that is a member of the Euro-zone.

The benefits for businesses from operating in the Euro-zone are clearly outlined by the European Commission (2003)[31] as follows:

> The cost of transferring money to do business in another country has come down and there is no need for businesses to take out insurance or increase their profit margin to protect themselves against the risks of exchange rate fluctuations. These costs were tantamount to a "tax" on doing business and used to amount to 1% of GDP. They have largely disappeared because more than 80% of the trade of euro-area countries is now with one another.

Companies in the euro area that trade with the rest of the world have the automatic advantage of using an international currency. They can often protect themselves against variations in exchange rates simply by billing their customers in euros. It is much easier to do that than it was in the past to persuade a client to pay in Greek drachma or Finnish markka.

Moreover, owing to the economic standards achieved with the adoption of the Maastricht criteria prior to adopting the single currency, businesses in the Euro-zone operate in an environment of relative price stability—with low inflation in other words. This enables essentially the conducting of more efficient trading transactions. This is further strengthened by the fact that Euro-zone businesses do not have to worry about exchange rate fluctuations and thus the degree of uncertainty is significantly lowered. In addition to these, the lower interest rates make investments more reasonably priced, and thus more affordable to businesses (and investors in general). In the long run, all these elements are bound to be translated into competition benefits which could, in turn, lead to higher economic growth and greater prosperity. In order, however, to ensure that business is not conducted at the expense of the consumers and the society at large, clear competition rules have been introduced to monitor the "game." These are discussed in the following section.

The Need for Regulation in Europe's Business Environment: The EU's Competition Policy

The Union's competition policy is aimed at guaranteeing that the European business environment is safeguarded by fair practices. Healthy competition is the cornerstone of this policy, which condemns anti-competitive practices, either on the part of businesses or on the part of national authorities. The authority responsible for overseeing the enforcement of competition policy in the EU is the European Commission. The Commission must ensure that the "game" is fair and that producers, suppliers, manufacturers, and traders in general do not restrict competition and do not act at the expense of the consumers.

The rules on competition adopted by the Community are laid down by Articles 81–89 of the EC Treaty (under Title VI of the Treaty: Common Rules on Competition, Taxation and Approximation of Laws). Four of these articles will be considered in this section (Articles 81, 82, 88, and 89), which relate to two of the main aspects of the EU's Competition Policy. These are the rules applying to undertakings and those applying to state aid.

Rules Applying to Undertakings

Rules applying to undertakings are concerned with keeping competition "clean" through three main channels. These are stopping restrictive agreements between companies, preventing companies from practicing abuses of their dominant position in a market, and controlling mergers.

As far as restrictive agreements are concerned, these relate, for example, to attempts by companies to fix prices (e.g., by means of cartels), to impose production (or delivery) quotas, voluntary restraints, collective boycotts, or even conclude market-sharing agreements. Such practices are outlawed and are thus prohibited by the Commission. In cases of infringement, the action is punished by imposing fines upon the violating party.

In 2001, for example, the car manufacturing company Volkswagen faced a fine of €30 million, which had been imposed upon it by the Commission. This was so because the company had practiced retail price-fixing back in 1996 and 1997, by asking German car dealers not to sell the VW Passat at discounted prices. This action kept the prices of that car artificially high in that period, and this distorted competition in the car market, acting at the expense of consumers.

As with regard to abuses of dominant position in the market, such action is again prohibited under the EC Treaty. Article 82 of the Treaty states in fact that "any abuse by one or more undertakings of a dominant position within the common market or in a substantial part of it shall be prohibited as incompatible with the common market in so far as it may affect trade between Member States."

Dominant position abuses may be practiced either by a single company that enjoys a great degree of economic power in a market or by a group of merging companies (either through a full merger or through a takeover). As a result of this, merger control also forms an important aspect of the rules that apply to undertakings. The Commission seeks to make sure that mergers do not lead to the creation of dominant positions in the market, so that it does not curtail competition (and competition gains).

Rules Applying to State Aid

The rules applying to state aid are contained in Article 87 of the EC Treaty, which clearly stipulates that in cases when aid given by a state to its companies distorts, or even threatens to distort competition, it shall be considered as incompatible with the common market. The main reason for this is that state aid usually tends to favor so-called "national champions" and gives these companies an unfair advantage over other ventures against which it competes.

There are, however, certain limited cases where state aid is not disallowed. These are, for example, cases related to the promotion of the development of certain activities, the development of certain backward regions, or the alleviation of damages caused by natural disasters. In general, forms of state aid that are seen as compatible with the internal market are closely connected to social concerns. An example of this is the granting of €1.89 million, in 1998, to Spain (the area of Doñana, Andalusia) in an attempt to boost small tourism businesses. This was essentially aimed at facilitating job creation in a relatively poor area of the Union.

Clearly, then, controlling business behavior in Europe's single market—by keeping competition free, fair, and "clean," through the EU's competition policy—is aimed at protecting the consumers and, to the extent possible, delivering benefits to them. The competition policy of the Union is thus closely linked to its wider social objectives.

Closing Case

The Free Movement of Goods: Extract from the Treaty establishing the European Community

PART THREE

COMMUNITY POLICIES

TITLE I

FREE MOVEMENT OF GOODS

ARTICLE 23

1. The Community shall be based upon a customs union which shall cover all trade in goods and which shall involve the prohibition between Member States of customs duties on imports and exports and of all charges having equivalent effect, and the adoption of a common customs tariff in their relations with third countries.

2. The provisions of Article 25 and of Chapter 2 of this title shall apply to products originating in Member States and to products coming from third countries which are in free circulation in Member States.

ARTICLE 24

Products coming from a third country shall be considered to be in free circulation in a Member State if the import formalities have been complied with and any customs duties or charges having equivalent effect which are payable have been levied in that Member State, and if they have not benefited from a total or partial drawback of such duties or charges.

CHAPTER 1

THE CUSTOMS UNION

ARTICLE 25

Customs duties on imports and exports and charges having equivalent effect shall be prohibited between Member States. This prohibition shall also apply to customs duties of a fiscal nature.

ARTICLE 26

Common Customs Tariff duties shall be fixed by the Council acting by a qualified majority on a proposal from the Commission.

ARTICLE 27

In carrying out the tasks entrusted to it under this chapter the Commission shall be guided by:

(a) the need to promote trade between Member States and third countries;

(b) developments in conditions of competition within the Community in so far as they lead to an improvement in the competitive capacity of undertakings;

(c) the requirements of the Community as regards the supply of raw materials and semi-finished goods; in this connection the Commission shall take care to avoid distorting conditions of competition between Member States in respect of finished goods;

(d) the need to avoid serious disturbances in the economies of Member States and to ensure rational development of production and an expansion of consumption within the Community.

CHAPTER 2

PROHIBITION OF QUANTITATIVE RESTRICTIONS BETWEEN MEMBER STATES

ARTICLE 28

Quantitative restrictions on imports and all measures having equivalent effect shall be prohibited between Member States.

ARTICLE 29

Quantitative restrictions on exports, and all measures having equivalent effect, shall be prohibited between Member States.

ARTICLE 30

The provisions of Articles 28 and 29 shall not preclude prohibitions or restrictions on imports, exports or goods in transit justified on grounds of public morality, public policy or public security; the protection of health and life of humans, animals or plants; the protection of national treasures possessing artistic, historic or archaeological value; or the protection of industrial and commercial property. Such prohibitions or restrictions shall not, however, constitute a means of arbitrary discrimination or a disguised restriction on trade between Member States.

ARTICLE 31

Member States shall adjust any State monopolies of a commercial character so as to ensure that no discrimination regarding the conditions under which goods are procured and marketed exists between nationals of Member States. The provisions of this Article shall apply to any body through which a Member State, in law or in fact, either directly or indirectly supervises, determines or appreciably influences imports or exports between Member States. These provisions shall likewise apply to monopolies delegated by the State to others.

Member States shall refrain from introducing any new measure which is contrary to the principles laid down in paragraph 1 or which restricts the scope of the articles dealing with the prohibition of customs duties and quantitative restrictions between Member States.

If a State monopoly of a commercial character has rules which are designed to make it easier to dispose of agricultural products or obtain for them the best return, steps should be taken in applying the rules contained in this article to ensure equivalent safeguards for the employment and standard of living of the producers concerned.

Question: How do the principles enshrined in Articles 23–31 of the EC Treaty lay provisions for overcoming the barriers (physical, fiscal and technical) which restrict the free trade of goods in Europe's single market?

Source: Consolidated Version of the *Treaty Establishing the European Community,* Office for the Official Publications of the European Communities, Luxembourg.

Chapter Summary

World War II had left Europe both economically and politically frustrated. In this setting, the development of Communist ideas found fertile ground, mainly in the USSR and in countries of the eastern and central parts of the continent. In an attempt to insulate the Western European front from such "threatening" ideological influences, the United States encouraged some West European nations to cooperate between them, initially in the form of jointly managing the funds given under the Marshall Plan.

In 1951, Germany, France, Italy, and the Benelux countries decided to cooperate economically with each other, establishing the ECSC (Treaty of Paris). The evolution of the Union from this original Community structure passed through a number of landmark phases, most notable of which were the creation of the customs union in 1957 (Treaty of Rome), the establishment of the common market in 1986 (SEA), as well as the movement toward the realization of an economic union in 1992 (TEU).

At the same time, the deepening of the Union, through its successive enlargements over the years (1973, 1981, 1986, 1995, and 2004), has caused a great degree of national and cultural diversity, which has greatly impacted upon business behavior in the single market. This diverse pattern has also been complemented by a lowering, or elimination in some cases, of barriers upon the free movement of goods, services, people, and capital. This increased freedom in Europe's single market has also had significant effects upon the ways in which businesses tend to behave, and the common economic policy of the EMU has posed further challenges upon them.

In light of these circumstances, the Union's competition policy has emerged. The objective of this policy has been to regulate the business environment, in an attempt to establish a policy that works for the benefit of the society, either through stopping restrictive agreements between companies, preventing companies from practicing abuses of their dominant position in a market and controlling mergers, or through applying rules concerned with the granting of state aid.

As a retrospective and conclusive remark, it can be outlined that the deepening and widening of the EU over the years resulted in considerable effects upon business behavior. Both the enlargement of the Union and the closer cooperation established between the member states (complemented by the gradual steps taken toward freeing up the movement of goods, services, people/workers, and capital) played a catalytic role upon the ways in which businesses tended to behave. This behavior often took the form of actions against fair-trading and, as a result of this, regulation was deemed as essential. This is why today the "game" is being governed by the EU's Competition Policy, as this has been laid down by the EC Treaty and is regularly overseen by the European Commission.

Review and Discussion Questions

1. What induced the beginning of cooperation between the states of Europe immediately after World War II? How determining was the role of the United States in this?
2. Clearly account for the three key milestones in the historical evolution of the EU (customs union, common market, economic union). What were the main achievements in each of these stages?
3. What is the importance of the institutional structure of the EU?
4. How does national and cultural diversity impact upon business behavior in the EU?
5. How do physical, fiscal, and technical barriers impact upon the free movement of goods in Europe's single market, and what is the importance of eliminating them?
6. Why have attempts to free up the services markets been met with protests?
7. What are the benefits that are expected to accrue to businesses, and to the economy at large, from freeing up the financial sector?
8. What are the benefits for businesses operating in the Euro-zone?
9. Why is it considered necessary to regulate the business behavior, and what are the main aspects of the Union's competition policy?

Endnotes

1. Under the Marshall Plan, financial assistance was also offered to Eastern European countries, but the countries rejected the offer. This rejection was mainly under the influence and driven by Soviet concerns and suspicions against this American initiative.
2. The OEEC was replaced in 1961 by the OECD (Organisation for Economic Co-operation and Development).
3. The Treaty of Paris was signed in April 1951, even though the ECSC began its operations in July 1952.
4. The Treaties of Rome were signed in April 1957, even though the EEC and Euratom did not begin operations until January 1958, when the Treaties became officially effective.
5. For a full version, see the Consolidated Version of the *Treaty of Rome* establishing a European Atomic Energy Community (1957), Office for the Official Publications of the European Communities, Luxembourg.
6. For a full version, see the Consolidated Version of the *Treaty of Rome* establishing an EEC (1957), Office for the Official Publications of the European Communities, Luxembourg.
7. This ambitious objective was outlined in Article 2 of the *Treaty of Rome* establishing an EEC (1957), Office for the Official Publications of the European Communities, Luxembourg.
8. The SEA was signed in February 1986 in Luxembourg and The Hague, by the Foreign Ministers of the member states. Nevertheless, it did not come into effect until July 1987, owing mainly to ratification problems in Ireland.
9. This figure has been obtained from European Commission (2003), Europe on the Move, *Going for Growth: The Economy of the EU*, Directorate General Press and Communication, Brussels.

10. Hititis, T. (2003), *European Union Economics*, Prentice Hall, London (p. 50).

11. The Treaty of Maastricht was signed in February 1992 and it came into effect in November 1993.

12. This absorption included five more Länder becoming part of the European Community.

13. For a full version, see the Consolidated Version of the *Treaty on European Union* (1992), Office for the Official Publications of the European Communities, Luxembourg.

14. McCormick, J. (2005), *Understanding the European Union: A Concise Introduction*, Palgrave Macmillan, Basingstoke (p. 110).

15. The Bolkestein Directive has been named after the former European Commissioner for the Internal Market, Frits Bolkestein.

16. The Bolkestein Directive has also satirically been called the "Frankenstein" Directive.

17. The Bolkestein Directive has also helped fuel opposition to the EU constitution, according to BBC News (16.02.2006), *Q&A: Services Directive*, http://news.bbc.co.uk.

18. Italy signed the Schengen Agreement in November 1990, Spain and Portugal in June 1991, Greece in November 1992, Austria in April 1995, whereas Denmark, Finland, and Sweden signed in December 1996.

19. European Commission (2002), *It's a Better Life: How the EU's Single Market benefits you*, Office for the Official Publications of the European Communities, Luxembourg.

20. Europa website, *The Schengen Acquis and its Integration into the Union*, http://www.europa.eu.int/scadplus/leg/en/lvb/l33020.htm.

21. The SIS was established in order to enable the exchange of information on people's identities and descriptions of objects that were lost or stolen. The aim was to combat, in this way, crime and terrorism.

22. Europa website, *Working in another Country of the European Union*, http://www.europa.eu.int/citizens.

23. European Commission (2003), Europe on the Move, *Going for Growth: The Economy of the EU*, Directorate General Press and Communication, Brussels.

24. For more information on these, look at European Commission (2002), *Functioning of EU Product and Capital Markets—Summary of European Commission Report*, http://www.europa.eu.int/comm/internal_market/en/update/economicreform.index.htm.

25. European Commission, *White Paper on Financial Services 2005–2010*.

26. European Commission (2002), *Functioning of EU Product and Capital Markets—Summary of European Commission Report*, http://www.europa.eu.int/comm/internal_market/en/update/economicreform.index.htm.

27. The exact date of the launch of the Euro was January 1, 1999. This is the date when the Euro became the official currency in the member states that adopted it, even though the first Euro notes and coins did not come into circulation until January 1, 2002. In this transitional period (from January 1, 1999 to January 1, 2002), the Euro was a so-called "virtual" currency, as all Euro transactions had to be made by using debit and credit cards, as well as by bank transfers.

28. The reason why Greece did not adopt the Euro in 1999, when the other eleven made the launch, was because it failed, at the time, to comply with the Maastricht criteria.

29. Even though the new ten members of the Union are committed to adopt the Euro in the near future, there is no fixed timetable for this. The countries can wait until they feel that their economies are ready for the transition. The countries must first join the Exchange Rate Mechanism (ERM), where they peg their national currencies against the Euro. Their currencies must remain stable within the margins set for a period of two years prior to adopting the Euro.

30. The ECB is based in Frankfurt, where its headquarters are found.

31. European Commission (2003), Europe on the Move, *Going for Growth: The Economy of the EU*, Directorate General Press and Communication, Brussels.

16

Doing Business in the Developing Countries

Rumen Gechev

Objectives

Through this chapter, the student will be exposed to:

- Learn about the specifics of the business environment in the developing countries
- Survey the existing and the potential business opportunities
- Be able to develop an appropriate entry strategy in correspondence with the country's or the regional peculiarities
- Examine the possible investment risk and to gain knowledge about how to minimize it
- Understand better the effects of the globalization on the developing economies.

Opening Case

Case: Green investments in Belize, Central America

Rio Bravo Carbon Sequestration Project between few American corporations and Belize generates mutually beneficial, environmental, social, and economic effects. In correspondence with the Kyoto Protocol Mechanism (1997) that allows trading of greenhouse emissions, highly industrialized countries have the opportunity to obtain such permissions against equal investments in various environmental projects. Large-scaled forestation is an excellent example for such projects. The US companies Wisconsin Electric Power Co., Synergy, Detroit Edison, Nexen, Pacificorp, Suncor, and Utility Tree Carbon, Co. have financed the forestation of 62,000 hectares with

24.5 million trees in the period 1995–2000. Within four decades, 2.4 million metric tons of carbon dioxide will be absorbed by this new forest.

For a developing country like Belize, this particular project has positive outcomes. Among these outcomes are:

1. Improvement of the domestic environment and stabilization of the microclimate
2. Preservation of the local bio-diversity
3. Attraction of more tourists in the newly developed natural park in the mountains
4. More than 200 new jobs
5. Production of wood material as a spin-off effect.

The US companies save money and "buy time" for the required improvements of their technologies in line with the higher environmental standards. It is cheaper for them to investment in projects like Rio Bravo than to make huge investment with sufficient return in the long term. Therefore, investing in environmental projects in the developing countries gives opportunity for better timing for the corporations' production strategy. Many Japanese and European companies follow this approach. Such joint projects benefit not only the investors and the developing countries—recipients of those investments—but the whole planet. It is one of the efficient tools in the combating of global warming caused by the greenhouse gases.

Question: Do you agree that compared to the investments in the traditional economic sectors (mining, metallurgy, chemical production), "green investments" in the developing countries have higher social and economic outcomes?

Source: Gechev, R. Sustainable Development: Economic Aspects (2005). Indianapolis: University of Indianapolis Press, pp. 218–220.

Introduction

The topic on the developing countries is among the most challenging in the theory and practice of International Business. The reason for this is that the differences among those countries are much more than their similarities. These countries are placed all over the globe, although most of them are located in the Southern Hemisphere. Despite its relatively small share in the world GDP, about 80 percent of the earth's population lives in countries categorized as developing. More than five billion people speak hundreds of languages and dialects and share different religions and attitudes. That group of countries includes national economies with vast natural resources (oil, minerals, and raw materials) and favorable climate conditions and economies without productive natural resources and unfavorable climates (desert and dry areas). Some of them are with relatively well-developed industry and infrastructure while the economies of others are current examples for the economic history from the end of nineteenth century.

There are business opportunities in every country regardless of its stage of development or location. Not surprisingly, you may find Colgate toothpaste in Malawi (Africa), Sony TV set in Nauru (the Pacific), Toyota cars in Burma (Asia), and Nokia cell phones in Belize (Central America). Some developing countries like China, India, Mexico, Brazil, and others, made substantial industrial progress during the last two decades and became a magnetic focus for trade and investments. Only China and India offer more than two billion customers with growing purchasing power and prove the high profitability and growth opportunities in the so-called "special economic zones."

The economic potential of the developing world is not to be underestimated. It is already a battlefield for many leading corporations and their subcontractors. However, these countries have more complicated and often unfavorable business legislation, a lot of bureaucracy, lack of infrastructure, currency exchange problems, or limited market demand. Nevertheless, you should be able to see the problems as a business opportunity if you gain enough knowledge and experiences on that specific issue.

Classification of the Developing Countries

Many definitions of the developing countries are in use in the specialized literature, including LDC, least developed countries, underdeveloped countries, Third-World economies, and poor countries. The World Bank divides the countries into four major groups, using the criteria of income per capita: (a) low income, (b) middle income, (c) upper-middle income, and (d) high-income countries. The UN operates with the following classification of the developing countries: (a) least developed (44 countries), (b) nonoil exporting developing nations (88), and (c) developing countries from OPEC (Organization of the Petroleum Exporting Countries)—13 member states. The UN is using two interdependent criteria: GDP per capita and the source of income (oil vs nonoil). The distinction is logical as far as that income depends on endowment of that particular natural resource rather than on the level of development. However, such approach raises questions about other highly valued natural resources like gold, silver, diamonds, and other minerals and raw materials. The Republic of South Africa (RSA) does not have crude oil export capacity but is endowed with diamonds and precious metals. The country is the world's largest producer of gold, platinum, and chromium. So, we may assume that the distinction between oil exporting and nonoil exporting countries does not really give an idea for the income per capita or the export/import potential.

The GDP is the most aggregated macro-economic indicator. There is a direct correlation between this indicator and the standard of living, the export and import potential, the competitiveness of the national economies, and so on. It can be easily proved by comparative analyses on appropriate statistical data. The GDP is a result of and at the same time a precondition for economic development. Nevertheless, this indicator should be used in broader aspects, like the structure of GDP (by sectors and products), the share of export and import, the structure of the export and import, the type of trade regime under which this GDP is realized, and so on. Also, other macro-economic and social indicators should be used for more reliable assessment about the business climate, its status, and its perspectives.

Nigeria is an oil exporting country with huge hard currency revenues but it is among the least developed countries in the world when measured for income per capita, standard of living, degree of social polarization, and so on. Although the country's oil exports' foreign exchange revenues reached $17 billion in 2003 (up 46% from 2002), the revenues per capita are barely $166 per capita or about fourfold below its level in 1980. Only 1 percent of the Nigerian population (the business and political elite) collects 80 percent of the export foreign exchange revenues.[1] Clearly, the huge production and export of crude oil (95% of the total export) does not guarantee better economic performance or acceptable standard of living. Other countries, with similar export capacity (Algeria, Libya, and Kuwait) are much better positioned in the UN list. Therefore, the rank of the country depends mainly on the efficiency of the export revenues "recycled" through the economy rather than on its absolute value.

The trend analysis for the GDP per capita is rather alarming for the LDC. As shown in the Exhibit 16.1, there was a reverse trend during the period 1980–2000. The 1970s were years of relative improvement, when the indicator rose from $142 to $370 in basic prices or by 62 percent. In the same low-income countries, the GDP per capita collapsed to $211 in 2000 or 57 percent below its 1980 level. In comparison, the same indicator rose by 59 percent in the high-income countries: from $11,483 in 1980 to $27,591 in 2000. This extremely dangerous trend continues through the beginning of the twenty-first century and the gap between highly developed and least developed countries has been widening with all economic, social and political consequences. In 2004, GDP per capita in the high-income countries is nearly $33,000, while GDP per capita in the heavily indebted developing countries is below $380.[2]

The UN model was further extended by the OECD, which includes a fourth category "newly industrialized countries" (NIC). This additional criterion helps to emphasize the higher level of industrialization in countries

Exhibit 16.1

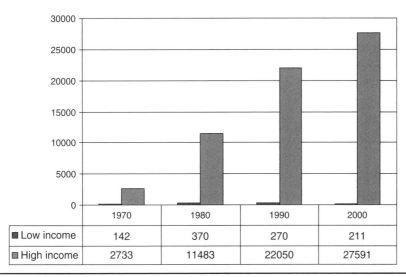

Trends in GDP per Capita in 20 High-income and 20 Low-income Countries, 1970–2000

	1970	1980	1990	2000
■ Low income	142	370	270	211
■ High income	2733	11483	22050	27591

Source: World Economic Outlook, 2005.

like Singapore, South Korea, and Hong Kong (now part of China). It is understandable why some experts and institutions have excluded Singapore and South Korea from the list of developing countries and have included them in the NIC.

The United Nations Development Program agency (UNDP) has developed more accurate index for measurement of the level of socio-economic development. This is the so-called "Human Development Index" (HDI) which incorporates economic and noneconomic indicators, like life expectancy, adult literacy rate, enrolment ratio in primary, secondary, higher, and tertiary education, and GDP per capita (in absolute value and as an index). The HDI has been in use since 1990. The last published report (2005), based on a survey of 175 countries, shows that the most developed nations are Norway, Iceland, Australia, Luxemburg, and Canada, while the least developed are Niger, Sierra-Leone, Burkina Faso, Mali, and Chad.

We believe that the HDI index is the most appropriate one for the objectives of the business environment research and the selection of suitable business entry strategy. The level of literacy, for example, affects directly the buying behavior and buying preferences, which in response define the chosen advertising techniques, branding, labeling, payment mechanisms, and so on. The education is of critical importance for the qualification of the labor force. The Exhibits 16.2 and 16.3 show data selected on the basis of

Exhibit 16.2

Human Development in Selected Countries: Human Development Index (maximum 1.000)

High (HDI > 0.800)	Medium (HDI 0.500–0.799)	Low (HDI < 0.500)
Argentina, Costa Rica, Chile, Uruguay, Brunei, Qatar, United Arab Emirates, Seychelles, Barbados, Bahamas, Cuba	Brazil, Egypt, Dominican Republic, Belize, Algeria, Kenya, Philippines, Cameroon, Libya, Peru, Syria, Gabon, Zimbabwe	Angola, Nepal, Chad, Ethiopia, Haiti, Nigeria, Laos, Pakistan, Cameroon, Uganda, Mozambique, Senegal, Sierra Leone, Yemen, Niger, Central African Republic, Burundi
Total: 54 countries	Total: 87 countries	Total: 34 countries, 30 in Africa, 3 in Asia, one in the Caribbeans (Haiti)

Source: Human development Report 2005, UNDP, accessed at: www.undp.org on January 17, 2006.

Exhibit 16.3

Classification of Selected Developing Countries by GDP per Capita, PPP/$ in 2003

Middle Income ($756–$9265)	Lowest Income (<$755)
Argentina, Peru, Venezuela, Uruguay, Belize, Colombia, Guatemala, Sri Lanka, Thailand, Swaziland, the Philippines, Tunisia	Tanzania, Malawi, Congo, Ethiopia, Sierra-Leone

Note: PPP/$- recalculated GDP based on purchasing power parity of the US$.
Source: Human development Report 2005, UNDP, accessed at www.undp.org on January 17, 2006.

HDI and income per capita respectively. It allows comparing the possible interdependencies between those indicators.

It is clear that the GDP per capita indicator must not be used as a single indicator when assessing the perspectives on market and investment opportunities. India, Indonesia, and Vietnam are in the group of low-income countries together with Bangladesh and Chad. The reality is that the first three countries are promising emerging markets with huge consumer base, growing middle class, and large-scale industrialization. Other countries like Pakistan, Bangladesh, Haiti, and Chad have simultaneously low income and low HDI. The data proves also that the endowments of natural resources are only a precondition for economic and social development. Nigeria has vast resources of crude oil but is in the bottom of the list of countries ranked by HDI or income criteria. Therefore, Egypt has more attractive business environment than Nigeria.

The developing countries can be categorized in correspondence with their structural differences. By our perspective, five main criteria could be used: (1) size of the country, (2) endowments with natural resources, (3) human resources and their characteristics, (4) economic structure, and (5) political structure and degree of dependence (independence).

The size of the country is viewed in two dimensions: size of territory and economic size (GDP, GDP per capita). These sub-indicators are not necessarily interrelated. You may have a country with relatively large territory but limited economic size—like Sudan. Argentina and Sudan have the same population (38 million people) and nearly the same size, 2.8 million square kilometers and 2.5 million square kilometers, respectively. In 2005, the GDP of Argentina (2005) was $537 billion, while the GDP of Sudan was only $53 billion. The same dramatic difference is in the GDP per capita, measured through the purchasing parity index (PPP): $12,106 for Argentina and $1910 for Sudan.

The endowments of natural resources are determined by the accessibility to natural resources. By accessibility we mean economic accessibility or the potential efficiency of extracting minerals and other raw materials. It includes also the arable land and climatic conditions. Some countries like Libya have plenty of crude oil accessible resources that form more than 90 percent of its export revenues. But the only arable land is in the coastal zone and the rest of the country is a desert area. The countries in the Caribbean do not have crude oil or mineral resources but enjoy favorable climatic conditions and exotic coastlines for the development of tourism. The geographic characteristics play an important role in the business investment process. Even the least developed countries attract foreign capital in the extraction industries if the natural resources are available.

The human resources with their quantitative and qualitative characteristics are probably the most important business decision factor. Usually, the size of the population is combined with additional parameters like the age structure, the level of literacy, qualifications, living habits, business culture, income per capita, propensity to consume and propensity to invest, and so on. Usually, these parameters are analyzed from the current trend's perspective as far as the foreign business activities are long-term oriented. India and China have similar size of the population (about one billion people) but Indian's GDP was $3.678 trillion (2005, PPP Index) while Chinese GDP was $8.158 trillion (2005, PPP Index). Therefore, with similar size and population, the two developing countries have substantial difference in the economic potential. The GDP per capita in China was $6200 and $3678 in India. China has superiority in other sub-indicators like level of literacy, labor qualification, labor motivation, and purchasing power.

The international marketers are interested in the differences in culture, including type of religion, beliefs, attitudes, traditions, history and historical relations with the neighboring countries and with the home country of the potential investor, and so on. Further in this chapter, some of these aspects will be a matter of more detailed analyses.

Also of importance are the decisions on where and how much to invest or export/import to/from depends on the structure of the economy presented by the sectors' share in GDP (agro, industrial, and services), by branches in the different sectors, by production (like car manufacturing, mineral extraction, bank services, food processing, etc.), commodity group structure of the export and import.

The economy in the developing countries is low in efficiency and vulnerable to external and internal fluctuations. There are a few determining factors, which make it possible:

- Production of low value-added commodities (natural resources, minerals, primary agro products, labor—intensive, and low-priced industrial products)
- Outdated technological base, little or even absence of investments in research and development, lack of government support for fundamental and applied sciences. Also, absence or insufficient protection of the intellectual property rights (both domestically and internationally registered)
- Low qualified labor, high illiteracy, and difficult (unaffordable) access to educational services
- Outsource of the most talented and young specialists toward the more developed countries (the so-called "brain drain phenomenon")
- Too much protectionism, a lot of bureaucracy, corruption, and deliberate complication of the import customs procedures
- Low or even absence of stimulus for foreign capital inflow
- Hard currency control and restrictions on the profit repatriation
- Lack of appropriate business infrastructure and logistical services
- Difficult entry and exit for the foreign investors, because of too extended license and concession requirements, leading to monopoly or limited competition

- Social polarization and extreme poverty. The purchasing power of three billion people (half the world's population) is less than $2 daily
- Too high hard currency indebtedness, which drains and diverts the scarce financial resources from investment in development to debt service
- Fragile democracy and underdeveloped legal system and law enforcement.

The so-called "digital divide" between the developed and developing countries is among the most alarming trends, which are currently taking place. This divide mirrors the deepening technological gap, especially in the modern computer and communication technologies. We know that the digital communication system is one of the most powerful tools for speeding up and widening the process of globalization. The access to reliable, fast, and cheap business communication is a precondition for successful business. The statistical data shows upstream trends in the number of computers and usage of Internet services from companies, institutions, and households in the industrialized countries. The average number of computers per 1000 people in the OECD countries is about 400 (nearly 600 in USA), while the same weighted average number in South America is 47, in Central America it is 31, and it is less than 10 computers in other countries like Kenya, Cameroon, Nigeria, Bangladesh, and Sri Lanka. Even in countries like China, which is becoming one of the major producers of computer hardware in Asia, this indicator is in the range of 20 units.

Nearly the same disproportion between the developed and the developing countries remains in the number of telephones per 1000 people. In South America that number is from 40 (Bolivia) to about 300 (Uruguay), while it is less than 20 units in some African countries like Ghana, Zambia, Egypt, Morocco, Zimbabwe, and others. The combined disadvantage of underdeveloped communication facilities and low access to computers still limits the attempts to better utilize the opportunity to mobilize the modern IT technologies as a vehicle for better adaptation to the new business realities.

Unfortunately, many of the poor countries stay far behind that trend because of different economic, political, and social factors. Although the prices of electronic products, including computers and the related services, tend to go down, the low-income countries do not allow the majority of families and the small- and medium-sized enterprises (SMEs) to use the advantages of the Internet for e-business and e-shopping. It is a serious problem when the exporters and investors assess the logistical opportunities for doing business in such countries.

How can these problems be solved and what is the role of the different stakeholders? These companies are state-owned monopolies in the majority of LCDs and the governments are using them as a cash cow for the state budget. The high profits, based on high service charges, are redirected to other government activities instead of being reinvested in modernization and further expansion. It prevents the local businesses and households from sufficient and cheap access to the advantages of the modern technologies. Not surprisingly, the state-owned companies use outdated equipment and do not have internal drive for quality improvements because of the monopoly position. By law, this most promising service sector is heavily protected by the governments and the entry of foreign business is virtually forbidden. The corruption is not to be underestimated when analyzing the factors which lead to unacceptable lack of innovation in that sector.

We share the understanding that the first step has to be privatization of the state-owned telecommunication companies. It explains why the WTO and the other international business institutions are placing pressure on such governments to privatize the telecommunication and Internet services and to open the doors for foreign investments and competition. Such investments may assure the availability of external hard currency and access to newest equipment and services. It would positively change the business environment toward more favorable conditions for doing business and in fact would generate even more government budget revenues derived by the increased production, higher foreign, and domestic trade turnover. The World Bank and its affiliated institutions have been implementing objective-oriented investment programs under very favorable conditions (long-term and cheap credits). These investments attract additional foreign and domestic private capital.

The development of that particular sector of the economy became a priority for some developing countries, like Costa Rica, Mexico, Brazil, Mauritius (Africa), Malaysia, India, and China. Without any doubt, it is a powerful factor for their increasing participation in the globalized world market. It is important to emphasize also that the development and the modernization of the communications and Internet services is not just an objective for that particular sector only. These facilities and services are required pre-conditions for establishing and maintaining a modern market economy. At the same time, it does not assume underestimation of the development of the other logistical elements or key industries. Even a perfectly modern communications and other e-business services would be useless if the particular country or region does not have an appropriate transportation system, customs and financial services, or the rest of the economy remains underdeveloped.

The modern market economy is unthinkable without the electronic banking system, e-commerce, e-business, access to large business data on Internet, and reliable communication in a real time. All these characteristics are essential competitive tools. Therefore, the overall business conditions and the availability of e-business methods are taken into account in the selection of suitable markets. In other words, the availability and accessibility of those services determine the entry strategy and the way the business will be done in the concrete conditions. At this stage, these conditions are unfavorable, especially in the poorest developing countries.

As we have noticed earlier, the economic reality in the developing nations is a result of combined internal and external factors. However, our objective is to explain how to do business in these real conditions, rather than discussing the concrete causes. The latter is a matter of different analysis and discussion. But we certainly can assume that the degree of the ratio between the external and internal problem-creating factors depends mainly on the domestic and the regional economic policies, respectively. Such an assumption is supported by the fact that several developing countries have chosen more liberal foreign economic policy and gradually opened their economy for trade and investments. Countries like South Korea, Singapore, Hong Kong (now part of mainland China), China, and Chile are convincing examples. China itself went through different stages of its economic policy after the World War II: from self-economic isolation and symbolic foreign trade to step-by-step liberalization since the change of its economic doctrine in 1978. Frankly speaking, the success stories in the LDCs are based on the degree of eliminating or easing the above listed barriers for competitive business and free interaction with the world market.

Despite its disadvantages, associated with absence of information about the distribution of income, the economic model of production, and self-

Exhibit 16.4

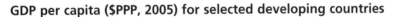

GDP per capita ($PPP, 2005) for selected developing countries

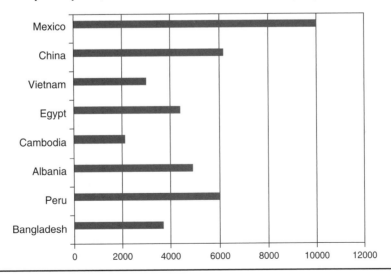

Source: World Bank (2005), accessed at: http://worldbank.org *on May 17, 2006.*

structure, the GDP per capita (recalculated through the PPP Index) gives enough ground to define what is the effect of the degree of liberalization on the path of development.

The classification of the developing countries is an open and dynamic system. Countries like China and Mexico used to be underdeveloped countries with inadequate economic potential. Thanks to their economic growth and active participation in the international division of labor, they have substantially improved their ranking as newly emerged industrialized economies. Unfortunately, the countries with very low income and low HDI tend to remain trapped in the vicious circle of poverty, weak economies, increasing indebtedness, corruption, and isolation from the foreign trade flow.

We shall emphasize that the categorization of the developing countries must be seen as a preliminary orientation or as a part of any concrete investment or foreign trade opportunity study. This is not "go" or "not go list." Every country has its advantages and disadvantages. The question is to what extent the character and the potential of your company is suitable to the concrete country conditions and how you can gain from these conditions?

Cultural and Political Factors

It is a common understanding that the cultural peculiarities are of high priority in the analysis of the business environments in various countries and regions. The developing countries are not an exception. The work of the international entrepreneur in those countries is even more difficult because of the extended variety of religions, languages, historical roots, ethnic groups, beliefs, and so on. For example, there are more than one thousand languages and dialects spoken in India. In fact, the official English language makes possible the communication between the people from different regions or ethnic groups in the same country. For the less-informed people, the Arabic language spoken in numerous Middle Eastern and Northern African countries is not the same. In fact, the citizens of Lebanon have difficulties understanding the Libyans or the Egyptians. When it comes to business negotiations, marketing research or contracting, the knowledge of the appropriate language must be at a professional level. It requires appropriate language proficiency of the company's field operatives. The use of local experts is highly recommendable. Well, it is true that most of the top managers in the developing countries speak English as a universal business language but it is also well known also that the use of the host country language(s) has its advantages. It is a must if your business activities require interaction with large number of consumers, producers, and/or middlemen.

We would like to underline that the language proficiency begins with the appropriate vocabulary and grammar but includes a crucially important additional element—the knowledge and understanding of the host country's culture. The language is the mirror of the culture, including the business culture. Therefore, the language proficiency must be viewed as a complex of components, which includes the other elements of the culture. The greater variety of languages in the developing world means also additional costs for labeling, translation, and interpretation. Certainly, it is not a major problem for the foreign businesses because those services are much cheaper than in the highly industrialized countries. Imagine what could be the difference in labor cost if you have to pay for the same volume of translation in Malaysia (Chinese and Malay) and in Canada (French and English). You should also keep in mind that, in general, the languages spoken in the developing world are with high context. It is especially true for the Arabic countries and the region of Latin America where these specifics should be taken into account.

Various studies highlight the differences and the intensity of the body language between the "Northern" and the "Southern" nations. Some personal business experiences come from Latin America. The people from that beautiful region of the world are very lively, easy to talk to, and very spontaneous. The expressions "language" and "body language" are indivisible. Some times it is difficult to separate the business matters from the personal, political, or every day life issues in the conversation, regardless if it is negotiation on a multimillion-dollar investment or interviews for marketing research.

Religion is probably the most important cultural component you must be careful with. There is no direct dependence between the level of income or level of economic development and the strength of the religious factor. The interdependence is much more complicated and is explained with a set of historical, political, moral, and other factors, which are not a subject in this chapter and which require special analysis.

The Muslim religion (Islam) in the Middle East, Northern Africa, Indonesia, and other parts of the world determines to a great extent the economic rules. Each group has its sub-groups and specifics. Turkey is a country where Islam has far less effect on the economic matters than Saudi Arabia, where Islam strongly modifies the economic rules. For example, the majority of women do not work, women are not allowed, or not encouraged to attend schools, and women may visit stores only for women and serviced by women. The Koran (the religious book of Islam) forbids the interests on money lending (the usury), and so on.

What is the practical meaning of these specifics? The marketing research, distribution, promotion, and selling of goods and services that target women have to be organized and executed differently. The door-to-door sales are not only prohibited but life threatening, especially if done by a male salesperson. Special stores for women have to be established and more attention has to be paid on the possibility to advertise before and sell such goods to male family members. It explains why the catalog sale for women's cosmetics, clothing, and jewelry is booming. By the way, it is also not appropriate to produce or sell male Investing in Emerging Markets T-shirts in Saudi Arabia or Iran because it does not coincide with their religious and moral norms. Because of the same reason, the entertainment industry (casinos, bars, night clubs, fashion shows, adult shows, etc.) is simply illegal and the entry is closed. The import of pork and alcohol beverages is also illegal in most of the Arab countries because of the same reason.

The religious rules in the moderate and conservative Muslim countries also affect the trade with nonsensitive commodities: labeling, promotion, and advertising. It has to be in harmony with the principles of the Koran. Frankly speaking, very few Western-made ads are usable under such conditions. Imagine that your bank would like to open a branch in the Middle East or you would like to get a credit from a local bank. In fact, how is the banking system performing if interest rates are not allowed? Well, the business is usually flexible enough when it comes to such problems. The problem is solved usually by the following mechanism: the borrower takes a credit and sells (with buying back option) appropriate volume of its shares, if it is shareholding company, to the creditor. When the principal is retired, the borrower buys back its shares but at a higher price. The same mechanism is used if other assets are used as collateral. At the end of the day, the creditor covers its expenses and gains profit.

It was just an illustration of the interrelations between religion and economy. The reason we picked up the Muslim religion is that under specific conditions it affects the economic organization, market institutions, and mechanisms. Most of these countries have impressive potential for economic development. The Middle Eastern countries are the main producers and suppliers of crude oil for the world economy; they actively participate in the WTO and their share in the foreign trade turnover is increasing. It is also an excellent springboard for re-export. May be the most developed re-exporting center in the region is Dubai which is a crossroads for traders from Europe and Africa. Speaking about Dubai, it is also important to mention that it is one of the seven United Arab Emirates (UAE), and it is not only a trade center, but a very progressive city where religion is not so strictly followed (i.e., there are many night clubs and alcohol is being served in restaurants, hotels, etc.) whereas the neighboring emirate of Sharjah is more conservative and religious rules are strictly followed (i.e., no alcohol is being served and there are no night clubs, etc.)

Some scholars argue that religion strongly affects the propensity to consume, in other words it limits the buying behavior. They often use the religions in South Asia (Confucianism, Hinduism, and Buddhism) as an example for the effect of the relationship between spiritual values and attitudes on the buying behavior. It may be true for some limited group of commodities, but in general we believe that such relation is strongly exaggerated. Our personal experiences in that region and the statistical data about the trends in consumption clearly indicate that the dominant variable is the income per capita, not the religion. The Indians, Pakistanis, Chinese, or Thais are eager to buy a car, TV set, a house, clothing, or good food as much as the Americans or the Germans. The way of doing business is much more influenced by the other cultural factors than by religion.

We argue that the material culture is more decisive in most of the cases. The fast economic growth in China, based also on technological innovation and infrastructure improvements (energy system, roads, communications), leads to higher demands of durable and nondurable consumer goods. The low consumption per capita in the developing countries, compared to the developed ones, is caused by the low income, not by any cultural differences.

The principal role of education on the business environment is the same everywhere, including the developing countries. On average, about 35–40 percent of the people in these countries are illiterate and only 1–2 percent of the young people in the LDCs have the opportunity to study at the university level. Unfortunately, this situation cannot be changed in the short run. The improvement of education needs long-term investments that very few low-income countries are willing to pursue and/or can afford. So, if you need to reach these customers or hire employees in the host country, you must adapt your policy to the host country realities. The use of Internet for marketing research or e-commerce in the poor countries is an impossible task. Even the use of TV, radio, and printed materials (newspapers and magazines, booklets) is useless in most of the cases. The foreign investors and the exporters need to be more creative and practical.

Exhibit 16.5 shows the differences between the developing countries based on culture segmentation. The power distance indicator is of interest for those who are involved in direct investment or trade negotiations. The power distance in India and Libya is much greater than in Costa Rica and RSA. The Chinese tend to avoid the uncertainty more than in Iran or Morocco. The individualism in Egypt is stronger than in Kuwait but lower than in Brazil.

It is important to know that the personal relationship in the Southern Hemisphere is incorporated in the business culture. Partnership and decision-making is based on such relationship. The approach "let's do the business first" would not work. In some cases, the relationship has to be established with the host country authorities. In Latin America, dinners and lunches with government officials are common practice. You will need serious contacts at a personal level with the government agencies and other institutions if you wish to do serious business in China, Vietnam, or Egypt.

The developing countries have their own manners and customs that affect the way the business is performed. For example, they make a clear distinction

Exhibit 16.5

Culture-based Segmentation

	Power distance	Uncertainty avoidance	Individualism	Masculine
Cluster I RSA, Mexico, Brazil, China, Costa Rica, Egypt	Medium	Low	Medium–low	Medium
Cluster II Malaysia, Uruguay, India, Turkey, Morocco	Medium–high	Medium–low	Varied	Medium–low
Cluster III Saudi Arabia, Iran, Kuwait, Indonesia, Sudan, Libya	High	High–low	Low	Low

Source: The method is based on the Hofstede's Value Dimensions.

between modern, modernization and westernization or Americanization. The technological and product innovation is a universal objective in all countries, regardless of their income level or cultural specifics. It is another issue that not all of them have the resources or the right policy to fulfill that goal. Iran, Tunisia, and Libya accept the modernization but reject the "cultural imperialism." Because of these differences in the values and attitudes, the food service retail chain McDonald's operates smoothly in many developing countries but its operations are unthinkable today in some Middle Eastern countries (i.e., Iran, Iraq) where the company is associated with the US politics and therefore is not acceptable. In Latin America and Southern Asia, the emblematic American companies like McDonald's or KFC are subject to angry attacks every time when the anti-globalization protests take place.

There are hundreds of different religions and religious beliefs you have to deal with around the world. What is known for sure is that there are no good and bad religions or cultures. The religions are simply different. As an international entrepreneur, you should learn about those differences and appropriately incorporate them in your business strategy.

The political spectrum of these more than 130 countries varies. What matters is not the name or the political belonging of the ruling party or coalition but rather their concrete economic policy assessed by such criteria like level of functionality of the market economy, the degree of trade and investment liberalization and profit repatriation, reliability of the legal system and its accordance with the international business law and business rules, membership and role in the international organizations, and of course the degree of political stability. During the last ten years, the foreign investments in China, ruled by the communist party (the only party in the country), are more than the investments in Eastern Europe. The leading companies from all over the world compete for market share there, despite the single party system. Kuwait does not have an electoral system at all and the Emir (the Ruler) appoints his government cabinet. Nevertheless, it is a more business-oriented country that offers much more opportunities than Bangladesh, with its democratically elected government. It does not substitute the classical rule that the modern market economy and the democracy are mutually exclusive.

Political factors determine the political risk and are incorporated in the business risk assessment. Various independent international agencies and consulting companies, like the Economic Intelligence Unit or the World Bank, publish regularly country reports with such assessments. There is no foreign investment with zero risk. The art of the business is how to minimize that risk and better utilize the country's business opportunities.

Entry Strategies in the LDCs

The basic entry strategies in the practice of international business are as follows:

- Direct exporting/importing
- Indirect exporting/importing
- Licensing
- Off-shore production (direct investments)
- Subcontracting
- Portfolio (indirect) investments.

We assume that the entry strategy, concerning the foreign trade turnover, includes the import because importing is as much international business as exporting. The choice of strategy depends on many factors, among them: the objectives of the concrete company, its business potential and level of competitiveness, its international business experiences, the qualification and the motivation of the top management, the business legislation in the home and the host country, foreign trade stimuli, tariff and nontariff system, profit repatriation opportunities and foreign exchange rules, government stimuli for direct investment and level of investment protection, taxation policy, access to natural and financial resources, strength of the environmental laws, and so on. The selection of the most appropriate entry strategy depends also on the favorable or unfavorable entry conditions for concrete countries or type of businesses.

The entry conditions are not yet equal despite the impressive steps toward the world market liberalization after the World War II and especially during the last decade. Many of the development countries are members of preferential regional trade zones. Mexico, for example, is a member of the North American Free Trade Agreement (NAFTA) together with the United States and Canada. The Mexican market is large enough (105 million people) for initiating export of goods or services. However, any exporter outside of NAFTA must compete with its North American rivals who enjoy zero or very low tariff and nontariff barriers. If the exporting product is nondifferentiated (the same product is offered by the regional companies), the best entry strategy would be direct investment. It could not only eliminate the expensive foreign trade barriers but could also open the doors for free entry into the whole regional trade organization. Therefore, the type of entry strategy depends on the possible membership of a given development country in regional economic and customs agreements and the character of those agreements.

The level of liberalization in NAFTA is at a much higher level than in CARICOM (Caribbean Community and Common market), MERCOSUR (Brazil, Argentina, Uruguay and Paraguay), or ASEAN (Association of Southeast Asian Nations). So, other things being equal, direct investment or export to a member country of highly liberalized regional market has its advantages in comparison with those with less liberalized economies.

In reality, the other things are not equal. There are plenty of factors that may overweigh the advantage or disadvantage of trading or investing in a particular regional economic agreement. The markets of India and China are much more protected than the markets of the Republic of South Africa or Chile. In China and India, the huge and fast growing domestic markets of a total of more than two billion potential consumers compensate the disadvantage of the higher import tariffs. In other words, the higher volume of sales and the huge absolute volume of profits can minimize the effect of the higher entry price. Or, the relatively higher imports tariffs are compensated with lower technical, warranty, or health standards, which allow for lower production cost and therefore high profitability.

Most of the small retail stores in Belize (Central America) give warranty on durable consumer goods usually for six months and the bigger retailers up to a year. The warranty for cars is from two to five times lower than in the developed countries, measured both as a time length of the warranty and/or the mileage. In such cases, the cost reduction for the exporters or producers is based on the lower expenses on supportive services (repairing, replacement, maintenance, etc.)

The choice between direct or indirect exporting depends on the parameters of the concrete business environment, including possible political factors. Some exporters prefer the so-called "regional approach." They export directly to their regional trade center in selected countries and then use local intermediaries for re-export to the neighboring countries. The selected country for regional trade center is usually one with the largest domestic market and/or with the most liberalized foreign trade regime and favorable trade relations with its neighbors. Such strategy minimizes the disadvantages of the establishment of numerous trade offices in an area with many countries with limited market potential. In addition, such indirect, regional approach eases the optimization of the logistical expenses.

The Procter & Gamble (P&G) Company uses a regionalized approach for the different parts of the world, like the one for Latin America.[3] It allows them to introduce regional branding on their products and also to use indirect export to countries where they decided not to have their own trade representatives because of the irrelevance of the cost compared to the relatively limited small markets in the Caribbean countries or Paraguay and Uruguay. In most cases, Guatemalan re-exporting companies cover the Caribbean area where P&G does not export directly. Of course, the direct exporting is not necessarily based on existence or absence of a country's representative office (company), although it is an established practice for the leading exporters. The example above illustrates the flexibility of the exporter in using different exporting strategies for markets with different size or importing rules.

Usually, the direct exporting to the developing countries is more difficult and often more expensive than the direct exporting to the developed markets. A number of factors such as very complicated import administrative procedures and heavy bureaucracy, underdeveloped wholesaling and retailing infrastructure, low density of population (few exceptions like the big cities), difficult conditions for marketing research, unfair competition, and so on have led to this. That is why the SMEs exporters to the developing markets minimize the risk and the export costs by using export intermediaries like Export Management Companies (EMC), Export Trade Companies (ETC), commission agents, and export agents.

Well, the use of such intermediaries requires price discounts, commissions, and so on but it usually pays the price. The small companies do not have the potential to do direct exporting and cannot afford the high cost of such exporting. In some cases, the SMEs use the established potential of the well-established exporting companies in the form of piggybacking. In fact, the exporter may use the piggybacking technique on leading domestic companies in particular developing countries. Some times, the piggybacking is realized in the form of the so-called "synergy," that is mutually planned branding and operating, including operational activities like promoting, advertising, utilizing the same distributive channels, and so on.

The cooperation between the Indian giant TATA Company and the British company Tetley is an excellent example. Among its many highly diversified industrial and trade activities, TATA is producing and selling millions of tons of high-quality tea, targeting both the huge domestic and the international markets. However, the Indian company does not have enough expertise in branding and packaging in line with the traditions and the specifics of the United Kingdom and other developed countries. This disadvantage is compensated by the use of Tetley's brand recognition and packaging experiences.

The Nepali producer of tea found that synergetic cooperation as a new piggybacking opportunity and initiated re-export operations through TATA's facilities in Calcutta, finding the best distributive channels for its exotic tea on the markets of India and beyond.[4] Finally, both companies gain from that synergy by combining its potential and expertise in mutually related marketing activities. The trade-off between price discounts and export costs usually favors the use of intermediaries. In fact, the exporters are free to change their entry strategies when they are ready for such a change.

The following are the factors to consider for the best entry strategy for the developing countries:

1. Company's characteristics
   - The type of its products and services
   - The qualification and motivation of its management
   - Export experiences and possible contacts with business counter partners in the host country
   - The availability of financial reserves for backing the higher risk of direct exporting.

2. The host country characteristics
   - Export/Import trade regime
   - Type of government
   - Government's trade and economic policy
   - Government's foreign policy
   - Favorability or restrictions toward the foreign business activities
   - Availability and reliability of the existing distributive system
   - Membership of regional custom and/or economic agreements
   - Level of corruption.

The type of commodity often predetermines the way of entry. If it is machinery and equipment, the most likely export is the direct one. Such delivery comes with training of the personnel who is going to use the technology, warranty agreement and maintenance responsibilities of the producer, delivery of spare parts, and so on. The branded durable consumer goods also tend to be exported directly. First, because the brand name is usually related to a well-established leading company which can afford such exporting. Second, the direct export is an additional assurance for them that the whole selling process and after-sale service will be in accordance with the company's quality standards. The Japanese company Matsushita produces extended line of various consumer and industrial electronic products. They are with pioneering technical solutions and of traditionally high qualities. The company is selling its products under several popular trade names like Panasonic, Techniques, National, Quasor, Victor, and JVC. It has its own agent companies in countries around the world—Americas (14), Europe (23), Africa (8), and Asia and Oceania (25).[5] These agent companies sell the company's product and coordinate and control the sales and services delivered by local authorized dealers. The popular trademarks are a result of huge investments in technology, qualification, research and development, and promotion. No one leading company with well-established brand names and trademarks may afford any compromises with the quality standards when doing business all over the globe. The developing countries are not an exception.

Usually, the exporters of technologies of complete industrial units to the LCDs take care of the appropriate qualification of the local labor. The importing countries prefer system delivery when it comes to huge national or regional projects. Further, the export product includes the production facilities, development of the production infrastructure, labor training, management of the start-up operation, new product marketing, and so on. A Japanese company has won an auction in Indonesia for building a cement factory near the capital Jakarta showing competitive advantage by offering a full package of products and services, although the offered price was higher than the one offered by the other competing suppliers from EU and the United States.[6] It is clear that such kind of entry strategy has to be direct.

It is well known that most of the developing countries have insufficient infrastructure. And the infrastructure is a determining factor when it comes to the decision if, how, and to what extent to invest in a particular country or region. The underdeveloped infrastructure and quality sometimes "force" local industries to require a "complex investment" or the establishment of an industrial park with various mutually supportive productions. Many foreign investors believe that this is the best way to assure the supply of raw materials, energy, components, and services necessary for the production of finished goods. Otherwise, the local suppliers often cannot meet the international quality standards; the risk of delayed deliveries is high and the delivery price might be too high because of the relatively low volume of production.

The great dependence of the domestic producers on foreign supply is a matter of another concern. They rely often on external financing, supply of materials and equipment. Any complication in that vulnerable chain, caused by insufficient hard currency reserves, government intervention, or unfavorable political developments, may create serious problems for the end producers. In other cases, the main obstacle could be the nonreliable distribution system or insufficient storage facilities. Therefore, the investment assessment in the LDCs has to be much broader and more detailed than the one in well developed market economies.

The industrial parks proved that this is one efficient solution of the above-mentioned logistical and industrial capacity problems. Not only the foreign capital, but also the host countries' governments and business organizations support or initiate their establishment. The Vietnamese industrial park (VSIP), the Iranian Pardis technological park (PTP), and the Indian Waluj are typical examples. Some of those parks have been in operation since the beginning of the 1980s and their number and activities is further increasing. Today, China has more than 270 such parks, Mexico more than 150. Waluj industrial park was created by the Industrial Development Corporation in the Indian state of Maharashtra, while VSIP is developed and managed by the Vietnamese government. The Mexican industrial parks are organized as a separate, nongovernmental organization.

What is common between them is that these are territorial areas with special preferences like free or cheap land, tax exemptions or tax preferences, independent and smoothly operating customs service, licenses issuing, construction permits, and so on. The infrastructure of that highly developed "Business islands" is often built with the financing from the host governments, from the international financial institutions or both. Some of the biggest parks are established as a result of close intergovernmental cooperation. The WUXI industrial park, near Shanghai, is a result of such cooperation between Singapore and China, has the internationally recognized ISO 9002 quality certificate, and delivers optimal conditions for the high-tech industries, including electronics manufacturing. Actually, the main objective in the establishment of such parks is the attraction of leading companies from the developed countries, which could play the role of locomotive for the whole economy.

These special zones are open for foreign and domestic companies. Such approach allows easier and faster transfer of technologies and managerial know-how and formation of different forms of cooperation, including joint ventures, strategic alliances, and so on. Waluj (India) has attracted giants like Johnson & Johnson, Goodyear, Colgate–Palmolive, Kenstar, and the domestic Bajaj Auto. As stated by Agosin and Mayer, such FDIs, including those in the industrial parks, attract domestic capital and improve the overall investment climate.[7]

The way of doing business with the developing countries also depends on the potential partner. Unlike the developed countries, the governments in the developing world directly control or indirectly influence most of the economic sectors. In fact, the utilities (transportation, energy production and distribution, ports, water supply, etc.) are public property. Therefore, entering these sectors must be done through an agreement with the governments. Most of the developing countries do not have the potential to implement huge infrastructural projects on their own. That is why their procurement policy is open for foreign companies. It is a profitable market for the exporters which often enjoy financial and political support and insurance from their own governments. The main players are the companies from the highly developed countries which can meet the high preliminary requirements of the host countries, including previous experiences, annual turnover, equipment, financing, qualified personnel, and so on. In most cases, only the companies from OECD member countries may fulfill these criteria.

Does it mean that these particular markets are closed for suppliers and investors from the LCDs? Of course not. There is a mutual interest of the establishment of a subcontracting system. So, companies from China, Bulgaria, or Brazil may participate in the execution of such projects by working under the umbrella of the "fat cats" from the OECD. Usually, such a subcontracting system is formed in consortiums, which compete in the international auctions. The main contractor gains from the cheapest delivery and services of the subcontractors, and the subcontractors gain on the piggybacking entrance to highly competitive markets.

Such projects (airports, ports, bridges, highways, energy plants, energy distributive systems, dams, etc.) are very profitable and may open the doors for other businesses in the host country. Often, construction companies from the less-developed countries and from the countries in transition use that subcontracting system to operate in the foreign markets. A Chinese company works on the construction of the new airport in Cyprus (EU member) and the Bulgarian company GlavBulgarstroy took part in a huge bridge construction in South Africa.

A company's readiness to go international depends on the qualifications and motivation of the top management. It is more difficult to do business in the developing countries because of factors such as much deeper cultural differences, language barriers, different life style, higher crime level, and higher personal risks. It is one thing if a UK company is doing business in Canada and a totally different story if the business has to be done in Morocco. The British managers must know Arabic or French, they must be aware of and follow some of the Muslim traditions, and their families need adaptation and need to overcome some life style differences. It is much more difficult to operate in a less predictable business environment where the exit is often as difficult as the entry. The uncertainty and the lack of experience are the most important problems. This explains why most of the companies begin their business activities indirectly or through the establishment of a partnership and joint ventures with domestic companies. After a certain period when they accumulate enough experiences and build self-confidence, the indirect entry can be transferred in direct operations.

Direct entry requires substantial preliminary investments. Therefore, the financial risk is much higher than in the indirect entry. Such entry requires primary marketing research, intensive on-the-spot business activities, establishment of a domestic subsidiary, branch, or representative office, assigning highly qualified personnel from the parent company and from the host country, and expenditures on legal registration and consultancy. Such investment may pay the price if the business initiative brings the fruits from the implementation of the investment plan. The problem may arise if the company's strategic objectives are based on misleading marketing research or if the investment climate of the host country is too vulnerable to unfavorable economic, social, or political developments. In such a pessimistic scenario, the possible exit would cause great losses unlike the indirect entry where such a problem can be easily solved by simply disconnecting the export or import.

Farmers from Western Europe, mainly from the United Kingdom, lost millions of dollars in investments in the agro and the food-processing sectors in Zimbabwe (Africa) during the last few years because Zimbabwe's political leadership has been forcing the previous owners out of the country. The losses for the foreign companies which used to operate in Iraq (Middle East, Asia) amount to tens of billions of dollars since 1992. The businesses which used to do indirect business there simply lost a market share. Unfortunately, the consequences for the companies which spent millions of dollars for retail property (land, buildings), equipment storages, raw materials, and so on are much more negative. One cannot escape the land or the other elements of the infrastructure in case of unfavorable developments.

The above cases do not prove that the indirect entry is more preferable and less risky than any other entry method. In fact, the direct entry gives many advantages and is widely and successfully used by hundreds of companies. Not only the leading international corporations but also many mid-size and even small companies operate directly in the developing world on their own or in cooperation with other partners. The various direct entries in infrastructural projects in Kazakhstan (Asia) are good examples. The French company Air France Europe has managerial contract with Almaty (the capital) Airport while the German company Tosehl rebuilt the runways. Another French company Generale Des Aaux invested $100 millions and maintains the water supply system of Almaty. The British company Galaher has built a new cigarette factory there. Often, companies from one developing country use a direct entry approach in another one. The Saudi Central

Asian Investment Company built a trading center and hospital complex in Kazakhstan for a total of $28 million. The state-owned Chinese CNPC established a joint venture with the domestic Aktobemunaigaz oil company for the development of the oil field and installation of oil pipelines to north-eastern China. The overall project, signed and guaranteed by the Kazakh's government, is for more than $9 billions.[8]

Direct entry might be preferable in some cases while indirect entry might have advantages in other cases. The decision on the entry strategy must be based on a careful and detailed analysis on all controllable and uncontrollable factors. Usually, the corporations from the developed countries insure their direct entries by appropriate insurance or political guarantees from the home and/or host government. It is a common practice when it is a huge regional or national project in the extracting industries, development of infrastructure or industry, which is in the priority list of the host government.

Costa Rica (Central America) is a typical case. Despite its relatively small population (four million people), the country is willing to become a regional center in the field of hardware and software industry. It has a GDP per capita of $4000 which is eight times less than the one in the United States, but multiple times higher than most of the other Latin American countries. The Costa Rican government supports these direct foreign investments by tax holidays, free land, encouraging custom's policy, and so on. Many leading hardware and software companies, including IBM, Dell, Apple, Compaq, Oracle, and Cisco also operate in this relatively small but fast-growing economy. Intel has one of its largest production facilities in Costa Rica. Foreign producers gain on the local preferential economic conditions and compete successfully in the regional and world markets.

Interaction with the World Market: Forms, Dependences, and Basic Trends

Exhibit 16.6 illustrates very well the correlation between the chosen model of economic structuring and the way of interaction with the world economy. We shall emphasize on the foreign trade and on export and the export potential in particular. It is not an underestimation of the role of the import but rather relies on the strong correlation between the level of economic development and the volume and structure of export. Clearly, it testifies about the achieved competitiveness and the ability to gain on the world division of labor.

Statistical data supports the assumption that the export potential varies substantially among the various developing countries. Latin America is well above the average. It means that the region is gaining market share and building competitiveness. Some countries from the region increased their

Exhibit 16.6

Annual Change of Export 1980–2003 (in percent)

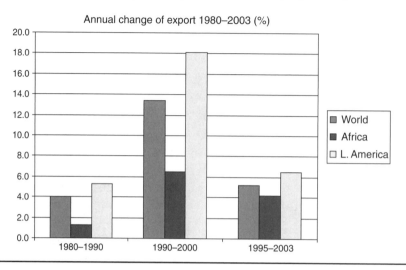

Source: Calculations based on data from IMF, ICT, WTO.

export impressively during the period 1990–2000: Costa Rica (32.9%), Mexico (32.3%), and Chile (20.6%). Brazil and Argentina is also among the fast-growing exporters with an average increase of 6.5–8.5 percent during the period 1995–2003. By estimation of the WTO, the total export from Latin America is $350.3 billion in 2002, which is five percent of the world export. The indicators for Africa are $140.1 billion and two percent. These figures have to be read carefully, because they exclude the intraregional trade. From that perspective, Latin America is a much better economically developed area with dynamic intraregional trade and cooperation.

Mexico is among the countries that have a well-developed economic model of mutually supportive industrial and agrarian sector. It is reflected in the export potential of that country which amounts to $161 billion in 2002. Such industrial goods as transport vehicle and equipment, IT products and electronic components, machinery, chemicals, and so on represent more than 60 percent of the export. Only the car export is $14 billion, plus additional 6 billion in other transport vehicles. The trade deficit of the country is $17.6 billion or 11 percent of the export.[9]

So far, the Asian developing countries show the highest dynamics of merchandise export growth, as seen in Exhibit 16.7. The Vietnamese increased their export by 640 percent for a period of ten years: from $2.6 to $16.5 billion. China and the Philippines gained export potential with about 380 percent, while India ended the period with an increase of 251 percent. Today, China is an export powerhouse with $325.6 billion of merchandise sold in

Exhibit 16.7

Merchandise Export Growth 1992–2002 (in percent)

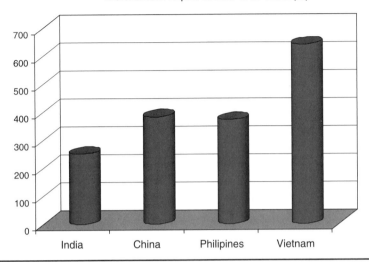

Merchandise Export Growth 1992–2002 (%)

Source: Calculations based on WTO data, 2004.

the world marketplace. The country had $30 billion merchandise foreign trade surplus in 2002. The export is a strong pro-growth factor in China. This country keeps annual economic growth of about 8–12 percent for nearly ten years. Today, the Chinese main export commodities are computers, telecommunication equipment, and consumer electronics (15%), electronic components (7%), miscellaneous manufacturing (22%), and clothing (18%). The basic trend is toward an increase of the export specialization in finished capital goods. Similar policy is led by Malaysia, Mexico, Costa Rica, and South Korea. Therefore, these sectors attract substantial foreign investment inflow. Many Japanese and US companies, producing consumer electronics, have transferred or developed production capacity in those countries because of the lower production costs and the highly qualified and disciplined labor.

The Chinese economic development deserves special attention as far as this is one-sixth of the world's population, the fastest growing economy with a persistently increasing export and import potential. The country is in a transition toward a market economy, and the economic success is actually based on that process since the reforms took place at the end of the 1970s. It became member of the WTO in 2001 and the membership definitely further accelerated the process of trade and investment liberalization.

The study of Shafaedin[10] exercises comparative analysis on the possible income of that Chinese WTO membership for the trade competition among the developing countries. An increased competition might be expected in the markets for clothing (India, Haiti, Thailand, Egypt, and Malawi), furniture (India, Indonesia, and Vietnam), electronics (Thailand, Malaysia, Mexico, and Malaysia) toys, and sporting goods (Sri Lanka and Pakistan). The main competition will be with the southeast Asian countries in the field of labor-intensive goods.

The exported merchandise per capita is another valuable indicator which allows us to compare the involvement of the different countries in the export activities regardless of the size of population. Mexico is a clear leader among the selected countries, followed by the Republic of South Africa and Argentina (Exhibit 16.8).

Further trade liberalization would move the prices on these products downward. In addition, this demand is highly cyclical, causing substantial changes in their price level. In most cases, the price trend is downward also. This assumption is well supported by the statistical data of the period 1965–2006. It explains why so often the developing countries that rely on such export face financial difficulties and debt service difficulties. Simply, the decreased revenues, even if the physical volume of exports were increased, squeeze the export revenues in hard currencies. We do not believe that the relative prices between industrial and low-processed products will change in the near future. Therefore, the Third-World countries will continue to suffer within the vicious circle of cheap exports and expensive import of industrial

Exhibit 16.8

Export per Capita in 2005 (US$) Legend: RSA—Republic of South Africa

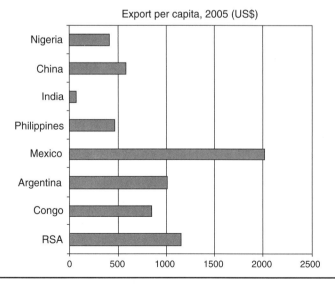

Source: Calculations based on WTO data, accessed at www.wto.org on January 3, 2006.

goods. Their call for "new economic order" is fully understandable. Yes, the trade liberalization may solve some of their problems and may create some growth stimulus, including attraction of additional foreign capital in the export-oriented sectors. At the same time, one should recognize the realistic danger of short-term imbalances for them, because of the eliminated protections on the weak local industries.

The investment flow plays an increasing role in the interaction between the developing economies and the rest of the world. The foreign investments in the developing countries are in three major forms: (1) direct investments, (2) portfolio equity investments, and (3) debt flows. Other things being equal, the direct investments are preferable because they are less vulnerable to the business cycle fluctuations in the mid and long run. The financial crises in Latin America and East Asia during the 1986–2006 proved that assumption. Those crises have slowed the direct investments but their effect was mainly on the portfolio investments, which are short-term oriented and are aimed toward fast speculative profits. The portfolio investments can be withdrawn very fastly, which lead to unexpected liquidity and other financial problems and misbalances in the host country (ies). By principle, such massive withdrawals lead to further irreversible deepening of the financial crisis. The Asian financial crisis in 1997–1998 is a typical example. An even highly industrialized country, like South Korea's banking and economic sectors went through very turbulent times. The consequences for the Asian developing countries were far more complicated and the recovery period was much longer.

Numerous studies confirm that the degree of the foreign investment effect on the domestic economy is quite different for the different types of investments. The study of Bosworth et al. covered nearly 60 developing countries from Asia, Africa, and Latin America.[11] Exhibit 16.9 shows the direct investments have the highest degree of positive effect. Every dollar of FDI attracts 80 cents additional domestic investments, while the foreign debt and the portfolio investments attract 50 and 10 cents, respectively.

We shall assume that the direct investments are preferable for the foreign businesses because of the relatively lower risk and the ability to manage the investment process in every stage. It is a win-win scenario for the host economies as well. Unlike the debt instruments, those direct investments increase the cash inflow in hard currencies that assist in the improvement of the balance-of-payments, stabilize the exchange market, and bring price stability. This is also the best hard currency back up for the import. In addition, these types of investments are usually made by companies with good world market positions and further generate hard currencies inflow based on the increasing exports. They also directly and indirectly open new jobs and increase the budget revenues (import duties, corporate and municipal taxes, environmental taxes, value-added or sales taxes, license

Exhibit 16.9

Foreign Investment Impact on Domestic Investments in LDC (in US $ cents)

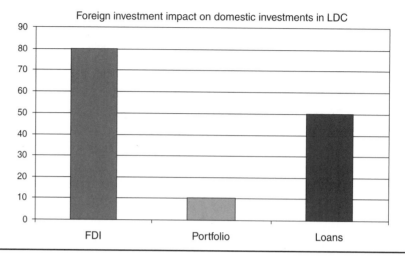

Foreign investment impact on domestic investments in LDC

Source: Calculations based on Bosworth et al.[11]

fees). The indirect effect is usually realized through subcontracting with the local suppliers of goods and services. The host countries also benefit from the increased competitive pressure on the local producers, if any, and urge them to catch up with the international standards. We share the understanding that it helps the developing countries to ease some social problems and to strengthen the market institutions and democracy.

The clear advantages of the direct investments should not underestimate the positive outcomes from the portfolio investments and the use of foreign debt instruments. The exact effects depend on the user of these instruments (private businesses or governments), their timing, and the reliability of the host country's financial system. If the governments assume the borrowing, it might have a contradictory effect. On the one hand, it helps the old debt service and lessens the possible crowding out effect if the government is forced to use the alternative domestic credit markets. On the other hand, it is further accumulating foreign debt or increased risk of unexpected withdrawals. Although your business could be in the real sector, a regular assessment of the domestic financial market is highly recommendable.

Many of the developing countries actively participate in different regional economic agreements as an intermediate or supportive step toward better access to the world market place. From that perspective, the regionalization is rather supporting than delaying the globalization. Several trade agreements are to be mentioned: ASEAN, Mercosur, Andean Pact, CARICOM, and the African Economic Community Treaty (ACT).[12] With no exceptions, all agreements reflect the wish to develop regional common markets for free movement of goods, services, and capital. Most of the developing countries have small domestic markets that do not allow them to achieve the economy of scale effect. From that perspective, the regional markets create the necessary conditions for the utilization of that effect. Why not look for direct access to the global markets? The answer is in the state of the developing economies and their incapability to compete with the developed market economies. The regionalization allows them to optimize the division of labor and to better utilize the capital allocation. There is a common understanding that the regional trade creates added economic effect, based on the increased exchange of intermediate goods. Usually, the countries from a particular region have similar economic structure and level of development that makes such cooperation easier.

The following are the economic outcomes from the regional economic cooperation between the developing countries:

- Economies of scale resulting from the interrelated domestic markets
- Lower costs on export/import because of the lower or eliminated tariffs and nontariff barriers (improved terms of trade)
- Better allocation of production, based on division of labor (specialization and cooperation)
- Better allocation of capital, building capacity to finance or co-finance larger investment projects at national or regional level
- Coordinated economic policy
- Stronger competition and stimulus for technological and product innovations
- Higher economic growth, higher employment and better standard of living
- Easier and more efficient interaction with the international organizations and institutions.

Unfortunately, the example of the integrated African economic group is different than those of Mercosur and ASEAN. The advantages of such integration remain mainly theoretical at this stage. The statistical data testify that there is no visible increase of the intraregional trade in any of the six REC agreements. Between 90 and 95 percent of the foreign trade took place with third parties. It means that the investors in that continent cannot rely much on regionalization of their business operations. They would rather rely on re-exporting to the developed countries. That is why the investors are interested primarily in such sectors of the economy like extraction of minerals (mining) and/or agro industry.

The failure in Africa is due to many factors, including the political instability and cyclical civil wars, high ethnic and religious tension, underdeveloped and/or nonreliable infrastructure (in large areas the only viable transportation is the expensive air transportation), nonconvertible currencies and lack of hard currency reserves, heavy bureaucracy and corruption, ineffective and wrongly applied highly protective foreign trade policy, failure (wrong priorities or policies) of numerous IMF programs and other international institutions for economic and financial stabilization), and so on.

We cannot agree more with assumptions, like the one of Yeats, that in the specific case of Africa the priorities of the regional economic cooperation should be aimed at the development of appropriate infrastructure and better-coordinated macro-economic policies, including financial stability, rather than the traditional boost of trade.[13] Clearly, the comparative figures below show that most of the African countries still rely on import protection—despite certain liberalization of its trade policy, increasing the share of open trade regimes from 23 to 43 percent and downsizing the restrictive regimes from 77 to 14 percent. Today, the share of the African open regimes is still three times lower than the share of the open regimes in the World Economy.

Sharer[14] argues that the poor African trade performance could be explained with the unfavorable import regime of the developing countries. He stresses that the US and the EU import tariffs for African export of raw agricultural products is two to three times higher than the import duties on industrial goods, 5–6 percent and two percent respectively. The duties on the processed agricultural products are even higher—up to 10 percent.

The nontariff barriers are of another concern. The highly developed countries continue to heavily subsidize its agriculture and extracting industries. Different quotas and standards are applied which create additional burden for such export. Today, the developing countries, including the ones in Africa, face extreme difficulties in dealing with nearly $400 billion worldwide in total subsidies. They erode the market competition and limit the potential for export from the less developed economies. We do not expect that the policy of subsidizing will change substantially in the near future. It is more realistic to believe that more significant steps will be taken in the direction of import liberalization. The EU and the United States have announced some unilateral steps, like gradual phase out of any quota restrictions on the importing of agro products till 2010 and further downsizing or even elimination of the customs duties. Such policy would be beneficial for the poor agrarian countries and would allow them to use the export as an engine for growth and better standard of living. In that respect, we see the increasing pressure from the WTO for multilateral agreements for such preferences.

However, the fact is that expected export increase of agro products and raw materials is achievable only if appropriate structural economic changes take place. The degree and the concrete shape of those structural changes have to be different for the various countries and regions. Some of the

Latin American countries like Brazil, Argentina, Mexico, Uruguay, Chile, and Venezuela have relatively well-developed industrial sectors. China and India in Asia also have a growing industrial potential. This is not the case of Africa, which exports the processed agro products and raw materials in primarily low quantities.

Chad is a typical example with 85 percent of the employment in the agrarian sector, 12 percent in the service sector, and only 5 percent in the lower end of the low-processing industrial sector. In 2002, the export of goods was only $65.1 million and consisted mainly of cotton ($48.4 million and natural gums, raisins, and balsams ($9.7 million). The country has small facilities for export production of some components for helicopters and airplanes—total value of $3.5 million. The import is $352 million and consists mainly of industrial products (machinery, parts, equipment, transport vehicle, chemicals, medication, etc.). The country has an astonishing trade deficit of $287 million or nearly five times higher than the annual export.[15]

Further analysis confirms that the limited local manufacturing does not have anything in common with the agro production. So, all the equipment (tractors, combines, irrigation facilities, vehicles, etc.) are imported. Chad illustrates the economic trap for many developing countries. There is an exit of that trap but it is unlikely that the trade liberalization alone would be capable to solve these problems. Obviously, it is a question of new economic policies that better integrate the agriculture and the light industries with the development of regional and domestic (where appropriate) production capacities for the necessary equipment and materials.

More profitable export of agro products and products of the extracting industry can be maintained only if the long-term trend of lower sale price is compensated with higher productivity. It is suggesting a serious and well-supported investment program. The absolute value of export has deteriorated in Niger, Burundi, Mauritania, and Cameroon in the period between 1992 and 2002. The worse case is Burundi, where the export in 2002 is barely 42 percent of the export in 1992, $30 million and $72 million, respectively.[16]

Africa is not an economically homogeneous continent. The level of economic development and the opportunities for doing business vary dramatically. The poorest and the most business risky area is tropical sub-Saharan Africa. Today, the annual GDP per capita (PPP adjustment, 1990 prices) is within the range of $1700 and what is even worse is that it tends to decline since 1985. For comparison, the GDP per capita in the nontropical Africa is about $7400 while in the five Northern African countries (Morocco, Algeria, Libya, Tunisia, and Egypt) it is $4371. The richest five African countries are the Republic of South Africa, Botswana, Seychelles, Namibia, and Tunisia where the GDP per capita is from $6764 (Tunisia) to $10,000 (RSA).[17]

This analysis emphasizes that Africa is a region which demands more attention from the international trade, financial, and industrial institutions.

There are still serious obstacles for development in South Asia and some Latin American countries. The call of the developing countries for "new economic order" is not yet fulfilled. The interaction of those least developed countries with the world market are too limited, often unfavorable or focused mainly on the natural resources. It is a problem not only for the LDCs. It limits the utilization of the potential business opportunities there, to the extent that at the end it affects the world economy.

Recently, the phenomenon of globalization attracts the attention as possible cure of the existing problems. At the same time, very prominent economists, politicians, and social organizations see the globalization as a process which will rather deepen the divide and further worsen the socio-economic conditions in the developing world, mainly in the least developed countries.[18] Generally, it is based on a free trade and high degree of economic interdependence. All the success stories in the Third World are a result of trade and investment liberalization. Therefore, the economic success supposes relatively free interaction with the world marketplace and free flow of goods, services, and capital.

The examples of China, Thailand, Mexico, Costa Rica, South Korea, and Malaysia are a good illustration. The extreme protectionism and isolation have not produced a single example of strong and viable economy in the whole human's economic history. And if the further liberalization and globalization of the world economy is seen as a major road toward better capital allocation and production efficiency then the speed and the mechanisms of globalization are subject to increasing discussion. The perspectives from leading economists, institutions, politicians, and businesses are often mutually exclusive. Some opponents of globalization see it as a disastrous trend for the developing world, while others argue that "the devil is in the details."

We share the understanding that globalization has to be seen as a gradual and well-balanced process instead of a "shock therapy" approach. Having in mind the substantial differences between the developed and the developing countries on the one hand and among the developing countries on the other, we do not believe that any "universal" mechanism or pace of globalization could be applied on a global level regardless of the above-mentioned specifics. It is quite understandable that the richest countries and the leading multinational corporations need an easier access to the natural and human resources and to domestic and regional markets. Using its powerful positions at the WTO and the other international institutions like IMF and the World Bank, they give continuous pressure for further downsizing and eliminating of the trade protection policies. This pressure is often applied as a precondition for further foreign debt service assistance.

The underdeveloped countries are not ready to compete with the highly developed producers and exporters. Their weak industries could face extreme difficulties if the liberalization takes place in short periods. In fact, the problem is not only with the time frame of the removal of the protectionist barriers but is mainly a structural problem. The international institutions and the governments should pay much more attention to the conditions and stimulus for mobilizing the foreign capital and expertise in the development of the real economy and better utilization of the natural resources if any. At the end of the day, a "free access" to those resources and the continuation of the common practice of concentration on the extraction industries and export of goods with low value added might worsen the conditions of those countries and make them more vulnerable to the world market fluctuations. From that perspective, globalization would be a success story only if it is seen not as a single act of import restriction removal but rather as a system of economic policies, covering the whole economy.

Closing Case

Indian's LIC company operates successfully in the developing countries

The Life Insurance Corporation (LIC) of India is one of the largest financial institutions in Asia. Its assets worth $100 billion in 2005 and continues to grow. The company has more than 130 million individual subscribers worldwide. It deals with life insurance, capital market services, pension funds management, and so on. In 2005, LIC distributed $253 million as bonuses to policyholders. No doubt, this is one of the most powerful financial intermediaries in Asia.

Despite the vast domestic market, based on a population above one billion, the company persistently extends its business mainly in the developing world. The low-income per capita, underdeveloped financial infrastructure and troubled economies are not an obstacle for LIC's foreign market expansion. Today, the company has branches in Nepal, Kenya, Fiji, Mauritius, Saudi Arabia, Oman, Sri Lanka, and many others. For example, 40,000 individual life insurance policies were sold (2005) in the small pacific state of Fiji. It generated annual revenues of $12 million in 2005.

The company has adapted its market entry strategy in correspondence with the domestic business environment and governments' regulations. In Nepal, one of the poorest Asian countries, LIC operates under the umbrella of joint venture with the domestic insurance company Vishal Group Ltd. LIC controls 55 percent of the shares, Vishal Group Ltd owns 25 percent and the remaining 20 percent were sold to individual investors.

The same approach was applied in other national markets, although in the different countries LIC penetrates different financial sectors. In Kenya, for example, LIC's activities were organized as a mutual fund. This fund has proved its efficiency in attracting small investors from both urban and rural areas of this African country. The attracted financial resources are reinvested in low-risk securities, mainly treasury bills and government bonds, or some quasi-government organizations like the Housing Authority.

Transnational corporations like LIC, British Petroleum, Royal Dutch Shell, and Coca-Cola proved that there are business opportunities in every single country. There are no "good and bad markets" but just markets that use different approaches. In addition, some market segments in the developing countries could be even more profitable than those in the developed countries.

Question: National Income per capita does not always characterize the real market potential in the developing countries. Discuss.

Source: LICI to provide life insurance in Nepal (Reuters, November 28, 2000), access at *http://www.rediff.com/money/2000/nov/28nepal.htm* on March 4, 2006; LIC India, accessed at *http://www.licifiji.com/aboutus.php* on March 6, 2006.

Chapter Summary

Third-World economy is quite heterogeneous. Different countries and regions follow different trends and patterns of economic growth and different degree of interaction. Unfortunately, there is a large group of countries which remain isolated from the main stream of increasing foreign trade turnover, deepening division of labor, and increasing productivity. Those countries have monoculture economies, chronic trade and financial misbalances, and mounting indebtedness. The standard of living is deteriorating in those countries, which results in very limited purchasing power and insufficient domestic demand. In most cases, the host government policies and business climate are unfavorable to foreign businesses. Nevertheless, it is possible to do business there despite the entry, economic, and other difficulties. Clearly, the traditional approaches are often useless, unless they are appropriately modified in relation to the particular environment. Usually, support and/or cooperation with the host and the home governments and business institutions are highly recommendable. Huge infrastructure projects of national and regional importance, co-financed from the international institutions and local governments, offer very good opportunities for direct investments.

Fortunately, there is large group of developing countries with impressive economic growth, increasing competitiveness, and incentives toward technological and product innovations. Most of these countries are members of WTO or are close to membership. The latter means that they lead foreign trade and investment policy, which can be characterized as of liberal type or less restrictive. Countries like China, Mexico, India, Brazil, and others attract the foreign exporters and investors who see widening business opportunities. They often enjoy a variety of government stimuli like tax holidays, low or zero duties on import of capital goods, free or cheap land for industrial facilities, unrestricted profit repatriation, and so on. The investors and the importers are gaining not only from the growing domestic markets but also from the access to the regional and the world market. Clearly, it is beneficial for both the foreign businesses and the domestic economies. At the same time, the specific cultural and political characteristics, as well as the problematic economic conditions demand enough knowledge, experiences, and appropriate business strategy. The process of globalization does not offer final results, it simply opens new opportunities.

Review and Discussion Questions

1. Comment on the reliability of indicators used for the classification of the developing countries.
2. Explain the key factors that lead to different levels of socio-economic development at a national and regional level. Discuss how the level of development modifies the business opportunities and practices.
3. Analyze the interdependence between the degree of trade liberalization and economic development.
4. Prioritize the factors which determine the investment inflow and outflow in the developing countries.
5. Some experts argue that the cultural and political factors in the LDCs have stronger influence on the business environment than in the highly industrialized countries. Comment on that assumption and explain how it affects the foreign business strategy.
6. Do you believe that the preferential access to the developed markets would solve the export problems of the developing countries?
7. Provide examples of success stories and failures of entry strategies in the LDCs.
8. Do you see the regional economic integration between the developing countries as a stage in the globalization process, or is it in fact a diversion from that process?
9. What makes the leading corporations and even mid-sized companies to conduct business in the LDCs instead of concentrating on the rich and highly demanding markets in the OECD? List the motivating factors.
10. The globalization is seen as a growth engine and vice versa—as a major threat to the economies of the developing countries. In your opinion, how does globalization affect the international business today and what are the expected outcomes in the short run and in the long run?

Endnotes

1. OPEC Revenues: Country details, Energy Information Administration, January 2004, accessed at www.eia.doe.gov.
2. World Development Indicators database, August 2005.
3. See for more details http://www.pg.com/latin/location.htm.
4. Information accessed at www.teaandcoffee.net/0200/tea2.htm.
5. Accessed at www.matsushita.com.
6. See Philip Kotler, *Marketing Management*, 11th Edition, Prentice Hall, 2003, pp. 219–220.
7. Agosin M. and Mayer, R. (2000) *Foreign investment in developing countries. Does it crowd in domestic investment*? UNCTAD Papers No. 146. Geneva: UNCTAD.
8. *Research & Analytical Papers*. Kazakhstan's Regions, Foreign & Commonwealth Office, UK, May 2000, pp. 13–33.
9. Ibid.
10. Shafaeddin, S. M. *The Impact of China's Accession to WTO on the Exports of Developing Countries*. Discussion Paper, No. 160, UNCTAD, June 2002.
11. Bosworth, B. P. and Susan, M. Collins 1999, "Capital Flows to Developing Economies: Implications for Saving and Investment," *Brookings Papers on Economic Activity*:1, Brookings Institution, pp. 143–69.
12. ASEAN was founded in 1967 by Malaysia, Indonesia, the Philippines, Singapore, and Thailand. Later on it was joined by Brunei (1987) and Vietnam (1995); CARICOM was established in 1973 by few Central American countries (Barbados, Jamaica, Guyana, and Trinidad and Tobago. Today, this agreement consists of 15 members and 5 associate members; Mercosur was created in 1991 by Brazil, Argentina, and Uruguay. It has two associated members (Chile and Bolivia) since 1996; ACT came into force 1994 with the main objective to strengthen the Regional Economic Communities, including the Arab Magreb Union, the Common Market for Eastern and Southern Africa (COMESA), the Economic Community of West African States (ECOWAS), the Southern African Development Community (SADC), and the Intergovernmental Authority and Development (IGAD).
13. Yeats, Al. (1999). What Can be Expected from the African Regional Trade Agreements?, World Bank's Working Paper, No. 2004, Washington, DC.
14. R. Sharer, An Agenda for Trade, Investment and Regional Integration, *Journal of Finance & Development*, IMF, Dec. 2001, Vol. 38, No. 4.
15. *International Trade Center (ITC)*, 2002, accessed at www.intracen.org.
16. WTO, 2004, accessed at www.wto.org.
17. See more details about the dispersion of economic potential in Africa: D. Bloom and J. Sachs. "Geography, Demography and Economic Growth in Africa" (1998, revised), *Harvard Institute of International development*, Harvard University, accessed at www.iaen.org.
18. See Stiglitz, J. *Globalization and its Discontents*. W.W. Norton & Company, Inc. (2002), NY.

Part B: A Potpourri of Cases

Air Arabia: Seeking Success in an Open Skies Market

Donelda S. McKechnie, Jim Grant and Mona Fahmi

The American University of Sharjah, UAE

Introduction

Air Arabia began operations in October 2003. The airline flies from Sharjah International Airport, in the United Arab Emirates, which is only 30 minutes from Dubai. Air Arabia's national affiliation is the Emirate of Sharjah. Its colors are red and white, its logo is the sea gull and its slogan is Pay Less... Fly More.

The mission of Air Arabia is 'to revolutionise air travel in the region through an innovative business approach offering superb value for money and a safe, reliable operation. To achieve this we will be known for our low fares, grow our business profitably, build motivated multi-functional teams, demonstrate the highest operational standards and manage our costs ruthlessly'.[1]

Following this strategic plan, the airline appears to have achieved success if profits earned and passenger numbers are any indication. However, since startup, their business plan has been to pursue a niche market using the low-fare, low-cost template made popular by South West Airlines. The question is whether this business agenda will continue to work for them in the future or whether they should alter their operations to include benefits more commonly delivered by full service carriers.

The Setting

United Arab Emirates is a small country nestled on the southern shore of the Persian Gulf. It is one of six including Saudi Arabia, Oman, Kuwait, Bahrain, and Qatar that form the Gulf Countries Cooperative (GCC).

587

The UAE is made up of seven emirates. The two most dominant are the oil-rich and more established Abu Dhabi and the westernized and rapidly developing world-renowned Dubai. Four are smaller and significantly less wealthy although each has an agenda for growth: Ajman, Umm Al Quwain, Ras Al Khaimah and Fujeirah. Sharjah is the seventh. It is distinct from the others for its adherence to traditional culture and values which are mandated through a dress code and strict laws prohibiting alcohol consumption within its boundaries. Each emirate functions to some extent as its own country, with its own ruler, cultural identity and government. The seven emirates together are ruled under the umbrella auspices of Abu Dhabi, which is the capital and acts in a federal capacity.

The 2003 projected UAE population figures[2] indicate that approximately 4,040,000 people reside in the country. Sharjah has an estimated 512,000 living in the urban areas. Ajman to the north has approximately 225,000 while urban Dubai to the south has less than 1.2 million. The percentage of population employed in the labor force ranges from 47 to 68 percent, depending on the emirate, with Sharjah at 56 percent and Dubai at 68 percent. Fujeirah and Ras Al Khaimah are lowest at 47 percent and 48 percent respectively. South Asians are the dominant demographic group with UAE nationals accounting for less than 20 percent of the total people.

Background

In early 2003, Sheikh Abdullah bin Mohammed Al Thani, Chairman of Sharjah Department of Civil Aviation, announced the startup of Air Arabia.[3] Investment was a share capital of 10 million AED ($1 US = approximately 3.66 Arab Emirates Dirhams) and operating funds of 50 million AED. It would fly from the easily accessible and under-utilized for passenger travel Sharjah International Airport. The first flight was in October of that year.

Initially, the airline made no comment about expected market positioning, routes, destinations, operations or fleet acquisition. Sheikh Al Thani explained that Air Arabia would offer a safe and efficient service at low price fares. Beyond that, all options were open, he said. At startup, Adel Ali, Chief Executive Officer, said the airline was being positioned as the 'people's airline' because it would serve the community. He acknowledged that the no-frills concept would require educating passengers. This type of service was not only new to the area but it was also counter to Arab culture which emphasizes hospitality.

Low cost operations, ticketless travel, small management team and working to slim margins were just a few of the plans to keep fares low, according to Adel Ali. Following this agenda, he predicted that the airline would break even by the end of its second year.

The Airbus A-320 was the aircraft of choice for Air Arabia. Its seating capacity is approximately 160 passengers for a single class, 3 and 3 configuration divided by a centre aisle. Early destinations for Air Arabia were 45 minutes to 4 hours flying time out of Sharjah. These included other countries in the GCC plus some destinations in the Middle East such as Lebanon and Jordan. The airline had one plane at launch and took delivery of a second less than a month later. Full fleet configuration was set at six A-320s by the end of 2004. Experienced pilots with Air Canada training were brought in to augment the flight deck roster.

Marketing efforts appeared to be minimal prior to launch. Little advertising was appearing in the catchment area and news of the startup was being passed by word of mouth. The reservations call centre opened less than 3 weeks prior to the first flight. The website for online bookings became available for use at about the same time. An independent market research study[4] found that only 46 percent of respondents surveyed in Sharjah had heard of the airline just days before the launch. However, 40 percent said yes they thought the airline would be successful while 35 percent said they did not know.

Distinguishing Low Fare from Full Fare

The distinction between a low cost carrier and one that is full service is the lower fares that derive from a low-cost operational structure. Comparatively, the characteristics are shown in Exhibit 1.[5] In sum, low-fare means no frills: few if any amenities are offered and transportation is point-to point.

The low-fare model is typically a niche strategy where the entire value proposition is intensely scrutinized and '... aimed at getting benefit from offer vacuums and from the service for pariah customers, starting from visiting friends and relatives, ethnic and leisure based movements and later climbing up to reach cost-conscious business travelers'.[6]

A low-cost airline will carve a new market space and take market share from a full service carrier when it begins operations. However, even though it is low cost and no-frills, pursuing a low-fare pricing strategy against a full-service incumbent will potentially put the new entrant at risk. To attract passengers, the no-frills operator's options include advertising and promotions targeted to the potential traveling public in the catchment areas surrounding secondary airports and building an in-flight culture of fun and excitement.

The airline industry regularly undertakes research about efficiency factors including punctuality, scheduling, seating, and routes. However, aside from the typical concerns, the traveling public will also consider a carrier's country-of-origin. In other words, associated with a national airline are expectations and reputation that contribute to the decision whether to buy

Exhibit 1

Characteristics of Low-fare and Full-fare Airlines

Low-fare Airline	Full-fare Airline
Simple brand—low-fare	Complex brand—price + service
Online and direct booking	Mainly travel agents
Reservations by telephone and Internet	
Simple ticket price structure and ticket less check-in	Complex fare structures
	Tickets produced for each booking
Use of secondary, low-charging airports (some exceptions) Located around major population centres	Focus on primary airports
High aircraft utilization—quick gate turnaround time	Lower utilization of aircraft
Do not interline; point-to-point service	Interlining important part of service; hub and spoke services
Offers non-stop routes	
Simple product—all additional services and facilities charged for, e.g., credit card bookings, late check-in, meals, etc.	Complex integrated service product(s), e.g. ticket flexibility, business lounges, frequent flyer program
Focus on ancillary revenue generation—advertising ('the plane as a billboard'), on board retailing (more common in Europe)	Focus on primary product
Mainly short-haul focus	Short and long haul
Common fleet type acquired at very good rates	Mixed fleet
Single type of aircraft	
Single class configuration	Cabins are usually divided into two or three classes to allow for different degrees of in-flight service
No complimentary in-flight meal service	Complimentary in-flight meal and drink(s)

Exhibit 1 *continued*

Low-fare Airline	Full-fare Airline
Aggressive yield management by implementing various price levels and capacities depending on load factors and when tickets are purchased	Yield management by filling up set-price classes in order of bookings
Minimum cabin crew on board	Cabin crew more numerous as required
Only operate core activities. Outsource most operations	Less outsourcing of operations

a ticket or choose another option. These factors apply to all carriers regardless of whether they are classified as low fare, full service or somewhere in between.

The Competition

The United Arab Emirates has an open skies policy. At the time that Air Arabia was entering the market, the emirate of Abu Dhabi was introducing its own carrier, Etihad Airlines and calling it the National Carrier of the UAE. It was positioned as full service with classes labeled Diamond, Pearl and Coral rather than First, Business and Economy. The Etihad launch was direct competition for the world renowned Emirates Airline, who take the position that they are "The Official Airline" named for their many sponsorship activities. Emirates Airline is successfully transitioning the low-cost model of the short-haul carriers, e.g., South West and Easy Jet into the full-service offering, long-haul industry. Under such operational guidelines, there is the expectation that ticket prices will be set to compete on the low-cost template.[7]

Also operating in the region is Gulf Air, a full-service carrier based in Bahrain but operating many flights out of Dubai and Abu Dhabi. Its destinations are regional and international. Gulf Air, in 2003, began reorganizing its operations and repositioning in the marketplace. Arab hospitality became the standard for the passenger services offered. Marketing greater comfort, more amenities and first-class meals appeared to position the airline closer to Emirates and Etihad on the full-fare/low-fare continuum. However, Gulf Air ticket prices were often less costly than the other two on the same routes.

Since Air Arabia entered the market in 2003, another emirate, Ras Al Khaimah has announced that RAK Airways will begin operations in 2007. Details about service have yet to be announced. Many of its expected destinations are currently part of the Air Arabia network. Virgin Airlines commenced flights between London, UK and Dubai in late March 2006, with the expectation that they will take 10–12 percent of the market. Low fare competition is coming from the no-frills carrier that is part of Indian Airlines. They will target the South Asian consumers.

Factors Affecting Passenger Choice

With only a few weeks to go before Air Arabia's first flight, a market research study was undertaken independent of the airline. Respondents were asked what factors they consider when choosing a full-service carrier and what factors they would consider if deciding to fly with a generic low-fare airline. Exhibit 2, below, identifies the eight factors and the percent of respondents who said these issues are important considerations. Factors are ranked ( ) with corresponding mean and standard deviation provided.

Questions about other passengers, seat spacing and entertainment relate to the regional culture. Social class is to a large extent rigidly observed in the UAE. Thus, who may be seated beside whom has the potential to cause upset if the aircraft has only one service class and reserved seating is not offered. Lack of amenities on board, seating space and little or no entertainment are counter to Arab hospitality standards. These also presented possible obstacles to attracting passengers.

Respondents were asked if they would consider flying Air Arabia and the results were cross-tabulated with responses to the eight factors for a no-frill

Exhibit 2

Factors Considered when Traveling any Airline or a Low-cost Carrier

	Any airline			No-frills			% of respondents who consider these factors important if they were flying Air Arabia
	% important	Mean	SD	% important	Mean	SD	
Ticket price	71 (3)	3.91	0.961	67 (2)	3.94	1.053	72
Other passengers	50 (7)	3.40	1.054	46 (7)	3.39	1.091	43
Punctuality	71 (2)	3.95	0.957	65 (3)	3.83	0.991	69
Flight timings	55 (5)	3.50	1.241	52 (5)	3.49	1.180	52
Airplane safety	77 (1)	4.22	1.063	74 (1)	4.18	1.057	77
Service on board	60 (4)	3.71	1.050	55 (4)	3.57	1.144	50
Seat spacing	51 (6)	3.48	1.095	50 (6)	3.43	1.102	48
Entertainment	43 (8)	3.21	1.182	40 (8)	3.12	1.234	41

airline. Interestingly, potential passengers put more emphasis on ticket price, punctuality, and safety if they were to fly Air Arabia versus any other no-frills carrier. Results closely aligned with percentages noted for any airline.

Marketing Air Arabia

The research indicated that Air Arabia had the opportunity to pursue a greater share of the market first, by creating awareness through increased promotions and, second, by addressing the factors that concern people when considering an airline. In the latter instance, it would be possible to exceed customer expectations by simply being punctual, pointing out the flight timing advantages in advertisements and using real-life passengers in media campaigns. The degree to which Air Arabia would be benchmarked against the established quality reputation of Emirates Airlines was unknown at startup and is not known today. This is a significant competitor given that Emirates aggressively pursues its markets through such activities as its recent announcement that they will sponsor the next two World Cup football (soccer) events.

In early 2005, Air Arabia introduced buzz marketing into its promotional efforts. The airline arranged 'ambassadorships' with the business student council of a local university. The young people were treated to familiarization trips on Air Arabia to experience the service. They then began a word-of-mouth campaign to promote the airline amongst their peers. In addition, students were hired as 'mystery shoppers' to assess both the on-ground and in-flight customer service activities. By mid-2005 Air Arabia began using South Park-type characters in its marketing campaigns. Depending on the destination being served, the characters are outfitted in the traditional dress of the country and are currently being integrated as a brand identifier. The airline continues to pursue the youth market; raffles for free tickets to the winner's destination of choice are held in the student centres of nearby universities.

The Future

Although Air Arabia faced competition when it started operations, it has successfully carved a niche in the marketplace.[8] At the end of its second year, management announced that the carrier had a reported profit of 32.1 million AED. 1.13 million passengers, an increase of 122 percent over its first year of business, had been carried on more than 9400 flights, up 90 percent year on year, to 23 destinations. Employee productivity also improved, when compared to the 2004 levels, by more than 11 percent. The airline appears committed to its mission statement that it will offer value and safety while costs are tightly controlled.

Thus, the low-fare, no-frills template appears to be successful in the region. Air Arabia has carved a niche in the marketplace and continues to fly from Sharjah which remains a secondary airport in the country. However, what of the future? Arguably it should not become complacent in an industry that is dynamic and volatile. Competition is intensifying as new entrants start operations on a seemingly regular basis. Thus, should Air Arabia continue with its current operation formula? Or should the airline begin to alter its business plan in anticipation of potential changes in the marketplace? If the latter is suggested, then what are the changes that senior management should consider?

Endnotes

1. http://www.airarabia.com.
2. http://www.uae.gov.ae/mop/UAE_figure/UAE_%2003.htm.
3. Sharjah launches national airline, Gulf News, February 5, 2003.
4. Fahmi, Mona, Khan, Marwish, and McKechnie, Donelda S. (2004). The Middle East's No-Frills Airline, unpublished data set.
5. Fahmi, Mona, McKechnie, Donelda, and Grant, Jim (2006) The low-fare, no-frills airline template arrives in the Middle East: Consumer views communicated, 11th Annual International Corporate and Marketing Communications Conference, Slovenia, pp. 246–251; Gilbert, David, Child, David and Bennett, Marion (2001) A qualitative study of the current practices of 'no-frills' airlines operating in the UK, *Journal of Vacation Marketing*, 7(4), pp. 302–315; Lawton, Thomas C. (2003) Managing Proactively in Turbulent Times: Insights from the Low-Fare Airline Business, *Irish Journal of Management*, 24(1), pp. 173–193.
6. Jarach, David (2004) Future Scenarios for the European Airline Industry: A Marketing-Based Perspective, *Journal of Air Transportation*, 9(2), pp. 23–39.
7. *Economist* (2005) EasyOz, Low-cost is coming to long-haul flights. Next could be low-fares, October 29, pp. 70–71.
8. Air Arabia reports profit of Dh32.1m, Gulf News, February 19, 2006.

Can Personal Agendas Produce Good Business Decisions: The Case of KYT Inc.[1]

Gary H. Kritz*, Marios Katsioloudes[†] and Samuel Wathen[‡]

* *Seton Hall University USA*
[†] *The American University of Sharjah, UAE*
[‡] *Coastal Carolina University USA*

The 26-year-old George Kathros, Executive VP of his family's company and future leader of the luxury cruise yacht division, has been living a lie. He is a homosexual; he knows he was that way and realized his sexual preference at the age of nine when he was repeatedly raped by an older cousin. He did not mind the abuse and knew that something felt right. He had always found his cousin attractive. In Turkey, homosexuality is a *yip*—that is, in its simplest terms, a societal no-no. His father rejected him when he announced his sexual preference at the age of twelve. He had never been his father's favorite son. That role was reserved for his older brother, Oropo. Oropo was always better at sports; he also had a way with the ladies. George had found everything awkward about the "other" sex. That was because he knew who he was at that early age. Even though George was no such in high school or college where he received a BS in Management and an MBA, his father did not treat him quite as well as his brother as indicated by Oropo's position in the company. Oropo had been sent to the United States for an education as George had been; yet, Oropo held a higher position in the company than George did. George's and his father's relationship did not worsen through these years, and George did get put in the family business in a fairly responsible position, but his personal life was never discussed again since his "coming out" at the age of twelve. George had been secretly very grateful to his father for being sent to the United States for his college education. It was in the States that he learned about gay community life and had had several relationships to explore his sexuality. He swore he would come back to the States to live somehow and still fulfill family obligations.

KYT Inv. has decided to expand its luxury yacht cruise business to North America. Through research, it has determined three possible cities in Florida that would potentially make an excellent base of operations. The three cities are Daytona, Fort Lauderdale, and Miami. George has been very involved in the research. His father has let him take the lead in this possible expansion because if it happens, George would be the leader of the operations and be based in one of the Florida cities. George sensed his father would like him "to be out of sight," yet still be perceived as a viable part of the company by the rest of the family. George also saw a great opportunity for himself personally. His preliminary research indicated some thriving gay community life in each of those cities. George knew that this was his opportunity to live his life as himself. He would not have to hide who he was, and he could prove to his father that he could be a successful business leader somewhat on his own. All he had to do was to determine which city would be the best for the company and for himself. No one would suspect a thing.

Company History

In 1949 Pamir Kathros started a sole proprietorship business specializing in the import and export of industrial goods. By 1952 this business was incorporated in Istanbul, Turkey, as Kathros Holding, Incorporated (KHI). The main business of KFH was still the import and export of industrial goods. Based on the explosive growth of tourism in Turkey, Pamir Kathors, one of the Co-CEO's of the company, and some of his board members decided to expand the operations of the business to include tourism and real estate. This event led to the founding of Kathros Yachting and Tourism, (KYT), a wholly owned subsidiary.

The main focus of KYT in 1964 was on the construction and chartering of commercial grade sailboats. The other two segments comprising this subsidiary were real estate sales and rental property management. KYT shared the same corporate building of Kathros Holding, Inc. and its subsidiaries.

KYT Today

Organizational Background

The organization's mission is based on the owners' honesty, dignity, and dedication to customer satisfaction. In 1991 Co-CEO Oropo Kathros, son of Pamir Kathros, stated, "KYT will provide the highest level of quality customer services at competitive prices, while setting the global standards in the luxury yacht charter industry."

The corporate culture of KYT and its parent company, Kathros Holding, Inc., remained unchanged until 1986. During the early years, KYT was tightly controlled by its founder, Pamir Kathors. According to George Kathros, 'after 1986, KYT's culture changed to become more relaxed and family-like. The current culture encourages individualism and empowers employees to achieve their goals. This type of culture provides employees with a "sense of belonging" that promotes morale, productivity, and innovation. The current culture, along with the growth of the company, has focused everyone on the tremendous opportunities that lie ahead in expanding the certain businesses to new markets beyond Turkey and Europe. Although some of the "old" culture still exists, family bickering is no longer allowed.'

Furthermore, George mentioned, "after finishing my studies in the U.S. and returning to Turkey, I had a long discussion with my father about running the business more efficiently and more professionally. I want to apply some of the concepts I learned from my business school education in the United States." His brother confirmed that information by saying, "My education is less than George's. That's why the family sent him to study in the U.S., so that he could return to help the family business grow by introducing new ideas. So far, we have been successful." The father, Pamir Kathros, stated that if they decide to expand into the United States, they would not face so many difficulties because, "my son, George, had studies in America and knows many people in our business who have also visited in Turkey. So, we can star in the United States since we already know several people."[2]

Organizational Structure

The KYT is a family owned and operated company having a traditional three-tiered organizational structure. On the first level are the Co-CEOs, Pamir Kathros and his eldest son Oropo. On the second level is George, the Executive VP. The third and lowest level is made up of three departments: Accounting, Operations, and Marketing and International Relations.

The operations department includes three yacht teams and a shore support team. A yacht team typically consists of a captain, engineer, cook, hostess, and two crewmembers. Each yacht team and its support team report individually to George Kathros. In addition to the organizational structure described above, there is a government contract advisor who is not in the chain of command. This advisor functions as an external consultant who reports directly to the CEO. According to the government external advisor, 'the organizational structure is function. The organization has good vertical and horizontal communications and encourages "open door" communication between all levels in the 23-person company.'

Strategy

Prior to 1986 KYT's major cash flows were generated from rental property management activities. Since 1987 all earnings have been re-invested in yacht construction and chartering. This strategy generated financial gains by allowing KYT to expand into new markets because of expanded customer bases due to higher demand during the late 1980s and early 1990s. In 1986 the Turkish government began subsidizing investments in the tourism sector. This subsidy along with KYT's friendly relationship with the Turkish shipyards provided an excellent opportunity for the company to move into the construction of more expensive yachts and luxury sailboats.

Although the Turkish government subsidy program began in 1986, KYT's first luxury yacht, the *Suheyla*, was completed in 1990. The four years from 1986 to 1990 were spent on feasibility studies, government bureaucracy, and the actual construction of the boat, which took two years. During 1990 construction began on two more yachts, the *Zeynep* and *Esra*, which were expected to be completed by the end of 1992 and launched by the summer of 1994. Failure to meet the contractual agreement, which requires KYT to operate four to five boats by 1994, will lead to a probationary period of two years by the Turkish government. During this probationary period KYT will be required to meet the new deadline imposed by the Turkish government.[3]

In order to expand its tourism strategy in the 1990s, the Turkish government provided additional investment allowances to the private tourist-related sector. A corporate tax exemption on investment was made available to corporations possessing Incentive Certificates. The investment allowances vary from 30 to 100 percent of the total fixed investment, given 100 percent allowance would be exempt from corporate tax until he recovered his total fixed investment (excluding land and certain expenditures). Generally, the percentage credit over the total fixed investment in ship/yacht building amounted to 30 percent. Also worth noting is that the investment allowance in the Black Sea region for agriculture, camping, river, and health (thermal) tourism is 50 percent (Under secretariat of Treasury and Foreign Trade, UTFT, 1992).[4] This is important for KYT because expansion in this area fits right into their business expansion plans and would allow dramatic savings in costs leading to greater profitability.

The following is a list of some of the selected priority sectors eligible for the corporate tax exemption granted by the Turkish government:

- Tourism facilities with investment certificates from the ministry of tourism (excluding yacht imports)
- Large-scale infrastructure investments in tourism areas
- Manufactures of wearing apparel, processors of leather, etc.

- Under the Build-Operate-Transfer (BOT) model a company constructing and operating its own buildings is eligible for a 50 percent contribution from the government to cover construction costs
- Ship and yacht building investments with fixed investments values over 10 billion Turkish lira
- Iron and steel product investments

Subsidies provided to the tourism sector by Turkey are unique, especially if one considers that similar subsidies are not a part of the government policies of countries such as Spain, France, Italy, and Greece. These countries are located in the same geographic area and compete with Turkey in the tourism sector.

Tourism is such a huge industry in the global marketplace that some countries attempt to increase tourism through business incentives and subsidies. KYT offers a prime example of how one company seized the opportunity to expand its current operation through Turkish incentives and subsidies designed to develop tourism in its country. In 1986 Turkey signed contracts with KYT and other tourism companies that included the following specific investment incentives.[4]

1. 100 percent of all income would be tax exempt until 1994.
2. All foreign purchases would be 100 percent free from tariffs and duty charges.
3. The government would cover 100 percent of all funds invested by the parent firm.
4. 10 percent of any additional funds invested by shareholders would be funded by the government.
5. There would be an exemption from all government related fees during the investment.

As mandated in its contract for government subsidies, KYT has to meet three requirements. First, the company has to have a fleet of four to five boats operating by 1994. Second, all expenses are to be documented in full and certified by government inspectors. Finally, KYT has to show revenue of one million in United States dollars by 1994.

Pamir and Oropo Kathros spent eleven months negotiating these contracts with a little input from George. Pamir and Oropo have extensive contacts in the government and were both very good at "greasing the squeaky Turkish government wheels" with saying the right things and offering some future benefits if the contract specifics were approved. Those benefits would include free vacations on the yachts for certain Turkish officials, their families, and friends. It was common in Turkey to offer such things as a way of doing business. The contract could save the company as much as 15 million in construction and tax savings. Pamir and Oropo received much of the family and community accolades for this deal even though George's input was really the key to getting the deal approved, George bided his time.

The tourism industry includes major segments such as recreational sports, conventions, historical tours, pleasure tours, vacationers, charters, health clubs, and resorts. Because the industry is so complex and the market so large, there are excellent opportunities in many niche markets. With tourism pumping an estimated $200 billion into the global economy annually, luxury yacht charters account for an estimated $500 million in annual revenues worldwide.

Niche Market Segment—Luxury Yacht Charters

The luxury yacht charter business includes four main categories: motorboats, sailboats, mega-yachts, and bareboats. Luxury yacht charters target a very special type of clientele with upper level income and high social status. The clients are usually well educated, demand excellent service, and are willing and able to pay premium prices for their charters but respect the tenets of fiscal conservatism.

With this in mind, bareboat chartering may exert competitive pressure due to its ability to provide similar experiences at significantly lower prices. A bareboat is usually shorter in length than most motorboats, sailboats, and mega-yachts with fewer crewmembers. Mega-yachts go to the other extreme by charging high prices with impeccable service. Motorboats and sailboats constitute the majority of the luxury yacht fleet. Motorboats may range from 30 to 130 feet in length and only cruise by engine power, while sailboats range from 35 to 125 feet in length and have a choice between engine cruising and sailing. Charters of this nature provide the privacy and serenity that the client expects. The experience is not directly comparable to other popular ocean-going tourism such as cruise ships, which broad hundreds of passengers.

KYT's Marketing Tactics

The operations of the marketing department are broker oriented. KYT has developed a broker network through contacts made at various charter and tourism expositions around the world. One such exposition is the Marmaris Boat Show, the showcase of mega-yachting, which has been the main element in developing KYT's success in the broker network business. The Marmaris Boat Show is an annual event that takes place in the city of Marmaris on the southeastern coast of Turkey. Generally, boat shows are the most economical way to develop broker contacts. Another element adding to the success of KYT's broker network is membership in the Charter Yacht Broker's Association (CYBA). This organization, formed by agents and brokers in the United States, usually sets the standards for the industry and dictates norms for services provided [3]

Broker network of KYT is quite extensive and can be found in countries such as France, England, Spain, Italy, Luxembourg, Switzerland, Denmark, and Germany. KYT's success has been mainly attributed to this highly sophisticated broker network which is responsible for the marketing of the luxury yacht cruises. The combined number of brokers in all countries is 82, and these brokers extensively promote KYT's charter yacht business. However, some of these brokers also negotiate with their respective countries to promote KYT's shipbuilding business. What makes KYT's broker network sophisticated are the computer, fax, and other telecommunications equipment that connects these brokers to KYT itself. Many European countries were lagging in the type of scheduling, pricing, and accounting software that KYT has. It made negotiations and pricing much easier for these countries especially with the different exchange rates for each country. The majority of KYT's clients are affluent and come from the aforementioned countries. For example, Princess Stephanie of Monaco and members of the royal family of Denmark have been clients of KYT. KYT's client referral system offers any client who introduces a new client to KYT one free cruise in the next season. Consequently, KYT has been successful in establishing repeat clients who provide feedback concerning their satisfaction with the cruise and the overall service they receive during the cruise. George Kathros has made it a habit at the end of each cruise to conduct a short interview with the clients to receive first-hand impressions.

A captain supervises the operation of each yacht. In addition to the captain, an engineer is responsible for maintaining all of the equipment and accessories, while a cook and hostess prepare three full-course meals each day. Two deck helpers generally perform all the other services required to meet the needs of the guests. All three vessels (with small variations) are designed to meet the following specifications:

- Range: 2500–3000 miles (under power)
- Fuel capacity: 9000 liters (approximately 2000 gallons)
- Water capacity: 20,000 liters (approximately 4500 gallons)
- Speed: 10+ knots cruising
- Power: Caterpillar 540 hp 3406 TC-AC
- Auxiliary: 2 × 20 KW (I IOV-220V-240V)
- Berths: *Suheyla*—12(16) in 6 cabins; *Zeynep* and *Esra*—8(12) in 4 cabins

- <u>Electronics</u>: depth gauge, compass, speed, wind, radar, echo-sounder, Loran and Chart-plotter, Sat-Nav, GPS, Cetrek 757, Autopilot, VHF, telephone, intercom, Fax machine.

Financial Information and Other Considerations

KYT is headquartered in Istanbul, Turkey. The Turkish lira is the currency of exchange. At the close of 1991, the United States dollar was equal to approximately 4,172 lira. The 1991 consolidated balance sheet and consolidated income statement figures are shown in United States dollars and provide information about the company's financial performance (Exhibits 1 and 2). Pricing is an area of concern for the company. Even though most clients earn above a certain income level, the long-lasting recession of the 1970s has led to decrease in revenues and profits slightly.

Exhibit 1

Consolidated Balance Sheet for 1991

Assets	USD
Cash	32,449
Account receivables	175,608
Inventory	1,374
Total current assets	209,431
Tied assets and investments	1,130,910
Fixed assets	670,039
Others	14,570
Total fixed assets	1,815,519
Total assets	2,024,950
Liabilities	
Account payable	105,263
Notes payable	20,427
Short-term debt	75,261
Total current liabilities	200,951
Long-term debt	126,645
Total liabilities	327,596
Equity	
Common equity	836,084
Retained earning	861,270
Total liabilities and equity	2,024,950

Exhibit 2

Income Statement as of December 31, 1991

	USD	%Sales
Revenues	1,104,844	100
Cost of service	146,625	13.3
General administrative and selling expenses	185,011	16.7
Other expenses	113,140	10.2
International expenses	12,650	1.1
Net Income	647,418	58.7

KYT Contemplates Entering Foreign Markets

With the rapid success of KYT's luxury yacht charter segment, KYT is now considering entry into a foreign market. The company is interested in operating three yachts and a shore support team in the Caribbean market. This plan will mirror KYT's Turkish operation and should generate similar revenues to support the expansion. The investment requirement will be substantial and financed from future retained earnings of KYT's operations.

Location

Due to KYT's success in the Mediterranean Sea, the company has decided to restrict its future locations to markets that offer similar characteristics such as a tropical area with a warm climate and serenity. Considering these characteristics and proximity to affluent economies, the Caribbean area appears to be the least risky new market according to George's research. (He made sure that he communicated to his father and brother that the Caribbean market was the way to go with a base of operations in Florida.) In an attempt to capture a major share of the luxury yacht charter business in the United States, KYT is considering three different Florida cities: Miami, Ft Lauderdale, and Daytona Beach. The company is investigating which of the three locations might be the most appropriate for its prospective Caribbean operations. Prior to making a decision, KYT analyzed the following information on the three alternatives.

Population

The population study was done by examining major American cities with populations over 200,000 and included both population in 1991 and the change in population from the last census. The study included tourists and conventioneers (US Department of Commerce, Bureau of the Census, 1990).

Comparison of Florida Cities under Consideration, 1991

City	Current population	Change since 1980 (%)	Unemployment rate (%)	Tourism	Income level	Number of competitors
Ft Lauderdale	1,653,058	+63	6.0	Strong and growing, younger people, average income	Average	4
Miami	2,007,350	+49	8.0	Strong but declining	Average to slightly above	2
Daytona Beach	310,600	+20	7.3	Somewhat strong but increasing rapidly	Average to above	0

Note: All three cities are non-union in yacht catering industries.

The Ft Lauderdale metropolitan area has a present population of around 2,000,000. This number represents an increase of about 100 percent over the 1980 population of 1,014,043. The tourism industry in Ft Lauderdale is incredibly strong. Although tourists come from all areas of the United States, below expectations, KYT's rates are based upon Western Mediterranean Terms (WMT), which are exclusive of all expenses except fuel, port dues, and crew. The rate for the Mediterranean operations is $16,000 per week, per couple. This rate also includes the 15 percent commission paid to brokers. KYT's rates have been consistently lower than its competitors as a result of the company's intent to operate at full capacity and its commitment to reduce costs. According to Pamir Kathros, "since entering the market, KYT has averaged ten to twelve weeks of occupancy per quarter year, which is well above its competitors' rate seven to eight weeks."

External factors contribute to the company's success. These factors include customer perception and satisfaction, new Yacht construction technology, changes in the exchange rates, and KYT's dependence on government subsidies (contracts). Furthermore, when comparing KYT to other competitors, such as Virgin Island Power Yachts and Nator Swan, several key success factors stand out. Based on an interview with George Kathros, the most important factor is KYT's customer service and satisfaction; the second factor is its advertising strategy. The third factor is KYT's established network of travel agencies and tourist brokers in Turkey and throughout the European continent. KYT heavily promotes its yacht cruises in many top travel magazines whose readership consists mostly of people with high income levels in countries such as England, France, Spain, Germany, Luxembourg, Switzerland, Austria, and Denmark.

KYT's internal working environment also plays a major part in its marketing strategy. Its internal environment displays the typical factors found in most successful customer service organizations. Quality of service is the most critical factor. KYT makes the effort to survey its customers' satisfaction after every trip. Then, KYT analyzes the date and implements changes. From a 1991 internal employee satisfaction survey that George initiated, it was discovered that the company's employee morale is very high because they enjoy what they do, are paid well, and have a say in what job responsibilities they each have. They are also asked by management what they think is needed to improve customer service. The organizational culture is such that there is a widely shared philosophy between management and employees, a view that people are a critical resource, and clear expectations about the direction of KYT. KYT management subscribes to Theory Y where workers are viewed as naturally motivated to work and play and where workers will exercise self-direction and self-control in the service of objectives to which they are committed.

KYT's Fleet

KYT's yachts are designed to offer elegance and high performance. The fleet offers accommodations of classic comfort, visions of pleasure and serenity, and exquisite craftsmanship throughout each boat. With six staterooms on the *Suhcyla* and four staterooms on both the *Zeynep* and the *Esra*, guests can enjoy the luxury of air-conditioned triple cabins with individual showers and toilets. Each suite also provides a number of luxury accessories such as stereo, TV, CD player, microwave, fax, telephone, refrigerator, freezer, ice machine, washer/dryer, dish washer, grill, and garbage disposal unit. In addition to the saloon, bar, and galley, the yachts are fully equipped with sports and leisure equipment including an Avon Searider, Windsurfer, Wetbike, water skis, diving equipment, fishing gear, and clay pigeon shooting. There are also several choices for relaxing. From the main mast deck settees, to the two rosewood floored upper decks, to the aft platform that contains an underwater lighting system for midnight swimming, guests can enjoy the Mediterranean weather in style and comfort.

Significant and increasing numbers of tourists come from Canada and Mexico. These tourists are primarily young people with average incomes. The population increase of 63 percent since the 1980 census has 6 percent of this population with incomes over $100,000.

Miami is a metropolitan area that has a population of about 2,007,350. Miami's population has grown more than 49 percent since 1980. Income levels of Miami's residents and tourists are average to slightly above average. The tourism industry is strong but declining. The population increase of

49 percent is comprised of 2 percent of this population with incomes over $100,000.

Daytona Beach has a population of approximately 500,000 in its metropolitan area. The city's population has increased from 258,300 in 1980 for a 100 percent rate change. Income levels of tourists and residents of Daytona Beach vary from average to above average. Tourism is somewhat strong but rapidly increasing.

Employment

The unemployment rate is examined in the three aforementioned cities.[5] In comparing these to the national average of about 6.9 percent, we find Ft Lauderdale to be the only location with a lower-than-average unemployment rate. Union possibilities are also examined in each city. None of these cities is considered a union stronghold. In fact, there does not appear to be a union for the yacht catering industries in the United States (Mayer, 1992).

Support and Personnel

The Caribbean business is to be managed by a separate division of KYT headed by one of the owner's sons as a division manager. As with the CEO and executive VP at KYT's headquarters, the Caribbean division manager will have a similar structure reporting to him. The manager will have an accountant, a marketing director, and the crews of the three yachts and shore support service reporting directly to him.

Market and Competition

Of the three cities considered, Ft Lauderdale has four of KYT's competitors operating in the area. Two competitors operate in Miami, while none exist in Dayton Beach. Despite the concentration of the competition in Ft Lauderdale, the city has all the necessary vendors and supporting companies needed to service a luxury yacht fleet. Also, Ft Lauderdale has the lowest unemployment rate which may have a negative impact on labor costs.

The following competitive pressures exist in KYT's external environment:

- Direct competition: motorboats, sailboats, mega-yachts, bareboats
- Indirect competition: cruise lines, rental properties, Club-Med, and so on.

Dealing with indirect competitors will be the least important factor due to the difference in the targeted clientele bases. Although bareboat chartering is considered an indirect form of competition, it is a low budget customer favorite due to its extremely low pricing structure.

Mega-yachts appeal to a different clientele as well. As a result of their premium price structure, mega-yachts compete in a different market niche. Thus, KYT's focus point will be on motorboats and sailboats.

Motorboats are vessels between 40 and 130 feet in length that cruise by engine power only. They include an extensive, full-service crew. They also have the advantage of speed cruising and more spacious accommodations. The sailboats that KYT will be competing against are mainly vessels between 35 and 125 feet in length and are often called motor sailors offering a choice between sailing and engine cruising. This is the category which KYT fits into, and where most of KYT's competitors are operating.

All four of the competitors in Ft Lauderdale are United States-owned family businesses, but do not provide as luxurious accommodations and amenities as KYT does. Competitors's pricing levels vary on a one-week cruise from $8000 to $14,000 per person. None of these businesses advertise at tradeshows, but they all advertise in the Yellow pages: the local travel section of the newspaper and some travel magazines such as *AAA Digest*. The Miami competitors are much closer to providing identical accommodations and amenities as KYT does with price packages for a one-week cruise at $14,000–$16,000 per person. The Miami competition is also family owned and promotes in similar media vehicles as the Ft Lauderdale competitors. However, KYT has discovered that one of the Miami competitors advertises in magazines of three major airlines that serve the Miami market: US Air, Delta, and American Airlines. None of the competitors have operations in any other countries and only have the one United States location in their respective Florida cities. Recent developments in Miami city government has made it rather difficult for foreign owners to start businesses in the city, especially service industries.

Daytona Beach's population increase of 20 percent since 1980 is comprised of only 1 percent of people who have incomes of over $100,000. The city is anxious to attract new businesses from any country. Dayton wants people to have the perception that the city is not inferior to its southern Floridaneighbors. According to reports from the Chamber of Commerce, the people want the world to know that Daytona Beach is just as sophisticated as Miami and Ft Lauderdale are with outstanding cultural amenities such as fine dining, shopping, museums, and performing arts venues. However, the shipping docks and slips have few service providers necessary to support KYT's business at the present time.

George was very anxious for a decision to be made. He had done his own investigation of gay life in each of the cities. The South Beach area of Miami was about to begin a complete makeover of economic development through the revitalization and renovation of many historic buildings and hotels.

The Chamber of Commerce was also anxious to bring major tourism back to South Beach through shops, restaurants, and a beach re-nourishment. George had found out that many gay people were living on the fringes of South Beach and were buying up property that had been undervalued and inexpensively priced due to the American economy's recession of the late 1980s and early 1990s.

Fort Lauderdale, known primarily as a major American college Spring Break destination, had begun to be disenchanted with the dependence on college students for most of their yearly revenues. From George's conversations with the Chamber of Commerce, the local merchants were seeking new customers who actually spent money and did not destroy property when they stayed in Ft Lauderdale. In the late 1980's Ft Lauderdale had begun to market itself to gay market segments touting the weather, beach, and lower property costs compared to Miami. Market research had already shown gay couples to have higher incomes than students—stayed longer in hotel rooms, spent more on clothing, food, drinks, and entertainment than college students—and were very quiet and respectful. Wilton Manors, a section of Ft Lauderdale, was becoming a gay housing community. Older aged permanent residents, retirees, and snowbirds, those who flock to warmer climates for two to six months of the year to escape the cold weather of the Northeast and Midwest, appreciated the culture and business gays brought to the area in terms of restaurants and shops. Gated communities were also springing up as older worn houses were being demolished to make way for the new money of those seeking warmer climates. There were three gay dance clubs and six gay bar that George already knew about.

George had also discovered that Daytona Beach properties were also inexpensive and that the local government was committed to making Daytona more than just a racetrack and Spring Break destination. Developers had already bought land along many of Daytona's waterways to develop shopping and entertainment centers. In addition, housing was inexpensive compared to South Beach and new gated housing communities were blossoming throughout the area to escape the crowded southeastern Florida coastline of high-rises and condominiums. There were also already two gay clubs and four gay bars in Daytona.

All George had to do was compare the cities in terms of whether each could support his family business. Personally, he felt he could not lose with any choice of the three Florida cities.

Appendix A
History of Turkey in Brief

Geography

Turkey is situated at the junction of Europe and Asia. The country covers an area of 300,000 square miles, approximately twice the size of the State of California. The European and Asian sides are divided by the Bosphorus, the Sea of Marmara, and the Dardanelles. There are numerous lakes and some, such as Lake Van, as large as inland seas. In the north the eastern Black Sea Mountain chain runs parallel to the Black Sea, and in the south the Taurus Mountains sweep down almost to the narrow, fertile coastal plain along the sea cost. The coastline of Turkey's four seas is approximately 2220 square miles.

History

Turkey has been called "the cradle of civilization," and by traveling through this historic land the tourist will discover exactly what is meant by this phrase. The world's first town, a Neolithic city at Catalhoyunk, dates back to 6500 B.C. From the days of its origin up to the present time, Turkey boasts of a rich culture that through the centuries has made a lasting impression on modern civilization. The heir of many centuries of cultures makes Turkey a paradise of information and cultural wealth. Hittites, Phrygians, Urartians, Lycians, Ionians, Persians, Macedonians, Romans, Byzantines, Seljuks, and Ottornans have all held important places in Turkey's history, and ancient sites and ruins scattered throughout the country give proof to each civilization's unique distinction.

Turkey also has a very fascinating recent history. Upon the decline of the Ottoman Empire, a young man named Mustafa Kemal, who was a soldier

609

by occupation but a great visionary in character, turned the defeat in World War I into a shining victory by liberating Turkey of all foreign invaders. Mustafa Kemal Ataturk founded the Republic of turkey on October 29, 1923. He led his country into peace and stability with tremendous economic growth and complete modernization. Through decades of change and growth, Turkey still boasts of this success by effectively living by its adopted motto of "Peace at Home, Peace in the World."

Population

According to 2000 census, Turkey has 58 million inhabitants, 41 percent of whom live in the countryside. The major cities are Istanbul (7.4 million), Ankara the capital (3.2 million), Izmir (2.7 million), Adana (1.9 million), Antalya (1.1 million), and Bursa (1.6 million).

Language

The Turkish language belongs to the Ural–Altaic group and has an affinity to the Finno-Hungarian languages. Turkish is written in the Latin alphabet and is spoken by some 150 million people around the world.

Religion

The Turkish population is 99 percent Moslem. Turkey is a secular state and guarantees complete freedom of worship to non-Moslems.

Tourism

In recent years Turkey has become a major tourist destination in Europe. With the rapid development of both summer and winter resorts, more and more people from all over the world are able to enjoy the history, culture, and beautiful sites of Turkey.

Agriculture

Agriculture plays a very important role in the Turkish economy. The main crops are wheat, rice, cotton, tea, tobacco, hazelnuts, and fruits. Sheep are Turkey's most important livestock, and Turkey is one of Europe's most important wool and cotton producers.

Natural Resources

The principal minerals extracted are coal, chrome (an important export), iron, copper, bauxite, marble, and sulfur.

Industry

Industry is developing rapidly and is directed mainly toward the processing of agricultural products, metallurgy, textiles, and the manufacturing of automobiles and agricultural machinery.

Political structure

The Turkish Republic is based on secular democratic, pluralistic, and parliamentary system. The National Assembly is elected by popular vote, and the nation is governed by the Council of Ministers headed by the Prime Minister. Turkey has aligned itself with the West and is a member of numerous international organizations, including the North American Treaty Organization, the Council of Europe, the World Bank, the International Monetary Fund, and the Asian Development Bank. Turkey is also an associate member of the European Union, and a founding member of the European Bank of Reconstruction and Development.

Appendix B
Economic and Financial Developments in Turkey Prior to 1980

From the early 1960s until 1974, the Turkish economy grew in real terms between six and seven percent per year. Those years were characterized by relative price stability, manageable budget deficits, modest levels of external debt, and a sound balance of payment position. Economic growth was achieved mainly through high levels of investment and consumption by the public sector. (Giannaris, 1988)

However, starting in the early 1970s the effects of sharp oil price increases as well as inflation, recession, and rising unemployment in the industrial countries adversely affected the Turkish economy. There was a sharp deterioration of the terms of trade and the balance of payments. Domestic factors complicated and compounded the difficulties associated with adverse external developments. Between 1974 and 1977 imports rose faster than GNP, mainly due to rising import prices, while exports stagnated due, in part, to world recession as well as an overvalued exchange rate of the domestic currency and inefficient pricing of agricultural exports.

According to Giannaris,[7] beginning in 1975, remittances of foreign exchange from Turkish workers abroad began to fall reflecting the increasing parallel market exchange rate differentials. The balance of payments deficit was financed almost exclusively through a reduction of reserves and in increase in various short-term obligations. The growing public-sector deficit was financed largely through borrowing from the Central Bank and, consequently, the money supply increased rapidly and inflation accelerated.

By the end of 1977, the principal economic problems facing Turkey included a severe shortage of foreign exchange, a large balance of payment deficit, a heavy burden of short-term external debt, a high rate of inflation, a large public-sector deficit, a slowing of growth, and increasing unemployment.

Appendix C
Economic Program of 1980 and Subsequent Developments

Efforts to stabilize the economy prior to 1980 proved to be inadequate in the face of the severity of problems. Measures taken to decrease the current account deficit during 1978–1979 had negative impacts on domestic production and employment.

In January 1980, a new set of economic reform measures were introduced with more reliance on market forces rather than direct government intervention. These measures included a flexible exchange rate policy; elimination of price controls, especially in state economic enterprises; a restrictive monetary policy; liberalization of foreign trade and payments regulations; an interest rate policy designed to encourage domestic savings; the introduction of a new foreign investment policy; institutional change designed to increase the effectiveness of the economic policy; and an introduction of investment opportunities for the tourist industry. On May 1, 1981, a daily adjustment of the foreign exchange value of the Turkish lira was introduced (UTFT, 1989).

Until the end of 1982, the Turkish economy showed an impressive response to the new economic measures. GNP grew in excess of 4 percent in both 1981 and 1982, and the annual increase in the wholesale price index fell from 107.2 percent in 1980 to 36.7 percent and 25.2 percent in 1981 and 1982 respectively. During the 1980s, Turkey staged a remarkable recovery from a severe economic crisis and succeeded in turning around a virtually unsustainable balance of payments situation. On the basis of a comprehensive adjustment program to stabilize and liberalize the economy, a sustainable pace of growth was attained, and considerable progress toward internal and external balance was achieved.

Incidentally, this comprehensive structural adjustment program, which enabled Turkey to achieve remarkable results in a relatively short span of time, was based on the principles of free market economy. Briefly, reliance on market forces, encouragement of the private sector, emphasis on export growth, import liberalization, encouragement of the tourist sector, and achievement of better internal and external balances were the main features of this process.[8]

A significant improvement was observed in tourism revenues, which went up by 59.6 percent as the number of tourist arrivals exceeded 4.1 million. Other invisible revenues also increased by 14 percent mainly because of the rise in revenues from contractors and freight services. On the expenditures side, interest payments and other expenses increased by 10 percent and 14 percent respectively, while the tourism expenditures declined by 20 percent.

Appendix D
Organizational Chart of KYT

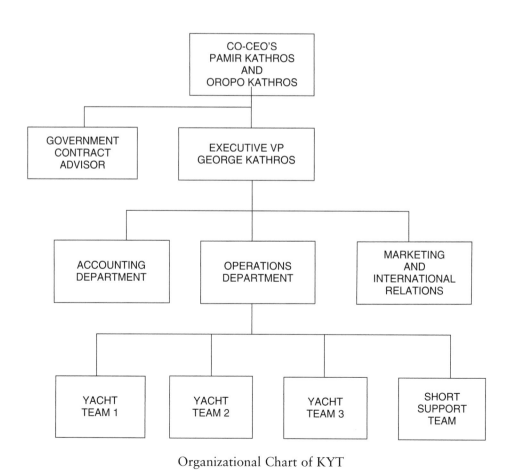

Organizational Chart of KYT

Endnotes

1. This case was prepared by Gary H. Kritz, Seton Hall University; Marios Katsioloudes, The American University of Sharjah UAE; and Samuel Wathen, Coastal Carolina University. It is intended to be used for class discussion rather than to illustrate either effective or ineffective handling of the situation. Presented to and accepted by the North American Case Research Association, (NACRA), for its annual meeting, November 2003, Tampa, Florida. All rights reserved to the authors and NACRA. © 2003 by Gary H. Kritz, Marios Katsioloudes, and Samuel Wathen.
2. P. Kathros, personal communication, August 30, 1992.
3. P. Kathros, personal communication, April 12, 1991.
4. Under secretariat of Treasury and Foreign Trade, UTFT, 1992.
5. US Department of Commerce, Bureau of the Census, 1990.
6. Mayer, 1992.
7. Giannaris, 1988.
8. UTFT, 1989.

Chicago Food and Beverage Company

IHRM and Expatriation Management: The Challenges of Managing International Assignments

Virginia Bodolica* and Marie-France Waxin†

* Université du Québec en Outaouais, Canada
† The American University of Sharjah, UAE

Case Description

The primary subject matter of this case concerns the management of expatriate managers with a particular focus on their recruitment and compensation. Secondary issues examined include the internationalization strategies of a multinational company and particularly the alignment of international strategy and headquarters' orientation regarding the international human resource management (IHRM) policy. The case has the difficulty level of six (appropriate for second-year graduate level). The case is designed to be taught in three class hours and is expected to require five hours of outside preparation by students.

Case Synopsis

The Chicago Food and Beverage Company (CFB Co.) is an American multinational with subsidiaries in North America, Europe, and Asia. The case is about the alignment of CFB Co. internationalization strategy and the orientation of the head office in regard to its IHRM policy and management of international assignments, with an emphasis on expatriates' recruitment and compensation. The case describes the international development of the company and the subsequent expatriation of Paul Fierman, the head of the Vietnam subsidiary. Paul's three-year mandate includes the preparation and execution of the strategy to synergize the three Asian subsidiaries (Singapore, Hong Kong, and Vietnam) with the collaboration of the head of the Pacific Rim, which should allow CFB Co. to conquer the Asian market. Six months after his arrival, Paul Fierman is disappointed by the financial conditions of his contract and by his relationships with local colleagues, not to mention the difficulties his wife has been having adapting to this new environment. The discussion of this case in class allows introducing and illustrating the theoretical concepts related to the following topics: (1) internationalization strategies and IHRM policies; (2) strategic management of international postings; and (3) advantages and disadvantages of different international compensation methods.

Evolution of Chicago Food and Beverage Company from 1960 to 1998

The CFB Co. is an American multinational which was established in Chicago in 1963. The company is specialized in the production of all kinds of fruit jams, canned fish, meat, vegetables, and non-alcoholic beverages. CFB Co. is primarily an American company and until 1985 it concentrated exclusively on the US market. Due to its reputation as a high-technology intensive company and its capacity to adjust to the changing market demands, CFB Co. grew rapidly. It expanded all over the US through its five national subsidiaries based in Chicago, New York, Atlanta, Los Angeles, and Portland. In 1985, CFB Co. became the fifth largest American producer in the food and beverage sector. In 2003 its revenues amounted to several billion US dollars (US$).

Since the long US recession of the 1980s, CFB Co.'s management wanted to expand abroad so that the company would not be so dependent on the already saturated domestic market. However, Mr. Brandon Long, CEO of the company since it was established, stubbornly opposed the idea. In late 1984, Mr. Long retired and was replaced by Mr. Bill Stevens who always dreamed of CFB Co. becoming a global power. With top management's approval, CFB Co.'s foreign expansion plans finally began and at the beginning of 1985 the company went international. The foreign expansion plans included two growth strategies: the company would either purchase small foreign enterprises operating in the same sector or establish joint ventures with foreign food and non-alcoholic beverage producers. CFB Co. expanded to Europe first, and, between 1985 and 1990, the company acquired three local enterprises in Belgium, France, and Germany.

Following that, from 1991 to 1998, CFB Co. turned towards the Asian market, installing three joint ventures in that region. According to CFB Co.'s managers, there was a huge potential for food processing and distribution in the Asian market because first, it accounted for over 60 percent of total world population, and secondly, Asian consumers' expenditures were increasing three times more rapidly than those of North Americans. Therefore, the company's expansion to this region was thought to be of crucial importance for its economic health. Thus, the first joint venture specializing in Asian fruit-based jam production was established in 1991 in Singapore and the second joint venture which was created in 1995 in Hong Kong produced canned fish, meat and vegetables; the third joint venture, started in 1998 with a Vietnamese subsidiary based in Haiphong, specialized in the production of all kinds of non-alcoholic drinks, fruit juices, and sodas. Although some of their clients are based in the neighbouring countries, each joint venture produces its own products which are basically distributed on the local market. There is no cooperation between subsidiaries since they are considered as completely independent entities from each other.

Creation of CFB Vietnam Joint-venture in 1998

The CFB Vietnam, created one year after the beginning of the Asian economic crisis, is a joint venture between CFB Co. (which owns 49% of capital) and a local state-owned enterprise (which owns 51% of capital). It was CFB Co's largest investment in Vietnam. The joint venture formula was chosen due to the mutual advantages it offered to the parties involved. On the one side, CFB Co. was gaining rapid access to the Vietnamese market, benefiting from the lands, buildings, and other infrastructure of the local enterprise and from the cheap national labour costs. On the other hand, the Vietnamese counterpart was benefiting from the accrued capital, high technology transfers, and American know-how. Therefore, the joint venture was rapidly granted with the licence to produce and distribute non-alcoholic drinks in the Vietnamese market. During its first year of functioning, the multinational invested more than US$ 2 million in bottling equipment. In three years, the subsidiary became the second biggest non-alcoholic beverage producer in Vietnam. It had only one competitor in the market: Vietnam Drinks Company, which was the national producer of all kinds of drinks and had its headquarters in Ho Chi Minh City.

The subsidiary is located in Haiphong, the third largest city in Vietnam after Ho Chi Minh and capital city of Hanoï. Haiphong is one of the three cities of the Northern economic triangle (Hanoï–Haiphong–Quangninh) and is very popular among foreign investors. CFB Co. management had chosen Haiphong for its economic dynamism and its accessibility to the sea, rail, and air transport. Haiphong represents a main gateway by the sea to the Northern provinces of Vietnam, facilitating fluvial commercial exchanges not only with the whole country but also with neighbouring countries. The subsidiary's activities, its production, bottling factory, and administrative buildings are all concentrated in one site situated at the Northern periphery of Haiphong. CFB Vietnam's primary mission was to produce exclusively for the national market, with an objective to export its products to neighbouring Asian countries over the next three years.

CFB Co. Restructuring in 2000

At the end of 1999, CFB Co. started to lose money in all of its foreign operations. National and international competition grew in all markets and consumers became quality-oriented. Even though the company's main operations in the US were still profitable, the figures were declining significantly as compared to the 1998 levels. The modest profits from the US plants were not enough to offset the losses reported abroad. In 2000, US headquarters analysed the situation and decided to undertake a radical strategic change. In order to reduce costs and achieve greater profits, the company's management decided to regroup its food and beverage production activities into three regional zones: United States, having its center in Chicago; Europe, with its regional center in Brussels; and Asia, with its center in Singapore. In other words, the subsidiaries which previously enjoyed exclusive rights in their respective local markets had to be integrated into "three regional networks: United States, Europe, and Asia". This strategy was expected to allow CFB multinational to find synergies within these three regional zones and thus to assure a significant increase in revenues per region. For instance, CFB Co.'s management wants the Vietnamese subsidiary to export its non-alcoholic drinks to the whole Asian zone, helped by the distribution systems of other regional subsidiaries from Hong Kong and Singapore. It is therefore necessary to create and implement common distribution and communication strategies. The main objectives are to reduce costs, to increase revenues, and to promote CFB Co.'s activities in the whole Asian region.

Changes in Expatriates' Compensation Policy in 2002

Back in 1985, when CFB Co. started its international expansion, the company did not have any experience in the field of expatriation management. Since the initial stage of foreign growth strategy, only a small number of expatriates were used. Therefore, the Chicago management team opted for a flexible expatriate compensation approach: the negotiation method. According to this method, each expatriate is handled case by case; the components included in the compensation package represent the final outcome of negotiations between the expatriate and the company. Moreover, this compensation formula is beneficial due to its administrative simplicity, requiring little information on costs of living and tax issues in host countries. Over the years, however, the multinational company penetrated several European and Asian markets and, therefore, the number of its expatriates increased considerably. Hence, starting in 1998, CFB Co. employed constantly about 25 American expatriates. With increasing expatriation development, the negotiation method became less effective, more time consuming, and rather expensive. In order to keep its costs under control, CFB Co.'s senior management decided that a significant change in its current expatriate compensation philosophy would be needed.

In 2002, Chicago human resources department (HR), which manages the company's expatriates, adopted a new and mixed compensation approach. In light of this approach, different compensation systems are proposed to senior and junior expatriates. Seniors, expatriates having more than six years of international experience, are compensated according to the international method. In this case, a specific international scale is applied to all senior expatriates. During their expatriation period, senior expatriates are compensated using the international compensation scale and once they are back in their home countries, they reintegrate the standard national compensation scale. Expatriate juniors, having less than 6 years of international experience, are compensated in line with the home country method, which uses the balance sheet approach. According to this method, the parent company allows its expatriate to make the same expenditures in terms of accommodation, goods, and services in the host country as those that would have been incurred in the home country had the employee remained at home. Moreover, the company commits to maintain the purchasing power of its expatriates in the host country, making some adjustments to the home compensation package in order to balance additional expenditures in the host country due to a higher cost of living index. The key purpose of this approach is to ensure that expatriate employees are no better or worse off as a result of an international assignment.

The summary of important events in the evolution of CFB Co. is presented in Exhibit 1.

Paul Fierman's Employment with CFB Co. and His Expatriation to Vietnam in 2004

Paul Fierman, a 34-year-old American, was appointed General Director of CFB Vietnam at the end of March 2004, with a mission to lead the subsidiary and to implement the new organizational strategy.

Exhibit 1

Summary of Important Events in the Evolution of CFB Co.

Year	Important event
1963	Creation of Chicago Food and Beverage Co., Chicago, United States
1963–1985	Expansion in United States, five American subsidiaries based in Chicago, New York, Atlanta, Los Angeles and Portland
1985	Beginning of the international adventure
1985–1990	Acquisition of 3 European local companies: Belgium, France, Germany
1991–1998	Conquest of the Asian market
1991	Joint venture Singapore
1995	Joint venture Hong Kong
1998	Joint venture Vietnam
1999	CFB Co.'s economic slowdown
2000	CFB Co.'s strategic change and restructuring; creation of three regional networks: United States, Europe, Asia
2002	Introduction of the new expatriates' compensation policy: the mixed compensation method
2004	Recruitment and expatriation of Paul Fierman to Haiphong (Vietnam)

Obtaining this expatriate position was not a difficult endeavour for Paul. In 1995, he earned his bachelor's degree in marketing from Johnson Business School, at Cornell University in New York. After graduation, Paul took a position as product vice-manager in the marketing department at the New York subsidiary of CFB Co. Three years later, he became carbonated non-alcoholic beverages' manager for the Eastern American region. After two years in this position, Paul was put in charge of both carbonated and non-carbonated non-alcoholic drinks in the US market. As a country manager, he was paid US$ 300,000 annual base salary and 10–15% commission on sales. Although Paul was satisfied with his job, he wanted to reorient his career towards general management positions in this company. Therefore, in 2002 he decided to undertake a full-time Master in Business Administration studies in international management at Harvard Business School in Boston. After completing his MBA, Paul wanted to come back to CFB Co., but in order be able to reach the pinnacle of his career, he thought he needed to acquire some international professional experience. The only international

Exhibit 2

Paul Fierman's Professional Evolution

Year	Professional evolution
1995	Bachelor's Degree in Marketing, Johnson Business School, Cornell University, New York
	Recruitment by CFB Co., New York subsidiary, product vice-manager
1998	Regional product manager: Eastern US markets, carbonated non-alcoholic drinks
2000	Country brand manager: US markets, carbonated and non-carbonated non-alcoholic beverages
2002–2004	Master of business administration in international management, Harvard Business School, Boston
2004	Expatriation to Haiphong, Vietnam

experience he had so far was a year spent in Oxford, Great Britain, as an exchange program student.

Paul Fierman's employment for CFB Co. can be summarized as follows (Exhibit 2):

During his MBA studies, Paul kept in touch with his former supervisor at his first position within CFB Co., Allan Roger, marketing director of the New York subsidiary. Just before graduating from his MBA, Paul called Allan to discuss about his potential return to the company. Allan, very enthusiastic about this perspective, told him:

> Mike Shannon, the expatriate Managing Director of CFB Vietnam, has just returned to the U.S. unexpectedly due to health problems. Since Mike's departure was not planned, the headquarters are desperate to replace him as soon as possible. If you are interested, you can send me your application for the position of Managing Director in Haiphong, and I will forward it to the General Manager in Chicago. In my opinion, Paul, you have a high professional potential in this company. Your lack of international experience is a problem. . . , but it does not mean that you would not be able to prepare and implement, in collaboration with the regional director of Pacific Asia, the new strategy aiming at integrating the three Asian subsidiaries. This expatriation would be an exceptional training experience for you, preparing you for a higher level managing position within the Chicago headquarters on your return to the U.S., three years later.

With his experience within CFB Co. and his high recommendations, Paul Fierman was a good candidate for this three-year expatriate position. He was perceived as a promising young manager due to his excellent academic background and the outstanding professional results he achieved during his employment within the company.

At that point, things went very fast. In March 2004, thanks to Allan's intervention and contacts, Paul met directly with the General Manager in Chicago. Two weeks later, a notice of approval had been sent to Paul from the Chicago HR department, officially confirming his managing position within CFB Vietnam. Robert Greenberg, managing director in charge of the Pacific Asia region, had been informed about Paul's nomination by Chicago's General Manager himself. One month later, in April 2004, Paul began his new position in Haiphong. Before his departure he spent a couple of weeks preparing his move and organizing the rental of his house in New York. His wife Carrie and their 7-year-old daughter Rachel joined him two months later in Haiphong. These two extra months gave Carrie enough time to have her dismissal accepted by her employer. In the meantime, Paul settled into their new Vietnamese house and enrolled their daughter at Haiphong international school. Before his departure, Paul bought three books on Vietnam in order to get some preliminary knowledge about the general business context of the country. However, his readings on culture and the economic and political history of Vietnam seemed to be too disconnected from today's business reality.

One week before his arrival in Vietnam, Paul had a 3-hour meeting with Robert Greenberg in New York. Robert showed him the outlines of the corporate strategy aiming at creating synergies among the three Asian subsidiaries. Since then, they never spoke to each other directly anymore.

Paul and Carrie's Frustration Six Months after Their Arrival in Haiphong

Six months after his arrival in Vietnam, Paul was feeling extremely frustrated. Sadly, he begins to explain to his wife Carrie:

> I have two big problems. My first one is related to the financial conditions of my expatriation contract. When I applied for this expatriation position in Vietnam, I expected to benefit from an excellent compensation offer, as all the other expatriates I had met before in the CFB Co. internal conferences had enjoyed. Although the final result of negotiations with the HR manager from headquarters varied from one expatriate to another, all of them were generally managing to negotiate at least double their previous salaries and lots of mobility, protection of purchasing power, accommodation, and hardship allowances. I thought that this expatriation to Vietnam would be not only a springboard for my career but also a good financial move. Unfortunately for me, the expected financial gain did not materialize. I am one of the five expatriates out of 25 who have less than six years of international experience. My compensation is therefore calculated according to the balance sheet approach.

Of course, the cost of living in Haiphong is significantly lower than in New York and the company had provided me with a nice house and a good company car. Nevertheless, I feel upset and frustrated. The expatriates from other multinational companies that I met in Hanoi and Ho Chi Min City enjoy better living conditions. In addition, they live in far more attractive cities than Haiphong. As I am the only American expatriate in CFB Vietnam, I feel isolated and frustrated. Since my arrival in Haiphong, I have practically worked alone in order to make the things work. The expatriates from CFB Hong Kong and CFB Singapore subsidiaries are all seniors, they are paid according to a far more advantageous compensation scale, plus they are living in very modern cities where all the usual distractions Americans are accustomed to are available. Furthermore, these two Asian subsidiaries employ several expatriates who are all collaborating closely in order to achieve their objectives together. Between Hong Kong and Singapore, the expatriates are used to pay each other regular friendly visits. My own salary does not allow me to enjoy the week-ends that my counterparts from Hong Kong and Singapore are enjoying.

Carrie was not surprised. She had many times noticed the sad mood of her husband in the past few months... She encouraged him to continue. *What is your other problem?*

My second problem is related to my work. I feel very frustrated by the results of my work in the subsidiary and the relationships I have with my Vietnamese colleagues. The financial situation of the subsidiary six months after my arrival is very bad: declining revenues, decreasing motivation of Vietnamese plant workers and staff, lack of cooperation on behalf of local management, etc. The implementation of the new organizational strategy is far from even getting off the ground! I have to handle all these problems alone. I have the impression that my work does not produce any of the expected results... What about you, Carrie, how do you feel?

Carrie's situation was hardly encouraging. Carrie seemed to be getting more and more depressed and irritated. Before their departure from US, she had been starting her fourth year of employment at the New York Stock Exchange as a financial analyst. Even though she liked her job and had good prospects for advancement in her career, she seemed enthusiastic to accompany her husband to Vietnam for the entire expatriation period. Thus, she could spend more time with their daughter. Carrie collected her thoughts and her courage and replied to Paul:

To me, who have never left the North American continent, Vietnam seemed to be an exotic country... and I thought, before our departure, that your expatriation would be a very new, enriching experience. However, this experience turns out to be hard to get through. Life here in Haiphong is not what I had imagined. Being used to work, I am getting bored staying home all day long. I also miss my family and friends whom we were used to visiting regularly in New York. Besides that, I have to admit that Haiphong's heat and humidity are really unbearable for me...And finally, I am also very worried for Rachel. The fact that she has arrived in the middle of the school year in the local Anglophone school prevents her from making any friends, as her classmates do not speak English outside the classroom. Rachel no longer wants to do her homework and cries every morning before going to school...We definitely cannot go on like this! What will we be doing, Paul? I hardly recognize our family, which is normally so happy.

Proposed Questions for Discussion:

Topic 1: Alignment of International Strategy and Headquarters' Orientation Regarding the IHRM Policy

1. Which internationalization strategies do you recognize in this case study?
2. What is the HRM orientation adopted by the headquarters? What comments can you make concerning this choice? What can you recommend to the company's headquarters in this sense?

Topic 2: Expatriation Management

1. Is Paul Fierman a good candidate for this expatriation position?
2. What comments can you make on the expatriation management in general? And what comments can you make on the expatriate recruitment policy in particular?

Topic 3: Compensation of International Staff

1. What are the different expatriate compensation methods you recognized in the text? What are the advantages and disadvantages of these different expatriate compensation methods?
2. What do you suggest to the US headquarters' human resources manager in order to improve the expatriate satisfaction/compensation?

Appendix 1
Map of Southeast Asia

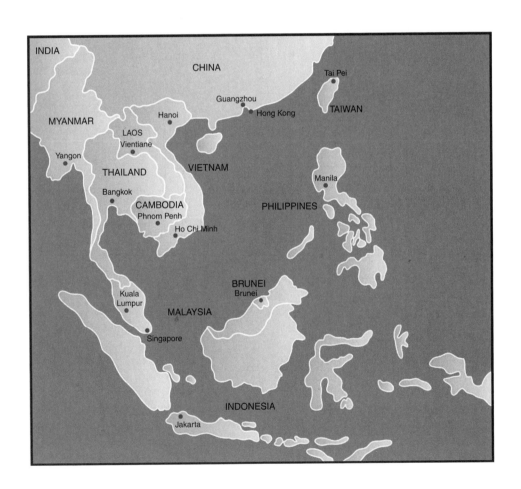

Appendix 2
Chicago Food and Beverage Co.'s Organizational Chart

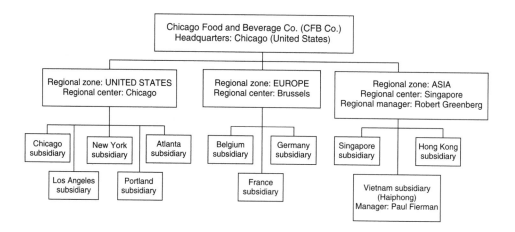

Appendix 3
Compensation Packages

Exhibit A

Annual Compensation Package of a Junior Expatriate Employees: Balance Sheet Approach

Employee: Paul Fierman
Position: General manager of CFB Vietnam
Country: Vietnam
Reason for relocation: New assignment
Effective date of change: 5 April 2004

Item	Total amount (US$)	Paid in US$	Paid in local currency VN dong
Base salary:	320,000	160,000	2,602,240,000
Hardship allowance (20%)	64,000	64,000	
Trip allowance	25,000	25,000	
Housing deduction	−22,000	−22,000	
Car deduction	−5,000	−5,000	
Tax equalization	−43,200	−43,200	
TOTAL	338,800	178,800	2,602,240,000

Cost of leaving allowance index—Haiphong: 84; New York: 100
Exchange rate—US$ 1 = 16,264 VN dong

Exhibit B

Annual Compensation Package of Senior Expatriate Employees: International Method

Employee:
Position: General manager
Country: Hong Kong
Effective date of change:

Item	Total amount (US$)	Paid in US$	Paid in local currency HK$
Base salary	400,000	200,000	1,560,000
Cost of living allowance	25,000		195,000
Overseas service premium (20%)	80,000	80,000	
Trip allowance	35,000	35,000	
Schooling allowance	10,000	10,000	
Tax protection	50,200	50,200	
Housing and car provided			
TOTAL	600,200	375,200	1,755,000

Cost of living allowance index—(Hong Kong): 110; New York: 100
Exchange rate—US$ 1 = HK$ 7.8

Making the Product-to-Service Transition in International Markets

Robert E. Bateman

The American University of Sharjah, UAE

Introduction

This case considers the challenges faced by a small business trying to change its business model to address shifts in the international marketplace. Names and other identifying information have been altered.

In the middle of 2005, George Cleary realized that his career was at a crossroads. His 15-year association with Advanced Software Analytics (ASA) had challenged his international management skills and created lasting friendships both within the company and among loyal customers around the world. But as the company considered changing its approach to international markets, Cleary became increasingly uncertain whether his own career interests were consistent with the strategic direction favored by the new CEO.

George was born in the US, but lived with his family in Japan for three years as a child. Most of his teenage years were spent in Germany. He joined the US Foreign Service shortly after completing an MBA with a concentration in International Business. Six years of service in embassies in three foreign countries had convinced him that working internationally was part of his identity. His action orientation and analytical skills helped him advance quickly—and even earned him an exceptional performance commendation—but that same energy often conflicted with the measured pace of a large bureaucratic organization. He left the government in 1990 and returned to the US, looking for a management role in the private sector that would allow him to use his knowledge of international markets. Friends working in a research center at a local university convinced him to join them in a small consulting company providing process analysis assistance to manufacturing companies.

The focus of the new venture was on a four-state region in the US, but George was soon bringing in small projects from international customers. His partners brought to the business their skill with application software used to analyze business processes. One particularly useful tool was the product of a small local company, ASA. Requiring some training and practice in its use, this software enabled a methodology which gave the consultants a rather unique entrée with clients. When the consultants began making their own modifications to the software, ASA approached the group about promoting the product as a sales agent and value-added-reseller. For three years, George had consulted and sold software, generating revenue in roughly equal measure from both activities.

Founded in 1986, ASA was the brainchild of an engineering professor at a nearby university. With the help of two graduate assistants, he had taken analytical methods previously applied by programmers on mainframe computers and put them in the hands of engineers and analysts working on desktop PCs. Although the niche occupied by ASA was fragmented and competitive, the software's relative ease-of-use attracted several large multinational companies which sought to improve the efficiency of their operations. Some purchased multiple software licenses.

A small and very flexible staff at ASA had handled sales, technical support, training and administrative functions for the first couple of years. By 1989, revenues were coming in through the efforts of independent sales agents, who received 35 percent of license fees as a commission. Due to the technical nature of the product and the need for training, however, the sales cycle was relatively long (6–8 months). Each license sale generated $15,000–$20,000 in revenues to ASA. By 1993, Cleary's group was one of the company's sales leaders.

The software also started to attract international interest. Three or four small consulting organizations or resellers in Europe and Asia contacted ASA about becoming distributors. A vice president had spent several weeks training one new distributor on-site, but this approach was not considered replicable or scalable. An attorney with international experience was hired to manage and oversee foreign markets, but his attention focused primarily on creating an appropriate legal framework for working with foreign sales partners. He developed a standard 30-page contract that covered most potential legal issues, but it did little to develop the sales capabilities or technical skills of distributors. In mid-1993, ASA hired George to begin building a distributor network that would allow the company to benefit from sales of software licenses abroad.

As a sales representative, George had encouraged ASA to sell its products to universities at reduced academic prices. The large pool of foreign students in US business and engineering programs became a source of potential distributors as they returned home with analytical skills and knowledge of the ASA software. Several individuals referred friends and former co-workers who also became distributors. By 1996, the company was selling software products and technical support through 30 independent representatives in Europe, Latin America and Asia. George recruited, trained and provided most sales support to the distributors, traveling frequently to meet and work with them individually.

Each distributor was a small, independent business. Few had more than four employees. Most were given exclusive rights to a specific market if they met agreed sales goals. Experiments with placing two distributors in the same market were discontinued when they led to price-cutting that undermined these already undercapitalized businesses. The image of ASA had probably suffered as well, as non-exclusive distributors used questionable tactics to lure customers from rivals. Some distributors focused on license sales and support; others offered consulting services and sold licenses bundled with analysis projects. All offered training services on their own account. Consulting projects were generally small (<$50,000), but some managers at ASA worried that distributor consulting allowed clients to obtain the answers they needed without purchasing the software. However, ASA also had a small number of consultants on its own staff to handle occasional customer projects in the US.

During its first seven or eight years, ASA had added staff when necessary and laid off employees during market dips. Headcount eventually stabilized at about 50 employees. With the exception of a small line-of-credit with a local bank, the company funded its expansion through sales growth, but cash shortages were a frequent source of concern. ASA sometimes made a small profit and sometimes incurred large losses. Although revenues had grown to more than US$ 7 million by 1996, the company continued to operate on a breakeven basis.

In the mid-1990s, however, the US market began to shift. Customers seemed less interested in purchasing traditional software, preferring instead "solutions" involving consulting, training, and software with custom interfaces tailored to specific requirements. This change in the market would have several implications. ASA began converting its US sales agents to employees, in part to bring the consulting activities of these independent operators into the company. In recognition of their contributions to the growth of ASA and the dedication of early employees, the founder awarded both groups with stock or options. Acknowledging the market changes, he expressed his desire that ASA would remain first and foremost a technology (or software) company.

By 1996, advances in software technology had also created the possibility for one application to work as a "plug-in" to another product, theoretically allowing customers to benefit from the advantages of both. Leaders at ASA saw the potential for its analytical tools to become more user-friendly by allowing customers to enter data using other, more widely-used software interfaces. In the view of company managers, this approach would allow ASA to move from selling niche products to a mass market. A multi-disciplinary team was soon working on this concept, coordinating both development of an integrated product and its introduction to the market. Because the new package was intended for sale through retail software outlets, George had been reluctant to allow distributors to sell it for fear that it would detract from their efforts to sell the higher-priced and more knowledge-intensive traditional products. Although this cannibalization of the distributor channel did occur to some degree, international sales continued to climb. In 1997, the new product was responsible for 27 percent of international sales and 10 percent of US revenues. However, limited marketing funds and lack of experience dealing with software reseller channels prevented the new product from ever reaching the shelves of computer stores.

Short on cash in late 1998, ASA agreed to be acquired by Tridemia, a consulting company six or seven times its size. Tridemia had been attempting to develop a software solution to facilitate its own process analysis methodology, but with little success. ASA products could support its consulting engagements with little modification. Flush with cash from a large, ongoing project, Tridemia spent lavishly to position itself as an up-and-coming high technology solution provider. Its consultants worked with ASA software developers to create custom applications that would generate interest from organizations hoping to better manage their research and development expenditures. Results were mixed, resulting in several pilot projects but few long-term engagements. However, more than $2 million in badly needed capital was injected into ASA. Meanwhile, the number of traditional ASA consulting engagements slowly increased, as did the average value of each project.

At their high point in 1997, international sales accounted for about one-sixth of ASA revenues. However, this number was somewhat misleading. US sales were shown as total revenues from which commissions, travel expenses and other costs were then deducted. International sales were based on fixed royalties remitted by the distributor for each license sold. After deducting operating costs, as much as 50–60 percent of international revenues remained as contribution to corporate overhead and profit. A "burdened" analysis by the accounting department in 1998 suggested that this contribution would be higher than US profits if internal resource usage was charged to each department. George took some pride in his care in limiting expenses and meeting his budget projections. Although domestic revenues were higher, he was pleased that international operations were highly profitable. In the technology boom of the late 1990s, however, interest in revenue growth eclipsed concern for profitability.

George anticipated the transition to services spreading to other world markets. Ken Palton, President of ASA, encouraged George to set up a subsidiary in Europe to promote software sales and provide the consulting services necessary to continue expanding ASA business there. As a vice president, George had been aware of the perilous state of the company's finances and was reluctant to move his family abroad. With the acquisition of ASA by Tridemia, however, ongoing financial support seemed more certain. In spring of 2000, George opened the offices of an international sales subsidiary in Frankfurt. Distributors in Europe soon responded to more attention from George with increased software sales. Small consulting projects began to come in. Established customers liked having a closer ASA presence and began to talk about larger engagements. George had a German attorney draw up employment contracts for two consultants who would join ASA Europe and bring 3 months worth of project business with them.

Unfortunately, the arrangement quickly began to unravel. Shortly after George left the US, Palton had been eased out as the management of ASA was consolidated with that of Tridemia. The President and CEO of the consulting firm had also supported the European initiative, but he too was replaced. The inability of Tridemia to attract follow-on consulting business in the US led to severe cost-cutting. George was brought back to the US almost monthly to help deal with downsizing, sales management changes, and other difficult leadership issues. Hiring of consulting staff in Europe was put on hold, and the two candidates were quickly retained by another firm. George improvised by outsourcing jobs to independent consultants and even customers with additional capacity, but less than 9 months after his departure the new CEO began asking him to return to the US. Although the new subsidiary was performing well ahead of its growth and profit projections, the new boss expressed concern with the high fixed costs of keeping George in Europe. Although he resisted the move for several months, the uncertainty was an ongoing strain on his family. In mid-2001, George returned to run ASA consulting operations. Shortly thereafter, a large European customer awarded the company a $400,000 project, one of the largest in its history.

A year later, ASA moved to a vertical market structure in which consultants were integrated into teams focusing on the needs of customers in specific industries. One of the verticals successfully developed a unique solution, building in part on earlier work by Tridemia consultants who had been laid off. In 2004, a single customer in this industry accounted for more than one-third of company revenues. Development resources were shifted to supporting specific applications for this client, resulting in several new spin-off products in non-traditional ASA markets. Some of these tools were marketed in specific industries by small dedicated teams, but others were simply placed on the website for purchase. Few found a real market beyond their initial application. Project size continued to grow in another of the verticals, where more than 80 percent of software sales resulted from consulting service engagements. A third vertical struggled to deliver its specialized projects, was downsized to a very small team, and eventually refocused on small, stand-alone software sales.

At the time of the restructuring, George asked to go back to international sales, hoping to reinvigorate the distributor network. The challenge proved to be more difficult than he expected, however. Software development resources were now focused on solutions for vertical applications. Traditional ASA products were updated infrequently. Distributors and established European customers complained that the software was becoming outdated, even as they saw other new ASA products appearing with new interfaces and capabilities. Some distributors began to question whether ASA would remain in its traditional market. Recruiting new distributors became more difficult.

By 2005, the only element of Tridemia remaining was its Board of Directors, which now controlled ASA. In January, a new CEO was appointed. This individual was a talented salesman with years of experience at ASA, who understood how to structure and sell solutions. His international experience was limited to short visits to client subsidiaries in the UK. Pointing to the slow decline in international revenues, he charged George to come up with a plan to fix it. Convinced that the traditional niche of ASA held little future promise, the CEO resisted suggestions that the company should devote more resources to updating the older software products. Providing comprehensive solutions would be essential internationally, as it had become in the domestic market.

George had talked with the new boss in the past about bringing some of the independent distributors into ASA, much as had been done with the US sales force. Laws in many nations treat a distributor's customer base as their own. Most of these representatives had also developed supporting training and consulting services, albeit on a small scale. Several of the most successful were interested in joining ASA, but each expected some compensation for merging their businesses into the US company. Not publicly traded and inconsistently profitable, ASA was unable to interest distributors in taking its stock in return. Because the company often struggled to meet its own cash requirements, outright purchase of distributor businesses was also unworkable. The Board instructed the CEO to pursue international growth without investing in another foreign company.

Europe accounted for almost 50 percent of international sales and was relatively advanced in its demand for solutions, so George felt that a presence there would be essential if ASA was to reverse the decline in revenues. One option he considered was to provide support to a consulting firm that would license the ASA name and trademarks, paying a share of project revenues in return. This alternative would require no investment from ASA, but its control would be limited. Of particular concern was the potential for channel conflicts between a licensee offering comprehensive solutions and distributors still trying to sell software.

One distributor with some consulting experience suggested that his business should be the licensee, but others in the region quickly expressed reservations. George felt that the new CEO favored this quick solution, but he knew that he would not want to deal with the potential channel conflicts if he had little control over the arrangement.

George wondered if he should invest in and set up a consulting company in Europe. His credibility and long-term relationship with the distributors would certainly allow him to manage their concerns. Returning to Europe would have a certain appeal as well. However, he was concerned that changes at ASA might once again put his family in an awkward position and put his investment at risk.

Questions

1. What challenges did George face in building international sales of ASA products? Do these factors continue to influence the choice of a future strategy?
2. Is the distributor network an asset or a liability in ASA's efforts to move to a service-based approach?
3. Can ASA build a solution-based business without investing its own resources? If so, how? If not, why not?
4. How would the shift to services change the cost structure of ASA? What impact should this have on the strategy selected?
5. What strategic approach would you recommend and why?
6. George's compensation at ASA had always been heavily weighted toward performance incentives based on revenue. If he decides to stay at ASA, what changes should George request in his compensation package as the company shifts toward services?

The Misadventures of an American Expatriate in Europe[1]

Marie-France Waxin and Virginia Bodolica*[†]*

* *The American University of Sharjah, UAE*
† *Université du Québec en Outaouais, Canada*

Introduction

On the morning of August 17, 2002, Jason Walter, CEO of Pharma First Europe (PFE), the European head office of Pharma First International (PFI), was on a flight back to Munich. He had just spent a week in Moscow, where the company was considering expanding its operations in the next 12 months. He was only a few hours away from his office in Munich, where he knew he would have to tackle issues that had been bothering him for some time. The flight would give him the opportunity to think things through before the important event that was to take place that afternoon: the managers' meeting for all of PFI's European subsidiaries. Jason was nervous and worried about this meeting.

Pharma First: From 1962 to 1998

Pharma First (PF) was founded in 1962, in Richmond (Virginia, United States). Originally a small pharmaceutical company, it quickly grew into a large multinational due to its capacity of innovation and flexibility.

In 1980, PF was diversified and its products targeted most segments of the pharmaceutical market: allergenic extracts, vaccines, phytoextracts, generic products, cosmetics and rapid diagnostic tests. With ten subsidiaries, PF covered the whole of the United States (US).

Between 1982 and 1993, PF bought eight local companies in Western and Central Europe. These acquisitions were small- and medium-size pharmaceutical companies that stood out on their local markets due to their dynamism and their capacity of innovation. The Munich subsidiary was the first one bought by PF; all the others followed. The last acquisition, in 1993, was the Danish subsidiary. In 1993, all the European subsidiaries were profitable and self-sufficient. Their managers and directors were all locals. When the American CEO wished to communicate with them, he would contact the head of each subsidiary individually. The Munich subsidiary, the first one bought, was thought of as the "psychological" base in Europe.

In 1995, PF decided on a new mission and focused its research and development (R&D) efforts on creating products of natural origins. In 1995, the company officially became Pharma First International.

By 1998, PFI was represented in nearly all European countries that were considered to be of strategic importance. The only market that had not yet been penetrated and that offered considerable potential for growth was the Community of Independent States (consisting of countries from the former Soviet Union, except for the three Baltic Republics: Russia, Ukraine, Belorussia, Moldova, Armenia, Azerbaijan, Georgia, Kazakhstan, Uzbekistan, Kirgizstan, Turkmenistan, Tajikistan). Powerful historical and cultural links existed between these countries, and PFI believed that creating a subsidy in Moscow would give access not only to the Russian market, but also to those of the other Republics of the Community. In fact, the strong political influence that Russia had exerted on the others and their coexistence for many years in one political and economic entity had resulted in the development of a feeling of brotherhood and a certain homogenization of their respective peoples. In addition, following the breakdown of the Soviet Union, many people had found themselves outside the borders of their countries of origin. Taking these elements into consideration, there were reasons to believe that, if the Russian market was conquered, growth in the other countries would come relatively easy, as products and marketing would need relatively little adaptation.

In 1998, PFI was a leader in the phytoextracts sector and provided for the production, the marketing and licensing of pharmaceutical specialties, mainly in the United States. The European subsidiaries kept on with their traditional production, but, more and more, they also produced locally some of the specialties of Pharma First US (PFUS).

In 1998, PFI's global sales figure had reached US$1.1 billion (PFUS: US$730 million; PFE: US$370 million); it held 7 percent of the American market and 8 percent of the European market. In 2002, the multinational had 5200 employees, 3420 of which was in the U.S. and 1780 in Europe. For the European subsidies, the repartition of the workforce was as follows: Munich, 150 employees; Berlin, 285; Denmark, 115; France, 345; Italy, 260;

Poland, 230; the Netherlands, 135; and Spain, 235. Twenty-five employees worked in the Munich head office, which had its offices attached to the subsidiary's office.

The Arrival of Jason Walter in Munich, the Birth of Pharma First Europe and the Conquest of the Russian Market

In June of 1999, the director of the Munich subsidiary retired. Since the successor that had been chosen for the position was not ready to undertake his new functions, Barry Gumpert, President and CEO of PFI, seized this opportunity to send his protégé, Jason Walter, on a 4-year mission (from June 1999 to June 2003). Jason's mandate was to temporarily fulfill the role of Director of the Munich subsidy, to train Thilo Rotenburger, the successor (what Jason did during the first six months of this mission), to found the European head office of PFE in Munich and to ensure that PFI's growth and R&D orientation policies were hatched in Europe. This orientation had been, since the early beginnings, the basis for the rapid growth and the successes of the company. Munich thus officially became the European center, even though the "European head office" merely consisted, then, of less than a dozen employees working in the Munich subsidy's buildings.

Shortly after his arrival, Jason decided to initiate business relations with Moscow. Since extraction and concentration were crucial operations for the development of products using medicinal herbs and since the legislation concerning traditional extraction methods, using organic solvents, were more restrictive in Europe than in the US, Jason decided, as the new CEO of PFE, to develop an innovative extraction method in collaboration with the Technological Institute of Moscow. This close scientific collaboration with Russian scientists had given the opportunity to study the needs of the Russian market and to analyze the advantages of setting up a new subsidiary in the area. After having studied various possibilities, Jason decided that the best way to penetrate that market was to acquire an existing pharmaceutical laboratory in Moscow. For this, Jason had the support of the US Head office. Negotiations with the Russian counterparts turned out to be lengthy and tedious, requiring much time and concentration from Jason. However, since this project was his main priority, he literally devoted himself to it. Between 1999 and 2002, Jason invested countless hours into this project. On this morning in August of 2002, things were looking up: the previous week's negotiations had been productive and, at last, the project seemed close to bearing fruit. Jason believed that, in less than one year, the pharmaceutical lab in Moscow would be a part of PFI, which would not only reinforce

PFI's position as a leader on the segment of natural origins products, but would affirm the company's international presence in a country the size of a continent. In that respect, Jason felt reassured.

Change in the European Strategic Orientation: The Creation of a Network Structure between the European Subsidiaries (2001)

However, Jason was a little worried about another important project: the creation of a network structure between the eight European subsidiaries. At the time of their acquisition by PFI, the subsidiaries produced and sold their own products on their respective local markets. As time went by, they began to produce some of PFI's specialties, which they did at a cost below that of the competition.

However, since 2000, there had been a shift: competitors' costs had fallen under those of the subsidiaries and PFE had had to lower its prices, which resulted in a diminution of profits. In 2001, the strategic committee had shown that, in order to reach the company's financial objectives, improve quality and clients' satisfaction and reduce the cost of production and marketing of their principal product, the subsidiaries needed to specialize themselves so that the main products' production costs would diminish.

At the end of 2001, the American Head office had decided then to create a network structure between its European subsidiaries, located in Germany (2 subsidiaries), France, Italy, the Netherlands, Spain, Denmark and Poland. According to this scenario, each subsidy would produce for all subsidiaries the main products for which it had a technological and economical advantage, and would keep producing the secondary and highly specialized products for its local market (products whose components were the main products). That strategy required that the subsidies be part of a large network and that the European managers cooperate as members of one unified team.

Yet, this morning, in 2002, these conditions were far from being met. In order to succeed in its restructuring, the company needed to unify the functioning of its European subsidiaries and to improve the cooperation and the cohesion between their managers. Implementing this strategy was of crucial importance, as it would allow PFE to respond in a unique way to the needs of pharmacists, doctors, and patients by offering a vast line of affordable medicines, on the entire European territory covered by the multinational.

Integrating the European team had thus become a strategic objective for PFI, and Jason had been given the mandate of implementing that decision.

The US Head office had consequently offered him a 2-year extension of his expatriation mandate (from June 2003 to June 2005). Jason had readily agreed, as he very much enjoyed his work and his life in Europe. This would be still the case for other three forthcoming years, he thought.

Recruiting Mike Harisson (2002)

When he agreed to the extension of his mandate, Jason had requested that the American Head office send him an assistant, someone highly qualified, who would be responsible for the "European network" project. The US Head office chose Mike Harisson, a very talented, very promising young manager. Two months after having met with the board of directors in Richmond, Mike and his family boarded the plane to Munich.

Mike's 2-year mandate (from January 2002 to January 2004), as decided by the US Head office, would, all under Jason's supervision, consist of three major parts. First, Mike had to design and implement the "European network" project, by creating a network for the European subsidiaries concerned with the production and commercialization of PFE principal products. Second, he had to develop organizational cohesion and facilitate communication between the European subsidiaries by creating and solidifying relationships between European directors. In the end, European directors were expected to form a unified team. Third, Mike was also responsible for organizing and implementing the training program integrating their new functions in the new organizational structure for the subsidiaries' managers.

Jason remembered the first impression Mike had given him when they were introduced, a little over a year ago in Richmond. Tall and athletic, the 35-year-old stood out amongst the other managers. Jason and Mike had had a brief talk, which had convinced Jason that Mike had more than good looks: he was assertive, determined and self-confident. "I'm good at what I do because I set out a goal, then I do everything I need to do in order to reach it," said Mike. "I excel at managing many projects simultaneously, especially when I don't have much time on my hands. I mobilize all resources and my whole team towards the common objective. This way of working has always allowed me to get fast results." Indeed, Mike had remarkable qualities that had undoubtedly fascinated, either consciously or unconsciously, all those people around him. Jason also had liked the way Mike had expressed his opinions in an honest, direct way; he had been impressed by the magnitude of his knowledge in the pharmaceutical field, his genuine interest for it and the originality of his ideas. Without a doubt, Mike was a very promising young man.

Mike had an excellent educational background. At Boston University, he had studied economics and international trade and then had done an MBA in strategic management. More importantly, he had worked wonders at the US Head office: he had successfully reorganized the American subsidiary that had been the least profitable, before designing and implementing a total quality management (TQM) program. These changes had resulted in lower production costs and remarkable quality improvements. The TQM program had been so successful that it had been implemented in all the other American subsidiaries. Moreover, Mike even had prior international experience: after his MBA, he had worked for 3 years at the American embassy in New Delhi as deputy economic counsel. He was then in charge of monitoring commercial trade and investment flows from the US to India, and of monitoring the macroeconomic situation of the country.

These professional qualities were the main reason why the CEO of PFI, Barry Gumpert, has chosen Mike for unifying PFE. Barry had implied that, if the project was successful, Jason could expect a high executive position in the US Head office. Jason was enthusiastic: Mike would help him reach the top.

A few months after Mike's arrival in Munich, Jason had spoken about the Russian project with the big boss. Barry took this opportunity to tell Jason that he strongly believed Mike was just what PFE needed: "Of all the high potential managers in Richmond," Barry said, "Mike was simply the best."

Mike's Difficult Start

Despite Mike's undeniable qualities, 8 months after his arrival in Munich in January 2002, no clear progress concerning the implementation of the network structure between subsidiaries had been recorded. In fact, Mike just did not seem to be efficient in the European environment. He was no longer the sharp, charismatic man that Jason had met in Richmond, and his mission was, at that point, a total failure.

In the first few weeks, when Jason had heard from subordinates and colleagues that Mike was having a hard time, he had thought it was due to a normal, temporary, phase of adaptation to the European ways of doing business.

In April 2002, Mike organized the "First Strategic Reflection Seminar on the Transformation of the European Structure." Just after this seminar, Mike had told Jason about his state of frustration and disillusion towards his new working environment:

> I just met with Dieter Hoffmann, director of the Berlin subsidiary, which is the most important in terms of employees and production. I invited him to stop by my office, as I wanted to know his thoughts on the proposed schedule for the networking of the subsidiaries and on the content of the

training seminar. I wanted to get him to trust me, so I asked him a few innocent questions concerning his family, his next holidays, before getting to the point. I also asked him to call me by my first name. Nevertheless, he kept a distant attitude throughout the whole conversation . . . I then asked about the work atmosphere at his company . . . You know what he said? "Everything's good", that's it. Can you believe it, Jay? I then told him that I would really appreciate if he would share his thoughts concerning the training program. You'll never guess what he did next: he gave me a suspicious look and asked me what I was expecting from him, exactly. Unbelievable!

Since June, Mike had been working on the design of the "Second Strategic Reflection Seminar on the Transformation of the European Structure." Mike had also organized this afternoon's meeting (about which Jason was so preoccupied) with the European subsidiaries' directors and top executives, where he was expected to present "The results of the first strategic reflection seminar on creating a network structure." However, Mike had called Jason in Moscow, yesterday, to tell him that today's presentation would not be "as good as he would have wished it to be" because he had not received all the directors' suggestions. The presentation would thus be shorter than he had planned. Mike had confided in Jason yesterday over the phone:

> I tried everything with them. I managed my way, which worked so well in Richmond: I delegated responsibilities; I gave them the freedom to manage themselves. But obviously, these methods don't work here. I tried to get closer to them . . . but every time I ask someone to come eat lunch in my office, they make up some excuse and decline the invitation. If our meetings last a few minutes longer than planned, they start to whisper and shuffle their agendas. I'm completely overwhelmed by the situation . . . Certain managers do not understand the company's objectives for restructuring. Other manager's may understand, but do not want to participate in the process. Then there are those who strive to hinder the understanding and participation of others in the company . . .

Mike still could not understand the European managers' reactions and knew that his own actions did not have the desired outcomes. Obviously, Mike really cared about his work. He knew that things were not as they should have been, but he just did not know what to do. Jason was worried: Was Mike really the man that everyone, at the US Head office, thought to be so extraordinary, so great? Jason was having doubts . . .

Jason was brought back to the real world by the captain's voice announcing their landing in Munich. A few minutes later, he was walking towards the parking lot where he had left his car, a week earlier. There would surely have been quite a bit of movement in the European office of PF because of the meeting today which would bring together the managers of all their European branches. Getting out from the airport, Jason drove on Schneider Straße reaching the PFE's offices in about 20 minutes. After having parked his car in the company's underground parking, Jason glanced at his watch: it was 12:45 p.m.

The Directors and Managers' Meeting for all of PFI's European Subsidiaries

Even though he was not hungry, he headed straight for the cafeteria, which was in the administrative wing of the company building. At this hour, all recently arrived managers should already be there: it was therefore a good opportunity to greet them in an informal context. He would use this chance to speak to Mike before his presentation of 2 p.m.

Indeed, they were all present, finishing their lunch and talking. Benoit Dupuis, director of the French subsidiary in Nantes, was the first person Jason noticed. "Salut Benoit, ça va bien?." Then "Hola Fernando, como estas?" ... "Wie geht's, Jurgen?" ... "Ciao Vincenzo, come va la vita?" ... "Hi Jacek!" ... "Pleased to see you, Hans!." Even though he knew the Polish and Danish salutations, he did not dare greeting managers who arrived from Warsaw and Aarhus in their respective mother tongues for fear of using improper pronunciation. Then, after having socialized a little bit with them, he scanned the room, looking for Mike without spotting him. He approached then his friend, Frans Klepzeiker, PFE's Human Resources Director. Frans, originally from Luxembourg but living in Munich for 15 years, had been working for the company for 5 years. Jason wanted to know whether Frans had seen Mike. "Oh, even on special occasions like today, Mike doesn't change his habits," responded Frans. "He never comes down to the cafeteria for lunch. He's surely in his office having his sandwich alone."

At 1:55 p.m. all the European participants were already present in the conference room. Where was Mike? Why was he not here checking out the technical aspects of his presentation? To hide his nervousness, Jason tried to concentrate on the plan of the meeting. "Summary of the first strategic reflection seminar: Network of European companies for better European performance" was the title of the presentation. Ten minutes later, at 2:05 p.m., Mike arrived in the room and headed directly for the podium. Jason heard a whisper from behind him: "Zu spät, wie immer, Ja! This is the American punctuality." How could Mike allow himself to be late, thought Jason.

Mike began his speech, thanking the managers for their attendance and their efforts to assure the project's success. He apologized from the start: his presentation of the results of the first strategic reflection seminar would be shorter than planned. Jason heard a few sighs in the room. Looking around at each participant, he noted many veiled smiles. At the end of his brief speech, Mike handed the presentation over to Jason, as CEO of PFE. Forty minutes later, the directors were already exiting the room.

The Discussion between Jason and Anja

At 3:30 p.m., the European managers had a scheduled workshop on "Total Quality Management at PFE," under Frans' direction. Mike attended this meeting. Jason decided to look for Anja Bonhage, his assistant manager, and get her impressions on Mike's first seminar. Frau Anja Bonhage was German from Freiburg. As effective as she was open-minded, she enjoyed an excellent reputation among the other local employees of the company. Indeed, many of them had made a habit of coming to talk to her about their little problems.

Shortly after Mike's arrival, Anja had begun to complain about the general decrease in morale of the European management team. She recalled to Jason the comments made by Danish and Dutch colleagues about Mike: according to them, his habit of working until late at night was a sign of inefficiency . . . or of serious problems at home, where he spent very little time. Otherwise, why would he stay at the office until midnight? But, since until this week Jason had been extremely busy with the Russian project, he had not listened to Anja's comments carefully. Anja, at her turn, did not dare to insist. Today, however, he was ready to listen to her. Jason came into Anja's office and asked her directly: "Anja, I am very worried. I absolutely have to find out how did Mike's first strategic seminar from April go?" To Jason, this first reflection seminar seemed to have generally gone well as he had not received any negative feedback about it so far. However, he had not participated, while Anja had. Anja collected her thoughts . . . and replied:

Mike has been more and more the object of criticism from the European directors. Many of them expressed their dissatisfaction with the poor organization of the first strategic reflection seminar. Vincenzo Cioli, the Italian manager, called to complain about the extremely strict timetable and the length of the work sessions, without even any coffee breaks. Pablo Perez, the director from Madrid, came by this morning to ask for Mike to be replaced; in his opinion, his post should have been filled by a person with a better understanding of the European environment. Further, Herr Rotenburger, the director of the Munich subsidiary, just called me to complain of Herr Harrison's embarrassing and inappropriate management style; he added that this opinion was shared by all his colleagues. Indeed, what bothers them, he said, was that Mike persists in making the rounds of all the employees throughout the whole working day, to ask them to tell him their ideas, give him advice or suggestions, without ever being able to find solutions on his own.

But things did not stop there. Anja continued:

European managers say that Mike's ideas and proposals lack clarity and that European collaborators cannot understand neither what they are told nor what they need to do in order to facilitate the integration process set by Mike. Finally, many managers are frustrated at the lack of respect shown to them by Mike. Among other things, Mike has an annoying tendency to call employees by their first names. Overall, the European employees feel that the company operated well before Mike's arrival and that Mike is not the reason for their exceptional performance. Managers believe that Mike should let them manage themselves during the integration process. The problem seems to be that every manager has his own opinion on the subject.

Jason looked more and more worried. Anja hoped she had not said too much.

The Discussion between Jason and Mike

6:00 p.m. All the European managers had left now. Mike came back to his own office and Jason intercepted him. In the hallway, Mike, looking more preoccupied than ever, told Jason without preamble:

> I sent each European manager who had attended the first strategic reflection seminar a structured questionnaire asking for their feedback and their proposals about the implementation of the network strategy, and the production and distribution of the main products. The questionnaire also asked them for their opinion about the training seminar on multifunctional teams. Some of them, particularly the French, sent me their comments in the form of text written on several pages. These pages contain nothing but negative critiques and unattainable proposals. As for the Danes, I still have not received any answer; every time I called them, I was told that they were still talking about it. The Italians, on their end, would have preferred that I personally explain the questions from the questionnaire in person in Italy. In Italy! Can you imagine! The Spaniards have not responded at all and I don't think they ever will: they categorically refuse the very idea of reorganization. They don't even want to broach the subject of abandoning production of their basic product line, a line they produce at a loss! They're afraid to lose control over their local production. The Spanish director, the oldest of all the European directors, even threatened to quit! In fact, that would probably be best: a younger director would better understand the reasons for change! Given that I was lacking feedback from different subsidiaries, I was incapable of preparing a good summary of the results of the reflection seminar.

Suddenly, Mike smiled, trying to seem optimistic.

> They'll simply have to adapt to the unified image of PFE. I'm sure that soon enough, they'll realize that they have to adapt and do things our way, which worked so well in Richmond!

Jason realized that they absolutely had to speak in private about this project. He took an appointment with Mike for the next day at 10:00 a.m. in his office. The remarks of certain European managers at today's conference and his discussion with Anja about the first strategic seminar had perturbed him. Before meeting with Mike tomorrow, Jason wanted to discuss the situation with his friend, Frans Klepzeiker, HR Director, in whom he had complete trust.

The Discussion between Jason and Frans

He knew that Frans would give him his honest opinion. As soon as he found Frans in his office, Jason went straight to the topic that interested him: "Frans, I absolutely need you to give me information. Tell me, the first strategic reflection seminar, how did it go?" Frans seemed hesitant, unsure how to respond. Actually, Frans seemed to have been waiting a long time to talk about Mike and his project. All Jason had to do was encourage him. "I'm listening, Frans, go on . . . "

> Well, generally, nothing extraordinary, but it was a good beginning. However, there were several small problems during the seminar. First of all, according to Mike's initial proposal, the seminar was supposed to end on Saturday evening. Once they had arrived, the Dutch, the Danes and the French announced to Mike that they would be leaving on Friday evening. Mike took this as a total lack of cooperation on their part. Saturday morning's workshop was very important to him. As a result, he reorganized the schedule so that the content of Saturday's workshop could be fit into the three regular weekdays, Wednesday, Thursday, and Friday. These three days were thus extremely busy. However, the French and the Spaniards had been counting on this seminar to meet and secure contracts with the other managers, who they only rarely ever saw. They complained that the tight schedule prevented them from doing so. Also, a member of the Danish management team asked many, many questions to Mike during his presentation, which visibly irritated him. Finally, the Italians absolutely wanted to meet you personally to talk about their personnel problems at the Milan branch. However, you were in Russia. Mike proposed to them that they discuss it the following week by phone, but this did not assuage them at all. This time, they didn't believe that Mike took the Italian branch seriously.

Frans was on a roll.

> In the end, there were many complaints. Some managers went to see Heidi to tell her that the seminar had been nothing but an incredible bombardment of information; others, like the Danes, accused Mike of not having furnished enough background information, assuming that they already had it. The German directors were very unhappy about the change in the schedule: they went so far as to ask to come back to the initial schedule and to continue with those that would still be present, a proposition that sparked a general feeling of uneasiness among the participants. Mike refused, stating that he wanted everybody in attendance. Everyone had something to say about this. In fact, this must have been quite unpleasant for Mike, who had gone to a lot of effort to organize the whole thing.

Jason was irritated. "Frans, I would have preferred if you had talked to me about all this earlier!" His response was not encouraging either: "You didn't seem to have any time to devote to the matter, you were too busy with the negotiations with the Russian partners."

The Discussion between Jason and Heidi

On the way to his desk, Jason passed by Mike's desk that happened to be in the same hall as Jason's. Heidi had helped Mike's family find a furnished house in Munich. Mrs Harisson would call her from time to time to ask where to find certain things in Munich. Jason asked Heidi: "Do you know how Mike's wife is doing?"

> From what I gather, she does not like it here at all. Not knowing anyone in Munich and not speaking German, she feels isolated and lonely. She often tells me about her first experience living abroad in New Delhi, where she knew all the English communities and lead a happy, easy life. Here, she is sick of not working and is having trouble adapting to her new role as a housewife. On top of that she cannot find a school with American equivalence and programs for her 12-year-old son who only speaks a couple of words in German. He is starting to have serious communication and psychological problems. Until now, he has always been a brilliant student and a social boy but that is rapidly changing.

Today had been a long day for everyone. Jason did not want to delay Heidi at that time. He decided he would speak to her about Mike later on.

How to Save the Situation?

Jason entered his office, suddenly apprehensive. His discussions with Anja, Frans, and Heidi had stressed him out. The decisive moment was upon him: would he keep Mike in Munich or would he send him back to the home office? Until now, he had been able to cover for Mike's slip-ups and point his career in the right direction. However, he feared that Mike might now jeopardize the networking of the subsidiaries, which would negate all the efforts he himself had made in the past 3 years at PFE. Moreover, Jason had invested 9 years into PFI, during which he had had many professional successes; he could not let his career crash. After all, it was not his fault that Mike was not performing well in Munich and that there was more resistance to the changes by the European employees than expected. Jason now believed that Mike's aptness for this post had possibly been overestimated.

But could he really consider sending Mike back to the US? Barry, with whom he had broached the question, categorically refused to have Mike return to the head office. Jason could also lose face, because he was responsible for the integration of the European team, not to mention that the directors at the home office might think that Jason had been totally assimilated by the Europeans, that he had forgotten the American way of doing things and that he had mistreated their "star." On the other hand, it could not be all Mike's fault. Mike was loyal, competent and well intentioned. Jason could not allow himself to destroy Mike's career . . . He did not deserve that.

Jason knew that a decision needed to be made quickly, before it was too late. Without saying that the failure of a networking strategy would also jeopardize the company's conquest of a Russian market. Thus, the future of PFE was at stake . . . and so was Jason's career. How had he, Jason, lost control like this? How come he had not noticed Mike's difficulties during his European mission earlier? Now he had to think of a way to make the situation right again.

Tomorrow, at 10:00 a.m., he would be meeting Mike and his big concern was what to do about Mike's functions?

Questions

Theme 1: Global Management

1. What internationalization strategies do you recognize in this case?
2. What is the international HRM perspective adopted by PFI?
3. Your comments about that choice?

Theme 2: Mike's Mission and Profile, Staffing Processes

1. Was Donaldson a good candidate for this expatriated position?
2. What is Mike's professional mission?
3. What is the profile of the ideal candidate?
4. What is the actual profile of Mike?
5. Criticize the staffing process for Mike's international assignment.

Theme 3: Intercultural Dimensions, Intercultural Adjustment, Intercultural Teams

1. What are the intercultural dimensions you recognize in this case? For each dimension, give one example drawn from the text, and justify/explain why this quotation is related to this dimension.
2. What difficulties are encountered by Mike?
3. What are the advantages and disadvantages of multicultural teams?

Theme 4: Expat Management

1. Did Mike commit any mistake?
2. Did Jason commit any mistake regarding the management of Mike's assignment?
3. Did Franz commit any mistake regarding the management of Mike's assignment?
4. Did the US headquarter commit any mistake regarding the management of Mike's assignment?
5. You are a consultant to the American HQ: What are your recommendations to them?

Theme 5: Jason's Decision

1. You are Jason. You want the situation to be fixed in the next 6 months.
2. What will you do to save the "network project"?
3. What will be your action plan? (please argument and justify)
4. And what will you do of Mike?

List carefully your precise actions in chronological order. Justify your choices.

Endnote

1. A previous version of this case has been published in this online case journal (in French). The *Revue Internationale de Cas en Gestion* has authorized the authors to publish this case in English. Waxin, M.F. and Bodolica, V. (2005). Pharma First International. Les tribulations d'un expatrié Américain en Allemagne, *Revue Internationale de Cas en Gestion*, HEC Montréal, March, vol 3, no. 1, p. 12.

Appendix 1

PFI's Organization Chart (as in August 2002)

Exhibit 1

Organization Chart (as in August 2002)

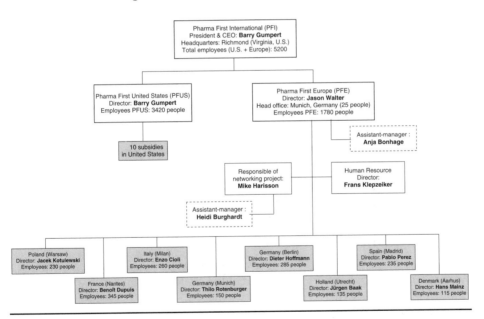

Appendix 2
Summary of the Important Events

Period	Important events
1962	Pharma First foundation in Richmond (Virginia, United States)
1980	Possession of ten diversified subsidiaries in United States
1982–1993	Purchase of eight local companies in Western and Central Europe
1995	New research and development mission; official creation of Pharma First International
1998	PFI, leader in the phytoextracts sector in United States
1999	Arrival of Jason Walter in Munich, creation of Pharma First Europe, project to conquer the Russian market
2000	PFI's economic slowdown
2001	PFI's strategic change
	Decision of creation of the network structure
2002	Recruiting of Mike Harisson
April 2002	First strategic seminar with all the European directors
August 2002	Meeting with all the European directors

Appendix 3
Map of Europe

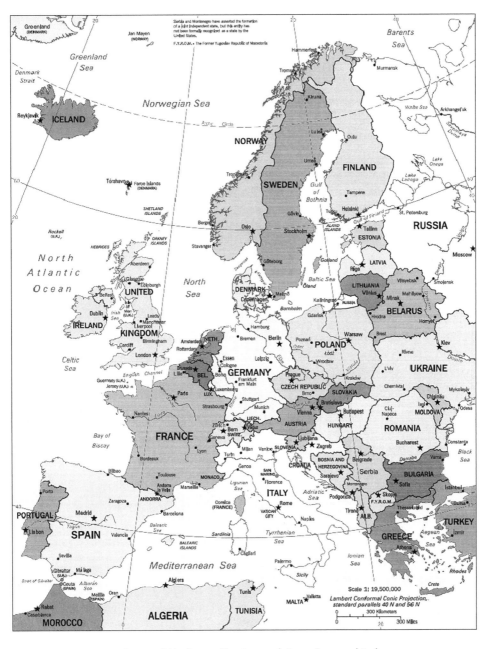

Source: http://www.lib.utexas.edu/maps/europe.html.

The UAE: An Information Society for Growth and Employment

Zeinab Karake Shalhoub

The American University of Sharjah, UAE

Introduction

The United Arab Emirates (UAE) has taken a quantum leap during the past 15 years in the direction of liberalizing its economy and diversifying it away from the oil-based sector. In 2005, the Networked Readiness Index, a joint project by INSEAD and the World Economic Forum, which evaluates the relative level of ICT development in 104 countries, ranked the UAE 23rd.[1] In 2006, the Index of Economic Freedom, a joint project by the Heritage Foundation and the *Wall Street Journal*, ranked the UAE 65th worldwide, 3rd among the Arab states after Kuwait which ranked 50 and Saudi Arabia with a rank of 62.[2] This index measures how well a country scores on a list of 50 variables divided into 10 areas of economic freedom. These include trade policy, banking regulations, fiscal burden, foreign investment codes, monetary policy, and black market. The various measures and incentives created by the government have helped the country move steadily and consistently into the direction of an information/knowledge based society. In this respect, and recently, the UAE has emerged as the forerunner in the Arab region and is among the top information technology (IT) users in the world, based on the classification issued by the US' IDC Group. In its global Information Society Index (ISI) for 2005, the World Times/IDC ISI ranks the UAE thirty-two (32) overall out of 53 countries, by evaluating 23 indicators measuring the capacity of a nation's citizenry to exchange information internally and externally. These 23 indicators are classified into four different categories: (1) computer infrastructure, (2) Internet infrastructure, (3) information infrastructure, and (4) social infrastructure.[3] The Index measures the country's achievements in IT and related fields, the

659

level of use and its readiness to cope with IT developments. Only four Arab countries are listed among the top 53 countries in IT readiness. The ISI establishes a standard by which all nations are measured according to their ability to access and absorb information and IT. While gross domestic product (GDP) measures economic wealth, ISI measures information capacity and wealth. The ISI is designed to help countries assess their position relative to other countries and to guide companies to future market opportunities.

Based on the ITU Digital Access Index (DAI) published in 2003,[4] the UAE is classified in the upper access category with a score of 0.64. The DAI index classifies countries into one of four digital access categories: high, upper, medium, and low. Those in the upper access category include mainly nations from Central and Eastern Europe, the Caribbean, Gulf States, and emerging Latin American nations. Many have used ICTs as a development enabler and government policies have helped them reach an impressive level of ICT access. This includes major ICT projects such as the Dubai Internet City (DIC) in the UAE (the highest ranked Arab nation in the DAI), the Multimedia Super Corridor in Malaysia (the highest ranked developing Asian nation), and the Cyber City in Mauritius (along with Seychelles, the highest ranked African nation). The DAI is a useful tool for tracking the future advancement of these ambitious emerging economies.

In the e-government domain, the UAE ranked number 38 globally on the United Nations e-government readiness index (0.535) of 2003, the first among the Arab countries and second only after Israel (0.663) in the Western Asia region.

While each of the above stated indices area treats a different facet of the information/knowledge based society, a degree of overlap and interdependence remains high among them. The following five fundamentals are identified and described, then later discussed in the case of the UAE (Exhibit 1):

1. *Hard Infrastructure.* This denotes hardware, telecommunications, networks, databases, telephones services, personal computers, main frame and supercomputers, and so on. In a nut shell, this constitutes the foundation over which all other components rest.
2. *Soft Infrastructure.* Also referred to as the policy and regulatory environment; this includes laws, regulations, intellectual property, cyber laws, electronic signature, and so on. The ICT environment cannot function harmoniously without this safety net.
3. *Talent Base.* This is related to skill development and human resources within the technology sphere, and is concerned with (a) efforts attracting a pool of talents from the region; (b) development of nationals within the local community; and (c) instituting IT training in the professional educational sector.

Exhibit 1

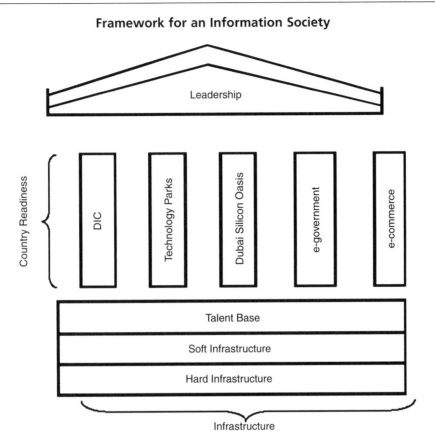

Framework for an Information Society

4. *Country Readiness*. While it is possible to have the hard and soft infra-structures in place, it is extremely challenging to control the elements of change in terms of societal acceptance and readiness. Country readiness is defined as "initiatives facilitating the change in the transformation process" into an information/knowledge society.

5. *Leadership*. This intangible component is the most important level of support in easing a country's passage into the information/knowledge arena; it has to come from the highest political levels in the economy. Support from the federal government is crucial for greasing the wheel of transformation process into an information/knowledge society.

Hard Infrastructure

To describe the technical infrastructure in the UAE, we will be looking at five main indicators: (1) fixed lines, (2) wireless technology, (3) Internet hosts, (4) Internet users, and (5) computerization. Up until 2005, public telecommunications services in the UAE were provided under monopoly conditions by the Emirates Telecommunications Corporation (Etisalat), headquartered in the federal capital, Abu Dhabi. Etisalat is a quasi-state company, with 60 percent ownership by the UAE government and 40 percent by individual UAE nationals, and is the second most valuable quoted company in the Middle East. The Corporation is ranked by *Financial Times* as one of the top 500 companies in the world in terms of market capitalization and the sixth largest in the Middle East. In its recent ranking the *Financial Times* ranks Etisalat 138 among the *Financial Times*' top 500 Corporations.[5] Business units and subsidiary companies provide Etisalat and clients with a whole range of services including voice, data, satellite, Internet, IT solutions and consulting, smart card manufacture, data clearing, submarine cable-laying, and maintenance and related telecommunications services. Etisalat serves over 4.8 million mobile customers in the UAE, a penetration rate of over 100 per cent. In 2005, Etisalat announced revenues of AED 12.9 billions and net profits of AED 4.3 billions.[6]

Incorporated in 1976, Etisalat was the sole provider of telecommunication services to individuals and institutions in the UAE up until 2005. To diversify its sources of revenue, the corporation has also invested in Thuraya Satellite, Zanzibar Telecom, Qatar Telecom, and Sudan Telecom. For the year 2001, Etisalat's silver jubilee year, the company surpassed targets and serviced a million customers in each of the fixed line as well as GSM businesses. In an effort to provide seamless communication around the globe, the Corporation now offers connectivity to 258 IDD destinations and 213 GSM roaming partners in 96 countries. The only networks independent of Etisalat are those operated by government departments with special needs such as the Ministry of Interior and Armed Forces/General Head Quarters. The oil companies such as the Abu Dhabi National Oil Company (ADNOC) now use Etisalat facilities but retain their own independent telecommunications facilities as a backup. During 2001, the Corporation launched nine new services and enhancements, including short message service (SMS) for prepaid mobile phones and prepaid service for fixed line. Etisalat is also employing a proactive approach to ready itself for opportunities that will arise through the convergence of Internet and mobile phones, namely wireless Internet. To achieve this, the corporation engaged in the development of infrastructure and value-added services. E-Vision, a cable TV and multimedia subsidiary, offers interactive services, through a fiber/coax network, to subscribers. High speed Internet (ADSL) and wireless Internet services (WAP) have also been introduced. The Thuraya Satellite has been launched and the services have already been introduced to the target markets (in 2005). Implementation of WAP and GPRS technologies has led to the migration to the 3G broadband mobile network. Etisalat has the second highest capitalization of any public company in the Middle East. It has a capital expenditure program expected to equal US$1.6 billion over the next 3 years.[6] Its wealth enables it to constantly expand its programs and implement technologies ahead of others in the region.

To summarize, the UAE has a modern telecommunications infrastructure, especially when compared to other countries in the region. It has frequently been referred to as the "most wired" state in the Middle East. The UAE residents have relatively unhindered access to all modes of communications that Western nations do.

Telephones

Within the UAE, Etisalat has a fixed exchange line capacity of 1.4 million telephone lines—100 percent digital—of which around 50,000 are ISDN in addition to the leased circuits. The number of telephone connections increased from 1,020,097 lines in 2000 to 1,052,930 in 2001, which represents a penetration of 34 lines per 100 inhabitants. The number for 2005 is estimated at 1,362,000, placing the country squarely at the top of the list in the Arab world, and among leading nations worldwide in telecommunications (Exhibit 2). During the year 2001, Etisalat announced a substantial reduction in its tariffs. The ISD tariffs were reduced by a whopping 34 percent on overage for 225 countries including some reduction of up to 79 percent. The proliferation of mobiles has decreased the dependency on payphones for many subscribers. Consequently, the number of payphones decreased from 28,839 to 28,623 in 2001 (Exhibit 3).[6]

Etisalat offers fixed line services over the next generation network (NGN), and has been migrating sections of its users onto the advanced network. The timeline for completion of migration is the end of 2007. By establishing NGN, Etisalat will be able to offer voice, video, and data over one single source, enabling true Triple-Play functionality.

Exhibit 2

Fixed Telephone Lines (Estimates from Etisalat)

Year	Subscribers (in thousands)
1997	835
1998	915
1999	975
2000	1020
2001	1053
2002	1120
2003	1195
2004	1277
2005	1362
2006a	1461

Exhibit 3	
Mobile Subscribers (Estimates from Etisalat)	
Year	Mobile Subscribers (in thousands)
1997	313
1998	492
1999	830
2000	1428
2001	1909
2002	2361
2003	2770
2004	3150
2005	3522
2006	3854

Wireless Communications

Etisalat was one of the first to introduce Mobile Telephones in the Middle East in 1982 and launched the GSM Service in September 1994. The subscriber base of 130,000 at the end of 1996 exceeded 3.5 million in 2005. The GSM service incorporates advanced digital communication technology with full roaming facility in countries where a reciprocal agreement is in existence. The unique feature of the GSM cellular service is the subscriber's identity module (SIM) card which is used to activate GSM handsets and provides unprecedented levels of security and privacy combined with high quality transmission. Etisalat offers a portfolio of rich services and is considered one of the most advanced countries in the application of wireless technology. Following is a description of applications offered to UAE residents.

- GSM International Roaming Service (GIRS) is a facility that allows subscribers to use mobile phones when they travel outside the UAE. This is possible because of roaming agreements between Etisalat and countries around the world.
- GSM Ishaar Package is a combination of three GSM value added services—GSM call waiting facility, GSM call conference, and e-mail notification on GSM handsets via SMS text. In addition, Etisalat's GSM fax and data service allows GSM customers (excluding WASEL) to send and receive fax and data using their mobile phones over the GSM network at speeds of up to 9600 bps within the UAE or while roaming. The service enables GSM users to work from home, hotels, or airport lobbies and to constantly keep in touch with the office, colleagues, or information sources. GSM users are able to send and retrieve fax and data from GSM, anywhere at any time. Conventional fax modem and

plug-in telephone are not required. The service is excellent for business travelers, executives, entrepreneurs, transports, couriers, and computer companies.

- Etisalat's Prepaid GSM Service, WASEL, ensures cost-effective and instant communication. The service is ideal for people who wish to keep in touch with their friends and relatives. International roaming is also available for WASEL customers. Furthermore, Etisalat's messaging service AL MERSAL for GSM, and WASEL customers, is a combination of voice mail, fax mail and short messaging service that includes SMS notification and SMS mail.

- RISALA (SMS mail) is a service that allows GSM and WASEL customers to send a short text message of up to 160 characters from their GSM handsets to other GSM subscribers within the UAE.

- Etisalat's SMS Breaking News Service provides the latest breaking news in politics, business, sport, or entertainment as it happens around the world. News content is provided as SMS alerts on GSM handsets. The service is available to GSM and WASEL Customers.

- Etisalat's EWAP Service and a WAP enable handset people in the UAE to have a more organized life. They can have the latest news, sports scores, or stock positions. They can check out airline schedules, make a booking, pay their bills, and carry out their banking all from their WAP enabled handset.

- GPRS or General Packet Radio Service is an innovative mobile data technology utilized for accessing information via GPRS enabled mobile phones. Etisalat has also launched prepaid GPRS, following the successful launch of post-paid GPRS at the start of 2002, which has so far attracted thousands of subscribers.

- SMS 2 Fax & SMS 2 e-mail is a unique and convenient way to send SMS text messages to a fax number and to an e-mail address. The facility allows GSM customers (post-paid & prepaid) to send a text message with a maximum of 160 characters from their mobile to a fax number and to an e-mail address. Mobile telephony has made giant stride in the UAE in a relatively short time, beating fixed-line telephony. The telecommunication sector in the UAE has undergone extensive development. At the end of 2001, there were 1.9 million GSM users indicating 62 percent penetration rate, which is compatible to the most advanced countries in the world. At the end of 2005, the number of mobile phone users rose to 3.522 million, or at more than 100 percent penetration rate. Compared to other countries of the Gulf Cooperation Council (GCC), which has a mobile penetration rate of 38.16 percent, the UAE penetration rate is more than double and stands on par with many Western European nations. Similarly, a 31.23 percent fixed line penetration rate and 39.11 percent Internet penetration rate place the country squarely at the top of the list, and among leading nations worldwide in telecommunications. In absolute numbers, the UAE, at 3.522 million mobile phones, accounts for slightly more than 13 percent of mobile phones in the Arab world.[7] In addition, the UAE mobile phone penetration rate is well above that of the world average, which stands at 26 percent.[8]

Internet

While the UAE's fixed line subscription grew at an average of 7.4 percent in the past 5 years (2000–2005), and mobile telephony grew at a whopping average rate of 109 percent for the same period, Internet users swelled by 99.2 percent on average during the same period. This was due to many factors, including proliferation of Internet cafes, lower subscription and connection fees, and the introduction of the Internet to all universities and many schools in the countries. At the outset, it must be noted here that individuals who accessed the Internet at least once (regardless of subscription and connection method) are defined as users, while mobile phone penetration is an indication of the number of individuals possessing a mobile phone subscription (an individual might possess more than one phone). The history of the Internet in the UAE goes back to the year 1995 when Etisalat started providing Internet services to all categories of users, including academic, business, industry, and home users. Since 1995, the number of Internet users in UAE has grown exponentially and reached 500,000 subscribers by the end of 2005. In March 2000, Emirates Internet and Multimedia (EIM) was established as a Strategic Business Unit within Etisalat to be the first Internet service provider (ISP) in the UAE. Even though a newly established unit, EIM has been playing a strategic role in quickly responding to the needs of Internet users; gaining a competitive edge by acquiring state-of-the-art Internet backbone and infrastructures, and enabling people of all walks of life to have access to the Internet. The UAE is the most wired nation in the Arab world and one of the top nations of the online world. With a customer base of about quarter a million, EIM has around 25 percent of Internet users in the Arab world. While the number of Internet subscribers is 500,000, the actual number of Internet users in UAE is about 1,500,000 users, and more than 39 percent penetration, putting the UAE among the top 18 most wired countries in the world, even ahead of some Western European countries.[6] In addition to the dial-up customers, in 2005, Internet was also used by 1280 leased line customers, more than 800 LAN connected subscribers, and 7511 Al Shamil subscribers.[6] Also, there were almost 1700 Business One customers and 7200 Web-hosting customers. Business One is a DSL service from EIM specifically developed for small sized and medium sized businesses. Its objective is to provide high speed Internet access and

Web presence quickly, easily, and cost-effectively. The EIM, recognized as the best ISP by the Middle East Information Technology Award for 2001, is dedicated to providing state-of-the-art and best of class services.

The number of Internet dial-up service during the year 2005 was 345,000 subscribers (Exhibit 4).[9] The recent trends in 2006 show a decline in the rate of growth because the market is perhaps approaching the saturation stage, and because the launch of prepaid cards and the sprout of Internet cafes give residents the option to dial-up access without having subscription to the service.

Al Shamil's total number of subscribers for this service was 7754 at the end of the year-end 2001; this number jumped up to 20,472 subscribers in 2002 and exceeded 45,000 subscribers in 2005. In 2002, Etisalat has upgraded their Internet access for home users by launching high speed access that enabled customers to enjoy speeds of up to 2 Mbps. The service went live early in 2003, offering customers the choice of 1 Mbps or 2 Mbps, up to six times faster than the existing Al Shamil service. The new Al Shamil 1 Mbps and 2 Mbps packages are targeted at domestic Internet users who use the Web extensively. These subscribers will have superior use of high bandwidth applications from video streaming to online gaming, whilst dramatically speeding up download times of large documents. Al Shamil Cable will utilize Etisalat's HFC (Hybrid Fiber Coaxial) cable infrastructure, which is presently used to deliver E-Vision's digital cable television services. It will complement the existing DSL infrastructure, which currently delivers high-speed Internet access to homes over copper telephone lines. A1 Shamil Cable is identical to the existing DSL package, but utilizes a separate network than the copper telephone lines. The key benefit of offering high speed Internet over the cable is that the service is not limited by distance, while it is not always possible to transmit high speed Internet over very long distances via

Exhibit 4

Internet Dial-up Subscribers (Estimates from Etisalat)

Year	Subscribers (in thousands)
1997	27
1998	66
1999	127
2000	209
2001	256
2002	286
2003	316
2004	335
2005	345

the current telephone network. In addition, EIM and E-Vision have intro-duced a bundled package (A1 Shamil Cable plus E-Vision's Basic Package).

Internet Web-hosting

At the end of 2005, the UAE had 31,000 Web-hosting customers, up from 4500 customers in 2001 (*www.etisalat.co.ae*). In October 2001, E-SHOP, an online virtual business center, was launched by Etisalat and is available free of charge to customers who can, following a registration process, access and view their bills online and settle outstanding amounts using their credit cards. In addition, they can subscribe to Star Services and track the status of their applications. E-SHOP is a practical demonstration of a successful implementation of e-commerce applications provided by Comtrust, Etisalat's business unit. The development of the telecommunication sector is a govern-ment priority and it is one of the fastest growing areas in the economy. The telecommunications market remains highly competitive, being dominated by government procurement.

Computerization

Computer utilization is on the rise with current computer users moving toward upgraded and higher capacity computers. At the time of writing, industry reports indicated that the UAE ICT sector has experienced a tenfold increase since 1997. Combined ICT spending by the GCC countries (includ-ing UAE) in 2001 was US$ 6.194 billion.[10] Statistics released by Madar Research indicate that in the six GCC states there are 121 users per 100 PCs, a ratio that appears to be set to change dramatically in view of the high computer literacy in the GCC region.[11] The positive growth forecast has generated great interest among PC vendors operating in the region as they can now look forward to expanding their customer base and increased IT spending. The Internet has been a driving force for many people to buy PCs, laptops, and notebooks. The excitement surrounding the Internet has become all-pervasive and is reflected in the general trend for individuals to own a PC and in the mushrooming of Internet cafes. Sooner or later, these new converts are going to become PC owners, slowly bridging the gap between PC penetration and Internet usage.

According to early forecasts by International Data Corp, the UAE crossed the 200,000 PCs a year mark for the first time in 2003. In value terms, this would be around $320 million, out of which the portable PCs accounted for $130 million. In 2002, the corresponding figures were $280 million and just over $100 million respectively.[12]

The UAE packaged software market is estimated at $190 million, and if combined with the market for customized packages then it could be as high as $550 million. Growth areas include a range of online services including tele-banking, financial and trading services, federal and local administration services, health care, insurance, electronic commerce, multimedia publishing, as well as services to the oil and telecommunications sectors.[13] Additionally, the UAE government has embarked on an ambitious e-government initiative aimed at improving government processes and service offerings by employing Internet and other technological solutions. The launch of tablet PCs, while still a niche product, holds the promise of firmer margins for vendors in the short term. Already, notebooks represent the highest growth category and are expected to expand by more than 25 per cent in 2006. Of the overall tally, notebook shipments in the UAE reached nearly 60,000 in 2002 for a total value exceeding $100 million, according to IDC.[14]

Supercomputing capacity in the Arab world were, and still are, primarily used in geophysical analysis associated with oil and gas exploration activities. The UAE is one of the four Arab countries owning supercomputers. The ADNOC has an SGI Origin 2000 (64 processors, 32 GB of memory and one terabyte of disk space) that enable the company to carry out large high-definition, comprehensive field reservoir simulations with great speed and precision. Abu Dhabi Company for Onshore Oil Operations (ADCO) has two SGI Origin 3000s, with 32 CPU, parallel processing supercomputers used for reservoir simulations. These offer 3-D seismic explanation to aid in the most advantageous placement of wells, thus maximizing oil and gas output. The ADCO has also created the first Virtual Reality Environment Center, which is powered by a 4 CPU, 8 GB SGI ONXY supercomputer designed specifically for heavy duty graphical output. Finally, Zakum Development Corporation (ZADCO), another oil company in Abu Dhabi, has one 16 CPU SGI Origin 2000 supercomputer machine and a multiprocessor SGI ONYX 3200. In general, the UAE has one of the most advanced automated systems in the private and public sectors, whereby all financial institutions, academic entities, governmental agencies, and public service departments are equipped with technology from Web fiber optic all the way to PCs, minicomputers, databases, and office tools.[15]

Other Indicators

- *Comtrust.* While the dot com bubble may have burst, the digitization of the economy and commercial transactions is slowly but surely gaining momentum. As businesses face increasing competition, they are forced to enhance the quality of service to improve response time and curtail costs. e-Commerce helps to achieve all this. Comtrust is Etisalat's brand name for the business unit dedicated to the development of e-commerce in the UAE. Against all odds and global depression in this sector, Comtrust has enjoyed years of substantial growth, developing new alliances and establishing networks to lay the foundation for future growth. In August 2001, the Central Bank of the UAE decided to link Comtrust's e-commerce systems with its UAE exchange network. This link helped facilitate payments for goods and services through direct debit requests processed in a secured environment and transmitted over the Internet. Online payment services are at the heart of Comtrust's activities with more and more organizations opting for these services to support their online business. Financial transactions made through Comtrust have seen a sixfold increase during 2001 (*www.etisalat.co.ae*).

On June 12, 2006, Dubai e-government in association with Dubai Municipality, Etisalat, and Commercial Bank of Dubai has announced the launch of its direct debit payment system aimed at facilitating direct debit payments capitalizing on Internet banking channels. The launch of direct debit is an important evolution in the online payment scenario in UAE and will lead to a quantum jump in increasing online payment transactions for government institutions and large corporations through extension of B2B and C2B payment transactions utilizing the existing IT infrastructure of banks.

- *EBTIKAR*. This is a sophisticated, state-of-the-art cards manufacturing unit set up by Etisalat in 1996 to tap the exponentially growing card/applications market. This is the only factory of its kind in the Middle East which has its own manufacturing and personalization center for a variety of cards—memory cards, microprocessors, and magnetic cards for multimedia applications within diverse industries such as telecommunications (pay phones, GSM, Internet, and WAP), social security, health, and so on. EBTIKAR also attend to the pre-personalization requirements of clients such as the art-work and design of the cards. Prepaid cards provide a popular currency for the communication culture encouraged in the UAE. The production of prepaid cards, smart cards, and GSM SIM cards in Etisalat's EBTIKAR Card Systems has nearly doubled from 45 million cards in 2000 to 82 million cards in 2001. The number of 2002 surpassed 110 million cards. The capacity has been enhanced from 70 million cards per year to 250 million cards per year. Ebtikar's business clientele has expanded both nationally and internationally over the past 4 years (2001–2005). International clients now include Omantel, Zanzibar Telecom (Zantel), Nation Link (Somalia), and Mobitel (Sudan). In UAE, Ebtikar boasts prestigious clients such as Thuraya, Dubai Economic Department, Dubai Municipality, and Sharjah Police. The Corporation realizes the potential of card business and its contributory value of facilitating e-commerce, mobile, and international telephony.

In April 2005, Etisalat introduced the latest developments in manufacturing cards like 3G cards and the latest technology implemented in manufacturing WASEL and GSM cards, all of which reflect Etisalat's success in offering best services for its customers. The new SIM card has an EEPROM memory capacity of 64 Kb and it supports GSM functionality. These features make it an ideal SIM card platform to migrate from 2G to new 3G services. As the new SIM card complies with both GSM and 3G requirements, all the mobile services offered today can be accessed with this new card. The card enables the operator to offer a wide range of value added services such as m-commerce, m-banking, as well as information, entertainment, and gaming services. The 3G is a multi-application and multi-standard card supporting both ETSI and ISO standards. This makes it easy to implement different types of services on a single card. 3G cards offer an open application toolkit platform to develop new applications and services.[16]

- *Data services.* The demand for data services continues to grow, 44 percent in 2001, primarily through ATM, Frame Relay, leased circuits, and ISDN connections. Revenues from data services contribute up to 7 percent of total revenues of Etisalat. The major drives of growth were ISDN facilities, SMS and Al Mersal messaging services, ADSL services, and EMIX. Data services are expected to continue to grow due to tariff reductions and introduction of new services. Virtual private networks (VPN) has shown much promise. During the year 2001, the ISDN basic rate service was at 2954 connections, and increased to 4565 in 2002 and 4259 in 2003 (latest figures available). The growth rate of ISDN service is likely to be affected when the public acceptance for ADSL AL Shamil increases more.
- *EMIX emirates.* Internet exchange-EMIX is the first network access point (NAP), private or public in the Middle East, and one of the first NAPs in Africa and Asia. The stated mission of EMIX is to become the regional hub providing all neighboring countries with access to the Internet via fiber optic at competitive prices. EMIX is developing its network to meet ISP's current and future requirements in the region by increasing its bandwidth which has reached 1.1 Gbps in 2003. In addition to Etisalat's own EIM, other customers include ISPs from Pakistan, Zanzibar, Sudan, Kuwait, and Oman.
- *Etisalat Internet Data Center (eIDC).* In a bid to gain market share in the international hosting market, EIM, the ISP business unit of Etisalat announced in July 2002 the launch of their hosting service. Co-location and telehousing are the first Internet hosting services to be offered under the "EIM Hosting Service brand."

The EIM Hosting Service offers a set of services named "remote hand service" such as power cycling, environmental control, and tape backup insertion. These are just a few of the options available. As more companies move to the UAE to conduct business, they will find an e-infrastructure that supports the most demanding of requirements. The EIM Hosting Service allows companies from around the world to place their servers in a controlled environment close to their customers in the Middle East. This will dramatically reduce the time it takes for regional customers to access the sites and will increase reliability. The new service is targeted at large corporations who rely heavily on their Internet presence in the region and need to ensure a minimal risk of "downtime" or security threats. In addition, companies use this service for disaster recovery. The EIM Hosting Service also provides physical security such as restricted access to the site and CCTV, which is heavily deployed to protect the servers. A controlled operations environment in which to operate the servers keeps the servers at exactly the correct temperature with fire protection systems in place to guard against damage. The eIDC has been established in two locations, Abu Dhabi and Dubai, as a best of breed physical and technical environment to provide centralized redundant repository for secure data processing, storage management, and dissemination of data for telecommunication. Services offered at both locations include secure housing option with a virtual data center, high availability storage option with guaranteed quality service, content hosting distribution option, utilizing clusters deployed at regional data centers for quick response, consultancy option, systems security option, and secure solution with VPN hardware and software. In addition, eIDC offers application option and WAP content and applications to its customers.

- *Emirates Data Clearing House (EDCH).* The aim of (EDCH) is to provide an efficient means of exchanging billing and accounting data (TAP files) between the GSM service providers as per the GSM MoU standards. The EDCH eliminates the need for each GSM operator to establish multiple electronic links with every roaming partner (multiple destinations). Instead, EDCH provides a single point of support to service providers, and offers a range of services associated with international roaming. The EDCH, the only such facility in the region, is being increasingly used by international GSM operators, and currently serves around 16 operators in 12 countries handling around 136 million calls during a year.

Investments

- *Thuraya Satellite Telecommunications Company.* Thuraya offers cost-effective satellite-based mobile telephone services to nearly one-third of the globe. Through its dynamic dual mode handsets and satellite payphones, Thuraya enhances freedom of movement and connectivity. Thuraya's US$1 billion regional mobile telecommunications via satellite (GMPCS) system will help meet the need for affordable, high quality mobile phone services to urban hubs as well as remote communities. Through partnership with leading national telecom and mobile communications companies, Thuraya provides blanket-to-blanket coverage to more than 110 countries in Europe, the Middle East, North and Central Africa, the CIS countries, and South Asia: a landmass inhabited by an estimated 2.3 billion people. Subscribers can access Thuraya's mobile satellite system through service providers, who are either national GSM network companies or local telecom operators. Thuraya in fact complements national GSM networks, allowing subscribers to remain connected to their national mobile networks, and to access Thuraya's system whenever their preferred national network is out of reach. Thuraya offers satellite, cellular (GSM) service, and location determination system (GPS) in a single dual mode handset that is lightweight, elegant, and easy to use. The dynamic handset offers voice, data, fax, and short messaging services. Thuraya was founded in the UAE in 1997 by a consortium of leading national telecommunications operators and international investment houses. The turnkey project was built by US satellite manufacturer Boeing Satellite Systems, formerly Hughes. The Thuraya-1 satellite was successfully launched on board a Sea Launch Zenit-3SL rocket from the equator in the middle of the Pacific Ocean on October 21, 2000. The launch was a record success, as it was the first satellite initiated from the Middle East and also the satellite was the heaviest to be launched ever.

The Thuraya system includes a second satellite which was launched in early 2003 while a third satellite is contracted to Boeing Satellite Systems to expand system capacity. The Primary Gateway in Sharjah, UAE, serves the entire Thuraya coverage area, and plans are underway to establish additional national gateways at other locations as necessary. After the successful launch of its first satellite in 2000, Thuraya has made considerable progress in preparation for a full service launch, driven by the advantages associated with geostationary satellite systems such as lower cost per minute, wide area coverage, and long life of satellite. Thuraya has already signed about 70 Service Provider Agreements and launched its services in several countries including UAE, UK, Italy, Sudan, Qatar, France, Romania, and Denmark. Thuraya mobile phones are dual mode in that they can operate as a GSM phone when there is a GSM signal. In addition, Thuraya phone offers voice, fax, data, and short messaging services and can even pinpoint its position using the GPS facility.

- *E-Vision*–Emirates Cable TV Multimedia (LLC)—The end user services for Internet, telephony, and entertainment are breaking loose from their dependency on distribution network. In the future, advanced television sets, hybrid terminals, and hand held equipment would be used for making calls, watching videos and television programs, accessing the Web, and even as a computer. The Emirates Cable TV and Multimedia (LLC), branded as E-Vision in UAE, is a strategic investment that has made significant progress over a period of less than 5 years. Currently, E-Vision offers 200 national and international television channels, ranging from movies to sports and documentary to music E-Vision officials have recorded a 1500% sales increase between 2000 and 2005. With the growth in the cable and satellite market of the UAE, the company now holds a 60% market share. E-Vision currently broadcasts almost 200 channels in 21 languages, with integrated packages including Showtime, Orbit, Pehla, and Firstnet. E-Vision is planning to invest Dh2.5 billion in 15 years. According to industry analysts' IMS Research, worldwide shipments of digital cable and DTH set-top boxes are set to increase by 15% over the next 5 years; this means 74.8 million units will be sold by the end of 2010, and estimates this market is forecast to reach over 41 million households.[17] E-Vision is investing in the future of the community; it has created two exclusive channels e-junior for children and e-xplor as a documentary channel that are tailor made to the tastes and requirements of its customers in the UAE. E-Vision provides the highest quality services on the first fully digitalized cable telecommunication system in the regions, utilizing hybrid fiber coaxial network and transmitting programs with enhanced picture quality. The network that is owned by Etisalat and partially leased to E-Vision has already reached several thousand homes in Abu Dhabi, Dubai, and Sharjah. E-Vision is now focusing on its programming and marketing efforts and has entered into agreements with re-sellers like Jumbo Electronics and Eurostar. In addition, it has entered into co-marketing agreements with National Bank of Abu Dhabi and Standard Chartered Bank. In 2002, E-Vision introduced "pay-per-view" (PPV) services, on around 16 channels.
- *E-Marine*—Emirates Telecommunication Marine Services (FZE)— E-marine is a wholly owned subsidiary of Etisalat, which operates two cable ships, *Umm Al Anber* and *C.S. Etisalat*, for submarine cable installation, repair, and maintenance projects. Because of E-Marine's extensive experience in local and international submarine cables and because of its geographically strategic location, regional customers find its services reasonably priced and of high quality. Recently, E-Marine has started focusing its resources on the oil and gas sector and has successfully completed a major project in submarine power cable installation for Zadco.

In line with its customer-centric orientation ad strategy and being cognizant that security and privacy are of paramount concerns to its customers, on June 3, 2006 Etisalat announced the availability of free software for Internet users in the UAE to alert them against Internet Dial scams. Once downloaded and installed the software automatically launches every time users start their computer. It will monitor any dial-up attempt made by the PC and alert users if there is an unauthorized attempt to dial a number outside a "safe" list of numbers. When such suspicious activity is detected a pop-up window will warn users with an alert message stating the identity of the number that their modem is attempting to dial.

Soft Infrastructure

The government of the UAE has been a leader in creating the right and appropriate soft infrastructure, including the legal and regulatory environments, in order to ensure success for its IT initiatives. A number of laws were enacted and passed during the past decade, with the objective of fostering a safe environment for businesses and investors. In 1992, the UAE federal government passed three laws in regard to intellectual property—a copyright law, a trademark law, and a patent law. These three pieces of legislation have made the UAE largely clean of selling pirated computer software because of a strong enforcement policy. In addition, the UAE is a member of the World Intellectual Property Organization (WIPO) and has joined the Paris Convention for the Protection of Industrial Property. The UAE has fully ratified the Agreement on Trade-Related Aspects of Intellectual Property Rights (TRIPS Agreement), which is one of the main agreements of the World Trade Organization (WTO). The primary difference for the UAE in terms of copyright law as compared to other nations is that any published material must have a registered copyright before being commercialized in the country. In 2001, a new law was issued in Dubai relevant to the use of computers in criminal procedures. Pursuant to this new law, Dubai Law No. 5 of 2001, documents with electronic signatures will be admissible as evidence in criminal investigations. The provisions of the law acknowledge signatures of individuals acquired through the use of computers and other means of IT for purposes of proof in criminal cases. In addition, in 2002, and in an attempt to regulate electronic transactions and boost users' confidence, another law was issued for the state of Dubai, Law No. 2 of 2002, concerning electronic transactions and commerce. The Electronic Transactions and Commerce Law abides by international principles associated with e-commerce and dealings and the latest development in this field. The 39 article law is a combination of the United Nations guidelines and local qualifications and is intended to: (1) smooth the progress of e-correspondence through trusty e-books; (2) eliminate any impediments to e-commerce and other e-transactions; (3) smooth the submission of e-documents to government departments and institutions; (4) trim down the number of submissions of e-correspondence and amendments thereto; (5) set standardized criteria for certification and security of e-correspondence; (6) raise the public's confidence in security and soundness of e-books and correspondence; and (7) improve the development of e-commerce and other transactions, locally and internationally, through using e-signature.

Federal Law No. 1 of 2006 concerning Electronic Transactions and Commerce Law and Federal Law No. 2 of 2006 (the Cyber Crime Law) were issued earlier in June 2006 under the decree of President His Highness Sheikh Khalifa Bin Zayed Al Nahyan. The new laws lay the foundation for legitimizing e-commerce and fighting misuse of cyberspace and new technologies. The federal laws reflect the UAE government's commitment to provide legal protection for Internet related investments and ensure that the legal system meets the challenges of the digital economy. The new laws represent a bold initiative from the UAE government. For the implementation of these laws to be effective, however, it is critical for the corporate community to be aware of their implications. Only then will the efficiency of the laws be tested.

The Federal laws have introduced a number of international standards while at the same time extended the relevance of existing laws to the electronic domain. With the rising threat of cyber crimes, especially identity theft, it is important to raise awareness about the legal recourse that companies have in the event of any incident. The new legislation provides a sound platform on which to build the regulatory framework. It does not, however, address some aspects of e-commerce and electronic transactions such as privacy, jurisdiction, data protection, domain names, and decency. The UAE government needs to promulgate more cyber laws to fill gaps in the existing legislation so that the legal system is able to meet the needs of the evolving digital economy.

The law creates a business and regulatory environment in which technology, electronic commerce, Internet, and media companies will be able to operate globally out of the UAE with significant competitive advantages over local and regional competitors.

In November 2005, a new initiative to create industry standards for commercial websites was announced. The Arab Internet Standards Organization (InterStandards) initiative has the mission of accelerating the development of the region's Internet industry by developing a set of new standards in e-marketing, e-design, e-content, e-security, and e-solutions for commercial websites.[18]

Supported by DIC and eHosting DataFort (eHDF), the initiative seeks to structure these benchmarks through a certification program that adheres to British Standards Institution (BSI) standards. The standards will be promoted among the industry through a comprehensive marketing program to be conducted in association with DIC and eHDF.

InterStandards will have five standardization modules:

1. e-design and structure module
2. e-marketing module
3. e-media/content module
4. e-security module
5. e-solutions/Web coding module.

These standards will act as guidelines for quality in the Web development sector and serve as unified industry benchmarks for evaluating Internet websites. They will also help create a rich environment for the Internet industry to thrive and grow and help accelerate the development of the Internet industry in the UAE and the region. It is expected that InterStandards will address the various inadequacies plaguing the Arab world's Internet industry. Very few Internet portals in the world follow the right standards for structure and design. Poor online payment security in the world and lack of online product lines and fulfillment logistics on Internet portals are hampering the development of e-commerce. Very few portals follow industry regulations for traffic analysis and banner management to create a proper e-marketing medium. Very few portals also offer genuine content and use the right technology. This new initiative will work to address and drive quality in each of these areas.

InterStandards promises to bring wide-ranging benefits to users and developers of websites. The standards will increase confidence levels for users while certified websites will be able to drive traffic and raise advertising revenue for their site. Advertisers will have access to more credible e-marketing data through audited website traffic statistics while content providers can tap into enhanced opportunities for digital branding and web development. The standards are also expected to raise the quality of e-payment and e-security systems, and e-marketing solutions deployed on the web. These in turn will have several spinoffs for retailers, logistics providers, and the credit market, all stimulating the growth of the entire value chain of the Web-based industry.

Talent Base

It is well known that the transition to an information/knowledge economy can generate demands on the educational system beyond the mastery of basic subject matters, numerical proficiency, and literacy. Success in the knowledge economy requires behavioral skills such as the ability to think critically and be equipped for lifelong learning—much of it is informal—a constant upgrading of skills. The success of worthy regional IT initiatives depends not only on setting up IT councils, investing in Research & Development (R&D) of the new information infrastructure, or creating the right legal environment. These are necessary but not sufficient conditions. It is equally, if not more, important to improve the skills of the human resource component in the country. Developing human capacity and creating human resources must be a primary task for the UAE; however attractive it is, in the short term, to import skilled labor instead. To help narrow the gap between the educational system and the requirements of skills needed in the workplace, and in its efforts toward the development of skilled labor force, a number of initiatives to attract and develop skilled workers undertaken by the federal and local governments recently are worth mentioning here. Efforts of the government have been aimed at three different, but complementary, directions: (1) attracting a pool of skills from the region; (2) developing the national talents through a sound educational system; and (3) promoting executive training programs. As mentioned earlier, one of the primary goals of the UAE government is economic diversification into the non-oil sector. Therefore, the government has implemented policies and programs to encourage citizens to pursue higher education, specifically training in engineering and IT. Primary, secondary, and higher education is provided gratis to all Emirati citizens. Currently, Emiratis comprise only between 15 and 20 percent of the population and even less of the labor market. Furthermore, the IT labor market is composed primarily of expatriates. Over the last decade, the UAE has become the hub for telecommunications and IT in the Middle East and is therefore attracting IT professionals from around the globe. The UAE is very receptive to inflows of educated business people (both men and women). As a result, the expatriate community is one of the largest in the world, proportional to the population. What makes the UAE attractive to IT professionals is the proximity of the country to India and Pakistan, from the East, and Egypt and Jordan from the West; countries with abundant IT skills. An exact estimate of the number of local IT professionals entering the market each year is unknown; however, there is not a significant risk of "brain drain." Considering the UAE is the hub of IT in the Middle East, the opposite is true. More college graduates shun the private sector and prefer to join family businesses or seek work in the public sector. Emiratis make up almost 70 percent of the government labor force while expatriates primarily populate the private sector. To meet the challenge of the evolving telecommunications and computer industries in the UAE, the government places a strong emphasis on education. The UAE authorities officially recognize only six universities, even though 33 private universities reside in the country. The UAE students comprise only about 10–15 percent of enrollment. In addition to these higher education institutions, Etisalat has placed much importance on the development of engineering education and training facilities, particularly in the field of communications, in order to encourage the reliance on indigenous sources. In this direction, Etisalat College of Engineering has remained dedicated to the engineering education of Emiratis and has already produced more than 300 graduates. This institution has served as an important source of national engineers who are appointed in management cadres in the corporation and some are sent abroad for postgraduate specialization. Exhibit 5 shows the number of students graduating in the various IT fields, from the major universities and colleges in the UAE.

By developing and instigating a number of initiatives, the UAE has made a great progress toward executive training in IT and related fields in the past few years. One such initiative is Knowledge Village (KV). The KV is an ambitious initiative, undertaken by the Dubai government, aimed at building a vibrant connected learning community that will develop the region's knowledge workforce and catalyze new economic growth and development. The KV, with facilities covering an area of a million square feet, provides a complete environment and infrastructure for a variety of organizations

Exhibit 5

IT Graduates in the UAE

Graduation Year	University	Number of Graduating Students in a Certain Major				Higher Diploma	Diploma	Certificate Program
		MIS	Computer Science	Computer Engineering	IT			
1997–1998	HCT					70		249
	UAE University		2					
1998–1999	HCT					141	171	525
	UAE University		95					
1999–2000	HCT					176	201	305
	UAE University		131					
2000–2001	Sharjah University	50	20					
	HCT	17		1	28	171	314	593
	UAE University		174					
2001–2002	Sharjah University	61	24	35				
	HCT	23	13	27	61	222	330	856
	UAE University		139					
2002–2003 (Fall 2002)	Sharjah University	74	28	33				
	HCT	13	7	13				

to create and disseminate knowledge, and to help SMEs. Construction of the physical infrastructure was completed in 2004, and currently houses a diverse community of knowledge focused organizations. These include a Media Academy, an Innovation Center, eLearning institutions, institutions that provide graduate and postgraduate education, R&D organizations, a multimedia library, corporate training institutions, scientific and technology institutes, certification and testing organizations, and incubators. One of the key objectives of the KV is to raise the abilities of the region's knowledge workforce to compete and innovate in the global economy. The learning community at KV will facilitate increased access to world-class learning opportunities in a variety of disciplines for student and corporate communities. The Village will have a "brick-and-click" infrastructure that supports both traditional and new modes of learning. Members of the learning community will have access to a host of shared facilities. These include modern classrooms and computer labs, a multimedia library, auditorium and conference facilities, IT and media laboratories, retail area, and dormitory.

One of the first projects at KV was the setting up of Dubai Police's E-TQM College that was inaugurated in October 2002. Dubai Police has been at the forefront of Dubai's drive toward e-government. With the E-TQM College, it is taking the lead in eLearning, which helps the workforce better negotiate the learning curve involved in providing e-government services. E-TQM will provide total quality management courses online to professionals in both private and government sectors and to SMEs. Another KV based project is the agreement announced in September 2002 between Purdue University and the Village, and which calls for Purdue to offer its top ranked International Executive MBA program to the Gulf region's KV. The International Master in Management (IMM) program is a collaborative executive program jointly offered by four leading business schools in the United States and Europe. Apart from Purdue University, these include the Netherlands based Tias Business School, The Budapest University of Economic Sciences and Public Administration, and the Europe based ESCP-EAP. The program is ranked 17th worldwide among Global Executive MBA programs. Another skill development initiative was undertaken in June 2002, when DIC announced its joint venture with e-College from the United States to form "Knowledge Access," a company that will make education more accessible to the Gulf region and surrounding areas. Knowledge Access is located in DIC and provides technology and support services for academic institutions and corporate training organizations to build full online programs. An important initiative in the "skill development" category is the "Mohammed Bin Rashid Establishment for Young Business Leaders" (the Establishment) which is responsible for co-ordinating a comprehensive program that aims to favorably impact and influence the perception of UAE nationals toward entrepreneurship and lower the barriers of entry for new entrepreneurs. The Mohammed Bin Rashid Establishment for Young Business Leaders was launched on June 12, 2002, as the first initiative of the Dubai Development and Investment Authority.

During 2006, three of the leading universities in the world (George Mason, Sorbonne, and INSEAD) have started or are in the process of starting new campuses in UAE. In 2005, George Mason University opened a satellite campus in UAE. It is in the process of building a permanent campus, Emirates Highway, at the Umm Al Quwain-Ras Al Khaimah border to be opened in 2009. The Ras Al Khaimah campus is currently offering four undergraduate degree programs, BS in Biology, BS in Business Administration, BS in Electronics and Communications Engineering, and a BS in Nursing. All credits earned at the campus will be fully transferable to George Mason University in the United States.

France's Sorbonne University will open its first venture outside France this October (2006), when it opens a branch campus in Abu Dhabi. An agreement signed between the French Education Minister and the UAE Higher Education Minister that Abu Dhabi will invest between US$20 and $30 million to set up the UAE campus of the Sorbonne. The Sorbonne campus in Abu Dhabi will initially enroll 200 students with a goal of building its capacity to 1500 over the first 3 years. The university will utilize a secular liberal arts curriculum with a focus on French language, history, geography, literature, and philosophy.

The latest development is a new agreement between INSEAD Business School and the Abu Dhabi Education Council where the two parties signed a Memorandum of Understanding (MoU) outlining plans for the establishment of an INSEAD campus in the Emirati capital. According to the agreement, INSEAD–Abu Dhabi will, by October 2006, be offering executive business education classes while also placing a strong emphasis on conducting research.

Country Readiness

As stated earlier, country readiness is defined as "initiatives facilitating the change in the transformation process" into an information/knowledge society. In this section, a number of initiatives are presented and their impacts are discussed.

Dubai Internet City[19]

Dubai Internet City's (DIC) objective is to nurture the growth of the new economy and the IT industry as a whole, by providing a cutting-edge, high bandwidth, Internet services and telecommunications, intelligent infrastructure, real estate, company registration, and facilitation, to support any level of service a client might wish to use for efficient operations. The City, which completed its first phase (in 2001) in a record 364 days, gives tenants a technology platform fit for the twenty-first century. It also fulfils the vision of the government of the UAE to provide the e-world with a world-class ground base for every virtual company. The DIC has already attracted more than 700 firms, mostly international companies operating in various IT industry sectors. The number of companies applying to work in the City has run well beyond preliminary expectations. The interest of the international IT industry in the City culminated in decisions by many leading firms, such as Oracle, Cisco, Microsoft, Siemens, and IBM, to set up their facilities there. The City is well equipped to play a pivotal role in supporting and promoting IT related activities within a vast geographical area covering the Gulf, Middle East, the Indian Subcontinent, Central Asia, North and South African countries. The City is also keen on creating an ideal environment for growth and flourishing of IT projects—an environment wherein software and multimedia developers, IT firms, communications companies, service providers, and suppliers all work side by side, thereby providing a solid base, not only for the growth of operations of each company within the City, but also for the creation of new business opportunities. Companies operating within the City enjoy a set of investment promotion incentives including 100 percent foreign ownership of projects, corporate tax exemptions, streamlined government procedures, 50 years land lease contracts, competitive prices for rendered services, cost-effective business sites, in addition to facilities for financing, training, education, and research. The initial DIC complex was established at an estimated cost of $272 million, provided by the Dubai government in the form of land in a prime area of Dubai; in addition, the Dubai government is the guarantor of a $500 million loans put together by a consortium of banks for the purpose of completing the infrastructural support for the project; this will ultimately act as an "incubator" for e-commerce in the region. It is estimated that private investors, representing 700 firms, some of them from American, European, Asian, and Australian business communities, would spend three times the amount contributed by the Dubai government to set up their own businesses at the complex. In terms of eligibility, all Information Communication and Technology (ICT) companies who would like to expand their operations to cover the footprint of DIC. Benefits from the DIC project have many spillover effects; for partners, it enhances the chances of success, raises credibility, helps improve skills, creates synergy among client-firms, facilitates access to mentors, information, and seed capital. In addition, DIC offers more than 1000 different services to their clients. According to Dr. Omar Bin Soleiman, at an early stage in the project, initial investment was set at 500,000 dirhams; but in an effort to help young entrepreneurs, this requirement was reduced to 1000 dirhams.

The most benefits, though, DIC offers those businesses opportunities for acquiring innovations and interacting with other businesses that might support, complement, or even compete with them in the same market. From the government's perspective, DIC helps promote regional development, generate jobs and incomes, and becomes a demonstration of the political commitment to SMEs. As for the local community, in addition to job creation, DIC has created an entrepreneurial culture, especially among young university graduates. Law No. 6 of 2002 was enacted covering the establishment and protection of the DIC's telecommunications network. Issued on November 10, 2002, the 12 article legislation has set out missions the DIC should carry out in co-operation with other concerned authorities to provide telecommunications services to individuals and companies via a fiber optic network, and land and air stations.

Technology Parks

Technology parks are part of urban development plan and encompass a university; research laboratories, which may be associated with firms or research institutes; new technology firms, including start-up SMEs; testing and analytical facilities; a variety of services for technology transfer; and financing association; and governmental agencies. The first of its kind in the Gulf region, announced in February 2005, the Dubai Biotechnology and Research Park (DuBiotech) is a science and business park dedicated to the biotech industry, set within a free zone infrastructure. DuBiotech has two main areas of interest. The first is the Foundation for Research and Innovation (FRI) which will be the main arm focusing on government funded R&D. The FRI will initially focus on medical research and genetics, plant biotechnology encompassing food and agricultural biotech, environmental biotech, and equine related biotechnology. Other areas include drug discovery, stem cell research, infectious diseases, and forensic research. The second arm of DuBiotech aims to set up a biotechnology industry cluster with the appropriate infrastructure, facilities and service for incubators, R&D labs, biotech related educational institutions, suppliers, biotech related manufacturing companies, and organizations from other sectors in the industry. The benefits of the park are manifold. First, it provides tenants with technological support, involving ready access to relevant and up-to-date technological knowledge, through contact with a university research center. This is what is referred to as "technology brokering." Secondly, the Park will support its tenants by establishing and providing business linkages, advice and services as well as general assistance. The latter function, in particular, could cover a wide range of contacts, ranging from basic building refurbishment and maintenance, secretarial and administrative services, advanced business and financial counseling to accessing sophisticated research equipment and instrumentation. The Park is envisioned simultaneously as an effective instrument for local development and technology transfer, stimulators of innovation, and seedbeds for new business enterprises. It is hoped it will create enormous success in employment creation, new technology generation, and as catalyst for enterprises. The Park has been designed and developed after years of extensive research, and as part of phase one it is located in Jebel Ali Free Zone, covering a land area of 3 square kilometers. The Park is a clear indication of the UAE, in general, and Dubai, in particular, strategic focus on its role as an international IT center. Through this project, the country will utilize the gains made in both technology and knowledge-based systems in a specific and focused way, which when channeled and applied to industry will benefit the region as a whole. The Park will enhance the development of the knowledge based economy, providing a wide range of opportunities for technology companies. It is designed to develop industrially based knowledge economy "clusters." These clusters are developed in strategic industrial sectors that will stimulate economic growth and ultimately boost the competitive edge in the region. Clusters will include a range of R&D and product development companies, laboratories, incubators, training institutes, technology transfer, and technology acceleration organizations. The focus of the Park will center on "demand-driven" industrial technologies, such as desalination; companies providing services associated with industrial technology from across the United Kingdom, Switzerland, Japan, USA, and Korea have also expressed interest and will potentially bring with them a range of activities that include laboratory services, renovation services for industrial plants, university research and technical services and engineering, and R&D projects. The Park will also focus on attracting business accelerators, consultancy firms and venture capital groups in addition to manufacturing and industrial companies. High tech services such as design, consultancy, prototype production of incubated innovations, industry, and spinoffs will also hold viable positions in the Park. In addition, environmental companies will focus on water resource management, biosaline products and technology, pollution management and control systems, recycling industries and "clean energy" industries such as solar and wind technology.

Health technology businesses will concentrate on Biotech products and processes, pharmaceuticals and medical devices, and equipment. The Park is in the process of forming strategic alliances with a number of local universities and research institutes. International organizations such as the International High Technologies Consortium from Russia have indicated their interest. The Park is also in the process of forming strategic ties with potential investment organizations and banks. Renowned services sector in the country is also expected to see business increase as the Park develops.

Furthermore, the type of industrial companies in the Park will potentially provide benefits to both the UAE and the region in terms of the study of pollution, improved safety automation with tailor-made intelligent control systems, and an improved supply of components through central warehouses for desalination and other industries and components. Especially important for long term development of the country and the region are the employment opportunities that the Park will offer. In line with Dubai's focus as a proponent of the high tech and new education strategy, and with the cooperation of universities locally and throughout the region, skilled national graduates in specialized industries will be able to find lucrative employment in the Park's industries. The Park will not only raise the expectations, skills, and abilities of the region's workforce, utilizing local talent as a source of long-term competitive advantage, but also bridge the gap between industrial viability and the application of knowledge.

Dubai Silicon Oasis

On December 29, 2002, General Sheikh Mohammed bin Rashid Al Maktoum, then Dubai Crown Prince and UAE Defense Minister, announced the establishment of the Dubai Silicon Oasis (DSO) for the global semiconductor industry. Spread across 6.5 million square meters, DSO will also encompass the US$1.7 billion Dubai factory of Communicant, the joint venture between Intel, the Dubai government, and the German government of Brandenburg State. Germany's project cost US$1.35 billion, and the DSO construction will begin within 6 months after finalizing the designs by experts including designers of other silicon parks. The Oasis was launched in January 2005 and production should commence by 2007. In collaboration with the German IHP technological center, an Institute of Technology will be set up at DSO to train and develop local technical expertise. The DSO will offer several programs with initial focus on communication and system-on-chip design complemented on technology management. Dubai Silicon Incubation Centre (DSIC) at DSO will provide a facility for broadband and wireless incubation for the development and commercialization of intellectual property and will help create regional enterprises at the top end of the technology spectrum. The incubation center will partner with several high-end global R&D centers and educational institutions. A portal will be based at DSO to provide career management and recruitment services to the global semiconductor industry professionals. Around 320 companies will be able to access it. As for the agreements with Communicant project partners, it is reported that 240 UAE nationals will be provided with masters studies in microelectronics within 10 years and another 250 nationals will be trained over a period of 12 years in Innovations for High Performance (IHP) microelectronics and the Germany-based company (Communicant) on two-year contracts (www.dso.ae).

Electronic government

The UAE has, in the past 3 years, made momentous advances in bringing its services online, for both business and individual users. Behind this evolution are two aspects fundamental for the development and success of e-government initiatives in the developing world: the political determination of UAE leaders and the availability of pertinent resources. In this section, we will cover (1) the e-government initiative at the federal level and (2) the e-government initiative in Dubai. The e-government project of the UAE government was initiated by His Highness Sheikh Hamdan Bin Rashid Al Makhtom, UAE Minister of Finance and Deputy Ruler of Dubai. e-Government applications were spearheaded by the Ministry of Finance and Industry since 1997. These services are aimed to reduce bureaucracy and allow customers to complete their services at a faster rate. The following are some of the services that are currently in place:

- *Websites development.* This is the first step toward being a customer focused government. Information and services pertaining to each ministry is posted on the UAE government's website. The general public or businesses can interact and transact their needs over these websites. This website is developed, maintained, and hosted by the Information Systems Department of the Ministry of Finance. The introduction of these websites became the catalyst for the integration of various government services offered by various ministries. By just clicking to a single website (www.uae.gov.ae), the public can navigate through the entire federal government and also understand the various services offered by the different ministries. Important information is always updated. Recently, this website has undergone major improvements in terms of design, look, and content.
- *Electronic mail(e-mail).* Electronic mail was introduced to improve communication between employees and also to reduce paperwork in an effort to make a transition to "paperless" offices. Almost all employees have an e-mail account and this has tremendously improved cycle time for making decisions. In some ministries, e-mail has replaced the normal "internal memo" as a formal tool for information dissemination throughout the Ministry. The introduction of electronic mail has also created much needed awareness concerning the importance of "IT" in creating an effective government. This transformation of mind-set has become one of the most important impetuses for introducing government wide e-government initiatives.

- *Financial applications.* Similar to other governments all over the world, the traditional accountability on "control and measure" lies with the Ministry of Finance. Thus, this became one of the important applications introduced to automate financial services provided by the Ministry. The Ministry is currently using a central financial system using NCR UNIX Platform. This system is now undergoing major changes as the Ministry of Finance is introducing the new "Performance Base Budgeting System" where accountability is now decentralized. All financial processes will be re-engineered and "financial personnel" re-trained on how to operate this new system. This is a classic example where "IT" is used as a tool in re-inventing government. All financial processes have been re-engineered and, currently, the appropriate IT applications are being evaluated. The e-Dirham, which became functional and online in 2003, is a payment tool devised by the Ministry of Finance and industry in order to facilitate collection of federal revenues, providing the government with a secure payment method and providing the public with a convenient payment tool. The e-Dirham card which is readily available all over the UAE not only improves the financial transaction but also provides "on-site" transfer of payments between the public and the government agencies. Front service government employees do not have to burden themselves with the security of "physical money" and with this system the government could balance the revenue by the end of the day without looking at the physical books. The e-Dirham has its own secure payment system guaranteed by the government and the payment card can be used for any government services. This project has been very successful and the UAE has had enquiries from many other countries in the region to implement similar systems.
- *Electronic transaction.* Since the UAE government has gone deep into implementing the e-government project, the Ministry of Finance and Industry started to offer online services to its customers and the public through the new electronic services which are e-procurement and eSinaee, where the customer can register, select the service, apply, fill in the forms, upload the documents and pay online using the e-Dirham card, and finally receive the services. The e-procurement provides a mechanism for government agencies and businesses to transact electronically. The Ministry is in the midst of further reviewing the "supply-chain process" within the government. By re-engineering the supply chain systems, the Ministry will eventually create a total "electronic procurement" where this application will be linked to the government financial and asset management system. The eSinaee is an application specially introduced to manufacturing entities within the UAE. This will allow factory owners not only to have the latest information regarding industrial promotion, but also to apply for tax exemption and other

industrial services. The introduction of all the above services has created awareness on the importance of IT for making government administrative services more efficient and effective. More importantly, this has paved the path for the introduction of the overall e-government implementation phase, learning from what has been learned from the initial application implemented. Among those is the importance of having an overall e-government strategy in place. Given the commitment from the highest authority in e-government, a high steering committee has been formed to drive this project. One item was clear among the members of this committee and that is "IT" should be used as a tool to re-invent and reform current "management" of the government. The federal e-government project adds to the convenience, accessibility, and quality of interactions between the federal government, businesses, and the people residing in the UAE. More importantly, e-government will improve information flows and processes within all government ministries.

Criteria for evaluating e-government progress are levels of integration and customization of basic e-services on a single government gateway. Dubai's performance in these areas is notable. The Dubai government has a Web portal, at www.dubai.ae, which allows access to services of various government departments, and is working on integrating these services in order to present them on a single user-friendly or user customizable interface. The portal was launched in October 2001, and has undergone several improvements since. The portal included a comprehensive list of online services available through Dubai government websites, a search facility, and downloadable application forms for government services, an ePay service, as well as eJawaz which allows the users to use all public services without having to register with each relevant government department separately. ePay allows users of government services to pay all charges electronically through a single site. Dubai portal has the infrastructure required for the integration of all government services, but many government departments have not yet made full use of this infrastructure. The Dubai e-government initiative, which was launched in 2000, has accelerated adoption of e-services by many government bodies to an extent that the UAE ranks 21st worldwide in a United Nations report which evaluated e-government performance of 190 countries in 2003. The initiative—the most advanced of its kind in the Arab world—marked a new phase, characterized by a strong drive toward improving the UAE's ability to provide government services through the Internet. As the initiative has gained momentum, increasing the pace at which government services have been coming online, wider segments of the households, businesses, and government sectors are feeling the benefits. The online availability of government services has made it much easier to access related information and has drastically reduced the time required—by businesses and individuals alike—to carry out transactions with government bodies. The benefit to government comes in terms of increased efficiency, and ultimately reduced expenses on provision of public services. One indicator is the percentage of basic public services available.

To summarize, the systems and processes of government are being re-engineered to capitalize on the potential benefits of new ICT applications. This process re-engineering has re-defined the way each government department performs its tasks in the new ICT environment. Specifically, the introduction of e-government has provided the following outcomes:

- Innovative services
- Managed government information as a strategic resource
- A government that is closer and more transparent to the people and businesses
- Functional integration within the government
- Effective information flow to facilitate policy development and implementation

To manage the e-government project effectively, the initiative has been phased out into three:

1. Creating an e-government strategy (completed in June 2003)
2. Contracting out the chosen e-government application (completed in November 2005)
3. Implementing the chosen e-government application (in progress).

Leadership

The leadership of the UAE federal government has been very supportive in the quest of creating an information/knowledge based economy. All the initiatives covered in the previous sections were instigated by the government and supported both politically and financially by the top political leaders of the Emirates. In summary, recent efforts at diversifying the economy in the direction of an information society have been largely successful, and proved UAE's leadership's true commitment to building a "high tech" economy based on information and knowledge. In addition to the superb job the UAE political leaders are doing in encouraging and driving the development of the information/knowledge society in their country, they are ready to help a lending hand to other Arab less unfortunate economies. At the Arab ICT Summit in Dubai (October 13, 2002) General Sheikh Mohammed bin Rashid Al Maktoum, then Dubai Crown Prince and UAE Prime Minister, urged Arab governments to find adequate means to fill in the wide digital divide between the Arab world and the West, emphasizing that Arabs have ample human and financial resources to do the job. Sheikh Mohammed pledged to put the UAE IT and communications know-how at the disposal of Arab countries to serve Arab development projects. "We are not short of anything... and we have plenty of opportunities to build a better future for our Arab generations," states Sheikh Mohammed. Locally, the UAE had come a long way in the path of IT and its investment, thanks to the creative e-initiatives being undertaken by Dubai, in particular. However, the country is still at the beginning of the road and must carry on with firm resolve and persistence. Sheikh Abdulla, the UAE Minister of Information, states that IT and communications are of vital importance for the UAE for two main reasons: first, political leaders pin high hopes on technology to develop human resources to tackle the imbalance in demographic structure and the second factor is that technology contributes in resolving the social problem of employment of women in the GCC. The Arab Human Development Report for 2002 cited major problems facing the Arab world from poverty, corruption, illiteracy to bureaucracy; there are technological challenges arising from low income, absence of regulations, low spending on scientific research in addition to the worse condition of the IT infrastructure.

Conclusion

The UAE is one of the leading Arab countries in terms of integrating knowledge and information into its economic, legal, cultural, and societal modules. It is ranked 32nd overall out of 55 countries on the World Times/IDC ISI Index. In terms of economic modernity and openness, the UAE is ranked 24th worldwide, the second Arab country after Bahrain, on the Index of Economic Freedom. At the federal and state levels, co-ordinated policies have been developed in order to ensure that the information requirements of the various departments and groups of people who use and generate information in the respective sectors of the economy are met. As mentioned above, Federal Law No. 1 of 2006 concerning Electronic Transactions and Commerce Law and Federal Law No. 2 of 2006 (the Cyber Crime Law) were issued in June 2006 under the decree of President His Highness Sheikh Khalifa Bin Zayed Al Nahyan.

In general, efforts at the federal and state levels are geared toward: (1) providing guidelines for action toward the promotion and development of systematic levels of information services, and in keeping with the country's social, economic, cultural, scientific, and technical development goals; (2) making available frameworks for the formulation and proper execution of plans regarding information support and integration; and (3) helping ensure the provision of policy instruments which would strengthen the activities and co-ordination mechanisms in information related activities.

In summary, a number of policies, laws, and initiatives created have, wholly or partly, addressed the following: (1) the role of information and communications technology in the country's development; (2) the co-ordination of national information related activities; (3) the dissemination and diffusion of information and knowledge; (4) the information content and applications developments; (5) the role of the private sector in information creation, analysis, synthesis, and dissemination; (6) the federal regulatory framework and legal structure; and (7) the involvement in international and regional co-operation.

Question: What is the future of this IT society? What does the UAE need to do for the future to stay competitive in the region and be competitive in this global environment?

Endnotes

1. Dutta, Soumitra (2005). The Network Readiness Index: 2005. Published by the World Economic Forum, Geneva: Switzerland.
2. The Heritage Foundation/WSJ (2006). Economic Freedom Index. Published by The Heritage Foundation, NE Washington, DC.
3. IDC/World Times (2005). Information Society Index: Measuring the Global Impact of Information Technology and Internet Adoption. Published by World Times, USA.
4. ITU (2003). ITU Digital Access Index: World's First Global ICT Ranking. Published by ITU, Geneva: Switzerland.
5. AMEInfo (2006). Etisalat reaches out as key DSS Sponsor. July 5, 2006. Retreived on July 10, 2006 at http://www.ameinfo.com/ 90732.html.
6. Etisalat Annual Reports (2001, 2002, 2003, 2004 and 2005). Published by Etisalat, United Arab Emirates: Dubai.
7. Madar Research Group, Quarterly Report. December 2005–January 2006 issue. Published by Madar, UAE: Dubai.
8. ITU (2005). "What is state of ICT access around the world?" World Summit on the Information Society, Tunis 2005.
9. Consult Etisalat's website at www.etisalat.co.ae.
10. WITSA (2002). "WITSA 2002 global IT excellence award," Retrieved on June 29, 2006 at http://www.witsa.org/awards02/ceremony.
11. Madar Research Group, Quarterly Report. December 2004 issue. Published by Madar, UAE: Dubai.
12. Gulf News (2002). "IDC projects the number of PCs in the GCC," December 19, 2002, p. 6.
13. Gulf News (2005). UAE leads Arab world in fighting software piracy. Published August 31, 2005.
14. IDC, 2003. Global IT Economic Outlook: A Snapshot of the Global Economy and IT Markets, 3Q02. Published by IDC, USA.
15. Karake Shalhoub, Z. and Al Qasimi, L. (2003). The UAE and Information Society. A 40-page report prepared for ESCWA, United Nations and presented in February 2003, United Nations. Published by the United Nations, Geneva: Switzerland.
16. Etisalat Annual Report (2006). Published by Etisalat, UAE: Dubai.
17. Gulf News (2006). "Dubai Studio City to be base for Arabian Travel TV," 13/08/2006.

18. AMEinfo (2005). Arab Internet Standards Organization (InterStandards), a new initiative to create industry standards for commercial websites, announced. Retrieved on June 25, 2006 at http://www.ameinfo.com/72462.html.

19. Information in this section is based on a personal interview with Governor Dr. Omar Bin Soleiman who was the CEO of DIC in 2003.

Index

Note: Cases are in **bold**, locators are normal.
   Graphs and charts locators are in **bold**, entries are normal.
   Discussion sections are capitalized.
   All main headings are capitalized.
   All subheadings are not capitalized unless it is entered in the text as capitalized.